The DYNAMICS *of* Family Policy

Also Available from Lyceum Books, Inc.

Advisory Editor: Thomas M. Meenaghan, *New York University*

Advocacy Practice for Social Justice, 2E
Richard Hoefer

Policy, Politics, and Ethics
Thomas M. Meenaghan, Keith M. Kilty, Dennis D. Long, and John G. McNutt

Social Work Practice with Families: A Resiliency-Based Approach, 2E
Mary Patricia Van Hook

Child and Family Practice: A Relational Perspective
Shelley Cohen Konrad

Theory and Practice with Adolescents
Fred R. McKenzie

Adoption in the United States
Martha J. Henry and Daniel Pollack

The DYNAMICS of Family Policy

Alice K. Butterfield
University of Illinois at Chicago

Cynthia J. Rocha
University of Tennessee

William H. Butterfield, Professor Emeritus
Washington University in St. Louis

LYCEUM BOOKS, INC.
Chicago, Illinois

© Lyceum Books, Inc., 2010

Published by

LYCEUM BOOKS, INC.
5758 S. Blackstone Ave.
Chicago, Illinois 60637
773+643-1903 (Fax)
773+643-1902 (Phone)
lyceum@lyceumbooks.com
http://www.lyceumbooks.com

All rights reserved under International and Pan-American Copyright Conventions. No part of the publication may be reproduced, stored in a retrieval system, copied, or transmitted in any form or by any means without written permission from the publisher.

7 6 5   15 16

ISBN 978-1-933478-13-5

Library of Congress Cataloging-in-Publication Data

Butterfield, Alice K.
  The dynamics of family policy / Alice K. Butterfield, Cynthia J. Rocha, William H. Butterfield.
    p. cm.
  Includes bibliographical references and index.
  ISBN 978-1-933478-13-5
  1. Family policy—United States. I. Rocha, Cynthia J. II. Butterfield, William H. III. Title.
  HQ536.B886   2010
  362.82'5610973—dc22

                                      2009005229

To my children, Sarah Spatz, Joanna Gioia, Joshua, Adam, Michael, and Leah Johnson: Thanks for all you have taught me about being family. To Bill, my husband, colleague, and mentor: Thanks for your constant support. To my parents, Wilfred and Mary Ann Kessler: Thanks for raising me to "see what needs to be done and then figure out a way to do it."

—AKB

To my daughter, Clarissa Rocha, and my husband, Bill Hnath, and in memory of my parents, Ernest and Joyce Gasperson.

—CJR

To Alice, my wife who had the vision for this book, and to my mother, Velma Walker, and my father, William Butterfield, who lived lives that taught me the value of family and to care for others. And to the National Institute of Mental Health and the GI Bill, which made it possible for me to get an education that I otherwise could not have afforded.

—WHB

Contents

Tables, Figures, and Boxes		xi
Preface		xv
Acknowledgments		xxvii
1	Valuing the Family	1
	Important Themes for Family Policy	2
	Changing Demographics and Social Trends	7
	Devolution	11
	Privatization and Managed Care	12
	Policy Analysis and Advocacy	13
	The Relationship between Policy and Practice	14
	For Further Reading	15
	References	16
2	Policy Dynamics and Family Policy Analysis	18
	Problems, Values, Power, and Politics	19
	Preparing for the Open Window: Guidelines for Policy Research	28
	Family Impact Analysis	33
	Summary	43
	For Further Reading	44
	References	45
3	Advocating for Families	47
	The Debate over the Role of Advocacy	48
	Levels of Practice and the Place of Advocacy	50
	Planning an Advocacy Campaign	55
	Skills for Implementing an Advocacy Campaign	60
	Breaking out of the Cause-versus-Function Debate	87
	Summary	90

	For Further Reading	90
	References	91
4	Family Poverty	95
	Defining and Measuring Poverty	96
	The Distribution of Income and Wealth	103
	Exits from Poverty	108
	Experimental Measures of Poverty	112
	Family Well-Being and Quality of Life	114
	Poverty Is Political	119
	Summary	125
	For Further Reading	126
	References	126
5	Theories of Poverty for Family Policy	130
	Types of Poverty Theories	131
	Theories of Poverty	136
	The Theories Families Live By	151
	Summary	153
	For Further Reading	154
	References	155
6	Welfare, Food, and Housing	158
	Welfare-to-Work Policy	160
	Food Policy	166
	Housing Policy	175
	Summary	193
	For Further Reading	195
	References	196
7	Work and Employment	202
	Globalization and the U.S. Labor Market	204
	Economic Recession	217
	Unemployment Policy	223
	The Minimum Wage and Earned Income Tax Credit	231
	Summary	240
	For Further Reading	241
	References	242
8	Health Care	247
	Health Disparities	249
	Health Care Policy	261
	Mental Health Services	273
	Summary	282

	For Further Reading	282
	References	283
9	The Care and Support of Children	289
	Working and Caring for Children	290
	Child Care	293
	Divorce and Child Custody	302
	Policies for Child Care and Support	306
	Summary	316
	For Further Reading	317
	References	318
10	Family Violence	323
	Defining Family Violence	325
	Trends in Family Violence	327
	Intimate Partner Violence and Child Abuse	332
	Violence Against Women	335
	Child Maltreatment	338
	Maltreatment of the Elderly	351
	Summary	354
	For Further Reading	355
	References	356
11	Marriage as Family Policy	359
	Marriage and the Family: In Flux or Deteriorating?	360
	Marriage, Common-Law Marriage, Domestic Partnerships,	
	and Civil Unions	363
	Same-Sex Marriage	369
	Promoting Marriage as Public Policy	373
	Summary	377
	For Further Reading	378
	References	379
12	Family Caregiving and Aging Policy	382
	Changing Patterns of Family Living	384
	Policies for Family Caregiving	392
	Old Age, Survivors, Health and Disability Insurance	400
	Summary	407
	For Further Reading	408
	References	409
13	Family Policy in a Global Context	413
	Devolution in the Global Context	414
	Family Well-Being from a Global Perspective	417

Implications of the Global Economy	421
Summary	422
For Further Reading	423
References	423
Appendix A. Preparing a Good Fact Sheet—the Basics	425
Appendix B. The Policy Brief	427
Appendix C. Guidelines for Testifying before a Committee	433
Index	435
About the Authors	445

Tables, Figures, and Boxes

Tables

2.1	Defining Homelessness as a Social Problem in the United States	23
2.2	Families as a Social System	34
3.1	Ten Steps in an Advocacy Campaign	57
3.2	Policy Advocacy for Homeless Shelter and Services in St. Louis	65
3.3	Types of Ballot Initiatives	77
4.1	Poverty Guidelines, 2007	100
4.2	People with Income Below Specified Ratios of Their Poverty Thresholds by Selected Characteristics, 2006	101
4.3	Percentage Share of Aggregate Incomes by Quintiles, 1967–2005	105
4.4	Income Mobility for White and Black Families, 1968–1998	107
4.5	Changes in the Distribution of Wealth, 1962–2004	107
4.6	Elements of the Current and Proposed Poverty Measures	115
4.7	Households with Satisfactory Ratings on Summary Measures of Well-Being by Income Quartile, 1992–1998	120
5.1	Barrier Theories and Psychology of the Poor Theories	132
5.2	Views of the Poverty Personality	135
5.3	Analysis of Exits from Welfare	137
5.4	Key Elements of Social Capital Theory	143
6.1	Where People Are Staying after Losing Their Homes	192
7.1	Comparison of General Motors and Toyota Auto Manufacturing in the United States	212
7.2	Type of Industry and Number of TAA-Certified Workers	228
7.3	Family Structure and Earned Income Tax Credit, 2008	239
8.1	Conceptual Framework of Community Effects on Health	260
8.2	Average Premium Increase Due to Parity	278

9.1	Parental Child Care Arrangements for Preschoolers Living with Mother, by Age and Employment Status of Mother	294
9.2	Families with Employed Mothers Who Pay for Child Care, Spring 2005	295
9.3	Average Weekly Child Care Expenditures of Families with Employed Mothers That Make Payments, Spring 2005	296
9.4	Children Living with Mother and in Self-Care by Age of Child, Family Income, Poverty Level, and TANF Assistance Status, Spring 2005	297
9.5	Children in Self-Care by Age of Child, Residence with Mother or Father, and Marital Status of Mother, Spring 2005	298
9.6	Use of Title XX Funds, by Expenditure Category, 2001	309
10.1	Victim-Offender Relationships in Nonfatal Violent Victimizations, by Victim and Gender, 1993–2004 (Average Annual Rate per 1,000 Age Twelve and Older)	327
10.2	Trend Data for Children Who Are Victims of Child Maltreatment, 1990–2005	328
10.3	Average Annual Nonfatal Intimate Partner Victimization Rate per 1,000 by Gender and Age Group, 1993–2004	331
10.4	Comparison of VAWA Enacted and Authorized Funding Levels, 2002–2004	337
10.5	The 2004 Survey of Adult Protective Services for the Fifty States, the District of Columbia, and Guam: Type of Abuse, Perpetrators, Types Substantiated, and Reporters	352
11.1	Household and Family Characteristics of Married-Couple and Unmarried-Partner Households for the United States and Puerto Rico, 2000	362
11.2	State Marriage Laws	372
12.1	Comparison of Seven Elements of Social Security Privatization Proposals	405
13.1	Comparisons of Social Indicators in the United States and Selected Industrialized Countries	418
13.2	Household Income Inequality Adjusting for Taxes and Income Transfers	419

Figures

4.1	Number in Poverty and Poverty Rate, 1959–2006	99
4.2	Family Poverty Gap and Family Poverty Rates, 1959–2005	102
4.3	Income and Poverty Rate, 1987–2006	104
4.4	Family Income Inequality, Gini Coefficient, 1947–2005	105

4.5	Number of People Entering and Exiting Poverty, 1996 and 1999	109
4.6	Episodic Poverty Rates, 1999	110
4.7	Chronic Poverty Rate, 1996–1999	111
4.8	Official Poverty Rate Compared to Alternative Measures, 1999–2006	116
4.9	Poverty Lines for Four-Person Families, 1947–2003	117
4.10	General Indicators of Household Well-Being by Race/Hispanic Origin of Householder, 1998	119
7.1	Unemployment Rate for All Workers (Aged 16+)	221
7.2	Unemployment Rates for Men and Women	222
7.3	Unemployment Rates for Workers with Different Levels of Education	223
7.4	Unemployment Rates for Workers of Different Ages	224
7.5	Purchasing Power of Minimum Wage, Adjusted for Inflation in 2008 Dollars, 1960–2009	234
7.6	The Federal Earned Income Tax Credit, 2007	238
8.1	Percent of U.S. Population without Health Insurance, 1987–2006	250
10.1	Nonfatal Violent Victimization Rate by Victim-Offender Relationship and Victim Gender, 1993–2004	326
10.2	Number and Rate of Victims of Child Maltreatment, 1990–2005	327
11.1	Measurement Framework for Conceptualizing and Defining Healthy Marriage	374
12.1	Percent of Individuals Sixty-Five Years of Age and Older Below Poverty by Race	403
13.1	Percent of the Population in Relative Poverty in Selected Industrialized Countries	420

Boxes

1.1	Family Values: Actions Speak Louder Than Words	3
2.1	Preparing for the Open Window: Guidelines for Policy Research	29
2.2	Family Impact Analysis	39
3.1	Examples of Coercive Strategies to Bring Change	63
3.2	Coalition Building in an Intra-institutional Domestic Violence Policy Intervention	67
3.3	Example of Using Interest Groups to Build a Coalition	72
3.4	Steve Goldsmith's Twelve Media Tips	80

3.5	Guidelines for Writing an Opinion Editorial	82
3.6	John Emerson's Review of Software for Electronic Activism	84
3.7	The Internet as a Tool for Social Activism	87
4.1	Critique of New Census Report on Measuring Poverty	121
6.1	Food Stamps and Staying Housed	171
6.2	Doubling up and Homelessness	178
6.3	Substandard Housing	180
7.1	Part-Time Employment and Job Retraining	208
7.2	Case Study of Auto Assembly Plants	213
7.3	Frances Perkins: A Social Work Policy Entrepreneur	232
7.4	Working Overtime without Overtime Pay	233
8.1	Emergency Room Visits and the Uninsured	252
8.2	Accessing Health Care through the Emergency Room	257
9.1	Parenting and Work	299
10.1	The Co-occurrence of Child Abuse and Intimate Partner Violence	332
10.2	Legal and Legislative History of Child Protection	339
10.3	Foster Care Drift	343
12.1	Multigenerational Caregiving	389

Preface

This book was born of our struggle to find materials to teach courses on child and family policy. Over the years, we looked for literature that covered family policies, including how to analyze and change them. We wanted to provide a comprehensive view of family issues, but we also searched for material that could give our students the perspective of real people facing real problems, and that incorporated a policy practice approach. One night, on our way to a policy conference in South Carolina, we sat drinking coffee at a Waffle House. As our conversation drifted from our research on homelessness and the working poor to the situations that we were facing in our families, we realized that we had to write this book. We believed that it was important to write a family policy book that presented the issues from a scholarly perspective but included methods and tools for developing and changing policies to support family well-being.

It was an important moment in our lives—one that set us on a course to write this book. But at that time many years ago, little did we know that we would personally experience many of the family issues discussed in this book: divorce and remarriage, blended families, chronic illness, caring for elderly parents and dealing with their deaths, adult children returning home with grandchildren in tow, child care issues, adoption and issues involving legal guardianship, and problems accessing health care. As we navigated our way through the policy maze of various systems in attempts to help our immediate and extended families, we became even more interested in writing a book that dealt with the issues facing families today and the policies that help or aggravate those issues. As social workers, we also understood the challenges that emerge when a person does not understand the way in which micro-level family issues intersect with broader macro-level policy. Social workers who do not understand the programs and policies that guide and limit practice are at a disadvantage in helping the families that they serve. It is doubly difficult to meet human needs in a policy environment that is fragmented and not focused specifically on families. Moreover, the policy-making environment is dynamic and ever changing—due in part to power issues and political processes that typically reflect the values of dominant groups in society, rather than the diverse types of families whom the policies are supposed to benefit. This disconnection between decision makers, interest groups, and consumers led us to look seriously at the dynamic processes of policy development, implementation, and policy change.

Over the years, our research has brought the lived experiences of families to our attention. The three of us have interviewed numerous individuals who have shared their experiences and stories of homelessness, the transition from welfare to work, family violence, the difficulty of accessing health care and child care, family caregiving across the life span, unemployment through plant closures, food insecurity, and substandard housing. More often than not, many of these issues are intertwined in the daily struggles of American families. We have included some of these stories in this book to illustrate the way in which policy affects families Our hope is that by offering a look into the lived experiences of real people, combined with serious discussion of the issues and an analysis of the policies, this book will help students, social workers, and other human service professionals better understand how to serve families through advocacy and policy practice.

We faced several challenges in trying to write a book on family policy. The first challenge was defining the family. In this regard, we determined that a functional approach to family well-being more clearly represented ways to support families than a structural approach that fails to value families in all their diversity—whether rich or poor, young or old, of one race or ethnic background or more than one. The work of other scholars and the demographic changes taking place in the United States show that diverse family forms represent not only the experience of family for the majority of Americans but also the changes in family structure that take place over the life span. For example, cohabitation, marriage, divorce and remarriage, adoption, kinship care, and the death of a spouse all create structural changes in the family. Thus, viewing families in all their diversity is an integral part of our approach to understanding family policy. Within this concept of the family, we also pay special attention to poor and working poor families, including families of color who face discrimination and experience health disparities and other forms of inequality. Our attention to diverse family forms means that the book also covers policies that are most likely to benefit middle-class and wealthy families, such as the Child and Dependent Care Tax Credit, the Family and Medical Leave Act, and Social Security retirement benefits.

The second challenge was defining family policy. Although the United States does not have a comprehensive body of family policy, in actuality, *all policy is family policy.* It would be impossible, however, to cover every U.S. policy in one book. To address this dilemma, we selected several broad policy areas that particularly pertain to families: welfare, food, and housing policy; work and employment policy; health care, child care, and child support; family violence; marriage policy; and policies related to old age and caregiving for the elderly. It was our aim not only to cover major policies that typically gain attention in most policy books but also to look at less-known policies that support families in all their diverse forms. The discussions of the demolition of public housing and the escalating homeownership crisis due to subprime mortgages in chapter 6, the effect of globalization on white-collar employment in chapter 7, and marriage policy in chapter 11 are examples of our attempt to look at new and emerging issues related to family policy.

The third challenge was writing a book that would do more than explain, discuss, and analyze family policy. Knowledge is important, but in order to take action, students and professionals should have practical tools and methods at hand for advocacy and policy practice. Part of our goal was to demystify the complex and fragmented world of policy making in such a way that readers would not only be convinced of the need for advocacy, but also become engaged in developing and changing policy as part of their lifetime professional work. To meet this challenge, we drew on the World Wide Web, which opened our eyes to the dynamic world of policy making. Readers will find many references to materials on the Web. In addition, chapter 2 provides guidelines for policy research, part of which requires use of the Web to examine government legislation, decisions of the courts, and the views of conservative and progressive policy think tanks. Other chapters discuss some of the concepts and theories that lie behind good policy analysis and offer practical tools for policy practice. For example, chapter 3 offers detailed instructions for mounting a large- or small-scale advocacy campaign; chapter 4 presents the idea that poverty is political, as illustrated by various measures of poverty; and chapter 5 looks at contemporary theories that take into account the dynamic nature of poverty and combine both individual and structural causes in explaining poverty. In addition, sprinkled throughout the chapters are useful online tools that pertain to specific areas of family policy.

In this era of globalization, our last challenge was placing family policy in a global context. Policy in the United States is focused on individuals. Families, in all their diverse forms and structures in the United States, are not at the center of policy development. As a result, policies are fragmented, without a coherent focus on the family system. Individualistic culture also affects the way in which self-sufficiency is perceived. The family is outside the purview of government, and policy should not interfere with family life. Families are responsible for their own well-being and the care of their children and elders, and for decisions concerning education and work. This view perceives social problems as personal problems that are within the control of individuals and tends to blame individuals for their low status in society. For example, individual explanations of poverty see failure to marry as a principal cause of welfare dependency and emphasize marriage as a way out of poverty. Child poverty is attributed to the failure of parents to marry rather than to poor education, unemployment, or the lack of affordable child care. Of course, single parenthood does not always lead to poverty, and a person's single status often results from economic insecurity rather than the other way around. Research on the outcomes of welfare reform indicates that families cannot control how much money they make in the market economy, but the belief is that the marketplace, acting essentially alone with few and limited social programs, can cure social ills. Nonetheless, investment in a globally competitive marketplace to the detriment of the domestic family safety net puts family stability at risk. To place these issues in context, chapter 13 offers a comparative and international perspective on family policy. Many other industrialized countries espouse more progressive policies than the United States because of their investment in the social economy, which supports families and increases citizens' abilities to compete in the global marketplace.

Although there are many policies affecting families, there is no clearly defined or comprehensive set of policies that one can point to as *family policy* in the United States. In order to address this situation, the first three chapters provide conceptual and practical tools for analyzing policy and advocating policy change. In chapter 1, we introduce several themes related to family policy and some of the issues affecting families today. The chapter outlines the changing demographics and social trends that influence the structure of the family and discusses how these changes result in different family needs. We also look at the considerable trends toward devolution, the privatization of service delivery, and managed care, which have marked the past several decades of policy development and implementation in the United States. Chapter 1 also introduces the topics of policy analysis and advocacy. In the dynamic environment of policy making, policy development is less often based on rational decision making, and more often influenced by the values and politics of various power holders and interest groups.

Chapter 2 starts where policy analysis begins—with the task of defining social problems. It is difficult to come to a consensus on the nature and definition of social problems because values, power, and politics interact in the dynamic policy-making environment. Here we outline in some detail the multiple-streams framework, which captures the process of moving social issues onto the public agenda and is a useful lens for understanding the dynamic processes of policy making. We also present a modified version of family impact analysis for analyzing family policy. This policy analysis method is particularly useful because it places families in the center of policy analysis and considers their perception of a problem and how they are affected by a particular policy. This chapter includes guidelines for policy research, a practical method for policy research.

Once policy analysis is completed, advocacy for policy development or change is the next step. In the absence of comprehensive family policy, there is a need for a more inclusive view of family well-being than that promoted by the numerous—yet limited and fragmented—policies and programs for families in the United States. Advocacy for a holistic and comprehensive approach to family policy is sorely needed. Social workers and other human service professionals are in a unique position to advocate and work for comprehensive family policy. They participate in the delivery of family services and programs and know the ways in which policy and programs affect family well-being. Although most social workers are involved with families and every day their work translates policy into practice, typically they do not see themselves as policy advocates even though they may well understand the limits and the opportunities inherent in the social programs in which they work. At the organizational level, workers have taken on a role in implementing policy for families, rather than the role of creating family policy. This observation is meant to challenge readers and the profession as a whole to put the business of managing and implementing the nation's fragmented and incomplete social welfare system in its due place. Social work and other human service professionals constitute an interest group. We have lobbyists, political action committees, and a presence in Congress and every state legislature, and as policy practitioners, we are uniquely positioned to influence change in the dynamic policy-making process. The challenge for social work and other human service professions is to make family policy central to their mission—to wield the power of their numbers and knowledge—to advocate family well-being on a wider scale.

Chapter 3 discusses these issues as part of the cause-versus-function debate of case advocacy versus cause advocacy. We show how advocacy fits in the continuum of service delivery and policy making by describing client-centered advocacy and system change advocacy at the organizational, grassroots, and legislative levels. A policy-practice framework is offered as a way for every practitioner working with families to make advocacy part of his or her work. We present the advocacy campaign, a strategic planning tool for helping students and policy practitioners organize for social change. Selected advocacy skills and tactics that we think are central to implementing an organized advocacy effort are presented. The chapter includes a detailed outline for developing a policy brief that can be used by advocates and organizations lobbying for a proposed policy position.

The next two chapters provide readers with a conceptual basis for understanding and analyzing family policy. Since family well-being often depends on whether a family is living in poverty or near poverty, chapter 4 provides readers with an in-depth view of family poverty. This chapter emphasizes the various ways that poverty is measured, and how measuring poverty is political and value based. Our discussion illustrates the way in which the same set of statistics can be used to support very different policy positions, depending on the values and policy preferences of advocates. Chapter 5 provides a discussion of theories of poverty. Some theories of poverty emphasize individualistic causes of poverty; others emphasize structural causes of poverty. We have selected contemporary theories of poverty that attempt to integrate both individual and structural causes of poverty. Taken together, chapters 4 and 5 help readers understand poverty and near poverty as the backdrop behind many of the policies outlined in following chapters.

Chapters 6 through 12 describe social issues affecting families and critically review selected social policies that apply to families in the areas of welfare, food, and housing; work and employment; health care; the care and support of children; family violence; domestic partnerships and marriage (both heterosexual and same sex); and aging, as well as multigenerational caregiving across the life span. Each of these chapters covers a wide range of policies affecting families. Some of the policies we have selected are commonly known because they are a basic part of the social welfare system; others are less well known but are nonetheless important for social workers and other helping professionals to know about. Many chapters include case illustrations of how policies are experienced by families. These stories bring to life some of the intended and unintended challenges that policies create for families. These stories also emphasize what poor and near-poor families have to go through to obtain assistance and support.

The final chapter puts family policy and family well-being in a global context. In order to test normative claims regarding social welfare in the United States, we examine how other countries are dealing with the global marketplace and compare the United States with other industrialized countries on key indicators of family well-being.

As we put the final touches on this book, we were ever so much reminded of the fact that policy making is political. The November 2008 elections had just occurred. Pundits and policy makers across the political spectrum view the election as historic. Barack Obama was elected in a landslide victory as the first African American president in the country's history. Voters across the United States cast their ballots in record numbers not seen for at least forty years. Approximately 133.3 million Americans cast their votes, accounting for an estimated turnout rate of 62.5 percent. An unprecedented number of newly registered voters, particularly young people, African Americans, and Hispanics, went to the polls. Voter registration campaigns were an essential part of the effort. According to the Pew Charitable Trusts (2008), "Youth mobilization efforts by nonpartisan youth voter registration organizations Declare Yourself and Rock the Vote has resulted in 10,650 downloaded voter registration forms since beginning their online outreach in late 2003." The Obama-Biden ticket won the electoral vote by 365 (52.9%) to 173 (45.7%). Several of the states that went to Obama had not voted Democratic for decades: the state of Virginia voted Democratic only once since 1952, Indiana voted Democratic only once since 1940, and North Carolina voted Democratic only once since 1964. The margin of winning votes in these states ranged from 25,836 votes in Indiana and 13,993 votes in North Carolina to 202,115 votes in Virginia. The election is also historic in terms of the wins of Democratic candidates in races for the Senate and House of Representatives. Democrats hold a wide majority in both houses of Congress, with 60 seats to 40 seats in the Senate, and 256 seats to 178 seats in the House. These numbers signal the end of a nearly twelve-year domination of Congress by Republicans.

Grassroots democracy through citizen-initiated ballot-based measures also played an historic role in the election. As we discuss in chapter 11, voters in California passed an amendment to the state constitution that makes same-sex marriage illegal. Voters in Arkansas passed a statute that forbids unmarried cohabitating couples—whether heterosexual or same sex—to foster or adopt children. In South Dakota, voters defeated an initiative banning abortion that strategists had hoped would challenge *Roe v. Wade* in the Supreme Court. Other value-based and hot political issues such as assisted suicide, marijuana use, and stem cell research found their way onto state ballots for direct policy making by the voting public. Thus, whatever one's political persuasion, the 2008 election ushered in a new era in politics and policy making at the federal level. All in all, voters voted for change.

President Barack Obama and Vice President Joe Biden face some of the most daunting domestic policy challenges since the Civil War–era election of President Abraham Lincoln and the Great Depression election of President Franklin D. Roosevelt. As of early 2009, the U.S. economy is in shambles, the effect of subprime mortgages in the inflated homeownership market and its domino-like effect on Wall Street. Even the mammoth $700 billion bailout bill designed to rescue banks and financial institutions from collapse has not calmed the stock market. Stocks are down as much as 40 percent from their worth about a year ago in late 2007. Massive bailout costs make for a challenging policy-making environment for spending in areas such as job creation, health care reform, and education. As discussed in chapter 7, the U.S. economy is in one of the worst recessions since the Great Depression. And even though the National Bureau of Economic Research officially declines to define a depression, some financial analysts warn that "a few poor policy decisions could put us in a depression" (Bennett, 2008).

To deal with these ominous economic conditions, Congress passed the American Recovery and Reinvestment Act, which was signed into law on February 17, 2009, by President Obama. To comply with the rules of the legislation, $787 billion must be spent quickly over the next two years in order to infuse dollars into the economy and thereby counter the effects of the recession. The legislation promises to protect up to 3.5 million jobs through federally funded construction projects. It offers immediate tax relief to consumers to increase spending and provides billions of dollars for fiscal relief and federal programs, of which $288 billion (37%) is for tax cuts, $144 billion (18%) for fiscal relief to states and local governments, and $357 billion (45%) for federal spending and federal social programs. The spending allocations related to some of the policy areas featured in this book include the following:

- ✓ Tax relief for individuals: $237 billion, including a $15 billion expansion of the child tax credit, $6.6 billion for homeowner tax credit ($8,000 refundable credit for first-time homebuyers for purchase of homes in 2009), and $4.7 billion for expanded earned income tax credit for workers with three or more children
- ✓ Health care: $147.7 billion, including $86.6 billion for Medicaid, $24.7 billion to provide a 65 percent subsidy for health insurance premiums for unemployed persons under COBRA, and $2 billion for community health centers
- ✓ Education and services for children and families: $90.9 billion, including $2.1 billion for Head Start, $2 billion for child care services, $13 billion for low-income public school children, and $70 million for education of homeless children

✓ Aid to low-income workers, the unemployed, and retirees: $82.5 billion, including $40 billion to extend unemployment benefits, $3.95 billion for job training through workforce investment programs, $1.2 billion for dislocated worker services, $500 million for supportive services in employment and training, $1 billion for the expansion of services provided by nonprofit organizations in communities experiencing economic downturn, $120 million for community service employment of low-income seniors, $19.9 billion for food stamps, $150 million to food banks, $100 million for food for seniors, and $100 million for free school lunch programs
✓ Housing: $12.7 billion, including $4 billion to upgrade public housing, $2 billion for Section 8 rental assistance, $1.5 billion for rental assistance, $2.25 billion in tax credits for low-income housing construction, and $1.5 billion for homelessness prevention

Economists are divided on whether the economic stimulus is large enough to make a difference. Is another $500 billion needed? Will short-term gains be offset later by the increase in the deficit? Some even question whether the stimulus plan was even needed (Izzo, 2009b). The latest prediction from economists is that the recession will end in September 2009 when the economy begins to benefit from the spending of stimulus dollars. "By December [2009], the economists on average expect the unemployment rate to reach 9.5%, up from the 8.5% reported for March. They do see the rate of decline slowing, forecasting 2.6 million job losses in the next 12 months, compared to the 4.6 million jobs lost in the previous period" (Izzo, 2009a).

In this uncertain economic environment, what is the future of family policy in the United States? The only prediction we can make is that policy in general is entering a period of rapid and perhaps far-reaching change. The *Progressive Agenda for the States 2008* (Horn, 2007) contains fifty policy tool kits and sixty-three model bills. It is an excellent resource on the policies presented in this book, as well as policies on the environment, consumer protection, the budget and taxation, elections, civil rights and liberties, education, and criminal justice that relate to the well-being of families.

Just prior to the November 2008 election, the Center for Law and Social Policy released the *CLASP Federal Policy Recommendations for 2009 and Beyond: An Overview*, which outlines three basic areas of policy focus for Congress, the new president, and many federal agencies and departments: (1) basic supports for families with children living in concentrated areas of poverty, (2) a strong and modernized safety net of programs and services to help families and individuals who face heightened risk in a global economy, and (3) attention to work and employment issues, including job training, better jobs, and improved wages. To address these basic areas, the Center for Law and Social Policy (2008) outlines ten specific agenda items for future policy change. It gives us particular satisfaction, as we write the final paragraphs of this book, that these agenda items reflect major content areas covered in the following chapters:

- ✓ Commit to cutting poverty in our nation by 50 percent within ten years, overhaul the federal poverty measures, and create measures to address issues of well-being beyond income status.
- ✓ Create a guarantee for child care for all families at or below 200 percent of the poverty threshold and provide substantial new funds to help states improve the quality of child care and to remove barriers to access for underserved families.
- ✓ Reverse the funding cut to the child support program and require the distribution of all child support collected to families and children.
- ✓ Adopt realistic child support policies for low-income non-custodial fathers and expand assistance to low-income fathers to strengthen families.
- ✓ Improve the child welfare system so that we do as much to prevent child abuse and neglect as we do to ameliorate the harm of such maltreatment.
- ✓ Transform and fund at a scale comparable to the GI Bill workforce education and training programs to help low-income individuals with few skills advance economically, increase our nation's productivity, and secure a better future for children.
- ✓ Provide government leadership to improve job quality through wages, benefits, paid leave, and predictable and responsive schedules so that workers can meet both work and family responsibilities and advance to meet new challenges.
- ✓ Invest in building the youth service delivery capacity in communities of high youth distress in order to reconnect disconnected youths.
- ✓ Improve the Temporary Assistance for Needy Families Program (TANF) and other safety net programs so that all families have necessary work supports and TANF focuses on positive outcomes for families and reducing poverty.
- ✓ Expand the earned income tax credit and make other tax credits refundable so that low-income families can benefit from them.

We encourage readers to reflect on these basic areas of possible future policy change.

It is our view that substantial policy change is likely in many areas related to family policy in the United States. As American families face the complex challenges of economic recession, it is time for policy that puts families at the center and promotes the well-being of families in all their diversity. Valuing the family challenges us to advocate for family policy and to find new ways to teach families how to organize and advocate on their own behalf. This book provides students and policy practitioners alike with the information and tools necessary for successful advocacy for family policy. We hope that this book becomes a useful text for child and family policy courses in social work and other human service programs. The way that we have structured the book makes it suitable for graduate and advanced undergraduate courses that emphasize policies for children and families, policy analysis, and policy practice. It can also be used for foundation social policy courses in social work education. We hope that readers will consider this book a start in their journey toward advocacy and policy practice—whether they plan to work at the micro level directly with clients, at the mezzo or organizational level, or at the macro level in policy analysis and practice.

REFERENCES

American Recovery and Reinvestment Act of 2009. Pub. L. No. 111-5, H.R. 1, S. 1. (2009).

Bennett, D. (2008, November 16). Depression 2009: What would it look like? *Boston Globe*. Retrieved April 13, 2009, from http://www.boston.com/bostonglobe/ideas/articles/2008/11/16/depression_2009_what_would_it_look_like/?page=full

Center for Law and Social Policy. (2008, October 16). *CLASP federal policy recommendations for 2009 and beyond: An overview*. Retrieved on November 9, 2008, from http://www.clasp.org/publications/clasp_fedpolicyrecommendationsfor2009andbeyond.pdf

Horn, B. (Ed.). (2007). *Progressive agenda for the states 2008: Leadership for America*. Washington, DC: Center for Policy Alternatives.

Izzo, P. (2009a, April 9). Economists see a rebound in September. *Wall Street Journal*. Retrieved April 13, 2009, from http://online.wsj.com/article/SB123921340472201877.html

Izzo, P. (2009b, March 11). Obama, Geithner get low grades from economists. *Wall Street Journal*. Retrieved April 13, 2009, from http://online.wsj.com/article/SB123671107124286261.html

Pew Charitable Trusts. (2008). *Unprecedented number of young voters register to vote in key battleground states*. Retrieved November 9, 2008, from http://www.pewtrusts.org/news_room_detail.aspx?id=18188

Acknowledgments

Many people have contributed to the development of our thinking in writing this book. In particular, we would like to thank Tom Meenaghan of New York University for his detailed critique of the manuscript. Tom pushed us to look more closely at the issues of power and politics, and their effect on family policies in the United States. David Follmer of Lyceum Books stayed with us and was supportive of our work as policy changes occurred and necessitated updating of the manuscript. We greatly appreciate the excellent copyediting work of Sonia Elizabeth Fulop. This is a better book because of her attention to detail. We are also in debt to our students at the University of Tennessee at Knoxville and the University of Illinois at Chicago. They were essential in providing feedback on the methods of policy practice and policy analysis that are featured in this book. Finally, we want to thank Andrea McCarter, Helo Oidjarv, and Clarissa Rocha, who served as our research assistants.

CHAPTER 1

Valuing the Family

This book is about valuing the family. It is not about family values. It is about valuing families no matter what their size, composition, structure, or race/ethnicity, or the sexual orientation of their members. It is about valuing families whether they are rich or poor, old or young, childless or with children. Valuing families means recognizing that in a diverse society such as the United States, family structures and membership vary widely, and the values held by the many kinds of families are diverse. Even though the values held by families vary widely, we believe all families have core needs that should be supported by and reflected in the nation's policies. Broadly stated, these include policies that improve the well-being of families and their access to work, food, housing, and health care, as well as the care and support of children and the elderly. Attention to these core needs will strengthen families—however different from the "norm" they may be, and however different their value systems. Thus, we believe that valuing families in all their diversity is the starting point for sound public policy.

Valuing families means paying attention to their changing needs over the life span. Problems such as poverty, homelessness, illness, inadequate housing, unemployment, and abusive relationships may come and go, but these situations challenge the ability of families to provide adequate care and intergenerational support for their members. As pointed out by Early and GlenMaye (2000), "Rhetoric about 'family values' is of no help to families who face real-life dilemmas, but valuing families through recognizing and building on their strengths can assist families in improving their lives" (p. 118). From a social work practice perspective, the strengths approach is recommended, but such practice is constrained and even thwarted by policies and programs that are individualistic in nature, and not aligned with the diversity of family situations.

> The United States is a land of contradictions. The dominant culture holds the individual to be primary and at the same time claims to place the greatest value on the family. Despite the rhetoric of "family values," our nation's programs and policies—which typically are based on discrete categories of individuals—often fall short of providing the support needed to truly value families. By fragmenting families into mere groupings of individuals, programs and policies often fail to provide the support families need not just to survive but to thrive. Our emphasis on this fragmentation often ties the hands of agencies that want to provide services outside limited categories or creates a labyrinth of services far too complex for most families to navigate successfully. (Zahn, Hirota, Garcia, & Ro, 2003, p. 1797)

Thus, in view of the individualistic nature of policy in the United States, valuing families means that social workers and other human service professionals are duty bound to advocate policy change that puts the family at the center of policy discussions and proposals.

In real life, there is often a separation between the family values stance and the way families actually live their lives. Box 1.1 illustrates this disconnection in the context of marriage and the practice of family values. Our view is that valuing families is a universal perspective that supersedes political ideologies and nation-state differences. The true meaning of family values comes from actually placing value on the things that families *do* to provide physical, emotional, social, and financial support. This means that the actions of families—their love, caring, and commitment to the well-being of their members—are primary, and these should be valued over an emphasis on family structure.

Important Themes for Family Policy

This book has two main purposes. First, it is intended to serve as an introductory text on issues related to family policy. Second, it is intended to serve as a guide to readers who want to be able to analyze issues related to family policy and then engage in advocacy for policy change. In our quest to write a family policy book, we have drawn on the work of other scholars, activists, and policy institutes, including research reports, census data,

Box 1.1 Family Values: Actions Speak Louder Than Words

The disconnect between who values marriage and who actually practices it is especially striking. The 10 states with the highest divorce rates are all red or conservative states whose voters overwhelmingly support "values" candidates. Born-again Christians are as likely to divorce as other Americans, and the Bible Belt has the highest divorce rate in the nation. By contrast, the Northeast, noted for liberal politics and greater tolerance for alternative lifestyles, is the region where marriages are most likely to last. Massachusetts, the poster state for nontraditional family values with its legalization of same-sex marriage, has the lowest divorce rate in the country.

Educated elites are often accused of undermining the family with their liberal, relativist values. On average, it's true that affluent, highly educated Americans are far more likely than less-educated or lower-income Americans to see divorce, cohabitation and unwed motherhood as acceptable behavior. But in practice they are far more likely to marry, less likely to divorce and less likely to have kids out of wedlock than their poorer brethren.

We see the same pattern internationally. Germans are much more accepting of teenagers engaging in sex than Americans are. But Germany has much lower rates of teen pregnancies and teen births than the United States. Norwegians consider out-of-wedlock births much more acceptable than do most Americans and a higher proportion of children are born to unmarried women in Norway than in the United States. But unmarried Norwegian mothers are much more likely than their U.S. counterparts to live with the father of their child. On average, Norwegian children spend 90 percent of their youth living with both parents, while U.S. children average just two-thirds of their youth living with both parents. . . .

What really matters in family and community life are not the abstract principles people give lip service to but the real relationships they enter into and how they handle commitments, whether those commitments are legally recognized or not. In today's changing family and marital landscape, we should spend less time passing judgment on people's theoretical "family values" and more time helping people build healthy relationships in their daily lives.

Source: Coontz, S. (2005, May 13). Family values: Actions speak louder than words. *Seattle Post-Intelligencer.* Retrieved May 7, 2008, from http://www.stephaniecoontz.com/articles/article15.htm

government documents, books, and journal articles. Starting in chapter 2, the reader will encounter many tables and charts that are very detailed. The purpose of these tables and charts is to provide readers with enough information to move beyond the conceptual level of understanding family policy to the operational level, where they can analyze and engage in family policy advocacy.

As we studied family policy, nine important themes emerged. Here we provide a brief introduction to these themes so that readers will be aware of these topics when they are revisited in later chapters. At the end of this chapter, the last three themes—devolution, privatization and managed care, and policy analysis and advocacy skills—are addressed in detail because they are so central to policy development and implementation.

First, there is not a uniform definition of the family in the United States. Because there is not a uniform definition of the family, policy has tended to address the traditional nuclear family—the so-called benchmark family—and ignore other types of family units. Moreover, as the changing demographics of families in the United States today show, it is inappropriate to equate the term *family* with the two-parent intact nuclear family. Thus, we have adopted a functional definition of the family, which is based on what families *do* to care for and support their members.

The second theme that emerged from our research is the lack of consensus on what constitutes family well-being. Trzcinski (1995) points out that although "consensus seems to exist across ideological lines for the most commonly cited goals of family policy," which are to strengthen and support families and ensure family well-being, "this consensus is illusory and exists only when the concepts of strengthening, support, and well-being are not explicitly defined" (p. 20). Differences occur because values are interconnected with how people view the world, and based on their values, people make assumptions about how family life is or should be. These value-based ideas about family well-being often come from the subjective life history or life experiences of people. Since everyone does not share the same life experience, it is often difficult to step outside these experiences and the values embedded in them to consider policy for various types of families in different situations. Consequently, when dominant ideologies permeate policies and programs, they may or may not be in the best interest of many families, especially in light of the great diversity in the makeup of families in the United States.

The third theme of the book is that a comprehensive set of family policies does not exist in the United States. The United States is one of the only countries in the world whose constitution does not specifically use the word *family* (Bogenschneider, 2002). Neither federal nor state governments have explicit sets of policies that are considered family policy. Although policy makers pass legislation that responds to specific issues, these policies do not provide a comprehensive vision of family well-being. Policy makers find it difficult to agree on what conditions constitute social problems, which factors contribute to them, what values should drive decisions, and how society ought to officially respond. Considering this lack of a comprehensive family policy, we take the view that *all policy is family policy*, since all policy affects families in one way or another. In saying this, we understand that some policies have an obvious direct effect on families, while other policies indirectly affect the family unit, and still other policies seem to have little or no effect. We espouse the idea that all policy is family policy in an effort to emphasize the importance of looking seriously at all policies to see the extent to which they support or assist families in all their diversity. We also believe that this is an important mind-set for students and policy practitioners as they seek to advocate for and work with families.

The fourth theme is the disagreement about how much the government should intervene in the private affairs of the family. Many policy makers feel the family should be outside the purview of policy, and family well-being should be regarded as a private matter. Given the current political propensity to control family privacy in areas such as abortion and same-sex marriage, this argument seems, at best, disingenuous. Nevertheless, the argument about the private sphere of the family persists because family policy implies regulation and intervention in family life.

The fifth theme is the question of whether family poverty and family problems are due to structural factors or individual behavior. Are family problems caused by circumstances outside one's control or the result of one's own doing? Historically, this debate is known in social work as the difference between those who are "deserving" and "undeserving" of help. During times of wide-ranging crisis such as the Great Depression or, more recently, the impact of Hurricanes Katrina and Ike or the nation's economic turmoil following the subprime mortgage crisis, there has been public recognition that many problems are outside the control of families. In situations such as this, public opinion turns in favor of government intervention and action. Federal, state, and local government policies and programs are viewed as essential to restoring the economy and attending to people's needs through social programs. But at other times and in less crisis–oriented situations, the notion that family functioning is the purview of the family takes hold politically, and the dominant view is that little or no government intervention is needed or appropriate.

Family policy making is all the more difficult because of the rapidly changing nature of the U.S. population. The sixth theme is that families are in flux, changing in demographics, structure, issues of diversity, and development over the life span. Some of these demographic trends and issues are discussed in this chapter, and also in later chapters. In addition, the changing structure of families over the life span makes it difficult to develop a standard, coherent body of family policy that takes the changing nature of the family into account. In turn, the changing nature of the family is affected by policy, by changes in social norms, and by external factors. What results is a complex policy analysis and policy development situation, in which the formulation of policies that are responsive to family needs and supportive of family well-being is very difficult. As Kay (2006) points out, "dynamic models of complex systems are much more difficult to construct than static ones. The difficulty arises because there are several processes . . . going on at the same time" (p. 1). Thus, just in terms of addressing the rapidly changing composition of families in the United States, family policy making is necessarily a dynamic process.

The debate over the auspices of policy development and implementation is the seventh theme. Should the federal government mandate uniform policy standards? Or should states have the final say about how policy will be implemented in the local context? This concept is referred to as devolution. Devolution is often framed as a state's rights issue, and the argument centers on whether it is constitutionally appropriate for the federal government to implement broad social policy objectives. Recent court decisions in such areas as civil rights and educational standards appear to have established that the federal government has such powers. Sometimes, the devolution argument is framed as whether a broad set of federal social policies is appropriate when local conditions within states may differ radically. The recent efforts of the federal government to allow states to develop programs in the areas of welfare, health care, and child welfare seem to be examples of this view. Although policies are often established at the federal level, through devolution they may be altered when states and local governments are given leeway to develop their own programs that implement the federal policy.

Privatization and managed care are the eighth major theme of the book. The privatization of programs and services occurs when government contracts for services with nonprofit and business corporations to implement programs and services. Managed care is a market-based method of rationing benefits and services, and this approach is often used as part of privatization. In today's world, privatization and managed care are often used by all levels of government to implement programs and services.

Later in this chapter, we look more closely at privatization and managed care, and in various chapters of the book, we discuss how these processes affect the implementation of family policies.

The ninth major theme of this book is the importance of policy analysis and advocacy. The dynamic nature of policy making requires policy analysis and advocacy skills, which are directly tied to practice. In the absence of critical analysis, only superficial knowledge of policy and its relationship to family well-being is possible. Social workers are positioned to advocate policy that is tied to the real experiences of the families experiencing problems or the effects of current policy on families. Without advocacy, it is unlikely that citizens, social workers, and other human service professionals will be able to bring about the changes needed to develop policies that support and assist families. Instead, policy change will likely take place as the result of some crisis or because of the influence of powerful interests who may or may not be focused on improving family functioning.

Because of their importance to the overall purpose of this book, we conclude this chapter by highlighting the last three major themes. First, we look at changing demographics and social trends that are greatly affecting today's families. This is followed by discussions of devolution, privatization, and managed care. Policy analysis and advocacy are briefly covered, leading up to more detailed discussions in chapter 2 and chapter 3. Finally, we discuss why it is important for social workers and other human service workers to understand the relationship between policy and practice.

Changing Demographics and Social Trends

The family is a fundamental social unit. Families produce, nurture, and protect children. They educate and socialize future adults. They care for the disabled and the aged. Families engage in work and production. These basic roles and functions of the family have not changed dramatically over time. But the way in which families carry out these roles and functions has changed at different times in history. In pre-agricultural hunting-and-gathering societies, the good of the community overshadowed the well-being of the family. In agricultural societies, the extended family played a central role in farming and property holding. With industrialization and mass production, people flocked to urban areas and traveled across oceans for new jobs. Many families were no longer living in their place of origin, where they could rely on the extended family or the local community for support. Likewise, the twentieth century brought many economic changes in the United States. The booms and busts of the Industrial Revolution gave way to the globalization of industries, and a shift to a lower-wage service economy. The gap between the rich and the poor increased. Whereas a family's income once came from a single wage earner, it is now common for both parents to have to work to make ends meet. With both parents working, the need for child care outside the home has dramatically increased.

Family structure is also dynamic. It changes over the course of its members' life span. For example, family structure changes with cohabitation, marriage, childbearing, divorce, remarriage or the decision to remain single, and widowhood. Family roles also change as families experience life changes in terms of childbearing and caregiving responsibilities, illness and health, and job loss and employment. Families shape and, in turn, are shaped by changes in social norms related to single parenthood, interracial families, families headed by gay and lesbian parents, grandparents raising grandchildren, and the growing elderly population. All these and other economic, social, and demographic factors cause changes in the family. The following section briefly looks at changing demographics and family trends that support the need to rethink what the term *family* means in the rapidly evolving social and economic structure that now exists in the United States. A consideration of these trends is important to the development of policies that support and assist all types of families in the United States.

Family Membership and Structure

The U.S. Census Bureau (2005b) reports that "Family households represented 81 percent of households in 1970 and 68 percent of America's 113.1 million households in 2005" (p. 1). Of the households counted in the United States, only slightly more than half (52%) were headed by married couples. It also reports that between 1970 and 2005, the number of married-couple families with children under eighteen fell from 40 percent of all households to 23 percent. and, in many of these families, one or both of the biological parents of the children who lived in the household did not live in the household. Although the majority of children live with two married parents, 26 percent of all children lived with a mother only, and 6 percent with a father only. The percentage of families with children headed by one adult increased from 11 percent in 1970 to 16 percent in 2003 (Fields, 2004). More than 5 million couples reported they were not married; however, it is likely that this is underreported. Single-mother families increased from 3 million in 1970 to 10 million in 2003, while single-father families increased from fewer than half a million to 2 million.

Childbirth among teenagers steadily declined between 1970 and 1990, but the number of births among unmarried women increased. As a result of this trend, the number of children living with a single parent increased. Much of the increase is due to older unmarried women having children, and increases in the divorce rate, which rose rapidly throughout the 1970s and 1980s before leveling off somewhat in the 1990s. Another major change in family composition is the increase in families headed by gays and lesbians. The American Civil Liberties Union (2005) estimates that 7.8 million to 10.4 million people (3–4% of the population) identify themselves as gay, but some researchers have estimated the gay population to be nearer to 10 percent of the total population. In the 2000 census, 1.2 million people (600,000 households) identified themselves as living with same-sex partners. Estimates suggest that between 1 and 9 million children live with one gay parent or more (American Civil Liberties Union, 2005). Same-sex partnerships, gay and lesbian parenting and custody, and adoption by gay and lesbian individuals are politically divisive issues. The courts and federal and state legislatures are grappling with the civil rights of gay and lesbian partners in employment, parental custody, hospital visitation, benefits, and financial matters.

An additional 3.9 million families are multigenerational households. Some consist of one parent or more, and grandparents and/or other relatives and children. In others, the parents of the children are absent. In 2003, there were 3 million sub-families—mainly multigenerational families consisting of elderly parents supporting their adult children and grandchildren, or young adults with children taking care of their parents (U.S. Census Bureau, 2005b). The number of grandparents raising grandchildren increased from 957,000 in 1970 to 1.4 million in 2003 (U.S. Census Bureau, 2005a). Another demographic trend is the increase of one-person households from 16.2 percent in 1970 to 26.4 percent of all nonfamily households in 2005 (U.S. Census Bureau, 2005b). Much of this increase in one-person households is accounted for by delays in marriage and greater life expectancy for the elderly.

Race and Ethnicity

Between 1990 and 2000, the overall U.S. population increased 13 percent. The number of Hispanics increased 57 percent, blacks 16 percent, Asians 52 percent, and Native Americans 16 percent, and the white non-Hispanic population increased 3 percent (U.S. Census Bureau, 2001). It is predicted that major population changes will occur by 2050. The white non-Hispanic population, which constituted 69 percent of the population in 2000, will make up only 50 percent by 2050. Blacks will increase from 13 percent to 15 percent of the overall population, and Hispanics from 13 percent to 24 percent (U.S. Census Bureau, 2004). The U.S. Census Bureau (2005b) released data in 2005 showing that "among people 15 and older in 2005, 56 percent of non-Hispanic whites and 58 percent of Asians were married and living with a spouse. . . . The proportion married and living with a spouse was 31 percent for Blacks and 46 percent for Hispanics" (p. 5).

Education

As the racial and ethnic composition of the population changes, it is likely that this will have an impact on individuals' levels of education. Education affects the life chances of individuals. In 2004, 87 percent of young adults age eighteen to twenty-four had obtained a high school diploma or a General Equivalence Diploma (GED). However, there were substantial differences by race and ethnicity. Ninety-two percent of whites held a diploma by age twenty-four, compared to 83 percent of blacks and 70 percent of Hispanics (Federal Interagency Forum on Child and Family Statistics, 2006).

Similar differences hold for college degrees. Twenty-eight percent of all U.S. adults attained a bachelor's degree by the age of twenty-nine in 2004. Thirty-four percent of college degrees were granted to whites. Blacks lagged behind at 18 percent, and Hispanics at 10 percent. These differences in educational attainment affect the ability of heads of households to support their families. Fifteen percent of all children have a parent who has not received a high school diploma. For children with foreign-born parents, that number increases to 43 percent. The income of individuals with a high school degree is almost double the income of those who drop out of high school, and on average, college graduates make more than double the income of high school graduates. Since families of color currently experience three times the rate of poverty as white families, a major increase in the ethnic and racial diversity of families has implications for family policy. In this changing demographic context, if there is no serious policy development in the areas of education and professional training, it is likely that a large proportion of families will experience increased economic stresses in the coming decades. This is cause for even more concern when one considers the negative trend toward inequality in the distribution of income and wealth, and the impact of globalization on income and job opportunities.

Devolution

Devolution is the process by which government establishes broad policies and then delegates, by statute or regulation, the responsibility for implementing and administering those policies to a lower-level governmental body or private entity. Devolution is a major force affecting the development of policies supporting family well-being in the United States. Because of devolution, federal influence over policies that have an impact on family well-being has diminished over the past three decades. Through devolution, states have assumed much of the responsibility for both policy creation and the implementation of family policy and programs. Devolution decentralizes government responsibility to the state or local level. Broad policy may be created at the federal level, but state and local governments have authority to shape—and the responsibility to partially pay for—social welfare services.

Devolution has its pros and cons. On one hand, it provides states with the opportunity to create innovative programs for families from a local grassroots perspective. Under the guidelines of broad federal mandates, states can tailor social policy and programs to local conditions. On the other hand, by relinquishing responsibility to the states, the federal government is limited in guaranteeing entitlement, or the rights of individuals to assistance through state-specific programs and policies. Moreover, the tradeoff is that although states have more decision-making authority, less money comes from the federal government to fund programs. The result is that some states are more progressive in their support for families, while others invest less in family programs and services.

The budget for funding many of the programs that assist families is funneled down to states and local governments through federal departments. Often funds are distributed through block grants or through grants to and/or contracts with public agencies and private for-profit or nonprofit organizations. A block grant is an intergovernmental transfer of money from the federal government to a regional or local body. Within general guidelines established by Congress and the executive branch, block grants give discretion to local bodies in the way that the money is spent. Block grants are commonly used to fund health, education, child welfare, community development, and many other types of programs. Opponents argue that block grants reduce the federal government's responsibility for social welfare, while proponents argue that block grants allow state and local governments to better assess local needs. Another criticism of block grants is that strong federal oversight is needed to ensure equity and fairness in the distribution of resources. Historically, most federal programs were funded by matching state and federal funds, but the process of devolution has increased the use of block grants. While there are drawbacks to both of these strategies, they do provide opportunities for social workers to influence policy development close to home. Since devolution brings decision-making authority down to state and local governments, social workers and other human service professionals have greater access to decision makers.

Privatization and Managed Care

Another important trend is the privatization of service delivery. Through privatization, programs are operated by for-profit and nonprofit organizations rather than by government agencies. Privatization can result from devolution or direct funding by federal, state, or local governments. Privatization is based on the belief that private corporations are more innovative, efficient, and effective in providing services than government bureaucracies. Like devolution, privatization presents its own set of political challenges. As the privatization of services has increased, a whole host of agencies have received government funds, and this has increased the complexity of the service delivery system. Critics challenge the movement toward privatization, especially when contracts for social services are given to large for-profit organizations. By definition, a for-profit organization is one that expects to make a profit that will be funneled back to the owners or shareholders of the company or corporation. The assumption is that for-profit corporations increase profits by reducing services or raising fees—both of which may negatively affect potential service users. Cost reduction also implies fewer available services, a dilemma that is at the very heart of the for-profit controversy. A recent example of how privatization can negatively affect service delivery relates to for-profit companies that own nursing homes. According to Duhigg (2007), "By many regulatory benchmarks, residents at those nursing homes are worse off, on average, than they were under previous owners, according to an analysis by *The New York Times* of data collected by government agencies from 2000 to 2006. The *Times* analysis shows that . . . many other nursing homes acquired by large private investors have cut expenses and staff, sometimes below minimum legal requirements."

Managed care is often related to privatization. Managed care is a market-based approach to service delivery that attempts to contain costs by targeting and rationing services. Companies and nonprofit corporations use managed care as a financial accountability method when they sign a contract for services with government. Managed care is widely used in many areas of family policy, including health care, mental health services, and child welfare.

Policy Analysis and Advocacy

Despite the complications of privatization and managed care, there are many opportunities for advocacy within organizations that contract for services with government agencies. Many policies can be changed at the agency level, particularly since so much decision making is left to the agency responsible for implementing government-funded programs or services. Thus, advocates may focus on changing the practices of an agency based on the organization's policies, which may or may not be formalized. Often policy is informal—that is, based on the culture of the organization, traditional ways of doing things, or the agency's desire to standardize delivery of services, regardless of the diversity of needs of the population being served (Ezell, 2001).

Advocacy that is not based on a critical analysis of the policies or issues affecting families can lead to the development of ineffective or misguided interventions. In chapters 2 and 3, we spend some time explaining policy analysis and advocacy. According to Meenaghan, Kilty, and McNutt (2004), there are two traditions in policy formation. One tradition relies heavily on a rational problem-solving approach, while the other stresses the impact of political forces and power. A rational approach to policy making is based on the assumption that scientific inquiry will provide policy makers with unbiased information about problems and possible solutions for family problems. Research will provide information that is inclusive of all family forms, and policy makers will use this information to make decisions. If this assumption were always true, then a rational approach to policy decisions would be sufficient. In reality, however, it is nearly impossible to account for all of society's values, take all possible policy alternatives into account, weigh the consequences of each alternative for all groups affected, and make a rational decision about which policy options are best.

An alternative view is that policy making is not a very rational process. Policy making is, rather, primarily a political process. For example, studies commissioned by the legislative and executive branches of government—and to a lesser extent the judicial branch—are often totally ignored by policy makers. This happens even when studies are based on fact finding and rational analyses of the options and possible solutions to the problems (e.g., Brodkin & Kaufman, 2000; Quinn & Magill, 1994). Indeed, there is rarely consensus about the problems confronting society and what, if anything, should be done about them. DiNitto (2006) contends that political conflict raises questions about how rational policy decisions can really be made in a society where few values are agreed on by all, and whose members cannot always agree on what the problems actually are, and when policy makers and elected officials may be more interested in reaping rewards for themselves, such as power, status, or reelection.

Issues of power and status in the policy-making arena are extremely important to the dynamics of the policy process. How do problems and issues get on the public agenda? Who has power in the policy-making process? What special interests do they represent? Can these interests be divorced from the policy-making process? Karger and Stoesz (2007) suggest that since the 1970s, social welfare policy has largely been shaped by values that emphasize individualism, work, and the unregulated use of the market rather than on a rational set of assumptions guided by reliable research. The interests being served by the values inherent in a given policy decision are important because these dictate the way in which services are delivered and resources are distributed. If social policies are shaped by the values of those in power, then it is possible to define problems according to the beliefs and values of largely privileged individuals who tend to look at issues from the perspective of people with similar resources, education, and opportunity structures. Certain values are seen as optimal, and if families deviate from the norm, their problems are seen as either less important or created by their own individual shortcomings. Welfare reform is a good example of this. Although the ultimate goal of welfare reform was to move people off welfare and into work, the kinds of jobs available and the necessity of a living wage associated with the work were not a top priority. Health benefits and access to affordable quality day care were also secondary considerations at best. Thus, although the *need* may be defined rationally, the *values* of different actors shape how the problem is defined, and how the solution is viewed when a policy is proposed. Who gets what—and how they receive it—becomes largely a discussion of who is at the table and who is making the decision. It is also important to understand that forces beyond the control of the policy makers may play a major role in determining what policies can be developed.

The Relationship between Policy and Practice

It is important for social workers to understand the limitations that policy puts on practice and the ways in which policy and practice are inextricably connected. The topics in this book are used to explore the challenges that workers confront when assisting families. Our discussions attempt to make explicit the connection between practice with families and the wide range of policies that inform, guide, and regulate that practice. Every day social workers and other human service workers experience the limitations of policy as they assist families to maneuver their way through a fragmented system of policies and programs dealing with separate yet overlapping problems. Often the family is not the focus of the policy. Rather, individuals with presenting problems are the focus, and the family unit is considered secondarily, or not at all.

Thus, without an understanding of how policy shapes practice and ways to advocate better services, helping professionals are likely to experience powerlessness and frustration in their work (Lewandowski, 2003). Understanding the linkage between policy and practice is not enough. Workers need information on how to analyze policy and how to advocate for families, both individually and systemically. And before they become active in advocacy, social workers need to feel a sense of efficacy (Hamilton & Fauri, 2001). This book presents skills for analyzing policies and programs, and for advocating for families at multiple levels of the organizational and political spectrum. Taken together, the various chapters of the book provide not only conceptual tools for understanding and analyzing family policy, but also practical skills for advocating and developing policies that value the family in all its diversity.

For Further Reading

Albrecht, G. (2002). *Hitting home: Feminist ethics, women's work, and the betrayal of family values.* London: Continuum.

Descartes. L. (2008). *The changing landscape of work and family in the American middle class: Reports from the field.* Lanham, MD: Lexington Books.

Hawkins, R. L. (2005). From self-sufficiency to personal and family sustainability: A new paradigm for social policy. *Journal of Sociology and Social Welfare, 32*(4), 77–92.

Jones, R. P., & Cox, D. (2006). *American values survey.* Retrieved July 23, 2009, from http://media.pfaw.org/pdf/cav/AVSReport.pdf

May, P. J. (1986). Politics and policy analysis. *Political Science Quarterly, 106*(3), 453–477.

McMillen, J. C., Morris, L., & Sherraden, M. (2004). Ending social work's grudge match: Problems versus strengths. *Families in Society, 85*(3), 317–325.

Sherraden, M. S., Slosar, B., & Sherraden, M. (2002). Innovation in social policy: Collaborative social policy. *Social Work, 47*(3), 209–221.

Wiseman, D. G. (Ed.). (2008). *The American family: Understanding its changing dynamics and place in society.* Springfield, IL: Charles C Thomas.

REFERENCES

American Civil Liberties Union. (2005). *Too high a price: The case against restricting gay parenting.* Retrieved May 7, 2006, from http://www.aclu.org/Files PDFs/thap2005.pdf\

Bogenschneider, K. (2002). *Family policy matters: How policymaking affects families and what professionals can do.* Mahwah, NJ: Lawrence Erlbaum.

Brodkin, E. Z., & Kaufman, A. (2000). Policy experiments and poverty politics. *Social Service Review, 74*(4), 507–532.

DiNitto, D. (2006). *Social welfare: Politics and public policy* (6th ed.). Needham Heights, MA: Allyn & Bacon.

Duhigg, C. (2007, September 23). At many homes, more profit, less nursing. *New York Times.* Retrieved September 25, 2007, from http://www.nytimes.com/2007/09/23/business/23nursing.html?ex=1348200000&en=ba37662b895c6589&ei=5088&partner=rssnyt&emc=rss

Early, T. J., & GlenMaye, L. F. (2000). Valuing families: Social work practice with families from a strengths perspective. *Social Work, 45*(2), 118–130.

Ezell, M. (2001). *Advocacy in the human services.* Belmont, CA: Wadsworth.

Federal Interagency Forum on Child and Family Statistics. (2006). *America's children in brief: Key national indicators of well-being, 2006.* Retrieved May 7, 2007, from http://childstats.gov/americaschildren/edu.asp

Fields, J. M. (2004). *America's families and living arrangements: 2003* (Current Population Reports P20-553). Washington, DC: U.S. Census Bureau. Retrieved May 7, 2006, from http://www.census.gov/prod/2004pubs/p20-553.pdf

Hamilton, D., & Fauri, D. (2001). Social workers' political participation: Strengthening the political confidence of social work students. *Journal of Social Work Education, 37*(2), 321–332.

Karger, H., & Stoesz, D. (2007). *American social welfare policy: A pluralist approach* (5th ed.). Boston: Allyn & Bacon.

Kay, A. (2006). *The dynamics of public policy.* Northampton, MA: Edward Elgar.

Lewandowski, C. (2003). Organizational factors contributing to worker frustration: The precursor to burnout. *Journal of Sociology and Social Welfare, 30*(4), 175–185.

Meenaghan, T. M., Kilty, K., & McNutt, J. (2004). *Social policy analysis and practice.* Chicago: Lyceum Books.

Quinn, L. M., & Magill, R. S. (1994). Politics versus research in social policy. *Social Service Review, 68*(4), 503–520.

Trzcinski, E. (1995). An ecological perspective on family policy: A conceptual and philosophical framework. *Journal of Family and Economic Issues, 16*(1), 7–33.

U.S. Census Bureau. (2001). *Table 1: Population by race and Hispanic or Latino origin, for all ages and for 18 years and over, for the United States: 2000.* Retrieved May 7, 2006, from http://www.census.gov/population/cen2000/phc-t1/tab01.pdf

U.S. Census Bureau. (2004). *Table 1a: Projected population of the United States, by race and Hispanic origin: 2000 to 2050.* Retrieved May 7, 2006, from http://www.census.gov/ipc/www/usinterimproj/natprojtab01a

U.S. Census Bureau. (2005a). *CH-7. Grandchildren under age 18 living in the home of their grandparents: 1970 to present.* Retrieved May 7, 2006, from http://www.census.gov/population/socdemo/hh-fam/ch7.pdf

U. S. Census Bureau. (2005b). *Families and living arrangements in 2005.* Retrieved March 1, 2008, from http://www.census.gov/population/pop-profile/dynamic/FamiliesLA.pdf

Zahn, D., Hirota, S., Garcia, J., & Ro, M. J. (2003). Valuing families and meeting them where they are. *American Journal of Public Health, 93*(11), 1797–1799.

CHAPTER 2

Policy Dynamics and Family Policy Analysis

In a complex industrialized country such as the United States, the unequal distribution of resources means that some families need more support than others. When families are unable to develop resources and need help doing so, the lack of government involvement in family life puts pressure on family systems. Families are expected to care for their young without adequate or accessible day care. They are expected to obtain self-sustaining jobs in a job market that relies on low-wage employment. They are expected to stay healthy without health care. To understand problems such as these, policy practitioners use tools known as policy analysis frameworks. These frameworks guide them in analyzing policy, presenting alternative proposals, and advocating policy change. This chapter provides two frameworks for policy analysis—the multiple-streams framework for understanding the dynamic processes of policy making, and a modified framework for family impact analysis for understanding the effect of policies on family functioning.

This chapter begins with a discussion of how social problems are identified and defined by a society. To understand the ways in which problems, values, power, and politics interact as part of the dynamic processes of policy making, we review the multiple-streams framework based on John W. Kingdon's (2003) work in political science and public policy. His research provides insights for understanding how problems, policy, and power are joined together in the process of creating sometimes unexpected and often quite unpredictable policy outcomes. The multiple-streams framework provides some explanation of the dynamic process of developing policy solutions and explains the seemingly unplanned and unpredictable nature of policy development. Why do some issues get on the policy agenda and others never make it? Who or what influences policy, and when and how?

Kingdon's work helps us understand and analyze the sometimes illogical, often confusing, potentially inaccurate, and relatively ambiguous side of policy development. Here we provide a policy analysis tool that we call guidelines for policy research. These guidelines underscore the role that power, politics, and values play and guide students as they prepare for advocacy in the dynamic environment of policy making and policy implementation. The guidelines use the multiple-streams framework to organize the process of gathering information.

The last half of the chapter features a modified version of family impact analysis, which is based on the work of Karen Bogenschneider at the Policy Institute for Family Impact Seminars at the University of Wisconsin–Madison. In contrast to the analytical frameworks listed in the suggested readings at the end of this chapter, family impact analysis is unique in its ability to take the social environment into consideration and analyze and evaluate policy in terms of its relationship to family functioning. By examining the effect of policies on the family unit and taking into account the complexities and the diversity of various family forms, family impact analysis puts families and the way that they experience policies at the center. To help students and practitioners understand the importance of analyzing policy from a family-centered perspective, we discuss the social construction or the meaning of policy from the viewpoint of those most affected by the problem and its policy solutions. We believe family impact analysis will give students and practitioners a grasp of the impact of policy on the family. Such information can be used to educate policy makers and create or revise and improve policies that promote healthy family functioning.

Problems, Values, Power, and Politics

The process of understanding social problems and developing policy solutions is not an exact science. Problems, values, power, and politics come into play in the imperfect world of policy development. Despite evidence that may be available about the untoward effects of a social problem or the negative effect of a certain policy on families, voters and decision makers are influenced by how a social problem is defined, and the values, power, and politics at play in selecting a policy solution. Values are not separate from power, power is not separate from politics, and politics is based on values. All interact within and across the spectrum of policy-related activities—from problem definition and advocacy to the passage of legislation, and throughout implementation. Values, power, and politics play a part in the multiple, ongoing, and sometimes simultaneous events that occur during the policy-making process. The interaction of these three rudimentary elements in policy development creates a dynamic, and a somewhat unpredictable, course of action. The reader may wonder how these factors can be separated in enough detail so that we can understand the distinct role of problems, values, power, and politics, and at the same time, the dynamic interaction among them. We start at the place where policy analysis begins: defining the problem.

Defining the Problem

What is a social problem? In a classic article, Herbert Blumer (1971) offers a theory about the nature of social problems that is still relevant today. Writing from a social psychology perspective, he contends that social problems are *time, place, and context bound*. A social problem does not exist unless it is recognized as such by society. Many dire social conditions go unnoticed by society, and even noticed problems sometimes fail to gain social recognition. In addition, a problem is acknowledged or not acknowledged as a social problem in different cultures, locales, regions, or nation-states, and at different points in time or history. Social problems go through a process of *collective definition*—that is, society (the public) identifies and gives meaning to social problems.

The theoretical idea that social problems are time, place, and culture bound is built on three major points. First, social problems always exist as a fact of collective behavior. This means that social issues such as poverty, juvenile delinquency, or child abuse, for example, *always* exist in society to a greater or lesser degree. Second, a given social issue must be recognized as a public problem. This means that recognition of the problem must reach some level of public consciousness. This may occur, for example, when a social problem (1) affects a significant number of people, (2) affects a number of significant people (power holders, heroes, celebrities), or (3) threatens mainstream or middle-class lifestyles.

Another part of the public definition of social problems is that they move in and out of public consciousness—that is, public interest in a given social issue ebbs and flows. An issue comes into public consciousness and retreats from public attention to reappear when events lead to a "new" or increased public recognition of the problem. Like the tide, a problem recedes from public consciousness when society views the problem as dealt with or solved at some level. At later times, the problem can resurface and is recognized again as a social problem when new information brings it to the attention of the public, or other factors push it into public awareness.

This approach to understanding social problems differs from the typical idea that social problems exist as objective conditions as dysfunctions, pathologies, and deviances, which are intrinsically harmful to society. If it were possible to identify social problems objectively, then entirely rational means could be used to identify the conditions that cause problems and proposals could be developed to solve them. Unfortunately, rational thought cannot adequately detect problems because, for example, some dysfunctions and deviances are tolerated, while others are not. In addition, standardized benchmarks are inadequate when it comes to identifying a problem as a social problem in one country or culture as opposed to another, or during different time periods. Another flaw in the rational assumption that social problems exist as objective conditions is that the type and characteristics of persons and rates of incidence or prevalence are related to whether society considers a given situation a problem. Finally, an objective definition of a social problem assumes that identifying the problem and describing it will lead to effective and remedial treatment. Thus this definition of the nature of social problems draws a fine line between public health and social problems in terms of the solution. Polio and smallpox, for example, fall in the public health category because of the development of vaccines. On the other hand, diseases such as HIV/AIDS are seen as social problems, in part because of the ways in which the virus is transmitted, and because no medical cure has been found. In addition, an objective approach to defining social problems also ignores the reality of value conflicts and power plays among various interest groups that see problems differently. For example, an analysis of the current global financial crisis reveals numerous examples of special interest groups and powerful individuals stalling efforts to prevent the abuses taking place in the subprime mortgage markets. Berner and Grow (2008) report that in 2003, the attorneys general of Iowa and North Carolina "traveled to Washington with a stern warning for the nation's top bank regulator" (p. 36). Their efforts and the efforts of groups throughout the country were essentially rebuffed by federal and state officials, who saw their concerns to be in conflict with federal policy encouraging homeownership.

Understanding the collective process by which society comes to define a given issue as a social problem is the first step in understanding the dynamic process of policy analysis. Values lie at the heart of defining and analyzing social problems. The values of society are the ground upon which an issue either emerges to be identified as a social problem or fails to gain attention from society. Thus, a preliminary step in defining a social problem is clarifying the values held by dominant and minority groups in society, and analyzing whether these values support identification of the issue as a social problem. Clarifying values means becoming familiar with the way in which issues that go against or concur with traditionally held values will be perceived. If society's values are in a state of flux or alteration, social issues may be compatible with or contradict values held by the majority of the public.

Thus, the emergence of a social problem depends on different factors—usually a combination of factors—that align the issue with the values held by the society's power holders. Sometimes conflict brings an issue to the forefront through agitation, violence, or nonviolent protests. Attention from the media, endorsements by celebrities and charismatic leaders, political campaigns, voters, policy analysis, and advocacy by interest groups, organizations, and government bureaucrats all play a role. However, each problem context is different—bound by time, culture, and the place of society—and the policy solutions proposed by power brokers also are different.

The same problem can also be defined at different times in history. Take, for example, the problem of homelessness, which emerged as a "new" social problem on America's streets in the mid-1980s. If we define homelessness as a lack of shelter, we can identify groups of people throughout American history who did not have a place to live. Table 2.1 shows how people without housing were defined differently during different periods of American history. At times of economic prosperity in the years following World Wars I and II, blame was laid upon the individual for his or her problem, but during the Great Depression, for example, blame was laid upon the structure of society. In more recent U.S. history, the term *homeless* was neutral in terms of placing blame, but only at this point in history was federal legislation passed to deal with the social problem defined as homelessness.

What we can be sure of in this dynamic environment of defining and redefining social problems is that once a social problem is defined, professions, bureaucracies, and service systems develop around the problem area. According to Gusfield (1989), social problems are a unique product of the modern welfare state:

> The idea of "social problems" is unique to modern societies. I do not mean that modern societies generate conditions which are problem-laden and cry for reform and alleviation while primitive and preindustrial ones do not. I do mean that modern societies, including the United States, display a culture of public problems. It is a part of how we think and how we interpret the world around us, that we perceive many conditions as not only deplorable but as capable of being relieved by and as requiring public action, most often by the state.

POLICY DYNAMICS AND FAMILY POLICY ANALYSIS   23

Table 2.1 Defining Homelessness as a Social Problem in the United States

	Colonial Period (1700s)	Civil War (1860s)	Progressive Era (1890–1912)	Great Depression (1920s–1940s)	Post–World War II (1950s)	Social Movements (1960–1970s)	Reagan Era (1980s)	Economic Expansion (1990s)
Who was affected?	Widows Orphans Mentally ill Disabled Victims of Indian Wars	Unemployed men Orphans Victims of cholera epidemic	Unemployed single men Disabled, Alcoholics The elderly Unwed mothers	Unemployed single men Families with children Youths	Unemployed single men Alcoholics	Unemployed single men Runaway youths Battered women	Unemployed single men Runaway youths Battered women Mentally ill Vietnam veterans Bag ladies Single mothers with children	Unemployed single men Runaway youths Battered women Dually diagnosed Middle-aged women People of color
Who was considered to be homeless?	Worthy poor	Tramps (men "tramping" home from Civil War)	Unworthy poor	The unemployed	Skid Row bums	Deviants Hippies Abused women Runaways Children who were kicked out of their homes	People who did not have a place to live	People who did not have a place to live
Whose fault was it?	No one's	The system's	The individual's	The system's	The individual's	The system's	No one's	No one's
What was the service delivery response?	Outdoor relief Families paid by local governments to take in the needy	Indoor relief Institutional care (asylums, orphanages, workhouses, poorhouses)	Ethnic and religious institutions City missions	Federal funding for local shelters City planning Public job programs (CCC, WPA, TVA, REA)	Skid Row: (cheap hotels, flophouses) Salvation Army, Full Gospel missions	Skid Row Runaway shelters Safehouses	Emergency shelters Transitional housing Housing vouchers	Emergency shelters Transitional housing

The concept of "social problem" is a category of thought, a way of seeing certain conditions as providing a claim to change through public actions. (p. 431)

Table 2.1 also shows the societal responses that occurred through the development of institutions, services, and policies to serve homeless persons throughout U.S. history. Gusfield (1989) refers to those professions that serve social problems as the "troubled persons" professions, which "live *off* social problems as well as *for* them." These include "counselors, social workers, clinical psychologists, foundation administrators, operators of asylum-like centers, alcohol rehabilitation specialists, researchers, and the many jobs where the task is to bring people who are seen as trouble to themselves or to others into the stream of 'adjusted' citizens" (p. 432). Defining drunkenness as alcoholism, for example, required the development of a body of knowledge and people with the skills and knowledge to help alcoholics. Treatment centers and recovery systems were developed, and all these institutions required a group of people to administer these programs and services. The same can be said of juvenile delinquency with its juvenile justice system, domestic violence and battered women's shelters and services, and abused children and the foster care system. Morgan (1980) refers to this process as the *depoliticizing* of problems, in which the psychologizing or medicalizing of phenomena emphasizes the individual's role in the problem rather than the structural or institutional role of society in contributing to the problem. Others such as Frances Fox Piven and Richard Cloward (1977) and Gerald Rothman (1984) have written classic works on the social control function of social welfare institutions.

The Dynamic Policy Process

Once a social problem is defined by society, the problem itself, alongside values, power, and politics, plays a role in creating dynamic processes that surround and permeate policy making as society attempts to deal with the problem. The challenge is sorting out these dynamics and, at the same time, showing how they interact. In policy analysis, this is part of understanding how long-standing policies came to be and new ones are developed. Sorting out the policy process is not easy. The policy arena is not static. It is dynamic. Policies change, and the process of policy change and development starts and stops. There are false starts. There are episodic advances, setbacks, and setbacks or advances again. There are times when new policies seems to appear or policies change—as if by political magic—without a long, drawn-out advocacy effort. These ambiguities and complexities occur across the legislative, regulatory, and implementation continuum.

John W. Kingdon's (2003) pioneering work, *Agendas, Alternatives, and Public Policies,* provides a policy analysis model that sheds light on the role that values, power, and politics play in the complex and ambiguous process of policy making. Kingdon's model starts with the assumption that much more is known about existing legislation than is known about how that legislation came to be. He is not referring to what might be called the history of the policy; he is referring to the process that brought the policy idea to the attention of policy makers in the first place. How did the policy issue get on the public agenda? How did the policy solution turn into "an idea whose time [had] come"? Kingdon sees the whole of policy making as a set of processes that range from setting the agenda and specifying policy alternatives from which to choose to decision making by an authoritative body such as the legislature and implementation. His work focuses, however, on the first two: setting the agenda and choosing between policy alternatives.

How do policy ideas get on the public agenda? Three things contribute to this: an increase in problems that strain the system; the cumulative effect of knowledge offered by academics or other types of policy specialists; and political processes such as election promises, public opinion polls, and changes in administrative officials. Each of these three areas—problems, policy proposals, and politics—operates as a separate stream. Thus, the model of analysis is typically referred to as the multiple-streams framework. These multiple streams all play a role in generating specific policy proposals:

> Ideas float around in a "policy primeval soup" in which specialists try out their ideas in a variety of ways—bill introductions, speeches, testimonies, papers, and conversation. In that consideration, proposals are floated, come into contact with one another, are revised and combined with one another, and floated again. But the proposals that survive to the status of serious consideration meet several criteria, including their technical feasibility, their fit with dominant values and the current national mood, their budgetary workability, and the political support or opposition they might experience. Thus the selection system narrows the set of conceivable proposals and selects from that large set a short list of proposals that is actually available for serious consideration. (Kingdon, 2003, p. 21)

Policy players who affect this process include those inside and outside government. Participants inside the federal government include the president, cabinet officials, political appointees and bureaucrats serving in the executive arm of government, elected officials serving in the legislative branch, and the Supreme Court and other judges and officials working in the judiciary. Participants outside government are academic researchers, the media, interest groups, policy think tanks, lobbyists, political parties, and the public. Whether located inside or outside government, those actively attending to the policy problem through research, policy analysis, legislative proposals, or advocacy are called the policy community.

Proposals, policy alternatives, and solutions—which are influenced by all these actors—float about in what Kingdon (2003) calls "policy streams." "In contrast to a problem-solving model, in which people become aware of a problem and consider alternative solutions, solutions float around in and near government, searching for problems to which to become attached or political events that increase their likelihood of adoption" (p. 172). A "policy window" opens, often unexpectedly—or to put it another way, the agenda changes, and suddenly for a short time, there is an opportunity for policy development or policy change. At this point, advocates seize the moment and try to create a change in public policy. Policy windows are often unpredictable and exhibit a sort of illogical randomness, particularly when openings come about because problems in the "problem stream" escalate or events in the "political stream" occur. When a policy window opens, these dynamic processes connect problems to solutions, and vice versa. Solutions previously associated with one problem become the solution for another problem; problems previously associated with a given solution become the problem attached to a different solution. One participant in this process offered insight into this arbitrariness:

> Government does not come to conclusions. It stumbles into paradoxical situations that force it to move one way or another. There are social forces that you can identify, but what comes out of them is just accident. . . . Which idea gets struck by lightning, I can't tell you. I've been watching this process for twenty years and I can't tell you. I can't tell you why an idea has been sitting around for five years, being pushed by somebody, and all of a sudden it catches on. Then another idea with the same kind of advocates, being pushed for those five years, won't catch on fire. You have an element of chance. (p. 189)

Policy entrepreneurs are at the heart of these dynamic processes that couple problems with different solutions and vice versa. Policy entrepreneurs can be found within and across the entire policy-making arena. They are lobbyists, elected officials, advocates, and ordinary citizens. Entrepreneurs are always championing their policy proposals; their voices are heard. They push and pull. Most of all, policy entrepreneurs do their homework. They have analyzed existing policies and developed alternative proposals. When the policy window opens, they are ready with policy proposals in hand to mobilize other actors, such as the media, voters, interest groups, and government officials.

The opening of the policy window is somewhat predictable when legislation comes up for renewal, so policy entrepreneurs in government are well positioned to modify existing legislation, write regulations, or attach new policy to broader pieces of legislation. For example, in the 1980s, in a case that illustrates the dynamic processes behind the passage of legislation to aid the homeless, members of the House of Representatives were policy entrepreneurs who held congressional committee meetings in shelters and soup kitchens to draw attention to the issue.

> The federal homeless policies have really been a result of the efforts of policy entrepreneurs within Congress, particularly the House leadership, Congressman Bruce Vento, Congresswoman Mary Rose Oakar, Senator Slade Gordon, and Housing Chairman Henry Gonzalez. These "entrepreneurs" have generally been responsible for generating the policy alternatives which eventually were adopted and for linking these proposals to broader pieces of legislation which would be accepted. These efforts were not the self-maximizing actions which would characterize the policy formulator described in the political science literature. [This] suggests that the notion of legislators offering policies in exchange for electoral support and/or power and prestige is too simplistic and that the existence of federal legislation to aid the homeless is a result of legislators' personal, moral commitments to assisting the homeless and willingness to invest political resources in legislative proposals which would do so. (Arnold, 1989, p. 56)

Kingdon's model has been applied as an analytical framework by health and education scholars in areas such as health insurance flexibility accounts (Laraway & Jennings, 2002), health coverage for Medicaid-eligible children (Sardell & Johnson, 1998), school reform in Chicago (Lieberman, 2002), and provision of preschool for all children in Illinois and California (Kelly, 2005).

Zahariadis (2007) provides an excellent summary of the multiple-streams framework, which is based on Kingdon's original work, as well as the subsequent work of other policy analysts who have modified it for domestic and foreign policy analysis. He discusses several important concepts that have been used to critique and refine the multiple-streams framework "to explain the entire process of policy formation" (p. 80). He also points out that there is *interdependence* among the multiple streams. For example, in the case of the Bush administration's War on Terror, sometimes there is a search for a rationale to justify the policy, and the policy solves no problems:

> Edelman (1988) goes so far as to argue that solutions create problems. Consider for example, the decision in 2003 by the Bush administration to go to war in Iraq. Whereas the initial rationale had to do with what was claimed to be the clear and imminent danger posed by Saddam Hussein's possession of weapons of mass destruction, subsequent rationalizations emphasized connections with terrorists, the liberation of Iraq, or democratization and nation building. The solution remained the same—depose Saddam—while the problem constantly drifted in search of an anchor. As insiders (such as Paul O'Neill, President Bush's former Secretary of the Treasury, and Richard Clarke, former counter-terrorism czar) later pointed out, the administration was fixated on Saddam long before the attack (Suskind, 2004; Clarke, 2004). The question was not whether, but when and how to do it.... If many policy analysts readily accept the assumption that people don't have to be rational—they only need act *as if* they are rational—they can also accept the assumption that streams don't have to be independent—they only need flow *as if* they are independent. (Zahariadis, 2007, pp. 81–82)

Preparing for the Open Window: Guidelines for Policy Research

Policy entrepreneurs need to be ready to act when a policy window opens. The window opens only for a short time, and even then, the opportunity for policy change is short lived. What can advocates do to be ready when the policy window opens? Being ready means doing one's homework—understanding the problem and policy area in detail, building relationships within the policy community, and developing proposals with policy options—in advance of the opening of the window.

To help students understand what it means to be ready for the opening of the window and subsequent policy change, we developed the guidelines for policy research (box 2.1), from Newton's (2007) case study assignment. Our experience in the classroom suggests that the guidelines help students untangle the dynamic processes at play in a policy area that interests them. The guidelines put students in touch with the policy community at work on

Box 2.1 Preparing for the Open Window:
Guidelines for Policy Research

Guideline 1: Policy Research from Academic and Government Resources

Purpose: Guideline 1 is designed to help you identify key sources of information in your chosen policy area. It will also help you decide which policy topic you want to focus on for your policy analysis assignment. The steps outlined will help you begin to focus on the issues in the policy area that you have chosen. **To begin:** Select a policy topic in consultation with the instructor. Your topic should be related to a social problem or issue related to family well-being.

Develop an annotated bibliography, in which references are formatted in APA style and each reference is followed by a short summary (100–200 words). Your annotated bibliography should include the following materials:

1. Academic Policy Resources: Academics and researchers play a role in policy making through policy research and program evaluation. Go to the library and find four articles from academic journals, book chapters, or books that discuss the problem or issue you have chosen. Be sure to include books and articles that consider the policy issues involved in your selected problem area.
2. Government Resources: Government also plays a role in policy making through research, official reports, and legislation. Identify the relevant government agencies, state and federal legislative bodies, and judicial decisions that are involved in the policy area. Identify two or more relevant government reports, documents, or laws related to your policy area.
3. Summary of Policy Issue: Based on the academic and government material that you have reviewed, write down your initial ideas in the area of policy that you have selected.

Guideline 2: The Policy Community: Policy Institutes, Media, and Internet

Purpose: Guideline 2 will help you understand policy making by those outside academia and government who advocate for different policy directions. **To begin:** Use the Internet to identify three to five groups that make up the policy community outside academia and government.

Identify and discuss the activities of the groups you have chosen. These groups supply information and also monitor the policy field.

1. Policy Group Presence on the World Wide Web: Groups can include nonprofit organizations, policy institutes, professional associations, informal groups, and business or labor associations. Include an international organization that is involved in the policy area. The media (newspapers, magazines, radio, and television) is also part of the policy community. Identify five groups that hold different views of the policy issue you have selected.
2. Media Accounts: Has this policy area been in the news recently? Why or why not? Locate and summarize at least two newspaper or popular magazine articles. Radio interviews, blogs, and film documentaries and other media reports also may be used.
3. The Nature of Each Group: In one or two paragraphs, outline the basic facts about each group or organization, including its location and Web site address. How is the group organized, who supports it, and how is the organization funded? Add a list of relevant reports or documents from each group or organization to your working bibliography.
4. Each Group's Stance on the Policy Issue: Summarize the position that each group takes in relation to the policy. Note differences in the policy views held by different groups or organizations. Which group or organization has had the most influence in shaping policy?
5. Analysis of Policy Stance: Compare the information that you obtained from the policy institutes, the media, and the Internet to the information you found in books, journal articles, and government documents. How do the views of policy institutes or the media challenge, affirm, or provide a complementary argument to the views held by those in academia and government?
6. Refining the Policy Analysis: Taking into consideration the new information you have obtained, refine your understanding of the policy issue. Refine the focus of your policy analysis. Note any information that may be important for you to obtain through further research.

Guideline 3: Policy History and Evaluation

Purpose: Guideline 3 will help you understand the background or history of your selected policy area. It will also help you explore the ways in which policy is evaluated. **To begin:** Examine the academic books and journals, government documents, and materials that you gathered from the Internet, the media, and policy institutes and organizations for information on the history of the policy, and the ways in which the policy is evaluated. Note the policy's relationship to families, including the effect of the policy on poverty, women versus men, people with disabilities, special populations, and other vulnerable groups.

Summarize the basic history of the policy. Indicate the ways in which the implementation of the policy has been monitored and evaluated.

1. History of Government Policy: What has been the basic chronology of events that led to the development of the policy? If your policy area is not official government policy, outline current issues or events that may bring the problem or policy issue to the attention of policy makers. Summarize two key government reports in your policy area and show how they shaped or are shaping the policy area.
2. Aggregate Spending: Is funding information available in your policy area? Is information available on trends in funding in the policy area or its programs? If information is available, provide summary tables or graphs for spending in the policy area or programs related to the policy area. Provide an analysis of funding or gaps in funding in relation to your policy area.
3. Evaluation Measures: Identify the types of statistical measures or other types of evaluation that are used to monitor the implementation of the policy. What does evaluation show about the outcomes of the policy or its performance? What is not known about the implementation of the policy? Briefly summarize issues related to evaluation in your selected policy area.
4. Situating Policy in the Global Context: Identify and briefly outline the way in which globalization, global policies, or the policies of other countries affect the policy area.

the issue, and this demystifies what is going on in the policy area. Students gain an understanding of the work of academic researchers, advocates, and policy analysts in think tanks, and past and current legislation, executive orders, and judicial decisions. Particularly important is the requirement to explore liberal and conservative views and values in a given policy area, because understanding opposing values, beliefs, and policy views is important when one is developing defensible policy alternatives. Overall, the guidelines help students begin a systematic process of gathering information and understanding the dynamic processes of policy making. Students gain an understanding of the kind of research and analysis process carried out by a government researcher, a practitioner in a human service agency, or an analyst working for a policy institute or a citizen group. As will be discussed in chapter 3, using the guidelines to gather information is also a first necessary step in planning an advocacy campaign.

Guideline 1 provides a view of the selected policy area from academic and government sources. This involves obtaining material from academic resources such as journals and books, and from government documents such as reports, legislation, and court decisions, and developing an annotated bibliography of major books, articles, and reports on the policy topic. An initial hypothesis or policy argument based on these sources forms the basis of a beginning understanding of the policy area and issues.

Guideline 2 provides more of a real-time view of the policy than is typically available from academic and government sources. Here, the use of the Internet provides a bird's-eye view of the role of the policy community in shaping public policy. Understanding the policy community means investigating the place and policy positions of the media, political parties, citizen groups, membership associations, advocacy organizations, and foundations. As students begin to see the ways in which conservatives and liberals approach the same issue from different values and power bases, policy institutes and think tanks emerge as enormously important actors within the policy community. Debates and commentaries by local, state, and federal officials, as reported in the news media, blogs, and other Web sites, are important in understanding the values and ideologies that critically affect policy making. Guideline 2 also details how to evaluate the content of Web-based material. A supplementary book that is particularly useful for comparing and contrasting liberal and conservative views is *Conservative Social Welfare Policy: A Description and Analysis* by Leon Ginsberg (1998).

Guideline 3 helps students develop a detailed understanding of the background of the policy, a chronology of its history, and its outcome. Guideline 3 challenges students to look at aggregate spending levels and evaluation measures that apply to the policy area. Basic components include assessing aggregate spending levels and statistical measures used to evaluate policy outcomes, deciphering budget allocations, and looking up implementation rules and regulations that apply to current policy. For example, this guideline might help students understand how devolution, privatization, and funding reductions have fundamentally changed the way the policy has been implemented since the beginning of the welfare state in the United States in the 1940s. Finally, guideline 3 challenges students to understand the selected policy area in relation to globalization and the policies of other countries.

These guidelines for policy research are exercises to help students develop a position paper arguing for or against a certain policy. At the conclusion of each guideline, students are asked to develop and refine their policy hypothesis or argument. The final result is a position paper with a defensible argument for policy development or change. Individuals working in the family policy field must develop convincing arguments, and also the ability to defend those arguments. Since arguments are defended through evidence, not simply through people's opinions or assertions, the guidelines help students develop arguments and draw on research findings to support specific policy decisions. This must be done, however, with the understanding that evidence is often not sufficient for policy change. As illustrated by the multiple-streams framework, agenda setting and policy alternatives are driven primarily by values, power, and politics.

We turn our attention now to the importance of developing policy that is responsive to family well-being. It is important that students, policy analysts, and policy entrepreneurs consider the impact of proposed and existing policies on family functioning. To address this, we have selected family impact analysis as the second framework for family policy analysis and advocacy.

Family Impact Analysis

As we indicated in chapter 1, we believe that, in essence, every policy is family policy. Health, education, housing, transportation, the environment, social services, the tax system, trade and labor policy, and economic policy all affect family well-being. Family impact analysis critically examines the past, present, and probable future effects of a policy, program, or service on family stability, family relationships, and family members' abilities to carry out their responsibilities. It examines how program goals may be counterproductive by inadvertently producing negative consequences for families. Family impact analysis can be differentiated from other types of policy analysis because the framework keeps the family at the center. This method assesses policy from a family perspective and judges the effects of policies and programs on family functioning and family well-being. It identifies which types of families may be affected differentially by policies and programs. Family impact analysis recognizes that policy created by the dominant culture may indeed undermine the subjective health and well-being of families not belonging to dominant groups in society. It can also be used to assess how implementation of federal regulations or agency policies affects families. The method also allows for an examination of the pressures exerted on families from a variety of sources, including policies that are not normally considered to directly influence families, such as labor market shifts and trade policies (Rocha & Strand, 2004).

Families as Social Systems and Subjective Realities

In order to undertake family impact analysis, one must have an understanding of families as social systems and their objective and subjective realities. How do families perceive the systems with which they interact? How do they understand the pressure exerted on them by policies and institutions that lie outside the family system? Looking at families as social systems is a helpful way to begin to conceptualize the varying layers of institutions and policies with which families interact. According to Zimmerman (1995), family systems theory looks at families as systems composed of interdependent components in interaction with each other and the environment. All systems are characterized by four basic properties: task performance, interdependence of their component parts, boundaries, and equilibrium and adaptive tendencies. Table 2.2 shows these four properties and how they relate to families as a social system.

Table 2.2 Families as a Social System

Properties of Systems Theory	Families as Social Systems
Tasks are performed to meet the needs of family members and the larger environment.	Tasks performed by families include care of members, procreation, socialization, social control, morale and motivation, and production and consumption.
All parts of the family system are interdependent.	Family relationships are based on shared values and normative expectations, which vary by social class and culture.
Boundaries differentiate systems from one another and their environment.	Boundaries are the demarcation lines that separate the family system from its environment (e.g., schools, religious organizations, work).
Equilibrium and adaptive tendencies ensure system viability.	Equilibrium and adaptive tendencies include a range of possible states in which families can function and adapt. Environmental conditions affect all systems: resources, culture, economy, violence. Specific conditions shaping family systems are policies and programs in child care and health insurance, and other policies that assist in family well-being.

The level of effectiveness at which a family can perform within its social system depends, in part, on its stage in the life cycle. Different life cycle stages interact differently with the environment. From an ecological perspective, the relationships that families have with their environment are like a balance within a circle of relationships. Within the circle, the integration of these relationships means that "nothing in the circle can change without every other thing in the circle changing" (Trzcinski, 1995, p. 10). If the environment changes, the quality of family life also changes. Families and their environments cannot be considered apart from one another, and families develop through interactions with their environments. Environments also present families with challenges that threaten their equilibrium and adaptive capacities. Thus, policies create environmental conditions that affect how easy or how difficult it is for families to live and thrive. When policy fails to consider the interrelationships between families and their environments, it may unequally affect families within and across different cultures and classes, because family policy exists within society as an ideal and stems from the values of those who make decisions. From an ecological perspective, however, those undertaking policy analysis should understand the diversity that exists among families and how the dominant culture disparately affects the environments faced by families.

Symbolic interaction theory can be used to understand family functioning. Symbolic interaction deals with a person's subjective experience within the context of objective reality. People live in a symbolic as well as a physical environment and acquire in their minds complex sets of symbols known as cognitive frameworks. According to symbolic interaction theory, if a person defines his or her situation as real, it is real in its consequences. Through interactions with their environments, families form a conception of themselves, which is tied to the community and larger society. Early socialization experiences are also very important in shaping adult attitudes. The context in social interaction refers to culture and places families in a society with others on the basis of characteristics unique to certain people. Culture is both a subjective and objective expression of self, subsuming racial and ethnic rituals, symbols, language, and ways of behaving (Zimmerman, 1995). Situations are significant for the subjective meaning a situation has for families, including family policies and programs. Since families live in symbolic as well as physical environments, both of these environments give subjective meanings to policies and programs.

Symbolic interaction relates to our discussion of family policy by directing us to look at the ways in which families perceive policies and programs and their effects. If families do not perceive a policy or program as contributing to their well-being, then it doesn't. Some scholars question symbolic interaction theory's assertion that there is more than one "objective" reality. However, these scholars fail to tell us who decides which reality is objective and which is subjective. For example, the dominant cultural reality may not be the objective reality faced by all families.

The Social Construction of Knowledge

Few dispute the notion that meaning is produced through social construction (Glassner, 2000). But what is constructed, and what is objective? Politicians, the media, advocacy groups, and other organizations help construct the meaning of social phenomena—but in each case, reality is based on the experiences of those who participate in the construction of meaning. Whether families affected by policies are included in the political, media, or advocacy groups that construct policy is the question. Those in power may be so affected by the dominant culture that it is difficult for them even to know what questions should be asked. Nevertheless, there are real costs to having only partial and distorted knowledge. First, learning from groups outside the mainstream of policy making helps one realize the partiality of one's own perspective. Second, misleading and incorrect knowledge leads to poor social analysis and "the formation of bad social policy—policy that then reproduces, rather than solves, social problems" (Anderson & Collins, 2001, p. 15).

Uehara, Sohng, Bending, Seyfried, Richey, Morelli, and associates (1996) suggest that researchers must be constantly aware of how their own values, beliefs, behaviors, and customs may distort communication and promote domination. Therefore, constant introspection and self-reflection are essential. This goes beyond simple reflection on cultural differences to a critical analysis of the social, political, and cultural forces that maintain patterns of intergroup domination and inequality. It also means including those who represent different cultures, races, ethnicities, sexual orientations, and family lifestyles in the critical analysis of social policy. Advanced policy analysis also takes a social constructionist approach in reframing social problems and related policies. A good example of such a theoretical discussion is an article called "The Feminizing of Neglect," which takes race and gender into account in observing how child care is constructed and the possible feminizing of child neglect (Turney, 2000). Another scholarly article looks at how the social problem of divorce has been constructed by organizations promoting conservative values as a moral breakdown of society, with children as victims. Coltrane and Adams (2003) discuss how this construction of divorce masks the issue of gender inequality in contemporary society.

How might the world be different if policy makers were to acknowledge and value the experiences and thoughts of those typically excluded from mainstream policy discussions? This question reflects the importance of taking into account the differential impact of the experiences of families who have been traditionally excluded from power. Many groups whose experiences have been vital to the formation of American society have been left behind in the construction of knowledge. The result is that our knowledge is distorted and incomplete (Anderson & Collins, 2001). In order to reconstruct knowledge so that it is inclusive of more than the "objective" reality of the dominant culture, the experiences of marginalized and excluded groups should be placed at the center of policy analysis. When this is not done, marginalized groups are typically judged by the experience of the dominant society, rather than understood on their own terms. This establishes a false norm by which all groups are judged. Such exclusionary thinking is increasingly being challenged by scholars and teachers who want to include the diversity of human experience in the construction and transmission of knowledge. When the experiences of excluded groups are made more visible and central in the construction of knowledge, the policy perspective shifts toward a better understanding of the intersection of race, class, and gender in the experiences of all families, including those with privilege and power. By shifting the center, policy makers are more likely to create policy that serves the best interests of a diverse array of families. This kind of policy making is more feasible than before because of advances in technology. For example, on January 29, 2009, his first full day in office, President Barack Obama signed a memorandum on transparency and open government to make the work of government more transparent, accountable, and responsible to the people of the United States. The Open Government Initiative Web site encourages the participation of ordinary people from all walks of life to help develop open government policy. The online process of brainstorming is followed by discussion and results in the collaborative crafting of policy proposals. The initiative promises to reflect a great diversity of ideas and perhaps shift the center of policy making toward the lived experiences of people (White House, 2009).

The Eight Steps of Family Impact Analysis

Family impact analysis is useful for analyzing policy through the eyes of families in need of a policy solution. The framework helps analysts look at how families understand policies and their effects. Family impact analysis is based on the work of Karen Bogenschneider and Heidi Normandin, who direct the Policy Institute for Family Impact Seminars at the University of Wisconsin. The Web site of the institute (http://familyimpactseminars.org)

provides many resources on family impact analysis, including sample analyses using the framework to assess various policies and their effects on family well-being, and a detailed policy analysis tool by Ooms (1995). The Web site includes over one hundred briefing reports and newsletters written specifically for state policy makers, and more than twenty reports written for federal policy makers. There is also policy impact data, a checklist for family impact analysis, and more than one hundred links to policy Web sites that help bring a family perspective to policy making. What is unique about the work of Bogenschneider and her colleagues is their effort to hold family impact seminars for state legislators, governors, legislative aids, and agency staffers, and to schedule them at times she calls "sensitive periods," when policy change is likely to happen due to pending legislation. In Wisconsin, for example, a family impact seminar, "held the day before the vote on Wisconsin's welfare reform legislation, attracted 28 state legislators.... One legislator remarked that the seminar helped him decide how to vote and that he was able to use information from the seminar in the assembly floor debate the next day" (Bogenschneider, Olson, Linney, & Mills, 2000, p. 332). The critical point of scheduling such seminars is based on the theoretical concepts of Kingdon's work outlined in the previous section of this chapter.

Our modified framework for family impact analysis based on the work of Gross, Bogenschneider, and Johnson (n.d.) and Spakes (1983) is shown in box 2.2. To clarify the various components of analysis, we identify eight steps involved in the process. First, the problem is examined to ascertain the types of affected families, and the effect on family well-being. In general, policies are selected for analysis because a problem has been identified. In this context, the term *social policy* includes all government and agency actions that affect any part of the family system, family relationships, and families' quality of life. The boundary of family policy encompasses "all actions, large and small, formal and informal, intentional or unintentional, which directly or indirectly affect the health, welfare and economic well-being of families" (Spakes, 1983, p. 53). Therefore, policy analysis can encompass policies, programs, regulations, agency procedures, and program evaluation. This is why the definition of the problem is so important. In order to assess what specific policies are affecting the problem, it must be defined in somewhat narrow terms.

Once the problem is identified, the analyst must obtain a deep understanding of the policies related to the problem. Policy clarification covers the origin of the policy; its history, original goals and purpose, and level of origination; and the impetus for its creation. Policy practitioners also

Box 2.2 Family Impact Analysis

STEP 1: PROBLEM ANALYSIS

A. The type of family or group affected
B. The ways in which the type of family or group is affected

STEP 2: POLICY OR PROGRAM SELECTION AND DESCRIPTION

A. The history of the policy/program
B. The policy/program intent (i.e., its stated and unstated goals and purposes)
C. How the policy/program was created and at what level of government

STEP 3: THE IMPLEMENTATION PROCESS

A. Rules and regulations
B. Resources and funding mandates
C. Other critical factors
   1. Agency characteristics
   2. Political conditions
   3. Economic and social conditions

STEP 4: EXAMINE THE SOCIAL ENVIRONMENT

A. Social and economic changes occurring independently
B. Conditions that may directly or indirectly interact with the policy/program

STEP 5: ANALYSIS OF FAMILY FUNCTIONS

A. Family types being affected by or using the policy/program (e.g., two parent, single parent, child-free)
B. Life stages of families being affected by or using the policy/program
C. Other family system characteristics
   1. Demographic characteristics of families
   2. Economic characteristics of families
   3. Characteristics of neighborhoods/communities in which families live

STEP 6: ANALYSIS OF IMPACT ON FAMILY FUNCTIONING

A. Family functions potentially affected by the policy/program
   1. Family structure and membership
   2. Effect of the policy/program on four main family functions: family creation, economic support, child rearing, and family caregiving

> B. Family well-being measures used to measure the impact of the policy/program
>   1. Health/mental health indicators
>   2. Economic distress indicators
>
> **STEP 7: ANALYSIS OF IMPACT**
>
> A. Select most appropriate questions and principles
> B. Select methods of quantitative analysis and/or methods of qualitative analysis
> C. Gather, review, and analyze data
>
> **STEP 8: DEVELOP POLICY/PROGRAM IMPLICATIONS**
>
> A. Assess likely effects of the policy or program on different types of families
> B. Evaluate the implementation process of the policy or program
> C. Indicate the potential impact of the policy or program as experienced by families
> D. Make policy/program recommendations
> E. Disseminate results to policy makers or practitioners who can apply the results to policy and program implementation

need to understand the implementation process. Often overlooked as a part of policy analysis, implementation is important because it often changes the original intent or purpose of the policy. Written standards or rules and regulations that outline and clarify how the enacted policy is to be implemented should be reviewed. Often, rules and regulations appear in the form of executive orders that define how the administrative arm of government understands the policy and intends to implement it. These orders, rules, and regulations may elaborate on the original policy, alter its intent, or change it in some other way. For example, agencies of the executive branch of government such as the U.S. Department of Health and Human Services and the Department of Education must transform the policy into a workable program. They issue rules and regulations for states to follow in order to implement the enacted legislation. When policies are developed that require resources, but sufficient resources are not allocated, this is called an unfunded mandate. If the agency lacks sufficient resources to implement the policy, the original intent may be subverted or altered.

As shown in table 2.2, family impact analysis is really distinguished from other forms of policy analysis and program evaluation by its examination of the social environment and its analysis of family function (step

4 and step 5). The analyst looks directly at conditions in the environment that may affect family functioning and takes into account social changes that may be occurring independent of the policy. Related conditions are other factors in the social environment that interact with the policy, or that act independently to produce impacts mistakenly attributed to policy. A well-constructed family impact analysis must take into account the social and economic environment outside the actual policy area. For example, shortly after the passage of the Personal Responsibility and Work Opportunity Reconciliation Act in 1996, the U.S. economy experienced a major economic expansion. Many people who had exited welfare were able to get jobs. Although the expansion was unrelated to the new policy, reformers lauded the numbers of welfare recipients who found jobs. When the boom was over in 2001 and the country experienced increased unemployment and more instability in the labor market, many welfare recipients lost their jobs and again had to rely on government assistance (Jindal & Winstead, 2002). Was job attainment due to welfare reform, economic expansion, or a little of both? In this case, family impact analysis could be used to tease out which outcomes were related to welfare reform, and which to an upswing in the economy.

The analyst must also examine the way in which the policy affects family functioning, including anticipated or possible effects. A list of possible indicators or measures can be used to evaluate the types of families most likely affected by a given policy. These indicators could be family structural issues, or positions in the life cycle of socially or financially vulnerable families. Impacts could include financial stress, changes in family membership, or changes in relationships or nurturance. Independent or intervening factors affecting the impact of policy on families could be internal family relationships, informal social networks, or neighborhood environments. These are only a few of the potential outcomes and family factors that can be accounted for by family impact analysis.

At this point, the analyst assesses the potential outcomes on family functioning and family well-being that can be attributed to the policy or program. Here it is important to consider the impact of the policy on the four major areas of family functioning: family creation (e.g., marriage, divorce, bearing children, adoption, and foster care), economic support, child rearing (socialization for the next generation), and family caregiving (e.g., family assistance for those with disabilities or in ill health, and the elderly). For example, the policy could cause financial stress, changes in family structure or relationships, changes in the physical and mental health of family members, or changes in the family's ability to care for its members. Next, the family policy analyst is ready to choose the most appropriate questions and methods to assess the policy's impact. Both qualitative assessments and quantitative indicators of the social environment and family functioning can be employed. Qualitative methods can include interviews and focus group discussions. For quantitative research, the policy or program is the independent variable, while relevant factors in the social environment and within the family are covariates. Specific impacts on the family must be narrowed down so that they can be used as the dependent variables in quantitative analysis. Sometimes existing research can be used to analyze the potential impacts of programs or policies on families, and at other times, original research must be conducted.

At this point, family impact analysis is carried out much like a program evaluation. However, whereas program evaluation looks at whether the stated program goals and objectives are being met, family impact analysis focuses on the effects of policies on families (Bogenschneider, 2002). It also focuses on the family, the interrelatedness of policy with the family, and the impact of policy on the family. With data and the overall analysis in hand, the researchers can then use this information for advocacy in policy making and policy implementation. Results are shared with relevant stakeholders, policy analysts, legislators, consumers of services, the media, program directors, and others. This involves publishing results and making recommendations for policy change or building support for current policy.

Overall, family impact analysis is a useful tool for assessing the impact of policy on family functioning and well-being. For example, using the previous example of welfare reform, it is possible to examine how the implementation of welfare reform (step 3) affects family well-being (step 6). The analyst might start by looking at work requirements for welfare recipients and thus focus the analysis on working families. Understanding how welfare implementation has affected working families requires taking several related variables into account, including unemployment rates, wage rates, and the availability of day care (step 4). The analysis would look at whether the welfare-to-work families are headed by single parents or dual-earner couples, and the number of children in the home (step 5). It would also assess the impact of welfare reform on family well-being by examining specific family-level characteristics, such as the relationships between spouse and children, and whether the family has adequate income for the basic necessities of food, clothing, and housing (step 6). Family impact analysis tries to assess the potential benefits to and/or stressors on the family system that result from the policy. Instead of simply assessing welfare-to-work policy based on the number of families who leave the welfare rolls or simply gain employment, the analysis focuses more generally on family well-being (step 7).

At this point, students and family practitioners are probably thinking, "How can I use this framework?" The analysis model presented here can easily be utilized by agencies, advocacy groups, and community organizations. There is often a need for an expert in analysis that requires quantitative or qualitative methods, but even so, analysts must be aware of their assumption of authority and expertise and be willing to take a backseat to the community. Government statistics from the Census Bureau and the Bureau of Labor Statistics are easily found on the Internet. Statistics are already analyzed in tables and summary reports. Depending on the policy and the problem, much may have been written on the subject, statistics already published, and outcomes noted for families in a given locale. It may be a matter of putting it all together to present in a way that makes sense to decision makers.

Agencies can also take the lead in facilitating family impact analyses with stakeholders, board members, and local leaders. Change can take place at many levels of government; it does not have to be at the federal level. Many decisions that affect families come from the local level: city council, boards of education, planning commissions, and the like. Local family impact studies are important because they are somewhat more likely to be used, especially when community leaders and advocates are involved in the process. The likelihood that a policy brief will influence a policy decision increases as the distance between decision makers and families decreases (Spakes, 1983). The real challenge is following the guidelines for family impact analysis—keeping the family at the center of the analysis so that the issues, indicators, and impacts that reflect the diversity of the community are at the forefront.

Summary

The way in which a social problem is defined and the interests served by differing definitions of the problem are important in policy analysis. In order to account for the role of problems, policy solutions, and politics in the policy-making process, family policy analysis requires a dynamic perspective. Issues of values and power—as well as what interest groups and other stakeholders inside and outside government stand to gain or lose—must be taken into account. This chapter presented the multiple-streams framework as a way of understanding the course of interaction among problems, policy solutions, power, and politics in the setting of public policy agenda. Guidelines for policy research were presented to guide students in gathering and organizing information for policy practice and policy analysis. It is important to analyze policy from the perspective of families, who may perceive policies and programs differently than policy makers or political power holders. A modified family impact analysis was offered for analyzing complex social problems, and for helping legislators understand the differential impacts of policy on different types of families. Family impact research can also be used by communities and neighborhoods to provide information and advocate policy alternatives at local and state levels. The next chapter provides specific strategies for persuading decision makers to utilize the results of policy analysis.

FOR FURTHER READING

Amy, D. J. (1984). Why policy analysis and ethics are incompatible. *Journal of Policy Analysis and Management, 3*(4), 573–591.

Bogenschneider, K. (1995). Roles for professionals in building family policy: A case study of state family impact seminars. *Family Relations, 44*(1), 5–12.

Caputo, R. K. (1989). Integrating values and norms in the evaluation of social policy: A conceptual framework. *Journal of Teaching in Social Work, 3*(2), 115–131.

Copeland, V., & Wexler, S. (1995). Policy implementation in social welfare: A framework for analysis. *Journal of Sociology and Social Welfare, 22*(3), 51–68.

Durning, D. (1993). Participatory policy analysis in a social service agency: A case study. *Journal of Policy Analysis and Management, 12*(2), 297–322.

Gormley, W. T., Jr. (1987). Institutional policy analysis: A critical review. *Journal of Policy Analysis and Management, 6*(2), 153–169.

Juviler, P., & Stroschein, S. (1999). Missing boundaries of comparison: The political community. *Political Science Quarterly, 114*(3), 435–453.

Lightfoot, E. (2003). The policy transfer model: A tool to help social workers engage in successful policy making. *Social Policy Journal, 2*(1), 21–34.

Lind, A. (2004). Legislating the family: Heterosexist bias in social welfare policy frameworks. *Journal of Sociology and Social Welfare, 31*(4), 21–35.

McPhail, B. A. (2003). A feminist policy analysis framework: Through a gendered lens. *Social Policy Journal, 2*(2–3), 39–61.

Meenaghan, T. M., Kilty, K., & McNutt, J. (2004). *Social policy analysis and practice.* Chicago: Lyceum Books.

Policy Institute for Family Impact Seminars. (2000). *Checklist for assessing the impact of policies on families.* Retrieved December 18, 2008, from http://www.familyimpactseminars.org/fi_checklist_aipf.pdf

Shulock, N. (1999). The paradox of policy analysis: If it is not used, why do we produce so much of it? *Journal of Policy Analysis and Management, 18*(2), 226–244.

Stone, D. A. (1989). Causal stories and the formation of the policy agenda. *Political Science Quarterly, 104*(2), 281–300.

Stout, K. E., & Stevens, B. (2000). The case of the failed diversity rule: A multiple streams analysis. *Educational Evaluation and Policy Analysis, 22*(4), 341–355.

References

Anderson, M., & Collins, P. (2001). Shifting the center and reconstructing knowledge. In M. Anderson & P. Collins (Eds.), *Race, class, and gender: An anthology* (4th ed., pp. 13–21). Belmont, CA: Wadsworth.

Arnold, C. A. (1989). Beyond self-interest: Policy entrepreneurs and aid to the homeless. *Policy Studies Journal, 18*(1), 47–66.

Berner, R., & Grow, B. (2008, October 20). They warned us: The watchdogs who saw the subprime disaster coming—and how they were thwarted by the banks and Washington. *Business Week*, pp. 36–42.

Blumer, H. (1971). Social problems as collective behavior. *Social Problems, 18*, 298–306.

Bogenschneider, K. (2002). *Family policy matters: How policymaking affects families and what professionals can do*. Mahwah, NJ: Lawrence Erlbaum.

Bogenschneider, K., Olson, J. R., Linney, K. D., & Mills, J. (2000). Connecting research and policymaking: Implications for theory and practice from the Family Impact Seminars. *Family Relations, 49*(3), 327–339.

Clarke, R. (2004). *Against all enemies*. New York: Free Press.

Coltrane, S., & Adams, M. (2003). The social construction of the divorce "problem": Morality, child victims, and the politics of gender. *Family Relations, 52*(4), 363–372.

Edelman, M. (1988). *Constructing the political spectacle*. Chicago: University of Chicago Press.

Ginsberg, L. (1998). *Conservative social welfare policy: A description and analysis*. Chicago: Nelson Hall.

Glassner, B. (2000). Where meanings get constructed. *Contemporary Sociology, 29*(4), 590–594.

Gross, E., Bogenschneider, K., & Johnson, C. (n.d.). *How to conduct a family impact analysis*. Retrieved April 25, 2008, from http://www.familyimpactseminars.org/fi_howtocondfia.pdf

Gusfield, J. R. (1989). Constructing the ownership of social problems: Fun and profit in the welfare state. *Social Problems, 36*(2), 431–441.

Jindal, B. P., & Winstead, D. (2002, June). *Status report on research on the outcomes of welfare reform*. Washington, DC: U.S. Department of Health and Human Services. Retrieved May 8, 2006, from http://aspe.hhs.gov/hsp/welf-ref-outcomes02/index.htm

Kelly, B. (2005, March). *John Kingdon's theory at the state level: A look at preschool for all in Illinois and California* (CROCUS Working Paper No. 5). Retrieved September 4, 2007, from http://www.crocus.georgetown.edu/reports/CROCUSworkingpaper5.pdf

Kingdon, J. W. (2003). *Agendas, alternatives, and public policies* (2nd ed.). New York: Addison-Wesley.

Laraway, A. S., & Jennings, C. P. (2002). Health Insurance Flexibility and Accountability Demonstration Initiative (HIFA): A policy analysis using Kingdon's policy streams model. *Policy, Politics & Nursing Practice, 3*(4), 358–366.

Lieberman, J. M. (2002). Three streams and four policy entrepreneurs converge: A policy window opens. *Education & Urban Society, 34*(4), 438–450.

Morgan, P. (1980). The state as mediator: Alcohol problem management in the postwar world. *Contemporary Drug Problems, 9,* 107–136.

Newton, J. (2007). *Policy case study.* Retrieved May 23, 2007, from http://www.yorku.ca/jnewton/Assignments.htm#overview

Ooms, T. (1995, October). *Taking families seriously: Family impact analysis as an essential policy tool.* Washington, DC: Family Impact Seminars. Retrieved May 4, 2008, from http://www.familyimpactseminars.org/pf_fis02suppreport.pdf

Piven, F. F., & Cloward, R. (1977). *Poor people's movements.* New York: Vintage Books.

Rocha, C., & Strand, E. (2004). The effects of economic policies and employment assistance programs on the well-being of displaced female apparel workers. *Journal of Family Issues, 25*(4), 542–566.

Rothman, G. C. (1984). *Philanthropists, therapists, and activists.* Cambridge, MA: Schenkman.

Sardell, A., & Johnson, K. (1998). The politics of EPSDT policy in the 1990s: Policy entrepreneurs, political streams, and children's health benefits. *Milbank Quarterly, 76*(2), 175–205.

Spakes, P. (1983). *Family policy and family impact analysis.* Cambridge, MA: Schenkman.

Suskind, R. (2004). *The price of loyalty.* New York: Simon and Schuster.

Trzcinski, E. (1995). An ecological perspective on family policy: A conceptual and philosophical framework. *Journal of Family and Economic Issues, 16*(1), 7–33.

Turney, D. (2000). The feminizing of neglect. *Child and Family Social Work, 5,* 47–56.

Uehara, E., Sohng, S., Bending, R., Seyfried, S., Richey, C., Morelli, P., et al. (1996). Toward a values-based approach to multicultural social work research. *Social Work, 41*(6), 614–621.

White House. (2009). *Open government initiative.* Retrieved July 21, 2009, from http://www.whitehouse.gov/Open/

Zahariadis, N. (2007). An assessment of the multiple streams framework: Structure, limitations, prospects. In P. Sabatier (Ed.), *Theories of the policy process* (pp. 65–92). Boulder, CO: Westview.

Zimmerman, S. (1995). *Understanding family policy* (2nd ed.). Thousand Oaks, CA: Sage.

CHAPTER 3

Advocating for Families

Chapter 1 of this book provided an overview of the overarching environment of family policy and a discussion of demographic trends related to families in the United States. Chapter 2 presented two approaches for analyzing family policy: the multiple-streams framework, which accounts for the dynamic processes of policy development, and a policy framework for family impact analysis. This chapter focuses on advocacy. Advocacy is part of the lifeblood of effective service delivery and policy making. We begin with a discussion of advocacy from three perspectives. First, we briefly look at an ongoing debate about the role of advocacy as a tool of service delivery. In discussing the advocacy roles of social workers and other human service workers, we examine the long-standing cause-versus-function debate on the role of the profession. We address the questions, Should social work's primary role be one of active engagement in social reform and policy change? Or should social work's primary role be one of helping improve the functioning of persons and families in society? In the context of this debate, we examine different levels of practice and the place where advocacy fits in the continuum of service delivery and policy making. Client-centered (or case) advocacy and policy practice (or class advocacy) are two forms of advocacy that are used to support or change policy in various settings.

Planning an advocacy campaign is the focus of the middle section of this chapter. Here we present a strategic planning method for mounting advocacy efforts by students, citizen groups, organizations, community coalitions, and others. Many different skills and tactics can be used as part of an advocacy campaign. Although a full discussion of advocacy skills and tactics is beyond the scope of this book, we present those that we think are central to an organized advocacy effort. We cover the politics of persuasion, task forces and coalitions, lobbying, print media, and activism on the Internet. The concluding part of this chapter discusses the development of policy practice, which we see as an important advancement in breaking the historical deadlock created by the cause-versus-function debate.

The Debate over the Role of Advocacy

A fundamental question behind much of the debate about advocacy in social work is what the role of the profession should be. Stripped to its bare essence, the question is whether the primary social work role should be taking on a cause for reform or helping people function in society by dealing with their emotional, behavioral, and interpersonal issues. Should the focus be on advocating change in organizational, governmental, and societal systems that negatively affect individuals, families, and larger groups in society? Or should the focus be on changing the client, whether the client is an individual, family, or group?

The issue, known as the cause-versus-function debate, has gripped the profession since its beginning. Porter Lee's (1937) book *Social Work as Cause and Function* started the debate. An overview of this ongoing debate can be found in an excellent article by Mimi Abramovitz (1998) entitled "Social Work and Social Reform: An Arena of Struggle." Other useful sources are Abramovitz and Bardill (1993) and Jarvis (2006). In terms of family policy, Karen Haynes (1998) summarizes the issue very well:

> "What do private troubles have to do with public issues?" We must define private troubles as public issues right now. . . . Does it make any sense for clinicians to spend hundreds of hours to keep a family together, only to watch public policy rip them apart again? Is it reasonable to work to empower parents to address the issues facing them and then leave them with outdated and punitive policies that may destroy them? If we are willing to devote everything it takes to keep a family functioning and intact, then we must also be willing to turn our efforts to advocacy in the political arena. (p. 504)

A vivid example of what Haynes is talking about is immigration policy. Under current policy, any child who is born in the United States is automatically a citizen and has the right to stay in the United States. But if the parent of the child is living illegally in the United States, the parent can be deported, while the child is eligible to remain in the United States. In cases of children born to one parent who is a U.S. citizen and one who is not—whether they are married or unmarried at the time of the child's birth—parents and children can be separated. Take the case of Janina Wasilewski. As a student activist in the Polish Solidarity labor movement, she feared the police and took refuge in the United States in 1989. She applied for asylum, but by the time immigration authorities took up her case in 1994, Poland was no longer classified as politically unsafe. Wasilewski claims that she did not understand what she was doing when, through her lawyer, she promised to leave the country voluntarily. Over the next thirteen years, she married, gave birth to a son, and started a home cleaning business in the Chicago suburbs. According to an article in the *Chicago Tribune*, "Wasilewski tried to correct her immigration status in 1998, but that only put her back on the government's radar, leading to the deportation proceedings that culminated in her tearful departure from O'Hare International Airport" (Hundley, 2007, p. 12). Her Polish émigré husband was given citizenship a few weeks afterward. The Wasilewski couple decided that Janina should take their six-year-old son with her to Poland. Although immigration policy requirements were met, the disruption of family life was severe and unwarranted. Some policies, although designed to solve one set of social problems, work against family well-being.

Haynes argues that there is a need to define private troubles as public issues by quoting Harry Specht, whose book *Unfaithful Angels: How Social Work Has Abandoned Its Mission* (Specht & Courtney, 1995) challenges the direction of social work education and practice:

> If we, as a country, are to solve our major social problems, we must focus our efforts on the primary source of those problems—on the community, or perhaps more correctly, on the absence of community in American lives. To develop healthy communities we must build community systems of social care that will eradicate highly fragmented social services, education, child care, public health, recreation, job training and development, and criminal justice arrangements. The major objective of such a system will be to help Americans to learn to live with, care for, and love one another. That is a very tall order. But it is a mission worthy of and appropriate for our profession. (Haynes, 1998, p. 508)

The cause-versus-function debate has an effect on social work education and the type of skills students take with them when they graduate. For example, the Alliance for Children and Families is an organization with the mission of strengthening the capacity of 350 nonprofit child-and-family organizations to serve and advocate for children, families, and communities. A recent Alliance report found "that many agencies have difficulty recruiting new social workers to work in community centered programs. More than 60 percent of the agencies surveyed felt that MSW and BSW graduates were not adequately prepared for community work. Factors contributing to these deficits include curricula overly focused on individuals and not enough on understanding families and the role of community in their lives, as well as faculty who are uninvolved in field education and unfamiliar with new community strengthening approaches" (Johnson, 2004, pp. 320–321). An overview of the levels of service delivery illustrates the importance of advocacy across all areas of practice.

Levels of Practice and the Place of Advocacy

Where does advocacy fit into the continuum of service delivery and policy making? Basically, there are two levels of service delivery. The first level focuses on the client, and the second level on larger systems that affect clients. We will discuss these two levels in detail, but first it may be helpful to briefly consider different ways to think about service delivery and how these ways interface with policy and policy practice. Wyers (1991) identifies five modes of policy implementation and development, four of which are applicable to our discussion. At level 1, the direct service practitioner is a policy conduit. Most of the worker's attention is on improving client outcomes through service delivery. As policy is translated into practice with clients, the worker keeps note of the impact of the policy and provides feedback to policy makers on the effect of the policy and changes that may be needed. At level 2, the direct service practitioner is a change agent in the internal work environment of the agency. Here the policy practice focus is on the impact of agency policies on service delivery. Practitioners are also attentive to the absence of policy addressing client needs and work to amend and develop agency policies. At level 3, the policy practitioner is a change agent in activities outside the employing organization and its work-related client system. This involves both direct and indirect methods of advocating change, including many skills associated with the policy expert role. At level 4, the policy practitioner is a policy expert. Here the work includes developing social policy and being involved in all phases of the policy making and advocacy processes. Work typically involves interaction with community groups, political parties, legislators, and other elected officials.

In practice, most service delivery situations do not fall neatly into one of the four categories, but using Wyers's categories helps when it comes to thinking about the target of the intervention and an individual worker's role in that intervention. Using Wyers's framework, the family practitioner who is doing an analysis of the service delivery situation would address the following questions:

1. Can the client's problems be addressed by existing policies and procedures?
2. If current policies and procedures are not adequate, will modifications and adjustments to agency policy and services be sufficient to address the client's situation?
3. If agency-level intervention is not sufficient, does the policy practitioner need to involve other organizations in addressing the client's situation?

These questions can quite often be addressed by a practitioner providing direct services to a client or, in the case of the third question, by the practitioner or the practitioner's agency in working to bring about policy change in larger systems. There are still further questions that an analyst should consider that move beyond the level of an individual worker's focus on a specific client's situation. They include questions such as the following:

1. Are there other issues not specifically related to the client's situation that should be addressed to improve the community or to meet the needs of families and children? Although individual workers may become involved in bringing about policy change, the focus of policy practice is separate from the primary work role and shifts toward his or her responsibility as a member of the community who is advocating changes that are believed to be needed.
2. Are the policy issues to be addressed and the changes needed sufficiently complex to justify the use of workers who are trained advocacy experts to develop an intervention designed to bring about system-level change? In this case, it is unlikely that an individual worker will function alone. It is more likely that the worker will assume the role of a policy expert as an employee, or as a volunteer, within an agency or interest group working to bring about the desired change.

In order for readers to better understand advocacy at these various levels, the next section discusses two levels of advocacy: the first is what is called client-centered or case advocacy; the second is class advocacy.

Client-Centered Advocacy

Client-centered advocacy is a complex process that requires specific skills in obtaining resources, negotiating systems, and using appropriate interpersonal communication skills, as well as knowledge of the skillful arts of negotiation and mediation. Client advocacy is focused on helping a particular client. Clients can be individuals, families, groups, or organizations. Freddolino, Moxley, and Hyduk (2004) outline four distinct models of client-centered advocacy. The first involves advocating for clients who are at risk. The focus is on protecting the client from harm. Examples of this level of client advocacy are arranging for foster care for an abused child or obtaining housing for a homeless family. The second form of client-centered advocacy is focused on obtaining needed services or resources that will improve client functioning. In this form of activity, the policy practitioner seeks out services and resources and delivers them to the client. This form of advocacy requires the worker to know bureaucratic procedures and policies and, if necessary, to take action on behalf of the client in larger systems. At an individual level, examples would be helping a client find and get welfare services, food, or Social Security and Medicaid benefits. At the group level, it might involve enrolling a family in a health insurance program, or helping families find day care services. At the organizational level, it might be writing a grant proposal to fund a needed client resource.

The third form of client-centered advocacy changes the worker's focus from obtaining services and resources to teaching the client how to secure his or her own services or resources. For example, this type of advocacy would involve teaching clients how to navigate through bureaucratic structures, informing them of agencies that can help them and how to obtain those services. At an individual level, examples might be coaching a client to apply for and participate in job training. At the group level, it might be teaching parenting skills to a group of families or holding a class for several families on housing vouchers, and then teaching them how to apply for housing. At the organizational level, an example would be training a day care center representative to apply for state subsidies for low-income families.

The final type of client-centered advocacy identified by Freddolino et al. (2004) involves seeking to increase clients' control of the services they receive by empowering them to gain control over their situations by helping them develop skills in organizing with others to identify and develop service options. This type of advocacy is distinguished from the previous three types in that although the worker's focus is on teaching a client a set of skills, the skills that are taught are not designed to benefit only the client but rather are designed to train the client in policy advocacy that leads to system change. In other words, the intent of this kind of advocacy is to turn the client into a policy advocate.

Class Advocacy

From the above discussion, it is apparent that the worker who delivers services to individuals and families must possess a broad set of skills and knowledge about services and resources and be able to teach them how to advocate new policy or policy change. However, helping individual clients may not be an adequate approach. Many social problems are caused by or exacerbated by structural problems occurring in organizations or in society as a whole. Others are caused by traditions or values held by some of the systems with which individuals and families interact. When advocacy skills are used to assist a larger number of people as members of a group or class of people, then workers are engaging in class advocacy, or policy practice, as it is called from a skills-based perspective. At this level, the target of service delivery is not the individual client but rather the policies that have an impact on the client system.

Intervention through class advocacy involves policy practice at the internal, external, and expert levels of Wyers's framework. Bruce Jansson (2003) defines policy practice as "efforts to change policies in legislative, agency, and community settings, whether by establishing new policies, improving existing ones, or defeating the policy initiatives of other people. By this definition, people of all ideological persuasions, including liberals, radicals, and conservatives, engage in policy practice. People who are skilled in policy practice increase the odds that their policy preferences will be advanced" (p. 13).

Class advocacy takes place at many levels. It may target legislative bodies ranging from the U.S. House of Representatives and the Senate to the fifty state legislatures, to county, city, township, and village governments—all of which enact laws or statutes. Other public bodies such as school boards and water and sewer districts also enact regulations that become public policy. Policy practice may target the executive and administrative bodies charged with establishing regulations designed to implement laws. Once published, regulations become the basis for policies that agencies and organizations develop to comply with the rules and regulations. As we discussed in chapter 1, privatization is a major way that public policies and legislation are implemented through for-profit and nonprofit organizations. Thus, whether policies are implemented through public or private organizations, these organizations also establish policy in a wide variety of areas not specifically under the purview of public policy bodies, and the policies they establish may also be a target of advocacy at the class level.

The federal Medicare drug program is a good example. The Medicare prescription drug coverage provides insurance coverage for prescription drugs. Once the legislation was enacted into law by Congress, regulations were developed by the Department of Health and Human Services. After the regulations were published in the *Federal Register,* the department then contracted with private insurance groups, which established their own individual policies regarding which drugs they would provide to Medicare clients who signed up for benefits. These policies are referred to as formularies and differ by the private providers that offer them. The system is so complicated that the Department of Health and Human Services has established an online Formulary Finder, which can be found at http://formularyfinder.medicare.gov/formularyfinder/selectstate.asp. Users enter information regarding the state they live in and the drugs they use, and the Formulary Finder generates a list of providers that offer all the drugs and a list of providers that offer some of the drugs. The list also tells the user if the provider company has any restrictions on the use of the drugs.

To illustrate the process, let's see what happens when the list of drugs commonly taken by a diabetic with high blood pressure and living in the state of Illinois is entered into the system. The computer program lists 123 providers that offer all of the drugs and 21 providers that offer some of the drugs. However, such a complex system is far from ideal. First, many elderly people do not know how to use a computer or have access to the Internet. Second, the Medicare recipient still has to decide which plan to choose. Knowing which plan is the best plan requires a level of knowledge far beyond that of the typical consumer. It also is doubtful that a knowledgeable health care provider would be able to provide patients with enough information to make a wholly informed choice.

Changing federal and state government policy is difficult, though not impossible. However, if the funds needed for services delivery come from the federal or state government—or the policies that need changing were established at that level—then advocacy must be targeted at that level. Wherever the effort to influence policy is targeted, practitioners need to have specific knowledge about the policies they wish to influence, and the ability to draw on many different advocacy skills. A comprehensive skills-based manual for practitioners working in nonprofit organizations is Robert Smucker's (1999) *The Nonprofit Lobbying Guide,* which is available online. An outstanding resource for those who want to engage in federal and state advocacy is the Alliance for Children and Families' Mission-Based Advocacy Toolkit. The Toolkit, developed by the Alliance for Children and Families (2006) with funds from Rockefeller Brothers Fund, is available at http://www.alliance1.org/Public_Policy/advocacyr3.pdf

Planning an Advocacy Campaign

How should policy practitioners go about developing an organized plan for advocacy? Do advocates or groups of advocates take the time to develop an organized plan? Are they deliberate about assessing their opponents, collaborating with like-minded groups, and deliberately selecting tactics? Or do they start with action that is familiar or convenient? Do they start advocating on an issue, improvising and inventing next steps in response to the success or failure of the actions that came before? All too often, the latter situations may be the case. In our work as educators in Ohio, Illinois, and Tennessee, we have observed many groups of social work students in their efforts to work on advocacy projects with local agencies and organizations. In most cases, when students contact agencies or organizations and offer to participate in advocacy work as part of their class project, they find that the advocacy effort has a goal and a general plan that involves the use of various types of advocacy skills. But the groups and agencies involved in advocacy do not have a well-developed plan guiding their advocacy work over the short or long term. In these situations, we have found an assignment that we call the advocacy campaign very useful. It takes advocacy to a level beyond the grab-bag approach of selecting advocacy tools and tactics as the need appears. Rather, an advocacy campaign requires advocates to develop a sort of strategic plan for advocacy that guides the action overall, while still allowing for adjustment and change in the use of advocacy skills and tactics.

The advocacy campaign is a tool for developing an organized plan for advocacy. Table 3.1 shows a ten-step process for developing an advocacy campaign. Since policy practice involves analysis and research, step 1 is conducting advocacy research. As we discussed in chapter 2, the guidelines for policy research and the family impact analysis are useful methods for researching and analyzing family policies. Here, we will assume that policy practitioners have done their homework: they have completed a policy analysis and have taken a position on the issue. Steps 2 through 10 guide the development of a strategic plan for policy advocacy. These steps involve planning a change strategy, selecting tactics, implementing the campaign, and evaluating its outcomes.

The right column in table 3.1 lists the ten steps in the advocacy campaign. The left column lists resources available at the Community Tool Box for developing an advocacy campaign. We developed this table from resources in the Community Tool Box (2007), a Web site that was created and is maintained by the Work Group on Health Promotion and Community Development at the University of Kansas. The Community Tool Box provides over 6,000 pages of practical information to support advocacy work in promoting community health and development and is an invaluable guide to policy practice.

Steps 2 through 8 outline a strategic planning process designed to maximize the possibility of a successful advocacy campaign. Planning begins with the development of mission, goals, and objectives for the campaign, and exploration of alternative ways to fulfill the campaign's objectives. Next, the process involves designing the overall campaign; identifying resources and assets that will help make the campaign a success, potential allies and opponents, and targets of the change process and agents of change; choosing the strategies and tactics that will be used; and developing an evaluation plan. Key components of these steps include developing outcome objectives, identifying the targeted systems, deciding on the action steps required to bring about the change, and identifying the types and sources of resources. Finally, there are always consequences—both intended and unintended—to social action, so advocates must think through the consequences of the proposed alternatives, especially those that will facilitate the desired outcomes and those that will inhibit them or prevent them from being achieved. A good advocacy plan includes plans for countering forces that work to prevent the desired change. The last two steps involve implementing the advocacy campaign and evaluating it. Evaluation involves both evaluating the process of carrying out the plan and determining the extent to which the campaign's objectives have been achieved.

Table 3.1 Ten Steps in an Advocacy Campaign

Step	Community Tool Box Resources
1. **Conduct Advocacy Research** A. Gather initial information about a social problem or policy issue. This includes research to understand the problem and policy context. B. Define the problem. This three-step process involves becoming aware of the issue, refining the problem within the small group/organizational context, and determining problem priorities.	Chapter 31: Conducting Advocacy Research How to Conduct Research Conducting Studies of the Issue Gathering Data on Public Opinion Studying the Opposition Requesting Accountability Demonstrating Benefit or Harm
2. **Develop the Mission, Goals, and Objectives for the Campaign** A. The mission statement tells what the campaign is about. It is a broad statement that provides a general direction for the task group's work (i.e., what the campaign is about). B. Goals provide a general direction and commitment to action but are rarely achieved. C. Objectives are relevant, attainable, measurable, and time-limited outcomes to be achieved.	Chapter 30: Principles of Advocacy Overview: Getting an Advocacy Campaign off the Ground Survival Skills for Advocates Understanding the Issue Developing a Plan for Advocacy
3. **Design the Advocacy Campaign** A. Determine community and system changes (i.e., new or modified programs, policies, and practices) the group hopes to bring about. Include the specific changes (e.g., new hiring policy) sought by the advocacy campaign. B. Determine the action steps required. (Who will do what by when to bring about the specific changes to be sought?)	Chapter 18: Deciding Where to Start Designing Community Interventions Participatory Approaches to Planning Community Interventions
4. **Identify Resources and Assets** A. Identify the number and kind of people who are available and committed. B. Identify the financial resources available. C. Identify the communication technologies, facilities, and other material resources available. D. Identify information and ideas that could be helpful. E. Identify other assets that can be used to support the effort.	Chapter 7: Encouraging Involvement in Community Work Developing a Plan for Increasing Participation in Community Action Promoting Diverse Group Participation Contacting Potential Participants Writing Letters to Potential Participants Contacting Potential Participants Involving Key Influential Persons Involving People Most Affected

Table 3.1 Ten Steps in an Advocacy Campaign—(*Continued*)

Step	Community Tool Box Resources
5. **Identify Potential Allies and Opponents** A. Identify likely allies and how they will support the effort. B. Identify likely opponents and how they might resist or oppose the effort. 　1. State the likely purposes of the opposition. 　2. Outline tactics that may be used by the opposition. 　3. Indicate how the opposition can be countered.	**Chapter 30: Principles of Advocacy** Recognizing Allies Identifying Opponents Encouraging Involvement of Potential Opponents & Allies
6. **Identify Targets and Agents of Change** A. Describe the targets of change in light of anticipated allies and opponents (i.e., those whose behavior should change). Indicate how conditions should be changed to affect their behavior. B. Describe agents of change (i.e., those who can contribute). Indicate how conditions should be changed to support their engagement in the effort.	**Chapter 18: Deciding Where to Start** Identifying Targets and Agents of Change: Who Can Benefit and Help **Chapter 6: Promoting Interest in Community Issues** Developing a Plan for Communication Using Principles of Persuasion Preparing Press Releases Arranging News and Features Stories Preparing Columns and Editorials
7. **State the Strategies and Tactics of the Campaign** A. Identify those strategies that will be used. Based on the particular situation/context, state the specific strategic goals and tactics that will be used. B. Review whether the planned strategies/tactics meet the group's criteria and situation. Consider whether they: 　1. Fit the group's style. Are group members comfortable with the approach? 　2. Use available resources and allies. Do they take advantage of the group's strengths? Engage its allies? Deter opponents? 　3. Are flexible. Do they permit adjustments with changing situations? 　4. Are likely to work. Do they bring about the desired effect with the issue and with opponents?	**Chapter 33: Conducting a Direct Action Campaign** Writing Letters to Elected Officials Writing Letters to the Editor Filing a Complaint Seeking Enforcement of Existing Laws Using Personal Testimony Lobbying Decision-Makers Conducting a Petition Drive Rules for Legislative Advocacy Relationships with Legislators Registering Voters Conducting a Public Hearing **Chapter 34: Media Advocacy** Working with the Media Making Friends with the Media Using Paid Advertising Meeting the Media Changing the Media's Perspective

8. Describe the Evaluation of the Advocacy Campaign A. Clearly state what indicators will signify success (e.g., in bringing about community and systems changes; in achieving longer-term outcomes). B. Describe how measures of success can be obtained (e.g., review records; interviews). C. Indicate how the initiative will make sense of the results (e.g., how data will be analyzed; how those affected will be involved in interpreting the information). D. Describe how the information will be used to improve the effort (e.g., feedback will be provided to leadership and membership; retreats to review progress and make adjustments)	Chapter 36: Introduction to Evaluation A Framework for Program Evaluation: A Gateway to Tools Developing an Evaluation Plan Chapter 38: Some Methods for Evaluating Community Initiatives Measuring Success: Evaluating Comprehensive Community Health Gathering Information: Monitoring Your Progress Rating Community Goals Rating Member Satisfaction Constituent Survey of Outcomes: Ratings of Importance Reaching Your Goals: The Goal Attainment Report Using Behavioral Surveys Conducting Interviews with Key Participants Gathering and Using Community-Level Indicators
9. Implement the Advocacy Campaign	
10. Evaluate the Advocacy Campaign	Chapter 39: Using Evaluation to Understand and Improve the Initiative Providing Feedback to Improve the Initiative Communicating Information to Funders for Support & Accountability

We have used this template for teaching students the process of planning, implementing, and evaluating advocacy campaigns for more than ten years with much success (see Rocha & Johnson, 1997). Student projects have targeted social problems and policies at the organizational, community, and legislative levels. Organizational-level projects have included working with public housing tenants to change a local HMO's health care policies, and increasing access for persons with disabilities at the University of Tennessee. Projects targeting the community and state levels have included changing bus routes in an inner-city neighborhood and empowering parent groups to contact legislators to change day care legislation. In some cases, students successfully carried out advocacy across all levels—from client-centered to community to legislative advocacy. Cynthia Blumenthal, Ron Dixon, Rex Fields, Gloria Mikells, Chris Nergaard, and John Ziegler, MSW students at the University of Illinois–Chicago Jane Addams College of Social Work, worked with state representative Constance A. Howard (D-IL) on House Bill 4098 for automatic expungement of some felony and misdemeanor offenses in the state of Illinois. The advocacy project was designed to empower individuals eligible for expungement, raise community awareness, and lobby for legislative change. Client-centered advocacy included walking two clients through the complex process of applying for the expungement of their criminal histories. Community-level advocacy included designing a fact sheet, distributing 5,000 flyers to public housing residents, and conducting workshops. At the legislative level, students traveled to the state legislature, met with key lawmakers, and held a press conference. In 2000, this project won the Influencing State Policy (ISP) Award Influencing State Policy. Influencing State Policy sponsors an annual student/faculty contest with prizes up to $1,000. Students must demonstrate how they have actually influenced a policy in their state. Examples range from initiating legislation on rape and assault law enforcement to organizing a Hispanic community, drafting HIV education bills, protecting the rights of mobile home owners, and assisting NASW chapters with their legislative agendas. Each year, ISP honors the winners at the BSW and MSW levels with certificates, plaques, and a cash award at a national conference. ISP encourages students and faculty to visit their state legislatures. Each year ISP also awards a $2,000 award for a PhD dissertation that is focused on a state social problem, program, or policy. "Policy affects practice and practitioners affect policy" is the motto of ISP. These words highlight the active role that all social workers must play in advocating for their clients. Legislation affects social workers and their clients, and if professional social workers and students stay on the sidelines, others who are less committed to social work values will certainly make the final decisions on social policies. Information on the policy contest is available online at http://www.statepolicy.org

Skills for Implementing an Advocacy Campaign

Implementing an advocacy campaign is a political process. By this, we mean that agencies or governmental bodies typically need to be persuaded to change. Sometimes the need for change—and its concurrence with society's values or the values of dominant stakeholders at the time—is so apparent that it can be accomplished through a rational presentation of the need for change, and an implementation plan that is acceptable to the change target. More typically, however, change requires a shift in the balance of power or resources within the change target. Advocacy campaigns then need to develop power to influence change. This section of the chapter focuses on several skills that are important in implementing an advocacy campaign, particularly those that we think are essential to effective advocacy.

The Politics of Persuasion

When one is working on an advocacy campaign, it is important to consider whether collaborative or confrontational strategies or tactics should be used. There are strong and conflicting opinions on this issue. Some advocate persuasion or providing rewards as the preferred strategy; others believe that coercive approaches are necessary (for an in-depth discussion, see Kriesberg, 1998). Regarding persuasion techniques, Bruce Jansson (2003), a leading author on policy practice, writes: "In friendly communications, policy advocates try to decrease opposition to a proposal with conflict-reducing techniques" by stressing commonalities with the audience or engaging in "win-win negotiations that emphasize shared interests" (p. 249). Thus, the main tenets of the friendly approach to negotiation are the following:

- Rather than staking out a point, advocates encourage mutual discussion of the situation.
- Advocates present the message in such a way as to get the audience to acknowledge that he or she would also benefit from the proposal.
- Rather than moving toward rapid closure, advocates move the discussion toward brainstorming, in which each of the parties in the discussion imagines alternative positions.
- Negotiators stress win-win solutions to underscore the desire to reach a conciliatory solution, offering to compromise, if necessary.
- Negotiators and the opposing party conclude the process of win-win negotiating with heightened respect for one another.

Even though a friendly approach seems generally preferable, it is not always possible. Jansson (2003) suggests that advocates first attempt conciliation to see if the opposing party will engage in collaborative problem solving. He outlines the following characteristics of cases in which collaborative problem solving is successful:

- Relations between parties are amicable.
- In the past, the issue at hand has generally been discussed with low levels of conflict and mutual concessions.
- At the outset, neither party in the negotiation has a fixed or rigid position (a position that is based on ideology or self-interest).
- Neither party in the negotiation attaches symbolic meaning to the issue or outcome (e.g., viewing loss or victory "as having extraordinary consequences").
- Onlookers or followers "do not pressure the parties to best each other."
- Both parties in the negotiation "value conciliation."
- "Low conflict and mutual concessions reinforce a win-win" negotiating style.

One important aspect of using friendly persuasion is diagnosing the beliefs and value premises, hopes and fears—both positive and negative factors—that motivate people to support or reject a policy. Another important aspect is evaluating the target group's degree of motivation and level of involvement in a specific topic and the extent to which the social context may influence their response to policy change. Factions within the target audience should be evaluated separately, but advocates can still identify and appeal to common values, hopes, and aspirations.

Because they may not have the resources to employ such strategies, policy practitioners use rewards less often. However, in practice, there are still many examples of this approach. For example, in an instance of interorganizational change, professors David L. Cronin and Harriet K. Switzer sought out a donor with a lifelong interest in Native Americans. By getting the donors to offer a substantial endowment, they were able to persuade the George Warren Brown School of Social Work at Washington University in St. Louis to establish the Kathryn M. Buder Center for American Indian Studies, even though the school had no history of curriculum development in this area (Martin, 2007).

Sometimes, for change to take place, confrontation is necessary. Coercive strategies should be used only when cooperation and negotiation have not worked, or when political and ideological factors, discriminatory attitudes, or hard-and-fast traditions make decision makers unwilling to consider policy alternatives. Coercive strategies can range from getting negative information published in the media to sit-ins, strikes, public demonstrations, and the use of the courts to compel policy change. Box 3.1 shows Donna Hardina's report on several of these strategies, including a hunger strike by students advocating free speech at Fresno State University in California.

Box 3.1 Examples of Coercive Strategies to Bring Change

On November 10, 2004, the Campus Peace and Civil Liberties Coalition at California State University, Fresno sponsored a presentation by Gary Yourofsky, an animal rights advocate previously affiliated with People for the Ethical Treatment of Animals (PETA). On the day of the event, the Campus Police demanded that the room location be changed and raised concerns about security. The event took place without incident. A week later, Ruth Obel-Jorgensen, an MSW student and President of Campus Peace, was asked to come to the campus police station to respond to police chief's concerns about another guest speaker. Ruth was told that in the future all speakers would be screened by the chief for security reasons.

During two meetings with University officials, Ruth and Donna Hardina, Campus Peace Faculty Advisor and ACOSA member, were told that undercover officers were present at the Yourofsky presentation. A number of explanations were offered: security concerns, intelligence gathering, and that the presence of uniformed officers would "inflame the crowd" of vegans who attended the event.

During Spring, 2005, Campus Peace and the American Civil Liberties Union filed a public records request with Fresno State and raised concerns with the University administration about the impact of this surveillance on student privacy and freedom of speech. The University refused to respond to the public records request. However, under pressure from local media, they eventually informed Campus Peace that six undercover officers (three University Police officers and three members of the county sheriff's department) attended the event for "security purposes."

In order to obtain accurate information about this incident and to lobby for changes in university policy, over a dozen members of Campus Peace staged a 48 hour hunger strike outside the University administration building, April 27–29, 2005. In addition to Ruth Obel-Jorgensen, the hunger strikers included several MSW students.

Immediately after the hunger strike, University President John Welty, issued a letter assuring Campus Peace that university police would not be permitted to conduct surveillance at university events unless required by law and approved by University administration. He also pledged to set up a task force to review police procedures. The Task Force, which included Donna Hardina, concluded its work in December, 2005. A variety of policies to protect the privacy of students, faculty, and university staff were recommended. These recommendations have been forwarded to the Faculty Senate and the University President for approval.

Unfortunately, the covert surveillance of the Yourofsky presentation was not an isolated event. There have been at least two previous incidents involving surveillance in Fresno that have been well documented. One of

> these events, the infiltration of a local organization, Peace Fresno, was described in Michael Moore's film, Fahrenheit 911. Currently, Campus Peace and Peace Fresno are waiting for several reports to be issued by California Attorney General's Office as to the legality of police infiltration of political groups and whether the state's anti-terrorism task force has provided information gathered through such surveillance to the FBI. Ruth Obel-Jorgensen (MSW, Fresno State, 2005) is now employed as a field organizer for the University of California Student Association.

Source: Hardina, D. (2006, Winter). Student action: Hunger strike for free speech at Fresno State. *ACOSA Update, 19*(4), 13. Retrieved September 9, 2007 from http://acosa.org/update_back.html

Another recent example of the media being used in an attempt to coerce change is a report, *The Scandal of Social Work Education*, released by the National Association of Scholars (2007) via the Internet. The purpose of the report is to coerce the social work profession to alter its values and code of ethics by involving and using the courts and legal system.

Task Forces, Coalitions, and Interest Groups

Individual efforts are generally more effective when policy practice is part of a larger group effort. That is why task groups and coalitions are so important in policy advocacy. Task groups and coalitions bring together a number of people interested in the same issue and provide additional resources for policy advocacy. In coordinated and strategic activities such as those outlined in an advocacy campaign, the work of task groups and coalitions is an essential part of planning, implementation, and evaluation. A task force is a time-limited, action-oriented committee that arises out of a crisis (see Johnson, 1994). A task force can be set up within an organization or as an interorganizational group with members representing different organizations. Interorganizational task forces are similar to coalitions, but in general, the term *coalition* implies a long-term relationship among participating organizations. Coalitions are "convening mechanisms" that allow organizations to interact and work together toward a common goal (Roberts-DeGennaro, 1987, p. 59). They are also strategic devices that leverage the impact of member organizations regarding an issue or a set of issues.

Table 3.2, based on Blumer's (1971) framework for defining social problems, illustrates the use of these two types of advocacy in a legal challenge

Table 3.2 Policy Advocacy for Homeless Shelter and Services in St. Louis

Stage	Policy Advocacy Process
Clarifying Values: What society values influence the issue? Were traditional values in a state of fluctuation?	Between 1981 and 1989, the rate of homelessness tripled from 5 people per 10,000 to 15 per 10,000. All types of people were homeless, including single women, men, two-parent families, veterans, people of color, and families with children. Policy analysts provided comprehensive and convincing arguments about the heterogeneous nature of homelessness and its relationship to poverty, personal disabilities, and the national shortage of affordable housing. During the 1980s, public attitudes toward the homeless were generally favorable.
Emergence: What brought the problem to public attention?	Reverend Larry Rice used his TV channel and other media to bring constant attention to the problem of homeless persons living in shelters. Camera crews would go with him on nightly winter trips to bring blankets and food to homeless persons living under bridges and in abandoned buildings in St. Louis. He organized nonviolent public demonstrations, for example, sleeping in a cardboard box in front of city hall.
Legitimation: Who were the important actors? Why did homelessness become a legitimate social problem?	Dan Glazier, Michael Ferry, and Sandra Farragut-Hemphill of Legal Services of Eastern Missouri and Ken Chackes of Washington University in St. Louis Law School filed a class-action lawsuit against the city of St. Louis. The lawsuit was based on a state statute from Missouri's colonial days that stated that "poor persons shall be relieved and supported by the county of which they are inhabitants."
Mobilization: What type of conflict occurred? How did conflict mobilize groups to redefine the problem? What policy was offered to solve it?	Mayor Vincent Schoemehl appointed a task force to study the problem. The task force consisted of representatives of the major social service agencies working with the homeless. The task force recommended shelter and services for the homeless. Expert testimony from both the legal and political systems aligned with that taken in the adversarial stance of the lawsuit.
Development: What developed as the solution? How did this solution resolve power issues among conflicting groups?	The case did not go to trial because the city of St. Louis and Legal Services of Eastern Missouri agreed to a court-ordered consent decree. The agreement mandated that the solution to homelessness in St. Louis included city-funded shelter beds *and* specific services such as crisis shelter, transportation, day center programs for women and children, and transitional housing. Legal Services was charged to monitor the consent decree.
Implementation: What policy emerged as the official solution? How was the plan modified or changed in implementation?	To comply with the consent decree, the city established the Homeless Services Network. Implementation occurred through a public-private partnership. The city contracted out the required provision of shelter and services to major social service agencies. Through purchase-of-service contracts and networking, a continuum-of-services model developed that won national awards for innovation.

concerning homeless shelter policy, programs, and services. In the mid-1980s, when homelessness was becoming a national issue, the government of the city of St. Louis refused to assume responsibility for providing a homeless shelter and services. This situation prompted Dan Glazier, a lawyer and a social worker at Legal Services of Eastern Missouri, to take the lead in filing a class-action lawsuit on behalf of homeless individuals (*Graham v. Schoemehl*, 1985). Based on a poor-law statute from Missouri's territorial days, the lawsuit argued that the city of St. Louis was responsible for caring for homeless persons.

In response to the lawsuit, and substantial media publicity as well, St. Louis mayor Vincent Schoemehl appointed a task force on homelessness to study the problem. The task force, which was comprised of key social service administrators, recommended solutions similar to those being sought by the lawsuit. As a result, the city reached a pretrial settlement that required that city funds and tax monies be used to provide shelter and services for homeless persons (Johnson, Kreuger, & Stretch, 1989). Not only did the court decree mandate an increase in shelter beds, but it listed additional homeless services to be provided (Chackes, 1987). These included a crisis-oriented reception center, transportation services, a day center for women and children, and transitional services (*Graham v. Schoemehl*, 1985). Next, the city privatized homeless services through a purchase-of-service model, which included a computerized bed-count system for keeping track of available shelter beds and referrals to shelters (Butterfield, 1995). As a means of coordination, the city organized a coalition called the Homeless Services Network, which developed a city-wide plan for coordinated homeless services (Johnson & Banerjee, 1992). In 1987, the city received the first of several national awards, the Innovations in Government Award from Harvard University. Their citation read in part: "The effectiveness of St. Louis' Network is clear: in 1986 of 2,600 calls to the intake center, 1,372 people were referred to shelters and 1,153 were referred to non-shelter services. Only 75 people who were seeking placement couldn't obtain it. In the first months of 1987, the Network succeeded in increasing their success rate to 98 percent placement. The multifaceted approach of the St. Louis Network is not innovative simply for its breadth of services, but for its ability to coordinate among them and offer homeless people a comprehensive support system" (Government Innovators Network, 2007).

For significant policy change to take place at the state or national level, it is nearly always necessary to use coalitions as a means of broadening and deepening resources and political influence that can be brought to bear. Beth Rosenthal and Terri Mizrahi (1994), at the Education Center for Community Organizing at Hunter College in New York City, have authored a

200-page practice manual on coalition building. This manual is an excellent resource for understanding and learning the skills of coalition building. Coalitions can be permanent or temporary. They may focus on issues or specific legislation. They can have both organizational and individual members. Formal coalitions may be more effective, but they are also more costly. Coalitions are usually formed by people or organizations that are affected by a policy issue and/or want to change a policy. A core group of people may decide to propose a strategy for coalition building to other organizations and key stakeholders. When this occurs, the basic procedure outlined in table 3.2 should be used to convince prospective coalition members of the need for advocacy. After the type of coalition is determined, the idea should be taken to key persons in the strongest potentially allied organizations. These key leaders can provide additional input, get involved, and become invested in the process. Meetings should be set to make a formal decision about whether to form a coalition.

Broadening a coalition simply as a way to include more people or organizations should be avoided when there is not agreement by the new members on the issues to be addressed. This weakens the coalition's position on the policy issue or problem area. It is generally better to start forming a coalition well before it is time to take final action on an issue. Decisions made because of the need to quickly develop a policy position often conceal differences between coalition members. Later, these differences may emerge at times when the coalition should be focusing its energy on presenting a united and coherent position on the needed policy change. Box 3.2 discusses Fran Danis's work in coalition building in an intra-institutional domestic violence policy intervention.

Box 3.2 Coalition Building in an Intra-institutional Domestic Violence Policy Intervention

Before I begin, I want to give you a thumbnail sketch about my background. I've been a practicing social worker for at least 24 years, 22 of those years have been spent working in the domestic violence movement. I worked as an organizer and the founder of a domestic violence program in Texas and was involved with the Texas Council on Family Violence, the statewide coalition of domestic violence shelter programs doing policy work. I've been on the board of a local grassroots rural shelter and have now evolved my practice into teaching and research and evaluation in the field of domestic violence. In many ways the development of the second wave of the feminist movement and my personal development as a social work professional are intertwined.

One of the reasons I was excited about participating in this particular panel discussion, is that I wanted to address the myths about working in the domestic violence field. Myth number one is that if we just provide counseling to all the battered women who need it, they'll see that their safety is at stake; they'll leave their abuser; they'll find a safe place to go; and that'll be the end of the problem. Many of us in social work are still looking at domestic violence as an interpersonal problem rather than framing it within the broader discussions of violence in our community and violence in the world. There are many structural reasons why women stay and these are challenges for us to address. For example, the lack of affordable day care and housing may be some of the practical reasons women don't leave.

I think that the second myth about addressing domestic violence is that it's mostly the work of people who work in community-based domestic violence programs. And by the way, people who work in those programs don't call themselves "caseworkers." They call themselves "advocates" for the most part, having embraced the community change perspective in doing this work. Because battered women and their children have multiple service needs, all social workers in all different fields of practice need to know basic information about safe screening, assessment and appropriate referral.

The numbers are staggering. Lifetime prevalence of domestic violence could be as high as 25–50% depending upon which study you look at. In the course of a year, 1.4 million women could be affected and need services relating to domestic violence. I'm using the term "battered women" because I personally take a gender-violence perspective. In the vast majority of cases, in fact 95% of reported cases are situations of male on female violence. We are not saying that men are not battered, or that women are never the primary aggressor, certainly that is the case with same-sex relationships, but I want to talk about the majority of situations.

When you look at the handout "The Continuum of Caring" we can identify all of the different services in the community that someone who's experiencing violence may need. Women can enter this delivery system at any point in the network. What's really exciting is that you'll find social workers in just about all of these different fields of practice and institutions in our society. In fact, social workers are the most common group that domestic violence survivors or victims will come into contact with. And, therefore we all need to have some basic information.

The myth that domestic violence is an interpersonal problem and that it is a social work clinician's job to address domestic violence needs further exploring. In fact, it is, I think, our macro skills that are most important in dealing with domestic violence. For the past twenty-five years advocates in the battered women's movement have used a variety of community-practice models that resulted in better public awareness about the issue, stronger criminal laws that hold batterers more accountable for their behavior, and the recognition that "behind closed doors" is a community problem that has consequences for all society. We now have increased federal, state, and local funding for shelters, programs and crime victims as a whole. We were very pleased that the federal Violence Against Women Act II was finally reauthorized, so that services and money can continue to flow from Washington to the states and directly to service providers and state coalitions. We've seen new and expanded services for battered women, child witnesses to domestic violence and for batterers themselves. Many communities now have "kids exchange" programs where parents can exchange children or have visitation in a safe, neutral, and supervised environment. These programs are a direct outgrowth of the battered women's movement. And we've seen better training for law enforcement and other entities in the criminal justice system. We've seen a lot of training for providers in the healthcare arena.

One of the things we learned dealing with the police and prosecutors and sheriffs' offices and courts and probation is that the criminal justice system is a collection of independent entities with independent leadership, independent leadership styles and so forth. Sometimes they can manage to put aside their turf issues and work together to enforce laws that hold batterers accountable. But at worst they're a collection of warring city-states of the 11th and 12th century. Organizing and pulling those folks together for a common purpose has been a challenge. In the early days of this movement, when we talked to the police, the court system, and the prosecutors, they were all pointing their fingers at each other. "I would prosecute if only police made arrests." "I would arrest if the DA's office would prosecute." The DA says, "The judge will just dismiss it, why should we even bother?" Or she will drop the charges. So what we've really learned out of that experience is the need to develop what we call "a coordinated community response" to domestic violence. This recognizes that no one entity, working alone, no matter how hard, can solve the problem of domestic violence by themselves. The blue handout, "Coordinated Community Action Model" shows that everyone has a role to play in this particular area: in the justice system, to hold batterers accountable, in the healthcare system, to do universal screening. The media can spotlight the issue and draw attention to the dynamics of domestic violence and not glorify violence and violence against women. The education system can help through informed teachers, counselors, and, of course, school social workers.

School social workers have a very important role to play in this arena. First, we know that witnessing domestic violence has tremendous impact and consequences for children, which can interfere with their ability to succeed in school. So school social workers must consider witnessing domestic violence as an underlying issue especially affecting children who are acting out aggressively (externalizing behaviors) or exhibiting internalizing behaviors such as being withdrawn and depressed. Secondly, when the battered women's movement began to do prevention work about 10–12 years ago, they jumped over the colleges and went right into high schools. And, lo and behold, it wasn't prevention work; we discovered this whole phenomenon of teen dating violence. School social workers have an important role in providing services to teens already in violent dating relationships and help students learn about healthy relationships. In Austin, Texas where I've been for the past 15 years, the local domestic violence and sexual assault agency, SafePlace, has been working with the school district to develop an anti-bullying and sexual harassment program that targets students in the 5th grade. The idea is what does a batterer look like at 11 years of age? He may look like a bully who just pulled up the skirt of a female student. Or maybe he has pulled a girl's hair. Teachers and other adults reinforce the use of violence by saying to girls who complain, "Oh he wouldn't be bothering you if he didn't really like you." How many girls have heard that over and over and over again? What message are adults sending? The message that girls hear is that violence and harassment is something boys do to show their love so don't complain about it. The school social worker may be the first adult that will listen to the girls' concerns and send a message about the inappropriateness of this behavior. I can't emphasize enough the important role social workers have in addressing domestic violence in schools.

While the role of the social worker within educational institutions is important, social workers can play an important role in developing coordinated community responses. Our expertise is needed as organizers, planners, advocates, case managers and coalition builders to participate in and to develop collaborations.

There are a couple of community organizing initiatives going on right now. The Family Violence Prevention Fund (http://endabuse.org/), based in San Francisco, has developed with the help of the Allstate Foundation, an "In Your Neighborhood" organizing kit to help people engage local communities against domestic violence. Since abused women often turn first to informal helping systems it's important to mobilize awareness and support among neighbors and friends. We need to stop avoiding discussions about abuse with our neighbors and co-workers because we don't want to embarrass them. They're a lot more embarrassed when they're standing on charges for murder. So, this project is about building the community's capacity to respond to domestic violence.

The Women's Center of South Eastern Connecticut has developed another community organizing project. They have developed a "Hairdressers Against Domestic Violence" project. This is a wonderful project that trains hairdressers to screen for domestic abuse and refer women to the local domestic violence agency. They train hairdressers on how to ask the question, how to be a good listener and how to refer.

The last thing I want to mention is that we need to concentrate on our efforts on our workplaces as well, especially those of us who work at universities. At the University of Texas at Austin, we pulled together representatives from the Dean of Students office, the UT police department, the student Health Center, Student Housing, the Employee Assistance Program, the Women's Center, International Student Office, the student Mental Health and Counseling Center, SafePlace (which is our local community-based domestic violence and sexual assault program); and the "Men Against Rape" student group. We brought these student groups and organizations together to develop an intra-organizational coordinating council on domestic and sexual violence. Is there domestic and/or sexual violence on our campus? Why should our 66,000 students, staff, and faculty be any different than any other community of 66,000? In fact, it's larger than the community of Denton, Texas where I started a shelter in 1980! The most exciting thing about this project so far is that we were able to come together and develop a plan and a grant proposal. They have just received Violence Against Women Act College Campus project funding for over $600,000 for two years to develop a comprehensive intervention program for victims on campus. I take great pride in being a mother of that, even though I have to start all over at the University of Missouri now.

If you're working as a manager or an administrator, you need to be thinking about workplace policies. This is another area that we're spending a lot of time on. Women are more and more likely to be stalked at their workplace by someone that they know and have been in a relationship with, or by someone who wants to be in a relationship with them. You need to organize the workers in the workplace. You could post pictures, walk people to their cars, or change work schedules. All this takes organizing, so go forth and do good things.

Source: Danis, F. (2002). Domestic violence from a macro perspective. *ACOSA Update,* 16(1), 10–11, 13. Retrieved September 9, 2007, from http://acosa.org/update_back.html

Interest groups are another kind of coalition. Interest groups are composed of membership organizations, political action committees, industries, citizen groups, and other organizations. Most people think of interest groups as large corporations and industries, such as the insurance industry, pharmaceutical companies, and the oil and auto industries, banding together to form powerful coalitions. While this is certainly true, there are other interest groups that are made up of citizens—human service organizations and social workers, to name a few—that work primarily for the betterment of society. Research on human service interest groups has identified several areas where highly effective interest groups differentiate themselves from less effective groups. In the legislative arena, highly effective groups develop consensus among different interest groups in order to reduce conflict, work with legislators on policy formulation, and use the media to influence public opinion. In the implementation process, highly effective interest groups work closely with the executive branch agencies, becoming involved in assisting with writing rules and regulations prior to their publication in the *Federal Register* (Hoefer, 2001; Hoefer & Ferguson, 2007).

Sometimes the interest group may have its own interest as well as that of the larger public good in mind. One such example is the Vancouver Citizen's Committee, which uses a variety of organizational and advocacy tactics to improve their community. Their online *Citizen's Handbook* is an excellent resource (Dobson, 2006). Another example is the effort of Local 880 Service Employees International Union and community organizers to unionize family child care providers in the state of Illinois, which subsequently led to the recognition of the union, improvement in wages, and health care coverage for the providers. Fred Brooks's report of this effort is described in box 3.3.

Box 3.3 Example of Using Interest Groups to Build a Coalition

I recently published a case study of Local 880 Service Employees International Union's (SEIU) organizing drive of family child care providers in Illinois. (Family child care is the care of unrelated children in the home of the provider). My data was collected in 2001 and documented the first 5 years of Local 880's remarkable success recruiting members, collecting over 2000 authorization cards, filing grievances, and winning a pay increase in 1999 through legislative lobbying. Among the keys to Local 880's success was their ability to utilize community organizing techniques, such as house visits and direct action campaigns, to build the child care union. This was impressive organizing, especially when you consider Local 880 accomplished all of this with a de facto union—the union was not recognized by the state as the bargaining agent for family child care providers. The union is de facto no more. Thanks to a successful election last week, Local 880 is now the official bargaining agent for over 49,000 family day care providers!

> Last week Local 880 capped their successful 10 year organizing drive by winning the largest union election in Illinois history. Family child care providers overwhelmingly voted to have Local 880 represent them in contract negotiations with the State. The union won 82% of 16,700 votes cast; only 359 votes were for no union representation. The election was sanctioned by Illinois Governor Rod Blagojevich's Executive Order issued in February authorizing a union election. The election was administered via mail by the American Arbitration Association. Local 880 says the first priorities for the new bargaining unit will be electing leadership and beginning negotiations with the state around health care coverage and pay increases. Some providers are reimbursed as little as $9.48 per child to care for a child all day long.
> The Illinois victory is the second biggest successful union election in the USA in over 60 years, surpassed only by SEIU 434B's victory in 1999 representing 75,000 homecare workers in California. Another unique aspect of Illinois victory was the infusion of community organizers the last several weeks of the drive. Local 880 is affiliated with the community organization ACORN. During the last few weeks leading up to the election ACORN contracted 50 organizers to assist Local 880 with door-knocking and telephone calls. This joint community and labor organizing blitzkrieg helped secure Local 880's wide margin of victory.
> The victory has implications beyond Illinois since SEIU and ACORN have a partnership and are replicating this organizing model in California, Maryland, Massachusetts, Michigan, Minnesota, New Jersey, Ohio, Oregon, Pennsylvania, Rhode Island, Washington, and Wisconsin. The union estimates there are over 500,000 family child care providers nationwide.

Source: Brooks, F. (2005). Union and community organizers join forces to deliver historical union victory in Illinois: Local 880 SEIU to represent 49,000 family child care providers. *ACOSA Update, 19*(2), 10. Retrieved September 9, 2007, from http://acosa.org/update_back.html

Lobbying

Lobbying is a specialized type of advocacy that focuses on influencing elected officials to support or oppose specific legislation or policy positions. Lobbying can be divided into two forms: direct lobbying and grassroots lobbying. Quite often the term *lobbyist* carries a negative connotation. Lobbyists are seen as extremely well-paid representatives of special interest groups whose purpose is to influence legislators to pass legislation benefiting the special interest groups. An example is the health insurance industry's successful effort to prohibit Medicare from negotiating group discounts on the prescription drugs that Medicare recipients use. Lobbying is also engaged in by individuals representing coalitions or grassroots interest groups interested in various kinds of policies. Constituents also try to influence elected representatives to work for their individual interests.

Lobbyists are an important resource for legislators. Lobbyists are important because they provide more information for decision making than any other source. However, if the information is, for all intents and purposes, biased or untrue, the lobbyist may no longer be welcome. Another important lobbying premise is ensuring that the policy change is morally and ethically justifiable. Effective lobbyists provide accurate information and are able to demonstrate that a substantial number of the legislator's constituents support the proposed policies and that opposing the policies will not damage the legislator's chances of being reelected. Lobbyist skills include providing information in a one- to two-page fact sheet. Legislators may deal with over a thousand bills during a single legislative session, so they don't have time to read complete research articles. It is useful to provide legislators with fact sheets with bullet points highlighting the important information and a short source list at the end (see appendix A).

A policy brief is another important tool for lobbying for policy change. A policy brief also presents the lobbyist's position on a proposed policy change but it is based on more extensive research on the issue than is represented by a fact sheet. Policy briefs can be submitted to legislators or other decision makers, but they are also useful for briefing journalists and informing the general public on the issues so as to gain support for policy change from a wider audience. Guidelines for developing a policy brief are shown in appendix B. Policy think tanks also develop quite extensive policy briefs with charts, diagrams, and statistics and post them on the Web for information and advocacy on specific policy issues. Good examples are located on the Web site of the Family Strengthening Policy Center (2009).

Testifying before committees is a formal type of lobbying. Legislative testimony can be used for many kinds of committees, including city councils, county commissions, and school boards. Regardless of the type of committee, the skills needed for testifying are similar. The types of testimony heard during public hearings range from detailed expert testimony using statistics to brief personal testimony of one's personal experiences. Each type of testimony is important because public officials often judge the significance of an issue by the number and type of comments they hear. Ineffective testimony can harm the possibility of legislative or regulatory change. Good testimony shows awareness of the issues, gives the reasons why a given proposal is better than other alternatives, and recommends a specific policy direction. All information should be accurate, as opponents will find flaws in misleading arguments. The testimony should be brief, focused, and clear, or the important policy message may not be understood.

Appendix C contains guidelines for testifying before committees developed from Sharwell (1982). A rule of thumb for writing and delivering legislative testimony is that a cover letter or introductory statement should be no more than seventy-five words. Closing remarks are no longer than fifty words, which includes thanks to the committee for hearing the testimony and contact information for further questions. Presenters should anticipate arguments and questions by the committee. Joking during the presentation is unwise, because everyone may not share the same sense of humor. Since the press is usually present for committee hearings, fact sheets with the important points highlighted should be prepared as press release handouts. If reporters are absent, handouts with other supporting material should be mailed or faxed to the media.

Lobbying is a type of advocacy. Typically, lobbying is a form of communication with elected officials or their staff. This is called direct lobbying, and it is meant to influence a piece of legislation by asserting a specific view on the policy or proposed legislation. When the issue is on the ballot or a referenda initiative, direct lobbying also refers to efforts to influence voters to vote for or against the proposed policy. Grassroots lobbying is the term used to describe efforts to influence the general public to contact officials about specific legislation, make their views heard, and take action on the issue. Such actions might include writing letters to elected officials, signing petitions, and making phone calls and personal visits (Alliance for Children and Families, 2006).

When public officials hear views from constituents, it can make a difference, because constituents vote. A well-written letter includes a summary of the writer's position on the issue, a clear statement of how the issue is affecting or will affect the person writing the letter, examples of how other people will be affected, and a description of the actions that should be taken to address the issue. It is also useful to credit the recipient for past actions that have appropriately addressed issues of importance to the writer. Form letters are less effective because, in practice, form letters are treated as petitions since all form letters are the same. Records are kept of the number of letters that are received. Although public officials receive hundreds of letters on various pieces of legislation, individual letters still count. Since there are thousands of pieces of legislation introduced during a congressional session, only a few letters may be written on a given piece of legislation. Two or three good letters from the legislator's district can help the legislator make a decision and may make a difference in how he or she votes.

Phone calls are another way to influence representatives. Staff usually record the caller's name, address, and position on the issue and determine whether the caller is a constituent. Callers to legislators should know the bill name and number, including the respective versions in the House and Senate, as well as any proposed amendments, and then briefly state their opinion about the legislation. Staffers keep a running record of constituent views and pass these on to their boss. Most elected officials now provide constituents with e-mail addresses that can be used to contact them. Because of the volume of e-mail received at the federal level, it is unlikely that a senior official or a legislator will read the e-mail. However, at the state and agency levels, it is not uncommon for officials to respond to their own e-mail.

Personal visits with policy makers are a good way to address policy issues. An appointment should be made in advance. Visitors should provide a written statement that identifies the policy issue (or if a legislative bill, the bill number and name) and concludes with a brief description of the constituent or organization's position. In conversations with lawmakers, Rocha (2007) found that "threatening an elected official with innuendo or direct comments about not voting for them in the next election" (p. 140) is not conducive to engaging in a discussion about voting in favor of a bill. While conflict may sometimes be effective as a part of group tactics, legislators often view negative comments as a personal attack. Finally, maintaining good relations with policy makers is important, because people are more likely to listen to someone they like. Also, policy makers who oppose a particular policy position and need to be convinced to support a particular policy issue at one point in time may be an ally on another issue at another point in time.

Direct Democracy

Direct democracy refers to the process in which citizens and interest groups organize to put legislation directly on the ballot for a decision by the voting public. One starts the process by obtaining the signatures of a large number of registered voters to petition the state to allow the proposed new law on the ballot of a general election. The attorney general of the state must certify that the required number of registered voters have signed the petition. Then, the proposed state statute is placed on the ballot, and voters vote yes or no. The resulting law is called an initiated state statute because it was initiated by the public and approved by voters. Table 3.3 shows seven different types of direct democracy that put issues on the ballot for democratic decision making: the legislatively referred constitutional amendment, the legislatively referred state statute, the initiated state

Table 3.3 Types of Ballot Initiatives

Types of Initiative	The Direct Democracy Process
Initiated constitutional amendment	An amendment to a state's constitution that comes about through the initiative process
Initiated state statute (direct and indirect)	A new law that a state adopts via the initiative process
Legislatively referred constitutional amendment	An amendment to the constitution that appears on a state's ballot because the state legislature in that state voted to put it before the voters
Legislatively referred state statute	A statute that appears on a state's ballot because the state legislature in that state voted to put it before the voters
Statewide recall	A process available in most jurisdictions whereby an elected official can be removed from office either for malfeasance or, in some jurisdictions, for any action the recall language specifies
Statute affirmation	A process only available in Nevada, in which voters collect signatures in order to place on the ballot a question asking the citizens of the state to affirm a standing state law; if a majority of voters affirm the law, the state legislature is then barred from ever amending it. However, citizens may themselves amend or repeal the law in the future through a direct vote of the people
Veto referendum	A vote that takes place when a group that opposes a new law enacted by the state government collects enough signatures within the statutory time frame in that state to place the new law on a statewide ballot so that the voters can either endorse it as a law or withhold their approval

statute (direct or indirect), the initiated constitutional amendment, the veto referendum (sometimes called the citizen referendum or the statute referendum), the statute affirmation (only in Nevada), and statewide recall (Ballotpedia, 2009). Ballotpedia.org, a wiki-type of Web page, keeps track of all of these types of ballot-based initiatives, including petition drives, their supporters, and their opponents. Direct democracy is an important and powerful method of social change because of its potential to change state statutes on a state-by-state basis. A chart of the direct democracy options available in each state is located at http://ballotpedia.org/wiki/index.php/Forms_of_direct_democracy_in_the_American_states.

Many of the issues taken directly to voters have a history in state legislatures and the courts, but advocates on one side or the other view either the current policy solution, or the absence of a policy solution, as unsatisfactory. Thus, the issues presented to voters are of great importance, highly value laden, and political. In addition, sometimes the real agenda of putting a measure on the ballot in one state is to force a change in federal policy should a state statute or constitutional amendment be challenged by the courts. If the new law is subsequently challenged by the courts, it may eventually find its way to the Supreme Court, thereby testing or challenging previous Supreme Court decisions or federal law.

The November 2008 election provides us with an excellent example of the use of direct democracy in the case of the South Dakota Abortion Ban Initiative, a constitutional amendment appearing on the ballot for the second time in South Dakota. The initiative would criminalize abortion, and doctors who perform abortions could be charged with a Class 4 felony, with a maximum punishment of ten years in jail and a $20,000 fine. According to the Ballot Initiative Strategy Center (2008), the proposed amendment set "exceptions for rape, incest, and the health of the mother that the previous version did not have. In reality, however, the legal requirements placed on the exceptions are so arduous that the exemptions are rendered virtually meaningless. For example, a woman who was raped and requests an abortion would be required by law to submit to a DNA test and allow the fetus to have a DNA test." Major organ failure was set as the standard for judging the effect of continuing pregnancy on the health of the mother. Although the restrictive ballot measure was defeated, with 55.3 percent (206,477 votes) voting against the measure, compared to 44.7 percent (167,518 votes) for it, the real agenda was to challenge the Supreme Court decision of *Roe v. Wade* (Walker, 2008). Some anti-choice groups disagree with this strategy, but this is clearly the agenda of Leslee Unruh, the leading antiabortion activist behind the proposed constitutional amendment in South Dakota: "The proposed ban also aggravates a rift among anti-abortion groups over strategy. Some groups prefer to incrementally increase restrictions on abortion and appoint more sympathetic judges. Unruh and her backers hope abortion rights groups will sue to overturn the measure if it passes, forcing the U.S. Supreme Court to reconsider Roe vs. Wade. Even if the effort fails again, Unruh said activists would try again at the ballot box in 2010. 'I'm not tired,' she said. 'We're going to continue. We believe in this' " (Riccardi, 2008).

We can expect that grassroots democracy through citizen-initiated efforts is likely to grow and intensify in importance as part of the dynamic policy environment of the future. Other recently attempted ballot-based initiatives have dealt with assisted suicide, marijuana use, stem cell research, energy policy, immigration policy, and affirmative action. Other illustrations of the dynamic policy making environment of direct democracy are the Unmarried Couple Adoption Ban, approved by voters in Arkansas (discussed in chapter 9), and Proposition 8: Eliminates Right of Same-Sex Couples to Marry, approved by voters in California (discussed in chapter 11). Students and practitioners of policy practice are encouraged to pay attention to the use of direct democracy as an advocacy tool for social change.

Using the Media

The ability to influence the media is an invaluable advocacy skill that cuts across all levels and types of advocacy. Radio, television, newspapers, photos, and film documentaries are several forms of media that can be used as tools for advocacy. Box 3.4 shows Steve Goldsmith's twelve general guidelines for working with the media.

The *Guide to Getting Good Media Coverage*, developed by the League of Women Voters of the U.S. and Michigan Public Policy Initiative (2001), is a simple and excellent guide to using the media. It includes samples and checklists that show how to put together effective press lists, deliver a speech, use television, write a press release, and prepare an opinion editorial or letter to the editor, and other methods of influencing the media.

It is important to understand that the likelihood that a message will get out to the public depends largely on the chosen media format. A person who is interviewed by the media has little control over what is reported. Facts may be reported out of context or distorted because the reporter misunderstood or misinterpreted what was said, and reporters rarely allow the person interviewed to check the story in advance of publication. According to Rocha (2007), "there are certain circumstances when it will be best to

Box 3.4 Steve Goldsmith's Twelve Media Tips

Here are a dozen pointers on getting into the news that I learned, painfully, over the decades of having my story ideas shot down by fish-eyed assignment editors:

1. Don't appeal to the reporters' altruism or friendship. Appeal to their hunger for a good story.
2. Don't give them enthusiasm. Give them ammunition.
3. A good news story is something new. Plus: surprising, fascinating, amusing or counter-intuitive—or has a direct and dramatic impact on the reader's or viewer's life.
4. Your opinions or feelings are not news—unless you are the Secretary of State and you have suddenly decided to break with the President's foreign policy.
5. Don't overlook the opportunistic nature of news. If your organization is active in part of Elbonia that just got devastated by a volcano, contact the news media at once! This is the moment when the public is interested in Elbonia. It won't be tomorrow.
6. Point #5 is more important than any 300-page strategic communications plan that gathers dust on a shelf. It means you have to follow the news and be quick on your feet.
7. Specifics are usually more effective than generalities.
8. Reporters feed on new, specific information. If nothing else, this can be a poll result, a survey, a research study, etc.
9. Journalism almost always requires the testimony of ordinary individuals who embody the story—a gay couple getting married, a flood victim, etc. Because of public suspicion over "unnamed sources," an individual (with rare exceptions) must give a name.
10. Don't ask the reporter to review the story in advance. You wouldn't want others to have that privilege.
11. News conferences, events and receptions are not, by themselves, news. Reporters have less free time than most people; don't ask them to waste it on something that won't produce a story. (And, while they are underpaid, they probably have had enough to eat, so free food isn't that much of a lure).
12. Before all else, remember Point #5!

Source: Alliance for Children and Families. (2006). *Mission-based advocacy: A toolkit for human service nonprofit board members and volunteers.* Washington, DC: Author. Retrieved July 21, 2008, from http://www.alliance1.org/Public_Policy/advocacyr3.pdf

write a press release or a letter to the editor, because the writer has more control over her or his written word. . . . One will have a greater likelihood of getting press attention by inviting a reporter to an event or scheduling an interview" (p. 44). Keeping this in mind, we offer more detailed information on using the media for advocacy through opinion editorials, letters to the editor, public service announcements, brochures, fact sheets, and newsletters.

Opinion editorials are generally written at the invitation of the newspaper editors. Op-eds, or commentaries, as they are often called, provide a great degree of autonomy over the written word than newspaper articles written by a reporter. Op-eds can also be submitted for publication, but usually few are selected for publication. It is good practice to call the editor to find out the word limit and whether the newspaper will accept unsolicited materials. Since editors of large newspapers receive several submissions a day, only a few are printed, and poorly written material is almost always rejected. Writers should establish themselves as experts on the topics or as the representatives of an organization. After a few successful submissions, editors may recognize the expertise of the writer and look more favorably on future submissions. Stoesz (1993) offers the following tips for writing op-eds. Writers should use a catchy title; a provocative style of writing; and correct grammar, spelling, and punctuation and should provide a brief biographical statement. The op-ed should present a clear and logical argument from a professional viewpoint, and arguments should be supported by case illustrations, facts, numerical data, and research. Writers should keep in mind that a well-told story may be more effective than the citation of statistics. Graphs usually have more impact than tables. The op-ed should conclude with a list of next steps or recommendations. Box 3.5 is a checklist of guidelines for writing an opinion editorial.

Like commentaries, letters to the editor and news releases offer the policy advocate a great amount of autonomy over what is printed. Letters need to be short—fewer than 300 words. Sometimes, when important issues are addressed and presented in a lively way, publishers will print a series of letters on a policy issue. For example, a letter was published in the *Knoxville News Sentinel* that focused on social democracies in Europe, and how those countries were able to provide health care, child allowances, and other programs for all members of the society (Rocha, 1997). Over the four- to six-week period that followed, citizens wrote letters in response, commenting both negatively and positively on the issue. News releases also give the writer a great deal of control over what is printed. Short news releases in

Box 3.5 Guidelines for Writing an Opinion Editorial

> **Writing Style**
>   Catchy title   _____
>   Provocative style of writing   _____
>   Grammar, spelling, punctuation   _____
>   Brief biographical statement   _____
>
> **Argument**
>   Clear and logical argument   _____
>   Professional values/viewpoint   _____
>
> **Data Support**
>   Case illustration   _____
>   Use of facts and research   _____
>
> **Resolution**
>   Sets a decision-making agenda   _____
>   Suggests steps needed to solve the problem   _____
>   Offers feasible recommendations   _____

Source: Adapted from Stoesz, D. (1993). Communicating with the public. *Social Work, 38*(4), 367–368.

print media will often be published without revision. However, a news release submitted to both radio and TV media will likely be revised.

Craig Miyamoto has produced an excellent Web site entitled "Things I've Learned about Public Relations: Helpful Information on Various Aspects of Public Relations and Communication." Regarding public service announcements, he writes:

> The first thing you should know is that radio and TV stations are obligated to run PSAs (public service announcements). The Federal Communications Commission renews their broadcast licenses only if they have demonstrated a fine record of public service. Broadcasters therefore need a thick file with thank-you letters praising the fine work they're doing on the community's behalf.
>
> Yes, they are obligated to run PSAs. But they are not obligated to run YOURS.
>
> Let's just talk about radio, if only because TV PSAs present a whole new set of problems to overcome (it's not unlike producing a Clio award–winning commercial) and quite frankly, although I've produced a few, I'm far from being an expert on TV PSAs.

So, what's the secret of writing effective PSAs? I have six rules: (1) Compel the audience to listen. (2) Empower the listener to take responsibility. (3) Make every word count. (4) Play with the listener's emotions. (5) Register the name of your organization. (6) Call for action. (Miyamoto, n.d.)

One downside of PSAs is that the policy advocate has no control over when PSAs will be aired. Thus, they may sometimes be scheduled at times when the targeted audience is asleep or at work.

Brochures and fact sheets can be used to create awareness of social problems or provide information about available resources and services. Newsletters are internal publications that organizations or coalitions use to communicate with members. According to Pick (1993), a secondary purpose of a newsletter is to inform politicians and the press of activities. Newsletters should be distributed to members, and to a mailing list of important leaders in the community, including city council members, public officials, administrators, and local newspaper editors. The organization's goals and a membership form should be included in each issue. The latest way of delivering newsletters is in an electronic format that uses e-mail to send them to members or other interested parties. Here we see the bridge between traditional print formats and electronic advocacy. The next section focuses on means of electronic advocacy. Since the availability of the Internet has mushroomed, so has the possibility of activism on the Internet.

Activism on the Internet

The Internet and other forms of modern technology provide a new venue for influencing public opinion and public policy (Hick & McNutt, 2002). Communication technology includes e-mail, online discussion boards, news groups, chat rooms, blogs, podcasts, and all types of personal, educational, business, and organizational Web sites. The advantage of these new modes of communication is the ability to gather information and disseminate it quickly to a large audience of general Internet users or targeted addressees (Hill & Hughes, 1998). Information accessible through the Web includes government documents, statistics, organizational literature and printed materials, pictures, in-stream videos, and graphics. The Internet allows access to vast amounts of information, including advocacy ideas and new and innovative practices.

The ability to tap information and communicate with others gives policy practitioners the opportunity to learn and acquire new skills from sites all over the world. The Web sites of nonprofit organizations, such as that of the Association for Community Organization and Social Administration (http://www.acosa.org), include excellent links for policy practice, advocacy, and other key issues in community and administrative practice. An important but often overlooked skill for electronic advocacy is the ability to critically evaluate Web pages. The Wolfgram Memorial Library at Widener University (2006) has a Web site with exercises, tutorials, and checklists to aid in evaluating the quality of information found on the Internet.

John Emerson's (2005) Web site entitled "An Introduction to Activism on the Internet" offers an excellent overview of electronic activism and advocacy tools, including e-mail, the Web, and other forms of new media (box 3.6). An inexpensive software product that can send e-mails to selected

Box 3.6 John Emerson's Review of Software for Electronic Activism

A number of for-profit companies provide readymade software systems for activists, non-profits, or political campaigns to manage their activist database online.

The systems have different feature sets, but each provides a combination of Web page management, email list management, and member database management. The systems often include ready-to-go, updated contact information for U.S. state or national officials. Some systems can also synchronize with an organizations donor database to allow targeted email messages to donors who match certain criteria.

When users input your zip code, their elected officials are identified, you can fax or email the text of a sample letter, or customize it.

In my opinion, the most powerful feature is the ability to email users based on their zip code. Using this, one can target key Congressional districts before a vote.

These systems are maintained on the companies' own servers, and can be managed and customized via a Web based interface. While some services may be available to very small non-profits at little or no cost, set-up and monthly fees often add up to tens of thousands of dollars per year.

Companies offering these services in the U.S. include:

- Blue State Digital, LLC at http://www.bluestatedigital.com/
- Convio at http://www.convio.com/site/PageServer
- Groundspring at http://www.groundspring.org/index_gs.cfm
- IStandFor at http://www.vshift.com/
- Kintera, Inc. at http://www.kinterainc.com/
- Adfero at http://www.adferogroup.com/

Source: Emerson, J. (2005). *An introduction to activism on the Internet.* Retrieved September 20, 2007, from http://www.backspace.com/action/

zip codes is offered by the Approved Association (http://www.approved association.com).

As for e-mail as an advocacy tool, there are a number of organizations that offer free Listserv services for activists. For example, phpList (http://www.phplist.com) is an open-source newsletter manager that allows activists to set up announcement lists on their own Web sites. Below are some tips for e-mail advocacy:

- It should immediately be clear what are you trying to communicate, what you are trying to do, and what you asking users to do. . . . Be honest about what you are asking them to do and why. . . . Demonstrate that you are doing something concrete that can have an impact. . . . If possible, include some good news.
- Do not send large images and attachments. . . . Make it easy to subscribe and unsubscribe. . . . Let your audience know what they are getting when subscribing to the e-mail list. . . . Feature an explicit link to your privacy policy.
- Segment your list if you have a large list of supporters. Create different messages for different audiences. . . . Write for e-mail, not for print. . . . Put your main point at the top. . . . Include an action component with everything.
- Follow up. . . . Give subscribers a sense of how many people took action and what the effects of that action were and thank them for taking action. . . .
- Be open and accessible and respond to users' questions and concerns. . . . Don't Spam. Only send e-mail to people who have agreed to receive it from you.

Web logs, or blogs, are another method of electronic advocacy and campaigning. In contrast to traditional campaigning, blogs encourage information flow between users, as "the blogosphere thrives on commentary and discussion and interlinking" (Emerson, 2005, p. 18). The popularity of blogs has prompted the creation of Web sites that monitor blogs for the popular topics and news of the day. According to the Pew Internet and American Life Project study, of the 120 million U.S. adults who use the Internet, 7 percent, or more than 8 million people, report that they have produced a blog or Web-based diary. The number of blog readers jumped from 17 percent of Internet users in February 2004 to 27 percent in November 2004—a 58 percent increase in blog readers in less than a year (Rainie, 2005).

Finally, viral marketing is another form of online advocacy. Viral marketing is based on the idea that if a recipient of a message or the viewer of a message or Web site finds the message of sufficient value or interest, he or she is likely to share the message with others. This is the electronic equivalent of using advertisements to get viewers or listeners to pass on message by word of mouth. Well-designed viral messages can spread rapidly and be very effective. One example is Amnesty International USA's (2007) "Conflict Diamonds," which is a dramatic video calling on people to stop buying diamonds mined in war-torn countries such as the Ivory Coast, in West Africa.

Some examples of other forms of Internet advocacy are SourceWatch and the Independent Media Center. As a collaborative project of the Center for Media and Democracy, SourceWatch (http://www.sourcewatch.org/index.php?title=Disinfopedia) aims at producing "a directory of public relations firms, think tanks, industry-funded organizations and industry-friendly experts that work to influence public opinion and public policy on behalf of corporations, governments and special interests." SourceWatch is based on Wikipedia's free software engine, which allows anyone to create and edit "wiki" encyclopedias online. Another resource is the Independent Media Center (http://www.indymedia.org), which is an organization of independent and alternative media organizations and activists originally founded to report news of the World Trade Organization protests in Seattle, Washington. The Independent Media Center features photos and audio and video reports, including documentaries, distributed by satellite to public access stations. The center uses a democratic open-publishing format, including a newspaper and a twenty-four-hour micro and Internet radio station. Its decentralized system consists of hundreds of independent journalists and media centers throughout the world.

As these examples illustrate, the Internet has become a major source of information and a tool for worldwide advocacy. Other new uses of technology that can be adapted for advocacy include YouTube, which is a free means for sharing digital video. At this writing, typing in the word *advocacy* in the YouTube search function brings up a list of 1,160 videos; the words *family advocacy* bring up a list of sixty-two videos. MySpace and Facebook are social networking sites that allow individuals to set up Web sites that can be used to network with others. One can find, for example, MySpace sites encouraging advocacy for persons with disabilities and federal prison reform. Box 3.7 provides a useful list of Web sites and alternative news sources of activism on the Internet from both liberal and conservative value bases. In summary, we can expect new technologies that will make advocacy even more electronic in the future.

> **Box 3.7 The Internet as a Tool for Social Activism**
>
> **Websites**
>
> MoveOn.org: **grassroots organizing** (mostly Democrats): http://www.moveon.org
>
> The Hunger Site (The Rainforest Site, The Breast Cancer Site, etc.): **fundraising** (can be done in many ways): http://www.thehungersite.com
>
> MeetUp.com: **organizing local face-to-face groups**: http://www.meetup.com
>
> Protest.net: **scheduling**: http://www. protest.net
>
> ActBlue: **political campaign fundraising**: http://www.actblue.com
>
> CT Citizens' Action Group: **local activism**: http://www.ccag.net
>
> **Alternative News Sources**
>
> There are many alternative news sources out there. Some have a partisan bias, like the following:
>
> **from the left...**
> Common Dreams: http://www.commondreams.org
> The Huffington Post: http://www.huffingtonpost.com
>
> **from the right...**
> Townhall.com: http://www.townhall.com
> NewsMax.com: http://www.newsmax.com

Source: Wronka, J. (2007). *Guide to activism on the Internet.* Retrieved September 22, 2007, from http://babsonlibrary.org/courses/activism.html#tool

Breaking out of the Cause-versus-Function Debate

Our discussion of advocacy revisits the opening theme of this chapter and the questions it raises regarding the cause-versus-function debate. The unanswered question is whether the primary role of the social work profession should center on reform or helping vulnerable people improve their ability to function in society. As we have presented the various types and levels of advocacy in this chapter, we have been struck by how much the idea of policy practice helps us break out of the cause-versus-function debate by bringing advocacy to center stage in the everyday practice of professional social work. Before we close this discussion of advocacy, which can be applied to the specific problems and family policies outlined in later chapters of this book, let us reflect for a moment on the recent development of policy practice in social work.

Policy practice is a relatively new emphasis in social work. Beginning in the 1980s, it was conceptualized as a problem-solving, action-oriented, and practice-oriented method for policy reform. In 1991, Wyers conceptualized policy practice as a way of combining social policy and direct social work practice. Not only should all social workers understand and analyze policy and its effects on clients, but all should participate in policy change. Figueira-McDonough (1993) can also be credited with helping to move the profession away from the dichotomous cause-versus-function debate. She challenged the profession to pay more attention to the goal of social justice (cause) and less attention to the client goal of self-determination (function). Others such as McInnis-Dittrich (1994) saw policy practice as an extension and application of the problem-solving approach used in direct practice. Summarizing the literature up to the mid-1990s, Iatridis (1995) provided five principles for incorporating policy practice into social work practice: (1) in order to understand the effects of social policy, one must analyze and assess the implementation of the policy; (2) direct services and social reform are linked through systems theory and person-in-environment approaches; (3) social work activities are bounded by the policies of organizations; (4) participation in policy making requires an action orientation; and (5) policy practice is concerned with improving social justice, fairness, and quality in the distribution of resources for improved individual well-being.

Although today there are some differences of opinion in the literature about the parameters of policy practice, there is general agreement that social work must educate students for advocacy. Policy is no longer simply the purview of policy experts. Policy practice skills should be found in the repertoire of every practicing social worker, and all social workers should begin to assume policy roles. Practitioners must be able to understand and analyze the effect of social policy, participate in the modification of social policy, and assist in the creation of new policy. It is, however, a challenge to integrate forms of policy practice, which emphasize social and organizational change, with direct practice, which focuses on individuals and families. Despite this challenge, 75 percent of direct-practice social workers perform some client advocacy as part of their jobs: negotiating services, arguing for clients' needs, and securing appropriate benefits. Social workers also think they should advocate more frequently than they do, citing bureaucratic restraints, heavy work demands, and a lack of advocacy skills and knowledge as reasons why they do not advocate as often as they should (Schneider & Lester, 2001).

There are other problems. Macro-practice concentrations that focus on training social work students as experts in policy analysis and political social work are few and far between. In schools of social work, macro concentrations typically feature blended combinations of policy, community organizing, social administration, management, and the like. To our knowledge, the pioneering certificate program in political social work at the University of Houston is still one of a kind. An evaluation of the program in 2001 found that about twenty students were attracted to the concentration each year. After graduation, they found jobs both in direct practice and administration/management and other forms of macro-oriented practice, with 39 percent working in direct practice and 61 percent in macro social work, compared to 75 percent and 14 percent respectively in a national study. Most importantly, in characterizing their perspective on social change, 67 percent identified social justice as their perspective, followed by feminism (66%), and a radical orientation and/or Marxism/socialism (10%). Of respondents who answered the qualitative questions on social activism, "most were not employed in what they considered a 'political setting,' but 78% thought they had support for their social justice beliefs on the job" (Fisher, Weedman, Alex, & Stout, 2001, p. 50).

Two recent studies discuss the political advocacy of social work practitioners and social work educators. A survey of the perceptions of state NASW chapter directors found that "members are more likely to participate when the specific issue is of personal importance or perceived as a problem by members. The second most common factor promoting participation was the ease of access to information and communication regarding an issue" (Hartnett, Harding, & Scanlon, 2005, p. 79). Constraints on advocacy set by employers were seen as a factor discouraging participation in advocacy activities. In Mary's (2001) study of sixty-three faculty members and field instructors at two universities, 95 percent agreed with the statement "Social work, in principle, is not separable from social reform" (p. 12). The study also found that social workers in macro positions were "more politically active, perhaps because their jobs require them to be involved in implementing and/or formulating policy" (p. 15). The Nancy A. Humphreys Institute for Political Social Work (2009), founded at the University of Connecticut in 1995, is making a concerted effort to address these issues by involving all social work students in policy practice and political social work. Efforts include training and curriculum in empowerment-based activities such as voter registration and other types of mobilization. In particular, the institute's mission is to increase the number of social workers who provide leadership in political campaigns, work for elected officials, and are elected to office.

Summary

Advocacy is an important part of social work and other human service professions that provide services for families and work to promote policies that support family well-being. This chapter framed the discussion of advocacy in view of the cause-versus-function debate, which challenges social workers in direct practice and those engaged in system reform to advocate for families. We examined different levels of advocacy and examples illustrating client-centered advocacy and class advocacy, which is targeted at system change. The chapter presented the advocacy campaign as a strategic planning method for organizing advocacy activities. Many different types of activities are useful in advocacy, and these can be applied at the organizational, community, and legislative levels, including local, state, and federal governments. We also briefly reviewed several types of advocacy tactics that can be used in implementing an advocacy campaign. These include persuasion, task forces and coalitions, lobbying, and various forms of the media, such as opinion editorials, letters to the editor, public service announcements, and various methods of electronic advocacy. Finally, we looked at the development of policy practice in social work as a way of breaking away from the cause-versus-function debate. The principles of policy practice are ways for all social workers and human service professionals to be involved in advocacy and policy change on behalf of and with families.

As we conclude this chapter on advocating for families, it is perhaps appropriate to turn again to the words of Porter R. Lee. In an address entitled "The Social Worker and Social Action" delivered at the New York State Conference on Social Work in 1935, Lee (1937) stated: "I do not believe that any social worker can afford to be apathetic towards the need for fundamental social readjustments in this country" (p. 268).

FOR FURTHER READING

Dobson, C. (2003). *The troublemaker's teaparty: A manual for effective citizen action*. Gabriola Island, Canada: New Society Publishers.

Ezell, M. (2001). *Advocacy in the human services*. Belmont, CA: Wadsworth.

Francisco, V. T., Fawcett, S. B., Schultz, J. A., Berkowitz B., Wolff, T. J., & Nagy, G. (2001). Using Internet-based resources to build community capacity: The Community Tool Box [http://ctb.ukans.edu/]. *American Journal of Community Psychology, 29*(2), 293–300.

Haynes, K. S., & Mickelson, J. S. (2000). *Affecting change: Social workers in the political arena*. Boston: Allyn & Bacon.

Hoefer, R. (2006). *Advocacy practice for social justice.* Chicago: Lyceum Books.

Jackson-Elmore, C. (2005). Informing state policymakers: Opportunities for social workers. *Social Work, 50*(3), 251–261.

Ortiz, L. P., Wirz, C., Semion, K., & Rodriguez, C. (2004). Legislative casework: Where policy and practice intersect. *Journal of Sociology and Social Welfare, 31*(2), 49–68.

Pidgeon, W. P., Jr. (Ed.). (2001). *The legislative labyrinth: A map for not-for-profits.* Hoboken, NJ: Wiley.

Rae, A., & Nicholas-Wolosuk, W. (2003). *Changing agency policy: An incremental approach.* Boston: Allyn & Bacon.

Seipel, M. O., & Brown, J. (2008). Promoting American families: The role of state legislation. *Families in Society, 89*(2), 174–182.

Teator, B. (2008). "Your agenda is our agenda": State legislators' perspectives of interest group influence on political decision making. *Journal of Community Practice, 16*(2), 201–220.

TreasuryDirect. (2008). *The debt to the penny and who holds it.* Retrieved July 20, 2008, from http://www.treasurydirect.gov/NP/BPDLogin?application=np

References

Abramovitz, M. (1998). Social work and social reform: An arena of struggle. *Social Work, 43*(6), 512–526.

Abramovitz, M., & Bardill, D. R. (1993). Should all social work students be educated for social change? *Journal of Social Work Education, 29*, 6–18.

Alliance for Children and Families. (2006). *Mission-based advocacy: A toolkit for human service nonprofit board members and volunteers.* Washington, DC: Author. Retrieved March 18, 2008, from http://www.alliance1.org/Public_Policy/advocacyr3.pdf

Amnesty International USA. (2007). *Conflict diamonds.* Retrieved September 14, 2007, from http://www.amnestyusa.org/diamonds/d4.html

Ballot Initiative Strategy Center. (2008). *South Dakota.* Retrieved November 7, 2008, from http://www.ballot.org/pages/south_dakota#

Ballotpedia.org. (2009). Forms of direct democracy in the American States. Retrieved July 22, 2009, from http://ballotpedia.org/wiki/index.php/Forms_of_direct_democracy_in_the_American_states

Blumer, H. (1971). Social problems as collective behavior. *Social Problems, 18,* 298–306.

Butterfield, W. H. (1995). Computer applications in social work. In R. L. Edwards, & J. G. Hopps (Eds.), *Encyclopedia of social work* (19th ed., pp. 594–612). Washington, DC: National Association of Social Workers.

Chackes, K. M. (1987). Sheltering the homeless: Judicial enforcement of governmental duties to the poor. *Journal of Urban and Contemporary Law, 31,* 155–199.

Community Tool Box. (2007). *Welcome to the Community Tool Box.* Retrieved May 10, 2007, from http://ctb.ku.edu/en/

Dobson, C. (2006). *The citizen's handbook: A guide to building community.* Retrieved May 15, 2006, from http://www.vcn.bc.ca/citizens-handbook/

Emerson, J. (2005, January). *An introduction to activism on the Internet.* Retrieved May 9, 2006, from http://www.backspace.com/action/

Figueira-McDonough, J. (1993). Policy-practice: The neglected side of social intervention. *Social Work, 38*(2), 179–188.

Fisher, R., Weedman, A., Alex, G., & Stout, K. D. (2001). Graduate education for social change: A study of political social workers. *Journal of Community Practice, 9*(4), 43–64.

Freddolino, P., Moxley, D., & Hyduk, C. (2004). A differential model of advocacy in social work practice. *Families in Society, 85*(1), 119–128.

Government Innovators Network. (2007). *Homeless services network.* Retrieved May 22, 2007, from http://www.innovations.harvard.edu/awards.html?id=3466

Graham v. Schoemehl, No. 854-00035 Consent Decree (Mo. Cir. Ct., 1985).

Hartnett, H., Harding, S., & Scanlon, E. (2005). NASW chapters: Directors' perceptions of factors which impede and encourage active member participation. *Journal of Community Practice, 13*(4), 69–83.

Haynes, K. S. (1998). The one hundred-year debate: Social reform versus individual treatment. *Social Work, 43*(6), 501–509.

Hick, S., & McNutt, J. G. (Eds.). (2002). *Advocacy, activism, and the Internet: Community organization and social policy.* Chicago: Lyceum Books.

Hill, K., & Hughes, J. (1998). *Cyberpolitics: Citizen activism in the age of the Internet.* Lanham, MD: Rowman & Littlefield

Hoefer, R. (2001). Highly effective human service interest groups: Seven key practices. *Journal of Community Practice, 9*(2), 1–13.

Hoefer, R., & Ferguson, K. (2007). Controlling the levers of power: How advocacy organizations affect the regulation writing process. *Journal of Sociology & Social Welfare, 34*(1), 83–110.

Hundley, T. (2007, September 23). Departed to a foreign land: For Illinois mom, Poland no longer feels like home. *Chicago Tribune,* p. 12.

Iatridis, D. (1995). Policy practice. In R. L. Edwards, & J. G. Hopps (Eds.), *Encyclopedia of social work* (19th ed., pp. 1855–1866). Washington, DC: National Association of Social Workers.

Jansson, B. S. (2003). *Becoming an effective policy advocate: From policy practice to social justice* (4th ed.). Pacific Grove, CA: Brooks/Cole.

Jarvis, C. (2006). Function versus cause: Moving beyond debate. *Praxis, 6,* 44–49.

Johnson, A. K. (1994). Teaching students the task force approach: A policy-practice course. *Journal of Social Work Education, 30*(3), 185–196.

Johnson, A. K. (2004). Social work is standing on the legacy of Jane Addams: But are we sitting on the sidelines? *Social Work, 49*(2), 319–322.

Johnson, A. K., & Banerjee, M. (1992). Purchase of service contracts for the homeless: The development of a city-wide network. *Journal of Applied Social Sciences, 16*(2), 129–141.

Johnson, A. K., Kreuger, L. W., & Stretch, J. J. (1989). A court-ordered consent decree for the homeless: Process, conflicts, and control. *Journal of Sociology and Social Welfare, 16*(3), 29–42.

Kriesberg, L. (1998). *Constructive conflicts from escalation to resolution.* New York: Rowman & Littlefield.

League of Women Voters of the U.S. & Michigan Public Policy Initiative. (2001, Spring). *Guide to getting good media coverage.* Retrieved May 8, 2006, from http://www.mnaonline.org/pdf/MediaGuide3.pdf

Lee, P. R. (1937). *Social work as cause and function and other papers.* New York: Columbia University Press.

Martin, J. (2007, April). Social work presents alumni, other awards. *The Record,* p. 7. Retrieved September 8, 2007, from http://record.wustl.edu/news/page/normal/9251.html

Mary, N. (2001). Political activism of social work educators. *Journal of Community Practice, 9*(4), 1–20.

McInnis-Dittrich, K. (1994). *Integrating social welfare policy and social work practice.* Pacific Grove, CA: Brooks/Cole.

Miyamoto, C. (n.d.). *Six steps to effective PSAs.* Retrieved September 14, 2007, from http://www.geocities.com/WallStreet/8925/writepsa.htm

Nancy A. Humphreys Institute for Political Social Work. (2009). *2007–2008 annual report.* Retrieved July 22, 2009, from http://web.uconn.edu/politicalinstitute/about/index.html

National Association of Scholars. (2007, September 11). *The scandal of social work education.* Retrieved September 15, 2007, from http://www.nas.org/nas-initiatives/CSWE-initiative/soswe_scandal/scandal_soc-work-ed_11sep07.pdf

Pick, M. (1993). *How to save your neighborhood, city, or town.* San Francisco: Sierra Club Books.

Rainie, L. (2005, January 2). The state of blogging. Retrieved September 23, 2007, from http://www.pewinternet.org/PPF/r/144/report_display.asp

Riccardi, N. (2008, October 27). South Dakota to reconsider vote on abortion ban. Los Angeles Times. Retrieved November 7, 2008, from http://www.latimes.com/news/politics/la-na-southdakota27-2008oct27,0,5945574.story

Roberts-DeGennaro, M. (1987). Patterns of exchange relationships in building a coalition. *Administration in Social Work, 11,* 59–67.

Rocha, C. (1997, August 24). Taxes could fund health insurance. *Knoxville News Sentinel,* p. F4.

Rocha, C. (2007). *Essentials of social work policy practice.* Hoboken, NJ: John Wiley & Sons.

Rocha, C., & Johnson, A. K. (1997). Teaching family policy and advocacy: A policy-practice course for direct practice students. *Journal of Social Work Education, 33*(3), 433–444.

Rosenthal, B., & Mizrahi, T. (1994). *Strategic partnerships: How to create and maintain interorganizational collaborations and coalitions.* Retrieved May 8, 2006, from http://www.hunter.cuny.edu/socwork/ecco/strategic_partnerships.htm

Schneider, R. L., & Lester, L. (2001). *Social work advocacy.* Belmont, CA: Wadsworth.

Sharwell, G. (1982). How to testify before a legislative committee. In M. Mahaffey, & J. W. Hanks (Eds.), *Practical politics: Social work and political responsibility* (pp. 85–98). Silver Spring, MD: National Association of Social Workers.

Smucker, R. (1999). *The nonprofit lobbying guide* (2nd ed.). Washington, DC: Independent Sector. Retrieved May 8, 2006, from http://wwww.independentsector.org/programs/gr/lobbyguide.html

Specht, H., & Courtney, M. (1995). *Unfaithful angels: How social work has abandoned its mission.* New York: Free Press.

Stoesz, D. (1993). Communicating with the public. *Social Work, 38*(4), 367–368.

Walker, C. (2008, October 18). *Abortion ban returns to ballot in South Dakota.* Retrieved March 1, 2009 from http://pewforum.org/news/display.php?NewsID=16703

Widener University. (2006). *Evaluate Web pages.* Retrieved January 10, 2006, from http://www.widener.edu/Tools_Resources/Libraries/Wolfgram_Memorial_Library/Evaluate_Web_Pages/659/

Wyers, N. L. (1991). Policy-practice in social work: Models and issues. *Journal of Social Work Education, 27*(3), 241–250.

CHAPTER 4

Family Poverty

As we discussed in the first three chapters, family policy and the programs that serve families are largely the product of politics. Through value-laden and political processes, power holders decide which aspects of family life are in need of attention and how resources to address family well-being will be distributed. This chapter and the next chapter, "Theories of Poverty for Family Policy," emphasize the ways in which poverty and theories about why people are poor are typically a part of political discussions that constrain the development of comprehensive family policy. These chapters set the stage for a more detailed look at specific policy areas that affect families and family well-being in the United States in chapters 6 through 12.

Why do we include a chapter on family poverty when not all policy for families is targeted at the poor? Given the broad range of policies that apply to families, we think it is important to help readers understand how complex and difficult it is to define the concepts that underlie family policy. To illustrate this, we use the measurement of poverty and of family well-being as an example. We have chosen the issue of defining and measuring poverty because many, but not all, of the policy areas discussed in the following chapters assume that measures of poverty and family well-being are a fundamental basis upon which the policy is developed. As our discussion will show, however, measuring poverty is in and of itself a political issue. Thus, examination of how poverty is defined and measured demonstrates the way in which values and politics can undermine the development of comprehensive family-related policies. This chapter also explains how poverty correlates with other issues that make family well-being and healthy family functioning difficult to maintain.

This chapter begins with an overview of the way poverty is defined and measured in the United States. This includes discussion of the poverty threshold and poverty guidelines, including the income-to-poverty ratio and the poverty gap, which shows how much a family's income varies from the poverty line. The distributions of income and wealth, or comparisons of the average or median income of the poor to the rest of the population, are other ways that poverty is measured. As part of our discussion, we report statistics on family poverty and exits from poverty. The middle part of the chapter looks at experimental measures of poverty that take relative and subjective definitions of poverty into account. In terms of family policy, an important measure of poverty is the deprivation index, which measures quality of life. The last part of this chapter is titled "Poverty Is Political." Here, we discuss the use of poverty statistics by conservative and liberal policy makers and think tanks. Our examples show how the same statistics on poverty can be used to promote different values and stances on policy alternatives—depending on the politics framing their use and the value differences that underlie the policy issue.

Defining and Measuring Poverty

The Social Work Dictionary defines poverty as "the state of being poor or deficient in money or means of subsistence" (Barker, 2003, p. 177). In economic terms, poverty refers to a lack of money or resources to provide for one's most basic needs. Narrowly defined, poverty refers to economic or material deprivation. If a family is poor, they are unable to meet their basic needs of food, shelter, and the like. The concept seems so straightforward that it appears that defining poverty would be a simple task. But in practice, it is very difficult to decide when a family is so economically or materially deprived that policies need to be developed to address their unmet needs. How do we know when an individual or a family is poor? It is difficult to apply a visual test to poverty. All members of society may not see it in the same way. Moreover, how we see poverty depends on how we measure it. Thus, our first task is to understand different ways in which poverty is measured.

Three approaches to measuring poverty are in common use. Absolute measures of poverty set uniform statistical standards for measuring the economic well-being of an individual, a family, or a country. Absolute measures are defined by statistics that determine a set yearly dollar amount above which a person is not considered poor and below which a person is considered poor. The dollar amount set by an absolute definition is only the minimal amount of money needed to provide for basic needs.

The second approach to measuring poverty is based on the concept of relative poverty. Relative measures compare poverty to the prosperity of the rest of society. Relative measures of poverty take regional and other differences in the cost of living into account, such as housing expenditures, state income tax levels, and costs associated with caring for children. One method of quantifying a relative definition of poverty is to define a percentage of the median or average family income and use this as the poverty level. According to Loeff (1986), "This measure was initially developed from the relationship that existed in 1965 between the 'absolute' poverty threshold and median income. . . . Under the relative poverty threshold, the incidence of poverty is reduced when the income of the poor increases faster than median income" (p. 3). In the United States, for example, the relative poverty line is typically set at 50 percent of the median income. It is updated yearly based on changes in the average income of the general population.

Finally, there are subjective measures of poverty. Subjective measures of poverty are an example of how social problems are defined in relation to time, place, and the context of society (see chapter 2). Opinion polls are one way to measure subjective views of poverty. Politics and values also play a role in shaping the way in which groups view poverty. In a recent testimony before the Subcommittee on Income Security and Family Support of the House Committee on Ways and Means, Patricia Ruggles captured this concept: "Most economists believe, as Adam Smith put it in 1776, that people can be considered poor if they cannot afford the things that 'the custom of the country renders it indecent for creditable people, even of the lowest order, to be without.' In other words, poverty is not just the inability to afford a subsistence diet; instead, the meaning of poverty varies from time to time and place to place" (*Measuring Poverty in America,* 2007). Subjective views of poverty influence the debate about the design of standardized measures of absolute and relative poverty for official use by society.

The Poverty Threshold

Since the 1960s, the United States has used an absolute definition of poverty known as the poverty threshold. The poverty threshold—or poverty line, as it is commonly called—was derived by Mollie Orshansky (1965), a statistician working at the Social Security Administration in 1964 (see also Fisher, 1997). The original poverty line was developed from the economy food plan—the cheapest of four food plans of nutritionally adequate diets prepared by dieticians at the U.S. Department of Agriculture. Based on survey data showing that families spent approximately one-third of their income on food in 1955, Orshansky multiplied the dollar costs of the economy food plan by a factor of three. She assumed that once families reached the spending limit for the economy food plan, they had to cut back on non-food expenditures at the same rate, so no specific dollar amounts were attached to non-food expenditures. Thresholds were based on family size, farm/nonfarm status, sex of the family head, number of children under the age of eighteen in the family, and whether or not adults in the household were over age sixty-five or of working age. The poverty thresholds were based on after-tax money, but they were applied to pre-tax income data because no other data were available. Orshansky reasoned that the measure would provide a conservative underestimate of poverty. Since Orshansky's model was adopted as the official poverty line, several minor changes have been made in the calculations. In 1969, a decision was made to adjust the thresholds only for price changes and not for changes in the general standard of living. This decision resulted in the indexing of the thresholds to the Consumer Price Index instead of by the per capita cost of the economy food plan. In 1981, differences for farm versus non-farm and female-headed versus male-headed families were eliminated.

The poverty line serves as a general social indicator for evaluating the economic health of people in the United States. By estimating the number of people who are poor each year, the poverty line measures the progress toward reducing economic insufficiency for the whole population and for specific groups. To determine the unemployment rate each year, the U.S. Census Bureau gathers statistics via the Consumer Price Survey, a monthly household survey of approximately 50,000 households. The March Demographic Supplement provides the income data for calculating poverty rates—that is, the number of people with incomes below the poverty line is divided by 1,000.

The overall poverty rate in the United States has fluctuated between a high of 22.4 percent in 1959 to a low of 11.1 percent in 1973, where they remained until about 1978. From 1979 to 1983, poverty rates steadily increased by about one-third, climbing from 11.4 percent to a high of 15.2 percent, followed by a decline to 12.8 percent in 1989. Beginning in 1989, poverty rates increased sharply, reaching 15.1 percent in 1993. Beginning in 1994, poverty rates declined slightly, reaching 11.7 percent in 2001. In more recent years, the poverty rate rose from 12.1 percent in 2002 to 12.6 percent in 2005, with a small decline to 12.3 percent in 2006.

When we look at rates for family poverty, we see a slightly different picture, with higher rates for families, and families of color in particular. Family poverty has fluctuated between a high of 20.8 percent in 1959 to a low of 9.6 percent in 2000. Family poverty declined to 9.9 percent between 1959 and 1974, rose to 13.1 percent in 1984, and fluctuated between 11.5 percent and 13.3 percent between 1985 and 1996. Starting in 1997, family poverty decreased, falling to 9.9 percent in 2001. Family poverty increased from 10.4 percent in 2002 to 11 percent in 2004, declining to 10.6 percent in 2006. Figure 4.1 compares the poverty rate and the number of people in poverty.

The Current Population Report shows differences in rates of poverty among certain subgroups of the poverty population, including children, female-headed households, and families of color. In 2006, children were overrepresented among the poor. The poverty rate for children was 17.1 percent, or 12.8 million children. That year, children under eighteen years of age made up 35.2 percent of the people in poverty, although they represented only 24.9 percent of the total population. "For related children under 18 living in families with a female householder with no husband present, 42.1 percent were in poverty compared to 8.1 percent for married-couple families. . . . Of related children under 6 living in families with a female householder and no male present, 52.7 percent were in poverty, over five times the rate of their counterparts in married-couple families (9.4 percent)" (DeNavas-Walt, Proctor, & Smith, 2007, p. 13). The poverty rate was higher for blacks (24.3%), Hispanics (20.6%), and Asians (10.3%) than for non-Hispanic whites (8.2%). Non-Hispanic whites made up 43.9

Figure 4.1 Number in Poverty and Poverty Rate, 1959–2006

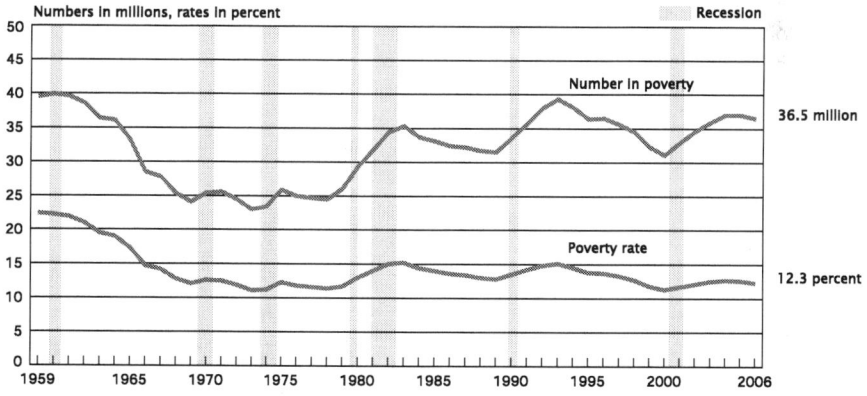

Note: The data points are placed at the midpoints of the respective years.
Source: U.S. Census Bureau. (n.d.). *Current population survey, 1960 to 2007 annual social and economic supplements.* Retrieved May 30, 2009, from http://www.census.gov/hhes/www/poverty/poverty06/pov06fig03.pdf

percent of the people in poverty, although they represented 66.1 percent of the total population of the United States.

Poverty Guidelines

Often the poverty line is confused with the poverty guidelines, the second type of federal poverty measure that is calculated each year. Poverty guidelines are an administrative version of the poverty line for families of different sizes. Although poverty guidelines are designated by the year they are issued, they are based on price changes for the previous year. Table 4.1 shows that the 2007 poverty guidelines set the poverty line for a family of three living in the forty-eight contiguous states at $17,170, and at $20,650 for a family of four (U.S. Department of Health and Human Services, 2007).

The poverty guidelines—or their percentage multiples—are used to determine financial eligibility for several federal programs. For example, families with incomes up to 130 percent of the poverty guidelines are eligible for Head Start, food stamps, and the Low-Income Home Energy Assistance Program. Eligibility for free and reduced-cost meals through the national school lunch and breakfast programs is set at 130 percent and 185 percent, respectively. Medicaid eligibility standards are set at 133 percent,

Table 4.1 Poverty Guidelines, 2007

Persons in Family or Household	48 Contiguous States and D.C.	Alaska	Hawaii
1	$10,210	$12,770	$11,750
2	13,690	17,120	15,750
3	17,170	21,470	19,750
4	20,650	25,820	23,750
5	24,130	30,170	27,750
6	27,610	34,520	31,750
7	31,090	38,870	35,750
8	34,570	43,220	39,750
For each additional person, add	3,480	4,350	4,000

Source: U.S. Department of Health and Human Services. (2007). Annual update of the HHS poverty guidelines. *Federal Register, 72*(15), 3147–3148.

and subsidies for prescription drugs through Medicare are set at 130 percent and 150 percent. To calculate the size and percentage of the poverty population that is eligible for these programs, the government uses the income-to-poverty ratio. The income-to-poverty ratio shows the depth of poverty—that is, how far below or above the poverty line household income falls, and how the level of poverty varies among different subgroups of the poor. Table 4.2 reports income-to-poverty ratios for 50 percent, 100 percent, and 125 percent of poverty thresholds by age, race/Hispanic origin, and family status in 2006. For example, the income of 12.8 percent of the U.S. population fell below the poverty threshold, and 16.8 percent of the U.S. population had incomes at or below 125 percent of the poverty threshold.

Table 4.2 People with Income Below Specified Ratios of Their Poverty Thresholds by Selected Characteristics, 2006

(Numbers in thousands, confidence intervals (C.I.) in thousands or percentage points as appropriate. People as of March of the following year)

Characteristic	Total	Under 0.50				Under 1.00				Under 1.25			
		Number	90-percent C.I.[1] (±)	Percent	90-percent C.I.[1] (±)	Number	90-percent C.I.[1] (±)	Percent	90-percent C.I.[1] (±)	Number	90-percent C.I.[1] (±)	Percent	90-percent C.I.[1] (±)
All people	296,450	15,447	457	5.2	0.2	36,460	676	12.3	0.2	49,688	768	16.8	0.3
Age													
Under 18 years	73,727	5,508	238	7.5	0.3	12,827	345	17.4	0.5	17,051	385	23.1	0.5
18 to 24 years	28,405	2,612	115	9.2	0.4	5,047	155	17.8	0.5	6,475	172	22.8	0.6
25 to 34 years	39,868	2,185	107	5.5	0.3	4,920	158	12.3	0.4	6,628	182	16.6	0.4
35 to 44 years	42,762	1,618	93	3.8	0.2	4,049	144	9.5	0.3	5,506	167	12.9	0.4
45 to 54 years	43,461	1,464	88	3.4	0.2	3,399	133	7.8	0.3	4,566	152	10.5	0.3
55 to 59 years	18,221	666	60	3.7	0.3	1,468	88	8.1	0.5	2,002	103	11.0	0.5
60 to 64 years	13,970	482	51	3.4	0.4	1,357	85	9.7	0.6	1,822	98	13.0	0.7
65 years and older	36,035	914	69	2.5	0.2	3,394	129	9.4	0.4	5,638	160	15.6	0.4
Race[2] and Hispanic Origin													
White	237,619	9,987	371	4.2	0.2	24,416	566	10.3	0.2	34,290	658	14.4	0.3
White, not Hispanic	196,049	6,917	311	3.5	0.2	16,013	465	8.2	0.2	22,432	544	11.4	0.3
Black	37,306	4,057	232	10.9	0.6	9,048	331	24.3	0.8	11,463	363	30.7	0.9
Asian	13,177	668	96	5.1	0.7	1,353	135	10.3	1.0	1,854	156	14.1	1.1
Hispanic (any race)	44,784	3,455	213	7.7	0.5	9,243	324	20.6	0.7	12,922	362	28.9	0.8
Family Status													
In families	245,199	10,341	378	4.2	0.2	25,915	581	10.6	0.2	35,810	670	14.6	0.3
Householder	78,454	3,156	110	4.0	0.1	7,668	185	9.8	0.2	10,531	226	13.4	0.2
Related children under 18	72,609	5,143	230	7.1	0.3	12,299	339	16.9	0.5	16,451	380	22.7	0.5
Related children under 6	24,204	2,231	154	9.2	0.6	4,830	221	20.0	0.9	6,291	249	26.0	0.9
Unrelated subfamilies	1,367	327	68	23.9	5.3	567	90	41.5	7.2	666	97	48.7	8.0
Unrelated individuals	49,884	4,779	139	9.6	0.2	9,977	218	20.0	0.3	13,213	263	26.5	0.4
Male	24,674	2,268	91	9.2	0.3	4,388	132	17.8	0.4	5,661	153	22.9	0.5
Female	25,210	2,511	97	10.0	0.3	5,589	152	22.2	0.5	7,552	183	30.0	0.5

[1] A 90-percent confidence interval is a measure of an estimate's variability. The larger the confidence interval in relation to the size of the estimate, the less reliable the estimate. For more information, see "Standard Errors and Their Use" at <www.census.gov/hhes/www/p60_233sa.pdf>.
[2] Federal surveys now give respondents the option of reporting more than one race. Therefore, two basic ways of defining a race group are possible. A group such as Asian may be defined as those who reported Asian and no other race (the race-alone or single-race concept) or as those who reported Asian regardless of whether they also reported another race (the race-alone-or-in-combination concept). This table shows data using the first approach (race alone). The use of the single-race population does not imply that it is the preferred method of presenting or analyzing data. The Census Bureau uses a variety of approaches. Information on people who reported more than one race, such as White and American Indian and Alaska Native or Asian and Black or African American, is available from Census 2000 through American FactFinder. About 2.6 percent of people reported more than one race in Census 2000. Data for American Indians and Alaska Natives, Native Hawaiians and Other Pacific Islanders, and those reporting two or more races are not shown separately.

Note: Details may not sum to totals because of rounding.

Source: DeNavas-Walt, C., Proctor, B. D., & Smith, J. (2007). *Income, poverty, and health insurance coverage in the United States: 2006* (Current Population Reports P60-233). Washington, DC: U.S. Census Bureau.

Although the poverty rate for people age sixty-five and older decreased slightly from 10.1 percent (3.6 million people) in 2005 to 9.4 percent (3.4 million people) in 2006, these figures mask the depth of poverty faced by many of the elderly poor: "The 65-and-older population was more highly concentrated between 100 percent and 125 percent of their poverty thresholds (6.2 percent) than below 50 percent of their poverty thresholds (2.5 percent). Among people 65 and older, 9.4 percent were below 100 percent of poverty, a 66.0 percent difference. The distribution was different for all people—12.3 percent were below 100 percent of poverty and 16.8 percent were below 125 percent of poverty, a 36.6 percent difference" (DeNavas-Walt et al., 2007, p. 16).

Another way to measure the depth of family poverty is to look at how much the dollar amounts of family income vary from the poverty line. This is called the poverty gap. Measuring the poverty gap is important because a family is considered poor regardless of whether their income falls one dollar below the fixed dollar amount of the poverty line or their income is many thousands of dollars below the line. Figure 4.2 shows the family

Figure 4.2 Family Poverty Gap and Family Poverty Rates, 1959–2005

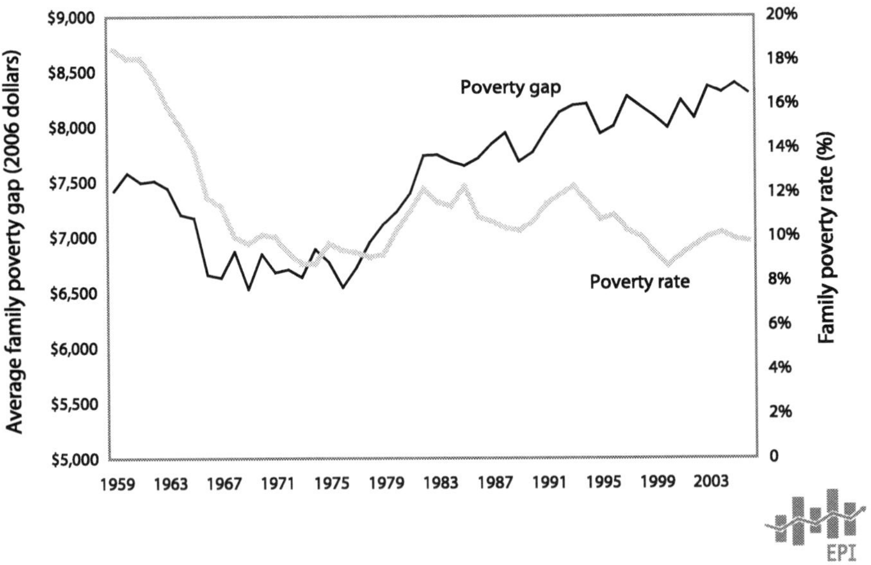

Source: Mishel, L., Bernstein, J., & Allegretto, S. (2009). *The state of working America, 2008/2009*. Ithaca, NY: ILR Press. Retrieved March 3, 2009, from http://www.stateof workingamerica.org/tabfig/06/SWA06_Fig6A.jpg

poverty gap from 1959 to 2005. For families with incomes below the poverty line, the average deficit was $8,125 in 2005, with the latest data showing an average family income deficit of $8,302 in 2006. This is the highest poverty gap on record, indicating that, on average, poor families are poorer now than they have been in nearly thirty years (Mishel, Bernstein, & Allegretto, 2007).

We can calculate the income deficit per capita by dividing the average deficit by the average number of people in that type of category. In 2006, the average family poverty gap was close to the average income deficit for families with single female heads of households ($8,859), married-couple families ($7,653), and families headed by a male with no wife present ($7,726). It was higher for single female householders ($2,743) than for married couples ($2,071). This is explained by the generally larger family size of married-couple households. For unrelated individuals of the same sex living together, the average deficit was $5,502, with males experiencing a slightly higher deficit ($5,832) in 2006 than the income deficit in unrelated female households ($5,244). For families with incomes above the poverty line in 2006, striking differences occur. The average income surplus for all families was $67,743, $75,461 for married-couple families, $34,995 for female-headed households with no male present, and $46,338 for single male–headed householders. The average for households made up of unrelated individuals was $30,400, $34,282 for male households, and $26,387 for female households (DeNavas-Walt et al., 2007).

The Distribution of Income and Wealth

The median or average income can also be used to compare the economic situation of the poor to that of the rest of the population. Figure 4.3 shows the median household income from 1987 to 2006 and the poverty rate for the same period. It also shows the income and poverty rate by racial/ethnic group. Economists use the Lorenz curve and the Gini index to calculate changes in the distribution of median income over time. The Lorenz curve shows the percentage of total household income received by each quintile of the population, starting with the poorest group. The Gini coefficient is a summary measure of inequality that is often converted to a Gini index for ease of use. The Gini index is the Gini coefficient expressed as a percentage. The Gini index ranges from a minimum value of 0.0, which means that the income of every family (household) is equal, to a

Figure 4.3 Income and Poverty Rate, 1987–2006

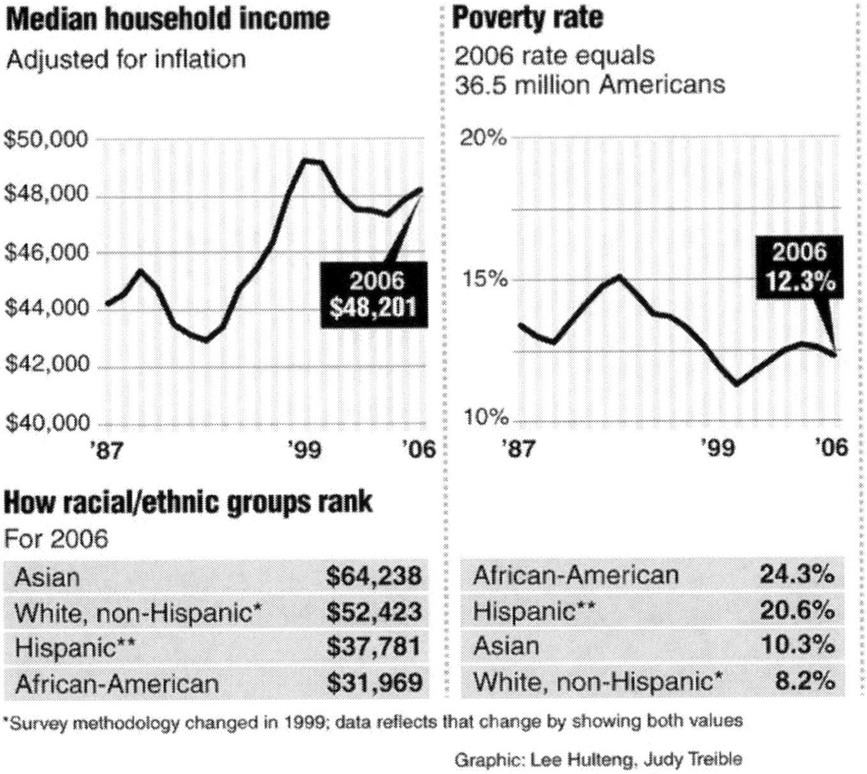

Median household income
Adjusted for inflation

[Line chart showing median household income from 1987 to 2006, with 2006 value labeled $48,201. Y-axis ranges from $40,000 to $50,000.]

Poverty rate
2006 rate equals
36.5 million Americans

[Line chart showing poverty rate from 1987 to 2006, with 2006 value labeled 12.3%. Y-axis ranges from 10% to 20%.]

How racial/ethnic groups rank
For 2006

Asian	$64,238
White, non-Hispanic*	$52,423
Hispanic**	$37,781
African-American	$31,969

African-American	24.3%
Hispanic**	20.6%
Asian	10.3%
White, non-Hispanic*	8.2%

*Survey methodology changed in 1999; data reflects that change by showing both values

Graphic: Lee Hulteng, Judy Treible

Source: Pugh, T. (2007, August 28). *Number of Americans without health insurance hits new high.* Retrieved September 6, 2007, from http://media.mcclatchydc.com/smedia/2007/08/28/20/389-20070828-POVERTY.large.prod_affiliate.91.jpg

maximum of 1.0, which means that only one family has any income and the income of every other family is 0. Figure 4.4 depicts the income inequality described by Mishel et al. (2007): "The Gini began to grow in the mid-1970s, and while it slowed in the 1990s, it continued edging up such that each year sets a new record for the highest level of inequality since the series began in 1947. The slower growth in the 1990s relative to the 1980s is due to the fact that the Gini gives greater weight to movements around the middle of the income distribution, whereas the 1990s inequality trend was largely driven by very large gains at the very top of the income scale" (pp. 58, 60).

Substantial income gains by the richest households have increased the gap between the rich and the poor. Table 4.3 shows the income gap between the rich and poor from 1967 to 2005 by aggregating census data

Figure 4.4 Family Income Inequality, Gini Coefficient, 1947–2005

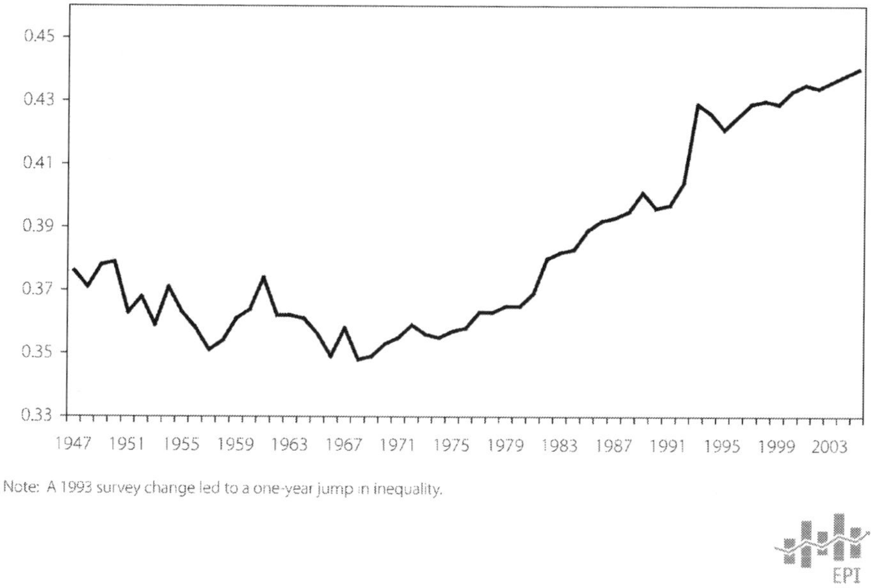

Note: A 1993 survey change led to a one-year jump in inequality.

Source: Mishel, L., Bernstein, J., & Allegretto, S. (2009). *The state of working America, 2008/2009*. Ithaca, NY: ILR Press. Retrieved March 3, 2009, from http://www.stateof workingamerica.org/tabfig/01/SWA06_Fig1L.jpg

Table 4.3 Percentage Share of Aggregate Incomes by Quintiles, 1967–2005

Year	Lowest Fifth (lowest income class)	Second Fifth (lower middle income class)	Third Fifth (middle income class)	Fourth Fifth (upper middle income class)	Highest Fifth (upper income class)
2005	3.4	8.6	14.6	23.0	50.4
2000	3.6	8.9	14.8	23.0	49.6
1995	3.7	9.1	15.2	23.3	48.7
1990	3.9	9.6	15.9	24.0	46.6
1985	4.0	9.7	16.3	24.6	45.3
1980	4.3	10.3	16.9	24.9	43.7
1975	4.4	10.5	17.1	24.8	43.2
1970	4.1	10.8	17.4	24.5	43.3
1967	4.0	10.8	17.3	24.2	43.8

Source: U.S. Census Bureau. (2006). *Selected measures of household income dispersion: 1967–2005*. Retrieved May 18, 2007, from http://www.census.gov/hhes/www/income/ histinc/p60no231_tablea3.pdf

on median income into quintiles (fifths) of the population. Quintiles can be used to see whether the proportion of the poor in the general population is growing or shrinking, the middle class is gaining or losing ground, or the rich are becoming richer. The use of median incomes as a measure shows that the top fifth (20%) of individuals commanded 44 percent of income in 1967, and that share grew to more than 50 percent by the year 2005. The bottom fifth commanded 4 percent of income in 1967, and that share decreased to 3.4 percent by 2005. All other categories (lower-middle, middle, and upper-middle classes) lost ground from 1967 to 2005. Thus, substantial gains in median income of the richest households have increased the gap between the rich and the poor. Periods of economic expansion since 1970 have disproportionately benefited the upper 20 percent of wage earners (U.S. Census Bureau, 2006b). Disparities in wealth also indicate a gap between rich and poor households. Statistics show that 1 percent of U.S. citizens own 40 percent of the property in the country, and 80 percent of U.S. citizens own only 16 percent. Racial inequalities in the distribution of wealth are also an issue. In 2002, the average Hispanic family in the United States owned eleven cents of wealth for every dollar of wealth owned by a non-Hispanic white family. The average share of wealth owned by an African American family was only seven cents per dollar of wealth. According to Michael Sherraden,

> Income inequality is different from asset inequality in both extent and meaning. As an example, we can look at US income and net worth inequality by race. The ratio of white to non-white income is about 1.5 to 1, which is a large inequality. This means that the typical white person in America has about 50 percent more income than the typical person of color (African Americans and Latinos are the largest non-white groups). However, the ratio of white to non-white net worth (total assets minus total liabilities) exceeds 10 to 1. . . . In other words, the typical white person has net wealth more than ten times greater than the typical person of color. (*Building Assets for Low-Income Families*, 2005)

Quintiles are used to show the movement of families from one income level to another. Table 4.4 shows the upward and downward mobility of white and black families from 1968 to 1998. Black families were more than twice as likely as white families to move from the top to the bottom income category; white families were more than twice as likely to move from the bottom to the top income category. Quintiles also help us understand the

Table 4.4 Income Mobility for White and Black Families, 1968–1998: Percent Moving from the Bottom 25% to the Top 25% and Vice Versa

	Bottom to top quartile	Top to bottom quartile
All	7.3%	9.2%
White	10.2	9.0
Black	4.2	18.5
Black-white difference	−6.0%	9.5%

Source: Mishel, L., Bernstein, J., & Allegretto, S. (2009). The state of working America. Ithaca, NY: ILR Press. Retrieved March 3, 2009, from http://www.stateofworking america.org/tabfig/02/SWA06_Table2.4.jpg

distribution of assets or wealth held by households. Table 4.5 shows that the top fifth of households accumulated 84.7 percent of all wealth in 2004, while "the middle fifth held a mere 3.8% (its lowest recorded share), and the bottom fifth actually had a negative net worth—they owed 0.5% of all wealth. Over the 1962 to 2004 period, the top fifth increased their share of wealth by 3.7 percentage points, while the bottom four-fifths gave up that

Table 4.5 Changes in the Distribution of Wealth, 1962–2004

Wealth class*	1962	1983	1989	1998	2001	2004	Percentage point change 1962–83	1983–89	1989–2001	2001–04
Top fifth	81.0%	81.3%	83.5%	83.4%	84.4%	84.7%	0.4	2.2	0.9	0.2
Top 1%	33.4	33.8	37.4	38.1	33.4	34.3	0.3	3.6	−4.0	1.0
Next 4%	21.2	22.3	21.6	21.3	25.8	24.6	1.2	−0.8	4.2	−1.2
Next 5%	12.4	12.1	11.6	11.5	12.3	12.3	−0.2	−0.5	0.7	0.0
Next 10%	14.0	13.1	13.0	12.5	12.9	13.4	−0.9	−0.1	−0.1	0.5
Bottom four-fifths	19.1%	18.7%	16.5%	16.6%	15.6%	15.3%	−0.4	−2.2	−0.9	−0.2
Fourth	13.4	12.6	12.3	11.9	11.3	11.3	−0.8	−0.3	−1.0	0.0
Middle	5.4	5.2	4.8	4.5	3.9	3.8	−0.2	−0.4	−0.9	−0.1
Second	1.0	1.2	0.8	0.8	0.7	0.7	0.2	−0.3	−0.1	0.0
Lowest	−0.7	−0.3	−1.5	−0.6	−0.4	−0.5	0.4	−1.2	1.1	−0.1
Total	100.0%	100.0%	100.0%	100.0%	100.0%	100.0%				

*Wealth defined as net worth (household assets minus debts).

Source: Mishel, L., Bernstein, J., & Allegretto, S. (2009). *The state of working America, 2008/2009*. Ithaca, NY: ILR Press. Retrieved July 22, 2009, from http://www.stateof workingamerica.org/tabfig/2008/05/04.jpg

percentage" (Mishel et al., 2007, p. 251). Thus, whether income or asset accumulation is measured, the gap between the rich and the poor is great, and economic inequality has been increasing over the past thirty to forty years.

Exits from Poverty

One of the purposes of this book is to look at poverty as a dynamic process in the lives of families. For example, families may be homeless, on welfare, or working poor or temporarily not poor and cycle between these broad categories over time. Here, we look at longitudinal research that can help us understand how families enter and exit poverty. Longitudinal data make it possible to measure movement in and out of poverty by the same people, and also to distinguish between short- and long-term poverty. Short-term poverty is often described as transitional, or intermittent episodes of poverty; long-term poverty is referred to as chronic poverty, or persistent episodes of poverty. According to Coulton and Chow (1995), research on the dynamics of poverty concerns the degree to which poverty is permanent. Key issues include the extent to which poor people remain poor over time and whether there is an intergenerational pattern to poverty. Most research on the dynamics of poverty uses longitudinal data from the Panel Study of Income Dynamics (PSID) collected by the Survey Research Center of the University of Michigan, or the Survey of Income and Program Participation (SIPP), collected by the U.S. Census Bureau.

The PSID is a random sample of families who have been interviewed yearly since 1968. The data set currently consists of 9,000 families, including the 2,900 original families and the families subsequently formed by their members, as well an over-sampling of 1,900 low-income families, and 2,000 Hispanic families added in 1990. Duncan, Coe, and Hill (1984) used the PSID to study the persistence of poverty. In their study, nearly one-quarter of the population (24.4%) fell below the poverty line for at least one year in the period from 1968 to 1978, of whom 13.5 percent were transitionally poor (poor for one or two years), 8.3 percent were intermittently poor (poor for three to seven out of ten years), and 2.6 percent were persistently poor (poor for eight out of ten years). Bane and Ellwood's (1986) analysis of PSID data from 1970 to 1982 found that nearly two-fifths of those who became poor in a given year also exited poverty within that year. Changes in earnings accounted for only half of all entries into poverty, but 75 percent of all exits. Using PSID data from 1970 to 1987, Stevens (1994) concluded that "exits from individual spells of poverty often do not imply permanent transitions out of poverty, with half of all those who escape poverty again falling below the poverty line within the next five years" (p. 37). Ruggles's (1990) review of PSID studies on the dynamics of poverty found that about 60 percent to 80 percent of the people who began a spell of poverty in one year exited poverty a year later. Long-term or persistent poverty is associated with female-headed households, people with low levels of education, African American adults and children, and people with disabilities. The evidence that poverty is intergenerational is limited.

The SIPP is a continuing national survey of approximately 14,000 to 36,700 interviewed households that began in 1983. Each panel lasts from two-and-a-half to four years, and a new sample is added every four months. In 1996, the SIPP was redesigned to include the over-sampling of addresses of those living below the poverty level in 1989. The strength of the SIPP data set is that each participant is interviewed every month for thirty-two months. This monthly measurement of average income allows for a more detailed measurement of chronic poverty than the yearly PSID survey. There are three government studies on the dynamics of economic well-being covering 1992–1993, 1993–1994, and 1996–1999 (Eller, 1996; Iceland, 2003; Naifeh, 1998). While all the studies are important in that they note entry and exit trends, we report here on SIPP data from 1996 to 1999, which covers the most recent period in which the poverty rate declined.

Figure 4.5 shows that almost 8 million people entered poverty and almost 15 million people exited poverty. Of those who were poor in 1996,

Figure 4.5 Number of People Entering and Exiting Poverty, 1996 and 1999

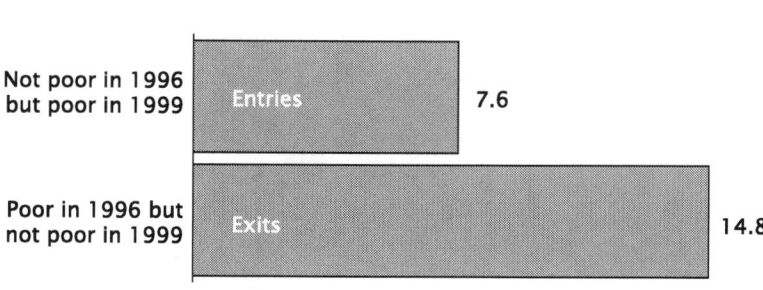

Source: Iceland, J. (2003, July). *Dynamics of economic well-being: Poverty 1996–1999* (Current Population Reports, Household Economic Studies, P70-91). Washington, DC: U.S. Census Bureau. Retrieved April 27, 2006, from http://www.census.gov/prod/2003 pubs/p70-91.pdf

65 percent were poor in 1997, 55 percent were poor in 1998, and 50 percent were poor in 1999. Of those who were not poor in 1996, only 3 percent became poor each year from 1997 to 1999. Seven percent of African Americans and 5 percent of Hispanics who were not poor became poor. The entry rate for married-couple families was about 2 percent, compared to nearly 7 percent for people in other family types. Figures 4.6 and 4.7 show episodic poverty rates (the percent of people who were poor for at least two months) and chronic poverty rates (the percent of people who were poor all forty-eight months) by family status, age, race/ethnicity, and residential location. Iceland (2003) reports: "Non-Hispanic Whites had lower [episodic and chronic] poverty rates than both Blacks and Hispanics. . . . Children had

Figure 4.6 Episodic Poverty Rates, 1999

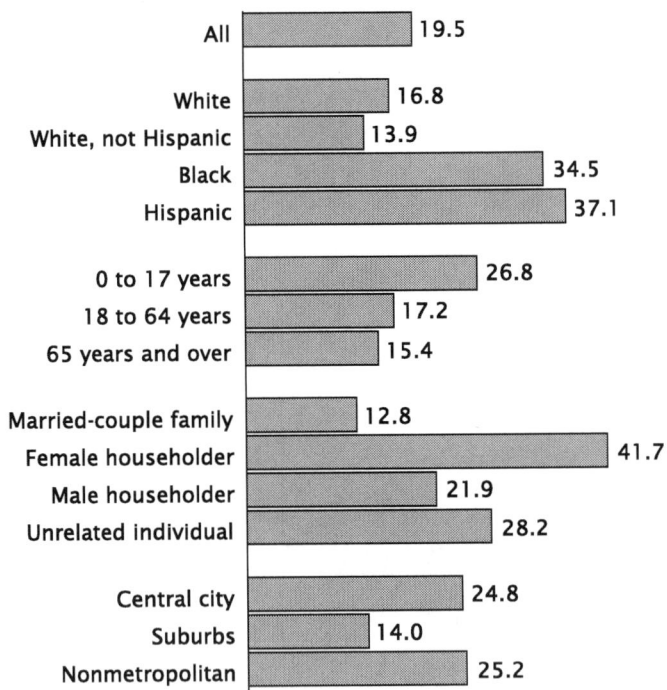

Source: Iceland, J. (2003, July). *Dynamics of economic well-being: Poverty 1996–1999* (Current Population Reports, Household Economic Studies, P70-91). Washington, DC: U.S. Census Bureau. Retrieved April 27, 2006, from http://www.census.gov/prod/2003 pubs/p70-91.pdf

Figure 4.7 Chronic Poverty Rate, 1996–1999

(Percent poor all 48 months)

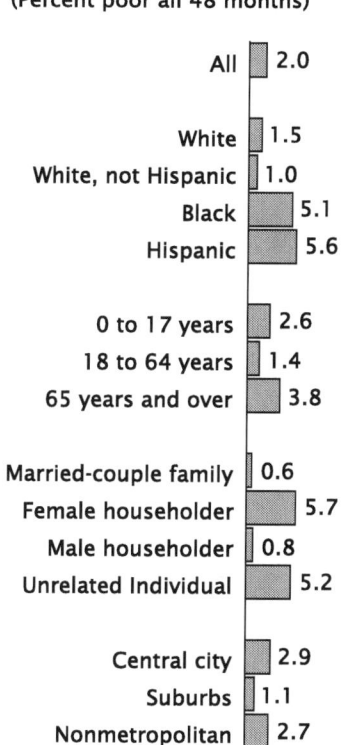

Source: Iceland, J. (2003, July). *Dynamics of economic well-being: Poverty 1996–1999* (Current Population Reports, Household Economic Studies, P70-91). Washington, DC: U.S. Census Bureau. Retrieved April 27, 2006, from http://www.census.gov/prod/2003pubs/p70-91.pdf

higher . . . episodic rates than adults 18–64 and those 65 and older, though the people 65 and over had the highest chronic poverty rates" (pp. 5–6). Married-couple families had lower rates of episodic, monthly, and chronic poverty. Female-headed families, unrelated individuals living in the same household, and those living in central cities had higher poverty rates. Over half (51.1 percent) experienced poverty spells lasting two to four months, 19.1 percent experienced spells lasting five to eight months, 9.2 percent experienced spells lasting nine to twelve months, 11.2 percent experienced spells lasting up to one year, 3.5 percent experiencing spells lasting up to two years, and 5.7 percent experienced spells lasting more than three years.

In summary, the evidence suggests that there is considerable movement in and out of poverty. For most people who become poor, poverty is a short-term situation. Those who become poor are similar to those who have difficulty moving out of poverty—female-headed households, people of color, and the elderly.

Now that we have examined the poverty threshold, the inequalities in the distribution of income and assets, and some findings from longitudinal studies on the dynamics of poverty, important questions remain. How well do absolute measures of poverty reflect the reality of poverty in the United States? Are new measures needed? If so, can family poverty be measured in ways that combine absolute and relative calculations? We turn our attention now to an extensive body of experimental research on alternative measures of poverty.

Experimental Measures of Poverty

Absolute measures such as the poverty line do not tell the complete story of what it means to be poor. According to Fisher (1995) the idea of an absolute definition of poverty is simplistic. In a paper on the historical behavior of poverty lines as absolute measures, he discusses a concept known as "the income elasticity of the poverty line" (p. 1). Empirical evidence of the poverty line in the United States before 1960, and similar evidence from Great Britain, Canada, and Australia, demonstrates that "successive poverty lines *developed as absolute poverty lines* show a pattern of getting higher in real terms as the real income of the general population rises." This results from societal changes in consumption and the standard of living:

> As technology progresses and the general standard of living rises, new items for consumption are introduced. They may at first be purchased and used only by upper-income families; however, they gradually diffuse to middle- and lower-income levels. Things originally viewed as luxuries—for instance, indoor plumbing, telephones, and automobiles—come to be seen as conveniences and then as necessities. In addition, changes in the ways in which society is organized (sometimes in response to new "necessities") may make it more expensive for the poor to accomplish a given goal—as when widespread car ownership and increasing suburbanization lead to a deterioration in public transportation, and the poor are forced to buy cars

or hire taxis in order to get to places where public transit used to take them. Finally, the general upgrading of social standards can make things more expensive for the poor—as when housing code requirements that all houses have indoor plumbing add to the cost of housing. (Fisher, 1996, pp. 2–3)

Given the technological change and innovation that have taken place in the United States, Fisher concludes that the fixed-constant-dollar poverty line used since the mid-1960s is inappropriate. An appropriate poverty line would rise in real terms over time in response to the general standard of living.

Dissatisfaction with the poverty line has been constant for more than one hundred years. Glennerster (2000) refers to the poverty line as "an 'official' definition in a time warp. . . . The debate has barely moved on in a century" (pp. 2–3). Researchers have criticized the poverty threshold both for underestimating and overestimating poverty. It underestimates poverty by not subtracting federal income taxes and Social Security taxes in the calculations. Underestimation also occurs because the amount of money used to estimate the food budget is not sufficient to provide a nutritionally adequate diet, and geographic differences in the cost of living are not taken into account. The poverty line overestimates poverty in the United States by tying it to the Consumer Price Index and ignoring substitutions that can be made by households to keep costs down. Overestimation also occurs because calculations do not include welfare benefits such as food stamps, Medicaid, and housing subsidies (Butler & Kondratas, 1987).

Academic and think-tank researchers began to pay serious attention to the formulation and proposal of alternative measures in the 1980s, resulting in a book entitled *Drawing the Line: Alternative Poverty Measures and Their Implications for Public Policy* by Patricia Ruggles (1990). This prompted a comprehensive examination of poverty measurement by the Panel of Poverty and Family Assistance of the National Research Council of the National Academy of Sciences. Citro and Michael's (1995) *Measuring Poverty: A New Approach* recommended a framework for the redefinition of poverty based on the cost of food, clothing, shelter (including utilities), and other minor expenses (e.g., household supplies, personal care, and non-work-related transportation). The portion of the family's income available for consumption would be used to decide whether the family was poor. For example, poverty measures would deduct mandatory expenses such as income and payroll taxes; work expenses, including work-related child care costs; out-of-pocket payments for medical care, including health insurance premiums; and child support payments to another household. Consumable income would include cash income and noncash government benefits such as food stamps, subsidized housing, and school lunches. Such experimental measures would adjust consumable income for geographic differences in housing costs and expand the definition of family to include cohabitating couples in order to account for the economies of scale in shared household resources and expenses. Finally, the panel recommended that agencies responsible for administering federal assistance programs consider using the proposed measure to determine eligibility for benefits and services.

Since that time, the Census Bureau and other researchers have analyzed data using various components of these definitions as experimental and alternative measures of poverty (Short, Garner, Johnson, & Doyle, 1999). Overall, experimental measures raise the poverty line. Table 4.6 compares the official poverty rate with all alternative measures proposed by the National Academy of Sciences. Figure 4.8 shows a comparison of the alternative poverty line as measured by the National Academy of Science and the official poverty line for 1999–2004. Figure 4.9 compares the official poverty line from 1947 to 2003 with the alternative National Academy of Sciences poverty threshold, a relative poverty line, and a subjective poverty line.

Family Well-Being and Quality of Life

Up to this point, we've been discussing poverty as a statistical concept. Looking at poverty as a statistical concept helps us understand the number of people who are poor, which groups are more disadvantaged than others, and the occurrence of poverty over time. However, economic dimensions of poverty do not tell us all we need to know about the reality of poverty. Citro and Michael (1995) point out that "Measures of other types of deprivation—psychological, physical, social—and the overlap with the economic poverty measure are also needed" due to the way in which the multidimensional nature of poverty affects family well-being:

> Many other dimensions of impoverishment can exist, from anxiety and fear about one's personal safety when living in a high-crime neighborhood or with abusive family members to suffering from inadequate medical care and from homelessness to loneliness to helplessness. These, too, need to be conceptualized, measured, and their prevalence recorded across groups and over time.

Table 4.6 Elements of the Current and Proposed Poverty Measures

Element	Current Measure	Proposed Measure
Threshold Concept	Food times a large multiplier for all other expenses	Food, clothing, and shelter, plus a little bit more
1992 level (two-adult/two-child family)	$14,228	Suggest within range of $13,700–$15,900
Updating method	Update to 1963 level each year for price changes	Update each year by change in spending on food, clothing, and shelter over previous 3 years by two-adult/two-child families
Threshold Adjustments		
By family type	Separately developed thresholds by family type; lower thresholds for elderly singles and couples	Reference family threshold adjusted by use of equivalence scale, which assumes children need less than adults and economies of scale for larger families
By geographic area	No adjustments	Adjusting for housing cost by regions and size of metropolitan area
Family Resource Definition (to compare with threshold to determine poverty)	Gross (before-tax) money income from all sources	Gross money income, plus value of near-money in-kind benefits (e.g., food stamps), minus income and payroll tax and other nondiscretionary expenses (e.g., childcare and other work-related expenses; child support payments to another household; out-of-pocket medical care expenses, including health insurance premiums)
Data Source (for estimating income)	March Current Population Survey	Survey of Income and Program Participation
Time Period of Measurement	Annual	Annual, supplemented by shorter term and longer term measures
Economic Unit of Analysis	Families and unrelated individuals	Families (including cohabitating couples and unrelated individuals)

Source: Citro, C., & Michael, R. (Eds.). (1995). *Measuring poverty: A new approach.* Washington, DC: National Academy Press. Information also available at http://www.census.gov/hhes/www/povmeas/povmeas.html

Figure 4.8 Official Poverty Rate Compared to Alternative Measures, 1999–2006

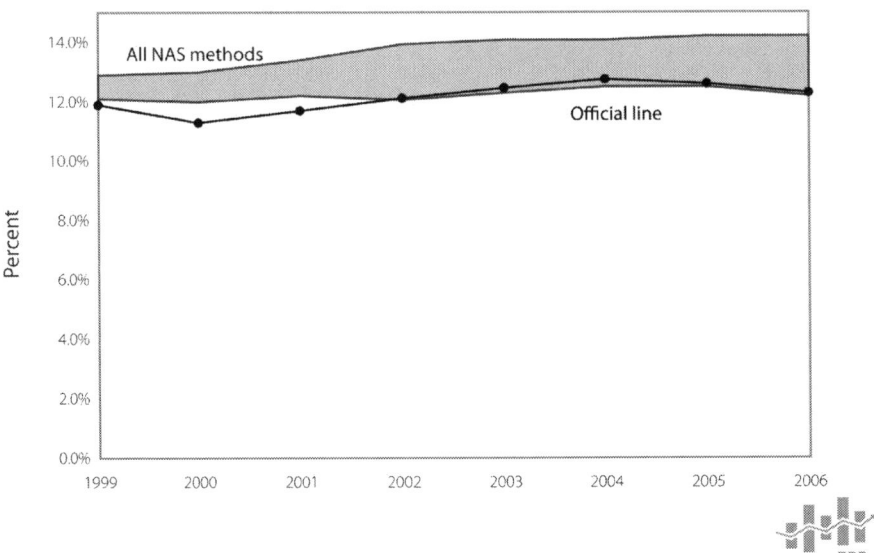

Source: Mishel, L., Bernstein, J., & Allegretto, S. (2009). *The state of working America, 2008/2009*. Ithaca, NY: ILR Press. Retrieved July 22, 2009, from http://www.stateof workingamerica.org/tabfig/2008/06/13.jpg

Also, we have not asked about the consequences of economic poverty in terms of other dimensions of impoverishment. . . . Economic poverty is linked to families' day-to-day lives—for example, to family violence, homelessness or frequent moves to different households, safety of their neighborhoods, or to access to friends, services, and jobs. Similarly, the consequences of economic poverty for access to health care, school achievement, prospects for employment, marriage, and parenting all deserve much more research attention. Also, we have not considered . . . how the consequences of economic poverty differ by an individual's age or other characteristics. These other, less easily quantified indexes of well-being that may or may not be associated with economic poverty are also deserving of study in order to have a fuller understanding of the lives of the poor and a more complete documentation of the consequences of living in poverty. (pp. 314–315)

Figure 4.9 Poverty Lines for Four-Person Families, 1947–2003

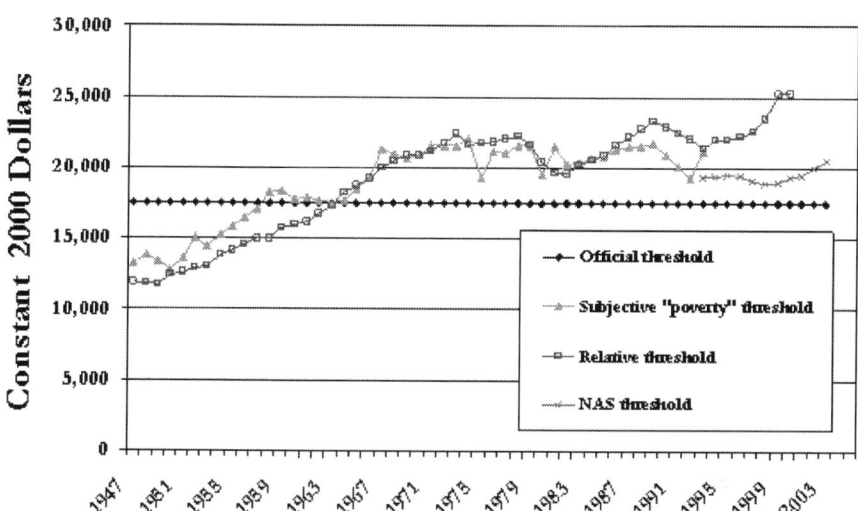

Source: Measuring poverty in America. Hearing before the Subcommittee on Income Security and Family Support of the House Committee on Ways and Means (2007) 110th Cong. (testimony of Patricia Ruggles). Retrieved September 12, 2007, from http://waysandmeans.house.gov/hearings.asp?formmode=printfriendly&id=6283

The concept of quality of life is a non-monetary measure that is not as well developed as the measures of poverty we have discussed, but it is useful for understanding family well-being and conveys a clearer picture of the impact of poverty on families than do straight income measures. The concept of quality of life helps us look at poverty in relative and subjective terms—that is, it helps us understand the well-being of poor families compared to the rest of American society, and how people view their quality of life. Understanding the concept of quality of life helps us in answering three questions: How well off are poor families in the United States? Do they have the minimum resources necessary for healthy functioning in American society? How do they view their quality of life?

To assess quality of life, researchers at the U.S. Department of Commerce developed the deprivation index based on three areas: ownership of or access to consumer durables, living conditions, and ability to meet basic needs (Bauman, 1999; Short & Shea, 1995). The deprivation index measures such things as housing conditions and expenses, crime and neighborhood conditions, health, clothing and transportation expenses, food expenses and food adequacy, minimum income and ability to meet expenses, access to help when one is in need, and consumer durables. Bauman's (2003) analysis of SIPP data is based on questions in several topical modules on extended measures of well-being:

> (1) whether the household possessed selected appliances and electronic goods, such as refrigerators, televisions, dishwashers, telephones, and computers; (2) housing conditions, including physical problems such as broken windows and leaky roofs, as well as the household's evaluation of warmth, space, privacy, overall housing repair, and other aspects of housing comfort; (3) neighborhood and community conditions such as the threat of crime, problems with traffic, abandoned buildings, relations with neighbors, police and fire protection, medical services, and quality of schools; (4) ability to meet basic needs, paying rent and utility bills, avoiding eviction, and having enough food in the household; and (5) whether help would be available from family, friends, or other sources if it were needed in the household. (p. 1)

Other data came from questions about financial assets, types of vehicles owned, child care arrangements, health status and disability, and children's well-being.

Figure 4.10 shows that race and ethnicity are important indicators of household well-being. Non-Hispanic white families fare better in all categories, with the most differences in the possession of a full set of appliances. Hispanics experience comparatively worse quality of life in terms of the need for housing repairs; Blacks are comparatively worse off in terms of ability to meet basic needs, fear of crime, and neighborhood conditions. Table 4.7 shows improvement in the quality of life from 1992 to 1998 in most measures of family well-being. Well-being of households in all quintile groups improved, with the exception of fear of crime. Here the data show stark differences in quality of life: "The lowest quintile was the one most affected by the increase in fear of crime. The percentage of households whose members felt safe to leave their homes fell by 5 percent in the lowest income quintile from 1992 to 1998, while it remained the same in the highest quintile" (Bauman, 2003, p. 16).

We believe there is a lot of work to do in developing valid measures of poverty. Current measures are reliable—that is, the same measures are reapplied year after year. However, in terms of having a valid measure of poverty, the numbers used to determine the official poverty threshold do not reflect the real income, assets, or expenses of poor households.

Figure 4.10 General Indicators of Household Well-Being by Race/Hispanic Origin of Householder, 1998

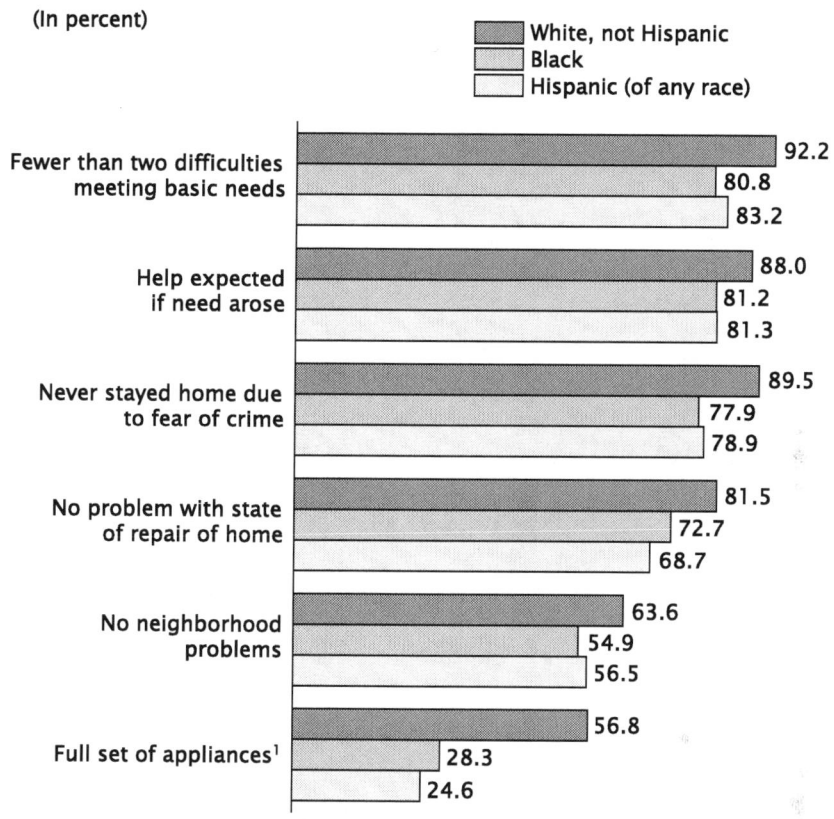

[1] A "full set of appliances" includes a stove, a refrigerator, a clothes washer, a clothes dryer, a dishwasher, and a telephone.

Source: Bauman, K. J. (2003). *Extended measures of well-being: Living conditions in the United States: 1998* (Current Population Reports, Household Economic Studies, P70-87). Washington, DC: U.S. Census Bureau. Retrieved September 12, 2007, from http://www.census.gov/prod/2003pubs/p70-87.pdf

Poverty Is Political

Poverty is political, and the debate about how to measure poverty is ongoing. We have already discussed some aspects of this debate, but in this part of the chapter we want to help readers better understand the politics of defining and measuring poverty. Recently, Bernstein and Sherman (2006) criticized the U.S. Census Bureau's (2006a) latest use of alternative

Table 4.7 Households with Satisfactory Ratings on Summary Measures of Well-Being by Income Quartile, 1992–1998

(In percent)

Measure of well-being	Household income quintile	1992	1995	1998
Experienced fewer than two difficulties meeting basic needs	Lowest quintile	79.9	81.8	83.0
	2nd quintile	83.4	87.9	86.1
	3rd quintile	88.3	91.4	90.7
	4th quintile	92.8	95.5	94.5
	Highest quintile	97.0	97.8	97.7
Never stayed home due to fear of crime	Lowest quintile	82.5	NA	77.2
	2nd quintile	87.9	NA	85.5
	3rd quintile	90.1	NA	88.7
	4th quintile	91.7	NA	90.6
	Highest quintile	93.9	NA	93.8
No problem with state of repair of home	Lowest quintile	63.5	NA	73.3
	2nd quintile	69.5	NA	76.7
	3rd quintile	72.9	NA	79.9
	4th quintile	77.5	NA	81.9
	Highest quintile	81.2	NA	84.1
Satisfactory neighborhood conditions	Lowest quintile	47.8	NA	58.7
	2nd quintile	50.2	NA	59.9
	3rd quintile	52.4	NA	59.4
	4th quintile	56.0	NA	62.4
	Highest quintile	62.6	NA	69.5
Possessed full set of appliances[1]	Lowest quintile	18.5	NA	23.0
	2nd quintile	30.5	NA	36.2
	3rd quintile	42.8	NA	49.6
	4th quintile	57.2	NA	64.0
	Highest quintile	75.5	NA	80.7

NA Not available.
[1] A full set of appliances includes a stove, a refrigerator, a clothes washer, a clothes dryer, a dishwasher, and a telephone.

Source: Bauman, K. J. (2003). *Extended measures of well-being: Living conditions in the United States: 1998* (Current Population Reports, Household Economic Studies, P70-87). Washington, DC: U.S. Census Bureau. Retrieved September 12, 2007, from http://www.census.gov/prod/2003pubs/p70-87.pdf

measures of poverty. Their concerns are highlighted in box 4.1. The cumulative impact of the changes in the measurement of poverty used in the government report lower the poverty rate by 4.4 percent—more than one-third—from the official poverty rate of 12.7 percent for 2004 to 8.3 percent in 2006. The alternative measure used by the Census Bureau is based on disposable income. Disposable income is the net income available for

Box 4.1 Critique of New Census Report on Measuring Poverty

Key Findings

- The Census Bureau recently unveiled new alternative poverty measures "intended to provide a more complete measure of economic well-being." The new poverty measures, which produce poverty rates as much as one-third below the official poverty rate, contain some features that have been characterized by poverty experts and past Census reports as flawed or incomplete.
- Unlike past Census reports on alternative measures of poverty, this report does not include a set of poverty measures that follow the recommendations of an expert panel of the National Academy of Sciences (NAS) and that are more complete than either the official poverty rate or the new measures. Poverty rates under the NAS measures are generally *higher* than the official poverty rate.
- The new measures are flawed (and biased downward) because, among other reasons, they do not account for families' expenses for child care and medical care and attribute major new categories of income (such as potential income from home equity) to families without making the adjustments to the poverty threshold necessary to create a consistent measure of well-being.

Source: Bernstein, J., & Sherman, A. (2006, March 28). *Poor measurement: New census report on measuring poverty raises concerns.* Retrieved September 13, 2007, from http://www.cbpp.org/3-28-06pov.pdf

spending after taxes and the purchase of essential needs such as food, clothing, and shelter. However, disposable income also includes such things as home equity, which hypothetically can be turned into cash if one borrows against the equity or sells one's home. The value of noncash benefits such as food stamps and other in-kind benefits is added into the calculation of disposable income.

Policy reports such as this suggest that it impossible to predict whether there will be a change in the official way that poverty is measured in the United States. What we can say is that alternative measures will likely increasingly find a place in discussions of poverty by analysts on both sides of the political spectrum. Thus, it is important to understand the significance of alternative measures of poverty and their place in politics and public discussion. An interactive Web page sponsored by the U.S. Census Bureau (2007) allows those interested in alternative definitions of poverty to develop their own measures and quickly analyze census data. By clicking on the variables that they would choose to include in an alternative definition of poverty, policy students, analysts, and advocates can use the Current

Population Survey Table Creator II to create tables for the poverty population in the United States, or by individual states. Data can be calculated for various types of households by such characteristics as age, race/ethnicity, gender, and worker status. The poverty line can be based on many different variables. Users can calculate an alternative poverty rate by including—or omitting—such things as taxes deducted from income, food stamps, housing assistance and other means-tested noncash benefits, work-related expenses such as child care, educational benefits, and means-tested tax credits such as the earned income tax credit.

The second point we want to emphasize relates to an overarching theme of this book: values, power, and politics all play a role in policy making. This is certainly the case in terms of how the statistics that result from measurements of poverty are used by analysts and politicians. Joel Best's recent book, *Damned Lies and Statistics: Untangling Numbers from the Media, Politicians, and Activists*, discusses how those who champion particular views or solutions to social problems are susceptible to presenting statistics in certain ways that support their value-based positions. According to Best (2001), "Although we sometimes treat social statistics as straightforward, hard fact, we ought to ask how those numbers are created. Remember that people promoting social problems want to persuade others and they use statistics to make their claims. Often, the ways people produce statistics are flawed; their numbers may be little more than guesses; or the figures may be a product of poor definitions, flawed measurement, or weak sampling. These are the four basic ways to create bad social statistics" (p. 32).

The discussion among public policy institutes that occurred in the weeks preceding and following the release of the Current Population Report in August 2007 is a good example. In "Politicizing Poverty," Bethany Stotts (2007) of Accuracy in Media reflects: "The poverty rate dropped to its lowest level since 2002 but don't expect to read any upbeat news stories on it. The number of people living below the poverty level of $20,625 per household of four declined by .5 million to 36.5 million persons nationwide. Yet in the face of what some would call positive news, others have fixated on the negative results of the census, such as the .5% increase in Americans without health insurance" (p. 1). Just a few days before the census report was released, Wade Horn, former U.S. Health Department assistant secretary in the Bush administration, confirmed that "The political reality [is] that poverty, believe it or not, in Washington, D.C.[,] . . . is a political issue. . . . There are those who like to see high numbers and those who like to see low numbers. Low poverty rates serve as a disincentive to growth of the welfare state, causing a decline in block grants. They also have the potential to decrease welfare, Medicaid, and SCHIP, government employees, to name a few. Increased poverty levels, in turn, spur on new funding" (Stotts, 2007, p. 1).

On the other side of the political spectrum, Robert Greenstein (2007), leader of the liberal think tank the Center for Budget and Policy Priorities, commented on the same statistics:

> The new Census figures are disappointing for the fifth year of an economic recovery—showing a significant decline in poverty for people over 65 but no significant decline in poverty for children or adults aged 18 to 64, and only a modest improvement in median income.... It is virtually unprecedented for poverty to be higher and the income of working-age households lower in the fifth year of a recovery than in the last year of the previous recession.... The latest evidence [is] that the economic growth of the past few years has been very uneven, with the gains concentrated among the highest-income Americans. Too many low- and middle-income families are not sharing in the gains. These figures are inconsistent with claims that the policies of recent years have produced an outstanding economic track record.

Why is the use of poverty statistics so politicized? It has to do with values. Liberal and progressive politicians and policy analysts believe that society has a responsibility to redistribute income through in-kind or money transfers to the poor. They believe that a capitalist market economy does not offer equal opportunities for all citizens to participate in economic growth and productivity. Some citizens cannot fully reap the benefits of the economy by making enough income to be non-poor. There are times when the economy is more robust than it is at other times, so families are vulnerable to unemployment during periods of recession or when factories close or illness strikes. Even during times of economic growth, some families are not competitive in the labor market. These might include those who suffer from discrimination, such as single parents and children, people of color, and those with low levels of education, disabilities, or mental health issues—or those with some combination of these characteristics. Thus, it is society's responsibility to provide social programs to partially support its most vulnerable groups. Readers are referred to the detailed analyses of progressive values and their historic impact on social policy offered by Wilson (1985) and O'Connor (2002).

Conservatives and right-leaning politicians and policy analysts take a different view. Their values center on the idea of "rugged individualism"—

that is, the belief that in a free market economy, individuals have freedom of individual choice and the opportunity to participate in the economy. If people participate in the economy and work hard, their lot in life will improve. When the economy does well, wages rise, and this, in and of itself, benefits those at the lowest economic levels. Conservative values place the responsibility for support and help on individuals and families. Government should not intervene in the family. Substituting in-kind or cash assistance through government programs creates welfare dependency. Readers are referred to the detailed analyses of conservative values and their historic impact on social policy offered by Lee (1985), Lo and Schwartz (1998), and Ginsberg (1998).

These value-based views about the role of government, individuals, and the family create the political environment that surrounds the measurement of poverty. Robert Rector (2007), a leading advocate at the Heritage Foundation, which is a think tank for conservative social welfare policy, summarizes conservative beliefs surrounding poverty: Poverty will remain politicized, he believes, because "what we will do as a society is invent new problems so that we can always have a large number of people 'in deprivation.' Otherwise, we really couldn't continue to fuel the growth of the welfare industry" (p. 2).

Just as we completed the writing of this chapter, we came across Rector's (2007) analysis of the same 2007 Current Population Report that we used to obtain current statistics on family poverty. Rector presents the census statistics and writes his analysis from a conservative point of view. In this chapter, we presented the same census statistics and wrote our analysis from a progressive point of view. If readers were to take the time to read Rector's analysis, we imagine that many would wonder if data from the same report were being reported. Some might even wonder if we were reporting poverty statistics from the same country at the same time in history. Reading Rector's online report would be a useful exercise in understanding the politicization of poverty and seeing the difference that values make in how statistics are reported for serious students and practitioners who are planning to engage more deeply in policy analysis and policy making.

The third point that we want to make in concluding this chapter is that policy analysts tie themselves to political candidates—either informally through their positions in policy institutes or think tanks, or formally as advisors to political campaigns and candidates. Policy think tanks, which generate much of the research on poverty and other social issues, can be liberal or conservative. Three leading liberal or progressive think tanks, for example, are the Brookings Institution, the Center on Budget and Policy Priorities, and the Urban Institute. Three leading conservative think tanks are the American Enterprise Institute, the Cato Institute, and the Heritage Foundation. While belief systems fall along a continuum from the far left to the far right, with left- and right-leaning moderates in the middle, it is fair to say that *values* underlie the type of policy analysis that professional policy institutes undertake and the views that they champion.

The 2008 campaign was no exception. The headline of a front-page article in the *Chicago Tribune* on September 17, 2007, read: "Obama's Policy Team Loaded with All-Stars" (Dorning, 2007, p. 1). The article reports that more than five hundred policy experts provided domestic policy ideas to the campaign, and more than two hundred provided proposals and ideas for foreign policy. What is interesting about the policy experts attached to Barack Obama's campaign is that they do not all follow progressive or liberal ideology. The article quotes Philip Zelikow, a former senior Bush administration official, and now a history professor at the University of Virginia: "If you guess that he's surrounded himself with people who are highly ideological, left-wing or dovish, you would guess wrong. . . . These folks cannot easily be typecast by ideology" (p. 17).

This is just one example, and there are similar stories behind other campaigns and political figures. There is a Web site called On the Issues: Every Political Leader on Every Issue (2007) that shows the policy position, voting record, and relevant quotes of every state and federal office holder, including all twenty candidates who sought their party's presidential nomination in 2008.

Summary

This chapter emphasized the importance of understanding the ways in which social indicators are developed and the ways in which social issues are measured. Defining and measuring poverty are not as simple as they may seem. Absolute, relative, and subjective measures of poverty can be used, and each type of measure reports different aspects of what it means to be poor. The United States uses the poverty threshold as the official measure of poverty, and the poverty guidelines as an administrative version of the poverty line to determine eligibility for government programs and services. We also provided information about other measures of poverty, such as median income, the income-to-poverty ratio, and the poverty gap, which shows how much a family's income varies from the poverty line. Poverty can also be assessed through comparisons of the distribution of income and wealth between the richest fifth of the population and the poorest fifth of the population. Researchers have also experimented with a wide range of alternative measures of poverty, including calculations that take into account in-kind benefits such as food stamps and housing assistance, home equity, taxes, and child care costs. In terms of family policy, an interesting measure of poverty is the deprivation index, which measures the quality of life from a relative and subjective point of view. Overall, the various definitions of poverty and the variables used to measure it matter greatly in officially determining who is poor and who is not.

This chapter concluded with a look at poverty statistics from a political perspective. Statistical data are neutral—that is, the same statistics can be used by advocates, researchers, politicians, and policy makers to promote policy stances on both ends of the liberal-conservative continuum. The way in which poverty statistics are used, however, largely depends on politics and the values held by those working to develop or change family policy.

Our final reflection is that the issues presented herein—poverty and its measurement, statistics and their use, and the influence of values and politics—remind us of the words of Mark Twain (1906): "Figures often beguile me, particularly when I have the arranging of them myself; in which case the remark attributed to Disraeli would often apply with justice and force: 'There are three kinds of lies: lies, damned lies, and statistics.'"

For Further Reading

Glennerster, H. (2000). US poverty studies and poverty measurement: The past twenty-five years. *Social Service Review, 76*(1), 83–107. Retrieved September 14, 2007, from http://sticerd.lse.ac.uk/dps/case/cp/CASE paper42.pdf

Ouellette, T., Burstein, N., Long, D., & Beecroft, E. (2004, April). *Measures of material hardship.* Retrieved September 15, 2007, from http://aspe.hhs.gov/hsp/material-hardship04/

Seccombe, K. (2002). "Beating the odds" versus "changing the odds": Poverty, resilience, and family policy. *Journal of Marriage and Family, 64,* 384–394.

Short, K., Garner, T., Johnson, D., & Doyle, P. (1999). *Experimental poverty measures: 1990 to 1997* (Current Population Reports, Consumer Income, P60-205). Washington, DC: U.S. Census Bureau.

Wu, K. B. (2001, May). *Older persons find it hardest to exit poverty.* Retrieved September 13, 2007, from http://www.aarp.org/research/assistance/lowincome/aresearch-import-333-DD61.html

References

Bane, M. J., & Ellwood, D. T. (1986). Slipping into and out of poverty: The dynamics of spells. *Journal of Human Resources, 21*(1), 1–23.

Barker, R. L. (2003). *The social work dictionary* (5th ed.). Silver Spring, MD: National Association of Social Workers.

Bauman, K. J. (1999). *Extended measures of well-being: Meeting basic needs, 1995* (Current Population Reports, Household Economic Studies, P70-67). Washington, DC: U.S. Census Bureau. Retrieved September 14, 2007, from http://www.census.gov/prod/99pubs/p70-67.pdf

Bauman, K. J. (2003). *Extended measures of well-being: Living conditions in the United States: 1998* (Current Population Reports, Household Economic Studies, P70-87). Washington, DC: U.S. Census Bureau. Retrieved September 12, 2007, from http://www.census.gov/prod/2003pubs/p70-87.pdf

Bernstein, J., & Sherman, A. (2006, March 28). *Poor measurement: New census report on measuring poverty raises concerns*. Retrieved September 13, 2007, from http://www.cbpp.org/3-28-06pov.pdf

Best, J. (2001). *Damned lies and statistics: Untangling numbers from the media, politicians, and activists*. Berkeley: University of California Press.

Building assets for low-income families: Hearing before the Subcommittee on Social Security and Family Policy, Senate Finance Committee. 109th Cong. (2005) (testimony of Michael Sherraden). Retrieved July 21, 2009, from http://csd.wustl.edu/Publications/Documents/P05-24.pdf

Butler, S., & Kondratas, A. (1987). *Out of the poverty trap: A conservative strategy for welfare reform*. New York: Simon and Schuster.

Citro, C., & Michael, R. (1995). *Measuring poverty: A new approach*. Washington, DC: National Academy Press.

Coulton, C. J., & Chow, J. (1995). Poverty. In R. L. Edwards (Ed.), *Encyclopedia of social work* (19th ed., pp. 1867–1878). Washington, DC: National Association of Social Workers.

DeNavas-Walt, C., Proctor, B. D., & Smith, J. (2007). *Income, poverty, and health insurance coverage in the United States: 2006* (Current Population Reports P60-233). Washington, DC: U.S. Census Bureau.

Dorning, M. (2007, September 17). Obama's policy team loaded with all-stars. *Chicago Tribune*, pp. 1, 17.

Duncan, G., Coe, R., & Hill, M. (1984). The dynamics of poverty. In G. Duncan (Ed.), *Years of poverty, years of plenty* (pp. 33–70). Ann Arbor: University of Michigan, Institute for Social Research.

Eller, T. J. (1996). *Dynamics of economic well-being: Poverty, 1992–1993: Who stays poor? Who doesn't?* (Current Population Reports P70-55). Washington, DC: U.S. Census Bureau. Retrieved September 12, 2007, from http://www.sipp.census.gov/sipp/p70-55.pdf

Fisher, G. M. (1995, August). *Is there such a thing as an absolute poverty line over time? Evidence from the United States, Britain, Canada, and Australia on the income elasticity of the poverty line* (Poverty Measures Working Papers). Retrieved September 17, 2007, from http://www.census.gov/hhes/www/povmeas/papers/elastap4.html#N_4_

Fisher, G. M. (1996, Summer). *Relative or absolute—new light on the behavior of poverty lines over time* (Poverty Measures Working Papers). Retrieved September 17, 2007, from http://www.census.gov/hhes/poverty/povmeas/papers/elastap4.html

Fisher, G. M. (1997, September). *The development of the Orshansky poverty thresholds and their subsequent history as the official U.S. poverty measure* (Poverty Measures Working Papers). Retrieved April 28, 2006, from http://www.census.gov/hhes/www/povmeas/papers/orshansky.html

Ginsberg, L. (1998). *Conservative social welfare policy: A description and analysis.* Chicago: Nelson Hall.

Glennerster, H. (2000). US poverty studies and poverty measurement: The past twenty-five years. *Social Service Review, 76*(1), 83–107. Retrieved September 14, 2007, from http://sticerd.lse.ac.uk/dps/case/cp/CASEpaper42.pdf

Greenstein, R. (2007, August 31). *Statement on the new Census Bureau data on poverty, income, and health insurance.* Retrieved September 16, 2007, from http://www.cbpp.org/8-28-07pov-stmt.htm

Iceland, J. (2003, July). *Dynamics of economic well-being: Poverty 1996–1999* (Current Population Reports, Household Economic Studies, P70-91). Washington, DC: U.S. Census Bureau. Retrieved April 27, 2006, from http://www.census.gov/prod/2003pubs/p70-91.pdf

Lee, D. R. (1985). The politics of poverty and the poverty of politics. *Cato Journal, 5*(1), 17–35. Retrieved September 16, 2007, from http://www.cato.org/pubs/journal/cj5n1/cj5n1-2.pdf

Lo, C. Y., & Schwartz, M. (Eds.). (1998). *Social policy and the conservative agenda.* Boston: Blackwell.

Loeff, J. (1986, April). The level and trend in poverty. *Social Security Bulletin.* Retrieved September 13, 2007, from http://findarticles.com/p/articles/mi_m6524/is_n4_49/ai_4516097

Measuring poverty in America. Hearing before the Subcommittee on Income Security and Family Support of the House Committee on Ways and Means (2007) 110th Cong. (testimony of Patricia Ruggles). Retrieved September 12, 2007, from http://waysandmeans.house.gov/hearings.asp?formmode=printfriendly&id=6283

Mishel, L., Bernstein, J., & Allegretto, S. (2007). *The state of working America, 2006/2007.* Ithaca, NY: ILR Press.

Naifeh, M. (1998). *Dynamics of economic well-being, poverty, 1993–94: Trap door? Revolving door? Or both?* (Current Population Reports P70-63). Washington, DC: U.S. Census Bureau. Retrieved September 12, 2007, from http://www.sipp.census.gov/sipp/p70-63.pdf

O'Connor, A. (2002). *Poverty knowledge: Social science, social policy, and the poor in twentieth-century U.S. history.* Princeton, NJ: Princeton University Press.

On the Issues: Every Political Leader on Every Issue. (2007). *Welfare and poverty.* Retrieved September 17, 2007, from http://www.ontheissues.org/Welfare_+_Poverty.htm

Orshansky, M. (1965). Counting the poor: Another look at the poverty profile. *Social Security Bulletin, 28*(1), 3–29.

Rector, R. E. (2007). *How poor are America's poor? Examining the "plague" of poverty in America.* Retrieved September 16, 2007, from http://www.heritage.org/Research/Welfare/bg2064.cfm

Ruggles, P. (1990). *Drawing the line: Alternative poverty measures and their implications for public policy*. Washington, DC: University Press of America.

Short, K., & Shea, M. (1995, November). *Beyond poverty, extended measures of wellbeing: 1992* (Current Population Reports, Household Economic Studies, P70-50RV). Washington, DC: U.S. Census Bureau. Retrieved April 28, 2007, from http://www.census.gov/prod/1/pop/p70-5orv.pdf

Short, K., Garner, T., Johnson, D., & Doyle, P. (1999). *Experimental poverty measures: 1990 to 1997* (Current Population Reports, Consumer Income, P60-205). Washington, DC: U.S. Census Bureau.

Stevens, A. H. (1994). Dynamics of poverty spells: Updating Blank and Ellwood. *American Economic Review, 84*(2), 34–37.

Stotts, B. (2007, September 7). *Politicizing poverty*. Retrieved September 16, 2007, from http://www.aim.org/briefing/3735_0_5_0_C/

Twain, M. (1906). Chapters from my autobiography. *North American Review, 186*. Retrieved September 16, 2007, from http://www.gutenberg.org/files/19987/19987.txt

U.S. Census Bureau. (2006a). *The effects of government taxes and transfers on income and poverty: 2004*. Retrieved September 17, 2007, from http://www.census.gov/hhes/www/poverty/effect2004/effectofgovtandt2004.pdf

U.S. Census Bureau. (2006b). *Selected measures of household income dispersion: 1967–2005*. Retrieved May 18, 2007, from http://www.census.gov/hhes/www/income/histinc/p60no231_tablea3.pdf

U.S. Census Bureau. (2007). *Current Population Survey (CPS) Table Creator II with customizable income and poverty definitions for the Annual Social and Economic Supplement*. Retrieved September 17, 2007, from http://www.census.gov/hhes/www/povmeas/povmeas.html

U.S. Department of Health and Human Services. (2007). Annual update of the HHS poverty guidelines. *Federal Register, 72*(15), 3147–3148.

Wilson, W. J. (1985). Cycles of deprivation and the underclass debate. *Social Service Review, 59*(4), 541–559.

CHAPTER 5

Theories of Poverty for Family Policy

As we showed in chapter 4, the definition and measurement of poverty are political. In this chapter, we extend our discussion of poverty and the politics that surround it to theories of poverty for family policy. To begin, we ask the following question: Why is theory important for family policy? Theory is important because it guides our understanding of social interactions and phenomena. Theory helps us to understand why social problems occur and why things happen. It helps us make sense of the world. Given a set of events in the past, theory also allows us to predict occurrences of behavior with some degree of accuracy. Theoretical models are "representations of selected aspects of social reality, the purpose of which is to facilitate understanding of the structure and dynamics of the phenomena they represent" (Gil, 1992, p. 20). According to Robbins, Chatterjee, and Canda (1998), theory is a way of understanding the relationship between sets of variables. Thus, not only does theory allow us to explain and predict human behavior, but it also allows us to explain and predict the impact of larger social structures on human behavior. In this context, social theory is a tool to help us understand the situation of the family and the impact of policies and the larger environment on the family.

To illustrate the place of theory in family policy, we will focus on selected theories of poverty in this chapter. First, we will provide a brief review of broad categories of poverty theory. Most analysts divide theories of poverty into two groups—those from the political left, which attribute the cause of poverty to society and its systems, and those from the political right, which attribute the cause of poverty to individuals and families. Following Mead (1994), we use the term *barrier theories* to describe the major components of structural theories of poverty, and *psychology of the poor theories* to describe theories that point to personal behavior as the cause of poverty.

We join Zelditch (1993) in arguing for an approach to theory development that integrates structural and individual causes of poverty. Integrated theories of poverty do not take sides in the long-standing macro-versus-micro debate—that is, the debate over whether the cause of poverty is situated within society, its policies, and its structures or poverty is solely due to the behavior, choices, and nature of individuals. Next, we will review four contemporary theories of poverty—structural vulnerability theory, assets for the poor theory, social capital theory, and social dislocation theory—in some detail. We have selected these theories because they integrate structural and personal causes of poverty, and there is a growing body of social science research underpinning each theory. These contemporary theories also provide some interesting insights into the dynamic nature of poverty in the lives of families and thus are particularly useful in explaining the role of theory in relation to family policy.

Finally, our discussion will set the stage for the upcoming chapters, in which we look more closely at family policies in specific areas such as housing, employment, and health. Here, we briefly discuss a key article by Kerry Daly (2003) entitled "Family Theory versus the Theories That Families Live By." This article provides a critical analysis of areas of family life that are overlooked in theorization about families. These areas may also be critical to understanding family poverty and the effects of policies on families.

Types of Poverty Theories

There are many theories about the nature of poverty. Historically, analysts have divided theories of poverty into three groups based on what they view as the cause of poverty—the individual, culture, and social structures (Popple & Leighninger, 1999). Individual theories assert that poverty results from characteristics inherent in the individual. These include such things as genetic disorders resulting in mental deficiency or mental illness, as well individual deficiencies in human capital—that is, a lack of knowledge, talents, skills, and the like. Like individual theories, cultural theories point to individual behavior as the cause of poverty. However, since culture is a compilation of individual behaviors, cultural theories ascribe the cause of poverty to group behavior, values, and norms. Structural theories are those that attribute the cause of poverty to the structure of society and its systems. These three categories of poverty theory roughly correspond to the micro, mezzo, and macro concepts used to conceptualize social work practice. Individual theories of poverty correspond with micro practice, cultural theories with mezzo practice, and structural theories with macro practice.

In an interesting article entitled "Poverty: How Little We Know," Lawrence Mead (1994) uses the term *barrier theories* to describe structural theories of poverty, which are usually championed by liberal and progressive theorists, and the term *psychology of the poor* to classify the theories of more conservative theorists, which point to personal behavior as the cause of poverty. These terms are instructive in helping us understand the broad theoretical categories of family poverty research. Table 5.1 summarizes the various explanations of long-term poverty that fit within these basic categories.

Table 5.1 Barrier Theories and Psychology of the Poor Theories

Barrier Theories	Psychology of the Poor Theories
Inadequate Labor Market • Dual labor markets • Minimum-wage work • Mismatch between the skills people have and the skills required by the labor market • Mismatch between where poor people live and where jobs are located • Unavailability of jobs • Underground economy	**Culture of Poverty** • The poor possess personal attitudes and beliefs that cause them to behave in certain ways (e.g., a weak work ethic, early childbearing) that contribute to persistent poverty. • The culture of poverty contributes to intergenerational poverty. • The poor have conventional values and beliefs but cannot enter mainstream society because of blocked opportunities.
Discrimination • Noneconomic barriers that occur because of race/ethnicity, age, gender, sexual orientation, and disabilities	**Individual Deficits** • Genetic defects • Psychological problems • Lack of human capital
Inequitable Distribution of Goods and Services • Lack of child care • Lack of transportation • Lack of health care • Unsafe neighborhoods	**Breakdown of Social Institutions** • Breakdown in the authority of public institutions in enforcing social norms • Breakdown of informal social authority • Disincentives to work generated by welfare

Source: Adapted from Mead, L. (1994). Poverty: How little we know. *Social Service Review, 68*(3), 322–350.

Barrier theories focus on the structure of society as the basis for poverty. Poverty is blamed on problems such as inequities in the labor market, discrimination, and imbalances in the distribution of goods and services. Problems include the inadequacy of the labor market in producing equity for all workers, low wages, and dual labor markets, which provide higher-paying jobs for well-educated workers, and minimum-wage and lower-paying service-sector jobs for unskilled workers. Many poor people work in the underground economy, or the secondary labor market. Other possible explanations for poverty include the unavailability of jobs, including a spatial mismatch between where poor people live and where jobs are located, and a skills mismatch between the skills people have and the skills required by the labor market.

Barrier theories also take non-economic barriers, such as race, age, and gender discrimination, into account in explaining poverty among people of color, women, disabled workers, and other vulnerable populations. These explanations for poverty include racism and subtler forms of discrimination not based on skin color. Barrier theories also attribute the cause of poverty to inequities in the distribution of goods and services, such as the lack of day care and transportation, as well as community factors, such as unsafe neighborhoods and poor schools.

Theories of the psychology of the poor emphasize family instability as the origin of poverty. The theory of a culture of poverty proposes that individuals who experience persistent poverty have a set of attitudes, behavior patterns, and values that are essentially different from those of people in mainstream society. The behaviors believed to be common to this "poverty personality" include early sexual activity and childbearing outside wedlock, abandonment of women and children, and impulsive and abusive parenting techniques. In addition, these families are often headed by single women. The theory of a culture of poverty also takes social and community factors into account. Accordingly, those who are persistently poor do not associate with society's institutions, for example, political parties, voluntary associations, and community organizations. The persistently poor also lack a sense of community outside the extended family. Other effects of the culture of poverty include strong feelings of marginality, helplessness, dependence, and inferiority (Popple & Leighninger, 1999). Culture of poverty theorists believe that these group personality traits cause people to stay poor or on welfare. When the opportunity to work arises, those entrenched in the culture of poverty fail to work, whereas those with a more mainstream psychology would see work as an opportunity to escape poverty. Once this poverty personality manifests itself, it becomes a part of the culture of the poor and is passed down from generation to generation.

Some psychology of the poor theories suggest that poverty is caused by individual deficits such as genetic defects, psychological problems, or a lack of knowledge or skills. As the major theory in this area, human capital theory posits that skill deficits, inadequate training, limited education, and inadequate family resources and assets negatively affect an individual's ability to compete in the job market (Becker, 1964). Race and gender can also be perceived as components of human capital, since wage differentials exist because of different amounts of investments in human capital (McConnell, 1984). Investments in human capital are made by the individual or family and include formal education and on-the-job training, choice of occupation, workforce participation, health investments, and the number of children one chooses to have. The underlying theoretical assumption is that it is the choices people make, rather than the barriers that persist in society, that cause some people to develop less human capital. Psychologically based theories also look at the breakdown of public and social authority in the enforcement of social norms and values (Murray, 1984). Examples of hypotheses related to the breakdown of public authority are the failure of criminal justice systems to enforce child support payments by absent fathers and the failure of public welfare programs to impose sanctions for failure to work. Examples of the breakdown of informal social authority are the lack of middle-class role models for children and promiscuity among adolescents in inner-city neighborhoods (Mead, 1994).

The Macro-versus-Micro Debate

Policy makers who adhere to the barrier-theorist point of view believe that solutions to family poverty require the reallocation of resources. Policies and programs that reduce inequality in the labor market are those that eliminate discrimination and redistribute goods and services to people who cannot compete in the market economy. Policy makers who ascribe to theories of the psychology of the poor believe that public welfare programs create dependency and poverty rather than alleviating or preventing them. They believe that individuals must take responsibility for their own failure to work. This debate is common among many professional disciplines, including sociology, political science, psychology, and social work.

According to Mead (1994), the components of the various barrier theories should be added together in multivariate analysis so that we can gain a better understanding of poverty. This is difficult, however, because many of the barrier theories compete with one another, and there is no simple way to separate one theory from the others. At the same time, the culture of poverty is hard to measure. Most research thus far has focused on what the poor believe about work and family. Since direct measures of a poverty personality have not been developed, it has not been possible to verify that such a thing exists. Table 5.2 illustrates the wide range of views about the psychology of the poor as conceptualized by some scholars. These sharply divided views are categorized on two important dimensions: motivation to work and commitment to conventional values.

How do we resolve this dichotomous categorization of theories of poverty? Zelditch (1993), a social psychologist, argues such a macro-versus-micro approach to theory development creates a false dichotomy that fails to link the structure of society to the actions of individuals. He argues that neither macro nor micro theories alone have very wide application, because they do not provide solutions to complex social problems such as inner-city poverty, dependency, family breakdown, and crime. The tendency to separate macro theories from micro theories sets them up as mutually exclusive alternatives, and as a result, several possibilities present themselves. In one scenario, macro and micro perspectives compete for

Table 5.2 Views of the Poverty Personality

	Strong Commitment to Conventional Values	Weak Commitment to Conventional Values
Strong Motivation to Work	Ellwood (1988) sees poor mothers as wanting to work, but low wages and the benefits of available jobs are unsatisfactory compared to welfare.	Murray (1984) sees poor mothers as economizers, but less moral, and likely to abandon self-reliance and become dependent if the government helps them unwisely.
Weak Motivation to Work	Wilson (1987) sees poor mothers as committed to work and family, but weighed down by structural disadvantages that prevent them from moving out of poverty	Hopkins (1987) sees poor mothers as not committed to mainstream values of work and family well-being because of their deprived upbringings.

Source: Adapted from Mead, L. (1994). Poverty: How little we know. *Social Service Review, 68*(3), 322–350.

dominance and causal explanations are reduced to either the macro or micro level. In another scenario, they are multiplied into micro, mezzo, and macro levels—each of which is believed to have a distinct theoretical structure. However, as Zelditch (1993) points out, the trend in theory development is toward the integration of macro and micro theories for explaining poverty: "The reduction of explanation is the wrong way to create a single theoretical structure—reduction of scope excessively narrows the subject; multiplication of levels creates a house without stairs between the floors. Integration into one theoretical structure is likely to be a more fruitful strategy for the future" (pp. 105–106).

Pertaining directly to our discussion of theories of persistent poverty, Mead (1994) also concludes that "long-term poverty probably never will be definitively explained . . . [but] the most persuasive constructions of the evidence will be those that combine a point of view with a recognition of multiple causes" (p. 344). In keeping with the idea that explanatory theories about complex social phenomena should integrate macro and micro perspectives, we have selected several contemporary theories of poverty that incorporate both concepts. These theories incorporate hypotheses that recognize both structural and individual causes of poverty.

Theories of Poverty

We turn now to contemporary theories of poverty that integrate components from barrier and psychology of the poor theories. Each theory integrates structural and individual causes of poverty, and each has been tested and refined by causal modeling and other forms of empirical research.

Structural Vulnerability Theory

Mark Rank developed his structural vulnerability argument through research on the dynamics of exiting welfare and repeat dependency. In *Living on the Edge: The Realities of Welfare in America*, Rank (1994) presented a statistical and ethnographic portrait of AFDC, food stamps, and Medicaid recipients in Wisconsin. His longitudinal study tracked a random sample of recipients at six-month intervals from September 1980 to September 1983 through the statewide Computer Reporting Network. In 1986, qualitative interviews based on a stratified random sample of fifty welfare recipients in one representative county were added. These interviews were supplemented by field observations of welfare offices, food pantries, and job training programs.

In order to understand structural vulnerability theory, let's look first at the exit and reentry rates of welfare participation. Rank calculated rates of welfare exits for a cohort of "new cases"—that is, people beginning their welfare spell at the same point in time. Exits from welfare differed among households headed by women, married couples, single individuals, and elderly individuals (table 5.3). The majority of all household groups (63%) went off welfare during the first eighteen months of use. Over the next eighteen months, there was a slow and steady increase in the proportion of individuals who exited: 69 percent at twenty-four months, 73 percent at thirty months, and 77 percent at thirty-six months. These results concur with other longitudinal studies that have found that most households on welfare utilize welfare for a very short time (Bane & Ellwood, 1986; Duncan, 1984; Plotnick, 1983). Rank (1994) concluded that "there is a downward trend in the likelihood of exiting over time in all household categories. That is, the longer a household remains on welfare, the less likely it is to leave" (p. 150).

What factors were associated with AFDC recipients' ability to leave welfare? Reasons for leaving welfare included an increase in income or assets above the eligibility limit (31.4%), a lack of children under the age of eighteen (15.1%), geographic moves (14%), changes in federal and state AFDC regulations (6%), and failure to provide information in order to remain

Table 5.3 Analysis of Exits from Welfare

Family Type	Percent Leaving Welfare							
	0–6 months	6–12 months	12–18 months	18–24 months	24–30 months	30–36 months	36–42 months	42–48 months
Headed by woman	25.26	35.48	44.86	52.41	58.98	63.79	67.22	70.07
Married couple	41.72	60.76	69.99	74.59	79.67	83.22	84.86	86.95
Headed by single individual	52.66	76.24	83.74	88.76	91.03	92.28	92.60	92.98
Headed by elderly individual	20.83	34.66	44.59	52.61	57.89	63.55	68.05	71.37
Total Sample	37.82	54.68	63.27	69.22	73.76	77.23	79.48	81.41

Source: Rank, M. (1994). *Living on the edge: The realities of welfare in America.* New York: Columbia University Press.

eligible (33%). Female-headed families were the least likely to exit welfare and also the most likely to repeat a welfare spell. Approximately 42 percent of female-headed families returned to welfare at some point during the thirty-month period, compared to 38 percent of families headed by married couples, and 26 percent of households headed by single individuals. Most households headed by elderly individuals left welfare because of death. Rank (1994) concludes: "The majority of households using welfare will generally do so for no more than one or two years. On the other hand, many of those exiting will return to the welfare rolls at some point in the future. These families are likely to weave in and out of poverty as their economic conditions improve or worsen. For those who remain on welfare for longer periods, the chances of exiting decrease. These are the individuals who may become locked in to the welfare system. They represent, however, a minority of households beginning a spell on welfare" (pp. 155–156).

These findings provided little support for the culture of poverty thesis or for negative behavioral effects associated with welfare. Those on welfare had lower childbearing rates than the general national and Wisconsin populations. There was also minimal indication of intergenerational welfare use. Only 18 percent of the Wisconsin sample recalled that their parents were ever on welfare, compared to 24 percent of a national sample (Rank, Cheng, & Cox, 1992). Welfare recipients were also found to embrace mainstream American values. Living on welfare was a constant struggle, and no one liked it. They valued education for their children. They dreamed of owning their own homes and getting out of poverty. And they were motivated to work—in fact, every welfare recipient interviewed in the study had a background of employment. Most recipients came from working-class backgrounds—some with extensive work histories, and others, especially women, with minimal work experience outside the home. They held blue-collar jobs in factories or were employed in the service economy or similar industries. Rank (1994) found that focusing on the attitudes, motivation, work ethic, and values of those on public assistance was not the answer: "Economic hardship, far more than welfare recipiency, influences family interaction and behavior among welfare families.... Public assistance is a by-product of that economic adversity. It alone does little to explain family dynamics" (p. 169).

At the same time, however, individual characteristics were clearly linked to the ability to leave welfare. Odds ratios showed that household heads who were high school graduates, white, employed, and not disabled had a much greater probability of exiting welfare. Why were people with these individual characteristics more likely to leave welfare? Rank's explanation linked the importance of individual characteristics to aspects of human capital theory. Because such a high percentage of welfare recipients left welfare after a relatively short time, deficits in human capital put people in jeopardy of adverse structural forces such as plant closings, recession, and changes in the labor market from a manufacturing to a service economy. Social forces such as increases in family breakups, lack of child support, and race and gender discrimination also put these households at risk of poverty. Political decisions resulting in the uneven or limited distribution of services such as health care, job training, birth control, and housing subsidies also played a part in increasing vulnerability:

> What I argue is that while these [human capital] characteristics alone do not cause welfare use, they place the individual in an economically vulnerable position when faced with a crisis such as loss of employment, changes in family status, illness and incapacitation, and so on. . . . Individuals and households lacking personal resources, human capital, and economic assets will have a more difficult time weathering such storms. As a result, they are more likely to turn to public assistance as a stopgap solution until they are able to get back on their feet. For some people, that period of time is short, while for others it may be longer. (Rank, 1994, p. 177)

Two other points are important in understanding structural vulnerability theory. First, the structural impact upon human capital deficiencies explains why some people lack human capital. Children born into working- and lower-class families enter life with fewer resources and opportunities, which, in turn, affects their life chances and outcomes (see Beeghley, 1989; Clignet, 1992). "Those whose parents are from a working or lower class are likely to remain working or lower class themselves. Similarly, those whose parents fall into the upper class are likely to remain upper class. To a great extent, differences in human capital are the result of familial social class differences. . . . Most agree that variations in economic and social class result in significant differences in resources and opportunities for children. These differences in turn affect children's future life chances and outcomes, including the accumulation of human capital" (Rank, 1994, p. 180).

The second point is that there are two levels in understanding economic vulnerability. The concept of human capital tells us who the winners and losers are in the economic game. However, we should not lose sight of the fact that "the more structural components of our economic, social, and political systems explain why there are losers in the first place" (Rank, 1994, p. 185).

Given that there is unemployment, given that there are periods of recession, given that there are low-paying jobs lacking benefits, given that there is occupational segregation in the labor market, given that there is a lack of affordable child care, given that there are no provisions to care for those who can no longer participate in the economy because of illness or incapacitation, someone is going to lose at this game. . . . Simply increasing individual human capital will shuffle persons up or down in terms of their positions in the competitive queue, but it will do little to change the overall rates of unemployment, low-paying jobs and so on. (Rank, 1994, pp. 183–184)

The concept of structural vulnerability provides important insights into the dynamic processes of poverty. A substantial portion of Americans will live in persistent poverty for many years, whether they are working full time, are on and off welfare, or are in and out of homelessness. Not only do constant economic battles define the struggle to survive on welfare, but they also precipitate welfare use. For the working poor, unexpected car repairs, accidents, or child care expenses may be all that's needed to push a family further into poverty. "However," as Rank (1994) points out, "when the unexpected occurs (as it often does), it can set in motion a domino effect touching every other aspect of [welfare] recipients' lives. One unanticipated expense can cause a shortage of money for food, rent, utilities, or other necessary items. The dominos begin to fall one by one" (pp. 56–57).

Assets for the Poor Theory

The theory of assets for the poor is important in helping us think about why people stay poor and are not able to leave poverty—sometimes for generations. In *Assets and the Poor*, Michael Sherraden (1991) began with the premise that no one likes welfare—not only the American public and liberal and conservative analysts, but welfare recipients as well. So, if no one likes AFDC or welfare, might it be useful to find out what makes people wealthy? What kinds of policies and programs have historically moved immigrant groups out of poverty or made people wealthy? Drawing from the literature in economics, sociology, and other social sciences, Sherraden found that people become wealthy through three important means—homeownership, pension funds, and savings accounts. The accumulation of wealth in each of these areas occurs through structures that allow individuals to save money and increase their capital investment. When an individual owns his or her own home, for example, home equity increases as housing prices rise over the long term. Interest-bearing accounts increase the amount of savings over time. And tax-deferred pension plans, most of which include an employer match, are invested in and produce high returns over the course of an individual's life span. Thus Sherraden hypothesized that leaving poverty for the long term requires mechanisms that allow poor people to accumulate tangible assets such as cash savings, stocks and bonds, and land.

In addressing the conservative view that public welfare entitlements cause dependency, Sherraden argued that public welfare programs such as AFDC were never designed to alleviate poverty. Rather, as the name implies, income maintenance programs provide just enough income or in-kind benefits to *keep* people in poverty. More importantly, eligibility criteria for income assistance programs typically forbid people to accumulate assets while receiving public assistance. Thus the structure of welfare programs affects individual behavior, but the behaviors of the poor are an effect rather than a cause of poverty. Individual behavior is a malleable variable based on one's social reality—that is, people act upon what they see as part of their future. In this regard, Sherraden hypothesized that allowing only the non-poor to accumulate wealth (income plus assets) not only results in great inequities in the distribution of wealth in the United States but has had a negative effect on the attitudes and behaviors of the poor. Thus assets are not simply stored income to be used for future consumption but have important effects on human behavior. He writes that assets provide stability in times of economic crisis. Assets are also important as capital for investment—which, in return, generates more income and asset accumulation. Because assets are stable over time, wealth accumulates and can be transferred to the next generation. Assets create a cognitive and emotional orientation toward the future. They enable focus and specialization, provide a foundation for risk taking, enhance personal efficacy, and increase social influence and political participation.

If these asset effects hypothesized by Sherraden are true, then the accumulation of assets by poor families is important in determining a family's opportunity structure and influencing behavior, and contributing to intergenerational well-being. For example, the welfare poor have a difficult time getting off welfare because historically they have not been allowed to accumulate resources before they leave welfare. In order to qualify for public assistance under AFDC regulations, families were not allowed to have assets and there was no transition period that allowed them to save money without negatively affecting their benefits. Without assets, it has been difficult for welfare and working poor families to get off and remain off welfare. "Working poor families have little cushion to protect them from poverty when a job loss, divorce, major illness, or other life crisis strikes. It is members of this group, without assets, who slip into hardship and public assistance, then work their way out again, accounting for the 'dynamic' nature of welfare recipiency in the United States. Without assets, children in these families are less likely to plan for the future and less likely to undertake a college education, perpetuating lower incomes and intergenerational finances removed from asset accumulation" (Sherraden, 1991, p. 128).

Individual development accounts, or IDAs, are the policy centerpiece for allowing poor people to accumulate assets. IDAs are earnings-bearing savings accounts in the name of an individual. IDAs are subsidized on a match basis—that is, for every dollar deposited by an individual, an equal or greater amount of money is put into the account. IDA funds are restricted accounts. This means that the money in the account can only be used for mechanisms that create assets over the long term—for example, homeownership, small business development, and higher education.

Michael Sherraden's work on assets for the poor is probably one of the most innovative and important new theories of social welfare. Work at the Center for Social Development at Washington University in St. Louis has influenced policy change at local, state, and federal levels since the mid-1990s. The center has also outlined new global initiatives for assets policy. The center's Web page provides excellent research reports on assets policy, as well as links to innovations in state and federal assets policy.

Social Capital Theory

Social capital theory is another theoretical perspective that combines micro and macro explanations for poverty. Table 5.4 outlines the major studies identifying key elements of social capital theory. We look first at the development of the concept by two major theorists: the late James Coleman, a sociologist at the University of Chicago, and Robert Putnam, a political scientist at Harvard University. Next, we review the work of other researchers who have made recent contributions to social capital theory.

James Coleman developed the concept of social capital by fusing theoretical explanations for the actions of individuals from two disciplines—economics and sociology. In proposing the concept of social capital, Coleman acknowledged the rational action theory of economists that each person has control over certain resources and interests in certain resources and events. He argued, however, that "social capital is a particular kind of resource available to an actor" (Coleman, 1988, p. S98). Compared to more tangible forms of capital such as physical capital (financial assets) and human capital (skills and knowledge), social capital exists in the structure

Table 5.4 Key Elements of Social Capital Theory

Author	Key Elements of Social Capital
Coleman, 1988	Obligations, expectations, and trustworthiness; information channels; norms and effective sanctions; intergenerational closure; appropriate social organization
Putnam, 1993, 1995, 2000	Trust, cooperation, long-term relationships
de Sousa Briggs, 1998	Social capital as leverage and social support
Temkin & Rohe, 1998	Sociocultural milieu and institutional infrastructure, neighborhood ability to act on common interest
Keyes et al., 1996	Long-term trust and relationships; shared vision, networking, economic incentives for mutual interest, financial nexus
Fukuyama, 1995	Spontaneous sociability, capacity to create new structures of cooperation
Fountain, 1998	Social capital as an enabler of innovation, collaboration to promote innovation

of relationships among individuals acting on their own behalf or acting as "corporate actors" on behalf of formal organizations.

Coleman (1988) identified three forms of social capital: (1) obligations, expectations, and trustworthiness of structures; (2) information channels; and (3) norms and effective sanctions. Obligations and expectations refer to one person doing something for another and trusting that he or she will reciprocate in the future. Social relations are also important sources of information. Norms and sanctions against violating them are another form of social capital. For example, norms that encourage young people to stay in school, refrain from sexual promiscuity, and avoid using drugs not only sustain certain actions but also inhibit others. In a study of public and private schools in Chicago, the effectiveness of norms imposed by parents on children depended on intergenerational closure—that is, parents knowing the parents of their children's friends (Coleman & Hoffer, 1987). "In the community . . . parents A and D can discuss their children's activities and come to some consensus about standards and about sanctions. Parent A is reinforced by parent D in sanctioning his child's actions; beyond that parent D constitutes a monitor not only for his own child, C, but also for the other child B. Thus, the existence of intergenerational closure provides a quantity of social capital available to each parent in raising his children—

not only in matters related to school but in other matters as well" (Coleman, 1988, p. S107).

Coleman also found that social capital is the context in which financial and human capital are transferred to the next generation. His study of the impact of financial, human, and social capital on the likelihood of students dropping out of school showed that three measures of social capital affected dropout rates. When other family resources were controlled for, the dropout rate for sophomores with two parents and one sibling, whose mothers expected them to attend college, was 8.1 percent; the rate for students with one parent and four siblings, whose mothers did not expect them to attend college, was 30.6 percent. Other important measures of social capital within families were the amount of time and attention given to children by adults, church attendance, and the number of times the family had moved.

> It is of course true that children are strongly affected by the human capital possessed by their parents. But this human capital may be irrelevant to outcomes for children if parents are not an important part of their children's lives, if their human capital is employed exclusively at work or elsewhere outside the home. The social capital of the family is the relations between children and parents (and, when families include other members, relationships with them as well). That is, if the human capital possessed by parents is not complemented by social capital embodied in family relations, it is irrelevant to the child's educational growth that the parent has a great deal, or a small amount, of human capital. (Coleman, 1988, S110)

Later, more advanced statistical analysis of the National Educational Longitudinal Survey confirmed that social capital interacts with financial and human capital to determine whether an individual stays in school: "In order to create well-being in children, financial and human capital must be accompanied by social relationships that allow resources to be transmitted to and used by children" (Teachman, Paasch, & Carver, 1997, pp. 1355–1356).

Robert Putnam's work spurred renewed interest in social capital theory. In his twenty-year study of regional governments in Italy, Putnam (1993) found that social capital was a necessary precondition for economic development. Differences in economic development between northern and southern Italy were tied to regional differences in voluntary group participation in soccer clubs, literary circles, choral societies, and other types of community organizations. Voluntary group participation was the fabric of social capital—that is, it resulted in "stocks of social capital, such as trust, norms, and networks [that] tend to be self-reinforcing and cumulative. Successful collaboration in one endeavor builds connections and trust—social assets that facilitate future collaboration in other, unrelated tasks" (Putnam, 1993, p. 3). In an influential 1995 essay entitled "Bowling Alone: America's Declining Social Capital," Putnam pointed out an acute decline over the previous two decades in the United States in participation in all kinds of organizations, particularly civic and educational associations (e.g., Lions Clubs, the Jaycees, the Red Cross, Boy Scouts, parent-teacher associations, unions). He argued that the precipitous decline in civic engagement negatively affects the level of trust and cooperation that exists in society.

Why is the level of trust and cooperation in society important? Trust and cooperation are a necessary precondition for economic development. For example, the dense social networks based on extended families and strong personal ties among immigrant groups and close-knit ethnic communities facilitate entrepreneurship in the establishment and operation of small businesses (Sanders & Nee, 1996). Rotating credit associations, in which participants make a monthly contribution to a joint investment fund and each group member, in sequence, uses the pooled money to start a small business or make home improvements, are another example of successful small group networks (Besley, Coate, & Loury, 1993; Velez-Ibanez, 1983). In his study of the "strength of weak ties" in the U.S. labor market, Granovetter (1973) found that even weak ties that connect people in different social groupings are important to job mobility. Those seeking employment were most likely to find a job through contacts with people they did not know well.

After Putnam linked social capital to economic development, several researchers started to test and refine social capital theory by identifying its dimensions at the individual, group, neighborhood, community, and organizational levels. Focusing on the micro-individual level, de Sousa Briggs (1998) identified two constructs of social capital—social leverage and social support. Social leverage is the type of social capital that helps one get ahead. For example, if a person knows someone who can provide job leads or a recommendation for a scholarship or loan, this enables socioeconomic mobility. Social support is the kind of social capital that helps one get by. For example, help from extended family members, friends, or neighbors to fix a flat tire, care for children, or borrow a little money makes it easier to manage life's challenges.

At the group level, Lang and Hornburg (1998) identify two main dimensions of social capital: "*Social glue* refers to the degree to which people take part in group life. It also refers to the amount of trust or the comfort level that people feel when participating in these groups. Social trust and group participation form a recursive relationship. The level of trust influences one's willingness to join a group. Likewise, group participation helps build trust. *Social bridges* are the links between groups. These links are vital because they not only connect groups to one another, but also give members in any one group access to the larger world outside their social circle through a chain of affiliation" (p. 4).

At the organizational level, research on nonprofit and for-profit businesses shows that social capital maximizes the group's ability to work together. Among organizations that develop low-income housing, the elements of social capital include long-term relationships of trust and reciprocity, shared vision, mutual interest, and financial nexus (Keyes, Bratt, Schwartz, & Vidal, 1996). What is more, "well-functioning partnerships, consortia, and networks are in and of themselves a form of social capital" (Fountain, 1998, p. 87). When organizations work together reciprocally for mutual gain, collaboration generates innovation: "In contrast to political and economic perspectives that emphasize individualism, closely held information, and autonomy, social capital is derived from those perspectives in which cooperation paradoxically enhances competitiveness, information sharing leads to joint gains, and the importance of reputation and trust ensure reciprocity and fair play within a given network" (Fountain, 1998, p. 86). Another element of social capital among organizations is called spontaneous sociability, which is "the capacity to form new associations and to cooperate with the terms of reference they establish" (Fukuyama, 1995, p. 27). The capacity to create new organizational structures of cooperation allows for the replenishment of the stock of social capital in the community.

At the neighborhood level, concepts of social capital help us understand the larger environment and how it contributes to increasing or reducing poverty. Temkin and Rohe (1998) identified three components of social capital that are important in stabilizing neighborhoods. Two of these components relate to the socio-cultural milieu of the neighborhood: loyalty and attachment to the neighborhood help it remain stable over time, and when a high proportion of people believe they live in a good place, the neighborhood is more stable. The institutional infrastructure of the neighborhood is also important. Neighborhoods with effective neighborhood organizations are more stable.

At the community level, two types of social capital have been identified. Bridging capital connects people who do not know each other together. Bonding capital brings people who already know each other together. Gittel and Vidal (1998) describe efforts to build these two types of social capital in an evaluation of the work of the Local Initiatives Support Corporation (LISC) with community development corporations (CDCs):

> Within low-income communities, the LISC demonstration sought to establish CDCs that crossed racial, ethnic, and class lines and brought residents together with business owners and managers from local nonprofit organizations such as hospitals and social service agencies. Across low-income communities, new linkages were attempted through coalitions of CDCs. In the metropolitan area, the program tried to strengthen bonds among members of private-sector and philanthropic organizations who already knew each other from other settings. Finally, if community residents and institutions were strengthened in these ways, they would have the opportunity to establish new bridges to outside resources also organized by LISC. In fact, a core aspect of the LISC demonstration was the fostering of bridges between the private sector in the larger metropolitan area and the newly organized CDCs. These new relations were intended to go beyond providing investment capital and charitable contributions to include technical and political support for the CDCs' efforts. (p. 4)

Social Dislocation Theory

William Julius Wilson, a black sociologist, took up the theoretical discussion of persistent poverty in urban ghettos in his 1987 book, *The Truly Disadvantaged*. Research from a liberal point of view on the social pathology of lower-class society had lain dormant since the 1960s, when critics charged that Daniel Patrick Moynihan's report on *The Negro Family* (1965) and the work of other urban analysts stigmatized racial minorities (see Clark, 1965; Rainwater, 1966). As a result, during the 1970s, the bulk of research on the ghetto family was carried out by minority scholars whose work emphasized the strengths of black families (see Hill, 1972; Ladner, 1978). By the 1980s, conservative views on the social pathology of the underclass dominated policy-making discussions (see Auletta, 1982; Murray, 1984). Liberals, in general, and white scholars, in particular, circumvented the policy discussion of the ghetto family by avoiding focusing on any negative behaviors that might cause their work to be interpreted as racist or blaming the victim. Many refused to use the term *underclass* to describe the atypical behavior and norms of inner-city families and individuals. Instead, they denied the existence of the urban underclass either by focusing only on positive aspects of minority families and communities or by overestimating racism as the cause of these problems. Thus William Julian Wilson's work is particularly important in that he reopened the discussion of the underclass from a liberal structural point of view. He called for "careful empirical research" that would "do more than simply react to what conservative scholars and policymakers are saying" (Wilson, 1985, p. 556).

Earlier, Wilson (1980) had written a controversial book entitled *The Declining Significance of Race,* in which he outlined the historical impact of slavery and racism on black Americans. He argued that in the period after the civil rights movement and desegregation, the significance of race had declined in comparison to economic class in explaining persistent poverty. In *The Truly Disadvantaged,* Wilson (1987) extended his discussion of the urban black underclass through data derived from a large-scale study of poverty in the inner city of Chicago. His research provided evidence that families in the inner city who are isolated from society's opportunity structures adapt to their impoverished lifestyle and exhibit behaviors that make it extremely difficult for them to escape poverty.

Social dislocation theory is grounded in evidence that poverty is geographically concentrated in urban areas. Geographic concentrations of poverty are urban areas of a city where the percentage of people living in poverty is extremely high, ranging from 40 percent to as high as 90 percent. The concentration of poor people in geographic areas of the city is attributed to urban industrial transition, changing labor markets, suburban growth, and the exodus of middle-class families from the inner city, as well as historical patterns of transportation and racial segregation. Within geographic concentrations of poverty, persistent poverty is attributed to an interconnection between employment barriers and the adaptation of the persistently poor to blocked opportunities. Concentrations of poverty impinge on family well-being because they isolate people from economic opportunities and mainstream ways of life. Social dislocation theory is built on several hypotheses.

First, social dislocation theory takes into account the movement of jobs out of the city as part of the process of urban industrial transition. Light manufacturing plants, heavy industry, and other types of factories close their doors or relocate away from the central city. This results in unemployment and underemployment. In particular, this loss of jobs in urban industrial areas contributes to widespread unemployment among black males. The closure and relocation of factories also erode the tax base. With less money to fund schools and other public programs, buildings deteriorate and services are cut back. Overall, the decrease of resources in the local economy negatively affects small businesses and community services. As new freeways and highways are designed to transport goods and services from the outer suburbs and new industrial parks, old transportation patterns tend to isolate old neighborhoods in decline (Kasarda, 1993).

The second hypothesis looks at the movement of middle-class blacks out of the city. Wilson attributes this to the development of new highway systems, urban renewal programs, and the unintended consequences of the civil rights movement. Prior to desegregation, lower-, middle-, and upper-class blacks lived side by side in the same sections of the city. After the civil rights movement, fair housing laws as well as affirmative action programs created an exodus of black professionals and middle-income and working-class individuals and families to jobs and better housing in the suburbs. In earlier years, these groups "provided stability to inner city neighborhoods and perpetuated and reinforced societal norms and values" (Wilson, 1987, p. 143). The migration of middle- and upper-class families from the inner city resulted in a lack of role models for youths and also made it more difficult to sustain basic institutions such as schools, small businesses, and recreational facilities.

The residents who were left behind in ghetto neighborhoods were the unemployed, single parents on welfare, criminals, and those with disabilities such as substance abuse and mental health problems. In this environment of blocked economic opportunities and social isolation, social pathology became normal. This included high rates of early sexual activity and out-of-wedlock births, absent fathers, and weak attachment to the labor force among single mothers and single fathers (see McLanahan & Garfinkel, 1993; Testa, Astone, Krogh, & Neckerman, 1993). Wilson found that ghetto residents were primarily individuals and single-parent families experiencing long spells of poverty and welfare dependency.

Social dislocation theory accounts for the increasing rates of out-of-wedlock births among black females in the inner city by focusing on the influence of male joblessness on family structure and married life. The theory posits that there is a shortage of marriageable men in the inner city. This shortage of marriageable men begins with the uneven ratio of male births to female births. By young adulthood, high black male mortality and incarceration rates have furthered the sex imbalance. Because of the movement of industry out of the inner city and subsequent high rates of unemployment among black males, data from 1950 to 1980 reveal "a long-term decline in the proportion of black men, particularly young black men, who are in a position to support a family" (Wilson, 1987, p. 83).

The final component of the theory asserts that geographic concentrations of poverty affect the people living in them. Wilson calls this the "concentration effects" of poverty. Concentration effects cause people to culturally adapt to the reality of blocked opportunities for employment, the absence of conventional role models, and the shortage of marriageable men. An example of this was found by Elijah Anderson, an ethnographic researcher who studied the sex codes and family life among inner-city youths ages fifteen to seventeen. In the face of the harsh economic reality of persistent poverty, young people stand to gain short-term benefits by engaging in a mating game and having children.

> The girl has her dream of a family and a home, of a good man who will provide for her and her future children. The boy, knowing he cannot be that family man because he has no job and no prospects yet needing to have sex with the girl in order to achieve manhood in the eyes of his peer group, pretends to be the good man and convinces her to give him sex and perhaps a baby. He may then abandon her, and she realizes that he was not the good man after all, but a nothing out to exploit her. The boy has received what he wanted, but the girl learns that she has received something, too. The baby may enable her to receive a certain amount of praise, a steady welfare check, and a measure of independence. Her family often helps out as best as they can. As she becomes older and wiser, she can use her income to turn the tables, attracting the interest of her original man or other men. (Anderson, 1993, p. 94)

Thus, Wilson's notion of an underclass—in which poverty is normal, work is unusual, children are born out of wedlock, and a father is absent—is distinctly different from culture of poverty theories. Earlier culture of poverty theories assumed that cultural traits have an autonomous character once they come into existence. Culture is learned and intergenerational; culture influences behavior even when chances for economic prospects increase. In contrast, the key concept in social dislocation theory is the social isolation of the ghetto environment, wherein countercultural behavior is an adaptation to the environment—a response to social and structural constraints and opportunities. "To emphasize the concept of *social isolation* does not mean that cultural traits are irrelevant in understanding behavior in highly concentrated poverty areas; rather, it highlights the fact that culture is a response to social structural constraints and opportunities. From a public-policy perspective, this would mean shifting the focus from changing sub-cultural traits (as suggested by the 'culture of poverty' thesis) to changing the structure of constraints and opportunities" (Wilson, 1987, p. 61).

The Theories Families Live By

As we have discussed, theory helps us explain and predict social phenomenon, and theories of poverty that integrate structural and individual causes provide comprehensive insights into the dynamics of poverty in the lives of families. At the same time, however, the lens of theory magnifies some things and necessarily minimizes others (Bahr & Bahr, 2001). This means that as theory focuses on certain economic conditions, cultural norms, or social behaviors, other aspects of family life fade in perspective or are left out of the picture entirely. This is particularly acute when we consider efforts to theorize about families. In a key article entitled "Family Theory versus the Theories That Families Live By," Kerry Daly (2003) of the University of Guelph provides a critical analysis of areas of family life that are systematically overlooked by theories about families: "In everyday life, there are many activities that take up considerable time, energy, and attention but that are poorly represented in our theorizing about families. In particular . . . (a) the realm of belief and intuition, consisting of emotions, religious and spiritual matters, and myth and folklore; (b) the world of material things and the activities of consumption; and (c) the coordinates of time and space as a means of understanding 'the here and now' of everyday family experience" (p. 772).

Part of the reason for the lack of theory about how families live their lives is the penchant of social scientists to study families through precise, empirical measures. Our usual and best statistical techniques require that the unit of analysis be independent, so in the case of the family, we are actually measuring individuals instead of the characteristics, attitudes, and behaviors of the family life. A second reason for this gap in family theory is that the family is studied by outsiders—usually academics and educators, who are the main consumers of their own research. Thus, there is an absence of theory of what it means to *be* a family, to *live* a family experience, and even to *do* family. Daly (2003) believes that "By more closely examining the everyday motivations, practices, values, and beliefs of family activity, we can build theories that can better serve to understand the puzzles of everyday living" (p. 773).

Before we move on to the following chapters, which focus on specific areas of policy that affect families, let's look briefly at these three areas that lack attention in family theory. First is the realm of belief, feeling, and intuition. Here, the approach of rational science, "which has shaped our way of seeing and theorizing, has resulted in a set of theoretical explanations that assume that families act in rational and predictable ways" (Daly, 2003, p. 774). Unpredictable events and inconsistent family behavior are not accounted for. Part of the reason lies in the realm of emotions, which, for example, may run in negative or positive cycles that affect the environment of the family. Contradictions in emotions that range, for example, from love to hate, from cooperation to competition, or from nurturance to a lack of attachment, are not adequately attended to by theory. Love is probably the most neglected emotion. Also in this category are spirituality and religion, and the role of the sacred realm in family decision making. According to Daly (2003), "Due in part to the politicization of religion and family values (Stacey, 1996) and the devaluation of religion in modernization . . . theories having to do with the spiritual or religious realm are often recessed in family theorizing" (pp. 776–777). Myth, folklore, and family stories are part of the cultural milieu that surrounds family decision making, and overall, these elements play a major role in the social construction of what it means to be family. "Family stories are one of the chief mechanisms a family uses for defining who they are as a family, including what they believe, what they value, and how they should act" (Daly, 2003, p. 777). In times of crisis, families fall back on family myths and ideologies to make sense of their situation and utilize these as guideposts for decisions about how to act or solve problems. If the crisis is new—and there are no family stories to guide behavior—new maps or guideposts develop that add myth and story to the old.

In the second realm of families as consumers of goods and services, theory has not accounted for the dominant role of consumption activity in the everyday lives of families. "Things shape values and beliefs in families, mediate family relationships, create conflicts in families, and are part of the process of identity work and dream management in families" (Daly, 2003, p. 778). In particular, the consumption of consumer goods relates to culture, social class, and upward mobility. How do families manage what they have? How do the production and consumption of goods and services relate to family life and living space within the home? How do these things contribute to or negatively affect play, leisure, child upbringing, and the use of family time? And finally, what meaning do families ascribe to consumption and the assets they may obtain?

The third neglected area of family theorizing is the location of family members in time and space. The elements of time and space relate to the way in which family life is structured, and also to the process of being or doing family: "Distance between the sites of home and work has a direct effect on time (how much is required to get to work); resources (the need for a car, energy costs); and emotional well-being (stress, anxiety, proximity to children during the day)" (Daly, 2003, p. 780). Smaller homes with communal space have given way to larger homes with increased individual space. As women's work moves outside the home, families are away from their homes and neighborhoods for much of everyday life. In general, families are smaller and houses are larger, and these changing patterns of work and household living—even the meaning of home (see Dovey, 1985)—are generally outside the realm of family theorizing. Only recently, for example, have models that begin with the family as the core unit of production, such as family-based community development, emerged (see Kordesh, 2006).

Where do these issues lead us in terms of family policy? The road is unclear and perhaps less traveled than we would wish. If Kerry Daly is correct that significant areas of family living and decision making are neglected in family theorizing, we can be quite sure they are also invisible in family policy making. In the chapters that follow, we look at policies in specific areas such as food and housing, work and employment, child care, and family violence. Some of Daly's neglected areas of family living are discussed in later chapters—but more as part of the problem than the policy solution. However, in many cases, we include illustrative cases that show how families experience policy, and although these illustrations do not address Daly's concern for more inclusive family theorizing, we hope that they add to our understanding of the need to see family policy and its impact from an insider's view—the view of families who experience them.

Summary

In this chapter, we reviewed four contemporary theories of poverty that integrate macro and micro perspectives. Mark Rank's theory of structural vulnerability helps us understand that people on welfare have the same dreams and values as the average American. Most come from working-class backgrounds—some with extensive work histories. Economic hardship influences their on-and-off welfare use. Michael Sherraden's theory of assets for the poor provides us with two insights about leaving poverty. Asset accumulation occurring through home ownership, pension funds, and profits from small business is historically tied to avenues of leaving poverty over generations. Moreover, allowing poor people to accumulate assets may have important behavioral effects in the short term—including the creation of a cognitive and emotional orientation toward the future, provision of a foundation for risk taking, and enhanced personal efficacy. The work on social capital by James Coleman, Robert Putnam, and others helps us understand the fabric of social relationships as resources for solving family problems, reaching group and organizational goals, stabilizing neighborhoods, and building communities. William Julius Wilson's social dislocation theory helps us understand persistent poverty in the inner city, where poverty is geographically concentrated. Here residents are socially isolated and blocked from mainstream opportunities and economic resources. As a result, the social fabric of family life and society breaks down, and cultural norms emerge that guide behavior outside mainstream society.

Lastly, this chapter looked at areas of everyday family life that are invisible in family theorizing: the realm of emotions, religion and spirituality, family myths, and folklore; families' acquisition and consumption of material goods; and the way in which everyday family living is set in time and space. By its nature, statistical research utilizes the individual as the unit of analysis within families, and thus it is difficult to holistically measure the behaviors, characteristics, and attitudes that define what it means to *be* family, *live* a family experience, or *do* family. These areas of everyday living are also invisible in family policy making. Nonetheless, it is important for readers to be sensitized to these issues as we move to looking at specific areas of policy that apply to families in the United States.

For Further Reading

Curley, J., & Sherraden, M. (2000). Policy lessons from children's allowances for children's savings accounts. *Child Welfare, 79*(6), 661–687.

DeFilippis, J. (2001). The myth of social capital in community development. *Housing Policy Debate, 12*(4), 781–806.

Kordesh, R. S. (2006). *Restoring power to parents and places: The case for family-based community development.* New York: iUniverse.

Kordesh, R. S., with Alejo, B. (2005, August). *Housing as a productive family asset.* Washington, DC: Annie E. Casey Foundation. Retrieved March 4, 2009, from http://www.aecf.org/upload/publicationfiles/housing%20as%20a%20productive%20family%20asset.pdf

Newby, R. G. (1989). Challenges and prospects of William Julius Wilson's The Truly Disadvantaged. *Journal of Sociology and Social Welfare, 16*(4), 3–6.

Page-Adams, D., & Sherraden, M. (1997). Asset building as a community development strategy. *Social Work, 42*(5), 423–434.

Popkin, S. J., Levey, D. K., Harris, L. E., Comey, J., Cunningham, M. K., & Burton, L., with Woodley, W. (2002, September). *Hope VI panel study: Baseline report.* Washington, DC: Urban Institute. Retrieved February 21, 2009, from http://www.urban.org/UploadedPDF/410590_HOPEVI_PanelStudy.pdf

References

Anderson, E. (1993). Sex codes and family life among poor inner-city youth. In W. J. Wilson (Ed.), *The ghetto underclass: Social science perspectives* (pp. 76–95). Newbury Park, CA: Sage.

Auletta, K. (1982). *The underclass*. New York: Random House.

Bahr, H., & Bahr, K. S. (2001). Families and self-sacrifice: Alternative models and meanings for family theory. *Social Forces, 79,* 1231–1258.

Bane, M. J., & Ellwood, D. T. (1986). Slipping into and out of poverty: The dynamics of spells. *Journal of Human Resources, 21,* 1–23.

Becker, G. S. (1964). *Human capital*. New York: Columbia University Press.

Beeghley, L. (1989). *The structure of social stratification in the United States*. Boston: Allyn & Bacon.

Besley, T., Coate, S., & Loury, G. (1993). The economics of rotating savings and credit associations. *American Economic Review, 83*(4), 792–811.

Clark, K. B. (1965). *Dark ghetto: Dilemmas of social power*. New York: Harper & Row.

Clignet, R. (1992). *Death, deeds, and descendents: Inheritance in modern America*. New York: Aldine de Gruyter.

Coleman, J. S. (1988). Social capital in the creation of human capital. *American Journal of Sociology, 94*(Suppl.), S95–S120.

Coleman, J. S., & Hoffer, T. B. (1987). *Public and private schools: The impact of communities*. New York: Basic Books.

Daly, K. (2003). Family theory versus the theories that families live by. *Journal of Marriage and Family, 65*(4), 771–784.

de Sousa Briggs, X. (1998). Brown kids in white suburbs: Housing mobility and the many faces of social capital. *Housing Policy Debate, 9*(1), 177–221.

Dovey, K. (1985). Home and homelessness. In I. Altman & C. M. Werner (Eds.), *Home environments* (pp. 33–63). New York: Plenum Press.

Duncan, G. J. (1984). *Years of poverty, years of plenty*. Ann Arbor: Institute for Social Research, University of Michigan.

Ellwood, D.T. (1988). *Poor support: Poverty in the American family*. New York: Basic Books.

Fountain, J. E. (1998). Social capital: A key enabler of innovation. In L. M. Branscomb & J. H. Keller (Eds.), *Investing in innovation: Creating a research and innovation policy that works* (pp. 85–111). Cambridge, MA: MIT Press.

Fukuyama, F. (1995). *Trust*. New York: Free Press.

Gil, D. (1992). *Unraveling social policy* (5th ed.). Rochester, VT: Schenkman Books.

Gittell, R., & Vidal, A. (1998). *Community organizing: Building social capital as a development strategy*. Thousand Oaks, CA: Sage.

Granovetter, M. (1973). The strength of weak ties hypothesis. *American Journal of Sociology, 78*(6), 1360–1380.

Hill, R. B. (1972). *The strength of black families*. New York: Emerson Hall.

Hopkins, K. R. (1987). *Welfare dependency: Behavior, culture, and public policy*. Alexandria, VA: Hudson Institute.

Kasarda, J. R. (1993). Urban industrial transition and the underclass. In W. J. Wilson (Ed.), *The ghetto underclass: Social science perspectives* (pp. 43–64). Newbury Park, CA: Sage.

Keyes, L. C., Bratt, R., Schwartz, A., & Vidal, A. (1996). Networking and nonprofits: Opportunities and challenges in an era of federal devolution. *Housing Policy Debate, 7*(2), 201–229.

Kordesh, R. S. (2006). *Restoring power to parents and places: The case for family-based community development.* New York: iUniverse.

Ladner, J. (Ed.). (1978). *The death of white sociology.* New York: Random House.

Lang, R. E., & Hornburg, S. P. (1998). What is social capital and why is it important to public policy? *Housing Policy Debate, 9*(1), 1–16.

McConnell, C. (1984). *Economics principles, problems, and policies.* New York: McGraw-Hill.

McLanahan, S., & Garfinkel, I. (1993). Single mothers, the underclass, and social policy. In W. J. Wilson (Ed.), *The ghetto underclass: Social science perspectives* (pp. 109–121). Newbury Park, CA: Sage.

Mead, L. (1994). Poverty: How little we know. *Social Service Review, 68*(3), 322–350.

Moynihan, D. P. (1965). *The Negro family: The case for national action.* Washington, DC: U.S. Department of Labor, Office of Policy, Planning and Research.

Murray, C. (1984). *Losing ground: American social policy, 1950–1980.* New York: Basic Books.

Plotnick, R. D. (1983). Turnover in the AFDC population: An event history analysis. *Journal of Human Resources, 18,* 65–81.

Popple, P. R., & Leighninger, L. (1999). *Social work, social welfare and American society* (4th ed.). Boston: Allyn & Bacon.

Putnam, R. D. (1993). *Making democracy work: Civic traditions in modern Italy.* Princeton, NJ: Princeton University Press.

Putnam, R. D. (1995). Bowling alone: America's declining social capital. *Journal of Democracy, 6*(1), 65–78.

Putnam, R. D. (2000). *Bowling alone: The collapse and revival of American community.* New York: Simon and Schuster.

Rainwater, L. (1966). Crucible of identity: The Negro lower class family. *Daedalus, 95,* 176–216.

Rank, M. (1994). *Living on the edge: The realities of welfare in America.* New York: Columbia University Press.

Rank, M. L., Cheng, L. C., & Cox, D. (1992, December 2). *The dynamics and determinants of intergenerational welfare use.* Paper presented at George Warren Brown School of Social Work, Washington University in St. Louis, MO.

Robbins, S. P., Chatterjee, P., & Canda, R. (1998). *Contemporary human behavior theory: A critical perspective for social work.* Needham Heights, MA: Allyn & Bacon.

Sanders, J. M., & Nee, V. (1996). Immigrant self-employment: The family as social capital and the value of human capital. *American Sociological Review, 61,* 231–249.

Sherraden, M. (1991). *Assets and the poor: A new American welfare policy*. New York: M. E. Sharpe.
Stacey, J. (1996). *In the name of the family: Rethinking family values in the postmodern age*. Boston: Beacon Press.
Teachman, J. D., Paasch, K., & Carver, K. (1997). Social capital and the generation of human capital. *Social Forces, 75*(4), 1343–1359.
Temkin, K., & Rohe, W. M. (1998). Social capital and neighborhood stability: An empirical investigation. *Housing Policy Debate, 9*(1), 61–88.
Testa, M., Astone, N. M., Krogh, M., & Neckerman, K. M. (1993). Employment and marriage among inner-city fathers. In W. J. Wilson (Ed.), *The ghetto underclass: Social science perspectives* (pp. 96–108). Newbury Park, CA: Sage.
Velez-Ibanez, C. G. (1983). *Bonds of mutual trust: The cultural systems of rotating credit associations among urban Mexicans and Chicanos*. New Brunswick, NJ: Rutgers University Press.
Wilson, W. J. (1980). *The declining significance of race: Blacks and changing American institutions* (2nd ed.). Chicago: University of Chicago Press.
Wilson, W. J. (1985). Cycles of deprivation and the underclass debate. *Social Service Review, 59*(4), 541–559.
Wilson, W. J. (1987). *The truly disadvantaged: The inner city, the underclass, and public policy*. Chicago: University of Chicago Press.
Zelditch, M., Jr. (1993). Levels in the logic of macro-historical explanation. In J. Huber (Ed.), *Macro-micro linkages in sociology* (pp. 101–106). Newbury Park, CA: Sage.

CHAPTER 6

Welfare, Food, and Housing

Although in theory, all policy is family policy, we know that some policy areas affect families more directly than others. More to the point, there is no comprehensive family policy in the United States, so we turn our attention in chapters 6 through 12 to selected policy areas that especially relate to the well-being of families. As we begin, we want to remind readers of the important themes of the book listed below. Our discussions in the following chapters will highlight these themes as they apply to and are illustrated by specific areas of family policy.

- There is not a uniform definition of the family.
- There is a lack of consensus on what constitutes family well-being.
- A comprehensive set of family policies does not exist in the United States.
- There is disagreement about how much government should intervene in the private affairs of the family.
- There is a debate over whether family poverty and problems are caused by individuals or by larger social systems.
- Demographic trends and the changing nature of the family make it difficult to develop comprehensive family policy.
- The devolution of federal policies affects policy implementation at state and local levels.
- Privatization and managed care play a major role in service delivery.
- The dynamic nature of policy making requires policy analysis and advocacy skills directly tied to practice.

This chapter starts with the family's basic needs. Basic needs can be defined as those that are minimally necessary to ensure the well-being of all types of families. We define basic needs as income, food, and housing, and this chapter looks at policies designed to address these basic needs. First, we discuss welfare-to-work policy. We begin with a brief historical overview of Aid to Families with Dependent Children, a major public welfare program that existed from the time of the Great Depression until 1996. This is followed by a discussion of Temporary Assistance to Needy Families, which replaced Aid to Families with Dependent Children (AFDC). We will compare the basic elements of the two programs and provide some information about the role and outcomes of welfare-to-work policies over the years.

Next, our discussion turns to food policy, which is designed to address the second basic need of families. Here we use the concept of food security to talk about hunger in the United States. Aspects of food security include access to food, taxes on food, and the community component of food distribution through food banks, food pantries, and soup kitchens. We discuss the Food Stamp Program, recently renamed the Supplemental Nutrition Assistance Program; Special Supplemental Nutrition Program for Women, Infants and Children; and the National School Lunch Program and School Breakfast Program.

The third basic need is housing. Here, our discussion begins with the issue of housing affordability and the housing affordability gap. We focus on the need for subsidized housing in the United States, and the issues related to the development of low-income or subsidized housing. At the policy level, we discuss federal housing assistance programs, including public housing, project-based Section 8, and Section 8 vouchers and certificates. Procedural barriers and housing preference rules limit access to public housing. Access to housing is also affected by the "one strike and you're out" policy of the Anti–Drug Abuse Act of 1998. We also discuss HOPE VI, a program designed to eliminate dilapidated public housing and redevelop urban areas with mixed-income housing. The chapter concludes with a discussion of the current mortgage crisis in America, which has affected the ability of working- and middle-class families to retain ownership of their homes. Current policies are inadequate for protecting homeowners from what has been termed the subprime mortgage crisis. We will briefly look at the situation of millions of homeowners who have lost their homes through foreclosure and examine the policies that have been proposed to support homeownership and protect homeowners in the future.

Welfare-to-Work Policy

Throughout much of the mid- to late 1800s, poor widowed and abandoned women and their children were taken to poorhouses and children were taken away from their mothers and put in orphanages (see Davidson, 1994). In 1935, Title IV-A of the Social Security Act authorized Aid to Dependent Children to assist states in providing relief to needy children. In keeping with the times, the cash grant program allowed mothers to stay at home to care for their children. In 1963, the program was renamed Aid to Families with Dependent Children. For more than sixty years, AFDC was the primary income maintenance program for families with children, and receiving benefits was referred to as being on welfare (Opulente & Mattaini, 1997).

AFDC eligibility criteria were strict. Children receiving benefits had to be deprived of at least one parent's support. Families could have only a very low income and virtually no assets. Despite such tight eligibility criteria, AFDC was a federal categorical program, which meant that all who qualified had a legal right to benefits. Through a combination of state and in some cases, local payments, a state could access unlimited federal matching funds to finance its AFDC program. Depending on the poverty level of the state, the federal match ranged from 50 percent to 78 percent. At the state level, benefits varied greatly, ranging from 17 percent to 77 percent of the poverty level. In 1993, for example, the maximum monthly payment for a family of three ranged from $121 in Mississippi to $850 in Alaska. However, the average benefit level reached only 47 percent of the federal poverty standards, so AFDC was never enough to raise a family's standard of living above the poverty line. More than 14 million individuals, including 9.5 million children and 5 million families, received AFDC. The popular belief was that welfare families drained the federal budget, but AFDC traditionally accounted for less than 2 percent of the annual federal budget.

In an effort to curb the perceived escalating growth of welfare caseloads in the 1980s, the Family Support Act of 1988 required states to provide at least six months of benefits to two-parent families in which the major provider was unemployed. It also required families to cooperate with the welfare department to establish paternity and child support and be willing to participate in job training programs. The Job Opportunities and Basic Skills Training Program (JOBS) was its welfare-to-work component. The goal of JOBS was to improve a family's ability to become self-sufficient through work readiness training, job search, community work, and on-the-job training. States were required to provide job training, education, and supportive services, such as child care and transportation, as well as health care, for one year after an individual became employed. JOBS represented a fundamental shift in thinking about welfare—one that encouraged teenage parents and others at risk for long-term dependency to gain skills that would help them move into work. Nonetheless, federal funding for JOBS was capped with a federal match for state expenditures, and many states could not afford to match federal dollars. This resulted in programs that varied greatly from state to state.

The next effort at welfare reform ushered in a new era in social welfare policy. Ellwood (1996) provides an insider's critique of the processes and politics involved in the passage of the Personal Responsibility and Work Opportunity Reconciliation Act of 1996, which replaced AFDC, JOBS, and emergency assistance programs with Temporary Assistance for Needy Families (TANF). TANF fundamentally changed the rules for receiving cash assistance:

- Recipients must work after receiving TANF for two years. The work participation rate mandates that 50 percent of adult-headed families receiving cash assistance must be engaged in work activities for at least thirty hours per week (twenty hours a week for single parents with a child under six years old). A separate provision requires states to have 90 percent of two-parent families engaged in work. Unsubsidized and subsidized employment, job search (for up to six weeks a year), and vocational education (for up to twelve months) count toward the first twenty hours of work per week.
- Transitional health insurance is provided for one year once the recipient finds work. States are also required to provide transitional child care for families transitioning off TANF cash assistance, but the amount of time for which states provide assistance ranges from one year to the time a child turns thirteen years old.
- There are tough new penalties for child support enforcement and uniform interstate child support laws.
- Teen parents must live at home and stay in school to receive benefits. States are responsible for locating adult-supervised settings for teens.
- States have the option to implement a cap on benefits for additional pregnancies after enrollment in TANF.
- There is a lifetime limit of five years for receiving TANF benefits.
- States cannot deny or reduce assistance under TANF to a single parent with a child under age six who is unable to comply with the work requirement because he or she cannot find child care. However, lack of child care does not stop the clock from ticking on the time limits on cash assistance.

- Individuals wanted in connection with a felony or parole or probation violation cannot receive TANF (or participate in other federal programs such as Supplemental Security Income and food stamps).

TANF takes away the entitlement status of AFDC and replaces it with block grants to states. Without entitlement status, cash assistance for poor families is not protected in the same way that it was under AFDC. Under the old system, the federal government paid 55 percent of all AFDC benefits, with no cap on the number of recipients. Under the new law, states receive a fixed sum of money from the federal government, regardless of the number of recipients. Grant levels do not increase unless there is a substantial increase in the poverty population. There is no increase during periods of economic recession; however, states may be eligible for a contingency fund if they experience high unemployment rates or large increases in food stamp caseloads. States are also permitted to cut their welfare spending up to 25 percent without suffering a penalty in block grant reductions.

Under TANF, states are no longer required to provide matching funds. Instead, grants are calculated so that each state receives an amount equal to the highest payments for AFDC, JOBS, and emergency assistance during the fiscal years 1995 or 1996, or an average of payments for 1992–1994. Then, states must pay a maintenance-of-effort requirement, which can be no less than 80 percent of their 1994 spending on AFDC benefits and administration, emergency assistance, JOBS, and child care programs. TANF is also very different from AFDC in that states have more power over which families receive benefits, and the types and level of assistance they receive. There are also incentives for removing people from the welfare rolls, including those who are not able to find work.

TANF was ushered in on the heels of an interesting form of devolution. Since AFDC was a federal entitlement program, the rules for welfare-to-work programs and cash assistance under AFDC were quite strict. State governors and others desired more flexibility in designing their welfare programs, and so they approached the Department of Health and Human Services for a waiver of federal AFDC policy requirements. Consistent with devolution, the idea was that states could better address local needs if they were given the opportunity to experiment and design their own welfare programs. As states rushed to obtain waivers, criteria were lax. In a hearing before the Human Resources and Intergovernmental Relations Subcommittee of the Committee on Government Operations (1994) of the U.S. House of Representatives, the process of receiving a waiver was reported to be rather ad hoc: "It soon became painfully obvious that the Department did not have any guidelines or criteria that it normally and regularly used in the review of waiver programs. It was a situation that if they felt they should give it, they would give it; and if they didn't, they would delay it" (p. 2). In his opening statement at the hearing, Chairman Edolphus "Ed" Towns (D-NY), a former social worker and community activist, predicted that "The expansion of the waiver process without clear criteria or priorities can result in a checkerboard of mini–welfare reforms all over the nation. On a national policy level, the expansion of waiver demonstrations allows states to opt-out of the national welfare strategy. Therefore, in its current form, the waiver process may actually undermine any attempt to form a national strategy which addresses poverty and welfare dependency" (Committee on Government Operations, 1994, p. 7).

By the time the Personal Responsibility Work Opportunities Reconciliation Act (PRWORA) became law, forty-two states had been granted federal waivers that allowed them to experiment with AFDC and modify its federal requirements. Some states tried out their experiments in a few counties and phased in their approaches over time, while others applied their demonstration projects statewide. Six types of AFDC waiver policies were granted: termination/reduction time limits, changes in JOBS work exemptions, JOBS sanctions, increases in earnings disregard, family caps, and work requirement time limits (Crouse, 1999). For example, Minnesota consolidated its AFDC and food stamp programs and increased the earned income disregard by nearly 40 percent. Officials in New Jersey set up a family cap program that disallowed additional AFDC payments for any child born into a welfare household.

With the passage of the PRWORA, states with waivers were allowed to follow the terms of their waivers even if their welfare-to-work policies and programs were inconsistent with the provisions of the new law. The vast majority of these states continued their demonstration projects as part of their state TANF programs. As the waivers expire, states adopt TANF requirements but can still offer variations in their programs as long as they use state funds to provide the additional services. The Assessing the New Federalism project at the Urban Institute has a longitudinal database that tracked state AFDC/TANF policies for all fifty states and the District of Columbia from 1996 to 2006. The Welfare Rules Database is a "comprehensive, sophisticated [resource] for anyone comparing cash assistance programs between states, researching changes in cash assistance rules within a single state, or simply looking for the most up-to-date information on the rules governing cash assistance in one state" (Urban Institute,

2008). Users may query the database for information on welfare rules across states, time, and geographic areas within states and different types of assistance units. Fact sheets and maps showing differences and similarities between state TANF programs are also available.

Personal Self-Sufficiency

The new welfare law stresses personal self-sufficiency through quick job entry and places an emphasis on job search assistance and job placement, with limited support for additional education and training. Since 1993, welfare caseloads have declined by 37 percent. Much of the decline has been attributed to federal waivers, provisions of the new welfare reform law, and a strong economy that lasted until the current recession. It is difficult to know how much of this decline was due to the economy and how much to welfare reform. Research has established that, regardless of welfare reform, approximately 30 percent to 50 percent of women who enter the welfare system for the first time stay for less than two years.

Families on welfare fall into three different groups. Job-ready individuals are likely to find employment with or without assistance from welfare programs. These families typically seek short-term assistance because of divorce, income loss, or the birth of a child. Families in the second group are likely to find work once they have received limited skills training and assistance in the search for a new job. Although approximately 90 percent leave welfare within five years, 45 percent return within a year, and 70 percent return within five years. The remaining 10 percent to 15 percent have considerable personal and family challenges that make the welfare-to-work transition more difficult. Welfare-to-work programs show substantial short-term success for the first two groups, but outcomes are weaker for more disadvantaged recipients.

An early review of several welfare-to-work programs found that many hard-to-reach recipients may not even participate in the programs because they have so few basic skills, health problems, chemical dependency issues, and other problems that require long-term solutions (Pavetti, Olson, Nightingale, Duke, & Isaacs, 1998). Accordingly, the two major challenges are moving families with no previous work experience into the labor force and helping those with personal and family problems find employment and stay employed. Other early research found that working recipients who left TANF rolls continued to live below the poverty level and experience grave financial distress (Parrott, 1998). Up to half of families who left TANF returned to the program at some point. State welfare reform outcomes from 1996 to 1999 reveal that 55 percent of former TANF recipients who exited welfare over a twelve-month period worked full time and earned between $7 and $8 per hour. Returns to welfare during the first year ranged from 25 percent to 35 percent. Respondents who had been off welfare between two and three years still only averaged earnings of $1,101 per month. Despite the fact that many former recipients had full-time jobs, annual earnings of the employed individuals who left welfare were so low that 57 percent to 67 percent used food stamps at some time during the first year. Over half of all welfare leavers had total incomes below the official poverty threshold. Of the eight states for which data were available, 24 percent to 44 percent of families reported not having enough food, 27 percent to 39 percent were behind on their rent, and 8 percent to 31 percent were unable to afford or get medical attention (U.S. Department of Health and Human Services, 2000).

A more recent study notes that 25 percent to 33 percent of welfare leavers return in the first year. Over half remain in poverty, and for all states, the overall average of earnings hovers near the poverty line. More than 25 percent of families experience food hardships at some point after leaving TANF, and the same percentage experience trouble paying rent and utility bills (Jindal & Winstead, 2002). At the same time, welfare caseloads declined to their lowest level in thirty years in 2001 (U.S. Department of Health and Human Services, 2004). Although incomes rose for single mothers in the mid-1990s to $23,000 in 2001, these increases were not enough to help the majority of single mothers leave poverty. These data lead to questions about the adequacy of TANF programs in assisting families to attain financial self-sufficiency over the long term.

Rebecca Blank, a leading poverty researcher and a member of the President's Council of Economic Advisors during the Clinton years, acknowledges positive outcomes among welfare leavers under the PRWORA. "It turns out that those who left welfare did well enough to surprise the skeptics, myself included, but it remains hard to identify all of the reasons" (Blank, 2006, p. 1). Changes in other policies also may have played a role. For example, the earned income tax credit was expanded, minimum wage increased in some parts of the country, and more attention was paid to child care subsidies and children's health programs in the mid-1990s:

> From a statistical viewpoint, it is hard to fully explain the major declines in caseloads and increases in employment. Most regressions explain—at best—one-third of the caseload and labor force change. My own interpretation is that we don't know how to adequately

specify the synergies that happened when all of these policy and economic changes pushed in one direction and were matched with a strong public message that welfare was going to be much less available in the future and that work was going to be the only choice for the long term.... "Were the women and children better or worse off?" While there is a lot of evidence that work has increased and that earnings on average rose more than benefits fell, the translation of these facts into a definitive statement about well-being is hard to make. More women are now working and poor, rather than nonworking and poor. (Blank, 2006, pp. 3–4)

Food Policy

Food is the second basic need of families. The relationship of food policy to family well-being helps us understand hunger. We will look first at the concept of food security and then look briefly at other issues such as access to food, taxes on food, and the role of voluntary or nonprofit agencies in dealing with food insecurity in the United States. This discussion is followed by a brief overview of the major federal food policies: food stamps; the Special Supplemental Nutrition Program for Women, Infants and Children; and the National School Lunch Program.

Food Security

As we discussed extensively in chapter 4, the poverty line is calculated based on a household's ability to purchase food for a minimally adequate diet. Thus, by definition, poor families are at risk of hunger. How prevalent is hunger in the United States? To answer this question, the U.S. Census Bureau conducted the first Current Population Survey Food Security Supplement in 1995. Consisting of interviews with approximately 45,000 households, the Food Security Supplement is the first comprehensive measurement of food insecurity and hunger in a nationally representative sample. Most American households—88 percent of approximately 100 million households—are food secure. The remaining 11.9 million households (12%) experience food insecurity. Most (8%) of these households are food insecure without hunger. About 4 percent, or one adult or more in 4.2 million households, are categorized as food insecure with hunger. About 800,000 households are in a category called food insecure with severe hunger, which means that children as well as adults are hungry. The prevalence of hunger is related to income and poverty, but the relationship is not exact. Not all poor households are food insecure, and only a small percentage of households with incomes below the poverty line experience actual hunger. Food insecurity is most likely among population groups that have high poverty rates, including African American and Hispanic households, households living in central city areas, and female-headed households with young children (Hamilton, Cook, Thompson, Buron, Frongillo, Olson, et al., 1997).

Hunger and food insecurity are related to the diets of poor families, which are likely to consist of meat, whole milk, fats, sugars, and refined grain products. These foods are high in calories but low in vitamins and minerals and therefore can cause obesity (Clarke & Mungai, 1997). Children, middle-aged and older adults, women, people of color, the poor, and the uneducated are most likely to suffer from diseases of obesity. Children from lower socioeconomic groups are more likely to be obese than children from moderate- and upper-income families. Poor women of color and children, who are the most likely to be overweight, are also overrepresented among food stamp recipients. Obesity is the leading cause of non-insulin-dependent diabetes mellitus, cardiovascular disease, hypertension, respiratory problems, arthritis, degenerative joint disease, and cancers of the colon, prostate, breast, and ovaries, as well as surgical complications that occur with each of these diseases. One cause of obesity is the fact that nutritionally dense foods such as fresh fruits and vegetables, whole grain products, and skim dairy products are more expensive than junk food. For example, milk is more expensive than soda, a loaf of whole grain bread is more expensive than white bread, and orange juice is more expensive than orange drink.

Access to food is another aspect of food insecurity. In the last twenty years, the retail food industry has gone through a massive restructuring process through leveraged buyouts, mergers, and the relocation of grocery stores to suburban areas. In part, these moves were caused by high insurance rates, low profits, and employment and security problems. In terms of food availability, quality, and prices, these market-driven changes in food distribution have a negative effect on low-income households living in inner cities and isolated rural areas. Whereas food is available in the suburbs through supermarket chains and discount food markets, food is available in most inner-city areas through a few small independently owned stores. These stores offer less variety in the type and brand of foods as well as the size and quantity of packaged foods. They also offer lower-quality foods and higher prices, particularly for produce, meat, and fish. A systematic study of city and suburban supermarkets in Wilmington,

Delaware, documents these issues. Field surveys, checklists, and observation showed that city stores have less square footage and fewer checkout aisles; less brand and product variety; poor appearance, condition of equipment, level of security; and many products past the expiration date. City shoppers also received fewer and less valuable store coupons than shoppers in urban areas (Curtis & McClellan, 1995).

Several states have policies that relieve the food tax burden for lower-income households by partially or wholly exempting food from sales tax (Johnson & Lav, 1998). Twenty-five states exempt food purchased from grocery stores from sales tax. Five other states tax food at a reduced rate. Six states fully tax food but offer credits or rebates to low-income households. The state of Georgia partially exempts food from sales tax and also offers a credit. Tax credits and rebates never fully cover the amount of tax paid on food, and most states limit these benefits to families with incomes below the poverty line. In order to receive tax credits, families must apply for the rebate. The remaining states tax food because of the need for revenue or a simplified administrative system. Taxes that are levied heavily on poor households are called regressive—that is, they take a disproportionate amount of the income of poor households compared to the income of non-poor households. For example, a family of four that spends the lowest amount for a nutritious diet in an average state spends $350 a year in taxes on food. This amount is close to a week's income for a family living at or near the poverty line. In addition, states that exempt food from sales tax must also decide whether local governments are required to do the same.

The community component of food security involves the extent to which voluntary nonprofit agencies provide food assistance within the local community. Thousands of voluntary nonprofit organizations such as regional food banks, local soup kitchens, and food pantries play an important role. Food banks are clearinghouses that receive bulk donations of mislabeled food, dented cans, and food with past-due expiration dates and, in turn, sell the food at an extremely low by-the-pound price to voluntary organizations such as soup kitchens and food pantries. These programs began to emerge during the late 1970s and quickly developed into a large national network of emergency food assistance organizations, which made a big difference in the distribution of food to the hungry. For example, between 1980 and 1990, the Greater Pittsburgh Community Food Bank experienced an 800 percent increase in the amount of food it distributed—from one million pounds of food in 1980 to that amount in the single month of May 1990 (Daponte, 1996).

Food pantries are local organizations that store small quantities of non-perishable food for distribution to needy families on an emergency basis.

Soup kitchens provide on-site meals to hungry people, and since running out of food at the end of the month is often a problem for both working and non-working poor people, it is not unusual to find both homeless families and those with homes using soup kitchens. Like soup kitchens, food pantries are voluntary organizations usually operated by churches, religious organizations, and self-help organizations. They are often formed by a coalition of one or more of these types of organizations. Because food pantries set up their own intake procedures and eligibility criteria, they are more flexible and less bureaucratic than government food assistance programs, and most programs use interviews and self-report to assess need. Volunteers at food pantries pack a three- to five-day supply of food in boxes or grocery sacks for on-site distribution to needy families. Recently, the U.S. economic crisis of 2008 redefined the meaning of "needy families" who visit food pantries. Across the country, the economy is "forcing tens of thousands of people to visit food pantries for the first time" (Morris, 2008). At the same time, food donations have dwindled. In Johnson County, Kansas, one of the wealthiest counties in the United States, "demand for free food . . . has spiked 50 percent from last year. Donations, meanwhile, have slowed to a trickle" (Morris, 2008). "The food-bank shortages are nationwide. The Community Food Bank of South Dakota in Sioux Falls, S.D., received 35% fewer donations from grocery stores last year. The Greater Chicago Food Depository, the nation's fourth-largest food bank in terms of the amount of food distributed, has 12% fewer donations this year than last" (Etter, 2007).

Federal Food Assistance Programs

The largest source of federal food assistance, commonly known as the Food Stamp Program, is simply referred to as food stamps. Food stamps are in-kind benefits. This means that instead of receiving cash, recipients use coupons or certificates to purchase foods for consumption. Recently, electronic benefit transfer cards, which function much like bank debit cards, have replaced coupons. Beginning October 1, 2008, the official name of the food stamp program was changed to the Supplemental Nutrition Assistance Program (SNAP). This name change took place as the program was reauthorized as part of the Food, Conservation, and Energy Act of 2008. The name SNAP highlights the program's new emphasis on meeting the nutrition needs of families during economic crises such as the 2008 recession and disasters such as Hurricane Katrina.

Food stamp policy is designed as a price support subsidy for farmers producing farm and agricultural products. Thus, unlike a typical welfare program, SNAP is administered through the Food and Nutrition Service of the U.S. Department of Agriculture. The policy's primary goal is food consumption, so food stamps do not limit the choice of foods purchased to those that are nutritious. Food stamps cannot be used to purchase hot foods; alcoholic beverages; or non-food items such as diapers, toilet paper, soap and cleaning supplies, vitamin and mineral supplements, tobacco, and pet food. The program is financed by the federal government through general revenues, which pays 100 percent of food stamp benefits and 50 percent of administrative costs. Remaining administrative costs are shared equally by state and local governments.

In 1964, the Food Stamp Act was passed as part of the War on Poverty to alleviate hunger and malnutrition among working and non-working poor people. The federal government determined the amount that people were charged for food stamps on the basis of their income, but states were allowed to determine eligibility. Poor people were required to purchase food stamps for a month at a time. The negative effect of this policy was that fewer people were able to receive federal food assistance because they could not afford to purchase a month's supply of coupons. However, since states with the lowest AFDC benefits had the largest federal food stamp allotment, the program was beneficial in equalizing the value of AFDC benefits from state to state.

During the Nixon administration, a broad coalition of agribusinesses, social service agencies, and churches advocated changes in food stamp policy. The effort successfully established national eligibility criteria, increased benefits and indexed them to inflation, limited the cost of food stamps to no more than 30 percent of household income, required able-bodied adult recipients to register for work, allowed the purchase of a portion of the monthly allotment of food stamps at one time, and increased outreach efforts. In 1977, during the Carter administration, recipients were no longer required to purchase stamps, and families with incomes above the poverty level were eligible to receive benefits. These policy changes resulted in an increase in the number of poor people participating in the program. Concerned with this increase, the Reagan administration supported cutbacks in food stamps through the Omnibus Budget Reconciliation Act of 1981, the Food Stamp Act Amendments of 1982, and the Continuing Resolution of 1984. New food stamp policies tightened income deductions by counting current and past income in calculations for food stamp eligibility, and increasing efforts to crack down on fraud and abuse. In 1985, the Food Security Act mandated states to develop a Food Stamp Employment and Training Program in an effort to reduce food stamp participation through employment. In 1996, the PRWORA prohibited undocumented immigrants and some legal immigrants from receiving food stamps, but these benefits were restored in 1998 to about one-third of those previously excluded. Within these eligibility guidelines, the PRWORA gave states new latitude in designing food stamp policies. Some states, for example, reduce food stamp benefits only for the head of household when he or she does not participate in employment and training programs; others disqualify the entire household. A few states disqualify recipients for failure to cooperate with child support, pay child support, and make minor children attend school (Gabor & Botsko, 1998).

Families are eligible for food stamps if their income is at or below 130 percent of the poverty level. Income eligibility levels are adjusted yearly in accord with the poverty line. Emergency food stamps are also available. For example, in the aftermath of Hurricane Katrina, the food stamp system operated under a different set of eligibility and benefit requirements. People who might not qualify for food stamps were eligible if their homes were damaged, they lost their income as a result of the disaster, or they had no access to bank accounts or other resources. Juwanda's story illustrates the importance of food stamps for people who are unable to work and find themselves in the precarious position of remaining housed (box 6.1).

Box 6.1 Food Stamps and Staying Housed

Juwanda has been moving around from relative to relative while she recovers from injuries sustained when she was hit by a drunk driver while walking home from nursing school. Food stamps play an important role in her plan to provide for herself and her daughter.

> I'm ready to call my worker and explain to her that at the end of the month if I could go, I have to be sent to another emergency shelter. I want to go now because my daughter is out of school and because I cannot continue living like this. . . . One always ends up doing more than the other when it comes to food. So that's why I told my aunt, "Don't worry about my food. I have my own food stamps. I'll furnish the food for my child and myself." It's just not working out right. Her family members come over and if they ask if they can have something and I tell them no, they verbally attack me. You know, they feel—she feels—their children can eat anything they want in that house even if it's mine. It's not right. Now I just finished the last of my food stamps last week so that we could have enough food to last us the rest of the month. All that food that I bought is gone because her family members came in and ate it all. So, now I'm willing to go back into emergency shelter with my daughter until I can find a place of my own.

In 2000, the U.S. Department of Agriculture spent $17.1 billion on the Food Stamp Program, down from a high of $24.6 billion in 1995 (Super, 2001). Participation decreased steadily from the mid-1990s until 2000 because of improved economic conditions and welfare reform restrictions that limited eligibility. After welfare reform, confusion about income limits and allowable deductions and changing eligibility rules contributed to lower food stamp participation rates (Zedlewski & Rader, 2004). In spite of this, in 2004, more than 26 million persons received food stamps—the highest number since welfare reform in 1996. And even though the number participating in the Food Stamp Program rose by nearly two million, the actual rate of participation among those eligible only rose from 53.2 percent to 53.8 percent (Sandstrom, 2005). Lack of information, low expectations of benefits, the hassle involved in the application and re-certification process, and stigma all contribute to low participation rates.

There is evidence that privatization is negatively affecting access to food stamps and other welfare programs. Indiana privatized its welfare system in twelve counties in 2007. Welfare offices were closed and case managers were laid off. They were replaced by a call-in center operating under contract for services with IBM and Affiliated Computer Services, a for-profit corporation. The Food Research and Action Center, an excellent policy institute on food security, summarizes some of the effects of the privatization of food stamps:

> When Muncie resident Pat Smith, who requires a special diet to prevent diabetes-related complications, didn't receive her food stamps in March, she called eight governmental agencies to inquire and complain. "Every time we got the same answer: I don't know when you're going to get them," she said. Smith isn't the only one complaining. The privatized welfare system, which started last fall in 12 counties, has been dubbed a failure by advocates for seniors, people with disabilities, and other low-income residents. Run in Marion through a call center operated by IBM and Affiliated Computer Services, the system replaced the network of county welfare offices and caseworkers. A "People's Town Hall" meeting is now scheduled for May in order to discuss the problems. Center Township Trustee Kay Walker, the meeting's organizer, tried to investigate individual cases where services weren't delivered or assistance recipients could not get through to the call center. "Every time we call the local office, they don't answer the phone," she said. "Every time we call Marion, they are busy or they don't return phone calls." Other cases include:

- Todd Barton's family, who went for weeks without food stamps and "skimped and scraped together little meals, whatever we could";
- U.S. Army veteran Charles Baxter, whose liver is failing; he hasn't "heard a thing yet" about his application for Medicaid, which he filed almost one year ago;
- Bobbi Brown and her son—both mentally challenged—who recently had their Medicaid and food stamp benefits cut.

A spokesperson for the state's Family and Social Services Administration said the state wants to help and takes every complaint seriously. ("Privatized System Fails," 2008)

The new SNAP legislation also makes benefit amounts slightly higher than has previous authorizations. More information is available on the Food and Nutrition Service Web site of the U.S. Department of Agriculture. The Congressional Budget Office predicts that food stamp usage in 2009 will reach its highest level since the program started in the 1960s. Escalating food and fuel costs, coupled with layoffs and unemployment, will cause the number of individuals using food stamps to reach 28 million in 2009, up from 27.8 million in 2008 and 26.5 million in 2007 (Eckholm, 2008). The Food Research and Action Center (2008) estimates that food costs for the thrifty food plan upon which the poverty line is calculated rose 10.3 percent between September 2007 and September 2008.

Special Supplemental Nutrition Program for Women, Infants and Children (WIC) is another federal food assistance program, originally authorized as an amendment to the Child Nutrition Act of 1966. WIC targets low-income pregnant women, postpartum and breastfeeding women, and at-risk children younger than five years of age. WIC's criteria for nutritional risk assessment also allow homeless and migrant persons to receive benefits based solely on their homeless or migrant status. WIC foods are purchased with coupons or vouchers or, in some states, with a check that can be used at authorized retail stores. WIC covers cereals fortified with vitamins and minerals, fruit juices high in vitamin C, eggs, cheese, infant formula, dried peas and beans, and peanut butter. Breastfeeding women can use coupons for tuna and carrots. All permitted foods are high in vitamin C, calcium, iron, protein, and other nutrients that may be missing from the diets of low-income families. WIC is managed at the federal level by the U.S. Department of Agriculture. Federal regulations require a determination of eligibility based on household income. WIC eligibility criteria, the income guidelines of which vary from state to state, are more generous than those of food stamps. Households with incomes up to 185 percent of the poverty line established by the federal poverty income guidelines are eligible.

Although WIC is similar to food stamps, there are several important differences between the two programs. First, WIC is a discretionary program, which means that the number of low-income people who can benefit from the program depends on the amount of funding allocated by Congress. Second, at the state level, SNAP is administered by the public welfare system, but WIC is administered by state health departments. Services are provided at approximately 10,000 clinics—the majority of which are state or local public health clinics—operated by 2,000 local agencies. Services are also provided at migrant and community health agencies, community action agencies, public housing sites, hospitals, Indian Health Service facilities, and mobile vans. Third, it is a comprehensive program that provides food assistance coupled with routine pediatric and obstetric care. A comprehensive health assessment is used to determine nutritional risk or medical conditions related to inadequate nutrition, and some programs train peer counselors to promote breastfeeding and paraprofessionals to serve as nutrition assistants. Most WIC programs have cooperative relationships with Medicaid and Head Start in order to offer comprehensive services. WIC offers health and social services for immunization, nutrition education, smoking cessation, and drug abuse treatment (U.S. Department of Agriculture, 1995).

The National School Lunch Program and the School Breakfast Program are federal programs that help reduce hunger in the United States. These programs provide food commodities and subsidies to reduce the cost of school lunches so that all school children can afford them. School lunches must meet at least one-third of the recommended daily allowances of vitamins and minerals; breakfasts must meet one-fourth of the recommended daily allowances of major nutrients. Certification is typically a simple procedure based on self-report of family income and handled by the local school district. Lunches are free for children from families with incomes under 130 percent of the federal poverty level and available at a reduced price for children from families with incomes between 130 percent and 185 percent of the poverty level. In schools that offer these programs, 56 percent of the students participate in the National School Lunch Program, and 19 percent in the School Breakfast Program.

Hunger produces negative behavioral effects in children. A large-scale survey in nine states found that 8 percent of American children under the age of twelve years experience hunger each year. Hungry children and those at risk of hunger are twice as likely as non-hungry children to be classified by parent and child report as having impaired functioning. Teachers report higher levels of hyperactivity, absenteeism, and tardiness among the hungry and those at risk than among not-hungry children (Murphy, Wehler, Pagano, Little, Kleinman, & Jellinek, 1998). According to data from the School Nutrition Dietary Assessment, nearly one-quarter of the children eligible for the program have not been certified, and of those certified, nearly one-quarter do not eat school lunches (Glantz, 1998). Nearly half of low-income children are not being reached, largely because parents and older children view the National School Lunch Program and School Breakfast Program more as welfare programs than as nutrition programs. Reasons for non-participation include the stigma associated with receiving free meals, poor food preparation, and the food choices that are offered.

Housing Policy

Housing is the third basic need of all families. In order to understand the complex housing policy in the United States, we will look at the housing affordability gap, which explains the disparity between the income of poor households and the cost of adequate market-rate housing. The housing affordability gap helps us understand the need for subsidized housing in the United States. Next, we provide a brief overview of three different subsidized housing programs for low-income families—public housing, Section 8 units, and Section 8 certificates or housing vouchers. Access to housing through these programs is complicated and difficult. Procedural barriers make it difficult to apply for housing assistance. Preference rules make it nearly impossible to obtain housing assistance for families with individual problems such as drug abuse, involvement with the criminal justice system, and unpaid debts to public housing authorities. Moreover, new federal law allows public housing tenants to be evicted if their guests or family members are involved in illegal activities—even those outside the control of the renter. We also discuss a major change in public housing policy: HOPE VI eliminates much of public housing through demolition and features the transformation of apartment complexes into mixed-income garden-style units and townhouses. Finally, we examine the most recent housing crisis, known as the subprime mortgage crisis, which has created a crisis in homeownership, particularly for working- and middle-class homeowners, and has caused a new wave of homelessness in the United States.

The Housing Affordability Gap

The housing affordability gap is caused by the absence of affordable housing (in constant dollars) for poor renters and the erosion of income among poor households. The shortage of affordable housing can be traced to massive cuts in federal funds for new housing construction that were made during the Reagan administration. Between 1981 and 1988, federally subsidized housing appropriations plummeted from $30 billion to less than $8 billion. Adjusted for inflation, this decrease represented more than an 80 percent decline in federal funding, which in turn drastically slowed the construction of new low-income housing. Between 1970 and 1980, for example, the number of occupied subsidized housing units rose from 1.0 million to 3.2 million, but by 1990, the total number was only 4.4 million (Dolbeare, 1991). Changes in tax laws also made it more difficult for private investors to profit from low-income housing development. Government policies affecting rent subsidies, credit allocation, and lending regulations—historically used to close the affordability gap between household incomes and housing expenses—were severely cut (Dreier & Appelbaum, 1992). Waiting lists for housing subsidies grew dramatically throughout the 1980s and 1990s. For example, the wait for public housing averaged ten years in Chicago, eight years in New York, and seventeen years in Miami. Many cities simply closed their waiting lists.

While these budget cuts and policy changes were devastating in and of themselves, the major cause of decline in the number of affordable units was the loss of low-income housing units on the private market. Beginning in the 1980s, landlords began selling off low-income property at tremendous profits. The effect of speculation in land and buildings increased the rent burden of poor people and led to displacement and homelessness (Tull, 1992). A variety of other market-driven forces contributed to both the deterioration and destruction of existing housing stock. These included under-maintenance, property tax delinquencies, mortgage foreclosures, eviction and eminent domain proceedings, arson, and demolition. The redevelopment strategies that followed, including gentrification, historic preservation, and the conversion of rental units to condominiums, transformed previously affordable housing into high-income properties in the private market. St. Louis, for example, blighted the entire downtown area and nearby neighborhoods for redevelopment. Under a state law known as Chapter 353, eminent domain procedures were combined with tax abatement strategies and private corporations were allowed to receive federal funds for redevelopment without paying federal relocation benefits to poor people who were displaced by the redevelopment process. The redevelopment process destroyed a large number of low-income units that met housing code standards. Many of these were spacious apartments previously occupied by families (see Johnson, 1992).

Rental costs as a portion of monthly income are typically more than double what the U.S. Department of Housing and Urban Development (HUD) considers affordable rent—30 percent of income. In 2001, for example, 35 percent of rental households paid more than 30 percent of their income for housing, and 21 percent paid more than 50 percent of their income. Fifty-six percent of very low-income households are severely burdened by the cost of housing and must pay 50 percent of their income for housing, with African American and Hispanic households paying the highest proportion of their income for rent (Powell, 2004). Thus, poor renter households are "shelter poor"—their housing costs are so high that they have little income left for other basic needs such as food, clothing, health care, and transportation (Mulroy, 1995). Poor families often must live in substandard housing because market-rate housing is so expensive.

Poor families often cope with the reality of a tight housing market and the affordable housing gap by "doubling up" with another person or family to offset rental costs and remain housed. Overcrowding is defined by HUD as more than one person per room. Between 1980 and 1987, there was a 98 percent growth in the number of households with related subfamilies, and a 57 percent growth in the number of households with unrelated subfamilies, comprising nearly 3 million households. By 1994, 2.8 million households consisted of related subfamilies, and 716,000 of unrelated subfamilies. White subfamilies comprised the largest share—2.4 million, with African American subfamilies disproportionately represented at 867,000, and Hispanic subfamilies at 709,000 (Rawlings & Saluter, 1995). Overcrowded housing conditions continue to disproportionately affect families of color. In 2000, 1.9 percent of non-Hispanic whites experienced overcrowding, and 0.6 percent experienced severe overcrowding, while 8.5 percent of African Americans were living in overcrowded conditions, and 3 percent experienced severe overcrowding. Rates for Hispanics were even higher, with 29 percent living in overcrowded conditions, and 21 percent experiencing severe overcrowding (Bennefield & Bonnette, 2003). Often, the hidden cost of living with extended family members is family friction, which leads to homelessness (see Johnson, 1989). Doubling up often occurs before a family becomes literally homeless. When families double up, they often violate the lease agreement of the host family. This is particularly a problem for "hidden homeless" families who are staying with extended family members or friends in subsidized housing. Nandita's story illustrates how overcrowding and eviction result in homelessness (box 6.2).

Box 6.2 Doubling up and Homelessness

Nandita's mother allowed her to return home at age eighteen on the condition she would help pay bills and get along with her stepfather. After her son was born, she went to school and her mother watched the baby. When the landlord found out that Nandita was living in the Section 8 apartment that he rented to her parents, he demanded that she and her two-month-old son leave. Later, he evicted Nandita's parents for violating their lease, and they also became homeless.

> *I asked my mom if I could move in with her. So she let me stay with her on the condition that I help her with the bills and try and get along with my stepfather. We agreed on that. And I did it. Then, the only problem that I had was the landlord. The landlord came by to pick up the rent one day and he found out that I was staying with my mom. He took all my things and threw them outside. And I didn't have anywhere to go. My mother was arguing with him—even my stepfather came to argue with him at one point. The landlord wouldn't agree on any kind of situation. He just picked up my things and threw me out. I was outside in the street. I slept outside for about a day and a half.*

Federal Housing Assistance

There are three major types of federally subsidized housing assistance: public housing; Section 8 units, which are set aside for low-income renters in privately owned apartment complexes; and Section 8 certificates or vouchers. In each type of program, rents are set at 30 percent of the renter's income and the difference is paid by the federal government. Although the federal government funds these three types of housing, the shortage of subsidies and public housing units means that only a small portion of the eligible poor receive assistance. Overall, about one-fourth of the poverty population receives housing assistance.

The first type of subsidized housing, called public housing, is built specifically for low-income residents. It is owned and managed by public housing authorities (PHAs), which are public or quasi-public organizations authorized by state or local law. Public housing includes a variety of architectural structures, including garden-style apartments, high-rise buildings, and smaller apartment units such as duplexes. Rental payments are used to cover operating and maintenance costs, and the federal government provides subsidies to the PHA to help cover operating costs. Subsidies are based on a formula that takes into account tenants' rental payments.

Nationally, there are approximately 1.2 million public housing units, and 550,000 are occupied by families with children.

The second type of subsidized housing is privately owned apartment complexes that receive Section 8 certificates as part of a federal financing package. In project-based Section 8, private developers build new housing in which all the units or a designated number of units are set aside for low-income households. Project-based Section 8 apartments are not administered by PHAs. Instead, owners contract directly with HUD, or with a state housing finance agency that acts as an intermediary. Rental payments go directly to the private landlords. The federal government guarantees rental payments on these units, and mortgages are insured by the Federal Housing Administration for time periods ranging from twenty to forty years. During the housing boom of the 1950s, developers were able to use their allotment of Section 8 certificates as collateral in obtaining mortgage loans to build large apartment complexes. This policy not only encouraged private development but also produced scattered-site units amid market-rate rentals in the same housing development. In this type of Section 8 program, subsidies are attached to the rental unit, so when a renter leaves his or her apartment, the subsidy stays with the apartment and is available for the next low-income renter. There are 1.4 million project-based Section 8 units, and approximately 500,000 are occupied by families with children.

The third type of subsidized housing is Section 8 certificates or vouchers issued by local PHAs. After 1983, the Reagan administration created what were called "walk-around" subsidies in order to give low-income households more choice about where to live and more access to the housing market. These certificates or vouchers are tenant based, which means that they are issued directly to renters. In theory, a renter may move from one market-rate unit to another and still receive housing assistance. Certificates and vouchers limit the amount of federal subsidy by capping it at 70 percent of market rate. However, the program allows low-income residents to spend more than 30 percent of their income on rent if the rents are higher than the fair market rate, or less than 30 percent of their income for rent if the rental unit is less expensive. This form of housing assistance has been popularized as a way of giving tenants choices about housing size and quality and neighborhood conditions. There are approximately 1.4 million tenant-based certificates and vouchers, and 900,000 are used by families with children. One downside of certificate and voucher programs is that they must be used within a certain period of time or returned to the PHA for reallocation to another household. More than half of the households that receive a Section 8 voucher in a given year return it unused because they cannot find an apartment to rent. In some cases, landlords are unwilling to rent to Section 8 tenants. In other cases, apartments are disqualified because rents are higher than the approved rent standard. In addition, sometimes inspection by PHAs fails and substandard housing is rented to voucher holders. Box 6.3 describes the situation faced by Phyllis, a woman living in substandard housing through the voucher program.

Box 6.3 Substandard Housing

Phyllis received a walk-around certificate for subsidized housing. However, despite the certificate, which makes housing affordable, her quest for decent housing continues. Phyllis has moved three times.

First one was Baldwin Street. That was a water problem. Water and roaches. Everybody's water from the third floor and second floor was coming down into my house. I bought a wet and dry vac. I could tell who was washing. The lady on the third floor used fabric softener. Crazy, but her water would come down through. The woman on the second floor, just bleach and soap powder; her water would come down dirty. Smelled like bleach and soap powder. Then in my bathroom, I would get peas, noodles, and stuff underneath my bathroom sink. I was taking a shower, and the wall—the wall was bubbly. You know, not bubble-bubble, but it was bubbling, so I knew it was gonna bust sooner or later. I just backed out of the shower—it busted! Okay, all this hot water comes in. This was subsidized housing, and the landlord kept saying he couldn't fix anything until he got his money from the state.

Phyllis was able to move with her certificate, but she's still frustrated. In her new apartment the ceiling has collapsed in two places and the landlord hasn't fixed anything. "I feel like I'm back where I started," she says.

Procedural Barriers and Preference Rules

Two other factors—procedural barriers and preference rules—make it difficult for poor families to obtain housing assistance. Procedural barriers make it difficult for poor families to apply for housing. The jurisdiction of PHAs generally follows city or town lines, but there are also regional or statewide PHAs. Throughout the fifty states, there are 2,000 PHAs that administer the Section 8 certificate program. Unlike applications for Social Security or unemployment compensation, which can be filed locally and allow people to remain eligible to receive benefits no matter where they live, the administrative maze through which subsidized housing is delivered requires individuals to file literally dozens of applications in order to maximize their chances of receiving housing assistance: "Complicating matters further, PHAs frequently require a separate application to be filed for their public housing and Section 8 project-based programs, in addition to the application for walk-around Section 8 certificates and vouchers. Then in addition to the tens or hundreds of PHAs at which one might wish to submit one or several applications, to receive a project-based subsidized unit at one of the potentially hundreds of privately owned and federally or state subsidized developments in an area, a separate application must be made to *each* project" (Sard, 1992, p. 193).

Beginning in 1988, federal preference rules required PHAs to provide 90 percent of available public housing units to those with urgent housing needs. Families with incomes up to 50 percent of the area median income were eligible for all programs and, in some cases, those with higher incomes could qualify. Federal housing laws also gave preference for subsidized housing to those who are homeless, involuntarily displaced, or living in substandard housing, or who paid more than 50 percent of their income for rent and utilities. Local PHAs set up ranking systems to prioritize among these various groups or set up local preference rules for subsidies not governed by the federal rules. Subsidized-housing owners and PHAs violated federal rules by discriminating against disabled and handicapped applicants, particularly those who were not mobility impaired. In 1994, these federal preference rules for families with urgent housing needs were reduced to 50 percent, and in 1996, they were eliminated altogether. The preference rules contributed to high concentrations of very poor unemployed families in public housing. Since poor families pay less in rent than higher-income families, the preference rules also contributed to lower operating revenues for PHAs to cover the costs of operating and maintaining public housing projects: "The preference rules were perceived to create social and fiscal problems for PHA's, particularly as the rules applied to public housing. PHAs complained the preference contributed to high concentrations of very poor, unemployed families, accompanied by increase in crime, drug-related activity, and welfare receipt in public housing. This, in turn, made public housing less attractive to families with higher incomes" (Daskal & Sard, 1998, p. 3).

Many PHAs have continued to use the federal preference rules for 50 percent of their available public housing units. For example, the New York City Housing Authority has continued to target 50 percent of available units, as required under the old rules, with those who are homeless given the highest priority. Working families with incomes between 51 percent and 80 percent of the area median income were given highest priority for the remaining units, followed by families with incomes between 31 percent and 50 percent of the median income. The argument was that through the use of "criteria such as employment status to accord priority to both working poor and working non-poor applicants, significant improvements in employment and income mix can be achieved, while continuing to maintain access to public housing for families with urgent housing needs" (Daskal & Sard, 1998, p. 7).

Historically, these changes in federal preference rules started a policy shift making federal housing assistance available to poor families at higher income levels. Federal law requires that housing applicants who meet certain criteria be placed higher on the waiting list and receive assistance before those who do not meet federal housing preferences. Preference is extended to applicants who have a severe rent burden (that is, rent plus utilities exceeding 50% of monthly income), are involuntarily displaced (by fire, threat of violence, or government action), or live in substandard housing (severe plumbing, electrical, or structural problems). Applicants are screened on other eligibility requirements, such as their ability to pay their bills and the absence of past debt to any public housing authority. Applicants cannot have a history of disturbing neighbors or damaging property or previously being evicted or terminated from a federal housing program. They must also not have a history of criminal activity, including drug-related offenses, and no one living in the housing unit can have a criminal history. Since the number of federal rent subsidies is far less than the number of people who need a subsidy to afford housing, eligible persons are typically placed on a waiting list. Public housing authorities maintain separate waiting lists for each federal housing program, and these lists can be very long—lasting years in some cases. Thus, preferences and priorities set forth in housing authority policies help some applicants obtain housing more quickly (Davis & Hammeal-Urban, 1999).

A recent law also makes it difficult to access subsidized housing. The "one strike and you're out" policy of the Anti–Drug Abuse Act of 1998 amended the regulations for public housing and Section 8. The law provides comprehensive policies "for denying admission to applicants who engage in illegal drug use or other criminal activity and for evicting or terminating assistance of persons who engage in such activity." The act requires each local PHA to establish standards that prohibit occupancy in any public housing unit or in the Section 8 program by anyone determined "to be using a controlled substance, or whose pattern of illegal use of a controlled substance or pattern of alcohol abuse would interfere with the health, safety or right to peaceful enjoyment of the premises by other residents" (*Federal Register*, 1999, p. 40262). The purpose of the law is to give more power to PHAs to rid the housing projects of criminal gangs and drug dealers.

The language of the law and the rules and regulations are purposefully vague in order to give housing authorities maximum control over administering the "one strike" policy. However, confusion about how PHAs determine that someone is using a controlled substance or has a pattern of alcohol abuse has created problems. There have been many court challenges to the law, generally filed by residents who have been evicted because of visitors in the household who have been arrested for illegal activity that the tenant believed he or she could not control. But according to the act, "any drug related criminal activity on or off such premises, engaged in by a public housing tenant, any member of the tenant's household or any guest or other person under the tenant's control, shall be cause for termination of tenancy." When the HUD issued the regulation for that section of the law, it was made clear that PHAs should have discretion in making decisions on an individual basis (Wilson, 2005). Although several plaintiffs have won cases in federal appellate courts, they have been overturned by the U.S. Supreme Court. Nevertheless, the number of lawsuits filed in connection with the ruling has caused local housing authorities to reevaluate some of their policies in order to avoid future lawsuits (Johns, 2002). Overall, however, federally funded housing policy has moved toward refusing access to those applicants who do not meet housing preference.

HOPE VI

Part of the policy solution to the increasing shortage of affordable housing since the 1980s was the promotion of homeownership for low-income families, including those residing in public housing. Through a program called Housing Opportunities for People Everywhere, HUD started to eliminate high-rise public housing complexes. HOPE VI, as it is commonly called, was also designed to revitalize public housing through management improvements and social and community support services to promote resident self-sufficiency (Public and Indian Housing, 2006). The objectives of HOPE VI are:

- to improve the living environment for residents of severely distressed public housing through the demolition, rehabilitation, reconfiguration, or replacement of obsolete projects (or portions thereof);
- to revitalize sites on which such public housing projects are located and contribute to the improvement of the surrounding neighborhood;

- to provide housing that will avoid or decrease the concentration of very low-income families; and
- to build sustainable communities.

Through HOPE VI, the projects—as public housing units in concentrated areas of poverty are commonly referred to—have been torn down, rehabilitated, and reconfigured into garden apartments, townhouses, and low-rise buildings.

HOPE VI began in 1992 as an Urban Revitalization Demonstration Project with $300 million appropriated by Congress. Unlike most programs, which require a two-step process of congressional legislation—one bill authorizing the legislation itself, and a second appropriations bill—HOPE VI operated for the next seven years through funding appropriations only. Most major policies operate through government regulations written by the executive branch, but HOPE VI was not administered by program regulation. Each fiscal year HUD administered HOPE VI grants through a notice of funding availability published in the *Federal Register*, and by executing a grant agreement with each recipient. The program was authorized for the first time in the Quality Housing and Work Responsibility Act of 1998, also known as the Public Housing Reform Act. Thus a new federal blueprint for low-income housing construction was adopted in dozens of U.S. cities: demolish public housing projects and develop mixed-income neighborhoods, with homeownership and commercial development mixed with public housing.

From 1992 to 2006, HUD awarded more than $6 billion through 446 HOPE VI grants in 166 cities. Like other federal policies implemented in recent years, HOPE VI operates largely through privatization by forging new partnerships between housing authorities and other agencies, local governments, nonprofit organizations, and businesses to leverage development funds and support services (Public and Indian Housing, 2006). The case of Chicago public housing illustrates the pitfalls and windfalls of using private developers to replace the demolished public housing projects.

As in many large cities, public housing projects in Chicago such as Robert Taylor Homes, Cabrini Green, ABLA Homes, Henry Horner Homes, and Stateway Gardens had become racially segregated ghettos of poverty and seedbeds of crime. In 2000, the city of Chicago, which had regained control of the Chicago Housing Authority through the courts, turned to private developers to implement federal housing policy through its ten-year Plan for Transformation. At the helm of the redevelopment effort was Habitat Co., a real estate firm appointed to desegregate public housing in 1995 by a federal judge. The Plan for Transformation, which combined public housing with market-rate condominiums for sale and commercial space, was conceived by the administration of Chicago mayor Richard Daley, Habitat, and federal officials from HUD. Of the 38,000 units held by the Chicago Housing Authority in 2000, 25,000 were to be rehabbed or torn down and replaced. In 2008, the *Chicago Tribune* investigated the results of the privatization plan. This included 7,186 new multi-family units (30% delivered, with 1,045 of these units delivered prior to the plan), 5,836 rehabbed multi-family units (45.1% delivered), 9,435 rehabbed senior units (94.3% delivered), and 2,543 rehabbed scattered-site units (100% delivered). "The sputtering effort also has translated into higher costs—with some public housing units totaling more than $300,000 to build, more than the price of a home in many Chicago neighborhoods" (Grotto, Cohen, & Olkon, 2008b, p. 22).

What went wrong? In 2008, the *Chicago Tribune* reported on the Park Boulevard complex that replaced the Stateway Gardens, a high-rise located across from U.S. Cellular Field, home of the Chicago White Sox. In the main, a privatized model of public housing development is contingent on developers making a profit. The city started tearing down the Stateway high-rises months before it even chose a developer.

- "The CHA practically gave away 7 acres at Stateway, paid to clean up the property and picked up the tab to tear down the high-rises. The city paid millions more for new roads, water pipes, and sewers."
- "Developers say the cheap land—$1 per year for 99 years—and other benefits are needed so they can compete with projects that don't include public housing."
- "The deal held out the prospect of staggering returns—$32 million in profits and fees according to project budgets—because it depended heavily on home sales rather than rental."
- "Commercial space represented another way for developers at Stateway to make money.... The development team ... leased that land from the CHA for 99 years in exchange for a one-time payment of about $200,000. It then built storefronts that were later sold ... for $4.2 million."
- "The construction of public housing was contingent on the sale of market-rate homes in the first onsite phase. Under the terms of its bank loan, the development team cannot lay the first brick for public or affordable housing until it has pre-sold half of the market-rate units for each building. So, when the housing market took a nose dive, so did the delivery of housing for the poor." (Grotto et al., 2008b, p. 23).

As we have pointed out, federal rules and standard policies are intrinsically slack in guiding privatization plans and implementation. Thus, one effort at privatization may be successful and another may fail. In Chicago, the Plan for Transformation worked better at Henry Horner Homes. There, residents fought displacement through the Sargent Shriver National Center on Poverty Law, which sued and won a consent decree that allowed residents to stay in buildings that were not demolished until new units were ready for occupation. All 464 families who stayed in that development now live in rehabbed housing. Also at Robert Taylor Homes, which is near the old Stateway site, development has focused on rental units, and 164 units of public housing have been constructed—more than three times the number completed at Park Boulevard (Grotto, Cohen, & Olkon, 2008a).

Overall, HOPE VI has transformed the federal policy approach to housing assistance and notably changed the physical space, shape, and location of public housing. Positive outcomes include the transformation of geographic locations and the correction of architectural flaws in the design of public housing. As a large-scale urban development effort, often-segregated public housing projects inhabited entirely by welfare and working poor families have been replaced with newly designed mixed-income housing and business development. Some public housing has moved to non-poor neighborhoods to promote scattered-site, mixed-income communities. Efforts have been made to develop positive incentives for resident self-sufficiency, including tenant councils and one-stop shopping centers for social and health services.

A negative aspect is the uprooting and long-term displacement of many families. Although some former residents obtained housing vouchers to rent apartments in the private market, lengthy construction schedules, readmission rules, and a shortage of new units suitable for larger families have prevented the return of many tenants to their former neighborhoods. Thus, despite its redevelopment success in transforming urban ghettos, "the original residents of HOPE VI projects have not always benefited from redevelopment, even in some sites that were otherwise successful. This can be partly attributed to a lack of meaningful resident participation in planning and insufficient attention to relocation strategies and services" (Popkin, Katz, Cunningham, Brown, Gustafson, & Turner, 2004, p. 3). Taken as a whole, HOPE VI promises only to improve the living conditions of a small number of low-income families. "This reality has occurred because the grants received by housing authorities have not been spent to replace public housing at a one-to-one rate.... The immediate option left for these families and individuals seems to be to pack up and move into another slum" (Cleveland & Frohock, 2002, p. 7).

Homeownership: The Subprime Mortgage Crisis

The discussion on housing policy in this chapter has focused on federal housing policy for the poor, as well as efforts through HOPE IV to offer homeownership opportunities to lower- and middle-income Americans. Here we discuss the recent foreclosure crisis that threatens the ability of lower-income working- and middle-class families to keep the homes they have purchased. This new crisis in homeownership developed out of a practice called subprime mortgage lending. Subprime-rate mortgages are loans that are given to families who are seen as too risky for a conventional loan, because their debt-to-income ratio is too high, their credit is not good enough for them to be considered for a prime-rate loan, or they do not have enough money for a down payment (Atlas & Dreier, 2007). These types of loans come with either a higher-than-normal interest rate or a low initial interest rate that jumps, or balloons, after a few years.

Although such lending began in the mid-1990s, subprime-rate mortgages surged between 2001 and 2006 for a number of reasons. First, interest rates began to fall after September 11, 2001, and this prompted lenders to offer mortgages to people unable to obtain conventional, or prime-rate, loans. At the same time, the Bush administration encouraged lenders to be creative in finding ways to get more people into homeownership. As the subprime market swelled, regulations were too lax to ensure good banking standards, which led mortgage brokers to engage in risky practices to increase the number of subprime loans. These included a dramatic increase in adjustable-rate mortgages, loans of 100 percent of the value of a home, inflated property appraisals, and high interest rates and fees. Once the subprime loan was made, lenders would sell the mortgages to Wall Street investors, who expected to make big profits on mortgage-backed securities when the balloon payments took effect (Rhodes, 2007).

The homeownership crisis began in 2006 when millions of adjustable-rate mortgages reached their balloon payment period, and millions of homeowners were unable to make the larger payments. In particular, the subprime lending crisis disproportionately affected families of color. Twenty-six percent of home mortgages obtained by white families were subprime, compared to 47 percent of home mortgages obtained by Hispanics and 53 percent of home mortgages obtained by African Americans—even after credit risk and individual credit scores are taken into account (Austin, 2008). By 2007, the homes of 2.2 million American families were in foreclosure and almost a half-million people had lost their homes (Christie, 2008; Kasperowicz, 2008). With so many homes in foreclosure, property values dropped and mortgage companies tightened their lending practices, which has made it difficult for middle- and upper-class homeowners to sell their homes. In addition, upper-income borrowers are having difficulty acquiring loans above $400,000, called "jumbo loans" because they exceed the limit that the nation's largest mortgage backers will fund. This wasn't a problem when the mortgage industry was flourishing, but now it is seen as a credit risk because banks and mortgage companies must find other sources to back the loans, such as mortgage-backed securities, which are currently in trouble because of the subprime-rate fallout (Rhodes, 2007).

Although the relationship between subprime lending, foreclosures, and mortgage-backed securities traded on the stock market is complex, it is important to understand this relationship in order to comprehend the monumental impact that homeownership policy has on the U.S. economy overall. At the center of the crisis are two quasi-private government enterprises. The first is the Federal National Mortgage Association (Fannie Mae), which was established in 1938 as part of Franklin D. Roosevelt's New Deal effort to finance homeownership for Depression-era Americans. In 1968, Fannie Mae was privatized by the Johnson administration in order to finance the Vietnam war. In 1970, the Federal Home Loan Mortgage Corporation (Freddie Mac) was authorized by Congress as a second government-sponsored enterprise, "which has the peculiar character of a profit-focused and shareholder-owned enterprise that existed for a public mission" (Blond, 2008).

Fannie Mae and Freddie Mac strayed from their social missions and came to hold $5.3 trillion in home loan debt—totaling nearly half the homeownership mortgages in the United States, or an amount equal to nearly half of the $9.5 trillion national debt. Their mandate is to maintain a market for mortgages—buying loans from banks, repackaging them as bonds, and selling those securities to investors with a guarantee that they will be paid.

> The real tragedy . . . is the betrayal of Fannie Mae's original mission to house the poor. If only Freddie and Fannie had used their profits to extend mortgage insurance and thus fixed-rate mortgages to the sub-prime classes, who only wanted to share in the wealth, then this recession need never have happened. You don't extend home ownership by concentrating on financing the middle class. (Blond, 2008)

The bailout of Fannie Mae and Freddie Mac came on the heels of the failure of a leading subprime mortgage lender, IndyMac Bankcorp, which required no proof of income for subprime loans. After a "run on the bank" in which depositors withdrew $1.3 billion, IndyMac was taken over by the

Federal Deposit Insurance Corporation at a cost estimated to range from $4 billion to $8 billion. Quickly following the federal takeover, the Federal Reserve issued new rules for mortgage lending, most of which went into effect in October 2009. For example, the length of fixed-rate mortgage payments must be advertised, mortgage companies will be required to credit the homeowner's account the day that the payment is received, brokers will be forbidden from coercing or encouraging appraisers to inflate real estate values, the pyramiding of late fees will be banned, and proof of income and assets for mortgages will be required (Aversa, 2008).

The Fannie-Freddie crisis occurred as investors lost confidence in the solvency of the two companies, and over a six-month period from January to July 2008, Fannie Mae stock prices fell 65 percent and Freddie Mac stock prices fell 75 percent. In mid-July 2008, the Bush administration proposed a bailout plan to extend each company's $2.25 billion credit line to up to $300 billion. Federal backing for the two companies would increase their current line of government credit and allow the U.S. Treasury to purchase equity capital in the companies—with the caveat of needed congressional approval. The Federal Reserve also announced its intent to loan money to the companies (Labaton, 2008).

Bernstein (2008) says it is ironic that what Alan Greenspan (2008) calls the "once-in-a century credit tsunami" is the result of federal housing policy that he and many others on both sides of the political aisle endorsed as a way to increase homeownership in the United States. When Greenspan, the chairman of the Federal Reserve from 1987 to 2006, testified at a hearing of the House Committee of Government Oversight and Reform, he was asked to identify when he realized that there was a housing "bubble," that is, that housing prices were inflated to an unprecedented level. Greenspan responded that he was aware of the situation as early as 2006. "Even more surprising, Greenspan explained that even after he realized there was a bubble, he never expected housing prices to decline so dramatically, because we had never had a nationwide decline in housing prices in the past" (Bernstein, 2008). This is in spite of the fact that, as we reported in chapter 2, state attorneys general of North Carolina and Iowa met with John D. Hawke Jr., "the nation's top bank regulator . . . [to] issue a stern warning . . . that lenders were pushing increasingly risky mortgages" at the same time that other state and local governmental bodies were actively attempting to rein in the lending practices of subprime lenders (Berner & Grow, 2008). All these efforts came to naught as federal policy makers and interest groups tied to the financial industry succeeded in beating back attempts to rein in the excesses of the subprime lending markets. The unintended consequence of these efforts is the current global financial crisis. One is tempted to attribute the situation to greed on the part of the financial community and to the lack of foresight of many policy makers. However, perhaps the problem is that economics is far from an exact science, and that lessons from the Great Depression were ignored by those responsible for today's economy and housing policy (Mankiw, 2008).

Questions asked during Greenspan's grilling on Capitol Hill support our view that policy making is primarily political, driven by values, and subject to ideology. "You had the authority to prevent irresponsible lending practices that led to the subprime mortgage crisis. You were advised to do so by many others," said Representative Henry A. Waxman of California, chairman of the committee. "Do you feel that your ideology pushed you to make decisions that you wish you had not made?" Greenspan conceded: "Yes, I've found a flaw. I don't know how significant or permanent it is. But I've been very distressed by that fact." Greenspan acknowledged that "he had put too much faith in the self-correcting power of free markets and had failed to anticipate the self-destructive power of wanton mortgage lending" (Andrews, 2008). This is a good example of well-meaning policy makers who were blinded by their value judgments on homeownership policy for lower- and middle-income families. Greenspan's entire testimony can be read at http://oversight.house.gov/documents/20081023100438.pdf.

Whatever the reason, the bailout of Freddie and Fannie and the takeover of IndyMac did not solve the financial crisis. We are now in the midst of a massive global financial crisis, the outcome of which is far from certain. Whether we are in the midst of a worldwide recession or depression is still a topic of political debate, but most economists are certain of two things. They believe that the global economic crisis started with homeownership foreclosures in the United States, and that it will last for several years.

A Homeowner Bailout?

Policy responses to the escalating rate of foreclosures have fallen largely along party lines. The Bush administration and Secretary of Treasury Henry Paulson have begun a program called HOPE NOW, which works with lenders and investors to freeze interest rates on adjustable-rate mortgages at the lower rate for a period of five years. Democrats in Congress have proposed one bill that would allow bankruptcy judges to amend the terms of home mortgages, and another that would make Wall Street and other investors liable for mortgage brokers and lenders who use illegal practices or otherwise steer borrowers toward higher fees and interest rates in order to provide loans that families cannot afford (Atlas & Dreier, 2007). Both types of plans have been criticized: liberals wish to reverse the 1980s deregulation of the banking industry with federal legislation to protect consumers, and conservatives believe that a voluntary approach is better for the economy than the long-term effects of new legislation and improved federal regulations.

On the heels of the massive bailout of Wall Street, policy discussions began to revolve around how to help "Main Street" (i.e., homeowners across America) avoid losing their homes. One policy option is called homeowner bailout. According to David Leonhardt (2008) of the *New York Times*, it is difficult to develop policy to support a one-size-fits-all homeowner bailout. There are two kinds of situations that need to be addressed. First, there are homeowners who cannot make their monthly mortgages, and second, there are homeowners who have no trouble making their monthly mortgage payments, but whose homes are now worth a lot less than the amount of their mortgage. The question is how to create policy that doesn't create an incentive for the second group of homeowners to risk walking away from their homes in order to obtain federal help. Why not help everyone? Leonhardt replies that such a policy response would be enormously expensive—probably costing trillions of dollars. The second part of his answer reminds us of one of the questions put forward by this book: Is poverty the fault of the individual or the system? Leonhardt believes that public policy to help Main Street should be designed in such a way that it doesn't reward individuals for the mistakes they made in buying homes that were more than they could afford. He suggests increasing or extending unemployment insurance benefits for those who have lost their jobs as a means of keeping people in their homes. Government could also take over the homes of homeowners who cannot pay their mortgages, or banks could retain ownership of the homes but allow the previous homeowners to stay in their homes for five years by paying rent at a lower rate than their current mortgage. This type of policy would not evict the homeowner immediately or flood the market with foreclosed homes all at one time. During their campaigns in 2008, John McCain and Barack Obama also had ideas. McCain's plan would have allowed the government to buy bad mortgages at their original value and provide new loans with lower fixed-rate mortgages. Leonhardt criticized this plan because it would essentially overpay the cost of the home at the expense of the homeowner, thus benefiting the bank. Obama offered a less ambitious ninety-day moratorium on mortgages, which might not make much difference but would forestall the foreclosure crisis.

These and future policy proposals are too late for those who have already lost their homes through foreclosure. According to the U.S. Conference of Mayors–Sodexho (2007), hunger and homelessness are on the rise in major cities across the country. The new faces of the homeless and hungry are previously middle-income, two-earner families who have lost their homes through foreclosure. Other factors that push middle-income families into homelessness include high utility bills, rising gas prices, and increasing unemployment, which rose from 5 percent to 5.5 percent in May 2008 (Armour, 2008). Where are people living after losing their homes through foreclosure? A comprehensive report from the National Coalition for the Homeless on foreclosure and homelessness provides data. Table 6.1 shows the results of an e-mail survey of 117 local and state homeless coalitions concerning where homeless people are staying after losing their homes. The largest percentages have doubled up with family and friends. Reports from local communities indicate that large numbers of the new homeless are living in their vehicles prior to entering emergency shelters. The report also includes policy recommendations for preventing homelessness because of foreclosure, including re-creating the Home Owners' Loan Corporation, a Depression-era government agency that bought delinquent mortgages and re-loaned money at lower interest rates and backed the loans with federal mortgage insurance. Other policy options include consolidating the Federal Reserve, the Office of the Comptroller of the Currency, the Office of Thrift Supervision, and the Federal Deposit Insurance Corporation—each of which is charged with monitoring banks and financial institutions. Comprehensive federal and state oversight are also needed to reduce predatory lending. "States have jurisdiction over the growing number of nonbank mortgage lenders (which accounted for about

Table 6.1 Where People Are Staying after Losing Their Homes

	California	Florida	Kentucky	Minnesota	Texas
Family/Friends	23%	29%	38%	38%	16%
Rental Home	18%	13%	25%	4%	37%
Emergency Shelter	15%	25%	19%	29%	16%
Transitional Shelter	16%	12%	0	8%	5%
On the Street	16%	17%	13%	17%	16%
Don't Know	3%	0	0	4%	37%
Other	9%	4%	6%	0	5%

Source: Adapted from Erlenbusch, B., O'Connor, K., Downing, S., & Phillips, S. W. (2008, April 15). *Foreclosure to homelessness: The forgotten victims of the subprime crisis. A national call to action.* Washington, DC: National Coalition for the Homeless. Retrieved July 20, 2008, from http://www.nationalhomeless.org/housing/foreclosure_report.pdf

40 percent of new subprime loans) without any consistent regulatory standards. States are responsible for regulating the insurance industry (including homeowner insurance), and do so with widely varying levels of effectiveness. It is absurd to have so many competing and overlapping agencies involved in regulating financial services institutions, particularly because they are often at cross purposes with one another" (Erlenbusch, O'Connor, Downing, & Phillips, 2008, p. 9).

At the local level, communities already experiencing a rise in homelessness through foreclosure are thinking creatively about how to join the foreclosure problem to a policy solution in the area of homelessness. In Ventura County, California, for example, more than one hundred foreclosed homes are vacant. Recently, nearly forty community officials, including representatives of banks and nonprofit and religious organizations, met to discuss the possibility of obtaining these homes from banks and turning them into homeless shelters, transitional housing, and long-term leased properties as part of the banking industry's requirement to reinvest in local communities through the Community Reinvestment Act (1977). "Officials said that such a program could not only get the homeless off the streets, but also stabilize real estate prices by lowering the number of unsold houses" (Wilson, 2008).

Summary

This chapter gave attention to policies that provide some assistance to poor families in meeting their basic needs of income, food, and shelter. It provided a brief discussion of Aid to Families with Dependent Children, which was the major welfare and cash assistance program for families since the Great Depression until 1996. Temporary Assistance to Needy Families replaced the AFDC entitlement program in 1996 with a system of block grants to the states, time limits, and work requirements. We discussed three groups of welfare recipients—those who are likely to find employment with or without assistance from welfare programs, those with limited job skills who are able to enter the workforce after receiving training, and those with health problems, chemical dependency problems, or other problems that require long-term assistance. Since TANF was implemented during a period of economic advancement in the U.S. economy, it is not clear how much of the reduction in the number of welfare families occurred through TANF and how much occurred because of increased opportunities for employment.

Food is one basic need of families. Our policy overview looked at the concept of food security and hunger, including access to food, taxes on food, and emergency food provided by the nonprofit sector through food pantries, food banks, and soup kitchens. Federal food policy through SNAP, WIC, and the National School Lunch Program and the School Breakfast Program were discussed, particularly in terms of the way in which these programs contribute to better nutrition for poor families.

The chapter also provided a discussion of public housing and two types of Section 8 housing: one in which the subsidy is attached to the housing unit, and one in which portable vouchers or certificates are transferred from one housing unit to another because they are attached to the eligible individual or family. Procedural barriers and housing preferences make it difficult for families with problems to access subsidized housing. For example, the "one strike" policy allows public housing authorities to evict renters when they, family members, or guests are involved in drug-related or other criminal activities. HOPE VI is a recent federal initiative with an emphasis on homeownership that was designed to eliminate blighted public housing through rehab and replacement alongside mixed-income housing. Private developers have been integrally involved in the construction of rehabbed and replacement public housing. Outcomes seem to indicate much-improved urban landscapes and less segregation of the poor, albeit at the cost of resident displacement and a decrease in the number of public housing units.

This chapter provided details of a critical disaster in housing policy known as the subprime mortgage crisis. We discussed the complex relationship between subprime lending, housing foreclosures, and the market-backed securities of Fannie Mae and Freddie Mac, which are traded on the stock market. This still-unfolding problem is affecting millions of middle-class, often two-earner working families, as well as many low-income first-time homeowners. The inadequacy of regulations for mortgage banks and lending institutions illustrates the need for federal policy regulations and oversight to protect consumers from predatory lending practices. In particular, our discussion of the now-global economic crisis highlights our view that policy making is primarily political and value based. Well-meaning policy makers can be blinded by their own beliefs and fail to see flaws in the policies they promote.

As the economic crisis grows, state and local communities across the country are seeing a surge in the number of homeless persons due to foreclosure, and we predict that middle-class homelessness will increase over the next several years. Community leaders and homeless advocates are looking at the feasibility of obtaining foreclosed properties from banks through the Community Reinvestment Act and turning them into shelters or transitional homes for the homeless. This is an example of how a problem in one area may become the policy solution in another area of policy development in the future.

FOR FURTHER READING

Brown, B., Noonan, C., & Nord, M. (2007). Prevalence of food insecurity and health-associated outcomes and food characteristics of Northern Plains Indian households. *Journal of Hunger and Environmental Nutrition, 1*(4), 37–53.

Depresz, L. S. (2008). The illusion of change, the politics of illusion: Evolution of the Family Support Act of 1988. *Journal of Sociology & Social Welfare, 35*(1), 105–132.

Fogel, S. J., Smith, M. T., & Williamson, A. R. (2008). A decent home for every family? Housing policy initiatives since the 1980s. *Journal of Sociology & Social Welfare, 35*(1), 175–196.

Hogan, S. R., Unick, G. J., Speiglman, R., & Norris, J. C. (2008). Social welfare policy and public assistance for low-income substance abusers. *Journal of Sociology & Social Welfare, 35*(1), 221–245.

Jacobson, M. (2007). Food matters: Community food assessments as a tool for change. *Journal of Community Practice, 15*(3), 37–55.

Johnson, C. C. (2002, May). *Defining eligible families in public housing and welfare: The traditions, values, and legalities of family form.* Blacksburg: Virginia Polytechnic & State University. Retrieved May 27, 2006, from http://scholar.lib.vt.edu/theses/available/etd-07312003-152427/unrestricted/Majorpaper2.pdf

King, R. F. (1999). Welfare reform: Block grants, expenditure caps, and the paradox of the food stamp program. *Political Science Quarterly, 114*(3), 359–385.

Meyers, M. K., Glaser, B., & Mac Donald, K. (1998). On the front lines of welfare delivery: Are workers implementing policy reforms? *Journal of Policy Analysis and Management, 17*(1), 1–22.

Miller, J. C., III, & Pearce, J. E. (2006, November). *Revisiting the net benefits of Freddie Mac and Fannie Mae.* Retrieved July 20, 2008, from http://www.freddiemac.com/corporate/reports/pdf/2006%20Pearce%20Miller%20report.pdf

Popkin, S. J., Gwiasda, V. E., Olson, L. M., Rosenbaum, D. P., & Buron, L. (2000). *Hidden war: Crime and the tragedy of public housing in Chicago.* Piscataway, NJ: Rutgers University Press.

Rocha, C. (2007). Food insecurity as market failure: A contribution from economics. *Journal of Hunger and Environmental Nutrition, 1*(4), 5–22.

Thompson, J. P. (1996–1997). The failure of liberal homeless policy in the Koch and Dinks administration. *Political Science Quarterly, 111*(4), 639–660.

Venkatesh, S. A. (2002). *American project: The rise and fall of a modern ghetto.* Cambridge, MA: Harvard University Press.

Vogt, R. A., Cassady, D., & Kaiser, L. L. (2007). Policy recommendations to improve the health of school-age children in the 2007 Farm Bill. *Journal of Hunger and Environmental Nutrition, 1*(4), 69–87.

References

Andrews, E. L. (2008, October 23). Greenspan concedes errors on regulation. *New York Times.* Retrieved October 26, 2008, from http://www.nytimes.com/2008/10/24/business/economy/24panel.html?bl&ex=1224993600&en=da694ed4921c5e8b&ei=5087%0A

Anti–Drug Abuse Act, Pub. L. No. 100-690, 102 Stat. 4181 (1998).

Armour, S. (2008, June 26). Hitting home: New faces join ranks of the homeless. *USA Today.* Retrieved July 17, 2008, from http://www.usatoday.com/money/economy/housing/2008-06-25-homeless-families-foreclosure_N.htm

Atlas, J., & Dreier, P. (2007). The conservative origins of the sub-prime mortgage crisis. *American Prospect, 18*(11). Retrieved June 15, 2008, from http://www.prospect.org/cs/articles?article=the_conservative_origins_of_the_subprime_mortgage_crisis

Austin, A. (2008). *Subprime mortgages are nearly double for Hispanics and African Americans.* Retrieved June 17, 2008, from http://www.epi.org/economic_snapshots/entry/webfeatures_snapshots_20080611/

Aversa, J. (2008, July 14). Fed ready to curb shady lending practices. *Daily Republic.* Retrieved July 20, 2008, from http://biz.yahoo.com/ap/080714/fed_mortgage_crisis.html?printer=1

Bennefield, R., & Bonnette, R. (2003, November). *Structural and occupancy characteristics of housing: 2000* (Census 2000 Brief No. C2KBR-32). Retrieved April 25, 2006, from http://www.census.gov/prod/2003pubs/c2kbr-32.pdf

Berner, R., & Grow, B. (2008, October 20). They warned us: The watchdogs who saw the subprime disaster coming—and how they were thwarted by the banks and Washington. *Business Week,* pp. 36–42. Retrieved July 20, 2009, from http://www.sabew.org/contest/2008/entries/5334END/The%20Watchdogs%20Who%20Warned%20Us.pdf

Bernstein, D. (2008, October 23). Greenspan's testimony today. *The Volokh Conspiracy.* Retrieved October 26, 2008, from http://volokh.com/posts/1224797890.shtml

Blank, R. M. (2006). Was welfare reform successful? *Economists' Voice, 3*(4). Retrieved May 13, 2007, from http://www.bepress.com/ev/vol3/iss4/art2

Blond, P. (2008, July 20). *They gave ordinary Americans a home. And then the roof fell in*. Retrieved July 20, 2008, from http://www.independent.co.uk/news/business/analysis-and-features/they-gave-ordinary-americans-a-home-and-then-the-roof-fell-in-872158.html

Child Nutrition Act, 42 U.S.C. 1771 (1966).

Christie, L. (2008). *Foreclosures up 75% in 2007*. Retrieved June 15, 2008, from http://money.cnn.com/2008/01/29/real-estate/foreclosure-filings-2007

Clarke, D. O., & Mungai, S. M. (1997). Distribution and association of chronic disease and mobility difficulty across four body-mass index categories of African-American women. *American Journal of Epidemiology, 145*(10), 865–875.

Cleveland, P. A., & Frohock, R. C. (2002). HOPE VI: HUD's program of false hope. *Religion & Liberty, 12*(5), 5–7. Retrieved April 28, 2006, from http://www.acton.org/publicat/randl/pdf/rl_v12n5.pdf

Committee on Government Operations. (1994). *AFCD waiver demonstration programs: Necessary flexibility or ad hoc decisionmaking?* Retrieved October 25, 2008, from http://www.archive.org/details/afdcwaiverdemonsoounit

Community Reinvestment Act, Pub. L. No. 95-128, Title VIII, 91 Stat. 1147, 12 U.S.C. § 2901 et seq. (1977).

Continuing Resolution of 1984, 7 U.S.C. 2011 (1984).

Crouse, G. (1999). *State implementation of major changes to welfare policies, 1992–1998*. Retrieved October 25, 2008, from http://aspe.hhs.gov/HSP/Waiver-Policies99/policy_CEA.htm

Curtis, K. A., & McClellan, S. (1995). Falling through the safety net: Poverty, food assistance and shopping constraints in an American city. *Urban Anthropology, 42*(1–2), 93–135.

Daponte, B. O. (1996, June). *Private versus public relief: Utilization of food pantries versus food stamps among poor households in Allegheny County, Pennsylvania* (Institute for Research on Poverty Discussion Paper No.1091-96). Madison: University of Wisconsin–Madison.

Daskal, J., & Sard, B. (1998, January). *Public housing admissions preferences: Recent changes in New York City illustrate the flexibility of existing rules*. Washington, DC: Center on Budget and Policy Priorities.

Davidson, C. E. (1994). Dependent children and their families: A historical survey of United States policies. In F. Jacobs & M. Davies (Eds.), *More than kissing babies: Current child and family policy in the United States* (pp. 65–89). West Port, CT: Auburn House.

Davis, J., & Hammeal-Urban, R. (1999, October 27). *Federal housing and domestic violence: Introduction to programs, policies and advocacy opportunities*. Retrieved April 25, 2006, from http://www.vawnet.org/NRCDVPublications/BCSDV/Papers/BCS8_FH.php

Dolbeare, C. (1991). Federal homeless social policies for the 1990s. *Housing Policy Debate, 2*(3), 1057–1094.

Dreier, P., & Appelbaum, R. P. (1992). The housing crisis enters the 1990s. *New England Journal of Public Policy, 8*(1), 155–167.

Eckholm, E. (2008, March 31). As jobs vanish and prices rise, food stamp use nears record. *New York Times*. Retrieved October 25, 2008, from http://www.nytimes.com/2008/03/31/us/31foodstamps.html

Ellwood, D. T. (1996). Welfare reform as I knew it: When bad things happen to good policies. *American Prospect, 7*(26). Retrieved April 28, 2006, from http://www.prospect.org/web/page.ww?section=root&name=ViewPrint&articleId=4940

Erlenbusch, B., O'Connor, K., Downing, S., & Phillips, S. W. (2008, April 15). *Foreclosure to homelessness: The forgotten victims of the subprime crisis. A national call to action*. Washington, DC: National Coalition for the Homeless. Retrieved July 20, 2008, from http://www.nationalhomeless.org/housing/foreclosure_report.pdf

Etter, L. (2007, May 22). Food banks go hungry; as manufacturers, retailers reduce waste, overstocks, charitable pantries suffer. *Wall Street Journal*. Retrieved October 25, 2008, from http://www.feedingillinois.org/news/articles/2007_05_22-wall_street_journal.pdf

Family Support Act, 42 U.S.C. 666 (1988).

Federal Register. (1999, July 23). One-strike screening and eviction for drug abuse and other criminal activity, *64*(141), 40262–40263. Retrieved February 21, 2009, from http://frwebgate.access.gpo.gov/cgi-bin/getpage.cgi?position=all&page=40261&dbname=1999_register

Food, Conservation, and Energy Act of 2008, Pub. L. No. 110-234, 122 Stat. 923 (2008).

Food Research and Action Center. (2008). *FRAC facts: Rising food costs and the thrifty food plan*. Retrieved February 21, 2009, from http://www.frac.org/pdf/thriftyfoodplanSEP08.pdf

Food Security Act, 10 U.S.C. 1001 (1985).

Food Stamp Act, Pub. L. No. 88-525, 78 Stat. 703-709 (1964).

Food Stamp Act Amendments, 7 U.S.C. 2011 (1982).

Gabor, V., & Botsko, C. (1998). *State food stamp policy choices under welfare reform: Findings of 1997 50-state survey*. Washington, DC: Health Systems Research.

Glantz, F. B. (1998). *Feeding the poor: Assessing federal food aid*. Washington, DC: AEI Press.

Greenspan, A. (2008, October 23). Testimony of Alan Greenspan. U.S. House of Representatives, Committee of Government Oversight and Reform. Retrieved July 21, 2009, from http://clipsandcomment.com/wp-content/uploads/2008/10/greenspan-testimony-20081023.pdf

Grotto, J., Cohen, L., & Olkon, S. (2008a, July 6). A housing site that worked for families. *Chicago Tribune*, p. 23.

Grotto, J., Cohen, L., & Olkon, S. (2008b, July 6). Public housing limbo. *Chicago Tribune*, pp. 1, 22–23.

Hamilton, W. L., Cook, J. T., Thompson, W. W., Buron, L. F., Frongillo, E. A., Jr., Olson, C. M., et al. (1997, September). *Household food security in the United States in 1995: Summary report of the Food Security Measurement Project*. Retrieved April 28, 2006, from http://www.fns.usda.gov/oane/MENU/Published/FoodSecurity/SUMRPT.PDF

Jindal, B. P., & Winstead, D. (2002, June). *Status report on research on the outcomes of welfare reform: A report to the congressional appropriations committees.* Washington, DC: U.S. Department of Health and Human Services. Retrieved May 1, 2006, from http://aspe.hhs.gov/hsp/welf-ref-outcomes02/index.htm

Johns, M. (2002). A "one strike" battle planned. *Residents Journal.* Retrieved October 23, 2006, from http://www.wethepeoplemedia.org/articles/maryjohns/onestrikebattle/

Johnson, A. K. (1989). Female-headed homeless families: A comparative profile. *Affilia: Journal of Women and Social Work, 4*(4), 23–29.

Johnson, A. K. (1992). Urban redevelopment law and the destruction of affordable housing. *Journal of Law and Social Work, 3*(1), 29–43.

Johnson, N., & Lav, I. J. (1998). *Should states tax food? Examining the policy issues and options.* Washington, DC: Center on Budget and Policy Priorities.

Kasperowicz, P. (2008). *U.S. foreclosures rise in December; reach 2.2 mln in 2007, up 75 pct from 2006.* Retrieved June 15, 2008, from http://www.forbes.com/markets/feeds/afx/2008/01/29/afx4584956.html

Labaton, S. (2008). Fed readies bailout of mortgage giants. Up to $300 billion for Fannie Mae, Freddie Mac. *Seattle Post-Intelligencer.* Retrieved July 17, 2008, from http://seattlepi.newsource.com/national/370666_mortgage14.html

Leonhardt, D. (2008, October 22). The trouble with a homeowner bailout. *New York Times.* Retrieved October 26, 2008, from http://www.nytimes.com/2008/10/22/business/economy/22leonhardt.html?pagewanted=1&ref=business

Mankiw, N. G. (2008, October 25). But have we learned enough? *New York Times.* Retrieved October 26, 2008, from http://www.nytimes.com/2008/10/26/business/26view.html

Morris, F. (2008, October 25). Economic woes hit nation's food pantries hard. *All Things Considered.* Retrieved October 25, 2008, from http://www.npr.org/templates/story/story.php?storyId=95849670

Mulroy, E. A. (1995). Housing. In R. L. Edwards & J. G. Hopps (Eds.), *Encyclopedia of social work* (19th ed., pp. 1377–1384). Washington, DC: NASW Press.

Murphy, J. M., Wehler, C. A., Pagano, M. E., Little, M., Kleinman, R. E., & Jellinek, M. S. (1998). Relationship between hunger and psychosocial functioning in low-income American children. *Journal of the American Academy of Child and Adolescent Psychiatry, 37*(2), 163–170.

Omnibus Budget Reconciliation Act, Pub. L. No. 97-35, 95 Stat. 357-933 (1981).

Opulente, M., & Mattaini, M. (1997). Toward welfare that works. *Research on Social Work Practice, 7*(1), 115–135.

Parrott, S. (1998). *Welfare recipients who find jobs: What do we know about their employment and earnings?* Washington, DC: Center on Budget and Policy Priorities.

Pavetti, L., Olson, K., Nightingale, D., Duke, A., & Isaacs, J. (1998). *Welfare to work options for families facing personal and family challenges: Rationale and program strategies.* Washington, DC: Urban Institute.

Personal Responsibility and Work Opportunity Reconciliation Act, 110 Stat. 2323 (1996).

Popkin, S. J., Katz, B., Cunningham, M. K., Brown, K. D., Gustafson, J., & Turner, M. A. (2004, May 18). *A decade of HOPE VI: Research findings and policy challenges.* Retrieved April 27, 2006, from http://www.urban.org/UploadedPDF/411002_HOPEVI.pdf

Powell, J. A. (2004, April). *Affordable housing in America: Issues and future needs.* Retrieved May 3, 2006, from http://www.kirwaninstitute.org/multimedia/presentations/AffHousingBreadPresApril282004.ppt

Privatized system fails to deliver food stamps in Indiana. (2008, April 28). *FRAC News Digest.* Retrieved October 26, 2008, from http://www.frac.org/digest/04.28.08.htm#9

Public and Indian Housing. (2006, March 7). *About HOPE VI.* Retrieved May 3, 2006, from http://www.hud.gov/offices/pih/programs/ph/hope6/about/

Quality Housing and Work Responsibility Act of 1998, Pub. L. No. 105-276 (1998).

Rawlings, S., & Saluter, A. (1995, September). *Household and family characteristics: March 1994* (Current Population Reports, Population Characteristics, P20-483). Retrieved April 25, 2006, from http://www.census.gov/prod/1/pop/p20-483.pdf

Rhodes, E. (2007). Growing mortgage crisis spreads to jumbo loans. *Seattle Times.* Retrieved June 17, 2008, from http://seattletimes.nwsource.com/html/businesstechnology/2003853935-jumbo26.html

Sandstrom, N. (2005, January 14). Number of food stamp participants increases. *Daily Illini.* Retrieved May 3, 2006, from http://www.dailyillini.com/media/paper736/news/2005/01/14/News/Number.Of.Food.Stamp.Participants.Increases-833312.shtml?norewrite&sourcedomain=www.dailyillini.com

Sard, J. (1992). Housing the homeless through expanding access to existing housing subsidies. *New England Journal of Public Policy, 8*(1), 187–200.

Social Security Act, 42 U.S.C. 301-1397jj (1935).

Super, D. (2001, July 10). *Background on the Food Stamp Program.* Retrieved May 3, 2006, from http://www.cbpp.org/7-10-01fs.htm

Tull, J. (1992). Homelessness: An overview. *New England Journal of Public Policy, 8*(1), 25–48.

Urban Institute. (2008). *Welfare rules database.* Accessed February 20, 2008, from http://anfdata.urban.org/wrd/wrdwelcome.cfm

U.S. Conference of Mayors–Sodexho. (2007, December). *A status report on hunger and homelessness in America's cities: A 23-city study.* Washington, DC: Author. Retrieved July 21, 2008, from http://www.usmayors.org/HHSurvey2007/hhsurvey07.pdf

U.S. Department of Agriculture. (1995, April 19). Special Supplemental Food Program for Women, Infants, and Children (WIC): Homelessness/migrancy as nutritional risk conditions. *Federal Register, 60*(75), 19487.

U.S. Department of Health and Human Services. (2000, December). *Status of research on the outcomes of welfare reform: A report to the congressional appropriations committees.* Retrieved April 28, 2006, from http://aspe.hhs.gov/hsp/welf-ref-outcomes00/index.htm

U.S. Department of Health and Human Services. (2004, November). *Temporary Assistance for Needy Families (TANF): Sixth annual report to Congress.* Retrieved September 4, 2005, from http://www.acf.hhs.gov/programs/ofa/annualreport6/ar6index.htm

Wilson, K. (2008, June 21). Foreclosures considered for homeless shelters. *Ventura County Star.* Retrieved July 21, 2008, from http://www.venturacountystar.com/news/2008/jun/21/foreclosures-considered-for-shelters/

Wilson, R. (2005). SAHA wrongly cited feds in eviction; Agency to weigh new drug policy in wake of zero-tolerance stance. *San Antonio Express News,* p. 3b.

Zedlewski, S., & Rader, K. (2004). *Recent trends in food stamp participation among poor families with children.* Retrieved May 17, 2007, from http://www.urban.org/uploadedpdf/311027_DP04-03.pdf

CHAPTER 7

Work and Employment

In chapter 6, we looked at policies in the areas of income, food, and housing that assist families in meeting their basic needs. The topic of this chapter is closely related to that of the previous chapter. Here, we focus on work and employment, rather than assistance through public welfare. The two chapters are tied together in that the 1996 welfare reform now requires families on public assistance to work. This chapter emphasizes problems and policies in work and employment that both poor and non-poor families face as they attempt to earn income through work.

The ability to secure jobs at a living wage is essential for family self-sufficiency and adequate family functioning. Yet over 50 percent of poor workers are employed in unskilled service positions, and almost 20 percent have jobs in the retail industry, where wages are generally low. Low-wage jobs, declining workplace benefits, reduced opportunities for training for higher-paying employment, and the decline in the value of the minimum wage all serve to reduce working families' abilities to remain self-sufficient. Historically, jobs in the industrial sector of the economy allowed unskilled workers in the United States to make a living wage. However, in recent years, the number of jobs in the industrial sector has decreased dramatically.

At the heart of these problems in the American workplace is globalization, which has brought about major changes in manufacturing and industry. Jobs in heavy industry and manufacturing have been replaced by jobs in the service sector of the economy. Service-sector employment grew from 92,292 million jobs in 1994 to 110,374 million in 2004, compared to employment in the manufacturing sector, which experienced a downward trend from 22,692 million jobs to 21,817 million jobs. By 2003, almost a quarter of all workers were employed in the low-wage labor market, including service, unskilled blue-collar, retail, and agricultural jobs. The service sector is expected to be the source of all growth in nonagricultural wage and salary employment between 2004 and 2014. The number of jobs in the service sector is anticipated to reach 129 million by 2014, accounting for almost four out of every five jobs in the U.S. economy (U.S. Department of Labor, 2005a, 2005b).

Critics disagree with the idea that the overall loss of jobs in the United States is due to firms seeking lower labor costs outside the country. In their view, the culprit is technological change. "Job churning" goes on regularly in the U.S. labor market as some jobs end and new jobs take their place. In the 1980s and 1990s, technological changes increased the demand for more skilled workers in the United States, but between 2000 and 2003, approximately 669,000 jobs in professional and business services, 433,000 jobs in information technology, and 109,000 federal government jobs were lost (Mishel, Bernstein, & Allegretto, 2005). During the Clinton administration, from 1992 to 2000, for example, 260 million jobs were lost and 280 million new jobs were created, for a net gain of 20 million new jobs. Each year, the United States loses about 35 million jobs for voluntary and involuntary reasons. Only about 1 percent of jobs go offshore, with the bulk of loss due to technology.

This chapter begins with a brief overview of globalization and how these changes have affected the availability of well-paying jobs in the United States. Understanding globalization and the changes it has created in the U.S. labor market is important for comprehending the relationship between private troubles and larger social issues. There are no easy explanations for the causes or the effects of globalization. What is clear, however, is that deindustrialization and the rise of the service economy are profoundly changing the lifestyles of working families. It is also clear that the brunt of this change is borne by American's skilled and semi-skilled blue-collar workers and those who find employment in the service sector of the economy.

Globalization has even more significant effects during an extended downturn in the economy, known as recession. In order to help readers understand the effects of a downturn in the economy, we discuss the problem of defining economic recession in the United States. In chapter 4, we pointed out that poverty is political in that how we view it depends on the way that it is measured and the way in which statistics are used. Here, we point out that determinations of whether the United States is in a recession are also political because of the way recession is defined and officially measured. In times of an economic downturn, researchers and policy makers have a hard time agreeing on whether the U.S. economy is in a recession. Indicators such as state budget shortfalls, public opinion polls, job loss, and the unemployment rate are used to judge whether the economy is moving toward recession. As we pointed out in chapter 2, it is important to consider the subjective realities of the family. If a family believes that a problem exists, then it is part of their reality. Public opinion polls usually show that people believe that the economy is in a recession well before government releases an official statement to that effect. Since high unemployment rates are one foreboding indicator of recession, we also discuss the way the unemployment rate is calculated and present rates by race, gender, and educational level over time.

In the last part of this chapter, we review employment-related policies, which we have divided into two categories: (1) policies that assist workers in finding employment after they become unemployed (unemployment insurance, notifications of plant closings, employment services, and programs that provide support and retraining for workers who have lost their jobs due to globalization) and (2) policies that provide income support for workers (minimum wage and the earned income tax credit).

Globalization and the U.S. Labor Market

Definitions of Globalization

Globalization has become such a major factor that we cannot have a discussion about the labor market in the United States without starting with the global marketplace. Before we begin our discussion, it is important for readers to understand some of the meanings of the term *globalization*. Globalization is complex. It encompasses the changing interaction and "co-evolution of millions of technological, cultural, economic, social and environmental trends" (Rennen & Martens, 2003, p. 137). A comprehensive discussion of the issue of globalization by Wells (2001) notes several different definitions of globalization.

- According to Keohane and Nye (2000), globalization is "the state of the world involving networks of interdependence at multicontinental distances. These networks can be linked through flows and influences of capital and goods, information and ideas, people and force, as well as environmentally and biologically relevant substances" (qtd. by Wells, 2001, p. CRS-2).
- Friedman (1999) views globalization as "the overarching international system shaping the domestic politics and foreign relations of virtually every country in the world" (qtd. by Wells, 2001, p. CRS-2). To Friedman, globalization is driven by free market capitalism. It is

the system that replaced the cold war system. Friedman's definition of globalization has six dimensions—politics, culture, technology, finance and trade, national security, and ecology—and via globalization, the boundaries between these dimensions are disappearing (Wells, 2001).

- The U.S. Department of Defense (1999) defines globalization as "the integration of the political, economic and cultural activities of geographically and/or nationally separated peoples—[it] is not a discernible event or challenge, is not new, but is accelerating. More importantly, globalization is largely irresistible. Thus, globalization is not a policy option, but a fact to which policymakers must adapt" (qtd. by Wells, 2001, p. CRS-1).

As these definitions indicate, globalization has many aspects. In this chapter, our focus is on economic globalization. In particular, we use the term to mean changes in the labor market, particularly those that have occurred since the 1980s. We believe that it is important to understand globalization not as a policy option or a policy area, but as a *fact to which policy makers must adapt*. Globalization affects policy, and policy affects globalization.

To help us understand the effects of economic globalization in the United States, we turn to Friedman (2006), who identifies three different eras of globalization. He terms these Globalization 1.0, Globalization 2.0, and Globalization 3.0. Globalization 1.0 began in 1492 with Christopher Columbus's journey between the Old World and the New World. His exploration reduced the size of the world from large to medium. This period of globalization was marked by "how much muscle, how much horsepower, wind power, or, later, steam power" a country had and how it was used. "In Globalization 1.0, the primary questions were: Where does my country fit into global competition and opportunities? How can I go global and collaborate with others in my country?" (Friedman, 2006, p. 9). Countries were the dynamic force in Globalization 1.0.

Globalization 2.0 began around 1800 and lasted until the year 2000, with brief intermissions caused by World Wars I and II. In this period, multinational corporations drove the integration of global markets, which reduced the size of the world from medium to small. This period was characterized by the exchange of goods, services, and information across the globe through advances first in transportation, by steamships and railroads, and second in communication technologies such as the telegraph, telephones, personal computers, satellites, fiber-optic cables, and the beginning of the Internet. "The big questions in this era were: Where does my company fit into the global economy? How does it take advantages of the opportunities? How can I go global and collaborate with others through my company?" (Friedman, 2006, p. 10). Companies were the dynamic force during Globalization 2.0.

Globalization 3.0 began about the year 2000 with the laying of fiberoptic cables around the world, widespread access to home computers, and the use of common software and the Internet. Friedman (2006) suggests that this new era of globalization is shrinking the world, making it *flat*. Although companies also benefit in this new era of globalization, its unique mark is the opportunity for individuals to play a role in globalization. "Every person now must, and can ask: Where do *I* as an individual fit into the global competition and opportunities of the day, and how can *I*, on my own, collaborate with others globally?" (p. 11). Individuals are the dynamic force in Globalization 3.0.

Our discussion focuses on the second and third waves of globalization because of the important effect they are having on the current labor market in the United States.

Globalization 2.0: Deindustrialization and the Rise of the Service Economy

Globalization 2.0 is represented by changes in heavy industry such as auto manufacturing. The period is marked by what is often referred to as deindustrialization: the loss of blue-collar jobs when heavy industries such as steel, rubber, and auto manufacturing are relocated overseas. The manufacturing and mining industries—once considered the most stable and best-paying employers for workers without a college education—lost approximately 2.2 million jobs between 1979 and 1995. Between 2000 and 2006, the United Sates lost an additional 3 million manufacturing jobs. The jobs lost in heavy manufacturing were union jobs that paid high wages of about $30 per hour, plus hefty benefit plans providing overtime pay, health insurance, and retirement pensions. In the past, it was common for young adults to get a job "at the mill," obtain on-the-job training, and stay until retirement. Union benefits gave unskilled and semi-skilled workers a solid middle-class lifestyle.

Globalization 2.0 placed less skilled and blue-collar workers in the United States in competition with workers in other countries. Heavy industries relocated overseas because of the reduced costs of labor in developing countries. The steel industry is a good example. In the early 1900s, steel mills drove the economy of Rust Belt cities such as Cleveland, Ohio; Gary, Indiana; and Philadelphia, Pennsylvania. By the 1970s and 1980s, the mills built at the turn of the century were outdated. Capital investment was required to install the latest technologies for producing steel and to comply with new laws designed to reduce pollution. In Cleveland, for example, steel mills lined the banks of the Cuyahoga River, which ran through the city. Pollution was so bad that the river caught fire several times. The passage of environmental policy that occurred after the Cuyahoga River burned illustrates the dynamic nature of policy making. It is a good example of how critical events in history can galvanize widespread support and open a window for policy change. In this case, the burning of the Cuyahoga River pushed pollution control into public consciousness in the 1970s, at a time when relatively few Americans were active in the environmental movement.

> Fires plagued the Cuyahoga River beginning in 1936 when a spark from a blow torch ignited floating debris and oils. The largest river fire in 1952 caused over $1 million in damage to boats and a riverfront office building. By the 1960s the lower Cuyahoga River in Cleveland was used for waste disposal, and was choked with debris, oils, sludge, industrial wastes and sewage. These pollutants were considered a major source of impact to Lake Erie, which was considered "dead" at the time. On June 22, 1969 a river fire captured national attention. Time magazine described the Cuyahoga as the river that "oozes rather than flows" and in which a person "does not drown but decays." This event helped spur an avalanche of pollution control activities resulting in the Clean Water Act . . . and the creation of the federal and state Environmental Protection Agencies. (U.S. Environmental Protection Agency, 2007)

Almost overnight, with the passage of environmental laws, business as usual changed. Pollution of America's rivers and waterways could result in fines up to $25,000 per day. As these changes unfolded in the United States, new steel-producing factories were being built in Japan, Korea, and, more recently, China. By 1982, Japan had become the world's top producer of crude steel, followed by China by 1998.

Other industries, such as the textile and apparel industries, were hit by the effects of trade liberalization and international trade agreements, which were also a part of Globalization 2.0. In 1993, the North American Free Trade Agreement (NAFTA) was signed by the United States, Canada, and Mexico. Since the United States previously had a trade agreement with Canada, evaluations have focused on the loss of manufacturing jobs to Mexico. From the mid- to late 1990s, overall imports from Mexico grew fastest in those sectors with the largest duty reductions under NAFTA (Avery, 1998). However, the decline actually began at least ten years earlier under other generalized tariff and trade agreements (Hinojosa-Ojeda, Dowds, McCleery, Robinson, Runsten, Wolff, & Wolff, 1996). For example, the apparel industry was affected by intermediate exports—goods that are exported to Mexico, processed, and then exported back to the United States. Levi Strauss, the company that made blue jeans since the Gold Rush days, closed the last of its sixty American factories in 2004. These factories paid about $14 per hour, plus benefits. Rocha and Strand (2004) used stratified random sampling and six-month follow-up interviews with 172 women who were sewing machine operators, fabric cutters, and laundry workers in a Levi Strauss plant in Tennessee that closed. None of the women were reemployed at a wage level equal to the wages they received at the plant. All but the women employed in higher-wage service jobs exhibited "increased levels of depressive symptoms associated with the wages of reemployment" (Rocha & Strand, 2004, p. 561). Single parents experienced the greatest financial difficulty and the greatest depression levels. Box 7.1 tells the story of Julie, who worked in a white-collar job until the company she worked for reorganized, and then she lost her job and

Box 7.1 Part-Time Employment and Job Retraining

Julie's situation illustrates the difficulties of corporate downsizing. After losing her job as a property manager, she returned home with her two children to live with her mother.

> Yes, I had a complete package—insurance, vacation, cost-of-living raises—everything that comes along with a full-time salaried job. The company was bought out by an organization that was doing a lot of restructuring, and . . . I no longer fit into their master plan. So, along with myself, a lot of people were laid off.

When she lost her job, Julie decided to go back to school part time. She has completed one year of college, so it will be several years before she finishes. In the meantime, she has several part-time jobs and no health insurance.

> I have several odd jobs I am doing. I take care of three children during the day besides my own, and every night I take care of an elderly gentleman who has Parkinson's disease, and on the weekends, I work at a restaurant. The biggest concern now is insurance, and that's mainly because if anything happens to me or the children, I don't have the means to pay for it. And with that comes my family having to suffer the cost of us not getting the proper health care because we can't afford to get it. Today, it could be a life-or-death situation. It's all in how much money you have. It could be something real simple, and if it's not taken care of initially, it escalates and you're up a creek.

health care benefits. Unable to find employment with commensurate wages and benefits, she works several part-time jobs. The question of how she will pay for health care if anything happens to her or her children is a constant stress.

Deindustrialization also illustrates how larger structural forces in society are a root cause of poverty. In America's older manufacturing cities, deindustrialization has had a domino-like effect in creating widespread poverty. As factories closed, city populations decreased. Public services in the inner core of cities diminished as businesses left, housing deteriorated, and schools that depended on property taxes for revenue lost funding. An article entitled "The Case of Baltimore: Deindustrialization Creates 'Death Zones'" (EIR Economics Staff, 2006) captures the reality of pre- and post-deindustrialization in the port and industrial city of Baltimore, Maryland. In its heyday, the Sparrows Point facility owned by Bethlehem Steel employed 260,000 workers and featured a state-of-the-art integrated steelmaking process for shipbuilding, rail tracks, aircraft, and the like.

> As the manufacturing jobs disappeared, so did the city's population: In 1950, the city had 950,000 residents; in the 2000 census, it has 651,000—a loss of about one-third. . . . Holders of the low-wage jobs in Baltimore are 71% African-American . . . [with] women filling 83% of administrative and personal service positions (e.g., hospital, health care workers, tourism). Of the women studied, 75% were the sole source of income for their households.
>
> The characteristics of these jobs dynamically interact with each other, and the environment at large, to create a "black hole" with such gravitational force that escape is virtually impossible: Low wages force such workers to seek second jobs, and work up to 60 hours a week, which takes many single mothers away from the home, precluding supervision of their children's schooling and social life; no benefits, no job training or opportunities for advancement; many jobs are part-time, with staggered shifts; and jobs like health aides may require hours of bus travel into the suburbs and back for just a few hours work. (EIR Economics Staff, 2006, pp. 10–11)

As happened in Baltimore, the industry shift to a service economy meant lower pay and fewer benefits for workers. A major issue was the loss of employer-provided health insurance. In non-standard jobs, health care benefits are lower, and only about 15 percent of women and 13 percent of men receive any employer-provided health care. Changes in heavy manufacturing also result in increased non-standard employment of temporary and part-time workers. During Globalization 2.0, manufacturing corporations typically contracted for parts and supplies from around the world and assembled the final product at a main factory. Union jobs were often lost to smaller firms that offered lower wages and part-time employment with minimal or no benefits. In 2003, part-time employees (those working fewer than thirty-five hours per week) constituted 17 percent of the workforce, or almost 20 million workers. This increase has been almost entirely involuntary, reflecting the preferred use of part-time workers by employers, not the preference of the workforce for shorter hours (Mishel et al., 2005).

The auto industry case highlights these and other complex issues related to the effects of Globalization 2.0 and deindustrialization on the U.S. labor market. In considering the idea that well-paying jobs have gone overseas, one needs to look a little closer at some other aspects of globalization. These include the considerable holdings of multinational U.S. corporations in the foreign auto companies, the return of auto manufacturing jobs to the United States in production facilities built by foreign companies, the inability of U.S. carmakers to compete because of high health care and pension fund commitments made through unionization, and the role of enormous tax subsidies from state and local governments to produce cars and trucks in the United States.

The first point is that U.S. automakers are multinational corporations that hold significant shares of stock or joint ownership in foreign car companies. So when one speaks of foreign automakers, it is not so simple to define what is foreign and what is not. A lengthy report on globalization and the transportation industry mentions just some of the partnerships, alliances, and joint ventures that have occurred over the past twenty-five years.

> The biggest of these moves, the Daimler-Benz acquisition of Chrysler in 1998, kicked off a new round of global consolidation. The acquisition was quickly followed by Ford's purchase of the car manufacturing division of Sweden's luxury carmaker Volvo. Volvo then bought Renault's U.S. Mack Truck Manufacturing business, and in turn gave Renault a 15 percent stock ownership stake in Volvo.... General Motors has alliances with three Japanese companies, owning 10 percent of Suzuki; 20 percent of Fuji Heavy Industries, maker of Subaru; and 49 percent of Isuzu ... [and] 20 percent of Fiat in Italy and all of Swedish Saab.... Ford owns 33 percent of the Japanese company, Mazda, and it has taken over Sweden's Volvo and Britain's Jaguar and Land Rover operations ... and has moved into India with 78 percent ownership in Ford India. (U.S. Department of Transportation, 2000)

More mergers and acquisitions have occurred since that time.

The second point is that although some auto manufacturing jobs went overseas, auto manufacturing has also come to the United States. Many foreign automakers have built production plants in the United States, mostly in the South and rural parts of the country. Analysts point out that, as a result, the industry has not really lost jobs. "Over the past 15 years, the number of people building autos and making parts in the United States has held just about steady, thanks to hiring by foreign automakers" (Speer, 2008). These boundaries have also been blurred by the export of autos made in the United States. "Two years ago, Nissan completed a $1.4 billion investment in a plant north of Jackson, Miss., providing jobs for 4,100 employees. It assembles several models, including the Titan pickup and the Armada sport-utility vehicle. Some are headed to markets outside the United States, including China, Taiwan, Mexico and Canada" (Freeman, 2006).

For the most part, foreign car production in the United States is not unionized, so wages per hour are lower. However, these wage differences are reduced by end-of-year profit-sharing bonuses that are based on auto sales in the United States. "Legacy costs" are partially to blame for making U.S. automakers less competitive in the global economy. American automakers are strapped with costs such as health care and retirement benefits that go on after workers retire. In addition, "with every plant closure, health-care costs rise because US firms carry an extra burden of coverage for retired workers. GM covered health care for 1.1 million people in 2005, almost 70 percent of whom were retirees or workers' family members" (Froetschel, 2007).

Table 7.1 shows a comparison of GM and Toyota production in the United States. Health care costs per vehicle in 2004 for GM were $1,525, compared to $201 for Toyota. The difference in retirees, who typically have higher health care needs, is staggering. GM has 460,000 retired workers compared to Toyota's 1,600. These legacy costs add up and contribute to an average labor cost of $73.73 per U.S. hourly worker at GM, compared to $48 at Toyota. A series of financial problems has plagued General Motors; the company reported a $38.7 billion loss in 2007. As a result, union contracts were renegotiated. Starting salaries for new hires decreased to about $17 per hour, and buyouts were offered to long-time employees. In a major change of policy, union negotiations with GM resulted in the development of a voluntary employees beneficiary association fund to move $51 billion in retiree health care costs off its books. GM will pay the United Autoworkers Union $34 billion in cash and stock to manage and cover retiree health care costs beginning in 2010. "The shift to a [voluntary employees beneficiary association] to pay retiree health care is the largest part of the 2007

Table 7.1 Comparison of General Motors and Toyota Auto Manufacturing in the United States

Data Reported	General Motors	Toyota
Vehicle Production in North America in 2005	4,856,000	1,558,828
Profitability per Vehicle	Loses $2,331 per vehicle	Makes $1,488 per vehicle
Number of Plants in North America	77 plants, all unionized. Plans to close 12 facilities by 2008	12, three unionized in Long Beach, California, Fremont, California, and Tijuana, Mexico
North American Workforce	White collar: 36,000 Production: 106,000 Retirees: 460,000	White collar: 17,000 Production: 21,000 Retirees: 1,600
Average Hourly Salary for Non-Skilled, Assembly Line Worker	$31.35 (includes idle workers still on payroll and those on protected status)	$27 (includes year-end bonus)
Health Care Costs per Vehicle in 2004	$1,525	$201
Average Labor Cost per U.S. Hourly Worker	$73.73	$48

Source: Adapted from Geng, D. (2005, December 19). *GM vs. Toyota: By the numbers.* Retrieved February 28, 2008, from http://www.npr.org/news/specials/gmvstoyota/

labor contract that will reduce GM's annual costs by $3 billion starting in 2010. But GM faces a liquidity crisis now that [will] ... require outside help for it to survive beyond 2009" (Shepardson, 2008). It received a cash infusion of $15.4 billion ("GM Gets Another $2B," 2009). The new contract also includes a moratorium on outsourcing and a "pledge to insource more than 3,000 [United Autoworkers Union] jobs" (United Autoworkers Union, 2008). Opponents argue that the voluntary employees beneficiary association shifts the risks of health care coverage to workers. From a family policy perspective, one has to ask why the U.S. auto industry doesn't push for national health care, since health care costs are one reason they have not been able to compete with foreign carmakers in their own backyard.

The last point underlying globalization is related to the production of foreign cars in the United States. Good Jobs First is a national policy resource center that promotes corporate and government accountability in economic development and smart growth for working families. The case in box 7.2 summarizes the financial assistance that Asian and European carmakers have received from state and local governments for infrastructure aid and extraordinary subsidies for the building of new auto production

Box 7.2 Case Study of Auto Assembly Plants

As the U.S. automakers have downsized their domestic manufacturing operations over the past two decades, foreign car makers have been opening one U.S. assembly plant after another. And in nearly every case, the Asian and European companies have received financial assistance from state and local governments eager for industrial jobs.

The first foreign automaker to set up shop in the United States was Volkswagen, which opened a plant in Pennsylvania in 1978. That venture, which fell victim to labor unrest, ended in 1988. The real invasion began in the early 1980s, at a time when Japanese producers were winning a steadily increasing share of the U.S. car market. To allay concern about the rising tide of auto imports, the Japanese decided to open production facilities in the U.S. This move was made all the more urgent by efforts in Congress to pass legislation mandating domestic content for cars sold in the U.S. market.

Honda began assembling Accords in Ohio in 1982. Nissan, which started producing trucks at its Smyrna, Tennessee plant in 1983, expanded to automobiles two years later. Toyota got involved in both a joint venture with General Motors in California and an operation of its own in Kentucky. Mazda announced plans in 1984 to build an assembly plant in Michigan, and Mitsubishi said it would produce cars in Illinois in a joint venture with Chrysler called Diamond-Star.

By the time of the Mitsubishi project, governments were lavishing large sums on the facilities, known as transplants. Illinois, hoping that the Diamond-Star plant would create a slew of additional jobs as nearby supplier companies sprang up, provided a package worth $249 million, the biggest in Illinois history and then the biggest package ever given an auto assembly plant in the U.S.

Such assistance was offered, even though many observers pointed out that the Japanese firms, concerned more about import controls than state and local taxes, would certainly proceed with their plans even in the absence of subsidies. Authors Martin and Susan Tolchin noted in their book *Buying Into America*: "There was nothing secret about these strategies: The Japanese encouraged their companies to invest abroad as enlightened policy, designed to stave off protectionism and save jobs."

By the 1990s the threat of protectionism had passed, yet foreign automakers continued to expand operations in the United States. The reason now was to bolster their ever-rising U.S. market share and to take advantage of what had become relatively inexpensive U.S. labor. The latter motivation prompted companies to shift their focus from the Midwest to "right to work" states in the South. Nonetheless, state and local governments continued to offer up lucrative subsidy packages, including the following:

- In 1992 South Carolina ushered in the new wave of investment by foreign carmakers in the South by offering BMW a package that was ultimately worth an estimated $150 million. A decade later, the state put up an additional $80 million in infrastructure aid when BMW decided to expand its operations in the state.
- In 1993 officials in Alabama lured a Mercedes-Benz facility, the first foreign auto plant in the state, with a package worth $258 million.
- In 1999 Alabama put together a $158 million subsidy deal to land a $400 million, 1.7 million-square-foot Honda plant. In 2002 state and local officials provided an additional package worth $90 million, including $33 million in tax breaks over 20 years, when Honda decided to expand the facility.
- In 2000 officials in Mississippi lured a $950 million Nissan plant with a $295 million subsidy deal. While the plant was still under construction, the company announced an expansion of the project that also involved an increase in the subsidy package to $363 million.
- When South Korean carmaker Hyundai staged a competition for a $1 billion plant, various states put together bids, but it was Alabama that won the contest in 2002 with a package worth $252 million.
- Commentators made much of the fact that when Toyota chose San Antonio, Texas in 2003 as the location for an $800 million assembly plant, the company had not selected the site with the most generous subsidy package. In another example of the fact that subsidies are not the most important factor in investment decisions, Toyota highlighted criteria such as access to the large Texas market for the pickup trucks that would be built at the plant. This is not to say that Toyota passed up all government assistance. The company received a package valued at $133 million, including $47 million in tax phase-ins and waived fees.

By the late 1990s there were signs that the big giveaway to BMW by South Carolina was exacerbating a fiscal crisis in the state. While the carmaker and other companies were enjoying minimal levels of corporate taxation, the state's schools were falling into greater disrepair and educational achievement was worsening. Funds for other government services such as highway maintenance and public safety were also in short supply, leading to tax increases for families. "The foreign companies that come in here don't care that the schools are terrible," one philanthropist told a reporter. "They just want the cheap labor. And the incentives are so extraordinary."

> It is only a matter of time before the other states that have given nine-figure subsidy packages to foreign carmakers also begin to wonder if they made the right decision for the long-term prosperity of their citizens. They may also realize that giveaways ultimately work against future corporate investments. A sign of this came in 2005 when Toyota rejected several subsidy-laden deals from U.S. communities and instead decided to build its next assembly plant in Ontario. The decision was said to be made because of the higher quality of the workforce in Canada.

Source: Good Jobs First. (2008). *Case study of auto assembly plants.* Retrieved February 29, 2008, from http://www.goodjobsfirst.org/corporate_subsidy/automobile_assembly_plants.cfm

plants in the United States. We point especially to the situation in South Carolina when BMW received $150 million in 1992, and another $80 million later, which, according to Good Jobs First, resulted in the state's schools "falling into greater disrepair and educational achievement was worsening. Funds for other governmental services such as highway maintenance and public safety were also in short supply, leading to tax increases for families."

Globalization 3.0: White-Collar Jobs Go Offshore

Globalization 3.0 began about the year 2000 and is characterized by many of the aspects of Globalization 2.0, such as outsourcing, which continues to be practiced not only by corporations, but by government as well. Take Boeing, for example. Twenty years ago, most of the parts for its aircraft were manufactured in the United States. Today, about 70 percent of its 727 Dreamliner airplane parts are made overseas, including major parts such as the fuselage, wings, and engine ("Dreamliner 101," 2007). Boeing also finds itself on the other side of outsourcing. The U.S. Air Force awarded a $35 billion contract to a defense contractor based in France to build 179 Airbus KC-30 planes to replace its outmoded fleet of aerial tankers. The contract also positions the Northrop and EADS group as a leading contender for two additional tanker contracts worth more than $100 million. The plane will be assembled in Mobile, Alabama, where a new factory will be built that will employ 5,000 people. Senator Richard Shelby (R-AL) has pointed out that Boeing and other aerospace companies outsource work to other nations. "We're in a global economy. . . . A lot of this work will be done in the good old U.S. of A" (qtd. in Johnsson &

Madhani, 2008, p. 16). The company estimated that had Boeing won the contract, 44,000 new jobs would have been created. This caused some members of Congress to raise concerns over outsourcing the contract. General Arthur Lichte, commander of the Air Force's Air Mobility Command, views the outsourcing decision differently: "This is an American tanker. . . . It's flown by American airmen. It has a big American flag on the tail, and every day it'll be out there saving American lives" (qtd. in Johnsson & Madhani, 2008, p. 16).

There is a new trend in Globalization 3.0 that has economists worried. In this wave of globalization, white-collar jobs are also moving offshore, as major corporations are eager to outsource white-collar jobs, which were once considered the mainstay of business at corporate offices. As many as 300,000 to 400,000 white-collar jobs are relocated overseas each year to countries such as India, China, Russia, Malaysia, and the Philippines. Any type of job that does not require personal contact can be outsourced, including back office work, call centers, customer service, computer programming, actuarial services, and medical diagnosis. "These services commonly known as 'business processes'. . . are among the fastest growing job categories in the United States. . . . It is significant that a substantial number of service activities might move offshore, because it was once thought that service jobs were the future growth area for developed country economics. By contrast, it was accepted that manufacturing would relocate to lower labor costs regions offshore" (Dossani & Kenney, 2004).

Generally, it is estimated that cost savings must be at least 40 percent to make it profitable for U.S. firms to outsource business processes services, but one Fortune 500 firm reports overall savings of 80 percent. For seven years, "General Electric, one of the pioneers of outsourcing service operations to India, has achieved an annual savings of $340 million per year" (Dossani & Kenney, 2004). Based on estimates from the U.S. Bureau of Labor Statistics, it is projected that as many as 3.3 million service-related U.S. jobs worth $136 billion in wages will move offshore by 2015 (McCarthy, 2002). Offshoring is a global trend that has moved high-tech jobs from India to China, from Western Europe to Eastern Europe, and from the United Kingdom to Japan. Analysts believe that in order to stay competitive, the United States has to follow suit. "Failure to do so likely will result in the loss of more jobs in the United States because of companies' diminished competitiveness" (American Electronics Association, 2004, p. 13).

As we shall see later in this chapter, the solution to Globalization 2.0 was job search and retraining, as well as temporary employment assistance for workers who lost jobs in industry and heavy manufacturing. In part, policy has bet on the availability of white-collar and high-tech jobs and the growth of the service economy as the future of the labor market in the United States. However, the rapid pace and changing nature of globalization makes recent predictions uncertain. At the beginning of the twenty-first century, analysts predicted that growth in the labor market through 2005 would be concentrated among occupations in the highest and lowest earnings quartiles: "Plenty of jobs will be available that require only short term training, but these jobs offer very low earnings.... Demand-side occupational projections suggest moderate- to long-term on the job training, or two or more years of post-secondary formal education, as the most certain path to employment offering family-sustaining wage and salary levels" (Bennici, Mangum, & Sum, 2000, p. 37). But now, the outsourcing of white-collar jobs makes it less certain that retraining programs are the answer for the future. "The classic solution to the problem of job loss created by technology has been to promote education and retraining programs. But if an unlimited supply of workers with similar skills is available at the end of a broadband wire for a tenth of the salary, the textbook economics remedy may not work" (Chanda, 2004).

Economic Recession

The aforementioned effects of the economic globalization on the U.S. labor market are even more critical in times of economic recession. What does it mean for the economy to be in recession? In order to answer this question, our first task is to understand the definition of economic recession and the way it is measured. Following this, our next task is to understand the unemployment rate, which is commonly used as one indicator of economic recession in the United States. These topics call to mind the debate about whether family poverty and problems are caused by individuals or by larger social systems. In periods of economic recession, less blame is placed on individuals as the cause of poverty, and more fault attributed to larger social systems.

The definition of recession commonly used today comes from one presented by economist Julius Shiskin in 1974 in the *New York Times*. Shiskin believed that three elements were important for determining whether the economy was in a recession: duration, depth, and diffusion. Duration was measured in terms of the rise in unemployment rate and the decline in nonfarm employment, and the decline in the dollar gross national product (GNP). Two business quarters of declining GNP indicated recession. Depth was measured by the change in the dollar GNP, the peak in unemployment rate, and changes in the consumer price index and the wholesale price index industrial commodities. Diffusion was measured by the percent of industries that were expanding. Despite Shiskin's insistence that all three elements were important, policy makers and pundits alike grabbed on to only one part of his definition, and over the years "the rest of his rules somehow dropped away" (Achuthan & Banerji, 2008). According to Mike Simonsen, co-founder and CEO of Altos Research (2008), "By now, everyone is familiar with the 2-quarters-negative-growth = recession 'definition' that 'they' use. It turns out, though, that this definition is garbage. Woefully inadequate and misleading." Furthermore, Solomon (2008) points out the powerful effect of the inadequate definition: "Ignorance about recessions has taken hold because of a simplistic idea that a recession is two successive quarterly declines in gross domestic product . . ., a measure of the nation's output."

Our purpose is not to argue the fine points of whether Shiskin's rule of thumb for measuring economic recession is correct, but to make two important points. First, the economic context has drastically changed since 1974; this is significant if, as we discussed in chapter 2, social problems are time, place, and context bound. In the 1970s, personal computers, the Internet, cell phones, and many other forms of technology were not part and parcel of the consumer environment. Global trade agreements such as NAFTA were not in effect. Deindustrialization had not become a major issue. The GDP has changed since 1974, and so on and so on. Certainly, a comprehensive definition of recession is needed in today's global economy. Second, we believe that Shiskin's three elements of duration, depth, and diffusion represent a more comprehensive definition of economic recession than the current definition, which only focuses on the duration of the economic downturn. The National Bureau of Economic Research has developed a multifaceted measure of recession that it calls the U.S. Business Cycle Expansion and Contractions. Founded in 1920, the bureau measures economic cycles since 1854 and is often regarded as "the arbiter of whether the country is in a recession" (Engstrom, 2008). According to the National Bureau of Economic Research (2003), "A recession is a significant decline in economic activity spread across the economy, lasting more than a few months, normally visible in real GDP, real income, employment, industrial production, and wholesale-retail sales. A recession begins just after the economy reaches a peak of activity and ends as the economy reaches its trough. Between trough and peak, the economy is in an expansion. Expansion is the normal state of the economy; most recessions are brief and they have been rare in recent decades." Engstrom asks the important question "So does the NBER say that the United States is in a recession? Well, that's not how the organization works. It is retrospective, waiting until sufficient data is available. It waits many, many months. Its last proclamation was in July 2003. It said that a trough had ended in November 2001, and it began in March 2001."

While the public waits for the official announcement that the U.S. economy is in recession, a variety of indicators are used to substantiate its onset. Some of these are state budget shortfalls, public opinion polls, job loss, and the unemployment rate. During 2008, for example, a survey of fifty state fiscal directors found that many states appeared to be in recession based on 2008 budget shortfalls, which, for example, reached $69 million in Delaware and $16 billion in California. Twenty-three to twenty-seven states predicted budget shortfalls totaling at least $39 billion for 2009 (Welsh-Huggins, 2008). Also, as we discussed in chapter 2, the social construction of knowledge takes into account the experience of those who are directly affected by policy. When people perceive something to be an issue, it is part of their subjective reality. "Whether or not the national economy is in recession—a subject of ongoing debate—is almost beside the point for some states" (National Conference of State Legislators, 2008). In the question of whether the United States is in a recession, the majority of the public believes that it is so. For example, exit polls taken after the 2008 primaries in Pennsylvania showed that nine out of ten voters believed that the United States was in an economic recession ("Pennsylvania Exit Polls," 2008).

The loss of jobs in the U.S. labor market is one indicator that the economy is in recession, or heading toward it. For example, the U.S. Department of Labor reported a loss of 240,000 jobs in October 2008, the tenth straight month of job loss. This brought total job loss to almost 1.2 million for 2008, the highest number in one year since the last economic recession in 2001. The October losses spread across many industries, including leisure and hospitality (16,000 jobs), construction (49,000 jobs), and manufacturing (90,000 jobs). Professional and business services lost 45,000 jobs. Job gain occurred only in a few sectors, such as government, health care, and accounting and bookkeeping. "In another sign of weakness, a growing number of workers were unable to find jobs with the amount of hours they wanted to work. Those working part-time jobs—because they couldn't find full-time work, or their hours had been cut back due to slack conditions—jumped by 645,000 people to 6.7 million, the highest since July 1993" (Goldman, 2008).

The unemployment rate is also an indicator of recession. In October 2008, the unemployment rate reached a fourteen-year high of 6.5 percent, rising from 6.1 percent over the previous thirty days. Nearly 10.3 million people were unemployed, which is also the most since late 1983. "Many economists believe the unemployment rate will climb to 8 percent by the end of next year before slowly drifting downward. Some think unemployment could even hit 10 or 11 percent—if an auto company should fail" (Aversa, 2008). Like recession, unemployment does not hit all parts of the country or all fifty states equally. The U.S. Department of Labor collects state-by-state data on unemployment rates; these are posted on the department's Web site at http://www.bls.gov/lau. In October 2008, for example, rates ranged from lows of 3.2 percent in South Dakota and 3.3 percent in Wyoming to highs of 8.7 percent in Michigan and 8.8 percent in Rhode Island.

The official unemployment rate is calculated from the Current Population Survey. About 60,000 households are sampled each month and are classified as either employed, unemployed, or not in the workforce. The Department of Labor defines the employed as all persons who did any work for pay or profit during the week of the survey, who did at least fifteen hours of unpaid work in a family-operated enterprise, or who were temporarily absent from their regular jobs because of illness, vacation, bad weather, strikes, or various personal reasons. The unemployed are defined as all persons who did not have a job at all during the survey week but made specific active efforts to find a job during the prior four weeks and were available for work, and all persons who were not working and were waiting to be called back to a job from which they had been temporarily laid off. Discouraged unemployed workers—defined as those who passively looked for a job or who want to work but are discouraged by their lack of success—are not counted in the official count of the unemployed.

The unemployment rate is one indicator of the status of the economy in the United States. Figure 7.1 shows the unemployment rate for workers sixteen years of age and older from 1948 to 2008. During periods of recession, unemployment rates are high. In the early 1980s, for example, the unemployment rate was over 11 percent. During the current financial crisis, it is expected that the unemployment rate will increase. The Bureau of Labor Statistics reported on October 3, 2008, that employment continued to fall in construction, manufacturing, and retail trade, while the number of jobs in mining and health care continued to increase. Nonfarm payroll employment declined by 159,000 in September, and the unemployment rate held at 6.1 percent (U.S. Department of Labor, 2008b). The Financial Forecast Center (2008) reported that the unemployment rate will approach 7.3 percent by May 2009.

Unemployment varies by age, by gender, and by education level. The next several paragraphs show these differences in the rise and fall of the

Figure 7.1 Unemployment Rate for All Workers (Aged 16+)

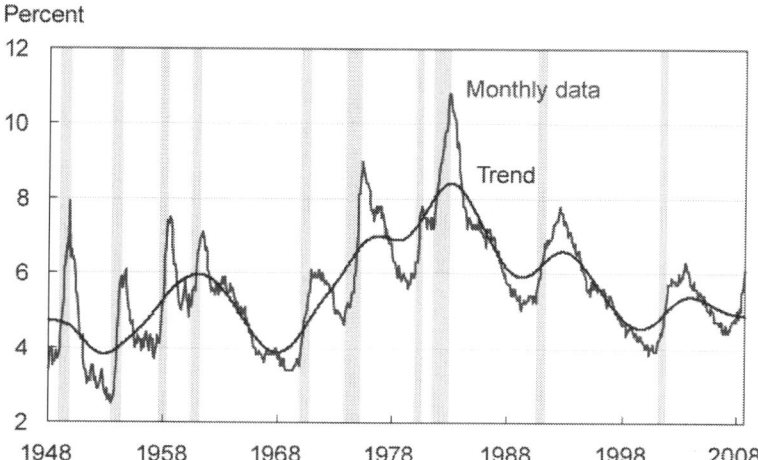

Notes: Data are seasonally adjusted. The trend was generated by using a Hodrick-Prescott filter with a smoothing parameter of 10^5. Shaded bars indicate recessions.
Source: Tasci, M., & Mowry, B. (2008, September 19). *Trend unemployment and what it says about unemployment patterns.* Retrieved November 4, 2008, from http://www.clevelandfed.org/research/trends/2008/1008/01ecoact.cfm

unemployment rate during times of economic recession and restarts in the growth of the economy. The trend data also illustrate differences that emerge over time. Figure 7.2 shows the convergence of unemployment rates for men and women:

> The unemployment rate for men and women . . . follows the countercyclical pattern, rising around the start of recessions and falling after the end of downturns. On the other hand, the overall trend in each of the two groups has been steadily changing over time. Until mid-1980s, the unemployment rate for women stayed consistently below that of men. Since then, the two unemployment rates have almost converged. One reason for this could be the higher labor force participation and higher educational attainment of women in the past two decades. These two potentially related facts created a female workforce with a stronger attachment to the labor market, whose unemployment profile increasing resembled that of men. One might even argue that the unemployment rate trend for men is now above the women's. (Tasci & Mowry, 2008)

Figure 7.2 Unemployment Rates for Men and Women

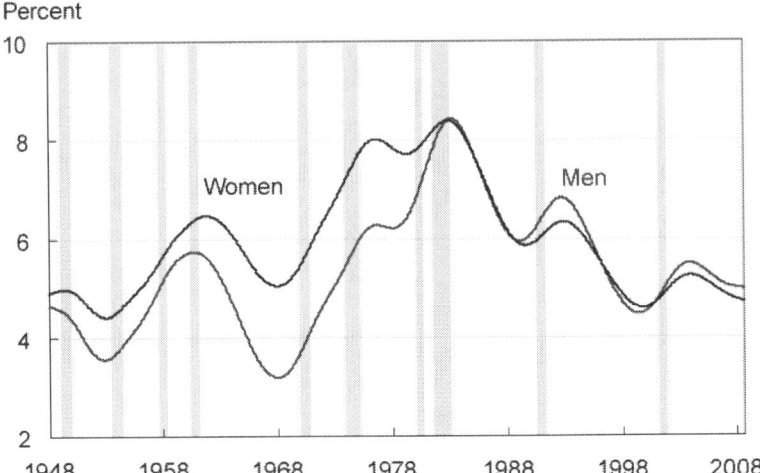

Notes: Data are seasonally adjusted. The trend was generated by using a Hodrick-Prescott filter with a smoothing parameter of 10^5. Shaded bars indicate recessions.
Source: Tasci, M., & Mowry, B. (2008, September 19). *Trend unemployment and what it says about unemployment patterns.* Retrieved November 4, 2008, from http://www.clevelandfed.org/research/trends/2008/1008/01ecoact.cfm

Levels of education interact differently with the unemployment rate. For example, Shettle (1997) reports that from 1973 to 1995, workers holding doctoral degrees in science and engineering have consistently had unemployment levels under 2 percent. As shown in figure 7.3, workers with advanced degrees have the lowest levels of unemployment.

Education does not appear to affect the basic countercyclical unemployment pattern. . . . As one might expect, years of schooling is negatively correlated with the unemployment rate. For instance, workers with at least a college degree have the lowest unemployment rate, around 2.4 percent on average since 1992. This compares with 3.9 percent for workers with some college, 4.8 percent for high school graduates, and 8.9 percent for high school drop outs. Even though we do not have a long enough time series to detect a clear cyclical pattern, we can see that over the last recession the behavior of the unemployment rates of workers with different levels of education fits the general picture. (Tasci & Mowry, 2008)

Figure 7.3 Unemployment Rates for Workers with Different Levels of Education

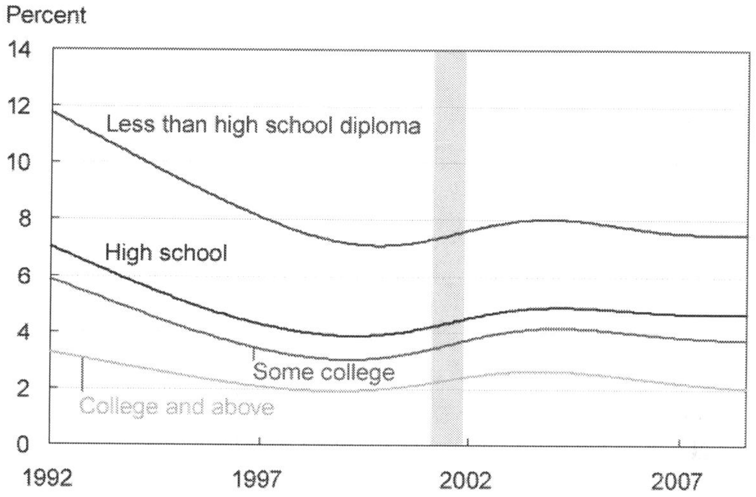

Percent

[Chart showing unemployment rates from 1992 to 2007 for four education levels: Less than high school diploma, High school, Some college, College and above]

Notes: Data are seasonally adjusted. The trend was generated by using a Hodrick-Prescott filter with a smoothing parameter of 10^5. Shaded bars indicate recessions.
Source: Tasci, M., & Mowry, B. (2008, September 19). *Trend unemployment and what it says about unemployment patterns.* Retrieved November 4, 2008, from http://www.clevelandfed.org/research/trends/2008/1008/01ecoact.cfm

Figure 7.4 shows that unemployment also varies by the age of the worker. "Because older workers are arguably more attached to the labor force and more experienced at their jobs, they are less likely to be let go in a downturn and more likely to be hired in a boom. This story likewise explains the higher unemployment rate of younger workers as well as its greater volatility" (Tasci & Mowry, 2008).

Unemployment Policy

As the previous discussions show, economic globalization continues to change the U.S. labor market. Currently, the U.S. economy is strapped by high unemployment rates and record numbers of job losses not seen since 1982 at the end of the last recession. Here we discuss the federal-state unemployment compensation program, an insurance program that provides temporary income support for previously employed workers. Our

Figure 7.4 Unemployment Rates for Workers of Different Ages

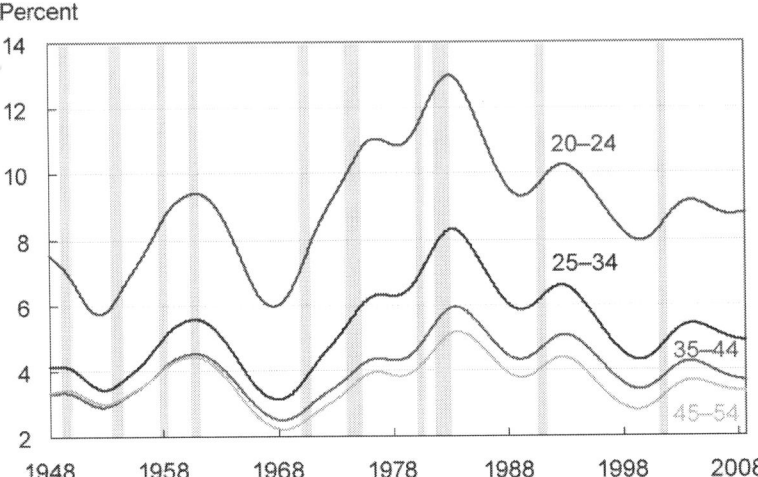

Notes: Data are seasonally adjusted. The trend was generated by using a Hodrick-Prescott filter with a smoothing parameter of 10^5. Shaded bars indicate recessions.
Source: Tasci, M., & Mowry, B. (2008, September 19). *Trend unemployment and what it says about unemployment patterns.* Retrieved November 4, 2008, from http://www.clevelandfed.org/research/trends/2008/1008/01ecoact.cfm

discussion also emphasizes policies that address job displacement due to globalization: the Trade Adjustment Assistance Reform Act of 2002 and the Worker Adjustment and Retraining Notification Act (1988). The Workforce Investment Act provides job search assistance, referral, and training for those seeking employment. Although deindustrialization is a structural cause of poverty, U.S. policy is focused on individuals and therefore represents a Band-Aid approach to the problems of globalization and economic recession.

The Federal-State Unemployment Compensation Program

Unemployment compensation is a federal-state program financed through federal taxes under the Federal Unemployment Tax Act (1939) and through state payroll taxes under the State Unemployment Tax Acts. Unemployment compensation is authorized under Titles II, IV, and XI of the Social Security Act of 1935. Unemployment insurance provides temporary and partial wage replacement benefits for up to twenty-six weeks for workers who become unemployed through no fault of their own and who are actively seeking a job. There is also a state-level program of thirteen additional weeks, but it is only available if the unemployment rate is high and certain other economic conditions are met. Whittaker's (2006) review of unemployment compensation programs found that no state offered this program. However, the QI, TMA, and Abstinence Programs Extension and Hurricane Katrina Unemployment Relief Act of 2005 set up a special federal trust fund for unemployment compensation systems in Alabama, Mississippi, and Louisiana, and the Katrina Emergency Assistance Act of 2006 extended Disaster Unemployment Assistance for an additional thirteen weeks.

Unemployment insurance is funded through the Federal Unemployment Trust Fund, which employers are required to pay into, and each state determines the maximum weekly benefit amount paid to the unemployed worker. Since benefits replace only a portion of lost income, "some workers—particularly higher-wage earners—receive less than 50% of their lost wages. Nationally, [unemployment insurance] replaced just over 47% of a worker's lost wages in 2003" (Economic Policy Institute, 2004, p. 7). This is called the replacement rate. The replacement rate is higher for women (49%) than for men because women generally earn less than men. The rate for Hispanics is 50 percent, for African Americans 49 percent, and for whites 47 percent. "Although the percentage of lost income replaced by UI benefits has remained fairly stable from 1988 through the present, the real replacement rate has actually fallen due to the fact that, as of 1987, UI benefits are now treated as income and are taxed fully by the federal government" (Economic Policy Institute, 2004, p. 7).

The number of workers receiving unemployment insurance is not indicative of the number of unemployed persons. In 2003, 41 percent of all unemployed workers received benefits, and of workers who lost their jobs, 71 percent received benefits. Monetary eligibility requirements, as well as requirements related to filing a claim with the state unemployment office, make some workers unable to obtain benefits. Excluded from compensation are those who do not file for benefits and those who have exhausted their benefits, have not yet earned benefit rights, or become unemployed due to their own actions. Workers must also actively seek employment during the benefit period. Benefits can be terminated if workers fail to meet any one of several criteria determined by the state. "Workers may fail to meet these criteria if they: limit their job search to part-time work in a state that requires workers to be 'able and available' for full-time work; fail to search for work in a given week; find a job; turn down a 'suitable' job offer;

or exhaust UI benefits because they received the maximum amount of benefits . . . or . . . the maximum number of weeks of benefits for which they were qualified" (Economic Policy Institute, 2004, p. 6). These criteria result in unfair treatment of some groups of unemployed persons. For example, only 18 percent of low-wage workers earning $8 an hour receive unemployment insurance. Rates for part-time workers at the same wage level are even lower (13%). Temporary workers typically fail to meet eligibility criteria (Economic Policy Institute, 2004).

In addition, the ability of state unemployment systems to pay benefits is strained because of the loss of employer Federal Unemployment Tax Act payments resulting from plant closings and corporate downsizing, which doubled between 1984 and 1995, and the increased number of workers applying for benefits. Another problem has been what is called SUTA dumping, which occurs when an employer forms a new company and transfers some employees to the new company. Since new companies are subject to lower state unemployment tax rates, opening a new company has been a way to avoid paying SUTA (state unemployment) taxes. It is estimated that states lose hundreds of millions of dollars in SUTA taxes each year: "States that have estimated losses from SUTA dumping are finding that their losses are in the tens of millions. Colorado estimates losses from SUTA dumping in excess of $40 million. California estimates its losses at $100 million in 2003. Michigan estimates that SUTA dumping costs it $60–$90 million a year" (National Employment Law Project, 2005). In 2004, President Bush signed the SUTA Dumping Prevention Act of 2004, which required states to have laws in place by 2006 to prevent this corporate business practice.

These data suggest that unemployment insurance is out of step with the changes brought about by globalization. Some policy alternatives being proposed include eligibility based on hours worked instead of earnings, consideration of a worker's recent job history in determining eligibility, and allowing part-time work while an individual is receiving benefits. It has also been recommended that benefits be increased by way of a raised maximum benefit cap, indexing of the benefit cap to state wages, and provision of dependency allowances that would raise benefits for families with children.

Trade Adjustment Assistance Reform Act of 2002

The Trade Adjustment Assistance (TAA) program is based on the premise that liberalization of trade benefits the country but imposes heavy costs on some individual workers who need assistance becoming reemployed. TAA was established by the Trade Expansion Act of 1962, authorized by the 1974 Trade Act, and amended several times. A key component of TAA is the provision of additional benefits for workers who need more than the six months of regular unemployment insurance after mass layoffs or plant closures. Originally, TAA assistance was added to unemployment insurance, raising benefit levels to 70 percent of the worker's average gross weekly wage for a maximum of fifty-two weeks. However, the 1981 Omnibus Budget Reconciliation Act reduced payments to the level of unemployment insurance, with TAA going into effect only when regular benefits are exhausted. Other revisions in 1998 required dislocated workers to register for training and participate in vocational training for up to eighteen months.

In 2002, President George W. Bush signed the Trade Adjustment Assistance Reform Act of 2002. Benefits include paid job training, financial assistance for job searches in other areas or relocating for employment to other areas of the country, a health care tax credit, and additional opportunities for older workers, for whom training may not be appropriate through the Alternative Trade Adjustment Assistance (ATAA) program. A two-step process is required to obtain TAA/ATAA reemployment services and benefits:

1. A group of workers must first file a petition with the U.S. Department of Labor's Division of Trade Adjustment Assistance requesting certification as workers adversely affected by foreign trade. If the group meets the necessary group eligibility criteria, a certification will be issued.
2. After a group certification is issued, each worker may then apply for individual services and benefits through the local One-Stop Career Center to determine individual TAA eligibility and ATAA eligibility for services and benefits. Workers age fifty and older may be eligible to receive benefits under either the TAA program or the ATAA program. All other workers may only apply for TAA benefits (U.S. Department of Labor, 2008a).

TAA targets workers who have lost hours and wages as a result of increased imports or the outsourcing of production. Workers are also eligible if the firm in which they are employed is a supplier or downstream producer to a firm whose workers are TAA certified. Between 1982 and 1987, the four industries with the greatest percentage of TAA-certified workers were the apparel industry, leather manufacturing, primary metals, and electrical machinery. Table 7.2 shows the number of certified TAA workers in various industries in 2006.

Table 7.2 Type of Industry and Number of TAA-Certified Workers

Type of Industry	Estimated Number of Certified Workers
Textile Mill Products	16,615
Electric and Other Electrical Equipment and Components, Except Computer Equipment	13,280
Transportation Equipment	12,012
Apparel and Other Finished Products Made from Fabrics and Similar Materials	9,935
Rubber and Miscellaneous Plastics Products	9,521

Source: U.S. Department of Labor. (2007). *Overview of Trade Adjustment Assistance program.* Retrieved March 1, 2008, from http://www.doleta.gov/tradeact/docs/Short ProgramOverview.pdf

The Consolidated Appropriations Act of 2008, signed into law by President Bush on December 26, 2007, was set to phase out and terminate TAA and the ATAA program by March 2009. However, in February 2009, Congress passed the American Recovery and Reinvestment Act of 2009, which authorized TAA until 2010 to cover at least 160,000 new workers who lose their jobs due to increased imports or factory relocation to foreign countries. The new legislation increases training funding up to $575 million, with an additional $86 million per year for administrative and case management costs to states. The law extends TAA coverage to service-sector workers and firms and creates a TAA for Communities program of strategic planning grants that give preference to small- and medium-sized communities negatively affected by foreign trade. The act also improves health insurance affordability and coverage and provides more flexibility in training options; for example, it allows recipients to use TAA benefits for higher education. These improvements are promising but do not address the development of new manufacturing jobs. As Dapice (2004,) has suggested, wage insurance would be better than Trade Adjustment Assistance: "Regardless of why people are losing their jobs, public policy could do much more to help the losers. The US government currently gives tax breaks to investment through accelerated depreciation. This is, in effect, a subsidy to capital. If it instead gave medical insurance subsidies to those who lost jobs, this would make the cost of labor cheaper. It would make it possible for a new firm to set up in a depressed area and enjoy lower labor costs, offsetting training and setup costs" (p. 2).

Worker Adjustment and Retraining Notification Act

The Worker Adjustment and Retraining and Notification Act (WARN) of 1988 is a little-known law with no teeth. This federal policy focused on individual workers requires employers with one hundred or more full-time employees to provide written notice sixty days in advance of a plant closing or mass layoff. The law requires that notice be given to workers, union representatives, local government officials, and the state's Dislocated Worker Unit or Rapid Response Team (U.S. Department of Labor, 2007). These units and teams have offices in each state; their main purpose is to provide information to displaced workers by advising and informing them about One-Stop's network of public and private employment services, which is part of the Workforce Investment Act, which is discussed later in this chapter.

WARN was vetoed by President Reagan and enacted into law without his signature after revision by Congress, which resulted in a watered-down version of the original bill, which would have required that dislocated workers receive severance pay. As a result, employers are able to decide whether they want to offer severance pay in the event of plant closing or mass layoff. If employers fail to notify workers of pending plant closing, the primary penalty is the payment of worker wages for each day that notice is not provided for up to sixty days before the plant closes, but only some employers comply (see Addison & Blackburn, 1994). "The main problem with WARN is that it was neither assigned enforcement nor oversight in the federal bureaucracy. Rather, the courts would be responsible for enforcement, and they would only have reason to act upon a [class action or individual] suit initiated by aggrieved workers" (Levin-Waldman, 1998, pp. 69–70).

The Workforce Investment Act

The Workforce Investment Act of 1998 is another good example of the rampant move toward devolution in federal policy. The act uses a local labor market approach to target business and job-seeker needs—an approach reflected by references to the unemployed as "customers," and by the requirement that service providers furnish information about placement success rates. States are required to develop five-year strategic plans to guide "workforce investment areas" managed by local workforce boards. Employment agencies, adult education, and literacy programs become a part of a one-stop system, with linkages to Trade Adjustment Assistance and the Adjustment Assistance program. The model uses a customer-based approach in which users utilize individual training accounts to select appropriate training from qualified providers. The idea is to promote individual responsibility and personal decision making.

Various federal agencies are required by Title I of the Workforce Investment Act to participate as One-Stop partners. State and local agencies, nonprofits, and community groups are represented. A Web page of the U.S. Department of Labor (2006) provides links to job training resources, including federal and state programs such as Job Corps and Vocational Rehabilitation, and other less well-known programs such as the Bureau of Apprenticeship and Training and the Veterans' Employment and Training Service. One-Stop is designed to bring knowledge of programs to job seekers and to integrate these programs and services through information sharing and networking. Overall, a One-Stop partner provides the following core services:

- A preliminary assessment of skill level, aptitudes, abilities, and support service needs
- Information on employment-related services, including local education and training service providers
- Help with filing claims for unemployment insurance and evaluating eligibility for job training and education programs or student financial aid
- Job search and placement assistance and career counseling
- Access to up-to-date labor market information on job vacancies, skills necessary for in-demand jobs, and information about local, regional, and national employment trends.

The act features a triage approach with services ranging from core services to intensive services, with job training as a last resort for people who are not able to find employment through core services. Intensive services include comprehensive assessments, individual employment plans, group and individual counseling, case management, and short-term prevocational services. Those who receive intensive services and still remain unemployed may receive job training, but that training must be tied to employment opportunities in the local area. Services may include such things as occupational skills and entrepreneurship training, skill upgrading and on-the-job training, job readiness training, adult literacy, and adult education. Low-income and welfare-to-work persons may be given priority status, support services such as transportation, and temporary income assistance while participating in job training (U.S. Department of Labor, 2006).

The Minimum Wage and Earned Income Tax Credit

The policies covered in this section are the minimum wage and the earned income tax credit, which provide income support for workers. Although these policies operate very differently, we have placed them together because they both relate to the level of wages of workers in the United States. As a requirement and directive for employers, the minimum wage sets a minimum standard that work is worth through the Fair Labor Standards Act of 1938. The earned income tax credit, which operates entirely through the income tax system, adjusts the difference between the poverty line and total income from work.

The Fair Labor Standards Act of 1938

The first federal effort to establish a minimum wage was the National Industrial Recovery Act of 1933, signed into law by President Franklin Roosevelt as part of the New Deal during the Great Depression. The act suspended anti-trust laws in an effort to promote less competition and increase wages. Through its Blue Eagle campaign, the National Recovery Administration encouraged businesses and industry to pay a minimum wage of $12 to $15 per week. It set the workweek at thirty-five to forty hours and, except in certain conditions, forbid the employment of youths under sixteen years of age. Two year later, the Supreme Court struck down these labor reform efforts as unconstitutional in *Schechter Poultry Corp. v. United States*, a case involving the slaughter of chickens sold to retail kosher butchers. The Supreme Court's decision and other rulings in the early 1900s were major roadblocks to the abolition of child labor and the establishment of fair labor standards, particularly for women.

After extensive legislative battles, Congress passed the Fair Labor Standards Act of 1938. The surviving bill had weathered nearly seventy-two amendments, most of which "sought exemptions, narrowed coverage, lowered standards, weakened administration, limited investigation, or in some other way worked to weaken the bill" (Grossman, 1978). Although the final legislation applied to only one-fifth of the labor force, it prohibited child labor and succeeded in setting the minimum hourly wage at twenty-five cents, and the maximum workweek at forty-four hours. An interesting story behind the passage of the Fair Labor Standards Act reminds us of the multiple-streams framework presented in chapter 2. In box 7.3, the words of Frances Perkins, a social worker who served as the secretary of labor under President Franklin D. Roosevelt, illustrate the way in which policy

Box 7.3 Frances Perkins: A Social Work Policy Entrepreneur

No top government official worked more ardently to develop legislation to help underpaid workers and exploited child laborers than Secretary Frances Perkins. Almost all her working life, Perkins fought for pro-labor legislation. Her autobiographical account of her relations with President Roosevelt is filled with the names of lawyers with whom she discussed legislation: Felix Frankfurter, Thomas Corcoran, Gerard Reilly, Benjamin Cohen, Charles Wyzanski, and many others both within and outside of government.

When, in 1933, President Roosevelt asked Frances Perkins to become Secretary of Labor, she told him that she would accept if she could advocate a law to put a floor under wages and a ceiling over hours of work and to abolish abuses of child labor. When Roosevelt heartily agreed, Perkins asked him, "Have you considered that to launch such a program . . . might be considered unconstitutional?" Roosevelt retorted, "Well, we can work out something when the time comes."

During the constitutional crisis over the NRA, Secretary Perkins asked lawyers at the Department of Labor to draw up two wage-hour and child-labor bills which might survive Supreme Court review. She then told Roosevelt, "I have something up my sleeve. . . . I've got two bills . . . locked in the lower left-hand drawer of my desk against an emergency." Roosevelt laughed and said, "There's New England caution for you. . . . You're pretty unconstitutional, aren't you?"

Source: Grossman, J. (1978). *Fair Labor Standards Act: Maximum struggle for a minimum wage.* Retrieved February 24, 2008, from http://www.dol.gov/oasam/programs/history/flsa1938.htm

entrepreneurs inside government prepare for the moment when the policy window opens.

The minimum wage is a wage level below which no employer can legally pay workers. The minimum-wage requirements of the Fair Labor Standards Act apply to all businesses that engage in interstate commerce; produce goods for interstate commerce; or handle, sell, or work on goods or materials that have been moved in or produced for interstate commerce. Businesses are exempt if they do not meet a $500,000 annual dollar volume test. There are also other exemptions that apply to delivery people and transportation businesses and employees who are salaried or are not paid by the hour. Regardless of the annual dollar amount earned by the business by which they are employed, employees are covered if they work in hospitals; institutions that care for the sick, aged, mentally ill, or disabled; institutions of higher education and other schools; or federal, state, and local governments. The Fair Labor Standards Act also allows businesses to require employees to work overtime, but in most cases the law requires employers to pay time-and-a-half for work over forty hours. The law, however, does not cover an employee who refuses to work more than forty hours a week, and firms that are exempt can force employees to work overtime without overtime pay. In box 7.4, Will, a delivery truck driver, is surprised to learn that the Fair Labor Standards Act allows his employer to require him to work overtime without overtime pay.

Box 7.4 Working Overtime without Overtime Pay

Will is a delivery man. His story is an example of the confusion that exists among the public about how protected workers really are on their jobs. Job protection is often taken for granted, but when workers are not protected, the maze of government policies makes it very difficult for workers to understand their rights and know what to do about injustices.

When they hired me, they told me they don't pay overtime. Everything is straight time, and they said there was no set schedule—that you worked until the day's deliveries were done. And they decided how many deliveries you were doing that day. I was so happy to have a job, I didn't care. I worked overtime pretty much every day. But after a few months of that, I started to get upset about it. You could tell them you didn't want to, but it didn't matter because you worked until the day's deliveries were done. I started thinking, How in the hell did they get away with this?

Eventually Will had enough. He started asking questions and tried to find out if it was illegal to force him to work overtime. He called the state Department of Labor.

People were called on the phone, and the people on the phone said very different things. Some people said what they were doing wasn't legal, and some said that what they were doing was legal ... very confusing. It was all very hazy. One day they were trying to send me out with more deliveries after I'd already worked eight hours and I told them no. They got very upset and there was a lot of yelling. But I told them I'd already worked my eight hours, I'd come in early that day, and when I left they said, "Okay, you're leaving the job site," and I was fired.

It makes me feel like the laws in this country are set up for business and not for workers. After I tried to read all the laws in "government speak"—you have to be a lawyer to understand it—it was perfectly clear that nothing was perfectly clear.

As mentioned above, the Fair Labor Standards Act establishes the minimum-wage requirement. The law, however, does not require that automatic cost-of-living increases be calculated in the formula used to determine the minimum wage. Each time an increase to the minimum wage is warranted, Congress must amend the Fair Labor Standards Act. Since the minimum wage is not adjusted for inflation, when the cost of living goes up, the real wages of workers decrease over time. Consequently, the rise in poverty level for workers in the lowest-paying occupations is largely due to the decline in the value of the minimum wage.

In order for us to understand how the value of the minimum wage has decreased over time, it must be compared in dollar amounts that have been adjusted for inflation. For example, when adjusted for the cost of living, the minimum wage of $1.00 in 1960 is the equivalent of $7.27 in 2008 dollars. Figure 7.5 shows the minimum wage from 1960 to 2008. From 1981 to 1989, there were no increases in the minimum wage, so after 1980, the minimum wage began to decline and reached an all-time low in 1988. Throughout the period of inflation from 1990 to 1995, there were only two increases in the minimum wage. This caused wages to decline in real dollars. Thus, even though the minimum wage was $5.15 an hour in 2000, it had less buying power than when it was set at $1.00 in 1960.

Figure 7.5 Purchasing Power[1] of Minimum Wage,[2] Adjusted for Inflation in 2008 Dollars, 1960–2009

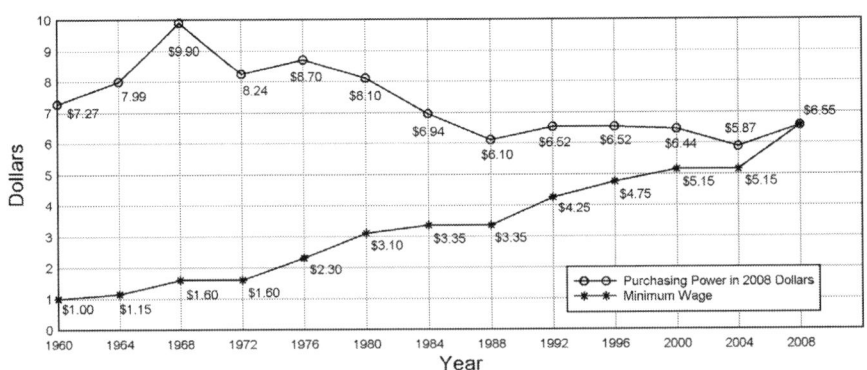

[1] Purchasing power was computed by Bureau of Labor Statistics (n.d.). *Inflation calculator*. Retrieved May 14, 2009, from http://data.bls.gov/cgi-bin/cpicalc.pl
[2] Data for minimum wage were retrieved from U.S. Department of Labor (n.d.). *Wage and hour division*. Retrieved May 14, 2009, from http://www.dol.gov/esa/minwage/chart.htm

In comparing the wages of families working for minimum wage to the poverty level (U.S. Census Bureau, 2006), from 1960 to 1980, the minimum wage was equal to the poverty line for a family of three, and slightly below the poverty line for a family of four. Although the poverty line continued to rise with adjustments for inflation after 1981, family income based on the minimum wage fell farther below the poverty line. By 2000, the annual income from full-time work at the minimum wage was $10,712, or $5.15 an hour. However, since the poverty threshold for a family of three was $13,728 per year ($6.60 per hour), a full-time minimum-wage worker earned only 78 percent of the poverty level, and a full-time minimum-wage worker earning $17,596 ($8.46 per hour) and supporting a family of four earned only 60 percent of the poverty level. By 2006, the poverty rate was $20,000 for a family of four, and the minimum wage was only 53 percent of the poverty level. Wages would not fall below the poverty line if the value of the minimum wage were automatically adjusted for inflation. This alone would keep full-time workers at or above the poverty line.

The majority of the American public supports adjusting the minimum wage for inflation, but other than during a short period of popularity in the 1970s, Congress has never seriously considered adjusting the minimum wage for inflation (Teixeira, 2006). And as globalization puts pressure on labor costs, it becomes even more difficult to adjust the minimum wage for inflation. Critics suggest that increasing the minimum wage will result in increases in unemployment and inflation. However, when the minimum wage was increased to its highest historical level at the time of the Clinton administration, the country also experienced the lowest unemployment rates. Since economic expansion in the late 1990s came on the heels of two relatively large increases, the argument that a higher minimum wage causes inflation or unemployment has little empirical support.

Thirty-two states have state minimum-wage levels higher than the federal level. California and Massachusetts have state minimum-wage rates of $8.00 per hour. The state of Washington has the highest minimum wage at $8.07 per hour and was the first state to automatically adjust its minimum wage for inflation. Arizona, Colorado, Florida, and Montana also adjust their minimum wage for inflation. Three states—Georgia, Wyoming, and Kansas—set the state minimum wage lower than the federal level. Kansas's minimum wage is $2.65 per hour, but the federal minimum wage is paid to workers covered under the federal Fair Labor Standards Act. Five states—Mississippi, Louisiana, Alabama, Tennessee, and South Carolina—have no minimum-wage laws (U.S. Department of Labor, 2008b).

In 2007, the Fair Minimum Wage Act increased the federal minimum wage. In terms of the dynamics of policy making, it is extremely interesting that Congress passed this new legislation by attaching it to the U.S. Troop Readiness, Veterans' Care, Katrina Recovery, and Iraq Accountability Appropriations Act (2007). In a display of political maneuvering, the minimum-wage legislation was attached as a rider to an Iraq spending bill that required immediate action by Congress and the president. In the language of politics, the term *rider* refers to the idea that a controversial bill is "hitching a ride" on a large or important piece of legislation making its way through Congress. Riders are a political tactic used by legislators. For example, appropriation bills are large *and* important pieces of legislation, and failure to pass them and get them signed by the president creates serious fiscal or programmatic problems for government. In the case of the Fair Minimum Wage Act, President Bush intended to veto stand-alone minimum-wage legislation, but he signed the Iraq and hurricane recovery legislation after tax cuts were included to offset the cost of increasing the minimum wage for small businesses.

The Fair Minimum Wage Act of 2007 includes a $2.10 per-hour phased-in increase to the federal minimum wage. The act raises the wage from $5.15 per hour prior to July 24, 2007, to $5.85 per hour up to mid-July 2008, to $6.55 per hour up to mid-July 2009, and $7.25 per hour after July 24, 2009. These wage increases, particularly the phase-in approach to raising the minimum wage over three years, are important. However, if inflation continues, it is likely that regular workweek wages at the minimum wage will result in income below the poverty level, especially for families with children. Even with these periodic increases, the wage is not adjusted for inflation and thus continually falls in its value. Because of this, there has been a growing movement in the United States to try to get local and state governments to increase wages to what proponents call a living wage. This campaign differs from the campaign for minimum wage because it looks at the cost of living in local areas and seeks to adjust the wage level of local government jobs, contracts, and other governmental financial assistance to local cost-of-living increases. Since the early 1990s, living-wage campaigns have successfully established more than 140 municipal and county living-wage ordinances (Living Wage Resource Center, 2008).

Maryland signed into law the first statewide living-wage bill on May 8, 2007 (Greenhouse, 2007). The law requires employers with state contracts to pay a minimum of $11.30 per hour in the urban Baltimore area and $8.50 per hour in rural areas. In 1994, Baltimore became the first city to establish a municipal living-wage policy. Currently, the highest living-wage policy in the nation is in Fairfax, California, and requires all businesses that receive government contracts to pay employees a minimum hourly wage of $13.00 with health benefits, and $14.75 per hour without health benefits. The Web site of the Living Wage Resource Center (2008) provides excellent resources on living-wage policies, and detailed legislative information about the passage of new living-wage laws in universities, cities and counties, and other government jurisdictions. The national living-wage movement is part of the work of ACORN, the Association of Community Organizations for Reform Now.

The Earned Income Tax Credit

The earned income tax credit (EITC), which operates through the federal income tax system, provides income support for poor working families. The EITC was initially enacted by the Tax Reduction Act of 1975 and was extended for the 1976 tax year by the Revenue Adjustment Act of 1975, which provided a wage supplement to low-income working families with children. The EITC is paid by the federal government in the form of a tax refund through the Internal Revenue Service. Rather than receiving a yearly lump sum of money upon filing income tax forms with the IRS, working adults who have children may parcel out the EITC as a part of their weekly or monthly paychecks, but few take advantage of this option.

The EITC is different from most income support programs. First, unlike other income support programs, such as TANF cash assistance or Supplemental Security Income, the EITC is not a safety-net or welfare program. Second, the EITC has been adjusted for inflation since 1987. Third, benefits under other programs tend to be largest for families with little or no income and decrease substantially or entirely as income from work falls farther below the poverty line. For families with very low earnings, the value of the EITC credit increases. This is the opposite of most means-tested programs, in which benefits fall as earnings rise. Figure 7.6 illustrates how the earned income tax credit works to adjust the income level of working families.

The EITC is $4,824 (forty cents per dollar up to $12,060 earned) for families with two or more children, $2,853 (or thirty-four cents per dollar up to $8,580 earned) for families with one child, and $438 for working single individuals and married couples with no children. To qualify for the EITC, childless individuals and couples must have a very low yearly income, and relatively few people apply. There is a maximum amount that families with children can earn at which they remain eligible for the maximum tax credit. The income cutoff point for the maximum EITC benefit is $18,750 for married-couple families regardless of the number of children in the family,

Figure 7.6 The Federal Earned Income Tax Credit, 2007

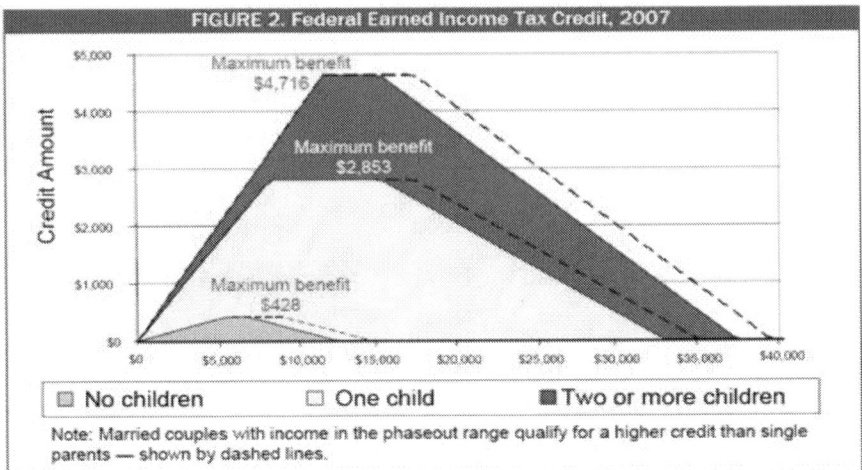

Source: Levitis, J., & Koulish, J. (2007, October 5). *A majority of states with income taxes have enacted state earned income tax credits: The federal earned income tax credit, 2007.* Retrieved March 2, 2008, from http://www.cbpp.org/10-5-07sfp.htm

and $15,390 for single-parent families regardless of the number of children in the family (FinPlan Divorce Planner, 2008). Table 7.3 shows the maximum federal EITC benefit for the 2008 tax year for various types of families.

The EITC has drawn criticism on the grounds of escalating costs. In 2004, the average benefit was $1,834, and one out of six people who filed tax returns received the EITC. Of those who filed for the EITC, 46 percent also filed for the additional child tax credit in 2004, with $895 as the average amount received. A total of $48.9 billion was claimed through the two programs in 2004 (Kneebone, 2007). The error rate—that is, the rate at which IRS forms contain inaccurate information—is higher for the EITC than for traditional social welfare programs. The error rate has declined, however, from 35 percent in the 1980s to around 30 percent in 2004, when the IRS required income verification from 300,000 families, and another 25,000 were asked to submit forms to prove their eligibility at the time of filing. One reason that low-income families do not receive the EITC is that they may not have adequate information about the program or may not understand the forms that must be filled out, and consequently they do not apply. The second reason is that proof of residency must be provided to show whether the children covered by the EITC were present in the home for specific periods of time. A certified statement of the children's resi-

Table 7.3 Family Structure and Earned Income Tax Credit, 2008

Type of Family Structure	Maximum Federal EITC Benefit	Amount of Yearly Income that Still Qualifies Family for Maximum Credit	Income Cutoff Point for EITC Eligibility
Married-couple family with two or more children	$4,824	$18,750 for married-couple family filing jointly	$41,646
Single-parent family with two or more children	$4,764	$15,390 for single parent family	$38,646
Married-couple family with one child	$2,917	$17,390 for married-couple family	$36,995
Single-parent family with one child	$2,872	$16,050 for single parent family	$33,995
Individuals and couples with no children	$438		

Source: Internal Revenue Service. (2008). *Earned income credit (EIC) for use in preparing 2008 returns.* Retrieved July 24, 2008, from http://www.irs.gov/pub/irs-pdf/p596.pdf

dency must be verified by someone other than the taxpayer, under penalty of perjury, and witnesses may be reluctant to sign such verifying statements on an IRS tax form.

An area of rapid policy change is the development of state EITC policy. Twenty-two states, the District of Columbia, and local governments in New York City and Montgomery County, Maryland, have EITCs. Four states developed EITCs in 2006, including some with state income taxes. A report from the Center on Budget and Policy Priorities, a liberal think tank, highlights the value of EITCs and the reasons why states are developing new policy in this direction. Since the federal EITCs end family poverty for more than 4 million people, about half of them children, state EITCs can increase this effect. EITC support to low-wage working families will help them stay in the workforce without receiving public assistance through welfare programs. State EITCs encourage participation in the workforce and bring the benefit of tax cuts to low- and moderate-income families. Finally, there is evidence that EITCs are used by families to increase their assets through debt reduction, education, and attainment of adequate housing (Levitis & Koulish, 2007, pp. 2–3).

From its inception, the EITC has benefited from widespread bipartisan support in Congress. Proposed initiatives include expanding the EITC so that working individuals and childless families can benefit from it as well. According to Jones (2004), who writes from the Hoover Institution, a conservative think tank, "the EITC is probably the most cost-effective antipoverty program the federal government operates. According to a report by the National Bureau of Economic Research, the EITC is inexpensive to administer relative to other income-support programs. One of the benefits of a system based largely on self-assessment (such as EITC) is lower administrative costs."

Summary

This chapter looked at work and employment policy in the United States in the context of economic globalization and deindustrialization. We looked at globalization as a fact to which policy makers must adapt. During what has been termed the second era of globalization, heavy industry jobs in auto manufacturing, textiles, rubber, and steel moved overseas. This caused a rapid loss of blue-collar jobs that pay a living wage through unionization. The effects of deindustrialization are felt most acutely in the urban centers of America's older industrial cities, resulting in the loss of the tax base, deteriorated housing, and social ills related to high concentrations of poverty. This period of globalization was also marked by the growth in the service sector of the economy and temporary and part-time employment. In the third and current era of globalization, these effects of globalization continue, but new aspects of globalization include the large-scale outsourcing of manufacturing parts that are returned to the United States for assembly. The individual's role in globalization is also highlighted in this era of globalization, as white-collar jobs in technology, call centers, customer service, accounting, and other back office procedures are also relocated overseas. Another phenomenon related to the current era of globalization is the return of some types of heavy industry jobs to the United States. We illustrated this with the example of foreign car manufacturing and tax incentives offered by state and local governments in rural and southern areas of the country. Although these jobs do not pay union benefits, end-of-year bonuses for production nearly close the gap between union pay and factory wages. At the same time, the costs of union benefits, particularly health insurance, have created a crisis for U.S. automakers in terms of their ability to produce cars priced competitively on the global market. All these changes in the U.S. labor market due to globalization are even more significant in times of economic recession. Officially measuring recession is a lengthy, retrospective process. Nonetheless, the general public, as well as state-level leaders, believes that the United States is in a severe period of economic downturn.

Two types of work and employment policy were discussed in this chapter. The first set of policies—unemployment compensation; the Worker Adjustment and Retraining Notification Act, which advises workers of plant closings; Trade Adjustment Assistance; and the Workforce Investment Act—addresses the needs of workers in finding employment. The second set of policies is the minimum wage and the earned income tax credit. These policies provide income and wage support for workers. Although the minimum wage is not indexed to inflation, recent changes that increased the minimum wage to $7.25 per hour after July 24, 2009, provide some relief for low-wage workers. Perhaps the most important employment policy that addresses family poverty is the earned income tax credit, which supplements the wages of working families with children through a tax credit filed through the Internal Revenue Service. Overall, however, our assessment of work and employment policies suggests that current policies are out of step with the effects of globalization on the U.S. labor market because of their emphasis on short-term training and partial replacement of lost income.

FOR FURTHER READING

Adams, S., & Neumark, D. (2005). Living wage effects: New and improved evidence. *Economic Development Quarterly, 19*(1), 80–102.

Caputo, R. K. (2006). The earned income tax credit: A study of eligible participants vs. non-participants. *Journal of Sociology & Social Welfare, 33*(1), 9–29.

Dehesa, G. de la. (2006). *Winners and losers in globalization.* Malden, MA: Wiley-Blackwell.

Lemert, C., & Elliott, A. (2006). *Deadly worlds: The emotional costs of globalization.* Lanham, MD: Rowman & Littlefield.

Mettler, S. B. (1994). Federalism, gender, and the Fair Labor Standards Act of 1938. *Polity, 26*(4), 635–654.

Meyer, B. D., & Holtz-Eakin, D. (Eds.). (2002). *Making work pay: The earned income tax credit and its impact on America's families.* New York: Russell Sage Foundation.

Nagle, A., & Johnson, N. (2006). *A hand up: How state earned income tax credits help working families escape poverty in 2006.* Washington, DC: Center on Budget and Policy Priorities. Retrieved February 22, 2009, from http://www.cbpp.org/3-8-06sfp.pdf

Stoker, R. P., & Wilson, L. A. (2006). *When work is not enough: State and federal policies to support needy workers.* Washington, DC: Brookings Institution Press.

References

Achuthan, L., & Banerji, A. (2008, May 7). *The risk of redefining recession: Pundits and even policy makers still cling to over-simplified definitions of recession. It's a dangerous misconception.* Retrieved November 4, 2008, from http://money.cnn.com/2008/05/05/news/economy/recession/index.htm?postversion=2008050612

Addison, J. T., & Blackburn, M. L. (1994). The Worker Adjustment and Retraining Notification Act: Effects on notice provision. *Industrial and Labor Relations Review, 47*(4), 650–662.

Altos Research. (2008, May 23). *When is a recession not a recession going to be a recession?* Retrieved May 23, 2009, from http://www.altosresearch.com/blog/archives/355-When-is-a-recession-not-a-recession-going-to-be-a-recession.html

American Electronics Association. (2004). *Offshore outsourcing in an increasingly competitive and rapidly changing world: A high-tech perspective.* Washington, DC: Author. Retrieved February 27, 2008, from http://www.aeanet.org/publications/IDMK_AeA_Offshore_Outsourcing.asp

Aversa, J. (2008, November 8). *Jobless ranks hit 25 million, most in 25 years.* Retrieved November 8, 2008, from http://news.yahoo.com/s/ap/20081108/ap_on_bi_ge/financial_meltdown;_ylt=An7HKZwFO9DAXM5_m4ZushUDW70F

Avery, W. P. (1998). Domestic interests in NAFTA bargaining. *Political Science Quarterly, 113*(2), 281–305.

Bennici, F., Mangum, S., & Sum, A. M. (2000). The economic, demographic and social context of future employment and training programs. In B. S. Barnow & C. T. King (Eds.), *Improving the odds: Increasing the effectiveness of publicly funded training* (pp. 19–48). Washington DC: Urban Institute Press.

Chanda, N. (2004, February 27). Outsourcing debate—part II. *YaleGlobal.* Retrieved February 26, 2008, from http://yaleglobal.yale.edu/article.print?id=3422

Consolidated Appropriations Act of 2008, Pub. L. No. 110-89 (2008).

Dapice, D. (2004, March 1). Outsourcing debate—part III. *YaleGlobal.* Retrieved February 26, 2008, from http://yaleglobal.yale.edu/article.print?id=3442

Dossani, R., & Kenney, M. (2004, February 25). Outsourcing debate—part I. *YaleGlobal.* Retrieved February 26, 2008, from http://yaleglobal.yale.edu/article.print?id=3406

Dreamliner 101: All about the Boeing 787. (2007). *Seattle Post-Intelligencer.* Retrieved February 29, 2008, from http://seattlepi.nwsource.com/boeing/787/787primer.asp

Economic Policy Institute. (2004, August). *Unemployment insurance issue guide.* Retrieved March 1, 2008, from http://www.epi.org/content.cfm/issueguides_unemployment_facts

EIR Economics Staff. (2006, January 6). The case of Baltimore: Deindustrialization creates "death zones." *Executive Intelligence Review, 33*(1), 4–26. Retrieved February 27, 2008, from http://documents.scribd.com/docs/2liwjoj6n5e052ncrgp8.pdf

Engstrom, T. (2008, November 4). The definition of recession changes this year. *Albert Lea Tribune.* Retrieved November 4, 2008, from http://www.albertlea tribune.com/news/2008/nov/04/definition-recession-changes-year/

Fair Labor Standards Act of 1938, 29 U.S.C. § 201 *et seq.* (1938).

Federal Unemployment Tax Act, Pub. L. No. 76-379 (1939).

Financial Forecast Center. (2008, October 17). *The U.S. unemployment rate forecast.* Retrieved November 4, 2008, from http://www.forecasts.org/unemploy.htm

FinPlan Divorce Planner (2008). Earned income tax credit. Retrieved July 24, 2009, from http://www.divorceplanner.com/webhelp/Divorce_Planner_2008/Taxes/ Credits/Earned_Income_Tax_Credit_(EITC).htm

Freeman, S. (2006, August 19). Detroit waves flag that no longer flies: Congress embraces jobs, growth created by foreign carmakers. *Washington Post.* Retrieved February 28, 2008, from http://www.washingtonpost.com/wp-dyn/ content/article/2006/08/18/AR2006081801384.html

Friedman, T. L. (1999). *The Lexus and the olive tree: Understanding globalization.* New York: Farrar, Straus and Giroux.

Friedman, T. L. (2006). *The world is flat: A brief history of the twenty-first century.* New York: Farrar, Straus and Giroux.

Froetschel, S. (2007, February 19). Globalization forces a health-check of US auto industry. *YaleGlobal.* Retrieved February 26, 2008, from http://yaleglobal.yale .edu/article.print?id=8785

GM gets another $2B in taxpayer loans, expected to scrap Pontiac. (2002). *USA Today.* Retrieved May 14, 2009, from http://www.usatoday.com/money/ autos/2009-04-24-gm-loans-chrysler-talks_N.htm

Goldman, D. (2008, November 7). *Jobs lost in 2008: 1.2 million.* Retrieved November 8, 2008, from http://money.cnn.com/2008/11/07/news/economy/jobs_ october/index.htm?postversion=2008110711

Greenhouse, S. (2007, May 7). Maryland is the first state to require living wage. *New York Times.* Retrieved March 2, 2008, from http://www.nytimes.com/ 2007/05/09/us/09wage.html

Grossman, J. (1978). *Fair Labor Standards Act: Maximum struggle for a minimum wage.* Online version. Retrieved February 24, 2008, from http://www.dol.gov/ oasam/programs/history/flsa1938.htm

Hinojosa-Ojeda, R. H., Dowds, C., McCleery, R., Robinson, S., Runsten, D., Wolff, C., & Wolff, G. (1996, December). *North American integration three years after NAFTA: A framework for tracking, modeling and Internet accessing the national and regional labor market impacts.* Retrieved May 21, 2006, from http://naid.sppsr.ucla.edu/NAFTA96/

Johnsson, J., & Madhani, A. (2008, March 1). Tanker deal loss staggers Boeing. *Chicago Tribune,* 1–16.

Jones, J. M. (2004). The mother of all tax credits. *Hoover Digest,* 2. Retrieved March 2, 2008, from http://www.hoover.org/publications/digest/3042856.html

Katrina Emergency Assistance Act of 2006, Pub. L. No. 109-176 (2006).

Keohane, R. O., & Nye, J. S., Jr. (2000). Introduction. In J. S. Nye & J. D. Donahue (Eds.), *Governance in a globalizing world* (pp. 1–41). Washington, DC: Brookings Institution.

Kneebone, E. (2007, April). *A local ladder for low-income workers: Recent trends in the earned income tax credit.* Retrieved March 2, 2008, from http://www.brookings.edu/~/media/Files/rc/reports/2007/04childrenfamilies_kneebone/20070416_zipcode.pdf

Levin-Waldman, O. M. (1998). Plant closings: Is WARN an effective response? *Review of Social Economy, 56*(1), 59–79.

Levitis, J., & Koulish, J. (2007, October 5). *A majority of states with income taxes have enacted state earned income tax credits.* Retrieved March 2, 2008, from http://www.cbpp.org/10-5-07sfp.htm

Living Wage Resource Center. (2006). *A compilation of living wage policies on the books.* Retrieved May 12, 2007, from http://www.livingwagecampaign.org/index.php?id=1958

Living Wage Resource Center. (2008). *ACORN's living wage Web site.* Retrieved March 2, 2008, from http://www.livingwagecampaign.org/

McCarthy, J. (2002, November 11). 3.3 million U.S. services jobs to go offshore. Cambridge, MA: Forrester Research. Retrieved February 22, 2009, from http://www.forrester.com/ER/Research/Brief/Excerpt/0,1317,15900,FF.html

Mishel, L., Bernstein, J., & Allegretto, S. (2005). *The state of working America: 2004/2005.* Ithaca, NY: ILR Press.

National Bureau of Economic Research. (2003, October 21). *The NBER's recession dating procedure.* Retrieved November 5, 2008, from http://www.nber.org/cycles/recessions.html

National Conference of State Legislatures. (2008, April 25). *Sluggish revenues at core of state budget woes.* Retrieved November 5, 2008, from http://www.ncsl.org/programs/press/2008/pr042508StateBudgetReport.htm

National Employment Law Project. (2005, March 31). *State SUTA dumping proposals. Many bills falling short at protecting state trust funds, workers and employers.* Retrieved March 1, 2008, from http://www.nelp.org/ui/state/funding/statesutadumping_.cfm

National Industrial Recovery Act, Pub. L. No. 73-67, 48 Stat. 195 (1933).

Omnibus Budget Reconciliation Act, 42 U.S.C. 8621 et seq. (1981).

Pennsylvania exit polls: 9 in 10 Americans think US in recession, Bush says "We're not." (2008, April 22). *Huffington Post.* Retrieved November 5, 2008, from http://www.huffingtonpost.com/2008/04/22/9-in-10-americans-think-u_n_98070.html

QI, TMA, and Abstinence Programs Extension and Hurricane Katrina Unemployment Relief Act of 2005, Pub. L. No. 109-91 (2005).

Rennen, W., & Martens, P. (2003). The globalization timeline. *Integrated Assessment, 4*(3), 137–144.

Revenue Adjustment Act of 1975, Pub. L. 94-164, 89 Stat. 970 (1975).

Rocha, C., & Strand, E. (2004). The effects of economic policies and employment assistance programs on the well-being of displaced female apparel workers. *Journal of Family Issues, 25*(4), 542–566.

Schechter Poultry Corp. v. United States, 295 U.S. 495 (1935).

Shepardson, D. (2008, November 5). Big 3, UAW ask for health trust help. *Detroit News Online*. Retrieved July 21, 2009, from http://lists.portside.org/cgi-bin/listserv/wa?A2=indo811A&L=PORTSIDELABOR&P=2178

Shettle, C. F. (1997). *S&E Ph.D. unemployment trends: Cause for alarm?* (Issue Brief NSF 97-318). Retrieved November 4, 2008, from http://www.nsf.gov/statistics/issuebrf/sib97318.htm

Shiskin, J. (1974, December 1). The changing business cycle. *New York Times*, p. 222.

Solomon, F. (2008, May 24). Recession: The forgotten indicia. *Market Movers*. Retrieved November 5, 2008, from http://www.portfolio.com/views/blogs/market-movers/2008/05/23/recession-the-forgotten-indicia

Speer, J. (2008, February 28). *Foreign automakers offset job losses in U.S.* Retrieved February 28, 2008, from http://www.npr.org/templates/story/story.php?storyId=5182166

SUTA Dumping Prevention Act of 2004, Pub. L. No. 108-295 (2004).

Tasci, M., & Mowry, B. (2008, September 19). *Trend unemployment and what it says about unemployment patterns.* Retrieved November 4, 2008, from http://www.clevelandfed.org/research/trends/2008/1008/01ecoact.cfm

Tax Reduction Act, Pub. L. No. 94-12. 26 U.S.C. § 1 et seq. (1975).

Teixeira, R. (2006, January 11). *Public opinion watch.* Retrieved May 21, 2006, from http://www.americanprogress.org/issues/2006/01/b1344313.html

Trade Act, Pub. L. No. 93-618C. § 2101 et seq. (1974).

Trade Adjustment Assistance Reform Act of 2002, Pub. L. No. 107-210 (2002).

Trade Expansion Act of 1962, Pub. L. No. 87-794 (1962).

United Autoworkers Union. (2008). *New contract protects UAW jobs.* Retrieved February 29, 2008, from http://www.uaw.org/contracts/07/gm/index.php

U.S. Census Bureau. (2006). *Table 1: Weighted average poverty thresholds for families of specified size 1959 to 2005.* Retrieved May 12, 2007, from http://www.census.gov/hhes/www/poverty/histpov/hstpov1.html

U.S. Department of Defense. (1999, December). *Final report of the Defense Science Board Task Force on Globalization and Security.* Washington, DC: Office of the Under Secretary of Defense for Acquisition and Technology.

U.S. Department of Labor. (2005a, December 19). Employment by major industry sector, 1994, 2004, and projected 2014. Service-providing sector and job growth to 2014. *Monthly Labor Review: The Editor's Desk.* Retrieved May 18, 2006, from http://www.bls.gov/opub/ted/2005/dec/wk3/art01.txt

U.S. Department of Labor. (2005b, December 19). Service-providing sector and job growth to 2014. *Monthly Labor Review: The Editor's Desk.* Retrieved May 18, 2006, from http://www.bls.gov/opub/ted/2005/dec/wk3/art01.htm

U.S. Department of Labor. (2006). *Workforce Investment Act One-Stop partners.* Retrieved March 2, 2008, from http://www.doleta.gov/usworkforce/onestop/partners.cfm

U.S. Department of Labor. (2007, July 20). *Rapid response services for laid off workers.* Retrieved March 1, 2008, from http://www.doleta.gov/layoff/workers.cfm

U.S. Department of Labor. (2008a). *Economic situation summary.* Retrieved November 4, 2008, from http://www.bls.gov/news.release/empsit.nro.htm

U.S. Department of Labor. (2008b). *Trade Adjustment Assistance (TAA) and Alternative Adjustment Assistance (ATAA) application process.* Retrieved March 1, 2008, from http://www.doleta.gov/tradeact/petitions.cfm

U.S. Department of Transportation. (2000). *The changing face of transportation.* Washington, DC. Retrieved February 29, 2008, from http://www.bts.gov/publications/the_changing_face_of_transportation/pdf/entire.pdf

U.S. Environmental Protection Agency. (2007). *Great Lakes pollution prevention and toxics reduction: Cuyahoga River area of concern.* Retrieved February 29, 2008, from http://www.epa.gov/glnpo/aoc/cuyahoga.html

U.S. Troop Readiness, Veterans' Care, Katrina Recovery, and Iraq Accountability Appropriations Act of 2007, Pub. L. No. 110-28 (2007).

Wells, G. J. (2001). *The issue of globalization—an overview.* Washington, DC: Congressional Research Service. Retrieved February 26, 2008, from http://digitalcommons.ilr.cornell.edu/crs/6/

Welsh-Huggins, A. (2008, April 25). *Many states appear to be in recession.* Retrieved November 5, 2008, from http://abcnews.go.com/US/WireStory?id=4722026&page=1

Whittaker, J. M. (2006, April 14). *Unemployment insurance: Available unemployment benefits and legislative activity.* Washington, DC: Congressional Research Service. Retrieved February 25, 2008, from http://digitalcommons.ilr.cornell.edu/crs/16/

Worker Adjustment and Retraining and Notification Act of 1988, Pub. L. No. 100-379 (1988).

Workforce Investment Act of 1998, Pub. L. No. 105-220. 29 U.S.C. § 794d (1998).

CHAPTER 8

Health Care

In this chapter we look at the problems and the policies in the dynamic policy-making environment of health and mental health care. We emphasize the role that privatization and managed care play in service delivery. Managed care originated in health care and now permeates service delivery. As readers will see, health care policy also illustrates the fact that a comprehensive set of family policies does not exist in the United States. Health and mental health care policy is not comprehensive by any means. Granted, federal entitlement programs such as Medicare and Medicaid still exist, but services are increasingly privatized and excessively fragmented, even among for-profit and nonprofit providers. A three-tiered health care system exists, but many people in the United States are left without access to health care.

As the only industrialized country without a national health insurance system, the United States spends more than twice as much annually per person for health care as other industrialized nations (Sullivan, 2002–2003). Yet the number of uninsured and underinsured families in the United States is increasing. These disparities result from the lack of comprehensive health care policy in the United States. Health disparities are also a symptom of the growing gap between the rich and the poor. Poverty, compounded by racial discrimination in its many forms, is detrimental to the health status of families. The death rates of people with low incomes are twice those of individuals with incomes above the poverty level. Poverty also hinders the life chances and intellectual development of children, particularly those who are adversely affected before birth because of their mothers' poor health and nutrition. For example, since the 1980s, as income inequality has increased, there has been a gradual increase in the incidence of low-birth-weight babies—from 6.84 per one hundred births in

1980 to 7.93 per one hundred births in 2003. Forty-nine percent of low-birth-weight babies have developmental disabilities, and 25 percent have severe disabilities. The United States ranks twenty-sixth in infant mortality in the world, and its average life expectancy is below the average of other industrialized countries (U.S. Department of Health and Human Services, 2005).

At the other end of the age spectrum, the aging of the American population increases the demand for health care. From 1950 to 2005, the population of individuals sixty-five years of age and older increased from 12 to 37 million, and by 2029, all the baby boomers will be sixty-five years of age and older. The total number of persons older than sixty-five is expected to increase to nearly 20 percent of the population by 2030. Overall, Americans are living longer and reporting better health than ever before. According to information taken from the United States Life Tables for 2004 from 1900 to 2004, life expectancy at birth increased from 48 to 75.2 years for men, and from 51 to 80.4 years for women, and average life expectancy reached an all-time high of 77.8 years in 2004 (Arias, 2007). However, life expectancy varies by race. In 2004, white males had a life expectancy of 75.7 years, and white females 80.8 years, while life expectancy for black males was 69.5 years, and black females 76.3 years. "Improved access to health care, advances in medicine, healthier lifestyles, and better health before age 65 are factors that account for decreased death rates among older Americans" (Sirven & Morrow, 2007).

The major purpose of this chapter is to help readers understand health care policies in the United States, and the disparities that exist in health care and service delivery. We begin our discussion by looking at issues that lead to health disparities, including access to health care, the high cost of medical care, efforts to contain medical costs through managed care, and uncompensated care that occurs through charity care and bad debt care by hospitals. Here, we offer a conceptual framework for assessing community effects on health, which takes into account the social and economic environment, the physical environment, and health services. This framework suggests that health disparities are rooted in the social, economic, and political environments of neighborhoods, communities, and government policy.

Next, our discussion focuses on Medicare, Medicaid, the State Children's Health Insurance Program, and community health centers. These policies finance health care and some mental health services. In the absence of national health care, devolution and privatization are a major component of health care services and programs funded by federal and state governments. As we will see, the involvement of for-profit business in public health care programs is extensive, and it is no longer easy to separate the work of for-profit organizations in health care delivery and services from government policy and programs. Finally, we look at policies related to community mental health centers, mental health parity, and suicide prevention on college campuses. The policy evolution of community mental health centers in the United States contrasts considerably with the history and the success of public health clinics. Our brief discussion of community mental health centers illustrates two important points in the dynamics of policy development. First, executive leadership at the top levels of government can move policy legislation forward at certain times in history. We highlight the way in which policy change has been promoted by power holders and policy entrepreneurs inside government who have experienced—or whose family members have experienced—problems such as mental illness, substance abuse, and mental retardation. We also reflect on the way in which legislative loopholes and changes in funding can substantially modify the original intent of the law and affect the scope of service delivery.

Health Disparities

Access to Health Care

Access to health care is a problem for the uninsured (those who lack health care insurance) and the underinsured (those who do not have adequate health insurance). Recent studies by the Institute of Medicine show that the lack of insurance has "a real and adverse impact, not only on the amount and quality of care ... but also on longevity and quality of life" (Gorin & Moniz, 2004, p. 344). Individuals who are poor and members of minority groups generally receive less primary health care. Those individuals who lack health insurance also do not have access to quality care. All these factors have been linked to poor health outcomes (Copeland, 2005). The U.S. Census Bureau's 2006 Current Population Report entitled *Income, Poverty, and Health Insurance Coverage in the United States* reports that the number of uninsured Americans rose from 44.8 million in 2005 to 47 million in 2006, which was the highest number ever recorded. The uninsured rate jumped from 15.3 percent of the population in 2005 to a record-tying 15.8 percent in 2006. For the second year in a row, the number of uninsured children increased by more than 611,000, for a total of over 8.7 million (DeNavas-Walt, Proctor, & Smith, 2007). Figure 8.1 shows trends in the

Figure 8.1 Percent of U.S. Population without Health Insurance, 1987–2006

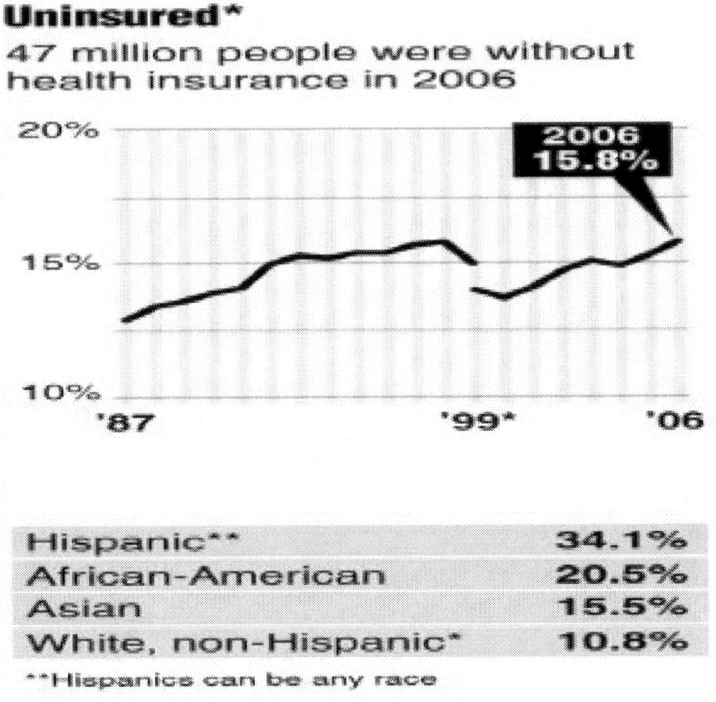

Source: Pugh, T. (2007, August 28). *Number of Americans without health insurance hits new high.* Retrieved September 5, 2007, from http://media.mcclatchydc.com/smedia/ 2007/08/28/20/389-20070828-POVERTY.large.prod_affiliate.91.jpg

number of the uninsured from 1987 to 2006. It also shows that the number of uninsured varies widely by race and ethnic background.

Nearly three of every four uninsured low-income persons in America come from working families (Kaiser Commission on Medicaid and the Uninsured, 2005). A decline in employer-based health insurance is the primary cause of the increase in the number of people who are uninsured. For all workers, employment-related coverage declined from 63 percent in 1993 to 45 percent in 2003. Some groups of workers are more adversely affected than others. For example, half of all white-collar and blue-collar workers have employer-provided medical insurance, compared to only 22 percent of service workers. Part-time workers, a growing proportion of the workforce, are least likely to have health insurance. Only 9 percent reported coverage in 2003 (Wiatrowski, 2004). For individuals with preexisting conditions such as a chronic illness or cancer, insurance is either unavailable or very expensive. A small portion of the growing number of uninsured workers consists of workers who refuse "consumer-driven" health insurance (Bownds, 2003). Families that opt out of employer-based insurance are usually low-wage workers who cannot afford to pay high insurance premiums or meet the cost-sharing requirements.

The underinsured are families covered by insurance policies that have extremely high deductibles, the dollar amount of expenses that need to be paid out of pocket before insurance coverage begins. Deductibles that range from $1,000 to $3,000 decrease costs to the insurance company, as well as the cost-sharing portion to the employer and the monthly premium to the worker. This type of health insurance is good for catastrophic illness, accidents, and major surgery, but it does not apply to regular physician care until the deductible has been met. Out-of-pocket expenses associated with health insurance also can deter low-wage workers from using their health insurance. In a study of public clinic utilization rates, Rocha (1996) found that over 45 percent of the patients had some form of insurance, but nearly 75 percent of privately insured patients made less than $20,000 per year. Consequently, they used public health clinics instead of private physicians. Overall, it is hard to gauge how many millions of families are underinsured, but this is a growing trend.

Hurley, Pham, and Claxton (2005) contend that a three-tiered system of access to health care is developing. Those with traditional health insurance are in the first tier. People covered by Medicaid, the government program that provides physical and mental health care for the poorest citizens, represent the second tier. Medicaid recipients do not have the same access to physician care as those with private insurance, but they have more access than the uninsured, who represent the third tier of health care access. The uninsured must rely on specialized clinics or wait until their condition is acute to use hospital emergency rooms. Free clinics, community health centers, and emergency rooms are the main suppliers of health care for this population. Third-tier health care is generally provided by doctors who donate part of their time. Services are sporadic, however, and rarely cover specialist or preventive care. Joanne's story in box 8.1 demonstrates the high cost of emergency room care for the uninsured. Her situation also illustrates the lack of continuity in care when one does not have access to a regular physician. Without ongoing care by one physician, it is more difficult to identify and treat serious illnesses.

Box 8.1 Emergency Room Visits and the Uninsured

Joanne is a single working mother of four children. Her story illustrates the problems faced by working poor families without access to regular health care. One serious illness can throw the family into a financial crisis. It took Joanne seven years to pay for one emergency room visit.

> We don't go to doctors. I haven't taken my kids to a doctor in years—ever since we've been off Medicaid. The main thing was the Medicaid. When you've got little kids, its terrifying not to have money to take them to the doctor. I haven't been to a doctor in years. Several years ago, when I took Katie to the emergency room, it was over $700. After being in the emergency room for four hours with all those tests—and they never did figure out what was wrong with her—I have to pay them twenty-five bucks a month. I think I'll be through paying them off this year sometime. I've been blessed that my kids are as healthy as they are, thank God, or we'd be devastated. I don't even want to think about it. That would truly sink our boat if anybody had a serious health problem.

The High Cost of Medical Care

As we have pointed out, the United States spends more money per capita on health care than any other industrialized nation in the world, yet it provides the smallest amount of social protection against health care costs (Organisation for Economic Co-operation and Development, 2004). Where does the money go? The bulk of investment in health care has been in research and technology—state-of-the-art equipment, information technology, research and development ventures, and specialized care—which have driven up consumer costs (Hurley et al., 2005). People with employer-based coverage have benefited most from these developments, and low-income families have paid the most to keep up with increased costs. Low-income families pay eight times the share of their income in out-of-pocket expenditures for the same access to private insurance that is paid by high-income families.

Insurance companies play a major role in the enormous increase in health costs. Between the mid-1980s and 1990s, insurance companies raised premiums 90 percent—a move that far exceeded wage increases. Private insurance companies are in business to make a profit, resulting in supplier-induced demand with little federal oversight. Private insurance companies are part of the dynamic policy environment of health care. They spend massive amounts of money on lobbyists and marketing, which drives up health care costs. The Foundation for Taxpayer and Consumer Rights (2006), a consumer watchdog organization, concludes that over 25 percent of every dollar spent on health insurance goes toward administrative costs, profits, and CEO salaries. The salaries of CEOs of pharmaceutical companies are also exorbitant. For example, in 2007 the total compensation of the CEO of Abbott Laboratories was $33,346,260, and that of Eli Lilly $13,011,390 (Companypay.com, 2009).

Overall, pharmaceutical costs are the fastest-growing component of health care. According to Angell (2004), Americans spend more than $400 billion a year on prescription drugs. Between 1980 and 2000, drug prices tripled. From 1997 to 2002, the prices of the forty-two drugs used most commonly by senior citizens increased at twice the rate of inflation, and the prices of ten of these drugs rose by four times the rate (Families USA, 2002). The health care industry's effort to generate greater profits is not the only factor contributing to the rising costs. Public policy has contributed to the problem as well. Legislation extended the patent life of brand-name drugs from eight years in 1980 to fourteen years in 2000, a policy decision that increased the time it takes for generic prescription drugs, which are cheaper than brand-name drugs, to become available to consumers.

Insurers, employers, and health care providers are shifting increasing health care costs on to consumers through higher co-payments for prescriptions, and to taxpayers in the form of higher Medicare and Medicaid costs. According to Gross, Schondelmeyer, and Purvis (2008), "Manufacturer prices for brand name drugs products most widely used by Medicare beneficiaries rose 7.1 percent in 2006 and 7.4 percent in 2007, the first two years of operation of the Medicare Part D drug benefit . . . [which were] . . . substantially higher than the rates of increase for manufacturer prices in the prior four years" (p. 4). "The cumulative effect of these price increases can be substantial. On average, manufacturer prices of the 169 most widely used prescription drugs that have been on the market since the end of 2001 have increased by more than 50.4 percent during the subsequent six-year period (2002 through 2007), compared with a general inflation rate of 19.0 percent" (p. 18).

Particularly for the poor and elderly, there are trade-offs between purchasing medicine, buying food, and paying utility bills. For those with mental health needs, the soaring cost of psychotropic drugs makes adherence to medication regimens less likely. The consequences for the severely mentally ill include increases in homelessness and incarceration. Hurley and colleagues (2005) believe a side effect of economic disparities in health care is that homeless shelters and local jails can be "characterized as the 21st century version of the state mental hospitals of 50 years ago" (p. 4).

One of the themes of this book is that family needs, family structure, and family functioning change over the life span. Needs related to health care are no exception. As Americans live longer, greater strain is placed on families as they care for aging family members. For families in poverty, the stress of caring for aging family members is greatest, because of costs associated with assisted living facilities, home health care, and increases in costs of Medicare. Increasing costs of paying for prescription drugs are also at a critical level. In particular, paying for prescription drugs is a hardship for older Americans. Although they comprise only about 13 percent of the population, older Americans use more than one-third of all prescription drugs, which adds up to 42 cents of every dollar spent for prescription drugs in the United States (McCloskey, 2000). On average, Medicare recipients pay $2,322 a year for prescription drugs, and the Congressional Budget Office predicts that the total amount for prescription drugs will increase from the $95 billion spent in 2003 to $284 billion in 2013 (Kaiser Family Foundation, 2003a, 2003b). Although retiree health plans offered by workers' previous employers have been the main source of covering the costs of prescription drugs not covered by Medicare, it is estimated that 22 percent of large employers will not continue to offer retirement health benefits to future retirees, and 85 percent of large employers report that prescription drug benefits will likely be reduced.

Low-income seniors face a double disparity in paying for prescription drugs. They are typically not covered by employer-related retirement health plans, and only about one-fourth of seniors on Medicare are also covered by Medicaid, with its prescription drug benefits. Mahan (2003) summarizes the situation:

> Only 27 percent of those in Medicare with incomes under 200 percent of poverty are covered by the Medicaid program; only 11 percent have Medicaid coverage for a full year. . . . Over a third of the nearly 18 million Medicare beneficiaries with incomes under 200 percent of poverty—less than $17,960 per year for an individual in 2003—do not have any source of prescription drug coverage. They must pay for the medications that they need out of their own funds. On average, they pay approximately $1,135 out-of-pocket for prescription drugs annually, which comes to over 6 percent of total annual income for an individual whose income is 200 percent of poverty. Their average out-of-pocket spending is lower than the overall per capita beneficiary drug spending because they cannot afford to purchase all of the drugs they need. Low-income Medicare beneficiaries [with incomes under 175 percent of poverty] without drug

coverage fill an average of 21 prescriptions a year, while their counterparts with coverage fill, on average, 31. For low-income seniors without drug coverage, increases in drug prices well above general inflation and their fixed real incomes often mean that some essential medications will go unfilled.

This is true even for many older Americans who worked for a substantial part of their lives, because although Social Security guarantees income at age sixty-two, and Medicare ensures health insurance at age sixty-five, Social Security benefits are based on previous income, so poor retirees are vulnerable to poverty in their later years. Overall, the care and support of an increasingly older population is an important issue facing American families. We address the issue of family caregiving across the life span in chapter 12.

Managed Care

Managed care as a method of service delivery was born of health care. *Managed care* is the term used to describe a market-based method of reducing the escalating costs of health care in the United States. Managed care introduced privatization and competition into health care in the United States. The basic premise of managed care is that market principles promote efficiency and cost containment in health care delivery and financing, replacing traditional fee-for-service care. Under managed care plans, providers are held responsible for providing cost-effective care, and financial incentives are given for not providing more care than is necessary. Health care providers are also rewarded when their patient population remains in good health, so less expensive, regular preventive visits to the family doctor reduce the need for hospitalization and expensive diagnostic tests and services. Overall, these elements of managed care are designed to reduce health care costs.

Since the mid-1990s, private insurance companies have aggressively promoted managed care. Health maintenance organizations (HMOs), which refer patients to a panel of doctors rather than giving patients an opportunity to select any doctor of their choice, were formed. HMOs allow private insurance companies to keep costs down by lowering premiums for enrollees. In this type of managed care approach, doctors are reimbursed according to a fee for service set by the insurance company. Physicians generally receive a payment in advance for the enrolled population, and in order to make a profit, the physician is responsible for keeping costs under the amount of money paid by the insurance provider.

Similarly, cost-containment efforts in behavioral health rely on managed care to replace traditional fee-for-service systems. This is true for mental health services provided through private health insurance and services funded through Medicaid. The trend, however, has been to separate mental health services from physical health services, with different access points, deductibles, co-pays, and service plans. A study of Medicaid participants in a managed care plan in Tennessee found many barriers to care, including access to mental health providers, problems obtaining medications, and termination of benefits. Respondents report feelings of hopelessness, loss of dignity, and an inability to access treatment and medications (Galambos, Rocha, McCarter, & Chansuthus, 2004). In general, state examinations of managed Medicaid programs focus primarily on cost reductions. Evaluations consist of provider surveys, rather than consumer perspectives. However, some states report potential access-to-care problems, greater use of emergency care, reductions in services, and major financial difficulties for community mental health centers (Manning, Liu, Stoner, Gray, Lurie, Popkin, & Christianson, 1999).

Uncompensated Care

Uncompensated care is another service delivery approach. To ensure public access to emergency services regardless of an individual's ability to pay, the Emergency Medical Treatment and Active Labor Act was passed as a part of the Consolidated Omnibus Budget Reconciliation Act (1985). Also known as the Patient Dumping Act, this federal law requires that all hospitals and outpatient clinics participating in Medicare provide appropriate medical screening to persons seeking emergency services and to stabilize patients before transferring them to another health care facility. The law, however, does not fund this mandate, so hospitals must absorb the cost of patients who can't pay for treatment. To offset losses, hospitals often charge uninsured patients much higher fees. This happens because in setting fees for patients without health insurance, hospitals are not bound by the lower fees that they have negotiated for patient care through Medicare, Medicaid, and private insurance companies.

Two types of uncompensated care are charity care and bad debt care. Charity care is related to an organization's tax-exempt status. The U.S. Internal Revenue Service instructs nonprofit organizations to provide charitable benefits to the communities they serve. Although this stipulation does not require hospitals to provide free or discounted care, they are obligated by law to give back to the community. Nationally, hospitals report providing 5.5 percent of their operating expenses for uncompensated care. Critics argue, however, that this figure is misleading. Hospitals count bad debt care, or patients' failure to pay for care, as part of their charity care because there are no national standards that clearly define what constitutes charity care. In Illinois, for example, hospital charitable spending averages less than 1 percent of hospital fees. Attorney general Lisa Madigan has proposed legislation that would require hospitals to spend at least 8 percent of their operating costs on charity care. Such care would provide discounts for care delivered to Illinois' 1.8 million uninsured (Rackl, 2006). Overall, an increasing number of uninsured individuals seek treatment in emergency rooms and community health clinics. But the kind of care received in emergency rooms is not complete, particularly if the situation is not seen as life threatening. Donna's story in box 8.2 strips away the illusion that people can access health care through emergency rooms.

Box 8.2 Accessing Health Care through the Emergency Room

Donna was having terrible lower abdominal pains and what seemed like a urinary tract infection and went to the student clinic. The clinic did a pelvic exam and could not find anything wrong with her and sent her home. The next night, the pain was so severe she went to the emergency room. There, they did another pelvic exam, took blood, and did a kidney scan. After several hours, the doctor returned and told her that her kidneys were okay but her white blood cell count was extremely elevated. There was an infection somewhere.

The emergency room doctor said, "My advice to you is to go see your general practitioner so he can refer you to a specialist." She told him she didn't have insurance and he said, "Well then, I would try to get some insurance because you really need to go see a gastro-intestinal specialist and an ob-gyn." She told him she didn't have a job that provided insurance and she couldn't afford it on her own. And then he said in the most sincere way, "Well then, you're pretty much screwed."

That was it, they told me to go home without knowing what was wrong with me. I was still in pain, I couldn't urinate, and I knew I had an infection, and they also knew it. They said I needed an ultrasound but wouldn't give me one. I guess it was too expensive. A $1,200 bill from the emergency room and no one could tell me what was wrong. Five months later, I found out I had a large fibroid tumor in my uterus, which could have been detected much earlier if they had done an ultrasound at the emergency room.

Cunningham (2006) points out that cuts in Medicaid and the State Child Health Insurance Program are likely to shift the cost of health care to hospitals in the form of uncompensated care. Public health crises such as epidemics and disasters do the same. Hurricane Katrina, for example, brought a catastrophic surge of uninsured patients into emergency rooms in Louisiana. Prior to Katrina, the state operated ten charity hospitals that were established in the 1930s during Governor Huey P. Long's populist rule. Louisiana funneled all federal and state aid for the uninsured and indigent to its charity system. Private nonprofit hospitals were not eligible for such assistance, which totaled $1.1 billion in 2004. Although state-run charity hospitals were long ago abandoned and replaced by nonprofits in other states, the flooding of hospital emergency rooms by the uninsured after a recent disaster is revealing. "In effect, Katrina blew the medically uninsured into the arms of the states' private hospitals, clinics and doctors. But state and federal funds to pay for their care did not immediately follow. By the end of [2004], the non-profit Ochsner Health System, New Orleans's largest private employer—with 7,100 workers, a 472-bed hospital and 25 clinics—had racked up a $70 million operating loss, 85% of that after the hurricane" (Smith, 2005, p. 1b). Part of this loss can be attributed to the fact that services to uninsured patients increased by two and a half.

Environmental Effects and Health Disparities

As we discussed in chapter 2, the family is embedded in larger social and economic systems in their environment. In terms of health disparities, the relationship between the environment and health reminds us of the debate about why people are poor. Neighborhood and community factors, organizations and institutions, racism, poverty policy, and the toxic waste left behind in the brownfields of deindustrialized urban areas create conditions that are external to the family. Health disparities occur when these larger systems do not support family well-being. In an attempt to document the causal relationships related to health disparities, researchers at PolicyLink (2002) interviewed forty key informants and reviewed over 140 studies and research papers. They found evidence that the expanding gap between rich and poor people contributes to health disparities in the United States. Race and ethnicity and neighborhood factors are also major determinants of health outcomes.

Racial discrimination triggers health disparities in several ways. Residential segregation affects people's health by limiting access to health-promoting resources such as grocery stores. The poor housing conditions, air quality, and water supplies in racially segregated neighborhoods, which contribute to health disparities, are the result of environmental racism. Chronic race-related stress is associated with institutional racism, as evidenced by low-quality education, a lack of culturally competent caregivers in hospitals and communities, and uneven diagnosis and treatment. In interviews conducted by PolicyLink (2002), "Interviewees . . . described how internalized racism, associated with a sense of hopelessness and inability to envision a positive future, contributes to mental health problems among people of color, in particular depression among women, violence and suicide in men, and substance abuse" (p. 10). Immigrant health is also negatively affected by low socioeconomic status. Latino interviewees reported difficulty accessing quality health care. Also reported were increases in asthma, hepatitis C, substance abuse, and domestic violence, and a decrease in health status among immigrants as they acculturate to life in the United States.

Health disparities are also determined by neighborhood effects, or geographic factors related to the communities where people live (see Ellen, Mijanovich, & Dillman, 2001). Although it is not clear exactly how neighborhood conditions contribute to ill health, poor outcomes in infant and overall mortality, child health and child development, adult physical health and health-related behaviors, and mental health are related to the neighborhood where a person lives. "Differences in health outcomes exist *even after* . . . known individual risk factors" are adjusted for (PolicyLink, 2002, p. 11). Children who live in geographically concentrated areas of poverty where the poverty rate reaches 50 percent or more are particularly at risk (see Coulton & Pandey, 1992).

The PolicyLink report offers a conceptual framework of community effects on health, which names and organizes various types of neighborhood factors that contribute to health disparities (table 8.1). The social, economic, and physical environments' effects on health can be positive (e.g., protective factors of economic stability, community cohesion, and quality services) or negative (e.g., racial segregation, lack of social support, and lack of access to services). The framework is designed to help policy makers and practitioners recognize three broad but interrelated categories of neighborhood characteristics related to health disparities:

- Social and economic environment: levels of poverty, racial and economic segregation, social networks, social organization, and political organization
- Physical environment: both the characteristics of the physical environment, such as air and water quality and housing conditions, and the relative connectedness of a community to resources and opportunities, based on location and transportation access

Table 8.1 Conceptual Framework of Community Effects on Health

		COMMUNITY CHARACTERISTICS	PROTECTIVE FACTORS	RISK FACTORS
RACIAL · ETHNIC · AND · ECONOMIC · INFLUENCES[1]	Economic Environment	**Employment, Income, Wealth and Assets** Quality and quantity of employment opportunities available to residents; the amount of collective wealth and assets in the community.	Living wage jobs with health benefits; safe workplaces. Savings, retirement, and homeownership provide economic stability.	Large numbers of community residents with low-wage jobs with no benefits and unsafe working conditions. Racial and economic segregation and concentrated poverty lead to higher stress and premature mortality.
		Neighborhood Economic Conditions Presence of commercial services including grocery stores, banks and restaurants.	Attracts public and private investment in services and infrastructure.	Disinvestment leads to loss of jobs, businesses, and decline in property values.
	Social Environment	**Cultural Characteristics** Values, attitudes and norms (related to a range of behaviors, including diet) deriving from race/ethnicity/gender, religion or nationality, as well as from other types of social and cultural groupings.	Cohesion, a sense of community, and access to key cultural institutions with healthy cultural norms/attributes.	Racism, language barriers, and acceptance of unhealthy behaviors. Absence of community norms and expectations that promote healthy behavior and community safety.
		Social Support and Networks Friends, family, colleagues, and neighborhood acquaintances. These networks exist within the community and beyond it, such as churches and clubs.	Social capital that can provide access to social supports and economic opportunities, as well as to certain health services and resources. Adult role models and peer networks are influential to young people.	Lack of social supports and role models. Residents do not have access to networks outside the neighborhood that can link them to employment and other key opportunities. Sometimes referred to as absence of "bridging" social capital.
		Community Leadership and Organization Level of capacity for mobilization, civic engagement, and political power.	Community leaders and organizations provide needed supports and services. Political power allows needed resources to be leveraged into neighborhood.	Lack of leadership, organization, and political power impedes the flow of resources needed for neighborhood problem-solving and hampers community leadership development.
		Reputation of the Neighborhood Residents' and outsiders' perceptions may affect behavior toward the neighborhood.	Neighborhoods perceived as "good" or "improving", with important social and economic attributes, are conducive to new investment.	Poor and "bad" neighborhoods are subject to negative stereotypes and discriminated against, limiting success of isolated improvement efforts.
	Physical Environment	**Environmental Quality** Air, water, land shared across a region.	Policies and practices that maintain a clean, healthy environment.	Presence of and exposure to toxics and pollution.
		Built Environment and Infrastructure Housing, parks and recreation, and workplaces.	Access to affordable, high-quality housing, local parks, and safe workplaces. Urban design that supports physical activity.	Exposure to lead paint, problems with inadequate sanitation and pest infestation, dangerous types of work and unsafe work environments. Urban design that inhibits physical activity.
		Public Safety The ways in which the design and social climate of communities influence safety, including the prevalence of crime and violence, traffic and pedestrian accidents.	Desired and necessary amount of police and fire protection. Little crime, lots of street/sidewalk activity and interaction.	Prevalence of violence breeds fear, isolation, and a reluctance to seek even needed services, as residents avoid leaving their homes and spending time outside.
		Geographic Access to Opportunities Throughout the Region Mobility and the ability to connect to resources within and beyond the neighborhood level.	Convenient location and mobility allow access to services, employment, cultural and recreational resources.	Isolation of homes from job centers, particularly areas without public transit access. Distance from recreational facilities or safe parks for health-promoting activities such as exercise.
	Services	**Health Services** Accessibility, affordability, and quality of care for individuals and families.	Necessary, accessible care delivered in a culturally sensitive manner in satisfactory health facilities with well-trained and culturally appropriate practitioners.	Lack of access to necessary healthcare services, while what is available is culturally inappropriate and of poor quality.
		Community and Public Support Services Neighborhood-level public services, including schools, parks, transit, sanitation, police and fire protection, and child care centers. Community institutions include churches, social clubs, and block groups.	Quality support services act as important neighborhood institutions providing needed services as well as venues for neighborhood meetings and leadership development.	Needed services are not available while those located in the neighborhood are undependable and of poor quality.

[1] Structural factors such as institutional racism and trends in the broader economic system have an overarching effect on how neighborhoods and regions develop, how people are distributed, and how public and private resources are allocated.

Source: PolicyLink. (2002, November). *Reducing health disparities through a focus on communities.* Retrieved July 29, 2006, from http://www.policylink.org/pdfs/Health Disparities.pdf

- Services: access to and quality of health services and other supportive public, private, and commercial services that contribute to healthy living

As the community effects on health framework illustrates, health policy takes into consideration much more than what is commonly considered under the health rubric. For example, an expanded discussion of the social and economic environment would include policies that affect such things as the lack of social capital or the existence of social networks outside the neighborhood, the scarcity of local leaders and mentors, and the absence of positive community norms. For example, the discussion of the physical environment would need to include a discussion of policies concerned with such things as lead paint, pollution, criminal activity, and unsafe working conditions. Although a discussion of all these aspects of the social, economic, and physical environments is not possible in this chapter, the health disparities framework is relevant to many of the policy areas that we discuss throughout this book. In particular, the framework provides a context for understanding the important role that programs and services play in reducing health disparities. The next section of this chapter looks at federal and state policies and programs that provide health care services to families in the United States.

Health Care Policy

Health care programs funded by federal and state governments include Medicare, Medicaid, the State Children's Health Insurance Program, and community health centers. Our purpose in discussing these programs is to familiarize readers with these major policy areas, including the role that managed care plays in the delivery of government-funded health care.

Medicare and Medicaid

Forty percent of all money spent on health care in the United States comes from governmental sources. The bulk of these federal dollars go to Medicare and Medicaid, two programs designed to help aged, poor, and disabled persons obtain access to medical care. Medicare and Medicaid are the most important health initiatives in American history. Introduced in 1965 as part of the War on Poverty, they were enacted into law as Titles XVIII and XIX of the Social Security Act of 1935. Initially, Medicare was designed to cover the hospital and medical expenses of retirees, but coverage was extended to disabled persons in 1972. Medicare benefits are tied to an individual's payroll tax contributions, so eligibility is contingent upon a person's workforce participation for at least part of his or her lifetime.

Medicare Part A provides hospital and some post-hospital services, such as skilled nursing facilities. Medicare Part A has no premium and comes with receipt of Social Security benefits at retirement. Medicare Part B is an additional public insurance program that covers the costs of outpatient services, such as physician fees and the cost of laboratory tests. In 2004, the premium for Part B was $66, and people could choose whether or not to participate. Medicare Part B did not pay physician co-pays, deductibles, or prescriptions drug costs, so many senior citizens opted to buy supplemental medigap policies provided by private insurance companies. Although premiums were relatively high for elderly persons on fixed incomes (e.g., $200 per month), medigap insurance traditionally paid all deductibles, co-pays, and prescription drug costs for families. In 2001, Medicare began providing Medicare + Choice plans (now called Medicare Advantage), which are similar to medigap policies and are administered by private insurance companies that contract with government to provide services through the private sector. Basically, Medicare Advantage plans provide all care through various types of managed care plans. Individuals can choose HMOs that have very low monthly premiums (e.g., $69 a month) and receive their care from physicians participating in a provider network. Or they can pick other plans with less expensive premiums, for example, plans that do not cover prescriptions. Over time, Medicare has become increasingly integrated as part of managed care plans through private insurance companies.

Beginning in January 2006, major changes occurred in the Medicare program that have affected millions of elderly and disabled Americans. Medicare Part D was added to the Medicare Prescription Drug, Improvement, and Modernization Act (2003) to provide assistance paying for prescription medications. The prescription drug benefit is voluntary and is provided by private insurers who contract with the federal government to provide coverage. Medicare estimates the average premium to be $35 per month, depending on the plan chosen, in addition to the Medicare Part B premium. Medigap policies no longer can provide prescription drug coverage; if people keep their medigap policy, they must pay both premiums. Medicare Part D requires a $250 deductible each year, after which Medicare pays 75 percent of drug costs up to $2,250. After drug costs reach $2,250, there is what has been termed the "doughnut hole." Individuals must pay the next $2,850 in drug costs before Medicare continues coverage. After that, Medicare covers up to 95 percent of all drug costs.

It was argued from a conservative point of view that the new legislation would give consumers more choice, but in practice, the multiplicity of choices offered to elderly consumers has created confusion and problems obtaining prescription drug coverage. Even our short description of the possible options here is confusing. Enrollees can now choose Medicare A; Medicare A and B; Medicare A, B, and D; or Medicare A, B, D and a supplement, or they can enroll in Medicare Advantage, which takes the place of A and B and offers drug coverage through a private insurance company that has contracted with the federal government to provide services. There are options to choose only Part D prescription drug plans for state and local areas, or to buy a supplemental Medicare Advantage plan plus a Part D drug plan.

There are a myriad of plans, and many of the supplemental plans incorporate drug plans in order to become more competitive. These plans take the place of the old supplemental insurance and form a complete managed care health insurance plan. This saves the Medicare recipient from having to deal with more than one company at a time. Some companies even pay the Part D premium to the government and fold that cost into the plan for the consumer (Centers for Medicare and Medicaid Services, 2006a). Some plans are very expensive, while others lower premiums by offering fewer benefits. Many elderly and disabled persons have difficulty maneuvering through the maze of numerous plans available to them. An article in the *New York Times* stated that the mix-ups occurring in the first weeks of the enrollment period had a particularly severe impact on low-income patients with mental illnesses (Pear, 2006). Since the new drug plans cover some prescriptions and not others, changes in drug regimens resulted in hospitalizations. Rising out-of-pocket expenses for prescription drugs are related to lower adherence to medication schedules.

Another concern is the situation of a low-income person whose income is not low enough to be eligible for Medicaid. What happens when prescription expenses reach the doughnut hole? Research suggests that most seniors benefit from modest savings on these new plans, particularly if they have chronic conditions for which they take prescription medication. But these savings will be short lived. For example, persons with high blood pressure, high cholesterol, or diabetes will have mounting drug costs that will push them into the doughnut hole within a few months. With the new benefits, chronically ill seniors might initially save more out-of-pocket money for drugs, but 35 percent of seniors who take more than three medications per month will likely be forced to pay 100 percent of their costs within a short time. The combination of premiums, deductibles, and co-payments, and the huge coverage gap of the doughnut hole, may leave many beneficiaries exposed to large and unaffordable costs (Gellad, Huskamp, Phillips, & Haas, 2006). Two recent polls found that a substantial number of low-income senior citizens and people with disabilities are not saving money on prescriptions. People who transferred from state Medicaid drug programs that had no co-payments now pay $1 to $5 per drug. Others who have been negatively affected include poor seniors who received drugs for free or at reduced cost from state programs or drug companies that no longer offer these programs, those with less expensive retiree insurance, and those who had few or no previous drug costs and are now paying insurance premiums (Wolf, 2006).

Medicaid, the program that provides medical care for over 52 million poor people, is funded through Title XIX of the Social Security Act. As the health care program for families on welfare, Medicaid covers four different categories of people: children, adults with dependent children, people with disabilities, and the elderly. Some Medicaid beneficiaries, known as "dual eligibles," are eligible for Medicare as well. Most live in long-term care facilities such as nursing homes and have no income or assets to pay for nursing home care. Medicaid pays their Medicare premiums and covers long-term care, dental care, and vision care, all of which are services that Medicare does not cover or for which it offers limited coverage. Among dual eligibles, more than one-third have a mental disability (34%), over one-fourth (27%) have diabetes, and nearly one-fifth (19%) reside in long-term care facilities (Kaiser Commission on Medicaid and the Uninsured, 2006b).

Medicaid is financed by the federal and state governments and is administered by the states. Federal minimum income standards vary for different groups, for example, pregnant women with children under the age of six with incomes at or below 133 percent of the federal poverty level, school-age children at or below 100 percent, parents with incomes at or below states' 1996 welfare eligibility levels (usually 50% of the federal poverty level), and most seniors and people with disabilities who receive cash assistance. States may raise these levels. For example, working parents in Maine may have incomes up to 157 percent of the poverty level, while those in Texas may have incomes of only 30 percent. Most states cover children at or below 200 percent of the poverty level. Within broad federal guidelines, each state determines the design of its program, benefits packages, and payment levels for coverage. Nearly 30 million people are enrolled in state Medicaid programs, but most Medicaid dollars are spent on the long-term care needs of the disabled and elderly. Although low-income children and families make up 75 percent of enrollees, they account for just 30 percent of program spending, the remaining 70 percent of which is spent on the disabled and elderly. In 2003, per capita spending was $1,700 per child and $1,900 per adult, while per capita cost was $12,300 for the disabled and $12,800 for the elderly (Kaiser Commission on Medicaid and the Uninsured, 2006b).

Federal expenditures for health care services and administration of the Medicaid program totaled $161 billion in 2003. Combined state and federal spending in 2003 totaled $275 billion, a 6.9 percent increase over 2002. Cuts in financing through the Balanced Budget Act of 1997 reduced federal subsidies, and economic downturns since 2001 also caused dramatic drops in state tax revenues. Rising costs and reduced public funds prompted many states to apply for Medicaid managed care waivers. Between 1993 and 1994, Medicaid managed care enrollment grew from 4.8 million to 7.8 million, a jump of 63 percent. Thirty-two percent of all Medicaid beneficiaries were in managed care plans in 1996 (Gold, Sparer, & Chu, 1996). By 2006, forty-seven states and the District of Columbia had managed care waivers or applications pending (Centers for Medicare and Medicaid Services, 2006b). Medicaid managed care programs are typically run by for-profit insurance companies that contract with the state to provide more cost-effective services than those provided by traditional Medicaid fee-for-service programs. But low reimbursement rates, paperwork, and excessive delays in reimbursement for medical services from state governments have led to a shortage of physicians who accept Medicaid. A quarter of the nation's physicians do not accept Medicaid patients, and about a third limit the number they will accept.

The Deficit Reduction Act

The Deficit Reduction Act (DRA) of 2005 is expected to reduce federal entitlement spending by $99 billion between 2005 and 2015. Most of the reductions will come from Medicaid to fill in gaps in Medicare coverage and to support safety-net providers. According to the Kaiser Commission on Medicaid and the Uninsured (2006a), many of the DRA changes in Medicaid policy will shift costs of care to Medicaid beneficiaries and limit health care coverage for low-income families. The major changes in reductions come from increasing premiums and co-payments for Medicaid recipients. For families (with children) earning over 150 percent of the federal poverty level, states may charge unlimited premiums and co-payments up to 20 percent of medical costs. For families with incomes between 100 percent and 150 percent of the poverty level, co-payments are set at 10 percent of the cost of service. For families below 100 percent of the poverty level, the law does not set any limits or amounts, so it is unclear if they will share increased costs or not. However, the law does state that cost sharing cannot exceed 5 percent of a family's income.

The DRA also targets reductions in emergency room services and prescription drug costs. States may charge higher co-payments for non-emergency use of emergency rooms and up to 20 percent of the costs of non-preferred prescription drugs. Finally, because the law shifts cost sharing from pharmaceutical companies to pharmacists, pharmacists could deny access to drugs if a Medicaid beneficiary cannot pay the cost-sharing amount at the point of service. Doctors also may refuse to provide services if co-payments are not received at the time of service, and states may terminate Medicaid coverage if beneficiaries are sixty days late on their premium payments. Cost sharing cannot be charged to pregnant women or children, or for emergency room visits, family planning, or hospice care. Benefit changes require states to offer some mandated services such as hospitalization and physician services but allow states to set limits on length of hospital stays or annual visits. Most savings come from tighter restrictions on asset transfers to family members or others at below fair market value within five years of an application for Medicaid.

The DRA allows states to replace the existing Medicaid benefits package for children and other groups with "benchmark" programs, which often do not cover key Medicaid services. Solomon's (2006) analysis at the Center on Budget and Policy Priorities found that the law specifically exempts elderly persons, pregnant women, people with disabilities, and some other beneficiaries from these new rules, so these individuals cannot be required to enroll in one of the benchmark plans. However, the Centers for Medicare and Medicaid Services has given states greater flexibility than Congress intended by allowing them to offer exempt beneficiaries the choice of enrolling in a benchmark package or remaining in regular Medicaid. Kentucky, Idaho, and West Virginia have already applied for benchmark programs. In implementing their plans, both Kentucky and Idaho have enrolled exempt beneficiaries in benchmark packages "without first offering them a choice between the benchmark package and regular Medicaid and without giving them a clear explanation of the differences between the two kinds of plans" (Solomon, 2006, p. 1). In Kentucky, for example, the state sent letters suggesting that recipients could opt out of the benchmark plan but would be required to pay higher co-pays if they did so. In Idaho, the information release for providers states that participants who are found to be eligible for Medicaid will be enrolled in either the basic or enhanced benefit package and does not offer the option of the regular Medicaid program.

Medicaid spending increases in the DRA include $2 billion for Katrina relief to pay the non-federal share for medical care under Medicare and the State Children's Health Insurance Program. There is also additional money for home- and community-based services for the elderly and disabled. This funding allows states to offer personal care and rehabilitation services to an estimated 120,000 enrollees. Other spending increases include demonstration projects based on a "money-follows-the-person" approach to move 100,000 individuals from nursing homes to community settings. Another 60,000 individuals will receive cash and counseling to test the viability of long-term community-based care services purchased on a predetermined budget.

Included in the DRA are two other important provisions: the Family Opportunity Act (2005) and health opportunity accounts. The first allows families with incomes below 300 percent of the poverty level to buy in to the Medicaid program. This provision is expected to provide medical care for an additional 115,000 disabled children, at a cost of $64 billion between 2005 and 2015. For as many as ten states, the five-year health opportunity accounts demonstration projects promote "fundamental policy change, where states would set up accounts for individuals to pay for medical services. However, after the money in the account is exhausted, beneficiaries could face additional cost sharing requirements to meet a deductible before they had access to full Medicaid benefits" (Kaiser Commission on Medicaid and the Uninsured, 2006a).

Consolidated Omnibus Budget Reconciliation Act

On April 7, 1986, the Consolidated Omnibus Budget Reconciliation Act (COBRA) became law:

> The law amends the Employee Retirement Income Security Act, the Internal Revenue Code and the Public Health Service Act to provide continuation of group health coverage that otherwise might be terminated.... COBRA provides certain former employees, retirees, spouses, former spouses, and dependent children the right to temporary continuation of health coverage at group rates. This coverage, however, is only available when coverage is lost due to certain specific events. Group health coverage for COBRA participants is usually more expensive than health coverage for active employees, since

usually the employer pays a part of the premium for active employees, while COBRA participants generally pay the entire premium themselves. Still, when an individual loses his/her job the person's ability to pay for health insurance is generally limited. (Employee Benefits Security Administration, 2008)

Thus, for practical purposes, the premiums are prohibitive. For example, a teacher recently resigned from a teaching position in a public school to return to employment in the private sector. He had been paying $54 per month. His employer had been paying the rest of his family's health care premium. However, when he resigned, his employer informed him that to continue his coverage for himself, his spouse, and their two children through COBRA, the premium for the insurance would be $1,110 per month. The feasibility of using the COBRA approach to health care is questionable. One can imagine that typically those individuals who leave a job that provides employer-based health care benefits would go to new jobs with similar benefits and wages. But when layoffs or underemployment make it impossible to obtain a new job that provides health care benefits, it is unlikely that an individual can pay such high health insurance costs out of a reduced salary.

State Children's Health Insurance Program

As a major health initiative for children, the State Children's Health Insurance Program (SCHIP) extends medical care to poor and near-poor children under the age of eighteen who are uninsured and not eligible for Medicaid. SCHIP was established under the Balanced Budget Act of 1997 as Title XXI of the Social Security Act. The legislation provided $40 billion in federal matching funds over ten years to help states expand health care coverage to uninsured children. The amount of matching funds given to state governments varied, depending on how each state designed and implemented its children's health care program. For example, on average, the state share of costs is 30 percent but ranges from 8 percent in New Mexico and 16 percent in Mississippi to 35 percent in New York and 37 percent in California. By the end of 2004, nearly 4 million children were enrolled in SCHIP programs, many of whom were previously outside the health care system. Compared to children with private health insurance, children enrolled in SCHIP were three times more likely to be Hispanic, and more than twice as likely to be in poor health (Byck, 2000).

SCHIP is a state-administered program, so states are allowed flexibility in designing and implementing their programs. Twenty states have created a new non-Medicaid children's health insurance program, twenty states and the District of Columbia have created a state program combined with a Medicaid expansion, and eleven states have expanded Medicaid only. Two states, Arkansas and Tennessee, phased out their Medicaid expansion programs in 2002. Medicaid expansions and non-Medicaid state programs are more likely than Medicaid-only programs to reach children whose parents are self-employed or employed in jobs without health insurance. Income eligibility levels and services vary by state. Most states allow recipients to earn less than 200 percent of the federal poverty level, but eligibility levels range from 140 percent in North Dakota and 185 percent in Oregon, for example, to 235 percent in Georgia, 300 percent in Maryland, and 350 percent of the federal poverty level in New Jersey (Henry J. Kaiser Family Foundation, 2006). It is estimated that these generally higher state eligibility levels exclude only about 23 percent of all uninsured children and only 16 percent of low-income uninsured children.

States market their new health insurance programs for children aggressively through media campaigns, outreach to child care centers and community-based programs, and the Internet. At the federal level, the Insure Kids Now! Web page features links to each state program, so consumers can easily find information about SCHIP programs in the state where they live (U.S. Department of Health and Human Services, n.d.). Still, many poor working families do not know about SCHIP. Others believe that they are not eligible for a federal health program because they work and are not on welfare. Rates of enrollment of citizen children with non-citizen parents are low because parents worry that participation may negatively affect their immigration status (Dubey, Hill, & Kenney, 2002). The American Academy of Pediatrics (2001) offers a comprehensive list of policy implementation and evaluation strategies, including coverage for immigrant children using state funds, simplified enrollment forms for coordination between state Medicaid and SCHIP, and linkage of children receiving school lunch subsidies with coverage.

Some states use SCHIP funds to offer health coverage for the entire family. For example, Ohio offers health coverage through its Medicaid expansion programs called Healthy Start for children up to age nineteen and pregnant women, and Healthy Families for both parents and children in families with incomes up to 100 percent of the poverty level. In July 2006, Illinois became the first state in the nation to provide affordable comprehensive health insurance for every child. Of the 250,000 children in Illinois without health insurance, more than half come from working- and middle-class families who earn too much to qualify for the state's SCHIP and Medicaid combination program, called Kidcare—but not enough to afford private health insurance. The All Kids and Family Care programs offer comprehensive health insurance to every uninsured child regardless of family income. Doctor's visits, hospital stays, prescription drugs, vision care, dental care, and medical devices like eyeglasses and asthma inhalers are covered. Parents pay monthly premiums, but rates for middle-income families are significantly lower than rates on the private market. For instance, a family of four earning between $40,000 and $59,999 a year will pay a $40 monthly premium per child, and a $10 co-pay per physician visit (State of Illinois & Blagojevich, 2005).

The Kaiser Commission on Medicaid and the Uninsured (2008) provides a short but detailed legislative history of SCHIP, which is a useful example of what it means to track legislation in Congress or provide a brief legislative history of related legislation and bills in Congress. The most recent action on SCHIP occurred in August 2007, when the Centers for Medicare and Medicaid Services, the federal agency that oversees SCHIP, sent a letter to state health officials to guide SCHIP implementation. Here we see the extraordinary power of the executive branch of government in guiding the implementation of federal legislation. The executive order requires states to

> show that they have enrolled 95% of the children under 200% of poverty who are eligible for SCHIP or Medicaid, and that private employer-based coverage for lower income children has not declined by more than 2 percentage points during the prior five years before they can consider an expansion beyond 250% of poverty. To expand to these higher income levels, states must adopt specific strategies to prevent substation of public coverage for private coverage or "crowd out" including a requirement that children be eligible for at least one year before they could be eligible for SCHIP. States were given 12 months to come into compliance. (Kaiser Commission on Medicaid and the Uninsured, 2008, p. 1)

In the fall of 2007, Congress passed the Children's Health Insurance Program Reauthorization Act with bipartisan support, but the legislation was vetoed by President Bush. The legislation put some limits on the expansion of SCHIP by prohibiting coverage for children whose families are at 300 percent of the poverty level, requiring additional verification of citizenship status, and obliging states to utilize best practices to eliminate "crowd out." It also encouraged premium options in children's health care and reduced the length of time that childless adults can spend on SCHIP from two years to one year. Funding for the expanded bill rested solely on increased tobacco taxes. On January 23, 2008, Congress was unable to muster the necessary two-thirds majority vote to override the presidential veto. According to Abramowitz and Weisman (2007), "The current confrontation stems as much from the White House's desire to use the bill reauthorizing the State Children's Health Insurance Program to advance Bush's proposals to expand health insurance coverage through tax breaks as it does from his budgetary concerns. The idea was a major focus of the State of the Union address, and Bush and his advisers tried throughout the spring to interest lawmakers in attaching the measure to an SCHIP bill." To preserve the current program, Congress passed the Medicare, Medicaid, and SCHIP Extension Act of 2007, which extended SCHIP until June 30, 2008. One of the early actions of the 111th Congress was to reauthorize SCHIP. It became law on February 4, 2009.

Public Health Clinics

The public health system is also a major provider of health care in the United States. The mission of the Health Resources and Services Administration, an agency funded under the Public Health Service Act (1944), is to ensure the support and delivery of primary health care services and the development of public health facilities. Since the community health center programs were launched in 1966, more than 1,000 federally funded community health centers have provided services for 14.3 million people. They provide primary health care to the uninsured, the homeless, and migrant workers, including health services in family medicine, internal medicine, pediatrics, obstetrics and gynecology; diagnostic services; preventive health services (prenatal services, well-child care, immunizations, cancer and other health screenings, family planning services, and preventive dental services); emergency medical services; pharmaceutical services; referrals to other medical and health-related providers, including service for substance abuse and mental health; case management; transportation and translation services; and patient education. The Health Resources and Services Administration manages most of the federal grants and programs, including maternal and child health block grants, community and migrant health center programs, the National Health Service Corps, the Comprehensive Perinatal Services Program, the Health Care for the Homeless Program, and the Ryan White HIV/AIDS Program.

With roots in the civil rights movement and the War on Poverty, health centers offer a unique approach to health care that integrates culturally competent patient care with public health and community-wide interventions. Over the past forty years, the centers have survived numerous policy changes and political challenges for continued funding and have been successful in expanding funding through direct appropriations, access to Medicare and Medicaid funds, and block grants (Lefkowitz, 2005). One reason for the success and growth of community health centers is their "ability to affect their physical, economic, and political environment" (Hunt, 2005, p. 340). Centers are tied securely to local neighborhoods by involving residents in community-based boards of directors. The law requires that the majority of board members be health center patients. The mission of centers also requires them to look beyond medical care to recognize the core economic and environmental factors that influence sickness and health. Implementation of this mission takes many forms, ranging from career ladder jobs for urban residents to well-water improvement and the establishment of food cooperatives in rural areas. Finally, health centers have been effective in advocating with local, state, and federal structures that oversee local conditions in the community.

As primary care providers, community health centers are charged with providing the four Cs of primary care: contact, continuous, comprehensive, and coordinated care (Starfield, 1992). To achieve comprehensive and coordinated care, the centers rely on collaboration and partnerships with hospitals and university medical centers, specialty physicians and other providers, networks and managed care, and innovative payment arrangements. This requires much coordination with other parts of the health care system, but generally "centers receive no additional financial resources to fund these levels of care, especially for their uninsured patients" (Zuvekas, 2005, p. 331). In 2004, 40 percent of health center patients were uninsured, and 36 percent were covered by Medicaid. From 1997 to 2004, the number of health center sites increased 58 percent, but uninsured patient care rose 90 percent during that same time period. Health centers have relied increasingly on Medicaid funding for patient care, which has grown from 15 percent of operating revenues in 1985 to 37 percent in 2004. Health centers are widely noted for providing quality care at lower costs, and for reducing health disparities among racial and ethnic minority groups, including lower infant mortality rates, tuberculosis case rates, death rates, and lack of access to prenatal care. The majority of patients who use health care centers are people of color, of whom 25 percent are African American and 33 percent Hispanic.

Current challenges include the Deficit Reduction Act of 2005, which imposes new citizenship requirements on Medicaid applicants. Since community health centers derive about one-third of their revenue from Medicaid, any eligibility changes affect cost reimbursements, as well as the number of uninsured individuals who may seek access to health care through public health clinics. And meeting the increasingly complex health needs of people who live in low-income communities requires high levels of case management through primary care programs (Rosenbaum & Shin, 2006). In the last days of the congressional session in 2008, Congress voted to suspend the roll call vote and instead allow simple aye or nay votes. Both houses of Congress unanimously reauthorized community health centers through the Health Centers Renewal Act of 2007, which was signed into law by President Bush on October 8, 2008. The law makes it easier for employees of community health centers to volunteer during times of disaster or public health emergencies such as flu pandemics. In addition, funding authorizations were increased from 2.1 billion in FY 2008 to $3.3 billion in 2012. For the first time, the law authorizes health centers with specific funding levels for each of the five years of reauthorization.

To assess what these costs mean in relation to funding costs for other proposed bills and legislation, we visited WashingtonWatch.com. Most readers are probably familiar with Wikipedia, the online encyclopedia that allows users to develop and edit its content. WashingtonWatch.com is also a wiki, with links to legislative Web sites such as the Library of Congress's Thomas. The wiki feature allows registered users to update information about pending legislation and also blog and post comments for or against the bill. This creates a very up-to-date picture of bills and the content of proposed legislation as it moves through Congress, including public views of that process. What we particularly like about WashingtonWatch.com is that the Web site estimates the average costs or savings of bills to the U.S. taxpayer. A simple drop-down menu shows the average estimated costs of bills or recently passed legislation. Costs per person, couple, household, and family, including the cost for larger families consisting of up to seven persons, are available. For example, the reauthorization of the Health Centers Renewal Act costs an estimated $101.94 per family of three in the United States, compared to $7,700.45 for the Consolidated Security, Disaster Assistance, and Continuing Funding Appropriations Act (2009) and $6.56 for the Reconnecting Homeless Youth Act of 2008.

Mental Health Services

In this chapter, our policy discussions on managed care and Medicaid have generally applied to funding for mental health services. We turn our attention now to policies specific to mental health programs. We cover community mental health centers, mental health parity, and suicide prevention on college campuses. The policy evolution of community mental health centers in the United States contrasts considerably with the history and noted success of public health clinics. The brief discussion that follows is intended to give readers some background in mental health policy. The mental health policies that are discussed illustrate the importance of leadership and power in the dynamic policy-making environment, and the role that funding plays in drastically changing service delivery within a given policy area.

The Mental Health Centers Construction Act

President John F. Kennedy championed the cause of mental disability. His mentally retarded sister, Rosemary, was institutionalized for most of her life after a "failed" lobotomy. Kennedy read the Final Report of the Joint Commission on Mental Illness, which outlined a detailed plan for creating a new system of care for the mentally ill. Kennedy hoped that such a system would replace state-funded asylums, or mental hospitals. His leadership came at a time when "no agency of the federal government devoted itself to [mentally retarded] children, no foundations took up their cause, and the tiny voice of nascent parents' movements barely made itself heard in the media and the corridors of power" (Shorter, 2000, p. 1). He appointed an interagency committee at the cabinet level and quickly proposed the Mental Retardation Facilities and Community Mental Health Centers Construction Act (1963). In a special message to Congress, "he emphasized the notion of community involvement and community ownership of the program. In addition, these mental health centers were to be comprehensive, providing services not only to the severely mentally ill, but also to children, families, and adults suffering from the effects of stress. These programs were to be comprehensive, coordinated, of high quality, and available to everyone in the population. In essence, where this country had failed to establish a comprehensive national health service or national health insurance system, the President was now proposing exactly that for mental health systems" (Cutler, Bevilacqua, & McFarland, 2003, p. 384).

The law ushered in a new era in mental health services in the United States by authorizing federal funds for the construction of a network of community mental health facilities. After Kennedy's assassination, funding was appropriated in 1965 to staff the centers for inpatient and outpatient care, crisis intervention, day treatment, and education. Amendments added alcohol and drug services in 1968 and mental health services for children in 1970. At that time, funding was increased from four years to eight years. "In addition, the government added a new priority of poverty as a main feature for competition for funding. The poverty area centers could get 90% of the costs of construction paid for by federal funds. The federal government would also pay for 90% of staffing costs for the first 2 years, 80% in the third year, 75% in the fourth year, and 70% for the remaining four years. This was a significant advantage for centers serving high poverty inner cities and rural areas" (Cutler et al., p. 386). Amendments in 1974 would have expanded services to children and the elderly, provided screening for admission to psychiatric hospitals, and mandated follow-up services to halfway houses, but these amendments were vetoed by President Gerald Ford. Soon, however, several factors began to affect the new system, including the reticence of states to pick up operating costs after the provision of federal money was to end, competition for state funds from state mental hospitals, and the community mental health center (CMHC) system's focus on prevention and the "worried well" rather than on the chronically mentally ill who had never received needed care or were being deinstitutionalized from state systems. Inflation also negatively affected funding levels, and after 1975, no new construction occurred. However, when the Social Security Amendments of 1972 defined mental illness as a disease, Medicaid dollars could be used to fund treatment, and CMHCs funded many of their programs through Medicaid fee-for-service reimbursements.

When President Jimmy Carter took office, First Lady Rosalynn Carter brought advocacy for mental health services back to the White House. In 1977, she was appointed active honorary chair of the President's Commission on Mental Health. She oversaw a twenty-person advisory board composed of social workers, medical experts, lobbyists, and psychiatrists who toured the nation, held public hearings, and sought the advice of community activists, doctors, legislators, and former mental health patients. She also developed thirty "special issue" task forces staffed by 450 volunteers. The outcome was a major report calling for massive policy change because, since the construction of the first CMHCs, the amount of community mental health services provided had increased dramatically, and a large number of persons with chronic mental illnesses still remained unserved. Racial and ethnic minorities, migrant workers, women, Vietnam veterans, the deaf, people with physical disabilities, and the urban poor numbered among those with chronic mental illness. In response, Congress passed the Mental Health Systems Act (1980) and authorized over $800 million in grants to existing community mental health centers. However, these federal grant monies for mental health services never materialized because Congress failed to pass an appropriations bill for funding the new law. President Reagan came into office in 1981 and recommended an immediate 25 percent cut per year in the budget for CMHCs, followed by similar cuts in subsequent years until the program was completely defunded. The Omnibus Budget Reconciliation Act (1981) eliminated all the federal initiatives for community mental health from the previous eighteen years.

As the Omnibus Budget Reconciliation Act consolidated federal mental health funding into block grants administered by state governments, CMHCs entered the world of block grants early on, and more recently, state managed care systems. By the 1990s, state governments began to scrutinize CMHCs and their programs in their efforts to apply for managed care Medicaid waivers. The future of mental health care services now seems to rest, for the most part, on Medicaid managed care and private insurance. These changes in funding have essentially altered the mission and purpose of CMHCs. Even the term *community mental health center* is no longer an official federal designation. In the absence of grants and direct federal funding, CMHCs struggle to provide quality care. As for-profit insurance companies sign contracts with states for managed care, business-oriented managers replace social workers and psychologists in the effort to turn clinics into profit-making ventures. According to Cutler and colleagues (2003),

> Some states, such as Massachusetts, Iowa, and Tennessee, grew weary of trying to keep up with the growing Medicaid fee for service explosion and picked up early on a growing trend towards managed care Medicaid waivers in the public sector. These states developed a capitation system to replace the existing overwhelmed fee for service system and one of them, Tennessee, put the whole thing up for bid to the managed care industry. One company came into control of all the so-called mental health carve out and proceeded to contract or not contract with whomever they pleased with the goal of saving money by providing minimal services. The results were disastrous, high functioning well-respected organizations were defunded over night throughout the state and patients with serious mental illness suffered enormously from the disruption. (p. 395)

Today, partially due to deinstitutionalization and the severe underfunding of the community mental health system, people with mental illness often end up homeless or in prison. One in five state prisoners is mentally ill, and a similar number of the homeless have mental health problems (Fellner, 2006; Martens, 2001).

Mental Health Parity

According to the National Alliance for the Mentally Ill, one in five adults (about 40 million Americans) experiences some type of mental illness in his or her lifetime. Although treatment can be funded by Medicaid managed care, private insurance can also cover mental health services. In the mid-1990s, debate about the financial inconsistencies associated with treatment of mental illness began to foment. Advocates behind the Mental Health Parity Act (1996) saw parity, or the notion that mental health and chemical dependency services should be covered by insurance companies at the same level as health care, as a way to bring equality to health care, and as a way to fight the stigma associated with mental illness (Tobin, 2005). Numerous groups opposed passage of the law. Insurance companies feared the high cost of mental health services. Businesses were opposed because of possible increased costs for health insurance. Others were concerned that parity would increase insurance rates and premiums. Insurance companies were also afraid that consumers would take advantage of treatment for mental health diagnoses such as caffeine withdrawal and mathematics disorder, which are listed in the *Diagnostic and Statistical Manual of Mental Disorders,* published by the American Psychiatric Association. Others argued that no change was needed: services and treatment for mental illness were adequate.

For ten years, the Mental Health Parity Act of 1996 pressed insurance companies to cover treatment for mental illness at the same dollar amount as for physical illness. Beginning January 1, 1998, the act required that the annual or lifetime dollar limit on mental health benefits be no lower than the dollar limit for medical and surgical benefits offered by group health insurance plans. The law applied to fully insured state-regulated health plans and self-insured group plans of large employers. These insurance programs had previously been exempt from state parity laws under the Employee Retirement Income Security Act (1974), which sets minimum standards for most pension and health plans in private industry.

Overall, however, the law was weak. There were many loopholes in the legislation that allowed insurance companies and businesses a way out of providing parity insurance. The policy exceptions given by law so weakened the Mental Health Parity Act that it did not benefit a large number of people. First, the act did not stipulate the amount, duration, or scope of mental health benefits, so cost shifting occurred through limits on hospitalization, prescription drugs, and outpatient care; raised co-payments and deductibles; and a changed definition of medical necessity (National Alliance for the Mentally Ill, 2006). Second, the law only applied to group insurance plans that offered mental health benefits *when the law went into effect.* Businesses with fifty or fewer employees were exempt, so small firms easily opted out. Lastly, the law did not apply to group plans if parity provisions would increase costs at least 1 percent. Larger firms had only to prove that parity would increase costs. According to Kjorstad (2003), the law's provisions were "easily circumvented, rendering it relatively ineffective as implemented" (p. 34).

Despite its weakness, the law was effective in raising awareness of the need for insurance coverage for mental health services, and in providing information on the cost of parity in cases in which insurance companies complied with the law. Forty-six states have enacted some form of parity laws, but coverage is uneven. Some states require mental health parity in services, which means that co-payments and deductibles, office visits, and lifetime and annual benefits for mental health, mental illness, and substance abuse must be equal to coverage provided for physical disorders and diseases. Other states have minimum mandated mental health benefit laws, which require some level of services. Still others have mandated mental health "offering laws," which allow health insurers to offer mental health or substance abuse benefits as an optional benefit that costs more but can be taken advantage of or rejected by the consumer. Some states also mandate that when insurers provide optional mental health and substance abuse benefits, these benefits must be at parity with physical health coverage (National Conference of State Legislatures, 2009).

An evaluation showed that cost increases are lowest in plans that include closely monitored managed care, and generous baseline benefits. Prior to the act, it was estimated that parity plans for substance abuse and mental health services would see premium increases ranging from 3.2 percent to 11.4 percent. Table 8.2 shows the average increase in parity plans, with full parity premiums averaging only 3.6 percent, most of which is due to mental health. Mental Health America, a policy think tank and advocacy organization, keeps up-to-date information on state parity laws on its Web site.

Table 8.2 Average Premium Increase Due to Parity

Type of Service	Average Premium Increase		
	Parity in Cost Sharing	Parity in Service Limits	Full Parity
Mental health/ substance abuse	0.4%	1.2%	3.6%
Mental health only	0.3%	1.1%	3.4%
Substance abuse only	0.1%	0.03%	.2%

Source: Adapted from Sing, M., Hill, S., Smolkin, S., & Heiser, N. (1998). *The costs and effects of parity for mental health and substance abuse insurance benefits.* Retrieved May 14, 2006, from http://www.mentalhealth.samhsa.gov/publications/allpubs/Mc99-80/prtyfnix.asp

When the Mental Health Parity Act became law in 1996, it included a sunset provision that stated that the law would expire on September 30, 2001. Although Congress has extended the legislation six times, advocates inside and outside government were never able to get stronger legislation passed. Over the years, the champions inside government were those who were seriously touched by the problems of mental illness and substance abuse in their personal lives. These included the late Democratic senator Paul Wellstone of Minnesota, whose brother was diagnosed with severe mental illness, and Republican senator Pete V. Domenici of New Mexico, whose daughter is atypical schizophrenic. In the House of Representatives, Patrick J. Kennedy (D-RI) acknowledged his treatment for alcoholism and addiction after a 2006 car accident on Capitol Hill, and Jim Ramstad (R-MN) recalled how he woke up in a South Dakota jail cell in 1981 after a blackout from alcohol.

After Wellstone was killed in a plane crash, Democratic senator Edward Kennedy of Massachusetts took up the fight and held town hall meetings around the country. Outside government, the National Alliance for the Mentally Ill, Mental Health America, former First Lady Rosalynn Carter, and Paul Wellstone's son, David, continued to advocate. After twelve years of advocacy, the break came. In September and October 2008, the crisis on Wall Street required congressional action to avert a collapse of the U.S. financial system. Amid this urgency, the policy window opened. Policy entrepreneurs seized the moment and attached the parity legislation to a $700 billion bailout bill. On October 3, 2008, Congress passed the Emergency Economic Stabilization Act of 2008, and just a few hours later, the legislation was signed by President George W. Bush.

Title V, Subtitle B, of the bailout bill is the Paul Wellstone and Pete Domenici Mental Health Parity and Addiction Equity Act of 2008. The legislation includes parity coverage for mental health treatment and substance abuse. The *New York Times* reports that five factors combined to allow the act to gain the necessary votes:

- Researchers have found biological causes and effective treatments for numerous mental illnesses.
- A number of companies now specialize in managing mental health benefits, making the costs to insurers and employers more affordable. The law allows these companies to continue managing benefits.
- Employers have found that productivity tends to increase after workers are treated for mental illnesses and drug or alcohol dependence. Such treatments can reduce the number of lost work days.

- The stigma of mental illness may have faded as people began to see members of the armed forces returning from Iraq and Afghanistan with serious mental problems.
- Parity has proved workable when tried at the state level and in the health insurance program for federal employees, including members of Congress. (Pear 2008, p. 1)

Behind the scenes, the lengthy process of passing mental health parity legislation "was forged in a highly unusual consensus-building process" (Pear, 2008, p. 2). In 2004, Senators Kennedy, Domenici, and Michael B. Enzi (R-WY) brought insurers and employers to the table with mental health advocates, and each side learned to trust each other. A major breakthrough came with the decision to drop the provision that would have required insurers to cover *any and all* conditions listed in the *Diagnostic and Statistical Manual*. "It was an incredible process," said E. Neil Trautwein, a vice president of the National Retail Federation, a trade group. "We built the bill piece by piece from the ground up. It's a good harbinger for future efforts on health care reform" (qtd. by Pear, 2008, p. 2).

The Garrett Lee Smith Memorial Act

On October 21, 2004, President George W. Bush signed the Garrett Lee Smith Memorial Act, the first piece of federal legislation dedicated solely to the prevention of youth suicide. The passage of the act illustrates how solving social problems requires long periods of advocacy and coalition building, but sometimes key pivotal events catapult legislation forward into public law (McMeel, 2005).

Efforts to enact legislation for suicide prevention began in the late 1960s. The federal government established a specialized unit devoted specifically to suicide and suicide prevention at the National Institute of Mental Health. In the 1980s, the Centers for Disease Control and Prevention focused on violence prevention and the increasing rate of youth suicide. It was not until the 1990s, through the newly established Substance Abuse and Mental Health Services Administration, that mobilization began to occur (U.S. Department of Health and Human Services, 2002). A series of alliances formed, including the National Youth Violence Prevention Resource Center, a partnership created by the Centers for Disease Control along with other federal agencies, and the Suicide Prevention Action Network USA. As the only suicide prevention organization specifically dedicated to prevention at the policy-making level, the Suicide Prevention

Action Network utilizes grassroots advocacy to raise support at the community level and awareness at the legislative level to push state and federal lawmakers into action.

In 1999, David Satcher, the U.S. surgeon general, produced the "Call to Action to Prevent Suicide," which was followed by Department of Health and Human Services steering group meetings with experts to refine the focus of the report's goals and objectives (U.S. Public Health Service, 1999). Results were widely disseminated, and public hearings were held to obtain knowledge and input from across the country. The outcome was the National Strategy for Suicide Prevention, a collaborative effort of the Department of Health and Human Services, the Centers for Disease Control and Prevention, the Health Resources and Services Administration, the National Institute of Mental Health, the Indian Health Service, and survivors, clinicians, researchers, and advocates (U.S. Department of Health and Human Services, 2002). This was the first time in history that such a collaborative approach among different executive agencies in the federal government was attempted.

It was, however, the death of Garrett Lee Smith that was the critical incident that opened a policy window and moved suicide prevention proposals forward in Congress. Garrett was the son of Senator Gordon Smith (R-OR). He committed suicide two days before his twenty-second birthday while away at college. Senator Christopher Dodd (D-CT) and Senator Smith proposed the Garrett Lee Smith Memorial Act, which combined two bills, the Campus Care and Counseling Act (2004) and the Youth Suicide, Early Intervention and Prevention Expansion Act (2004), which had already been introduced in Congress. The legislation passed by a recorded vote of 352–64 in the House and a unanimous vote in the Senate.

The Garrett Lee Smith Memorial Act was signed into law in 2004. It amended the Public Health Service Act of 1944 and created a new program at the Substance Abuse and Mental Health Services Administration. Congress authorized $82 million over three years for the program, with the first $11 million available in 2005. Grant applications focus on three areas: development and implementation of state-sponsored youth suicide early prevention programs, campus suicide prevention services, and evaluation and assessment of adolescents at risk of suicide for referral to mental health services in the community. Although the legislation did not provide funding for direct services and the hiring of mental health professionals in suicide prevention, it is an "important first step in establishing critical and needed support for mental and behavioral health services to students on college campuses" (American Psychological Association, 2004, p. 1).

Summary

This chapter has looked at various aspects of health care policy in the United States. The high cost of medical care has led to increasing numbers of uninsured and underinsured Americans. Costs for uncompensated care, or charity care, have continued to rise as hospitals are required to attend to the emergency care needs of uninsured and poor persons. Managed care is the method used by private insurance companies to control the rising costs of medical treatment, as well as by federal and state governments since the early 1990s. In this market economy approach to health care provision, the salaries of CEOs and the profits of insurance companies and pharmaceutical corporations have risen enormously, while employer-provided health care has declined. In addition, increasing health disparities among racial and ethnic groups are the result of the lack of access to quality health care; environmental racism related to poor housing conditions, air quality, and water supplies; and race-related stress due to low-quality education, a lack of culturally competent caregivers, and poor diagnosis and treatment. Living in concentrated areas of urban poverty also affects health by limiting access to grocery stores and health care facilities.

The chapter discussed several major federal policies and programs that are part of the health care system: Medicare, Medicaid, the State Children's Health Insurance Program, and public health clinics. In the area of mental health, we looked at the policy evolution of the community mental health centers, mental health parity, and legislation designed to prevent youth suicide. We also considered the importance of leadership and funding allocations to secure the implementation of policy. Two common policy themes emerged in this chapter. First, managed care is the major method of service delivery in both health and mental health care policy. As clearly evidenced by SCHIP and Medicare Part D prescription coverage, federally funded health care programs and services are implemented through managed care systems organized by states and private-sector organizations. Second, attention is being paid to health care policy in the United States, and the recent passage of the Paul Wellstone and Pete Domenici Mental Health Parity and Addiction Equity Act of 2008 provides some hope that a consensus-building process will be successful over time in leading to the passage of new legislation in the area of health care.

For Further Reading

Angel, R. J., Lein, L., & Henrici, J. (2006). *Poor families in America's health care crisis.* New York: Cambridge University Press.

Cooper, L., & Cates, P. (2006). *Too high a price: The case against restricting gay parenting* (2nd ed.). New York: American Civil Liberties Union Foundation. Retrieved February 22, 2009, from http://www.aclu.org/images/asset_upload_file480_27496.pdf

Crowley, J. E. (2003). *The politics of child support in America.* New York: Cambridge University Press.

Furman, R., & Shukraft, A. (2007). A qualitative study of letters to President Kennedy from persons with mental illness and their families: Using the research poem in policy oriented research. *Journal of Sociology & Social Welfare, 34*(4), 81–95.

Greenburg, M. (2007). Next steps for federal child care policy. *The Future of Children, 17*(2), 73–96

Kaiser Commission on Medicaid and the Uninsured. (2004, June). *Medicaid: A timeline of key developments.* Retrieved May 28, 2006, from http://www.kff.org/medicaid/medicaid_timeline.cfm

President's New Freedom Commission on Mental Health. (2003, July 22). *Achieving the promise: Transforming mental health care in America. Final report* (DHHS Pub. No. SMA-03-3832). Retrieved May 9, 2006, from http://www.mentalhealthcommission.gov/reports/FinalReport/downloads/FinalReport.pdf

Steimo, S., & Watts, J. (1995). It's the institutions, stupid! Why comprehensive National Health Insurance always fails in America. *Journal of Health Politics, Policy, and Law, 20*(2), 329-372.

Svihula, J. (2007). Political economy, moral economy and the Medicare Modernization Act of 2003. *Journal of Sociology & Social Welfare, 35*(1), 157–173.

Vladeck, B. C. (2005). Paying for hospitals' community service. *Health Affairs, 25*(1), 34–43.

References

Abramowitz, M., & Weisman, J. (2007, October 4). Bush vetoes children's health insurance plan. *Washington Post.* Retrieved November 4, 2008, from http://www.washingtonpost.com/wp-dyn/content/article/2007/10/03/AR2007100300116.html?hpid=topnews

American Academy of Pediatrics. (2001, May). Implementation principles and strategies for the State Children's Health Insurance Program. *Pediatrics, 107*(5), 1214–1220. Retrieved May 23, 2006, from http://aappolicy.aappublications.org/cgi/reprint/pediatrics;107/5/1214.pdf

American Psychological Association. (2004, September). *Congressional update: Garrett Lee Smith Memorial Act passes House and Senate.* Retrieved May 9, 2006, from http://www.apa.org/ppo/issues/eglsupdt904.html

Angell, M. (2004, July 15). The truth about the drug companies. *New York Review of Books, 51*(12). Retrieved May 22, 2006, from http://www.nybooks.com/articles/17244

Arias, E. (2007). United States life tables, 2004. *National Vital Statistics Reports, 56*(9). Retrieved March 12, 2008, from http://www.cdc.gov/nchs/data/nvsr/nvsr56/nvsr56_09.pdf

Balanced Budget Act of 1997, 47 U.S.C. § 309(j)(14)(A)-(B) (1997).

Bownds, L. (2003). Consumer-driven health plans: More choice is not always better. *Journal of Economic Issues, 37*(2), 425–433.

Byck, G. R. (2000). A comparison of the socioeconomic and health status characteristics of uninsured, State Children's Health Insurance Program–eligible children in the United States with those of other groups of insured children: Implications for policy. *Pediatrics, 106*, 14–21.

Campus Care and Counseling Act, S. 2215, 108th Cong., 2nd sess. (2004).

Centers for Medicare and Medicaid Services. (2006a). *Medicare and you, 2006.* Retrieved February 1, 2006, from http://www.medicare.gov/publications/pubs/pdf/10050.pdf

Centers for Medicare and Medicaid Services. (2006b). *Medicaid waivers and demonstrations list.* Retrieved May 22, 2006, from http://www.cms.hhs.gov/MedicaidStWaivProgDemoPGI/MWDL/list.asp#TopOfPage

Companypay.com. (2009). *Executive compensation: CEO salaries, bonuses, stock options.* Retrieved March 6, 2009, from http://www.companypay.com/industry index.asp

Community Mental Health Centers Construction Act, Pub. L. No. 88-164 (1963).

Consolidated Omnibus Budget Reconciliation Act, 2 U.S.C. 636, 641 (1985).

Consolidated Security, Disaster Assistance, and Continuing Funding Appropriations Act, Pub. L. No. 110-329 (2009).

Cooper, L., & Cates, P. (2006). *Too high a price: The case against restricting gay parenting* (2nd ed.). New York: American Civil Liberties Union Foundation. Retrieved February 22, 2009, from http://www.aclu.org/images/asset_upload_file480_27496.pdf

Copeland, V. (2005). African Americans: Disparities in health care access and utilization. *Health and Social Work, 30*(3), 265–270.

Coulton, C. J., & Pandey, S. (1992). Geographic concentrations of poverty and risk to children in urban neighborhoods. *American Behavioral Scientist, 35*(3), 238–257.

Cunningham, P. (2006). Medicaid/SCHIP cuts and hospital emergency room use. *Health Affairs, 25*(1), 237–247.

Cutler, D. L., Bevilacqua, J., & McFarland, B. H. (2003). Four decades of community mental health: A symphony in four movements. *Community Mental Health Journal, 39*(5), 381–398.

Deficit Reduction Act, 42 U.S.C. 1396p and 1396r-5 (2005).

DeNavas-Walt, C., Proctor, B. D., & Smith, J. (2007). *Income, poverty, and health insurance coverage in the United States: 2006* (Current Population Reports P60-233). Washington, DC: U.S. Census Bureau.

Dubey, L., Hill, I., & Kenney, G. (2002, October). *Five things everyone should know about SCHIP* (Assessing the New Federalism Policy Brief No. A-55). Retrieved May 2, 2006, from http://www.urban.org/UploadedPDF/310570_A55.pdf

Ellen, I. G., Mijanovich, T., & Dillman, K. N. (2001). Neighborhood effects on health: Exploring the links and assessing the evidence. *Journal of Urban Affairs, 23*(3-4), 391-408.

Emergency Economic Stabilization Act of 2008, Pub. L. No. 110-343 (2008).

Emergency Medical Treatment and Active Labor Act, Pub. L. No. 99-272 (1985).

Employee Benefits Security Administration. (2008). *FAQs about COBRA continuation health coverage.* Retrieved March 9, 2008, from http://www.dol.gov/ebsa/faqs/faq_consumer_cobra.html

Employee Retirement Income Security Act, 29 U.S.C 1001 et seq. (1974).

Families USA. (2002, June). *Bitter pill: The rising prices of prescription drugs for older Americans.* Retrieved December 19, 2005, from http://www.familiesusa.org/assets/pdfs/BitterPillreport74f9.pdf

Family Opportunity Act, 42 U.S.C. 1396p and 1396r-5, Chapter 6, Subchapter A (2005).

Fellner, J. (2006). *New data on the prevalence of mental illness in US prisons.* Retrieved May 18, 2007, from http://hrw.org/english/docs/2007/01/10/usdom15040.htm

Foundation for Taxpayer and Consumer Rights. (2006). *Health care: Get the pork out of health insurance.* Retrieved February 6, 2006, from http://www.consumerwatchdog.org/healthcare/healthcosts

Galambos, C., Rocha, C., McCarter, A., & Chansuthus, D. (2004). Managed care and mental health: Personal realities. *Journal of Health and Social Policy, 20*(1), 1-20.

Garrett Lee Smith Memorial Act, 42 U.S.C. 201 note, 290bb-36 note (2004).

Gellad, W., Huskamp, H., Phillips, K., & Haas, J. (2006). How the new Medicare drug benefit could affect vulnerable populations. *Health Affairs, 25*(1), 248-255.

Gold, M., Sparer, M., & Chu, K. (1996). Medicaid managed care: Lessons from five states. *Health Affairs, 15*(3), 153-166.

Gorin, S., & Moniz, C. (2004). Will the United States ever have universal health care? *Health and Social Work, 29*(4), 340-344.

Gross, D. J., Schondelmeyer, S. W., & Purvis, L. (2008). *Rx watchdog report: Trends in manufacturer prices of brand name prescription drugs used by Medicare beneficiaries* (Research Report No. 2008-5). Washington DC: AARP. Retrieved March 12, 2008, from http://assets.aarp.org/rgcenter/health/2008_05_watchdog_q407.pdf

Health Centers Renewal Act of 2007, Pub. L. No. 110-355 (2007).

Hunt, J. W. (2005). Community health centers' impact on the political and economic environment: The Massachusetts example. *Journal of Ambulatory Care Management, 28*(4), 340-347.

Hurley, R. E., Pham, H. H., & Claxton, G. (2005, December 6). A widening rift in access and quality: Growing evidence of economic disparities. *Health Affairs,* W5-556-W5-576. Retrieved July 21, 2009, from http://content.healthaffairs.org/cgi/reprint/hlthaff.w5.566v1

Kaiser Commission on Medicaid and the Uninsured. (2005). *Health insurance coverage in America: 2004 data update.* Retrieved May 6, 2006, from http://www.kff.org/uninsured/upload/Health-Coverage-in-America-2004-Data-Update-Report.pdf

Kaiser Commission on Medicaid and the Uninsured. (2006a). *Deficit Reduction Act of 2005: Implications for Medicaid.* Retrieved May 6, 2006, from http://www.kff.org/medicaid/upload/7465.pdf

Kaiser Commission on Medicaid and the Uninsured. (2006b). *Who needs Medicaid?* Retrieved May 6, 2006, from http://www.kff.org/medicaid/upload/7496.pdf

Kaiser Commission on Medicaid and the Uninsured. (2008). *State Children's Health Insurance Program (SCHIP): Reauthorization history.* Retrieved November 4, 2008, from http://www.kff.org/medicaid/upload/7743.pdf

Kaiser Family Foundation. (2003a). *Medicare and prescription drugs fact sheet.* Retrieved March 12, 2008, from http://www.kff.org/medicare/upload/Medicare-and-Prescription-Drugs-Fact-Sheet-Fact-Sheet.pdf

Kaiser Family Foundation. (2003b). *Medicare and prescription drug spending chartpack.* Retrieved March 12, 2008, from http://www.kff.org/medicare/loader.cfm?url=/commonspot/security/getfile.cfm&PageID=14382

Kaiser Family Foundation. (2006). *Statehealthfacts.org: Your source for state health data.* Retrieved May 3, 2006, from http://www.statehealthfacts.org/cgi-bin/healthfacts.cgi

Kjorstad, M. C. (2003). The current and future state of mental health insurance parity legislation. *Psychiatric Rehabilitation Journal, 27*(1), 34–42.

Lefkowitz, B. (2005). The health center story: Forty years of commitment. *Journal of Ambulatory Care Management, 28*(4), 295–303.

Mahan, D. (2003). *Out-of-bounds: Rising prescription drug prices for seniors* (Families USA Publication No. 03-106). Washington, DC: Families USA. Retrieved March 12, 2008, from http://familiesusa.org/assets/pdfs/Out_of_Boundsab79.pdf

Manning, W., Liu, C., Stoner, T., Gray, D., Lurie, N., Popkin, M., & Christianson, J. (1999). Outcomes for Medicaid beneficiaries with schizophrenia under a prepaid mental health carve-out. *Journal of Behavioral Health Services and Research, 26*(4), 442–450.

Martens, W. (2001). A review of physical and mental health in homeless persons. *Public Health Review, 29*(1), 13–33.

McCloskey, A. (2000, July). *Cost overdose: Growth in drug spending for the elderly 1992–2010.* Washington, DC: Families USA. Retrieved March 12, 2008, from http://www.familiesusa.org/assets/pdfs/drugoddofd.pdf

McMeel, L. (2005). *The Garrett Lee Smith Memorial Act: A policy analysis.* Jane Addams College of Social Work, University of Illinois at Chicago. Unpublished paper.

Medicare Prescription Drug, Improvement, and Modernization Act, 42 U.S.C. 1396kk-1 (2003).

Medicare, Medicaid, and SCHIP Extension Act of 2007, Pub. L. No. 110-173 (2007).

Mental Health Parity Act, 29 U.S.C. 1185a and 42 U.S.C. 300gg-5 (1996).

Mental Health Systems Act, 42 U.S.C. 9511 *et seq.* (1980).
Mental Retardation Facilities and Community Mental Health Centers Construction Act, 42 U.S.C. 2689 *et seq.*, 6001 *et seq.* (1963).
National Alliance for the Mentally Ill. (2006). *The Mental Health Parity Act of 1996*. Retrieved May 14, 2006, from http://www.nami.org/Content/ContentGroups/E-News/1996/The_Mental_Health_Parity_Act_of_1996.htm
National Conference of State Legislatures. (2009). *State laws mandating or regulating mental health benefits*. Retrieved July 21, 2009, from http://www.ncsl.org/default.aspx?tabid=14352
Omnibus Budget Reconciliation Act, 42 U.S.C. 8621 *et seq.* (1981).
Organisation for Economic Co-operation and Development. (2004). *OECD health data*. Washington, DC: Author.
Paul Wellstone and Pete Domenici Mental Health Parity and Addiction Equity Act of 2008, Title V, Subtitle B of the Emergency Economic Stabilization Act of 2008, Pub. L. No. 110-343 (2008).
Pear, R. (2006, January 21). Medicare woes take high toll on mentally ill. *New York Times*. Retrieved January 27, 2006, from http://www.nytimes.com/2006/01/21/politics/21drug.html?ex=1148443200&en=e9203906f7ca6d4a&ei=5070
Pear, R. (2008, October 5). Bailout provides more mental health coverage. *New York Times*. Retrieved October 29, 2008, from http://www.nytimes.com/2008/10/06/washington/06mental.html?ref=policy
PolicyLink. (2002, November). *Reducing health disparities through a focus on communities*. Retrieved May 14, 2006, from http://www.policylink.org/pdfs/Health Disparities.pdf
Public Health Service Act, Pub. L. No. 78-410 (1944).
Rackl, L. (2006, January 23). Madigan: Hike charity health care. *Chicago Sun-Times*. Retrieved May 7, 2006, from http://www.suntimes.com/output/news/cst-nws-hosp23.html
Reconnecting Homeless Youth Act of 2008, Pub. L. No. 110-378 (2008).
Rocha, C. J. (1996). Use of health insurance in county funded clinics: Issues for health care reform. *Health and Social Work, 21*(1), 16–22.
Rosenbaum, S., & Shin, P. (2006, March). *Health care centers reauthorization: An overview of achievements and challenges*. Retrieved May 6, 2006, from http://www.kff.org/uninsured/upload/7471.pdf
Shorter, E. (2000). *The Kennedy family and the history of mental retardation*. Philadelphia: Temple University Press.
Sirven J., & Morrow, D. (2007). Fly the graying skies: A question of competency vs. age. *Neurology, 68*, 630–631.
Smith, E. B. (2005, April 26). Katrina closures crowd hospitals that are open. *USA Today*, p. 1b.
Social Security Act, Pub L. No. 74-271, 49 Stat 620 (1935).
Social Security Amendments, 42 U.S.C. 1383(d)(2) (1972).
Solomon, J. (2006). *The illusion of choice: Vulnerable Medicaid beneficiaries being placed in scaled-back "benchmark" benefit packages*. Retrieved February 22, 2009, from http://www.cbpp.org/9-14-06health.htm

Starfield, B. (1992). *Primary care: Concept, evaluation, and policy.* New York: Oxford University Press.

State of Illinois & Blagojevich, R. R. (2005). *All Kids: Illinois' program to provide healthcare for all kids.* Retrieved May 2, 2006, from http://www.allkidscovered.com

Sullivan, K. (2002–2003). Understanding the health care reform debate: A primer for the perplexed. *Social Policy, 33*(2), 53–58.

Tobin, J. (2005). *The Mental Health Parity Act of 1996 and the Senator Paul Wellstone Mental Health Equitable Treatment Act of 2003.* Jane Addams College of Social Work, University of Illinois at Chicago. Unpublished paper.

U.S. Department of Health and Human Services. (2002). *National strategy for suicide prevention.* Washington, DC: Author.

U.S. Department of Health and Human Services. (2005). *Health, United States, 2005. With chartbook on trends in the health of Americans* (DHHS Publication No. 2005-1232). Retrieved May 22, 2006, from http://www.cdc.gov/nchs/data/hus/hus05.pdf

U.S. Department of Health and Human Services. (n.d.). *Insure kids now! Linking the nation's children to health insurance.* Retrieved May 10, 2006, from http://www.insurekidsnow.gov/

U.S. Public Health Service. (1999). *The surgeon general's call to action to prevent suicide.* Washington, DC: Author.

Wiatrowski, W. J. (2004, August). Medical and retirement plan coverage: Exploring the decline in recent years. *Monthly Labor Review Online, 127*(8), 29–36. Retrieved May 22, 2006, from http://www.bls.gov/opub/mlr/2004/08/art4full.pdf

Wolf, R. (2006, April 27). 1 in 5 pay more in Medicare Rx plan. *USA Today*, p. 1.

Youth Suicide, Early Intervention and Prevention Expansion Act, S. 2175, 108th Cong., 2nd sess. (2004).

Zuvekas, A. (2005). Health centers and the health care system. *Journal of Ambulatory Care Management, 28*(4), 331–339.

CHAPTER 9

The Care and Support of Children

In chapter 7, we looked closely at work and employment in the context of globalization and economic recession. Our review focused on policies that relate to unemployment, layoffs, job search, and retraining. We also looked at the minimum wage and earned income tax credit, which are two policies that provide minimum income support for workers. A major issue not previously addressed is working families' need for child care. This is an issue that particularly affects single parents who spend a major part of their time in the workforce in order to provide for themselves and their children. In many ways, the need for child care affects the family's ability to work and, conversely, the need to work affects the family's ability to care for children.

This chapter first addresses the issues and policies related to the care and support of children. We look at the ways in which parents seek to reduce child care costs and, at the same time, find quality care for their children. Many children are cared for by family members, and the working parents of small children often work different shifts so one parent can be at home with the children while the other works. Child care costs consume a large portion of family income, particularly among low-income or working poor families who do not receive subsidized day care for their children.

The next part of this chapter illustrates a major theme of the book: there is no uniform definition of the family. Families in the United States take many forms: heterosexual married-couple families with children, single-parent families, blended families, grandparents raising grandchildren, gay and lesbian couples with children, and so on. Consequently, we define families by their function, not by their structure. In this chapter, we look at structural changes in the family that result from divorce, and how divorce and child custody affect the care of children. We also review some effects of divorce on children and note recent changes in divorce law, as some states require the filing of joint custody plans and pre-divorce counseling. We also address gay parenting and adoption, especially as these issues relate to policies resulting from judicial decisions in these areas. We also look at the passage of the citizen-initiated statute on the November 2008 ballot in the state of Arkansas, an example of direct democracy. The Unmarried Couple Adoption Ban prohibits single parents from adopting children or serving as foster parents. At the other end of the spectrum of caring for children, new technologies related to sperm donation and surrogate parenting make nontraditional childbearing and parenting possible. We also discuss legal definitions of parenting roles that can be used in the United States and Canada to defend the legal rights of both heterosexual and gay and lesbian stepparents and other non-biological parents.

Lastly, our discussion looks at specific policies for child care and support, including child care block grants, Head Start, the child and dependent care tax credit, and child support paid by the non-custodial parent. These illustrate the wide range of policies that provide some relief for the growing costs of child care for working families. Overall, however, child care costs are borne by the family because child care is not included as a part of public education for all children in the United States.

Working and Caring for Children

The norms of work and child care are changing in the United States. These include the entry of women with children into the workforce and the work requirement for women receiving welfare benefits, the increasing cost of child care for working mothers, and the impact of divorce on parents' abilities to meet their child care responsibilities. We begin this chapter with a quote that we think captures the essence of some of the current major issues in child care: "Mothers face a damned if you do and damned if you don't set of choices, in which they are expected to bring home income but are admonished for leaving their children in the care of others" (Gerson, 1998, p. 13).

During the Industrial Revolution in the late nineteenth century, when families began moving to cities, it was considered best (from a child development perspective) for mothers to stay home with their children. At that time, non-maternal care was considered substandard care of last resort. These beliefs were tied to individualism, self-sufficiency, and the belief that mothers made the best caretakers for their children (Cahan & Bromer, 2003). For example, in the 1930s, the original purpose of the Aid to Dependent Children program was to support widows in child rearing until their children reached the age of eighteen. However, in the last twenty-five years of the century or so, beliefs regarding the place of work in the lives of women began to shift. The prevailing view now is that single women who receive public assistance should work as well as rear their children. At the same time, the public holds different beliefs regarding work among more affluent women who choose to rear children as their primary job. In general, non-working mothers are mainly married white women, and those with at least a year of college. There is no similar trend among mothers who are single, African American, and Hispanic, or among those who have not pursued education beyond high school (National Center for Policy Analysis, 2001). However, for many mothers in the middle class, the days when a single earner in two-parent families could provide an adequate family income have passed. As a result, two-earner families are common, and the number of full-time homemakers is decreasing.

For the past quarter century, mothers have entered the workplace in growing numbers. Between 1990 and 2006, the percentage of families with children under age six in which both parents were working increased from 54 percent to 61.6 percent (U.S. Census Bureau, 2006a). In 2000, three out of five preschoolers had mothers in the workforce, and 79 percent of mothers with children ages six to seventeen worked (U.S. Department of Labor, 2002). In 1950, 60 percent of married women stayed home to care for children, compared to only 15 percent by the end of the century (Gerson, 1998). Mothers in the workforce are not merely working for an extra income. Due to the changing economy, male earnings have stagnated. The decline of high-paying manufacturing jobs and the increase of low-paying service jobs have resulted in both parents working, and longer hours on the job. By 2006, married-couple families in which both parents work constituted 53.5 percent of all married couples in the workforce (U.S. Census Bureau, 2006b). Over half of the women who work bring home at least half of all household income. In two-paycheck families, one in four women earns as much or more than her husband. Most women in today's society realize the need to work, and most families depend on their earnings. Paid work for both parents in the family is the key determinant of whether their children live in poverty or in middle-class comfort. But there is a trade-off between the value of economic resources and the amount of time available for parent-child interactions (Hernandez, 2003). Parental working conditions and longer working hours spent away from home are associated with lower levels of verbal ability and higher levels of behavior problems in their children. For single parents, earning enough to make ends meet may mean having to take on more than one job, which increases time away from children and places stress on family functioning.

The need for single parents and for both parents in two-parent families to work has produced a generation of children who spend time at home without adult supervision. The term *latchkey kids* is used to describe these children. The U.S. Census Bureau (2000) estimates there are around 7 million latchkey children between the ages of five and thirteen. The situation of children caring for themselves is more prevalent for middle school children than for elementary school children: 9 percent of all children ages five to eleven care for themselves, as opposed to 41 percent of children ages twelve to fourteen, and 2 percent of five-year-olds as opposed to 48 percent of fourteen-year-olds. The Children's Defense Fund (2003) suggests the numbers are higher than the Census Bureau estimates. They estimate that half of all children ages twelve to fourteen are home alone for an average of seven hours per week.

Two reasons that the children of working parents are left alone are the rising cost of child care and the loss of subsidized assistance when children reach age thirteen. This growing problem is also due to the federal government's retraction of comprehensive child care services that were available to working families during World War II. Alston (2006) writes:

> Fathers had gone off to war, and mothers had gone into industry, making the tanks, planes, uniforms and bullets the soldiers needed. The children went home with keys on chains, ribbons, a piece of string tied around their necks. Some mothers chose to work the night shift, called the "swing shift" and tucked their children in bed, locked the door and went to the factory. The country's response was prompt and comprehensive. Programs were set up in factories, in schools and community centers, to gather in all the children whose parents were busy with the war effort. These programs closed promptly when the war ended, and women resumed their housewife roles.

Leaving children without adult supervision puts children at risk. Researchers have found that unsupervised children are more likely to be depressed, and more likely to experiment with cigarettes, drugs, and alcohol (Children's Defense Fund, 2003). Keeping children busy after school is the best way to avoid some of the potential pitfalls. The latchkey issue crosses class lines, but children from the poorest families are most vulnerable when they are left at home alone. Low-income children, who have the greatest need for after-school programs, are less likely to have access to constructive activities during their out-of-school time. After-school programs such as Boys and Girls Clubs may be available in poorer, more dangerous neighborhoods, but barriers to participation include the lack transportation to and from these programs, prohibitive costs, lack of comprehensive programming, and weak coordination with other youth services (Quinn, 1999).

Child Care

The Cost of Child Care

As the prior discussion makes clear, the increase in the numbers of families in which both parents work or the sole wage earner is a single parent puts pressure on families to find ways to minimize the risk to their children. They attempt to fill their need for the supervision and care of their children by using outside sources of child care. In seeking outside sources of care, they face two issues. The first is how to find care they can afford, and the second is how to find quality care. In order to understand how parents deal with the problems of child care, several factors need to be considered. Which caregivers do families use? How many families pay for child care? How much do they pay for child care? And what portions of the children needing care are left home alone? Table 9.1 shows the types of child care used by parents.

In 2005, parents reported needing child care for a total of 57,470,000 children. Of these children, 10,238,000 children (52.2%) under the age of five (U.S. Census Bureau, 2005a) and 17,012,000 children (44.9%) between the ages of five and fourteen (U.S. Census Bureau, 2005b) were cared for by a family member or other relative. Another 24.9 percent were cared for in some type of formal day care (U.S. Census Bureau, 2005a, 2005b). The rest were cared for in a variety of other types of settings. Most interesting is that 36.6 percent of the children under five had no regular arrangements for child care (U.S. Census Bureau, 2005a), and that 14 percent of the children over five were left home to take care of themselves (U.S. Census Bureau, 2005c).

Families have devised a variety of child care arrangements to control the growing costs of child care. Twenty-five percent of all working couples with children are "split-shift" couples: the mother cares for children while the father works, then the father cares for the children while the mother works. A review of the literature found that among married couples below the poverty level, low-income married mothers rely heavily on their husbands, who provide 42 percent of child care (American Psychological Association, 2006). This reduces child care costs but leaves less time for overall family relationships. The rate of split-shift couples among young dual-earner families with preschool children is twice that of other groups.

Single mothers in low-income families rely heavily on relatives to assist with child care. Depending on the age of the children, relatives living in the

Table 9.1 Parental Child Care Arrangements for Preschoolers Living with Mother, by Age and Employment Status of Mother

Age	Number of children	Designated parent[1]	Other parent[1]	Sibling	Grandparent	Other relative	Day care center	Nursery, preschool	Head Start	School	Nonrelative in child's home	Family day care	Other nonrelative in provider's home	Self-care	No regular arrangement	Multiple arrangements
Under 5	19,633	851	3,089	522	4,489	1,287	2,649	1,236	204	711	732	1,078	848	11	7,191	3,364
		4.3%	15.7%	2.7%	22.9%	6.6%	13.5%	6.3%	1.0%	3.6%	3.7%	5.5%	4.3%	0.1%	36.6%	17.1%
5–14	37,837	1,446	5,754	3,230	4,691	1,891	1,744	326	54	35,541	877	507	1,013	5,285		
		3.8%	15.2%	8.5%	12.4%	5.0%	4.6%	0.9%	0.1%	93.9%	2.3%	1.3%	2.7%	14.0%		

[1]Time in parental care is only shown for women who worked as employees or were in school.

Source: Adapted from U.S. Census Bureau. (2005). *Table 3A: Child care arrangements of grade-schoolers 5 to 14 years old living with mother, by employment status of mother and selected characteristics* (Survey of Income and Program Participation, 2004 Panel, Wave 4). Retrieved February 28, 2008, from http://www.census.gov/population/socdemo/child/ppl-2005/tab03A.xls; U.S. Census Bureau. (2005). *Table 1A: Child care arrangements of preschoolers under 5 years old living with mother, by employment status of mother and selected characteristics* (Survey of Income and Program Participation, 2004 Panel, Wave 4). Retrieved February 28, 2008, from http://www.census.gov/population/socdemo/child/ppl-2005/tab01A.xls

same house provide between 44.9 percent and 52.2 percent of primary child care for employed single mothers living below the poverty level. Table 9.2 shows that only about 35 percent of all child care is paid for by the child's parents. And when the mother's marital status is factored in, the percentage of parents paying for child care varies only slightly. However, when the amount parents pay for child care is considered, major differences emerge. Table 9.3 shows those differences. The average monthly family income of mothers who are married is nearly two-and-a-half times higher than that of families in which the mothers are widowed, separated, or divorced, and about three times that of families in which the women have never been married. Thus, even though the amount that unmarried women pay for child care is substantially less than that paid by married women, the percentage of their income allocated to child care is nearly double that of widowed, separated, and divorced mothers (10.6% vs. 5.6%), and that of never-married women is 2.2 times higher (12.3%).

Child care consumes a large share of the income of working poor families. According to the March 2002 Current Population Survey, 40 percent of working poor single mothers spend at least half of their cash income on child care. Among working poor married families, 21 percent spend

Table 9.2 Families with Employed Mothers Who Pay for Child Care, Spring 2005

		Making child care payments	
Characteristics	**Total**	**Number**	**Percent**
Families with Children under 15 Years	22,961	7,989	34.8
Marital Status of Mother			
Married	15,988	5,622	35.2
Widowed, separated, divorced	3,417	1,159	33.9
Never married	3,556	1,208	34.0
Age of Mother			
15–24 years	1,758	700	39.8
25–34 years	8,026	3,350	41.7
35+ years	13,177	3,938	29.9

Note: Omits families with no income.
Source: Adapted from U.S. Census Bureau. (2005). *Table 5: Families with employed mothers that make child care payments, by age groups and selected characteristics: Spring 2005* (Survey of Income and Program Participation, 2004 Panel, Wave 4). Retrieved February 29, 2008, from http://www.census.gov/population/socdemo/child/ppl-2005/tab05.xls

Table 9.3 Average Weekly Child Care Expenditures of Families with Employed Mothers That Make Payments, Spring 2005

Characteristics	Number (in thousands)	Average weekly child care expenditures (in dollars)	Average monthly family income (in dollars)	Percent of family's monthly income spent on child care[1]	Average monthly mother's income (in dollars)	Ratio of child care expenditures to mother's income[2]
Families with Children under 15 Years	7,989	107	7,261	6.4	3,521	13.2
Marital Status of Mother						
Married	5,622	116	8,944	5.6	3,915	12.9
Widowed, separated, divorced	1,159	89	3,639	10.7	3,185	12.2
Never married	1,208	83	2,908	12.3	2,008	17.9

Note: Average expenditures per week are among families making child care payments.

[1] Percent is a ratio of average monthly child care payments (prorated from weekly averages) to average family monthly income.
[2] Ratio is average of monthly child care payments (prorated from weekly averages) to mother's average monthly income, shown as a percentage.

Source: U.S. Census Bureau. (2005). *Table 6: Average weekly child care expenditures of families with employed mothers that make payments: Spring 2005. Survey of Income and Program Participation, 2004 Panel, Wave 4.* Retrieved February 29, 2008, from http://www.census.gov/population/socdemo/child/ppl-2005/tab06.xls

between 40 percent and 50 percent of their income on child care, and 23 percent spend more than half of their cash income on child care (Wertheimer, 2003). Single women earning minimum wage must spend half their earnings to pay for market-rate child care. Table 9.3 shows child care expenditures as a proportion of monthly earnings. The largest percentages of expenses are borne by the lowest-wage workers, who on average spend more than a third of their wages on child care. The second-highest category is single mothers, who spend on average 17 percent of their income on child care. Thus, those who can least afford it spend a higher proportion of their income on child care.

The percentages of children who have no child care but rather are left home to take care of themselves are both startling and disturbing (see tables 9.4 and 9.5). Also, the fact that a substantial number of people evidently did not provide information about children left at home alone

Table 9.4 Children Living with Mother and in Self-Care by Age of Child, Family Income, Poverty Level, and TANF Assistance Status, Spring 2005

Characteristics	Child 5 to 8 years			Child 9 to 11 years			Child 12 to 14 years		
	Total	In self-care		Total	In self-care		Total	In self-care	
		Number	Percent		Number	Percent		Number	Percent
LIVING WITH MOTHER	14,362	269	1.9	11,575	1,135	9.8	11,901	3,881	32.6
FAMILY INCOME (MONTHLY)									
Less than $1,500	2,160	43	2.0	1,696	156	9.2	1,678	413	24.6
$1,500–$2,999	2,971	65	2.2	2,347	189	8.1	2,343	621	26.5
$3,000–$4,499	2,392	27	1.1	2,000	212	10.6	2,010	615	30.6
$4,500 and over	6,519	125	1.9	5,257	566	10.8	5,699	2,188	38.4
Missing	320	9	2.8	275	13	4.7	171	44	25.7
FAMILY POVERTY LEVEL									
Below poverty level	2,543	62	2.4	2,070	175	8.5	1,963	450	22.9
At or above poverty level	11,498	199	1.7	9,229	948	10.3	9,767	3,387	34.7
100–199 percent of poverty level	3,493	59	1.7	2,629	190	7.2	2,606	671	25.7
200+ percent of poverty level	8,006	139	1.7	6,600	759	11.5	7,160	2,716	37.9
Missing	320	9	2.8	275	13	4.7	171	44	25.7
RECEIVED TANF									
No	14,103	266	1.9	11,359	1,116	9.8	11,710	3,834	32.7
Yes	259	3	1.2	216	20	9.3	191	46	24.1

Source: U.S. Census Bureau. (2005). *Table 4: Children in self-care, by age of child, employment status of mother, and selected characteristics for children living.* Survey of Income and Program Participation, 2004 Panel, Wave 4. Retrieved February 29, 2008, from http://www.census.gov/population/socdemo/child/ppl-2005/tab05.xls

Table 9.5 Children in Self-Care by Age of Child, Residence with Mother or Father, and Marital Status of Mother, Spring 2005

Characteristics	Child 5 to 8 years			Child 9 to 11 years			Child 12 to 14 years		
	Total	In self-care		Total	In self-care		Total	In self-care	
		Number	Percent		Number	Percent		Number	Percent
TOTAL	14,889	284	1.9	12,097	1,196	9.9	12,584	4,135	32.9
LIVING WITH FATHER ONLY	527	16	3.0	522	60	11.5	683	254	37.2
LIVING WITH MOTHER	14,362	269	1.9	11,575	1,135	9.8	11,901	3,881	32.6
MARITAL STATUS OF MOTHER									
Married	10,590	172	1.6	8,363	754	9.0	8,435	2,698	32.0
Widowed, separated, divorced	1,844	57	3.1	1,959	270	13.8	2,306	862	37.4
Never married	1,926	40	2.1	1,253	111	8.9	1,160	320	27.6

Source: U.S. Census Bureau. (2005). *Table 4: Children in self-care, by age of child, employment status of mother, and selected characteristics for children living.* Survey of Income and Program Participation, 2004 Panel, Wave 4. Retrieved February 29, 2008, from http://www.census.gov/population/socdemo/child/ppl-2005/tab05.xls

means that we cannot be sure how well the numbers reported reflect the true rate of children left home alone. For children under eight, income is less of a factor in the number of children left at home alone. People at the lowest income levels do leave more children at home (2.4%) than do people at higher levels of income (1.7%). Although the percentages are small, the number of children (459,000) left at home alone is still significant. The situation becomes even more serious when children over eight years old are involved. As income goes up, so does the percentage of children over eight left at home, with 33.8 percent of children in families with incomes less than $1,500 a month left at home. For families with incomes from $1,500 to $2,999 a month, the percentage is 34.6 percent; for families with incomes from $3,000 to $4,499, the percentage is 41.2 percent; and for families with incomes over $4,500 a month, the figure is 49.2 percent. Why higher-income families are more likely to leave their children at home alone is an intriguing question that deserves investigation. Table 9.5 shows that widowed, separated, and divorced women are the most likely to leave children to care for themselves.

Quality Child Care

Finding quality day care is a significant barrier to employment for low-income mothers. In general, women's decisions about whether and how much to work depend upon both the availability and cost of child care. Less than a third of Americans work the standard work schedule of Monday through Friday, 8:00 a.m. to 5:00 p.m. (Presser, 1998). One in five works evenings, nights, or rotating schedules. Among low-income families, these numbers increase to 50 percent. Even though up to half of the low-wage jobs require non-standard work schedules, most child care centers do not have weekend and evening hours, and those that do offer non-standard schedules are much more expensive. These barriers often cause poor workers to lose their jobs or severely limit employment opportunities, particularly among mothers who are young and single, who are members of a minority group, and who have low educational attainment (Hernandez, 2003). These barriers can be the difference between maintaining self-sufficiency and returning to welfare. As we discussed in chapter 6, there are many reasons why welfare leavers return, and problems with child care are one of the most important. The story in box 9.1 points out the challenges of a non-standard work schedule and how this affects children. Karen could not afford the cost of day care after she lost subsidized child care.

Box 9.1 Parenting and Work

When Karen was on welfare, subsidized day care was provided until she finished vocational school. When she finished school, she tried to work two jobs.

If I hadn't had Child Place, I couldn't have gone to school. I couldn't afford $500 a month and that's average—that was the average cost. I couldn't afford day care when I worked for the nursing service. I would work 11 p.m. until 7 a.m. I only did that when my daughter got old enough to be responsible. How old was she then? Fifteen. . . . It was so hard to do that. I would go home from that job and the kids would go off to school. Then, I would be at the clinic by 9 a.m. It would burn me out and I wouldn't have any energy when the kids got home. I would be sleepy and couldn't do anything with them. I'd be able to come home and fix them supper and fall into bed. I wouldn't spend time with them and their behavior went down. . . . Their grades were going down.

Karen made the decision to stop working nights, leaving her part-time day job as her only source of income. She suffers the consequences financially but feels better about her ability to parent.

I realized that they needed more of me and that I couldn't be gone that long from them without severe consequences—consequences that I couldn't live with. . . . It was a value decision.

In a study of centers serving children of all income levels, Phillips (1995) found that about 15 percent were low-quality settings that threatened the health or development of children, in which there were safety hazards such as broken glass, poor sanitation practices, unresponsive caregivers, and few toys. An equal percentage of child care settings were rated as high quality in promoting child development. Although the majority of child care centers (70%) were not dangerous to children, they also did not facilitate child development. Research studies consistently show that high-quality care enhances children's emotional, social, cognitive, and physical development, while low-quality care has negative effects on children, particularly if they do not experience secure relationships at home (Cahan & Bromer, 2003; Parcel & Menaghan, 1997). Research on the quality of child care programs indicates that child development progresses when there are fewer children per care group and when there are more adult staff members. Children also do well with caregivers who are sensitive and responsive to children, well educated, and well paid, so that staff turnover is minimal. Upper-income children are more likely than middle- or low-income peers to be cared for by trained, better-compensated, and more sensitive teachers in developmentally appropriate settings. One factor that characterizes low-quality child care programs is the high turnover rate of knowledgeable and experienced workers. The salaries of child care workers are, and have been historically, among the lowest of any profession. Low wages are associated with low-quality care and high staff turnover. High staff turnover rates have negative consequences for children by inhibiting stable and nurturing relationships with adults.

Another factor affecting the quality of child care is the caregivers' level of education and training. There is an emerging state-by-state movement to institute standards and training for child care workers, and several states offer tiered reimbursement rates for subsidized child care based on standards of accreditation. The Department of Labor funded a national initiative to develop paraprofessional child care workers through training and certification. The Quality Child Care Initiative was designed to make the child care industry one of professional service, stability, and career advancement. Over a three-year period, thirty-one states and the District of Columbia obtained more than $12 million to develop and implement a self-sustaining statewide system to educate child development providers using a registered apprenticeship model in partnership with local industries.

Comprehensive skill standards have been developed by the American Federation of Teachers (Education and Training Voluntary Partnership, 2003). The National Association for the Education of Young Children (n.d.) administers a voluntary national professional accreditation process for all types of preschools, kindergartens, child care centers, and child care programs for school-age children. High-quality programs are those in which the children are comfortable, relaxed, and involved in play; a sufficient number of adults with specialized training in early childhood development and education is present; and there are appropriate staff-child ratios for age-appropriate groups of children. High-quality programs also emphasize close communication between parents and staff. The National Association for the Education of Young Children also recommends two annual inspections from state licensing agencies, including one unscheduled visit.

Also linked to improving the quality of child care is the attempt to unionize child care workers, thereby increasing their pay and providing a benefits package. It is estimated that in the United States there are about 306,000 licensed family child care providers, who care for 1,080,000 children. Yet less than 5 percent are unionized. Brooks (2005) offers an informative policy case study of efforts to unionize child care workers in Illinois. After twenty years of organizing home care workers, Local 880 used its power and authority to organize a legislative campaign to allow child care workers to unionize. Through grassroots organizing in direct politics and coalition building, the union was able to influence state elections and get the issue heard by legislators. Local 880 won thirteen pay increases for Department of Human Services/Office of Rehabilitation Services workers and helped win an increase in the reimbursement rates for licensed child care providers in 1999 ranging from $13 to $18 per hour to $18 to $21 per hour. The union is involved in a long-term statewide campaign to win health insurance for its members. "The ultimate goal of 880 is to recruit over 50 percent of the 5,000 licensed family child-care providers who care for state-subsidized children" in Illinois (Brooks, 2005, p. 50).

As the victories won by the Local 880 in Illinois demonstrate, it is not realistic to expect that the problems of quality and affordability of child care will be resolved without the exertion of pressure on government. Thus, efforts to organize child care workers through the wielding of political clout are especially critical to federal child care policies. Similar efforts are underway in other parts of the country. Issues of low pay, lack of health insurance, and a sense that unions are not respected are also union labor issues, and major unions, faced with declining traditional membership, have started to compete for the right to represent child care workers. It is not easy to organize child care workers because they are often spread out among facilities, and their clients are often low- or middle-income parents. Organizing efforts are very active in Iowa, California, Pennsylvania, Massachusetts, Maryland, Michigan, Ohio, and Wisconsin. Unionizing child care workers seems to be most difficult in the South, the Great Plains and the Rocky

Mountain states, and also in Rhode Island. The American Federation of State, County and Municipal Employees has increased its organizing budget from 14 percent to 25 percent to target home health care, universities, and child care centers. The union's goal is to enroll 75,000 workers annually over the next few years (Haynes, 2001). Child care workers employed by both public (e.g., Head Start) and private facilities are targeted.

Divorce and Child Custody

There have been major changes in the structure of families over the last few decades. As women choose to postpone marriage or remain single and decide whether to become parents, there is a growing separation between marriage and parenthood. At the same time, the institution of marriage has been redefined as an emotional commitment that can change if feelings of love change. Although divorce rates have fallen from a high in 1980 (5.3 divorces per 1,000 marriages each year) to levels not seen since 1970 (3.6 per 1,000 marriages), divorce is still a major source of family instability. About 10 percent of the population is now divorced. This is up from 8 percent in 1990 and 6 percent in 1970 ("U.S. Divorce Statistics," 2008). Although marriage remains popular, and most who divorce will remarry, a substantial proportion of children will spend at least a portion of their childhood living with a single parent.

Under traditional divorce laws, husbands were responsible for alimony and child support, and the wife was the custodial parent responsible for children. The greatest share of property was given to the "innocent" party. No-fault divorce was instituted in California in 1969 under Governor Ronald Reagan. Since then, every state has signed into law some form of no-fault divorce. By the mid-1990s, couples could simply cite marital breakdown or incompatibility in all but twenty-two states, and in these states couples could choose fault or no-fault divorce (Hershkowitz & Liebert, 1998). Under no-fault divorce law, spouses are responsible for self-support, both are eligible for child custody, and both are responsible for child support. Property is divided equally, usually through the sale of the property, or one spouse can buy out the other's share.

Proponents of changes to the traditional fault-based divorce system believed that non-adversarial divorce, with its no-guilt and no-financial-gain provisions, would improve legal processes. But as early as the mid-1980s, the unintended consequences of no-fault divorce for women and children had become apparent. In a comprehensive analysis of these issues in the 1980s, Weitzman (1985) found that no-fault divorce had negative consequences on custody issues because the new laws made child custody the only sphere in which fault was relevant. Angry husbands and wives could raise child custody claims to embarrass or harass their spouse, and child custody suits were used in negotiations over property. As property was sold and divided, many children were uprooted from their homes. Since mothers made less money on average than fathers and were more likely to have custody of the children, divorced mothers were more likely to live in poverty. This problem of poverty among divorced parents is still relevant twenty years later. In 2003, most divorced families with children experienced enormous drops in income, which lessen somewhat over time but remain significant for years—unless there is a subsequent parental cohabitation or remarriage (Parke, 2003).

Children of divorced parents are 70 percent more likely to be expelled or suspended from school and twice as likely to drop out and also score somewhat lower on intelligence tests. Declines in income following divorce account for up to half the risk of children dropping out of high school, regardless of income prior to the divorce. Children's problems may also be due to conflict in divorcing families. Children living in high-conflict families are at an increased risk for a variety of problems, and so the problems of children in divorced families may be caused by conflict that precedes and accompanies marital dissolution. Whether due to a conflict between spouses that puts children in the middle or other divorce-related issues such as the slide into poverty for divorced single parents, divorce has negative repercussions for children. The effects of divorce on children often last through adulthood. For instance, adult children of divorce are more likely to experience depression and their own divorces—as well as earn less income and achieve lower levels of education—than adults whose parents remain married. However, if parents have conflict in their relationship, remaining married is not the answer either. In an analysis of research on marriage and divorce and their impact on children, the Center for Law and Social Policy found that chronic conflict between married parents is "inherently stressful for children, and children learn poor relationship skills from parents who aren't able to solve problems amicably. When parents have a highly discordant relationship, children are often better off in the long run if their parents divorce" (Parke, 2003, p. 6). Between 30 and 40 percent of divorces that involve children are preceded by a period of chronic discord between the parents. If this were to continue, children would do better if their parents divorced than if they stayed married.

Nationally, there has been some movement to return to traditional fault-based divorce or impose additional obstacles to the process of divorce. This movement was spurred by what has been seen as increasingly high divorce rates, the high rate of poverty in single-parent homes, and perceptions that the real victims of no-fault divorce are the children. Many states have proposed legislation to impose substantial obstacles to divorce, including bills that require divorcing parents to file a joint-parenting plan, allowing no-fault divorce only when the couple is childless, and requiring pre-divorce counseling and substantial waiting periods before a divorce is finalized. Other efforts are underway to support marriage, such as the requirement of premarital counseling before marriage licenses are issued. Nonetheless, divorce law reform will not stop parents from fighting and separating. Moving back to fault-based divorce policy probably would have little impact on these issues, but premarital and marital counseling may have a positive impact on child care and financial support. Poverty among divorced mothers might best be solved by efforts to directly address the issue.

Gay Parenting and Adoption

The discriminatory belief that gays and lesbians are not fit parents underlies public attitudes, policies governing judicial decision making in custody disputes, and laws concerning adoption and foster care. However, a review of studies spanning twenty years reveals normal child development patterns in gender identity and sexual preference, with the qualification that children of lesbian mothers have less sex-typed preferences for activities at school (Patterson, 1997). Another review of twenty-three empirical studies published between 1978 and 2000 looked at outcomes for 615 children of lesbian mothers or gay fathers. Children raised by gay parents did not exhibit adverse outcomes on emotional functioning, sexual preference, stigmatization, gender role behavior, behavioral adjustment, gender identity, and cognitive functioning compared to other children (Anderssen, Amlie, & Ytteroy, 2002). In general, population samples of children of gay men and lesbians are small and difficult to come by, and some studies lack good internal validity and have serious design flaws (Belcastro, 1997), but studies that have matched these groups of children with groups of children with heterosexual parents have shown no major differences on any of the measures used to assess the children. Based on research findings, the American Psychological Association, the American Academy of Pediatrics, the American Academy of Family Physicians, the National Association of Social Workers, and the Child Welfare League of America have all issued statements supporting second-parent and joint adoptions by gay and lesbian couples.

An excellent review of all the issues related to LGBT parenting, adoption, and foster care is provided by Cooper and Cates (2006). Graff (2002) concludes: "The results are quite clear: Children of lesbian or gay parents turn out just fine on every conceivable measure of emotional and social development: attachment, self-esteem, moral judgment, behavior, intelligence, likeability, popularity, gender identity, family warmth, and all sorts of obscure psychological concepts. Whatever the scale, children with lesbian or gay parents and children with heterosexual parents turn out equally well—and grow up to be heterosexual in the same overwhelming proportions" (p. 51).

Although the literature does not reveal serious negative risks for children who are adopted by same-sex couples and single individuals, states' responses to same-sex couples and individuals wishing to adopt or foster children vary widely. The Web site of the National Gay and Lesbian Task Force (2008) provides a map that shows which states have restrictions. Florida prohibits adoption by gay and lesbian individuals. Same-sex couples in Michigan and Mississippi cannot jointly adopt children. Utah restricts the right to adopt to married couples and prohibits adoption by cohabitating couples involved in a sexual relationship. A separate state statute allows only opposite-sex couples to legally marry, thereby effectively banning adoption by gays and lesbians. A directive issued in 1995 by the then director of the Nebraska Department of Social Service prohibits adoption if the prospective adoptive parent is known by the adoption agency to be homosexual or unmarried and cohabitating with another adult. It is unclear, however, whether this directive has been enforced. In Arkansas, an initiated state statute prohibits cohabitating couples— whether heterosexual or homosexual—from adopting or fostering children. The statute was put on the ballot through the direct democracy process, as described in chapter 2. Arkansas voters passed the Unmarried Couple Adoption Ban by an overwhelming 57 percent (579,695 votes) for, and 43 percent (437,720 votes) against.

As of February 2009, no other states specifically ban adoption by gay and lesbian individuals, but they must adopt as single parents whether or not they are in a relationship. State statutes are silent regarding the status of bisexual and transgender persons to adopt children. Where second-parent adoption (adoption of a child by the partner of the child's parent) is involved, the situation is somewhat different. Michigan, for example, has not recognized such adoptions since 2004. The courts in Ohio and Wisconsin have ruled that state law prohibits second-parent adoption by same-sex couples. Colorado, California, Connecticut, Vermont, the District of Columbia, Illinois, Indiana, Massachusetts, New York, New Jersey, and Pennsylvania permit gays and lesbians to adopt the children of their partners. In Maryland and fifteen other states, courts have ruled in favor of second-parent rights to adopt.

Another important issue related to the topic of lesbian and gay parenting is the use of new reproductive technologies. Arnup's (1999) detailed analysis reports that an increasing number of lesbian baby boomers over the past fifteen years have conceived children through artificial insemination by way of services offered at infertility clinics and sperm banks. Interpreting parental rights in cases of paternity that involve artificial insemination can be difficult, requiring new legislation, legal action, and advocacy. Gay men often serve as sperm donors and utilize surrogate parenting to have children. Since both single heterosexual women and lesbians as well as gay men use these new technologies, gay and lesbian rights may converge around the issue of parents' rights and sperm donation. Several legal arguments that have been used to defend the rights of stepparents in the United States and Canada could be used to protect the rights of gay and lesbian parents (Antoniuk, 1999). These include de facto parenthood, which refers to the role of a person who parents on a day-to-day basis; in loco parentis, which gives the non-biological parent the same rights as a biological parent; *equitable estoppel,* which gives a legally unrecognized parent the right to argue for legal parental status; and equitable parenthood, which could extend legal rights to gay and lesbian parents.

It is obvious that adoption by same-sex couples is controversial. However, it is also clear that, with some twenty-five states recognizing second-parent adoptions, the issue of adoption by gays and lesbians is much less controversial than that of same-sex marriage. Still, many same-sex couples wanting to adopt must overcome substantial social and legal barriers. In concluding this section, we can do no better than to endorse Polikoff's (1990) view: "When parents create a nontraditional family, that family becomes the reality of the child's life. The child may experience some stigma, but courts should delegitimize, not condone, disparaging community attitudes. The courts should protect children's interests within the context of nontraditional families, rather than attempt to eradicate such families by adhering to a fictitious, homogenous family model" (p. 482).

Policies for Child Care and Support

Our discussion turns now to several federal policies that assist families in acquiring child care and child support. Three types of policies provide child care assistance at the state and federal levels. The first is a block grant program that subsidizes the cost of child care for low-income working parents. It is designed to promote and maintain adult employment. The second is Head Start, which focuses on early childhood education and child development for poor children. Finally, the most universal policy is the child and dependent care tax credit, a tax policy that defrays the cost of child care.

Child Care Block Grants

The Child Care and Development Block Grant Act (CCDBG) of 1990 was first enacted as part of the Omnibus Budget Reconciliation Act of 1990. In 1996, the Personal Responsibility and Work Opportunity Reconciliation Act eliminated child care entitlements. Through welfare reform, the CCDBG was reauthorized and four other federal child care programs for low-income families and working families were consolidated into a single block grant to states. The CCDBG is the primary federal day-care subsidy in the United States. As we have discussed previously, block grants are fixed-sum federal grants that give state and local governments the flexibility to design and implement programs in response to local needs and conditions but also eliminate a person's right or entitlement to the benefit or service (Finegold, Wherry, & Schardin, 2004). In the case of CCDBG, the purpose was clear: "The child care provisions in [the Personal Responsibility and Work Opportunity Reconciliation Act] are . . . intended to streamline the federal role, reduce the number of federal programs and conflicting rules, and increase the flexibility provided to states" (Butler & Gish, 2003, p. i). In 1998, the Urban Institute undertook a study to see if the new system of block grant funding could meet the need for child care if states utilized all the available funds. Among the states that utilized the maximum level of block grant funding in FY 1997, the need for child care assistance could still only be met for about half of the low-income children needing assistance (Long, Kirby, Kurka, & Boots, 1998).

Prior to the Personal Responsibility and Work Opportunity Act, children were entitled to child care assistance if their parents were receiving AFDC and working or participating in job training. Provided that their income was less than 75 percent of the state's median income, low-income working parents could receive child care assistance if funds were still available after the AFDC population had been assisted. This translated into roughly 130 percent of the federal poverty level. The Personal Responsibility and Work Opportunity Reconciliation Act changed child care assistance programs for low-income families. It eliminated child care entitlements and consolidated four major sources of federal child care subsidies into a single block grant to the states. Thus, states no longer receive increased funding to respond to greater demand for child care if caseloads grow, or if more people engaged in work-related activities need child care. If the money runs out, not everyone who needs child care can get it, assistance levels are reduced, or eligible families are put on a waiting list. However, states also have the option of increasing the portion of their block grant used to cover child care and reducing the portion of the block grant for other types of TANF-related programs.

Children must be under age thirteen to be eligible. Subsidies decline as income rises, and parents must share the cost of care. Income eligibility levels vary by state. Each state sets its own eligibility and administrative requirements, so there is great variability regarding who can receive assistance, how much assistance can be received, and how subsidies are delivered. Some states provide assistance only to families at the minimal income levels required by federal law, but other states have increased funding to assist a larger number of working poor families with incomes up to 200 percent of the poverty level. Reimbursement rates to day care providers also vary widely, ranging from $59 per week in Alabama to $110 per week in New Jersey. Eligibility requirements may vary, so low-income working families cannot rely on the availability of subsidies. During economic downturns, changes in eligibility requirements often make families ineligible. Although in many states families are now required to recertify for benefits only once every six months, families become ineligible when state budget crises result in lower income eligibility requirements for day care subsidies. Paperwork and processing delays also lead to interruptions in day care assistance, creating a domino effect in cases of the loss of a job. Families cannot count on the subsidies because a change in work schedules or earnings can suddenly make them ineligible. Some families do not apply because of the bureaucratic red tape they encounter, or because they lack knowledge of the program. Even though they are eligible for the assistance, the use of subsidized day care among low-income families not affiliated with TANF is very low, ranging from 4 percent to 11 percent of those eligible. Depending on the state, only 7 percent to 43 percent of families leaving TANF who are eligible for day care assistance use child care subsidies (Zedlewski, Adams, Dubay, & Kenney, 2006).

The Social Services Block Grant (SSBG) of 1981, Title XX of the Social Security Act, also provides some funds for child care. Originally authorized with a $2.8 billion cap for social service spending by the states, the SSBG has been reduced several times by Congress. In FY 2003, $1.7 billion was appropriated. SSBG is a flexible source of funds that states can use at their own discretion to fund a variety of social welfare programs, including adoption services, protective services for adults and children, and special services for at-risk youths. Table 9.6 shows the use of Title XX funds by expenditure category in 2001. Since welfare reform, the grant has been reduced substantially, yet it still accounts for about 13 percent of federal child care expenditures (U.S. House of Representatives, 2004).

Table 9.6 Use of Title XX Funds, by Expenditure Category, 2001

Service category	Percentage of SSBG expenditures
Adoption services	1.3
Case management	6.5
Congregate meals	0.3
Counseling services	1.6
Day care—adults	0.9
Day care—children	7.6
Education/training services	0.3
Employment services	0.8
Family planning services	1.6
Foster care services—adults	0.3
Foster care services—children	10.1
Health-related services	0.9
Home-based services	7.6
Home-delivered meals	0.7
Housing services	0.3
Independent/transitional living services	0.1
Information and referral services	2.6
Legal services	0.6
Pregnancy and parenting	0.2
Prevention/intervention	7.7
Protective services—adults	5.7
Protective services—children	11.8
Recreation services	0.1
Residential treatment	4.0
Special services—youth at risk	2.3
Special services—disabled	8.3
Substance abuse services	0.6
Transportation	0.7
Other services	4.3
Administrative costs	10.1

Source: Gish, M. (2003, August 20). *Social services block grant (Title XX of the Social Security Act).* Retrieved March 4, 2007, from http://assets.opencrs.com/rpts/94-953_20030820.pdf

Head Start

Another federal child care program is Head Start. Head Start began in 1965 as a part of President Lyndon Johnson's campaign to fight poverty with economic, educational, and community action programs. Emerging child development theories of the time, combined with research showing significant delays among low-income kindergarten children, led lawmakers to develop Head Start as an educational preschool program. It was believed that poverty "deprived children of appropriate educational experiences as well as adequate care" and that the negative effects of this educational deprivation could be reversed if the federal government intervened to provide comprehensive preschool programs (McGill-Franzen, 1993, p. 85). Head Start sought the "maximum feasible participation" of parents by including them in almost every aspect of the program—from hiring staff to becoming teachers themselves. A half-million children were enrolled by the summer of 1965 (Cahan & Bromer, 2003). By 2003, over 900,000 were enrolled in Head Start, which was funded at $6.7 billion, or about $7,366 per child.

Since its inception, Head Start has been seen by lawmakers as a social welfare program, and it is administered at the federal level by the Department of Health and Human Services rather than the Department of Education, as one might expect. As a federal policy, Head Start has remained much the same since its inception, largely based on its reputation as a program that works. The Head Start Act was amended as part of Title VI of the Omnibus Budget Reconciliation Act (1981), with other amendments added by the Technology-Related Assistance for Individuals with Disabilities Amendments of 1993 and the Coats Human Services Amendments of 1998. Head Start targets the poorest children, with 90 percent of enrollments from families at or below the federal poverty level and families eligible for public assistance.

The idea of community and parent involvement as a route to better outcomes for impoverished children is central to the mission of Head Start. Local communities have the flexibility to develop full-time (all-day) or part-time (half-day) programs that operate year round, or for only part of the year like public schools. Head Start is implemented through grants to local organizations, including community action agencies, schools, for-profit and nonprofit agencies, government agencies, and tribal governments and associations. Low-income children and families are at risk for health and nutrition problems; lower reading, math, and general test scores; more problem behaviors; and low self-esteem. With the goal of eliminating or reducing these problems, Head Start is designed to offer comprehensive services. Offered on-site or often in partnership with local health clinics, the typical program offers nutrition (breakfast and hot lunches), hygiene education, medical services, dental health services, immunizations, social services, and home visits to help parents with parenting skills. Head Start also fosters leadership skills and self-esteem by working with parents to achieve their own goals and to participate in volunteer activities. Parents are viewed as the child's most important teachers, and as active participants in early childhood education.

Head Start's recent history provides an excellent example of the survival of a federal program from the long-reaching arm of devolution. From the beginning, grants for Head Start have been provided directly by the U.S. Department of Health and Human Services to local grantees. But with the Bush administration's FY 2004 budget proposal, states would have been given an opportunity to administer Head Start if they could provide evidence of coordination with other programs and services yet retain Head Start's focus on developing relevant skills and competencies (Gish, 2003). Alongside this across-the-board attempt to eliminate direct federal funding and devolve responsibility to the states, President George W. Bush planned to transfer the authority for Head Start from the Department of Health and Human Services to the U.S. Department of Education. Proponents argued that with the transfer of authority, states would be better able to coordinate Head Start with other services offering early childhood education and care. Opponents feared, however, that Head Start funds would be pooled with other preschool programs that were not targeted to low-income children and that standards would be lower because of the difference between many state early education standards and the Head Start Performance Standards (Waller, 2005). The National Head Start Association advocated the retention of federal control on the grounds that studies had not been done to assess whether the quality of the services would be maintained if Head Start became a state program. The association offered a number of convincing arguments, including the lack of state government funds for high-quality preschool education, the risk that services and the number of children in Head Start will be reduced due to less federal oversight and inadequate funding, the lowering of teacher standards and educational achievements, and an increase in state administrative costs. A major concern was the lack of direction to states for involving Head Start's 900,000 parent volunteers (National Head Start Association, n.d).

These arguments, combined with a swell of grassroots advocacy activities such as petition signing, letter writing, and meetings with elected officials by Head Start parents and volunteers, were successful in retaining Head Start as a program of federal grants to local agencies. In 2007, the Improving Head Start for School Readiness Act of 2007 reauthorized Head

Start with an emphasis on school readiness. Traditionally, Head Start did not have a great deal of impact on children whose mothers work. Table 9.1 shows that only about 1 percent (196,330) of the children whose mothers were working were enrolled in Head Start programs. However, in the post-1996 welfare reform era, when parents are required to work, the reauthorization addresses this problem by beginning to convert part-day programs to full-workday programs or converting part-day slots to full-workday slots. The Early Childhood Learning and Knowledge Center of the Administration for Children and Families is an outstanding online resource that provides information about the new law (see U.S. Department of Health and Human Services, 2008). The center's Web site offers an inside look at changes in policy from one authorization of a law to its new articulation. On the Head Start Reauthorization section of the Web site, the Head Start Act of 1998 is posted alongside the Improving Head Start for School Readiness Act of 2007. The new legislation is marked up in bold type so it is possible to see exactly how the old law and the new Head Start law are different. Head Start parents, advocates, and interested parties can ask questions about the new legislation and see the questions and responses of others. Head Start agencies will carry out a yearly self-assessment based on guidelines available in a new report entitled "A System of Designation Renewal for Head Start Grantees," which is also posted.

Child and Dependent Care Tax Credit

Tax credits are another type of approach used by the federal government to defray the cost of child care for working families. With the child and dependent care tax credit (CDCTC), families reduce their yearly income tax burden by a percentage of what they paid for child care during the year. The maximum amount that can be claimed is $3,000 for one child or $6,000 for two or more children. To qualify for the credit, the child must be under age thirteen. Single parents filing the tax return must be the heads of household, and two-parent households must file a joint tax return. Based on a family's adjusted gross income, the credit is a percentage of the amount of work-related child and dependent care expenses paid to a care provider. The percentage of child care expenses that can be deducted ranges from 20 percent to 35 percent, depending on income. As income rises, the percentage of credit falls. For up to $15,000, parents are allowed to deduct 35 percent. For each $2,000 earned above that amount, the credit is reduced by 1 percent, until income reaches $43,000. For income of $43,000 and above, the credit remains at 20 percent of a family's income (Internal Revenue Service, 2008).

The CDCTC is not a refundable tax credit like the earned income tax credit. For example, if a family only owes $500 in taxes, it doesn't matter if their credit is $1,000; the CDCTC reduces the amount of income tax by $500. An example provided by the IRS shows how the tax credit is figured. Jerry and Clara are married with two preschool children. One child stays at the neighbor's house while Jerry and Clara are at work; the other goes to a nursery school. During the year, Jerry and Clara paid total child care expenses of $6,200: $3,000 to the neighbor and $3,200 to the nursery school. Their adjusted gross income was $27,000. Jerry and Clara were only able to take the maximum of $6,000 for their two children, even though they paid more than that for child care for the year. Because their income was $27,000, they multiplied their $6,000 child care maximum by 28 percent (the percentage allowed for their income). This gives them a credit of $1,680, but since they owed $473 in taxes to begin with, they were only allowed to take that amount as their credit. If this were a refundable tax credit, like the EITC, they would have been given the additional $527. In an analysis of the CDCTC, the Urban Institute notes that although the credit is the single largest source of federal support for child care, it does little to aid the lowest-wage workers because they generally owe little, if any, taxes (Long & Clark, 1997). This makes sense if one looks at a higher-income family who also spends $6,000 on child care but earns $50,000. They would only be eligible for a 20 percent credit (or $1,200), but they would receive the entire amount of the CDCTC because they would also owe more income taxes. Thus, as a proportion of income, the CDCTC assists middle-income earners more than lower-wage workers.

Child Support

Nearly 23 million children, or about a third of all children under age twenty-one, lived with a custodial parent in 1998. Of the 14 million custodial parents, only 7.9 million (or 56%) received some type of financial assistance for their children from the non-custodial parent. The number of custodial parents with a child support award who received full payment of all support owed them in the previous year increased from 37 percent in 1994 to 46 percent in 1998, and to 45 percent in 2002 (Grall, 2003). Custodial parents who had never married were substantially less likely than custodial parents who had been married to receive the full child support payment owed them. In 2002, 32 percent of never-married custodial parents reported that they received full child support payments the previous year, compared to 49 percent of custodial parents who had been married. Custodial parents with at least a college degree are twice as likely as those without a high school diploma to receive the full amount of child support payments awarded to them. In 2002, among parents who were due child support payments in the previous year, only 28 percent of custodial parents without a high school degree reported that they received their full child support awards the previous year, as opposed to 44 percent of those with a high school degree, 46 percent of those with some college or an associate's degree, and 59 percent of those with at least a bachelor's degree.

The percentage depends upon the financial status of the parents. For example, only 30 percent of poor children receive any child support. Poor non-custodial fathers or mothers have little or sometimes no earnings from which to pay child support. Custodial parents are more likely to receive child support payments if the non-custodial parent is employed and has an adequate income. Child support orders make it nearly twice as likely that custodial parents will receive financial support (U.S. Census Bureau, 2003). "During the five year period covered by the initial FY 1995–1999 Strategic Plan, child support collections rose to over $15 billion and, for the first time, more children had paternity established than were born outside of marriage in a given year. Further, in FY 2003, during the five year period covered by the succeeding FY 2000-2004 Strategic Plan, $21.2 billion was collected on behalf of children. Similar gains were made in paternity establishments and the percentage of child support collections that actually went to the children on whose behalf the collections were made" (Administration for Children and Families, 2005).

Child support reduces poverty among children and makes up an average of 35 percent of income for poor families who are not on welfare (Sorensen & Zibman, 2000). The enforcement of child support as a way of alleviating poverty for women has been a policy agenda for more than thirty years through the Child Support Enforcement Program of 1975, the Child Support Enforcement Amendments of 1984, and Title I of the Family Support Act of 1988. In the early years, the law was focused on obtaining child support from non-custodial parents whose children were AFDC recipients, but in the 1980s, services were extended to non-welfare families as well. Beginning in 1982, federal tax refunds began to be intercepted to satisfy past-due child support, so many families receive a lump sum payment of child support when the non-custodial parent files an income tax return. In 1988, the Family Support Act began to require wage withholdings for non-payment of child support. In 1996, TANF furthered collection activities by mandating that states have laws revoking the professional, occupational, and recreational drivers' licenses of non-custodial parents who owe past-due child support, and setting up a national database to recover child support payments from non-custodial parents who live out of state.

Families receiving welfare must assign their rights to all child support received—up to an amount equal to monthly cash assistance—to the state. As long as the family is receiving cash assistance, child support payments are retained and split between the state and the federal government. Before TANF, states were required to distribute the first $50 in child support collection each month to the custodial family, and the state had to disregard this amount in their calculation of AFDC payments. Under TANF, states are still allowed to disregard the first $50, but since the federal government no longer funds this policy, there is a financial disincentive for states to release the money to families. Once the custodial parent leaves TANF, child support reverts back to the family, unless the state determines that the custodial parent owes the state for un-reimbursed assistance. If the support received by the custodial parent exceeds the established monthly support obligation, states are allowed to retain any additional money to satisfy arrearages owed. The implementation of child support enforcement policy may be one reason why some studies that measure the effect of child support find that it does not substantially reduce poverty among the lowest-income groups of women (Farrel, Glosser, & Gardiner, 2003; Rocha, 1997).

Child support payments are determined by the state where the non-custodial parent lives. The level of support varies from state to state. A child support calculator for each state can be found at http://www.alllaw.com/calculators/childsupport. One is struck by how the calculations used by each state differ. Most take into consideration the number of children the support is for, the wages of the custodial and non-custodial parent, the cost of health insurance, and factors in the cost of child support being paid by each parent to others. Some states also ask for the cost of day care and state and local tax payments, but other states require only minimal information. Mississippi, for example, asks only for the amount of income and other child support paid by the non-custodial parent. The result is that amounts of child support can vary a great deal from one state to another. We calculated the amount of monthly child support for one child using $3,000 per month as the non-custodial parent's income, and $2,000 per month as the custodial parent's income. The amounts of child support that the non-custodial parent had to pay ranged from $750 in California and New York to $410 in Mississippi.

Once the level of support is determined by the state or a court, the state assumes the responsibility for collecting the funds. Since not all parents are willing payers, each state has developed procedures to maximize the amount of the child support collected. Most child support enforcement efforts focus on welfare parents. Families can also contact the office of the attorney general or the state office of child support enforcement and report that they are not being paid child support. Despite these enforcement policies, the surest way for non-poor families to receive child support is to take non-custodial parents to court. However, the financial constraint of hiring a lawyer makes obtaining child support difficult and expensive.

Summary

This chapter addressed the issues and policies related to the care and support of children. Also, in many ways, this chapter illustrates a major theme of the book: that there is not a uniform definition of the family in the United States. Although the structures of families may differ, their functional need to work and at the same time care for and support children is essentially the same. Policies such as the Personal Responsibility and Work Opportunity Reconciliation Act, which eliminates welfare benefits as an entitlement and ties eligibility and assistance to participation in the workforce, create new demands for out-of-home care. Overall, however, the demand for child care is predicted to grow due to the movement of women with children into the workforce and the impact of divorce. Changing cultural norms also play a part in the need for child care. These include the creation of families through the use of reproductive technologies, surrogate parenting, and adoption; stepfamilies; and families headed by single parents and by same-sex couples. Thus, due to the changing work circumstances and structure of U.S. families, the degree to which policies can enhance and promote the well-being of children must be considered. The sum of these trends signals an urgent and increasing need for child care in the twenty-first century.

The movement of women into the workplace also creates new challenges for two-parent families. Since the well-being of children depends fundamentally on their mothers' circumstances in terms of marriage, education, income, and job security (Hernandez, 2003), the quality, price, location, and availability of child care and children's access to after-school activities are important areas of family life that are shaped by social policies and programs. While federal and state governments recognize the need for day care, almost no programs focus on children who are left at home alone. Thus, the latchkey child phenomenon is very much alive, and a substantial number of parents leave children at home to care for themselves. The number of children left home alone should be viewed as a national tragedy that cannot help but lead to poor outcomes for the children involved.

This chapter discussed several different policies and programs that provide some level of support for child care. Funding for child care block grants has decreased, with assistance provided for about half of the children in need. Head Start has survived recent federal policy change efforts to devolve it to a state-level program. Because of the variation in states' commitment to early childhood development, changing the funding of Head Start to block grants to the states would probably have reduced its scope and altered its approach to early childhood development. Instead, recent federal policy is designed to make the Head Start program more accessible to and useful for working parents through daylong and year-round programs. The only program approaching universal coverage is the child and dependent care tax credit, which refunds a portion of child care expenses through the IRS, but the tax credit is least effective in assisting the lowest-wage workers, who ordinarily owe little or no income tax. Finally, child support enforcement policy has improved over the last twenty years. Still, the enforcement of child support from non-custodial parents remains problematic for welfare recipients, who must assign their right to child support or a portion of child support payments to the state. In cases in which the non-custodial parent is marginally employed, child support is minimal or hard to collect, and attorney fees for collecting overdue amounts are prohibitive for those not involved in the welfare system.

Child care policy in the United States provides an excellent and obvious example of the devolution of federal responsibility to the states. With the exception of Head Start, subsidized child care is funded almost exclusively through block grants. There are no guarantees that poor families who need subsidized child care can receive it, and if all families who were eligible actually applied, there would not be enough subsidized child care to go around. This says something about the differences in states' commitments to provide additional monies for child care, and why critics of block grants argue for the federal government to remain involved. Yet, as we have seen in previous chapters, no program is exempt from devolution or privatization. The trend in the United States is to move social welfare programs out of the sphere of the federal government into state and local grant programs, and for private for-profit and nonprofit corporations to implement these programs within broad guidelines.

For Further Reading

Adams, G., & Snyder, K., with Tout, K. (2003). *Essential but often ignored: Child care providers in the subsidy system* (Occasional Paper Number 63). Washington, DC: Urban Institute. Retrieved May 4, 2008, from http://www.urban.org/UploadedPDF/310613_OP63.pdf

Crowley, J. E. (2003). *The politics of child support in America.* New York: Cambridge University Press.

Greenburg, M. (2007). Next steps for federal child care policy. *The Future of Children, 17*(2), 73–96.

Michel, S. (2002). *Child care policy at the crossroads: Gender and welfare state restructuring.* New York: Routledge.

Mooney, A., & Statham, J. (Eds.). (2003). *Family day care: International perspectives on policy, practice, and quality.* London: Jessica Kingsley.

Polakow, V. (2007). *Who care for our children? The child care crisis in the other America.* New York: Columbia Teachers College Press.

References

Administration for Children and Families. (2005). *Child support enforcement, FY 2004: Preliminary report.* Retrieved March 7, 2009, from http://www.acf.hhs.gov/programs/cse/pubs/2005/reports/preliminary_report/

Alston, F. K. (2006). *Latch key children.* Retrieved May 12, 2007, from http://www.aboutourkids.org/articles/latch_key_children

American Psychological Association. (2006). *Making "welfare to work" really work: Child care.* Retrieved May 29, 2006, from http://www.apa.org/pi/wpo/child.html

Anderssen, N., Amlie, C., & Ytteroy, E. (2002). Outcomes for children with lesbian or gay parents: A review of studies from 1978 to 2000. *Scandinavian Journal of Psychology, 43*(4), 335–351.

Antoniuk, T. (1999). Policy alternatives for a diverse community: Lesbians and family law. In T. R. Sullivan (Ed.), *Queer families, common agendas: Gay people, lesbians, and family values* (pp. 47–60). Binghamton, NY: Haworth Press.

Arnup, K. (1999). Out in this world: The social and legal context of gay and lesbian families. *Journal of Gay & Lesbian Social Services, 10*(1), 1–25.

Belcastro, P. (1997). A review of data based studies addressing the effect of homosexuals parenting on children's sexual and social functioning. In A. Sullivan (Ed.), *Same-sex marriage* (pp. 250–256). New York: Vintage Books.

Brooks, F. P. (2005). New turf for organizing family child care providers. *Labor Studies Journal, 29*(4), 45–64.

Butler, A., & Gish, M. (2003, April 7). *The Child Care and Development Block Grant: Background and funding.* Washington, DC: Domestic Social Policy Division, Congressional Research Service. Retrieved March 4, 2008, from http://www.senate.gov/~kohl/childcare2.pdf

Cahan, E. D., & Bromer, J. (2003). Trends in the history of child care and family support: 1940–2000. In R. Weissberg, H. Walberg, M. O'Brien, & C. Kuster (Eds.), *Long-term trends in the well-being of children and youth* (pp. 207–230). Washington, DC: CWLA Press.

Child Care and Development Block Grant Act of 1990, 42 U.S.C. § 9801 et seq. (1990).

Children's Defense Fund. (2003). *School-age child care: Keeping children safe and helping them learn while their families work.* Retrieved May 19, 2007, from http://www.childrensdefense.org/site/DocServer/keyfacts2003_schoolagecare.pdf?docID=593

Child Support Enforcement Amendments of 1984, 42 U.S.C. § 651 et seq. (1984).

Coats Human Services Amendments of 1998, Pub. L. No. 105-285 (1998).
Cooper, L., & Cates, P. (2006). *Too high a price: The case against restricting gay parenting* (2nd ed.). New York: American Civil Liberties Union Foundation. Retrieved February 22, 2009, from http://www.aclu.org/images/asset_upload_file480_27496.pdf
Education and Training Voluntary Partnership. (2003, September 9). *Skill standards for frontline workers in education and training: Paraprofessionals, paraeducators, teacher assistants, education assistants, child care workers working in general education, special education, early childhood care and education.* Retrieved April 29, 2006, from http://www.aft.org/pubs-reports/psrp/SkillStandards.pdf
Farrel, M., Glosser, A., & Gardiner, K. (2003, April 11). *Child support and TANF interaction: Literature review.* Retrieved August 18, 2005, from http://www.aspe.hhs.gov/hsp/CS-TANF-Into3/index.htm
Finegold, K., Wherry, L., & Schardin, S. (2004, April). *Block grants: Historical overview and lessons learned* (Assessing the New Federalism Policy Brief No A-63). Retrieved June 8, 2006, from http://www.urban.org/UploadedPDF/310991_A-63.pdf
Gerson, K. (1998). Gender and the future of the family: Implications for the post industrial workplace. In D. Vanoy & P. Dubek (Eds.), *Challenges for work and family in the twenty-first century* (pp. 11–22). New York: Aldine de Gruyter.
Gish, M. (2003, March 31). *Child care issues in the 108th Congress.* Retrieved May 29, 2006, from http://www.senate.gov/member/wi/kohl/general/child care.pdf
Graff, E. J. (2002). The other marriage war. *American Prospect, 13*(7), 50–53.
Grall, T. S. (2003). *Custodial mothers and fathers and their child support: 2001* (Current Population Reports P60-225). Washington, DC: U.S. Census Bureau. Retrieved May 19, 2007, from http://www.census.gov/prod/2003pubs/p60-225.pdf
Haynes, V. D. (2001). *Child-care workers seek better pay through unions.* Retrieved June 8, 2006, from http://archives.econ.utah.edu/archives/m-fem/2001m02/msg00033.htm
Head Start Act, 42 U.S.C. 9801 et seq. (1981).
Hernandez, D. (2003). Changing family circumstances. In R. Weissberg, H. Walberg, M. O'Brien, & C. Kerster (Eds.), *Long-term trends in the well-being of children and youth* (pp. 155–180). Washington, DC: CWLA Press.
Hershkowitz, D. S., & Liebert, D. R. (1998). *Divorce reform in California: From fault to no-fault . . . and back again?* Retrieved May 29, 2006, from http://www.library.ca.gov/crb/98/04/currentstate.pdf
Improving Head Start for School Readiness Act of 2007, Pub. L. No. 110-134 (2007).
Internal Revenue Service. (2008). *Publication 503, child & dependent care expenses, 2007.* Retrieved February 29, 2008, from http://www.irs.gov/taxtopics/tc602.html
Long, S. K., & Clark, S. J. (1997, October). *The new child care block grant: State funding choices and their implications* (Assessing the New Federalism Policy Brief No. A-12). Washington, DC: Urban Institute. Retrieved June 8, 2006, from http://www.urban.org/UploadedPDF/anf12.pdf

Long, S. K., Kirby, G. G., Kurka, R., & Boots, S. W. (1998). *Child care assistance under welfare reform: Early responses by the states* (Occasional Paper No. 15). Retrieved June 1, 2006, from http://www.urban.org/UploadedPDF/occa15.pdf

McGill-Franzen, A. (1993). *Shaping the preschool agenda: Early literacy, public policy, and professional beliefs.* Albany: State University of New York Press.

National Association for the Education of Young Children. (n.d.). *Promoting quality through accreditation.* Retrieved March 7, 2009, from http://www.naeyc.org/accreditation/

National Center for Policy Analysis. (2001, October 19). *Proportion of working mothers with babies decreases.* Retrieved August 18, 2005, from http://www.ncpa.org/iss/wie/pd101901c.html

National Gay and Lesbian Task Force. (2008). *Adoption laws in the United States.* Retrieved March 4, 2008, from http://www.thetaskforce.org/reports_and_research/adoption_laws

National Head Start Association. (n.d.). *Keep Head Start funding federal to local.* Retrieved May 29, 2006, from http://www.nhsa.org/download/advocacy/fact/HSFund.pdf

Omnibus Budget Reconciliation Act, Pub. L. No. 97-35 (1981).

Omnibus Budget Reconciliation Act of 1990, Pub. L. No. 101-508, 104 Stat. 1388 (1990).

Parcel, T. L., & Menaghan, E. G. (1997). Effects of low-wage employment on family well-being. *The Future of Children, 7*(1), 116–121.

Parke, M. (2003). *Are married parents really better for children? What research says about the effects of family structure on child well-being* (CLASP Policy Brief). Retrieved May 19, 2007, from http://www.clasp.org/publications/Marriage_Brief3.pdf

Patterson, C. (1997). Children of lesbian and gay parents: Summary of research findings. In A. Sullivan (Ed.), *Same-sex marriage* (pp. 240–245). New York: Vintage Books.

Perry, E. (2007, June 1). Gay adoption battle mirrors marriage war. *National Blade.* Retrieved March 3, 2008, from http://www.washblade.com/2007/6-1/news/national/10688.cfm

Phillips, D. A. (1995). *Child care for low-income families: Summary of two workshops.* Washington, DC: National Academy Press.

Polikoff, N. (1990). This child does have two mothers: Redefining motherhood to meet the needs of children in lesbian-mother and other nontraditional families. *Georgetown Law Journal, 78,* 459–475.

Presser, H. (1998). Toward a 24 hour economy: The U.S. experience and implications for the family. In D. Vanoy & P. Dubek (Eds.), *Challenges for work and family in the twenty-first century* (pp. 39–48). New York: Aldine de Gruyter.

Quinn, J. (1999). Where need meets opportunity: Youth development programs for early teens. *The Future of Children, 9*(2), 96–116.

Rocha, C. (1997). Factors that contribute to economic well-being in female-headed households. *Journal of Social Service Research, 23*(1), 1–7.

Social Services Block Grant, Title XX of the Social Security Act, Pub. L. No. 97-35 (1981).

Sorensen, E., & Zibman, C. (2000, March). *Child support offers some protection against poverty* (Assessing the New Federalism Policy Brief No. B-10). Washington, DC: Urban Institute. Retrieved June 8, 2006, from http://www.urban.org/UploadedPDF/b10.pdf

Technology-Related Assistance for Individuals with Disabilities Amendments of 1994, Pub. L. No. 103-218 (1994).

U.S. Census Bureau. (2000). *Census Bureau says 7 million grade-school children home alone.* Retrieved August 18, 2005, from http://www.census.gov/Press-Release/www/2000/cb00-181.html

U.S. Census Bureau. (2003). *Annual social and economic supplement: 2003* (Current Population Reports, Current Population Survey, P20-553). Washington, DC: Author.

U.S. Census Bureau. (2005a). *Table 1A: Child care arrangements of preschoolers under 5 years old living with mother, by employment status of mother and selected characteristics* (Survey of Income and Program Participation, 2004 Panel, Wave 4). Retrieved February 28, 2008, from http://www.census.gov/population/socdemo/child/ppl-2005/tab01A.xls

U.S. Census Bureau. (2005b). *Table 5: Families with employed mothers that make child care payments, by age groups and selected characteristics: Spring 2005* (Survey of Income and Program Participation, 2004 Panel, Wave 4). Retrieved February 29, 2008, from http://www.census.gov/population/socdemo/child/ppl-2005/tab05.xls

U.S. Census Bureau. (2005c). *Table 4: Children in self-care, by age of child, employment status of mother, and selected characteristics for children living* (Survey of Income and Program Participation, 2004 Panel, Wave 4). Retrieved February 29, 2008, from http://www.census.gov/population/socdemo/child/ppl-2005/tab05.xls

U.S. Census Bureau. (2006a). *R3202. Percent of children under 6 years old with all parents in the labor force: 2006.* Retrieved March 7, 2009, from http://factfinder.census.gov/servlet/GRTChart?_bm=y&-_box_head_nbr=R2302&-_req_type=C&-ds_name=ACS_2006_EST_G00_&-_grtChart=Y&-format=US-30

U.S. Census Bureau. (2006b). *R2304. Percent of married-couple families with both husband and wife in the labor force: 2006.* Retrieved February 27, 2008, from http://factfinder.dads.census.gov/servlet/GRTTable?_bm=y&-_box_head_nbr=R2304&-ds_name=ACS_2007_1YR_G00_&-_lang=en&-format=US-30

U.S. Department of Health and Human Services. (2008). *Head Start reauthorization.* Retrieved March 4, 2008, from http://eclkc.ohs.acf.hhs.gov/hslc

U.S. Department of Labor. (2002, February 27). *Strategic goal 3: Quality workplaces. Foster quality workplaces that are safe, healthy and fair.* Retrieved May 29, 2006, from http://www.dol.gov/_sec/media/reports/annual2001/goal3.pdf

U.S. divorce statistics. (2008). *Divorce Magazine.* Retrieved February 29, 2008, from http://www.divorcemag.com/statistics/statsUS.shtml

U.S. House of Representatives. (2004, March). *2004 green book: Background material and data on the programs within the jurisdiction of the Committee on Ways and Means* (WMCP 108-6). Retrieved June 1, 2006, from http://frwebgate.access.gpo.gov/cgi-bin/getdoc.cgi?dbname=108_green_book&docid=f:wm006_10.pdf

Waller, M. (2005, December). *Block grants: Flexibility vs. stability in social services* (Center on Children & Families Policy Brief No. 34). Retrieved May 29, 2006, from http://www.brookings.edu/es/research/projects/wrb/publications/pb/pb34.pdf

Weitzman, L. J. (1985). *The divorce revolution.* New York: Free Press.

Wertheimer, R. (2003). *Poor families in 2001: Parents working less and children continuing to lag behind* (Research Brief No. 2003-10). Washington, DC: Child Trends.

Zedlewski, S. R., Adams, G., Dubay, L., & Kenney, G. M. (2006, February). *Is there a system supporting low-income working families?* (Low-Income Working Families Paper 4). Washington, DC: Urban Institute. Retrieved June 8, 2006, from http://www.urban.org/UploadedPDF/311282_lowincome_families.pdf

CHAPTER 10

Family Violence

In chapter 9, we reviewed the issues and policies related to the care and support of children. Chapter 10 approaches family caregiving from the dark side. Here we look at family violence, which negatively affects the ability of the family to provide a supportive and caring environment for its members. This chapter also differs in that we look at family violence not only as it affects children, but also as it affects intimate partners, women, same-sex couples, and the elderly. The chapter highlights the pervasive way that social problems such as violence affect the family in its different forms, and even as family structure changes over the life span. Our discussion also illustrates the way that demographic trends and the changing nature of the family make it difficult to develop comprehensive family policy. Thus, this chapter covers a variety of policy areas, all of which address the problem of family violence.

Rather than use the term *domestic violence* or *domestic abuse* as the title of this chapter, we use the term *family violence* because it more comprehensively captures the different types of violence that occur in families in the United States. The chapter begins with a discussion of three categories of family violence: intimate partner violence, domestic violence, and child maltreatment. For example, the use of the term domestic violence usually means that abuse occurs among those who are intimate or share some form of family relationship in common living quarters. In a broader sense, however, domestic violence includes abuse by other individuals in the household and other family members, including adult children. Although a commonly held assumption is that domestic violence is heterosexual in nature, and that it is always the woman who is abused and the man who is the abuser, domestic violence also occurs in same-sex relationships.

Since violence affects different types of families, different family members, and families at different points in the life span, we present trend data on family violence from different sources that compare domestic violence, intimate relationship violence, and child maltreatment. These data show the complexity of family violence in relationship to gender, race and ethnicity, and age. Data are also presented on trends in intimate relationship violence and child maltreatment, trends in gay and lesbian intimate partner violence, and the co-occurrence of child maltreatment and other types of domestic violence. Thus, in order to provide readers with a comprehensive understanding of family violence, in the first part of the chapter we discuss the various definitions of family violence and present extensive data collected under the rubric of these various definitions.

The middle part of the chapter looks in more detail at violence against women and child abuse. Public awareness of both types of abuse emerged through social movements in the United States in the 1970s, followed soon by major legislation. Here, we draw distinctions between the role of the women's movement in bringing public attention to the problem of violence against women and the role of the modern child protection movement in the emergence of awareness of child abuse as a social problem. This comparison illustrates the emergence of social problems as an essential part of the dynamics of policy making. Readers are sensitized to the long-lasting policy effects of the various ways that social problems are defined by society.

In terms of federal policy to address family violence, our discussion covers the Violence Against Women Act, the major policy for addressing domestic violence in the United States. The law provides little support for gays and lesbians who experience family violence and for heterosexual males who are abused. Currently, the law diverts funding from services that focus on women's social, financial, and emotional needs to the criminal justice system for the prosecution of offenders. We then discuss the Child Abuse Prevention and Treatment Act of 1974, the Adoption Assistance and Child Welfare Act of 1980, the Adoption and Safe Families Act of 1997, and the Keeping Families Safe Act of 2003. Our discussion of child abuse policy illustrates two major themes of the book—the debate about whether problems are caused by individuals or by larger social systems, and the lack of consensus about how much government should intervene in the private affairs of the family. For example, in the many reiterations of federal child abuse policy since the 1980s, we see a pendulum-like swing between the policy goals of child welfare policy. During one historical period, policies emphasize family preservation services to reunite abused and neglected children with their families. During the next period, policies emphasize removing children from their families through foster care placement, termination of parental rights, and adoption.

A review of the history of child welfare policy helps us understand another theme of this book: the popularity of privatization in service delivery. Not only have lawsuits played an important role in bringing managed care into child welfare, but they have also been instrumental in establishing child maltreatment policies, and in interpreting the way that laws are implemented. Lastly, the chapter looks at the maltreatment of the elderly as a form of family violence and elder abuse policy. The Older Americans Act has resulted in the establishment of Adult Protective Services at the state level, which provides long-term care ombudsman programs and legal assistance. Since minimal federal guidelines are in place, elder abuse prevention and services vary greatly from state to state and are likely to be provided through private agencies that contract for services with government.

Defining Family Violence

We start with the problem of defining family violence. Within the broad category of family violence, three different terms are commonly used to label different types of violence: *intimate partner violence*, *domestic violence*, and *child maltreatment*. The use of these different terms not only raises definitional issues but also affects the way in which statistics on family violence are collected. These definitional issues and the complications they create in recording statistics on family violence can be seen in the figures and tables that follow. Our purpose in looking at data based on different definitions of family violence is to provide a conceptual framework for the policies covered later in the chapter.

First, intimate partner violence is violence that occurs among married and unmarried couples, both gay and heterosexual. Intimate partner violence is a subset of domestic violence. The term *domestic violence* is most commonly used to describe abuse that takes place within a shared domicile. Sugg, Thompson, Thompson, Maiuro, and Rivara (1999) define domestic violence as "physical and/or sexual violence between former or current intimate partners, adult household members, or adult children and a parent. Abused persons and perpetrators could be of either sex, and couples could be heterosexual or homosexual" (p. 302). According to most current definitions, this type of violence involves assault and patterns of coercive behavior, which can include psychological and economic coercion. This means that even if the relationship does not involve physical or sexual abuse, it can be abusive in other ways. Further confusing these terms is the lack of a clear definition of what constitutes intimacy. Sometimes the word *intimacy* is used to refer to sexual intimacy, but at other times it is used to refer to emotional intimacy, so one cannot always be sure how the term is being used. The terms *domestic violence* and *intimate family violence* are generally used to refer to family violence involving adults; however, "there is a recent trend for states to adopt legal definitions of domestic violence that include violence toward children (more than half of states now mention children in their domestic violence laws). This could broaden the definition to be violence between any of the following: husbands, wives, ex-husbands, ex-wives, partners, ex-partners, brothers, sisters, mothers, fathers, children, people who have lived together (which could include cousins, brothers-in-law, sisters-in-law, and caregivers), and people who are or have dated in the past" (Newton, 2001).

The term *child maltreatment* is used to refer to the neglect and/or physical, sexual, psychological, or emotional abuse of children. There are substantial differences among various statistical reports of child maltreatment because of differences in the age at which children are considered to be adults. For example, figure 10.1 shows the rates of violent family and nonfamily victimization for all people over the age of twelve from 1993 to 2004. Child maltreatment rates for the period 1990 through 2005 are shown in figure 10.2. However, figure 10.2 covers children through nineteen years of age, so we cannot be sure about the degree of data overlap in the two graphs. Table 10.1 summarizes the data shown in figure 10.1, and table 10.2 shows the information plotted in figure 10.2 as well as a substantial amount of additional information about the types of maltreatment and the age and gender of maltreated children.

Figure 10.1 Nonfatal Violent Victimization Rate by Victim-Offender Relationship and Victim Gender, 1993–2004

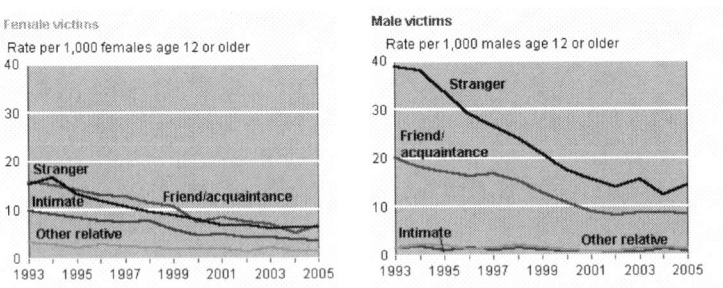

Source: U.S. Bureau of Justice Statistics. (2007). *Intimate partner violence in the U.S.* Retrieved July 21, 2008, from http://www.ojp.usdoj.gov/bjs/intimate/overview.htm

Figure 10.2 Number and Rate of Victims of Child Maltreatment, 1990–2005

[Graph: Number and Rate of Victims of Child Maltreatment, 1990-2005. Number of Victims (in thousands) values shown: 860.6, 1026.3, 1012.0, 906.0, 829.0, 872.1, 899.5. Victimization Rate (per 1,000) values: 13.4, 15.3, 14.7, 11.8, 11.9, 12.1. X-axis: 1989–2006.]

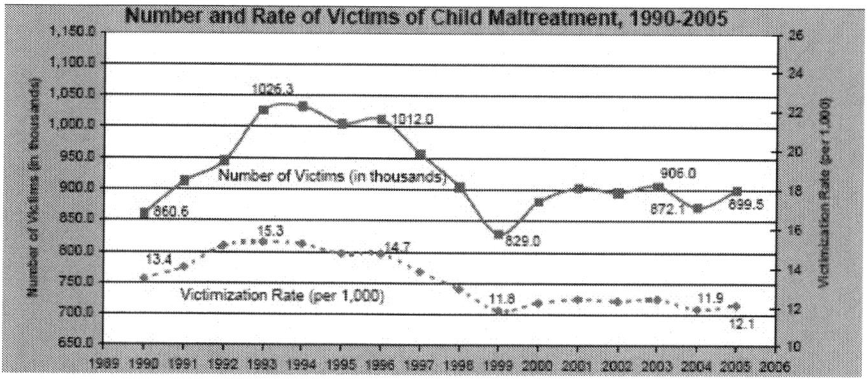

Source: Child Trends DataBank. (2003). *Child maltreatment.* Retrieved September 13, 2007, from http://www.childtrendsdatabank.org/indicators/40ChildMaltreatment.cfm

Table 10.1 Victim-Offender Relationships in Nonfatal Violent Victimizations, by Victim and Gender, 1993–2004 (Average Annual Rate per 1,000 Age Twelve and Older)

	Female		Male	
Victim/offender relationship	Rate	Percent	Rate	Percent
		100%		100%
Intimates	6.4	22.0	1.1	2.9
Other relatives	2.2	7.7	1.4	3.7
Friends/acquaintances	10.6	36.4	13.3	33.8
Stranger	9.9	33.9	23.5	59.6

Source: U.S. Bureau of Justice Statistics. (2007). *Victim/offender relationship in nonfatal violent victimizations, by victim and gender.* Retrieved September 7, 2007, from http://www.ojp.usdoj.gov/bjs/intimate/victims.htm

Trends in Family Violence

Since data on the trends of all forms of family violence are not available in one comprehensive study, we compare data on domestic violence, intimate violence, and child abuse from different sources. The data show trends in domestic violence and child abuse in relation to gender, race, and ethnicity.

Table 10.2 Trend Data for Children Who Are Victims of Child Maltreatment, 1990–2005

	1990	1991	1992	1993	1994	1995	1996	1997	1998	1999	2000	2001	2002	2003	2004	2005
Number of Victims	860,577	911,690	994,655	1,026,331	1,032,000	1,005,511	1,011,973	956,711	904,000	829,000	881,000	903,000	896,000	906,000	872,088	899,454
Rate per 1,000	13.4	14.0	15.1	15.3	15.2	14.7	14.7	13.8	12.9	11.8	12.2	12.4	12.4	11.9	12.1	
Gender (as % of all victims)																
Male	44	45	45	41	41	40	39	40	48	48	48	48	48	48	48	47
Female	50	52	51	47	46	45	43	44	52	52	52	52	52	52	52	51
Age of victim (as % of all victims)																
1 year and younger	13	14	13	12	12	11	11	11	14	14	15	16	16	16	17	—
2–5 years old	24	25	25	23	23	23	22	21	25	24	24	24	24	25	25	—
6–9 years old	22	23	23	21	20	2	21	21	25	25	24	24	23	23	22	—
10–13 years old	19	20	19	18	17	17	16	17	20	20	20	21	21	21	20	—
14–17 years old	14	15	15	14	13	13	13	12	15	15	15	15	15	15	16	—
18 and older	1	1	1	1	1	1	1	0	1	1	0	0	0	0	0	—
Race and Hispanic origin of victim (as % of all victims)																
White	53	56	53	51	48	47	50	49	56	54	51	50	—	—	—	—
Non-Hispanic white only	—	—	—	—	—	—	—	—	—	—	—	—	54	54	54	50
Black	25	27	27	25	25	24	22	22	25	26	25	25	—	—	—	—
Non-Hispanic black only	—	—	—	—	—	—	—	—	—	—	—	—	—	—	—	—
Hispanic	10	10	10	9	9	9	9	9	14	14	15	11	12	17	17	17
American Indian/ Alaskan Native	1	1	1	1	1	1	2	2	2	2	2	2	11	12	17	—

Non-Hispanic American Indian/Alaskan Native only	—	—	—	—	—	—	—	—	—	—	—	—	2	2	1	1
Asian/Pacific Islander	1	1	1	1	1	1	1	1	1	1	1	1	—	—	—	—
Non-Hispanic Asian only	—	—	—	—	—	—	—	—	—	—	—	—	—	1	1	1
Non-Hispanic Pacific Islander only	—	—	—	—	—	—	—	—	—	—	—	—	—	0	0	0
Multiple race	—	—	—	—	—	—	—	—	—	—	—	1	—	—	2	2
Unknown	1	2	2	1	1	2	3	3	2	11	7	6	—	—	—	—
Type of maltreatment (as % of all victims)																
Neglect	49	46	50	49	52	52	52	55	54	56	60	57	59	61	62	63
Physical abuse	27	26	23	24	24	24	24	24	23	21	19	19	19	19	18	17
Sexual abuse	17	16	4	14	14	13	12	12	12	11	10	10	10	10	10	9
Psychological or emotional abuse	7	6	5	5	5	4	6	6	6	8	8	7	7	5	7	7
Medical neglect	0	2	3	2	2	3	3	2	2	2	3	2	2	2	2	2
Other and unknown	10	13	21	17	16	17	19	12	26	28	17	20	19	1	15	15

Source: Adapted from Child Trends DataBank. (2003). *Child maltreatment*. Retrieved September 13, 2007, from http://www.childtrendsdatabank.org/indicators/40ChildMaltreatment.cfm

Age trends in intimate relationship violence and child abuse, and trends in gay and lesbian intimate relationship violence, are also provided.

Gender Trends in Domestic Violence and Child Abuse

Table 10.1 shows that 29.7 percent of the overall violent victimization of females was due to domestic violence and that 6.6 percent of all violence against men was domestic violence. The rates of child abuse from 1990 to 2005 were much higher than were domestic violence rates for adults. This is easiest to see if we compare the domestic violence rates for adults in table 10.1 with those for child abuse in table 10.2. When the mean for data in table 10.2 is computed for the period from 1993 to 2004, the rate for adult males is 2.5 per 1,000 and the rate for male children is 44.4 per 1,000. The rate for adult females was 8.6 per 1,000, and the rate for female children was 49.1 per 1,000. When viewing data on family violence, one has to be very careful because in some cases the data are for all domestic violence, and in others it only refers to intimate partner violence. For example, the U.S. Bureau of Justice Statistics does not provide data on adult domestic violence by race, ethnicity, and age trends, but rather only on adult intimate violence.

Racial and Ethnic Trends in Intimate Relationship Violence and Child Abuse

Trend data show that between 1990 and 2003, rates of nonfatal intimate partner violence for white females and males and black females decreased. However, from 2003 to 2004, the rate of nonfatal intimate partner violence for black females increased from 3.8 to 6.6 victimizations per 1,000 persons age twelve years and older. Although occurring at much lower rates, nonfatal intimate partner violence for white males also increased between 2003 and 2004, from .5 to 1.1 victimizations per 1,000 males age twelve and older (U.S. Bureau of Justice Statistics, 2007). Rates of child maltreatment are higher for nonwhite children than for white children. "Non-Hispanic black, American Indian or Alaskan Native, and Pacific Islander children have higher rates of reported child maltreatment than do other children. In 2005, non-Hispanic black children had a reported maltreatment rate of 19.5 per 1,000 children, Pacific Islander children had a rate of 16.1 per 1,000 children, and American Indian and Alaskan Native children had a reported maltreatment rate of 16.5 per 1,000 children, compared with 10.8 per 1,000 for non-Hispanic white children, 10.7 per 1,000 Hispanic children, and 2.5 per 1,000 Asian children" (Child Trends DataBank, 2007, p. 2).

Age Trends in Intimate Partner Violence and Child Abuse

Table 10.3 summarizes the data for adult intimate violence from 1993 to 2004. Between 1993 and 2004, for all age categories, nonfatal intimate partner victimization declined. In general, during that period, "females in the oldest (50+) and youngest age (12–15) categories were at the lowest risk of nonfatal intimate partner violence. For [2004], females age 20–24 and 25–34 were at the greatest risk of nonfatal intimate partner violence. Rates for males increased between 2003 and 2004, returning to levels last seen in 1996" (U.S. Bureau of Justice Statistics, 2007).

Table 10.2 shows the child maltreatment rates based on the number of occurrences in a population of one thousand. For the period from 1993 to 2004 they were 13.7 for children one year old and younger, 23.6 for children two to five years old, 20.9 for children six to nine years old, 19 for children ten to thirteen years old, 14.2 for children fourteen to seventeen years old, and 0.5 for individuals eighteen and older.

Table 10.3 Average Annual Nonfatal Intimate Partner Victimization Rate per 1,000 by Gender and Age Group, 1993–2004

	Females	Males
12–15	1.9	0.3
16–19	12.4	1.2
20–24	17.0	2.3
25–34	12.3	2.1
35–49	6.3	1.3
50–64	1.4	0.5
65 or older	0.2	0.1*

* Based on ten or fewer cases
Source: U.S. Bureau of Justice Statistics. (2007). *Intimate partner violence in the U.S. has been declining.* Retrieved September 7, 2007, from http://www.ojp.usdoj.gov/bjs/intimate/overview.htm

Trends in Gay and Lesbian Intimate Partner Violence

Federal statistics provide no information on the incidence of violence in gay and lesbian relationships. Citing numerous studies, Cahill, Ellen and Tobias (2002) report that "Preliminary studies of lesbian couples found that 22 to 46 percent of lesbians have been in physically violent same sex relationships and that one in four men from a sample of 2000 men had experienced domestic violence" (p. 158) and that the level of violence for lesbians is as high as or higher than that among other type of couples, and much higher for gay males than for other types of couples. In addition to the reasons given by heterosexual victims of intimate partner violence, gay and lesbian victims report that the following factors make their efforts to deal with violence in their relationships difficult:

- A dearth of resources, services, and education on GLBT domestic violence issues
- A fear of being outed
- Belief in the myth that same-sex relationships cannot be abusive, leading to a failure to recognize abuse when it happens
- Fear of homophobic reactions by service providers, police, and others
- Greater risk of losing children to a third party than heterosexual victims of intimate partner violence
- Fear of having to cut ties to one's community

Intimate Partner Violence and Child Abuse

It is impossible to separate intimate partner abuse and child maltreatment from each other; they are inextricably linked. Box 10.1 tells the story of Bonita, a twenty-eight-year-old woman who is the oldest of nine children, and her long history of childhood victimization. This case illustrates the co-occurrence of intimate partner violence and child abuse.

Box 10.1 The Co-occurrence of Child Abuse and Intimate Partner Violence

Bonita, a twenty-eight-year-old woman who is the oldest of nine children, has a long history of childhood victimization. This case illustrates the co-occurrence of child maltreatment and intimate partner violence. The pattern of physical abuse was so predictable that Bonita's mother would warn the children to go to their rooms when their father was coming home from work.

> We all would scatter upstairs and hide from him. But he would beat us. He would throw the milk crates at me, throw beer cans at me, throw me, pick me up to the ceiling and throw me onto the floor. Okay? And my brother, too. One time we didn't have no hot dogs in the house, and my father got really mad at him. Oooh, he kicked his legs like nothing! Today, he has the scar between his groins. You can see the scar coming down his leg from being kicked so much because

> *there was no hot. . . . "Why didn't you tell me we didn't have no hot dogs? God dammit." You know, cussing and what have you and this in Spanish. I mean it.*

Bonita's mother was also severely abused by her husband. Sometimes she fought back, but most of the time she would not talk to her children about the abuse, even though they urged her to leave him. Bonita couldn't stand her mother's reaction to the abuse and finally left home at age fifteen.

> *And then one time my mother had her twins—her first twins. Well, then they had an argument. Boy, my father pushed her onto the floor and got the chain out of the closet and started hitting her on the back.*
>
> *Okay? And then—what else? One time I came home from school, and I didn't really want to go to school, because I had a funny feeling there was gonna be a fight. So my mother went and got a knife and cut his groin. He got pissed—really upset—punched right into Mom. I said, "Mom, what happened? You and Daddy were fighting? You and Daddy were fighting? You and Daddy were fighting?" She said, "Yeah, baby. Just leave me alone, baby. Just leave me alone."*
>
> *And I would tell her at fourteen years, "Mom, you should get rid of Daddy, Ma. You know, Daddy's no good," and this and that. But yet she would keep him. Yes, he would stay with her. Yes, she would stay with him. I would be so mad, so angry at him and at her. I would tell her, "It's your fault—you're taking the abuse. And you live upstairs beaten by him and you just as bad as he is." And, she would have a nervous breakdown over him constantly. I couldn't stand that. That's why I left home, too. I couldn't stand that.*

Newton (2001) writes:

When describing the effects of domestic violence on children, it is important to note that domestic violence and child abuse are often present in the same families. Estimates are that more than 3.3 million children are exposed to physical and verbal spousal abuse each year. Exposure means seeing or hearing the actual abuse or dealing with the aftermath of the abuse. "In homes where domestic violence occurs, children are physically abused and neglected at a rate 15 times higher than the national average. Several studies have found that in 60% to 75% of families in which a woman is battered, children are also battered" [Osofsky, 1999, p. 34]. In addition, children living in households where domestic violence is occurring are at a higher risk for sexual abuse.

In a 1999 study from Johns Hopkins, it was reported that abused women are at higher risk of miscarriages, stillbirths, and infant deaths, and are more likely to give birth to low birth weight children, a risk factor for neonatal and infant deaths. In addition, children of abused women were more likely to be malnourished and were more likely to have had a recent untreated case of diarrhea and less likely to have been immunized against childhood diseases [Heise, Ellsberg, & Gottemoeller, 1999].

Most battered women take active steps to protect their children, even if they do not leave their batterer. Domestic violence can severely impair a parent's ability to nurture the development of their children. Mothers who are abused may be depressed or preoccupied with the violence. They may be emotionally withdrawn or numb, irritable or have feelings of hopelessness. The result can be a parent who is less emotionally available to their children or unable to care for their children's basic needs. Battering fathers are less affectionate, less available, and less rational in dealing with their children. Studies even suggest that "battered women may use more punitive child-rearing strategies or exhibit aggression toward their children" [Carter, Weithorn, & Behrman, 1999, p. 6].

When children cannot depend on their parents or caregivers—for emotional support and for practical support—their development can be seriously delayed or, in severe cases, permanently distorted. Children without an emotionally available parent may withdraw from relationships and social activities. Since childhood is the time when social skills and attitudes are learned, domestic violence can affect their ability to form relationships for the rest of their lives.

The effects of witnessing or experiencing violence at home vary tremendously from one child to another. The attributes that give a child the greatest chance of surviving unscathed are "average or above-average intellectual development with good attention and interpersonal skills. Also feelings of self-esteem and self-efficacy, attractiveness to others in both personality and appearance, individual talents, religious affiliations, socioeconomic advantage, opportunities for good schooling and employment, and contact with people and environments that are positive for development" [Osofsky, 1999, p. 39].

As these passages show, child maltreatment and other forms of domestic violence are inseparably linked. Nonetheless, the policies developed to deal with each of these manifestations of family violence have in large part ignored the link and consequently have developed policies focused on each problem separately. Because policies were developed separately, we separate our review of policies addressing child maltreatment from those that focus on other forms of domestic violence.

Violence Against Women

Intimate partner violence against women has existed for all of recorded history. An excellent chronology entitled "Herstory of Domestic Violence: A Timeline of the Battered Women's Movement" (Minnesota Center Against Violence and Abuse, 1999) can be found online. In many parts of the world, intimate partner violence has yet to be formally recognized as a social problem. In the United States, it was only recently recognized as a social problem deserving governmental intervention. In the 1960s and 1970s, the feminist movement successfully politicized and reframed intimate partner violence against women (then called domestic violence), which had previously been seen as a private or personal issue, as a public problem rooted in sexism, male dominance, and the powerlessness of women. Through the feminist movement, the issue of intimate partner violence against women became recognized as a national public social problem that affected women of all backgrounds—rich and poor, white and nonwhite, educated and uneducated. Consequently, women are the focus of intimate partner violence policies, and therefore there are few or no policies specific to males who are abused in heterosexual or same-sex relationships.

The Violence Against Women Act

The recognition of various forms of domestic violence, particularly intimate partner violence, as a social problem led to the passage of a series of laws and regulations designed to end violence against women. The first piece of legislation, the Family Violence and Prevention Services Act, was enacted as Title III of the Child Abuse Amendments of 1984. The law was amended by the Keeping Children and Families Safe Act of 2003. Administered through the Family and Youth Services Bureau of the Department of Health and Human Services, the law provides grants for temporary shelter and emergency services such as counseling, food, clothing, child care, and transportation for battered women. Ten percent of federal funding from this act goes to state coalitions to provide assistance on domestic violence policy and practice to local programs. Funds may also be provided for interdisciplinary collaboration among law enforcement, social services, health, and legal professionals. The act funds five national resource centers.

In 1994, Congress passed the Violence Against Women Act as part of the Violent Crime Control and Law Enforcement Act of 1994 (VAWA). The VAWA was the first comprehensive federal legislation to improve criminal justice and community-based services for domestic violence. The breadth of the social movement behind the VAWA was extraordinary. Congressional hearings were held in Utah, Maine, and Washington, D.C., as advocates presented testimony on the problem from a variety of perspectives. From volunteers of the Young Women's Christian Association to leaders of the right wing of the Republican Party to representatives of the American Medical Association—all were in full support of the proposed legislation. Senator Dianne Feinstein (D-CA) described lobbying for the bill as "a new kind of bipartisanship" (Sklar & Lustig, 2001). The enactment of the VAWA was hailed as a "success of historic proportions on various political and social fronts . . . undeniably a victory for feminism . . . also a civil rights victory" (Rivera, 1996, p. 464).

VAWA legislation created criminal penalties for gender-related violence and provided grants for states to address domestic violence and sexual assault. The law made it possible to enforce orders of protection across state lines and made it a federal crime for anyone subject to a protective order to carry a firearm or to violate a protective order even if both individuals are in another state. Its reauthorization in 2000 identified dating violence and stalking as crimes and provided additional resources to prosecute perpetrators and provide services to victims. It also promoted supervised visitation programs for children in families experiencing abuse and strengthened protection for women with disabilities, immigrants, victims of elder abuse, and college students. The Office on Violence Against Women administers grants from the Department of Justice to ensure better responses to violent crimes against women by criminal justice systems. It has awarded more than $1 billion in grant funds, including Services, Training, Officers, Prosecutors (STOP) grants to state, tribal, and local governments and to community-based agencies to train personnel, set up domestic violence and sexual assault units, assist victims, and prosecute perpetrators. More than 6,500 STOP subgrants have supported community partnerships among police, prosecutors, victim advocates, and others to address violence against women (U.S. Department of Justice, n.d.).

The VAWA has been reauthorized twice—both times with remarkable, nearly unanimous bipartisan support. It was authorized first as part of the Victims of Trafficking and Violence Protection Act of 2000, and then as part of a much broader crime bill, the Violence Against Women and Department of Justice Reauthorization Act of 2005, which authorized funding for programs at the Department of Justice until FY 2009. The history of this legislation illustrates the funding trade-offs that occur when bills are attached to larger pieces of legislation. Originally, the law was passed with specific funding levels for both the U.S. Department of Health and Human Services and the Department of Justice, but the Department of Health and Human Services received less funding than was authorized by Congress, and the Department of Justice received a considerably greater amount of funding than was authorized by Congress (table 10.4). Less funding for the Department of Health and Human Services has meant less capacity for dealing with the longer-term social and emotional consequences of domestic violence, including poverty and homelessness, posttraumatic stress disorder, and depression. Thus, greater funding levels for the Department of Health and Human Services are needed to fully provide comprehensive services for victims of domestic violence (Dakin, 2005).

In terms of the law enforcement, the result of the VAWA has been an increase in the number of crimes reported, cases prosecuted, and perpetrators sentenced. It is estimated, however, that only 7 percent to 14 percent of intimate partner violence incidents are reported to the police. Victims are more likely to report if the abuse is severe and if it is witnessed by a child or other relative. Abuse is less likely to be reported if the victim is in a long-term abusive relationship and is less educated. The fear of retaliation is a primary reason why victims of abuse do not call the police or follow through with criminal charges and protective orders. Recognizing this, many municipalities have begun to change policy to make intimate partner violence a crime against the state, rather than against an individual. This allows the district attorney to charge the abuser with a crime without requiring the victim to press charges.

Table 10.4 Comparison of VAWA Enacted and Authorized Funding Levels, 2002–2004

	2002 Authorized	2002 Received	2003 Authorized	2003 Received	2004 Authorized	2004 Received
Department of Justice	337.5	390.6	362.3	390.6	362.3	385.4
Health and Human Services	263.0	126.62	263.0	129.81	263.0	127.0

Source: Congressional Research Service. (2004). *Impact of the Violence Against Women Act*. Washington, DC: Author.

Child Maltreatment

Child maltreatment was recognized as a social problem much earlier than other forms of domestic violence. In the early part of the nineteenth century in the United States, poverty and child neglect were intertwined. Mothers who were too poor to care for their children were often sent to poorhouses. During the Progressive era of the late nineteenth century, reformers attempted to remove innocent children from the poorhouses but not necessarily unite or reunite the family. Instead, the primary aim was to remove children from the harmful influence of husbandless families (Davidson, 1994). In the mid-1800s, Charles Loring Brace, a Presbyterian minister and the founder of the Children's Aid Society, believed that the best solution for some of New York's 30,000 homeless children was removing them from foundling homes, orphanages, and street gangs and placing them in "morally upright" farm families. The narratives of adults who rode the orphan trains to new families show many different reasons for their situations—parental deaths, impoverishment among immigrant widows, inability to feed children, and children born out of wedlock, as well as neglect and abuse (Ayler, 2005). The orphan train movement, during which children were placed on trains and sent West to deserving families, is now viewed as the beginning of foster care in the United States. Between 1853 and 1930, the orphan trains took more than 150,000 children to out-of-home placements in more than forty-five states across the United States as well as Canada and Mexico. Some children were adopted; others worked as free or paid hired hands. Some found loving, caring new homes and families; others were abused and neglected.

It was not until the early 1960s that the modern child protection movement began with the research and writings on battered children of C. Henry Kempe and his colleagues. Speaking at a 1961 conference of the American Academy of Pediatrics in Chicago, the Denver pediatrician coined the term the *battered child syndrome,* which described a pattern of child abuse, and established a medical and psychiatric model of the cause of child abuse. They revealed that not all injuries to young children were accidental—and such injuries often led to permanent injury or death (Kempe, Silverman, Steele, Droegemuller, & Silver, 1962). This time it was not poverty, orphanhood, or immigration at the heart of child maltreatment, but physical injury. By 1967, Kempe's work had led all fifty states to pass child abuse reporting laws.

The complexities of the issue of child maltreatment can be seen in the various approaches that have been taken to deal with the problem. Since the mid-1970s, public policy has wavered between a child-centered approach focused on removal of children from their homes and placement in foster care and a family-centered approach focused on reunification with family or, where that is not possible, permanent placement through adoption. The child-centered approach is encapsulated by the phrase "the best interests of the child." It is based on the belief that it is the state's responsibility to intervene regarding the welfare of children when family systems fail. The family-centered or family preservation approach places high value on parental authority and the right to privacy, as well as the primary right of children to live in a family related by blood ties. The vacillation between the child-centered and the family-centered approach to child maltreatment occurred because as time passed, it became clear that whichever policy approach was currently being used was failing to reduce the levels of child maltreatment.

The Child Abuse Prevention and Treatment Act of 1974

Bartholet (2000) lays the blame for the inadequacy of the child welfare system on what he calls the "artificial narrowing" of child welfare that began with the election of President Richard Nixon. With the collapse of the War on Poverty, liberals in the early 1970s sought to build bipartisan support for new strategies to improve the lives of children in poverty. Senator Walter Mondale (D-MN) led the legislative effort that resulted in the Child Abuse Prevention and Treatment Act (CAPTA) in 1974, which started the current child welfare system. Box 10.2 shows the many legal and legislative events that gave rise to the contemporary child welfare system in the United States. Through its long history of legislative amendments, several later child welfare laws are connected to CAPTA.

Box 10.2 Legal and Legislative History of Child Protection

- In 1874, ten-year-old Mary Ellen was removed from her home and provided with protection from abuse by the New York court system. The case led in part to the founding of the New York Society for Prevention of Cruelty to Children.
- In 1839, the Pennsylvania court issued the *Ex parte Crouse* decision, which affirmed the responsibility of the government to care for society's children.
- The first juvenile court was established in Cook County, Illinois, in 1899. Early juvenile courts were concerned with keeping the streets free of poor and vagrant children.
- In 1912, as a result of President Roosevelt's 1909 White House Conference on Children, Congress created the United States Children's Bureau.

- In 1921, Congress passes the Sheppard-Towner Act, which established Children's Bureaus at the state level and promoted maternal-infant health.
- In 1944, the Supreme Court of the United States confirmed the state's authority to intervene in family relationships to protect children in *Prince v. Massachusetts*.
- In 1960, New York became the first state to adopt the Interstate Compact on Placement of Children. It established orderly procedures for the interstate placement of children and fixed responsibility for those involved in placing children.
- In 1962, C. Henry Kempe published the landmark article "The Battered Child Syndrome," generally regarded as one of the most significant events leading to professional and public awareness of the existence and magnitude of child abuse and neglect.
- In 1967, the Supreme Court of the United States issued a decision in *In re Gault* guaranteeing constitutional protection to children accused of crimes.
- By 1967, forty-four states had adopted mandatory reporting laws. The remaining six states adopted voluntary reporting laws. All states now have mandatory reporting laws.
- In 1974, Congress passed landmark legislation in the federal Child Abuse Prevention and Treatment Act. In 1974, the National Center on Child Abuse and Neglect was created to serve as an information clearinghouse.
- In 1974, Congress adopted the Juvenile Justice Delinquency Prevention Act and Family Education Rights and Privacy Act, which mandated support for juvenile delinquency prevention programs.
- In 1978, Congress passed the Indian Child Welfare Act. The act gave federally recognized Indian tribes and Native Alaskan villages jurisdiction over child welfare cases.
- In 1980, Congress passed the Adoption Assistance and Child Welfare Act of 1980, which was designed to remedy problems in the foster care system. In 1983, the act was amended to provide for special procedures before a child was removed and reunification strategies after removal. The act and its amendment essentially provided fiscal incentives to encourage states to prevent unnecessary foster care placements and to provide children in placement with permanent homes.
- In 1981, Title XX of the Social Security Act was amended to include the Social Services Block Grant to provide child protective services funding to states.

- In 1984, CAPTA was amended to include medically disabled infants, the reporting of medical neglect and maltreatment in out-of-home care, and sexual exploitation.
- In 1986, Congress passed the Child Abuse Victims' Rights Act, which gave child victims of sexual exploitation a civil damage claim.
- CAPTA was fully rewritten as the Child Abuse Prevention, Adoption and Family Services Act of 1988.
- In 1990, Title III was added to CAPTA for services for homeless families and families at risk of homelessness by the Stewart B. McKinney Homeless Assistance Act of 1990.
- In 1991, Congress passed the Victims of Child Abuse Act to improve the investigation and prosecution of child abuse cases.
- In 1993, the New York Supreme Court Appellate Division, in *In re Jamie TT*, found a constitutional basis for the representation of children in dependency cases.
- In 1993, as part of the Omnibus Budget and Reconciliation Act, Congress provided funding for state courts to assess the impact of the Adoption Act on foster care proceedings, to study the handling of child protection cases, and to develop a plan for improvements.
- In 1994, Congress passed the Multiethnic Placement Act. The act provided that adoption or foster care placements may not be denied or delayed based on race, color, or national origin of the individual or the children involved.
- In 1996, the CAPTA amendments of 1996 amended Title I, replaced Title II with a new Community-Based Family Resource and Support Program, and repealed Title III Services Regarding Children of Homeless Families or Families at Risk of Homelessness.
- In 1996, Congress replaced AFDC with Temporary Assistance to Needy Families. Although TANF made few changes to federal child protection programs directly, it affected child welfare services by changing programs upon which it had formerly relied.
- In 1997, Congress passed the Adoption and Safe Families Act of 1997. ASFA represented the most significant change in federal child welfare law since the Adoption Assistance and Child Welfare Act of 1980. Congress passed the Chafee Foster Care Independence Act in 1999. The Act provided funding and services for youths who have aged out of the child welfare system.
- In 2000, Congress passed the Child Abuse Prevention and Enforcement Act, which focused on improving the criminal justice system's ability to provide timely and accurate criminal-record information to agencies engaged in child protection, and enhancing prevention and law enforcement activities.

- In 2001, Congress reauthorized the Stewart B. McKinney Homeless Assistance Act as part of the No Child Left Behind Act. McKinney-Vento provided emergency assistance for homeless children and youths. It required schools to remove barriers to enrollment, attendance, and success for homeless youths in public schools.
- In 2003, Congress amended and reauthorized CAPTA by the Keeping Children and Families Safe Act of 2003.

Source: Adapted from Ventrell, M. (1999–2000). Evolution of the dependency component of the juvenile court. *Children's Legal Rights Journal, 19*(4). Retrieved May 24, 2006, from http://naccchildlaw.org/childrenlaw/childmaltreatment.html

As the primary federal legislation dealing with child abuse and protection, CAPTA positioned the federal government to assume a proactive role in the *detection* of child maltreatment, but a far less active role in the *prevention* and *treatment* of child abuse. Although some federal money for foster care was available through the Social Security Act Amendments of 1962, CAPTA increased incentives for states to place children in foster care as a protective intervention. CAPTA also required mandatory reporting, as it was believed that it would lead to early detection of symptoms and prevention of more serious injuries and fatalities (Hutchison, 1993). In order to receive federal funds, states are required to have personnel and facilities available for reporting, investigating, and treating child abuse, and each state develops its own definition of child maltreatment, covering four general areas.

- Physical abuse: shaking, slapping, punching, beating, kicking, and burning or severe physical punishment, and expulsion from the home or refusal to allow a runaway to return home
- Sexual abuse: involving dependent children and adolescents in sexual acts, including touching, fondling, and penetration; child prostitution; and exposure to child pornography
- Neglect: failure to provide for a child's basic needs such as food, housing, clothing, medical care, and education (includes emotional neglect)
- Emotional or psychological abuse: parental child abduction, intimate partner violence, or drug and alcohol abuse in the presence of the child, and threatening or intimidating a child by shaming or belittling him or her or calling him or her names

After CAPTA became law in 1974, the magnitude of child abuse reports was far greater than policy makers believed would occur. Protective service agencies were inundated with reports of child abuse. Instead of catching maltreatment early enough to prevent it, reporting laws increased child abuse caseloads and the required case investigations. Advocates continually sought increases in federal funds, but Congress failed to authorize significant funding increases for social services in several reauthorizations of CAPTA. Federal funding could not keep up with the growing needs of casework, and as a result, child welfare workers offered little more than superficial interventions (Jimenez, 1990).

Adoption Assistance and Child Welfare Act of 1980

By 1980, the child welfare system was blamed for allowing "foster care drift"—children spending years and years in foster care without permanency. Criticisms included the system's failure to monitor children in foster placements and to work toward the reunification of parents and children. Children entered care too easily, with little effort made to maintain them in their own homes, and foster care became permanent for many children. Services to help biological parents resolve the problems that necessitated placement were rarely provided (Stein, 2000). Norma's story in box 10.3 illustrates the problems of foster care drift, as well as the problem of who is defined as a family member for the purpose of obtaining custody. If their mother's partner had been able to keep the children initially, they might have been able to maintain the family unit.

Box 10.3 Foster Care Drift

Norma's biological father was an alcoholic, and her drug-addicted mother used to beat her. Norma first became homeless when she was seven years old and her mother abandoned her.

> I don't know my real mother. I got to meet her a couple of times, but I don't know her completely. She left me and my brothers and sisters at home one day, and she never came back. She just, like, picked up and left us all by ourselves in the house with no food, no nothing.... My older brother was eight, I was seven, my younger brother was six, and my little sister, she was—I'm six years older than her, so she was about a year and something.... And it was just us four in the house and we didn't know what to do.... By that time, we had a stepfather.

> *... My stepfather tried to stay with us, but the court said he couldn't have us, because he wasn't related to us and he wasn't married to my mother. So they split us up. My mother's sister took custody of me.*

Norma's little brother was sent to Puerto Rico, and she has never received any information about his whereabouts. Her baby sister was placed in foster care, and she saw her sister for the first time after she turned eighteen. Norma moved from foster home to foster home for eight years. At age eleven, she was placed with a foster mother whom she could relate to, but the agency still kept moving her around. Finally, her foster mother adopted her when she was fourteen years old.

> *Before she legally adopted me, she had me when I was going on eleven years old. I was already ten years of age, and about seven months. She took me—my mom, I mean, my foster mom. She'd already taken me, but since she was just taking care of foster kids, they would switch me around. But mainly they would leave me to her since they saw that I was great with her. I got along with her.... It came a point that the last time that they took me away from her, I got real sick, 'cause I wanted to be with her.... That was mainly all my life.... My teenage years weren't much, but right then I felt stable. I felt loved.*

In response to these concerns, Congress passed the Adoption Assistance and Child Welfare Act of 1980, which shifted funding away from foster care and toward permanency planning through prevention and reunification. The new law emphasized the preservation of the biological family and, if that could not be done, the creation of adoptive families. Only as a last resort were children to be placed permanently in foster homes. As a condition for federal funds, states were to make reasonable efforts to reunite parents, review each child's case no less than once every six months, and conduct a dispositional review at eighteen months. Although Congress authorized funding for preventive and reunification services, the amount actually appropriated was far short of what was authorized.

The Adoption and Safe Families Act of 1997

Seventeen years later, Congress passed the Adoption and Safe Families Act of 1997. ASFA shifted the emphasis of child welfare away from family preservation and reunification toward a concern for the child's safety by terminating parental rights more quickly, and moving children from foster care to permanent adoptive homes. Under certain circumstances, reasonable efforts to reunite families were no longer needed. Permanency planning could be bypassed in cases of extreme physical or sexual abuse or abandonment, cases in which parental rights had already been terminated for another child, and cases in which a parent was found responsible for the death of another child. The act changed the time limit for the court hearing on permanency from eighteen months to twelve months and allowed the state to petition the court to terminate parental rights for children who were in foster care for fifteen of the most recent twenty-two months.

ASFA introduced the first federal performance-based financial incentive in child welfare. Congress authorized incentive payments to agencies for terminating parental rights and finding successful adoptive parents within given time frames. The Adoption Incentive Award provided a financial incentive of $4,000 for each child adopted, and an additional $2,000 for each adopted child with special needs. States could opt to participate and also choose how to spend the additional resources. Managed care in child welfare also began during this time. Some states obtained title IV-E Child Welfare Demonstration waivers to experiment with managed care, including some performance-based financing. Tennessee and Florida, for example, were using fixed or prospective payment or blended per diem systems to pay contractors: "Under these models, private agencies receive a case rate for each client referred, and the rate represents the average cost of treating all referred clients. Such systems do not necessarily tie funding to a particular standard of performance by the agency or outcome for children. However, they may provide a fiscal incentive to promote improved outcomes in the areas of permanency and child well-being" (U.S. Department of Health and Human Services, 1997).

According to Stein (2000), the goals of the 1997 and 1980 laws were the same—and both were attainable under the previous law, if they were attainable at all. There were several impediments to these goals. First, if parents are to have a fair chance at regaining custody of their children, service provision must be intense. Child welfare workers need to have skills in service provision, brokering services, problem solving, and monitoring client progress toward goal attainment. However, only 15 percent of child welfare workers have any formal social work education. High turnover of workers and huge caseloads permit only superficial contact with clients. These same workers must petition the court and convince the court that allowing the parent-child relationship to continue is more detrimental than the consequences of terminating parental rights.

The Keeping Families Safe Act of 2003

Congress took action to address some of these problems with the Keeping Children and Families Safe Act of 2003. This reauthorization of CAPTA provides states with flexible funds to improve child protective services in areas such as intake, assessment, screening, and investigation; case management and service delivery; the tracking of reports of abuse and neglect through automated systems; and training for agency staff, service providers, and mandated reporters. The act also provides grants to provide financial assistance and services to facilitate adoption, provide public education, and enhance collaboration between the courts, departments of children's services, and the community-based agencies that provide services to maltreated children.

Each state must also submit a five-year plan with assurance that it is operating a child welfare system that (1) has a citizen review panel; (2) expunges unsubstantiated and false reports of child abuse and neglect; (3) preserves the confidentiality of reports and records of child abuse and neglect; (4) provides public disclosure of the facts of a case that results in child fatality or near fatality; (5) appoints a guardian ad litem to represent a child's best interests in court; (6) expedites termination of parental rights for abandoned infants; (7) does not require reunification of a child with parents who have committed certain crimes and makes conviction of certain felonies grounds for termination of parental rights. According to Davidson (2003), the reauthorization of CAPTA "potentially doubles the amount of state grant funds available, if Congress ever significantly increases CAPTA appropriations." Congress has never funded CAPTA adequately, but the FY 2005 and 2006 amounts are the most ever appropriated.

Lawsuits and Child Welfare

Federal and state legislation are not the only source of changes that have taken place in the development of child maltreatment policies in the United States. In addition to mandating state compliance with federal law, individual and class-action lawsuits have had some success in changing state child welfare systems. In 1980, attorney Marcia Lowry led the American Civil Liberties Union in a successful class-action lawsuit against New Mexico's child welfare system. Since that time, Children's Rights, an organization that she founded, has filed civil lawsuits against seven states and six local governments. Connecticut, Georgia, Illinois, Mississippi, Missouri, Nebraska, New Jersey, New Mexico, New York, Tennessee, Washington, DC, and Wisconsin have been the target of class-action lawsuits that allege heavy caseloads, foster care drift, inadequate supervision, and other problems in the child welfare system. Each defendant settled out of court—except for Washington, D.C., which went to trial and lost. Alabama, Illinois, Utah, and Washington have been sued by the Bazelon Center for Mental Health Law. Class-action lawsuits are extraordinarily expensive. New Jersey spent $1.2 million in private attorney fees and $1.2 million for case reviews by outside experts at the Child Welfare League of America and paid Children's Rights another $1.6 million in costs. Advocates argue, however, that the costs are worth it. The case against New Jersey ended with a commitment by the state to spend $320 million over the next three years on improving its child welfare system (Kelly, 2004).

Filing lawsuits to force change can be very time consuming. Cases tend to drag on—sometimes for years. In *Marisol v. Pataki* (1998), which lasted for thirteen years, Children's Rights sued both the New York city and state child welfare systems on behalf of more than 100,000 children in foster care. Legal complaints included the failure to investigate complaints of child abuse, provide mandated pre-placement preventive services before children enter foster care, and provide services for teens aging out of the foster care system. In 1999, a settlement mandated the creation of an advisory panel of experts to help the city implement necessary state reforms and a statewide data management system. In 2001, additional legal action was taken to address unresolved issues.

Critics of legal action as a solution to the woes of child welfare point out that court rulings end in rigid mandates that inhibit the longer-term remedies needed to permanently improve public agency performance. In 2001, *Brian A. et al. v. Sundquist et al.* required training for all case managers, smaller caseloads of ten to twenty children, reassignment of cases to other case managers within twenty-four hours of worker turnover, and placement of children within seventy-five miles of their home. The Tennessee appeals court also ordered a variety of other placement rules: children cannot be placed in more than two emergency or temporary placements in any twelve-month period, foster children cannot be placed with other children who are at high risk for violent behavior or perpetration of sexual abuse, foster homes may not have more than six children, children under age six may not be placed in a group home, and residential treatment facilities cannot have more than eight children. In Tennessee, a civil suit has literally stalled the system. Many children are being sent home—just to reenter the system again—because there just are not enough permanent placements available. Some group homes have closed, and others are having difficulty remaining financially solvent after downsizing. Gelles and Schwartz (1999) point out that it is the absence of a Supreme Court ruling on the federal guarantees to children in child welfare systems that has resulted in so many class-action lawsuits. They conclude: "In Alabama, for example, the state is obliged to provide more family preservation services; in Connecticut the state has been ordered to give more weight to child safety. Unfortunately, however, even class action suits have failed to provide a clear basis for the rights and best interests of children (or even reflect differing conceptions of children's 'best interests'). . . . Most observers would agree that the current system merely substitutes government neglect and mistreatment for parental abuse and neglect" (p. 110).

Attempts to increase the oversight of private agencies providing child welfare services sometimes lead to unexpected consequences. Through privatization, nonprofit agencies receive contracts from the state to recruit foster parents, provide training, and place children who are wards of the state in foster care. The contract for services also requires the agencies to monitor the individual cases of foster care children and provide services, which are often also privatized or contracted out by the lead foster care agency to other providers such as child psychologists. Recently, Catholic Charities of the Archdiocese of Chicago decided to end its foster care program, which provided services for about 900 children and jobs for more than 150 child welfare workers. This decision was made after a medical provider reported to the Illinois Department of Family Services that a foster parent forcibly placed a child's hands in a pot of boiling water. Catholic Charities was accused of gross neglect and of "using unqualified foster parents, not obtaining employment verification from the foster parent, placing children in homes without enough bedrooms, failure to perform home visits as often as required, inaction on reports of suspected abuse, failure to remove children at the request of foster parents, and lost or destroyed key records with respect to this foster home" (Hurley, 2007, p. 1). In an out-of-court agreement, Catholic Charities settled the $12 million lawsuit for an undisclosed amount. According to officials, the decision to end the foster care program was a fiscal one. The organization was unsuccessful in finding liability insurance to continue coverage of its foster care program. "For them to be pulling out of the business in a major city like Chicago is a major challenge for the field," said Mark Courtney, faculty associate at the Chapin Hall Center for Children at the University of Chicago. "It doesn't bode well for the public-private partnership that has existed in child welfare for 100 years. That's a big deal" (Associated Press, 2007).

Privatization and Managed Care in Child Welfare

Privatization has had a profound impact on the delivery of federal- and state-funded child welfare services. Private agencies have contracted for the majority of services formerly offered by public child welfare departments. Initiatives in Kansas, Missouri, Michigan, Maine, Missouri, Arizona, Arkansas, Illinois, Tennessee, and Florida are best known, but McCullough's (2004) analysis shows various types of managed care models widely used across the fifty states. Usually, in child welfare circles, managed care is called *privatization*. Florida uses the term *community-based care* to refer to its privatized partnerships with local nonprofit agencies. But other terms—such as *public-private partnerships, contracts-for-services,* and *performance contracting*—illustrate different aspects of managed care models being used by the states to deliver child welfare services.

Perhaps one of the most extensive examples of privatization is the system developed in Kansas. For that reason, we will discuss Kansas's attempt at privatization in some detail. Child welfare managed care began in Kansas through a civil suit filed against Kansas, which was later amended and joined by the American Civil Liberties Union in 1990 and resulted in an out-of-court settlement in 1993. Under court order to modify its child welfare practices, Kansas announced its intention to completely overhaul its child welfare system. By mid-1997, Kansas had privatized its three major child welfare services—family preservation, foster care, and adoption—by transferring them from the state to private agencies through contracts for services. Kansas's new service delivery model borrowed heavily from the managed care model of health care. Similar to the capitation payments in managed health care, the state agreed to pay contract agencies a set amount or "case rate" for services for each child or family. For example, contract agencies would receive $13,500 for each child in the adoption system. Agencies would receive half of the money when the child was referred to the private agency, one-fourth when the child was adopted, and the remaining one-fourth when the adoption was finalized. However, unlike the doctors who work with HMOs, the private agencies that contracted with the state had to accept all children and families referred by the state. Thus, what was implemented was a semi-privatized system (Belsie, 2000).

The Kansas chapter of the National Association of Social Workers (1997) spent over a year assessing the early outcomes of privatization through input from social workers and frontline service providers. Findings varied by type of child welfare service. Feedback to privatization of adoption services was generally positive, family preservation somewhat negative, and foster care generally negative. Several issues emerged from reports by child welfare workers. For example, it was found that some community-based agencies were closed and there was a drop in the number of foster care beds available when contracts were awarded to large service providers. A major issue was that mental health services were not being delivered. This occurred because state medical cards could not be used to pay for services for children in foster care and adoption. This resulted in children being reassessed and diagnosed with fewer mental disorders. Moreover, there was a disincentive for contract providers to pay for these expensive services out of case rate funds. The managed care system was confusing, particularly for workers and foster parents, as it was not clear who was responsible for the children—the state or the managed care contracting agency. In effect, privatization added another layer of bureaucracy to the state system. These difficulties resulted in high staff turnover and heavy caseloads, long hours, and large geographic service areas for workers. Many public welfare workers sought career changes and agencies had to hire recent social work graduates without experience in child welfare. This, as well as a lack of time for adequate planning, introduced new inefficiencies into the system.

Nelson's (2001) critique points out that the Kansas managed care model of privatization went against the principles of a family-centered approach to child welfare. Privatization did not work well from a strengths perspective—that is, in terms of developing partnerships with families, working toward empowerment, and integrating formal and informal supports. Unruh and Hodgkin (2004) explain that another problem with the Kansas model was the decision to contract separately for family preservation, foster care, and adoption, when, in fact, meeting performance outcomes depends somewhat on the performance of other service providers. In an evaluation comparing privatization in foster care and adoption in Kansas, Michigan, and Illinois, the Illinois model, which allowed for the most competition between public and private providers, ranked highest in adoptive placements and in eliminating ineffective agencies (Blackstone, Buck, & Hakim, 2004).

Kansas Action for Children (2003) reports that the unintended consequences include disruption of services and decreased continuity of care and longer stays in out-of-home care for children, and a confusing and complicated system of child welfare for all involved. To be fair, however, even the system's advocates admit that after several years of managed care, children in the state system are most often children with severe emotional and mental problems who are hard to place for adoption and the least likely to benefit from family preservation services. On the positive side, Kansas's regional approach to child welfare improved the balance of services between the state's urban centers and rural areas. The state has improved its rate of child adoption, and children are moving through the system toward adoption or reunification more quickly. More services are offered through the managed care approach than through the state's pre-lawsuit model. And data for evaluating the system are available so that providers can be held accountable for performance (Belsie, 2000).

Maltreatment of the Elderly

Elder abuse can involve any of the many forms of abuse and neglect inflicted on adults and children. We have chosen to discuss it separately, because, as has probably become apparent to readers, the policies developed to address domestic abuse only tangentially apply to the elderly. As we shall see when we discuss federal and state responses, attention to the maltreatment of the elderly has been limited, even though the maltreatment of the elderly is a major problem. Unlike intimate partner violence and child maltreatment, for which systems have been set up to collect and evaluate information, there is no national system for collecting information on violence to the elderly. The most recent and rigorous attempt to collect this kind of information is the 2004 Survey of State Adult Protective Services conducted by the National Center on Elder Abuse (2007) at the U.S. Administration on Aging. The survey attempted to collect 2003 data from all fifty states, Guam, and the District of Columbia; this is made difficult by the fact that only twenty-one of the fifty-two jurisdictions (the fifty states, Guam, and the District of Columbia) surveyed keep an abuse registry or database. Table 10.5 shows results from this survey. The survey showed that whereas there were 472,813 reports of suspected elder and vulnerable adult abuse in 1999, the number in 2003 was up to 565,747 in 2003. Only two-thirds of the states were able to separate data on elder abuse from data on abuse of adults in general, and in many cases, few states were able to provide the requested data. For example, only twenty-nine jurisdictions reported the total number of cases investigated (192,243), and only twenty-four jurisdictions reported the number of incidents of elder abuse substantiated (88,445, or 46% of cases of suspected elder abuse). Twenty-four jurisdictions also reported an elder abuse rate of 8.84 per 1,000 adults.

The most striking aspect of the data is how poor it is. It illustrates how differently states collect data on this phenomenon. This is a result of the fact that adult protective services have been established by states with little or no guidance from the federal government. Given the poor quality of the data, it is probably not appropriate to try to compare the data to the national data on domestic and intimate partner abuse. However, we can see

Table 10.5 The 2004 Survey of Adult Protective Services for the Fifty States, the District of Columbia, and Guam: Type of Abuse, Perpetrators, Types Substantiated, and Reporters

	Percent	# of Jurisdictions Reporting
Percent occurring in domestic settings	89.30	12
Victims		
Women	65.70	15
Men	34.30	15
White	77.10	11
African American	21.30	13
Other race	0.60	11
80 years of age or older	30.95	20
Perpetrators		
Women	52.70	11
Under age 60	75.10	7
Over age 60	24.90	7
Adult children	32.60	8
Other family members	21.50	10
Spouses/intimate partners	11.30	10
Types of maltreatment that were substantiated		
Self-neglect	37.20	17
Care giver neglect	20.40	16
Financial exploitation	14.70	19
Emotional/psychological/verbal abuse	14.80	19
Physical abuse	10.70	18
Sexual abuse	1.00	16
Other	1.20	9
Top five reporters of maltreatment		
Family members	17.00	10
Self	6.30	10
Law enforcement	5.30	10
Social service workers	10.60	9
Friends	8.00	9

Source: Adapted from the National Committee for the Prevention of Elder Abuse & National Adult Protective Services Association. (2007). *The 2004 survey of state adult protective services: Abuse of vulnerable adults 18 years of age and older.* Retrieved July 20, 2009, from http://www.ncea.aoa.gov/NCEAroot/Main_Site/pdf/APS_2004 NCEASurvey.pdf

that there are a substantial number of elderly people who are believed to be maltreated, and that financial exploitation is a major cause of the maltreatment that takes place. It is also interesting that only eleven states reported information on who reported the maltreatment, and moreover that of those providing data, none indicated that any of the maltreatment was reported by health professionals. This may be because the data collection is so poor, but it may also be a reflection of a failure to report abuse, the results of which can be devastating. "Despite the serious health implications of elder abuse and the high frequency of older persons' contact with physicians, health care clinicians detect and report abuse infrequently" (Rodriguez, Wallace, Woolf, & Mangione, 2006, p. 403).

The earliest legislation that addresses the issues of elder maltreatment can be found in the 1962 amendments to the Social Security Act, which allowed states to establish protective services for neglected and/or exploited adults. It also authorized the establishment of protective services for persons who have physical or mental limitations that make them unable to manage their own affairs. The Older Americans Act, which was signed into law in 1965, was the second law that had implications for the management of elder abuse in the United States. The original law did not directly address the issue of elder abuse, but Title VII, which was added in 1972, and subsequent amendments and reauthorizations have added language on elder abuse. Congress did not hold hearings on elder abuse until 1978, and legislation was proposed as early as 1980. However, it was not until 1992 that the National Center on Elder Abuse was established when

> Congress created and funded a new Title VII, Chapter 3 for prevention of abuse, neglect, and exploitation. Title VII Vulnerable Elder Rights Protection also includes provisions for long-term care ombudsman programs and state legal assistance development.
>
> In 2000, provisions were added to Title VII to encourage states to foster greater coordination with law enforcement and the courts.
>
> In the 2006 amendments to the Older Americans Act, new language was added to Title II and Title VII emphasizing multidisciplinary and collaborative approaches to addressing elder mistreatment when developing programs and long-term strategic plans for elder justice activities. New language in Title VII also expands the options for States and tribal organizations to use some portion of the Title VII allotments for detection, assessment, intervention in, investigation of, and response to elder abuse, neglect, and exploitation, in addition to prevention and treatment. And, for the first time, "elder justice" and "self-neglect" are defined in the OAA. (National Center on Elder Abuse, 2008)

As a result of the 1962 legislation, all states now have functioning adult protective service sections. However, since they were established with minimal federal guidance, the way in which they function varies greatly between states. The statistics reported in Table 10.5 clearly reveal the differences in the quality and extent of information that is collected by APS in various states. These vast differences are also reflected in the elderly abuse services offered by the states.

Summary

The term *family violence* describes many different types of domestic violence, including intimate partner violence, child maltreatment, and elder abuse. *Domestic violence* usually means abuse that occurs among those who are intimate or share some form of family relationship in common living quarters. However, in a broader sense, domestic violence includes abuse by other individuals in the household and other family members, including adult children. The general assumption is that domestic violence is heterosexual in nature, and that it is always the woman who is abused and the man who is the abuser. Due to the way in which violence against women emerged as a social issue and was recognized as a social problem in the late 1970s, early legislation and the Violence Against Women Act focus on women as the victims of abuse. There is little, if any, specific policy support that provides protection for gay and lesbian individuals who experience intimate partner abuse and for heterosexual males who are abused. Thus, the law does not take into account the actual realities of domestic violence in all its forms in this country. Although a more comprehensive VAWA has been enacted, the focus of funding is shifting from women's social, financial, and emotional needs to the prosecution of offenders.

Child maltreatment, or child abuse, was recognized as a social problem in the 1960s and became a public issue. The last thirty or more years of child welfare laws show a pendulum-like swing between policy that emphasizes child protection and child safety and the removal of maltreated children from the home and policy that emphasizes parental rights and family preservation through reunion of maltreated children with their parents. Child protection policies have viewed child abuse as an individual problem of family dysfunction, with little attention given to broader economic and social conditions that negatively affect child well-being. Many major pieces of child welfare legislation have been passed at the federal level, with amendments designed to refocus state efforts to address child abuse and neglect in its many forms. Lawsuits have also played a major role in shaping the interpretation of child welfare policy, largely through out-of-court settlements that set standards for the implementation of federal law in states in which the lawsuits are filed. There has also been a large-scale move toward privatization of services and a managed care approach to child welfare.

Elder abuse is the final form of family violence that this chapter addressed. The Older Americans Act and its amendments require states to develop offices of adult protective services, including long-term care ombudsman programs and state legal assistance. Minimal federal guidelines are in place, however, to ensure the quality and extent of information, and the type and range of services, provided. As a result, elder abuse prevention and services, as well as the requirements for reporting elder abuse, vary greatly from state to state.

For Further Reading

Bartholet, E. (1999). *Nobody's children: Abuse and neglect, foster drift, and the adoption alternative.* Boston: Beacon Press.

Brownell, P., & Podnicks, E. (2005). Long-overdue recognition for the critical issue of elder abuse and neglect: A global policy and practice perspective. *Brief Treatment and Crisis Intervention, 5*(2), 187–191.

DeMause, L. (1998). The history of child abuse. *Journal of Psychohistory* 25(3), 216–236. Retrieved May 25, 2006, from http://www.psychohistory.com/htm/05_history.html

Freundlich, M., & Gerstenzang, S. (2003). *An assessment of the privatization of child welfare services.* Washington, DC: CWLA Press.

Guggenheim, M. (2003). Translating insights into policy: Maximizing strategies for pressing adults to do right by children. *Arizona Law Review, 45,* 765–782.

Mellor, M. J., & Brownell, P. J. (2006). *Elder abuse and mistreatment: Policy, practice, and research.* New York: Haworth.

Meyer-Emerick, N. (2001). *The Violence Against Women Act of 1994: An analysis of intent and perception.* New York: Praeger.

Pleck, E. (2004). *Domestic tyranny: The making of American social policy against family violence from colonial times to the present.* Champaign: University of Illinois Press.

Podnieks, E., Kosberg, J. L., & Lowenstein, A. (Eds.). (2003). *Elder abuse: Selected papers from the Prague World Congress on Family Violence.* New York: Haworth Press.

Walton, E., Sandau-Beckler, P., & Mannes, M. (2001). *Balancing family-centered services and child well-being: Exploring issues in policy, practice, theory, and research.* New York: Columbia University Press.

References

Adoption and Safe Families Act, 42 U.S.C. § 671 *et seq.* (1997).
Adoption Assistance and Child Welfare Act of 1980, 42 U.S.C. §§ 620–628, §§ 670–676 (1980).
Associated Press. (2007, April 17). *Catholic Charities to drop large foster care program.* Retrieved February 26, 2008, from http://www.pantagraph.com/articles/2007/04/17/news/125477.txt
Ayler, D. B. (2005, December 25). *The orphan train collection.* Retrieved May 25, 2006, from http://www.orphantrainriders.com/
Bartholet, E. (2000). Reply: Whose children? A response to Professor Guggenheim. *Harvard Law Review, 113*(8), 1999–2008.
Belsie, L. (2000, August 3). Kansas' bold experiment in child welfare. *Christian Science Monitor,* p. 4.
Blackstone, E. A., Buck, A. J., & Hakim, S. (2004). Privatizing adoption and foster care: Applying auction and market solutions. *Children and Youth Services Review, 26*(11), 1033–1049.
Brian A. et al. v. Sundquist et al. No. 3-00-0445 (U.S.D.C. M.D. Tenn., 2001). Retrieved June 16, 2006, from http://www.vanderbilt.edu/VIPPS/C&FPC/TAC/settlement.pdf
Cahill, S., Ellen, M., & Tobias, S. (2002). *Family policy: Issues affecting gay, lesbian, bisexual and transgender families.* New York: National Gay and Lesbian Task Force Policy Institute. Retrieved February 24, 2009 from http://www.thetaskforce.org/downloads/reports/reports/FamilyPolicy.pdf
Child Abuse Prevention and Treatment Act of 1974, 42 U.S.C. § 5101 *et seq.* (1974).
Child Trends DataBank. (2007). *Child maltreatment.* Retrieved September 5, 2007, from http://www.childtrendsdatabank.org/pdf/40_PDF.pdf
Dakin, A. (2005). *Perpetrator accountability and services for victims: Implications of the funding inequities of the Violence Against Women Act of 1994.* Jane Addams College of Social Work, University of Illinois at Chicago. Unpublished paper.
Davidson, C. E. (1994). Dependent children and their families: A historical survey of United States policies. In F. Jacobs & M. Davies (Eds.), *More than kissing babies? Current child and family policy in the United States* (pp. 65–89). Westport, CT: Auburn House.
Davidson, H. (2003). *Significant new changes to the federal Child Abuse Prevention and Treatment Act: Practical implications for child and family advocates.* Retrieved May 31, 2006, from http://aia.berkeley.edu/media/pdf/davidson_capta_sen.doc
Family Violence and Prevention Services Act of 1984, 42 U.S.C. § 10401 *et seq.* (1984).
Gelles, R. J., & Schwartz, I. (1999). Children and the child welfare system. *Journal of Constitutional Law, 2*(1), 95–111.
Hurley, C. T. (2007, April 17). *A response to Catholic Charities dropping foster care.* Retrieved May 21, 2007, from http://www.chicagoinjurylawyerblog.com/2007/04/a_response_to_catholic_chariti.html

Hutchison, E. D. (1993). Mandatory reporting laws: Child protective case findings gone awry? *Social Work, 38*(1), 56–63.

Jimenez, M. (1990). Permanency planning and the Child Abuse Prevention and Treatment Act: The paradox of child welfare policy. *Journal of Sociology and Social Welfare, 17*(3), 55–72.

Kansas Action for Children. (2003). *A case for contract reform: The development of a single regional contract for foster care and adoption services in Kansas.* Topeka, KS: Author. Retrieved February 26, 2008, from http://www.kac.org/PDF/ContractReform.Report.pdf

Kansas Chapter of the National Association of Social Workers. (1997, October). *Kansans talk back: Early responses to the move to privatization of child welfare services.* Retrieved May 30, 2006, from http://www.socialworkers.org/practice/children/kansans.asp

Keeping Children and Families Safe Act, 42 U.S.C. § 5106(g) (2003).

Kelly, J. (2004, September). Class action? 13 lawsuits that reformed (or drained) child welfare. *Youth Today.* Retrieved June 16, 2006, from http://www.youthtoday.org/youthtoday/Sept04/story2_9_04.html

Kempe, C. H., Silverman, F. N., Steele, B. F., Droegemuller, W., & Silver, H. K. (1962). The battered child syndrome. *Journal of the American Medical Association, 181,* 17–24.

Marisol v. Pataki, 95-Civ-10533 (S.D.N.Y. 1998).

McCullough, C. (2004). *Financing and contracting practices in child welfare initiatives and Medicaid managed care: Similarities and differences.* Retrieved June 1, 2006, from http://www.cwla.org/programs/bhd/mhpubfinancing.htm

Minnesota Center Against Violence and Abuse. (1999, September). *Herstory of domestic violence: A timeline of the battered women's movement.* Retrieved January 13, 2009, from http://www.mincava.umn.edu/documents/herstory/herstory.html

National Center on Elder Abuse. (2006). *Fact sheet: Abuse of adults aged 60+ 2004 survey of state adult protective services.* Retrieved July 21, 2008, from http://www.ncea.aoa.gov/NCEAroot/Main_Site/pdf/2-14-06%2060FACT%20SHEET.pdf

National Center on Elder Abuse. (2008). *The Older Americans Act: Title VII, vulnerable elder rights protections, and Title II, elder abuse prevention and services.* Retrieved February 24, 2008, from http://www.ncea.aoa.gov/NCEAroot/Main_Site/Library/Laws/Older_Americans_Act.aspx

Nelson, K. E. (2001). Shaping the future of family-centered services: Competition or collaboration? In E. Walton, P. Sandau-Beckler, & M. Mannes (Eds.), *Balancing family-centered services and child well-being: Exploring issues in policy, practice, theory, and research* (pp. 359–376). New York: Columbia University Press.

Newton, C. J. (2001, February). *Domestic violence: An overview.* Retrieved February 23, 2008, from http://www.findcounseling.com/journal/domestic-violence/

Rivera, J. (1996). A promise to be fulfilled: The Violence Against Women Act and the construction of multiple consciousness in the civil rights and feminist movements. *Journal of Law and Policy, 4,* 463–512.

Rodriguez, M., Wallace, S., Woolf, N., & Mangione, C. (2006). Mandatory reporting of elder abuse: Between a rock and a hard place. *Annals of Family Medicine, 4*(5), 403–409.

Sklar, K. K., & Lustig, S. (2001). *How have recent social movements shaped civil rights legislation for women? The 1994 Violence Against Women Act.* Retrieved May 22, 2006, from http://womhist.binghamton.edu/vawa/doclist.htm

Stein, T. J. (2000). The Adoption and Safe Families Act: Creating a false dichotomy between parents' and children' rights. *Families in Society, 81*(6), 586–592.

Sugg, N. K., Thompson, R. S., Thompson, D. C., Maiuro, R., & Rivara, F. P. (1999). Domestic violence and primary care: Attitudes, practices, and beliefs. *Archives of Family Medicine, 8*(4), 301–306.

U.S. Bureau of Justice Statistics. (2007). *Intimate partner violence in the United States.* Retrieved September 7, 2007, from http://www.ojp.usdoj.gov/bjs/intimate/ipv.htm

U.S. Department of Health and Human Services. (1997, November 19). *Progress report to the Congress.* Retrieved June 1, 2006, from http://www.acf.dhhs.gov/programs/cb/pubs/congress/

U.S. Department of Justice. (n.d.). *About the Office on Violence Against Women.* Retrieved May 22, 2006, from http://www.usdoj.gov/ovw/about.htm

Unruh, J. K., & Hodgkin, D. (2004). The role of contract design in privatization of child welfare services: The Kansas experience. *Children and Youth Services Review, 26*(8), 771–783.

Victims of Trafficking and Violence Protection Act of 2000, 22 U.S.C. § 7101 et seq. (2000).

Violence Against Women Act of 1994, 42 U.S.C. § 13981 (1994).

Violence Against Women and Department of Justice Reauthorization Act, H.R. 3402, 42 U.S.C. § 14045 (2005).

Violent Crime Control and Law Enforcement Act of 1994, Pub. L. No. 103-322 (1994).

CHAPTER 11

Marriage as Family Policy

As we set forth to write this book, we were cognizant of the fact that marriage is not a topic usually covered by policy books. Yet our research convinced us of the importance of marriage as a dynamic area of contemporary policy change, and thus of the need to inform students and policy practitioners about marriage and family policy. In many ways, this chapter illustrates an important theme of the book: demographic trends and the changing nature of the family make it difficult to develop comprehensive family policy. The chapter also emphasizes what we see as the overriding purpose of family policy: valuing families in all their diversity. In chapter 1, we explained our emphasis on valuing families. We would add here that valuing families also means ensuring their rights—their rights to visit loved ones in the hospital, their rights to inheritance, their rights to support and parent children, and so on. Marriage is one mechanism for ensuring such rights, and in some states, other mechanisms such as common-law marriage, domestic partnerships, and civil unions also exist to partially protect these rights. Thus, our focus in this chapter is on federal and state policies relating to adult couples—whether heterosexual or same sex—who are living together in committed relationships regardless of marital status.

At the heart of the debate about marriage as public policy is whether the American family is in flux or it is deteriorating. In the first part of the chapter, we present some statistics that show that the makeup of families has changed markedly over the last sixty years. These changes in family structure help us understand the ongoing debate over the proper policy response to the changing nature of the family and help frame our discussion of the issues. We identify the meaning of marriage in contemporary society, and several myths about marriage that have not held to be true historically.

In order to help readers understand the various policy issues related to marriage, the next part of the chapter defines the types of unions officially recognized in the United States: legal marriage, common-law marriage, domestic partnerships, and civil unions. Our discussion shows that a substantial portion of unmarried-partner households do not use any of these legally sanctioned unions, and we briefly discuss why they do not use them or are prohibited from using them. In keeping with the book's focus on the changes in family structure that are taking place in American society, our discussion addresses these issues as they relate to heterosexual, as well as gay and lesbian, persons. In addition, our discussion sheds light on the policy issue of marriage versus nonmarital unions.

At the policy level, we provide an overview of federal laws and initiatives, including the Defense of Marriage Act (1994), which defines marriage as a heterosexual union and gives states the right to acknowledge or reject same-sex marriages performed in other states. However, much of the advocacy that surrounds marriage as public policy takes place at the state level, where the courts and state legislatures play a role in establishing marriage laws. In various states, grassroots democracy in the form of citizen-initiated state statutes and constitutional amendments is being used to challenge state laws and court decisions, and for the most part, these initiatives are designed to limit people's ability to marry or otherwise restrict individual rights. Thus, this type of direct democracy effort has the potential to profoundly affect the gay and lesbian communities, as well as unmarried cohabitating couples. Finally, we look at the promotion of marriage as public policy. Although traditionally supported by conservatives, this policy stance now has broader support among progressive scholars and child and family advocates because of research that points to the benefits of healthy marriages for families and communities.

Marriage and the Family: In Flux or Deteriorating?

There have been radical changes in the structure of families in the last sixty years. The U.S. Census Bureau (2000) reports that in the 1950s, 68 percent of males and 66 percent of females were married. By 2000, 58 percent of males and 55 percent of females were married. The tipping point came in 2005, when 51 percent of women above the age of fifteen were not married. "Marriage is no longer the social norm," reported Suzanne Goldenberg (2007) in the *Guardian*, a major British newspaper. Of all households in the United States in 2006, 49.7 percent were headed by married couples. Of these, only 21.6 percent were traditional married-couple households raising children under the age of eighteen (U.S. Census Bureau, 2006). Many families are blended in some way; these include families with stepparents, single-parent families, multigenerational families, and gay and lesbian and heterosexual cohabiting couples. Married-couple households are growing at a rate of less than 1 percent per year, while other types of households are growing at 3 percent per year (U.S. Census Bureau, 2004). By age thirty, half the women in the United States have lived with a partner to whom they were not married. The 2000 census identified 5.5 million unmarried-partner households. Of these households, only about 600,000 (11%) were same-sex unmarried-partner households (Simmons & O'Connell, 2003). More detailed information on the characteristics of married-couple and unmarried-partner households can be found in table 11.1. These statistics make it clear that family structure in the United States is rapidly changing. These changes are deeply disturbing to many and have led to efforts to strengthen marriage. "Proponents of strengthening marriage form a diverse group. Many are in religious communities, especially conservative Protestant denominations. Their aim is to rebuild a traditional model of lifelong monogamous marriage. Others—practitioners and professionals in various fields—are motivated by concerns about rising divorce rates or about the welfare of couples, individual adults, and children" (Nock, 2005, pp. 21–22). Proponents of this view are able to point to substantial bodies of research that show that individuals who are in healthy marriages reap economic, behavioral, emotional, and psychological benefits. They make the case that heterosexual marriage is the bedrock—the underlying social institution—that protects against crime, welfare dependency, and child neglect, particularly by fathers. This view supports the nuclear family and marriage as the right path for optimal family structure. In recent years, new policies supporting this view have been enacted into law. These policies were designed to promote and strengthen marriage, reward couples who marry, and endorse the traditional family as an anti-poverty solution.

According to family historian Stephanie Coontz (1997), this view of marriage is based more on myths than facts. The first myth is that the convention of marriage, defined as the sole union of one man and one woman, is the typical form of marriage that has existed throughout much of history. In fact, the definition of marriage as the sole union of one man and one woman is of recent origin, and many other forms of marriage have been more common over the ages. The second myth is that the institution of marriage has always been about love. In previous times, marriage was a way to cinch a business arrangement, increase military power, or enlarge the labor force. Marriage for love's sake is a radical new invention—only two hundred years old. The third myth is that the male-breadwinner family has

Table 11.1 Household and Family Characteristics of Married-Couple and Unmarried-Partner Households for the United States and Puerto Rico, 2000

Area	Percent of householders female		Percent of households with children under 18 years					
					Unmarried-partner households			
					Opposite-sex partners		Male partners		Female partners	
	Married-couple households	Opposite-sex unmarried-partner households	Married-couple households	Own children[1]	Own and/or unrelated children[2]	Own children[1]	Own and/or unrelated children[2]	Own children[1]	Own and/or unrelated children[2]
United States	12.9	46.4	45.6	38.9	43.1	21.8	22.3	32.7	34.3
Region									
Northeast	15.4	48.4	45.2	37.4	40.9	21.3	21.7	31.2	32.6
Midwest	11.1	45.8	45.1	38.7	43.9	22.3	22.9	32.8	34.7
South	12.6	46.7	44.4	39.7	44.0	22.1	23.9	34.4	36.1
West	13.4	45.0	48.5	39.2	42.7	20.8	21.1	31.5	33.1
State									
Alabama	11.7	48.2	43.1	41.6	46.1	27.8	28.3	36.8	38.1
Alaska	15.0	43.8	54.4	40.6	45.1	36.2	37.1	37.0	38.6
Arizona	12.7	44.6	43.5	40.5	44.3	22.5	23.0	33.1	35.0
Arkansas	9.9	44.4	41.9	41.8	47.6	26.1	26.7	36.2	38.2
California	14.0	45.3	50.9	41.4	44.4	19.6	20.2	32.8	34.3
Colorado	13.8	45.7	47.2	31.3	34.6	19.9	20.5	26.1	27.8
Connecticut	17.2	50.7	45.4	35.6	38.7	21.9	22.2	30.2	31.6
Delaware	14.5	48.6	42.8	39.9	44.1	18.4	18.9	29.4	31.8
District of Columbia	24.9	56.6	36.6	31.8	32.8	4.8	5.0	23.4	24.5
Florida	14.4	46.5	38.1	35.5	39.2	17.4	17.8	29.3	31.0
Georgia	14.1	48.9	47.3	42.2	46.1	21.1	21.6	34.4	36.2
Hawaii	13.9	45.2	44.8	35.8	39.0	20.7	21.3	30.6	32.6
Idaho	10.0	42.3	47.8	37.6	43.0	30.3	30.8	35.7	37.9
Illinois	11.9	46.2	47.3	38.3	42.5	23.5	24.0	35.6	37.0
Indiana	10.3	44.0	44.4	40.5	47.0	22.8	23.5	33.6	36.3
Iowa	10.0	44.6	43.4	37.5	43.0	24.9	25.4	33.8	35.5
Kansas	10.1	44.8	45.9	39.1	44.1	28.3	29.0	36.5	38.1
Kentucky	11.4	46.1	43.7	40.1	46.0	23.5	24.4	33.0	34.9
Louisiana	12.1	47.7	46.2	44.4	48.5	25.9	26.3	38.5	39.8
Maine	15.1	45.2	41.4	35.7	40.9	18.7	19.0	25.2	27.1
Maryland	15.0	49.5	46.4	38.1	42.1	23.3	24.0	31.7	33.3
Massachusetts	16.6	49.8	45.8	32.8	35.9	18.1	18.6	27.7	29.0
Michigan	11.3	46.9	44.8	40.1	45.3	22.8	23.6	33.2	35.3
Minnesota	11.4	45.7	46.9	35.4	40.2	17.2	17.9	26.8	28.5
Mississippi	12.2	48.9	45.0	49.2	53.4	30.7	31.1	42.0	43.8
Missouri	10.3	45.5	43.6	39.9	45.7	20.9	21.5	31.7	33.7
Montana	11.7	44.0	42.9	35.1	39.3	28.7	29.6	34.2	35.5
Nebraska	9.8	44.6	45.9	36.4	41.5	24.7	25.7	32.7	34.4
Nevada	13.9	41.9	44.5	36.1	40.2	24.7	25.3	35.4	37.5
New Hampshire	15.3	43.7	45.9	33.0	38.1	22.3	22.9	27.2	29.0
New Jersey	14.7	48.0	47.4	38.1	40.9	25.4	25.8	33.8	34.7
New Mexico	12.0	44.2	46.1	48.4	51.7	27.4	27.9	31.0	32.2
New York	17.5	50.1	46.4	39.2	42.2	21.3	21.7	33.1	34.3
North Carolina	12.3	46.1	43.0	38.4	42.9	25.2	25.9	33.3	34.7
North Dakota	8.8	43.0	45.1	36.9	41.5	21.4	21.7	34.4	34.7
Ohio	12.4	46.9	43.6	40.2	45.3	20.9	21.6	31.8	34.0
Oklahoma	10.6	45.1	43.4	42.1	47.2	26.7	27.3	35.0	36.9
Oregon	13.7	45.6	42.8	33.9	38.4	18.9	19.5	26.3	28.1
Pennsylvania	11.6	45.6	42.3	38.5	42.8	20.9	21.3	31.5	33.2
Rhode Island	16.6	50.4	43.6	37.1	40.1	20.5	20.6	27.3	28.6
South Carolina	14.2	47.8	42.6	41.9	45.7	26.8	27.2	37.1	38.8
South Dakota	9.9	44.2	45.2	42.1	47.4	33.2	33.9	41.4	42.3
Tennessee	11.3	46.3	42.5	39.1	44.3	23.9	24.7	33.4	35.4
Texas	11.5	45.2	50.2	42.9	46.8	26.7	27.3	39.2	40.9
Utah	8.9	41.9	55.5	42.2	47.2	29.7	30.2	40.6	42.3
Vermont	16.5	46.2	44.2	33.8	38.3	19.9	20.6	26.7	28.9
Virginia	12.6	46.5	45.3	35.0	39.6	19.8	20.3	31.2	32.7
Washington	13.3	45.9	45.8	35.1	39.7	18.1	18.6	26.7	28.2
West Virginia	9.9	43.7	39.5	40.2	45.6	27.6	27.9	34.9	36.4
Wisconsin	10.5	45.4	44.5	34.9	40.5	21.7	22.4	30.6	32.4
Wyoming	10.9	41.2	44.3	36.0	41.8	28.2	29.9	35.7	37.5
Puerto Rico	14.1	54.4	49.4	56.5	56.7	39.2	39.2	42.2	42.5

[1] Refers to own sons/daughters of the householder.
[2] Refers to own sons/daughters of the householder and other children not related to the householder.

Source: U.S. Census Bureau. (2003). *Married-couple and unmarried-partner households: 2002.* Retrieved July 22, 2009, from http://www.census.gov/prod/2003pubs/censr-5.pdf

always been dominant in the United States. Historically, only a small portion of households were wealthy enough for wives to stay at home and not contribute to household productivity. Rather, as we pointed out in chapter 8, most women worked side by side with their husbands on the farm or in the family business. The 1950s era of the stay-at-home mom was atypical in

American history, and by the 1970s, a large number of women had begun to join the workforce. By 2006, 53.4 percent of married couples were ones in which both husband and wife were working (U.S. Census Bureau, 2006).

On the other side of this value-based debate are those who believe that the attempt to make marriage the focus of family policy is misplaced and doomed to fail. Citing the body of statistics collected by the Census Bureau, those holding this view believe that the structure of families is in a period of rapid and profound flux. This view holds that alternative family structures are not pathological but rather represent over thirty years of reform helping liberate women from abusive relationships. Alternative family structures allow couples who consider marriage oppressive or choose not to marry for financial and other reasons to live together in committed relationships with less social sanction. Advocates for pluralism and diversity in family structure acknowledge the nuclear heterosexual family as a valid family form, but they see marriage-only policies as backward and stigmatizing for unwed mothers, gay men, lesbians, and cohabiting couples—many of whom are parenting children. They argue that the marriage-only view pursues a policy agenda that doesn't fit the current life situation of all families and thus is discriminatory and a threat to personal liberty.

According to traditionalist or conservative values, the family is deteriorating. According to progressive or liberal values, the family is changing. Both sides see the future of the American family as tied up in this cultural war over values. Do these changes represent decay or evolution? If, for example, the deterioration of the traditional family is leading to the unraveling of American society, then policy to shore up the nuclear heterosexual family and encourage its proliferation is needed. If, on the other hand, the family in flux is an indicator of the evolution of the family in American society, then policy is needed to support the changing structure of the family and ensure the survival of society. As we will see in this chapter, the future of marriage policy hinges on this debate.

Marriage, Common-Law Marriage, Domestic Partnerships, and Civil Unions

Here we will discuss federal and state efforts to develop policy concerning married and unmarried couples. However, before we can do that, we need to understand the current legal status of these various types of relationships. Four types of formal or quasi-formal couple relationships are recognized in the United States. They are marriage, common-law marriage, domestic partnerships, and civil unions. We will discuss each of these types of relationships and the laws and policies that frame them.

Marriage

Marital status is often the key to how families fit into the state and federal matrix of benefits, parental rights, and financial responsibilities. Marriage brings with it a host of legal rights and benefits. The General Accounting Office (1997) found 1,049 different laws in which rights, benefits, and responsibilities were determined on the basis of marital relationships. Marriage status plays a prominent role in federal law and benefit structures, particularly in policy areas such as Social Security, housing, and food stamps; veterans' benefits; taxation; and federal civilian and military service benefits. Marriage status is also a significant factor in legislation concerning employment benefits and related laws; immigration and naturalization; Native Americans and tribal authorities; trade, commerce, and intellectual property; financial disclosure and conflict-of-interest laws; criminal law and family violence laws; loans, guarantees, and payments in agriculture; laws concerning federal natural resources and related laws; and other miscellaneous laws. These thirteen categories of federal law are multiplied at the state and local levels.

In the United States, state laws govern who can marry and how marriage can be ended. Until recently, marriage was defined as a legally sanctioned union between a man and a woman. Two types of marriages are recognized in the United States. The first, religious marriage, is performed under the auspices of a religious body. The second is civil marriage, which is performed under the auspices of the state government. In many countries, couples who want to have a religious marriage must first have a civil marriage ceremony, followed by a separate religious ceremony. In the United States, couples must first get permission from the state to marry by applying to the state for a marriage license, which is approved after the couple complies with whatever regulations the state may impose. The state is the authorizing body. However, in practice the state usually delegates the authority to issue marriage licenses to a local governmental body such as a court or city government, or the courts that exist within the local jurisdiction. Once the license is issued, the ceremony can be carried out by a judge or other person licensed by the state to perform marriages. In the United States, the state often authorizes priests, rabbis, and ministers to act as agents of the state. They can then perform a ceremony that meets the requirements of the state and the religious body they represent. When the ceremony is completed, the couple is married in the eyes of both the church or Jewish law and the state. The rights, privileges, and responsibilities that come with marriage that are defined by law are enforceable through the state legal system. The states, however, do not enforce any religiously mandated requirements that are not a part of state law. For example, some religions forbid previously married members of their faith from remarrying, but state marriage statutes allow remarriage.

Common-Law Marriage

Common-law marriage is a carryover from English common law and is being phased out in this country. Only nine states (Alabama, Colorado, Kansas, Rhode Island, South Carolina, Iowa, Montana, Oklahoma, and Texas) and the District of Columbia recognize common-law marriages agreed to within their borders. Georgia, Idaho, Ohio, Oklahoma, and Pennsylvania only recognize common-law marriages entered into before a certain date. The status of common-law marriage in New Hampshire is only applicable in cases in probate court, and in Utah, such marriages are legal only if they are approved by a court order (National Conference of State Legislatures, 2009). Before a state will recognize a common-law marriage, a heterosexual couple must live together for a significant amount of time. They must consider themselves a married couple, which is signified by their use of the same last name, references to each other as husband and wife, and filing of a tax return as a married couple (a joint return, or an individual return on which they indicate they are married). In addition, for a common-law marriage to be legally valid, the couple must intend to be married. If a couple's union meets the requirements of a common-law marriage, and the relationship breaks up, either partner can use the state legal system to protect his or her rights. Generally, this means the couple is required to get a legal divorce. Common-law marriage is often problematic when a spouse dies and/or there are minor children involved. For example, if a spouse dies, the surviving partner must ask the state courts to declare that the relationship was a valid marriage in order to ensure the same legal rights and duties that would have resulted from a marriage ceremony. And if the partner tries to collect Social Security benefits for him- or herself or a minor child, a federal court must rule on whether a common-law marriage existed.

Domestic Partnerships

Until recently, unmarried individuals living together as couples in same-sex or heterosexual relationships did not have any legal recognition under state or federal law. Consequently, the rights, responsibilities, and legal protections available to married couples were not available to unmarried couples. This began to change in the early 1980s, when the term *domestic partner* was coined to develop a legal framework to define the benefits and responsibilities that accrued to unmarried adult couples living in long-term, dedicated relationships. In 1979, Tom Brougham, a City of Berkeley employee, tried to sign up for health and dental benefits for his life partner, Barry Warren. To Broughman, this represented

> an opportunity to test the new anti-discrimination legislation in a way that the city had not considered. Berkeley had resolved not to discriminate based on sexual orientation, but marriage was assumed to be the sole vehicle for providing benefits to committed couples. Since marriage was defined by state law, Brougham saw a contradiction that could not produce an equitable outcome for same-sex couples. So he started to think outside the box. In two letters dated August 21, 1979, Brougham described the problem and proposed a solution. In the first letter, he analyzed the effect of using marriage as the sole eligibility criterion and asserted that Berkeley had a responsibility to end uneven effects in its own programs and in its contracts with health care providers. In the second letter, Brougham proposed a solution: Berkeley could resolve the dilemma by creating a new category called "domestic partnership." (Traiman, 2008, p. 23)

The new category encompassed all the rights and responsibilities of marriage, differing only in the partners' sexual orientation. Both partners were to publicly and freely declare their partnership, commitment, and responsibility to each other.

In 1983, Leland Traiman, vice-chair of the city's Human Relations and Welfare Commission, was appointed to head the Domestic Partner Task Force to develop the policy. In July of 1984, the Berkeley City Council rejected the proposal on the grounds of financial costs, and consequently, all city council members who voted against the proposal were not reelected to office in the November 1984 election. In December 1984, the domestic partnership policy was passed. Originally, the city implemented only dental benefits and employee leave benefits. Eventually, "the city broke the resistance of its medical contractors through firmness and simply by guaranteeing to pay whatever excess costs they might incur. It soon became clear, however, that same-sex partners were no more expensive to care for than opposite-sex partners" (Traiman, 2008, p. 24). It is important to understand that although the term *domestic partner* originated in an effort to extend benefits to same-sex couples, what emerged was a policy that was sex neutral. This is important because the term as now used in many venues supporting domestic partner agreements can be used to describe both heterosexual and same-sex partnerships. In other words, any type of committed unmarried adult couple can apply for and receive the benefits that accrue from their relationship's legal designation as a domestic partnership. Willetts's (2003) study shows that domestic partnerships are being used by heterosexual unmarried partners as well as same-sex partners. In addition to same-sex unions' need for legal protection, unmarried heterosexual couples need this legal avenue to protect their relationships; this was true "particularly prior to the 1980s when cohabiters were regarded as 'legal strangers to each other' (Glendon, 1989, p. 253)" (p. 940).

Readers may wonder why unmarried heterosexual couples would need to or want to use the domestic partner option when they could simply marry to gain marriage's rights and privileges. Edin and Reed (2005) provide some insights into the reasons why low-income couples, especially those who have children, do not marry. Social and economic factors both play a role. Social factors include attitudes about childbearing, which no longer needs to go along with marriage; norms governing the standard of living necessary for marriage; the quality of relationships; aversion to divorce; and the inclusion of children from previous relationships on the part of both men and women. Economic barriers include the marriage penalty "tax" on welfare benefits, male unemployment, and low-paying unskilled employment. An increase in employment among unskilled women may also reduce the economic incentive for them to marry.

There is evidence that the instrumental value of marriage is declining, while the symbolic value of marriage is increasing. "The same couples . . . who believed their day-to-day lives would not change at all if they married went on to say that getting married would profoundly transform the meaning of their relationship, in no small part because they believe that marriage carries with it much higher expectations about relationship quality and financial stability than does cohabitation" (Edin & Reed, 2005, p. 121). Regarding the likelihood of marriage among disadvantaged couples, the "ideal remains largely unrealized because of the complexities of their lives" (Edin & Reed, 2005, p. 128). There are also many reasons why economically secure unmarried couples might not want to marry or remarry—for example, to honor their religion's doctrines—even if they are in a committed relationship. Still others may have incomes from sources that will end if they marry. For these heterosexual couples, domestic partnerships may offer many advantages.

Suffredini (2005) provides a good summary of the current status of domestic partnership laws and regulations. Employment-based benefits are usually given to domestic partners and their legal dependents. Although domestic partnership benefits differ from state to state, as many as eleven states, several municipalities, and thousands of private employers, including institutions of higher education, provide domestic partner benefits. At the same time, domestic partner benefits are weaker than those typically accruing to partners in civil marriage and do not include the 1,138 federal benefits offered to married partners.

Civil Unions

The terms *civil marriage* and *civil union* are sometimes confused. The term *civil marriage* refers to the non-religious marriage of a man and a woman performed by a licensed agent of the state, for example, a judge or a justice of the peace. Civil marriages are recognized in all states and by the federal government. The term *civil union* is a term that is reserved for marriages between same-sex partners. Suffredini (2005) clarifies this difference and outlines the protections provided by civil unions:

> The difference between civil marriage and civil unions is not merely a matter of semantics. Civil unions are different from civil marriage in fundamental ways, which can have direct implications on how courts apply the law to these unions and on how employers administer benefits programs.
>
> Civil unions provide only the state-level legal protections attendant to civil marriage. The federal benefits and protections that are provided to married couples by the federal government are not automatically guaranteed to couples who are in civil unions. These federal protections implicate almost every aspect of life and death:
> - eligibility for Social Security survivors benefits;
> - the right to inherit in absence of a will;
> - the ability to roll over a deceased partner's 401(k) plan without incurring substantial tax penalties; and
> - the exemption from tax on the value of health insurance for one's partner.
>
> These differences are substantial and, despite representations to the contrary by opponents of legalizing civil marriage for same-sex couples, many cannot be contracted for through wills, powers of attorney or other legal documents. (p. 9)

Civil unions came about as the result of a court decision in Hawaii. In 1993, the Hawaii Supreme Court ruled that statutes prohibiting a person from marrying someone of the same sex violated the state constitution. In response, the Hawaii legislature proposed an amendment to the state constitution that reserved marriage for relationships between a man and a woman but also recognized that same-sex partners should be given the same benefits as other couples. It is probably an understatement to say that these actions were the equivalent of a nuclear explosion. The decisions by the Hawaiian state courts and legislature unleashed forces that have led to extensive revisions in state and federal laws. These policy changes include the Defense of Marriage Act, which defines marriage as a heterosexual union, and the Federal Marriage Initiative.

Same-Sex Marriage

Within the gay and lesbian communities, there are two competing value-based views or ideologies about state-sanctioned same-sex marriage. Historically, gay rights organizations viewed marriage as an oppressive, sexist, and inherently heterosexual institution. They devoted little energy to the issue and remained suspicious of state-supported marriage but supported domestic partnership or civil union rights (Sullivan, 1997). Those holding this radical position objected to "same-sex marriage based on the notion that it subscribes to heteronormativity and is not a way of liberating individuals from oppressive attitudes and practices" (Yep, Lovaas, & Elia, 2003, p. 51). However, over the past twenty-five years, gay and lesbian groups have taken the position that the legal right to marriage is the linchpin of gay civil rights. Advocates of the assimilationist position have spearheaded efforts to establish legal rights to marriage. Assimilation in this context refers to the view that gays and lesbians are no different from heterosexuals and thus should have the same rights in marriage as those awarded to heterosexuals. Marriage is viewed as the ultimate form of acceptance and equality for intimate relationships and gives those who marry a higher societal status. The assimilationist view "supports same-sex marriage based on the premise that it will lead to more acceptable, equitable, stable, and healthier lives for gays and lesbians" (Yep et al., 2003, p. 52). Granting gay and lesbian individuals the right to marry will remove various forms of social stigmatization against them. As married gay and lesbian individuals are afforded all rights that opposite-sex marriages receive, they will be allowed to raise children in a "stable, socially sanctioned, highly functional and economically viable setting" (Yep et al., 2003, p. 52).

The Defense of Marriage Act

In response to the situation in Hawaii, the U.S. Congress took an unprecedented step and became involved in state marriage laws through the passage of the 1996 Defense of Marriage Act (DOMA). DOMA defines marriage as the "legal union between one man and one woman" and denies same-sex couples federal partner benefits, such as Social Security. DOMA also allows states to reject same-sex marriages performed in other states. Discrimination occurs when a distinction is made between people without regard to individual merit on the basis of class or categories such as race, religion, sexual orientation, disability, ethnicity, height, and age. Since DOMA was written specifically to support heterosexual marriage, DOMA discriminates against gay and lesbian persons on the basis of sexual orientation because it prohibits legal marriage for same-sex couples (Simpson, 2005).

According to Liu and Macedo (2005), the creation of DOMA was based on prejudicial beliefs that gay and lesbian individuals are not worthy of marriage and the rights afforded to heterosexual couples through marriage. However, rather than confront the issue of same-sex marriage directly, the Republican strategy behind the passage of DOMA was to "shift the focus of the debate away from homosexuals and toward children; instead of advancing a morally perfectionist case against gay marriage, they relied on what seemed to be less controversial and more widely acceptable claims about children's welfare" (Liu & Macedo, 2005, p. 211). For example, unable to find any evidence that gay marriage causes direct harm to children, Senator Rick Santorum (R-PA) insinuated that gay marriage would indirectly destabilize the institution of marriage and separate marriage from parenthood. He cited findings of higher rates of cohabitation, out-of-wedlock births, and family dissolution in four European countries that have legalized civil unions (Denmark, Norway, and Sweden) and gay marriage (the Netherlands). His remarks are captured in the *Congressional Record* (2004): "Sweden allowed same-sex unions. There are 8 million people in Sweden. How many same-sex unions? There were 749. Is it worth it that now 60 percent of first-born children born in Sweden are born out of wedlock? Is this worth it? 749? By the way, the break up rate of those marriages is two to three times what it is in traditional marriages. Is it worth it?" The senator's argument was based on a faulty understanding of the Swedish divorce statistics, which show that these dissolutions were associated largely with heterosexual couples and extramarital sex— not the result of problems in the 749 gay marriages. Although based on incorrect facts, the strategy was a political success.

Since DOMA does not allow same-sex couples to marry, the law may be open to judicial review. Three basic issues have been identified as grounds for legal review. Clarkson-Freeman (2004) argues that in passing DOMA, Congress misused Article IV, Section 2, of the United States Constitution, the full faith and credit clause, which requires state courts to recognize, honor, and enforce the actions of other states. Of only four cases ever drawing on the clause, DOMA was the first case in which Congress limited the application of the full faith and credit clause (Johnson, 1997). In a Congressional Research Service Report for Congress, Smith (2004) identifies two other possible reasons why DOMA may face legal challenges: DOMA might "impose a special disability on homosexuals not visited on any other class of people" (p. 3) and in *Lawrence v. Texas* (2003), the U. S. Supreme Court extended the right to privacy to protect "consensual homosexual sodomy." In his report, Smith concludes that none of these arguments is compelling. Others disagree, so it is likely that at some point the legality of DOMA will be challenged. The depth of opposition to same-sex marriage is illustrated by the fact that in 2004, Congress tried to pass an amendment to the U.S. Constitution entitled the Federal Marriage Amendment, which would have forbidden same-sex marriages in the United States. Forty-eight senators voted for the amendment, but that was twelve votes short of the sixty votes required for passage. At the state level, Super DOMA legislation designed to prohibit the legal recognition of all forms of same-sex relationships (domestic partnerships, civil unions, gay marriage, etc.) has been proposed by various state legislatures.

Despite these indicators of opposition to same-sex marriage, gay and lesbian couples have made gains in having same-sex marriage and civil unions recognized, though not without losses and setbacks. Rothblum (2005) provides an overview of the legal status of same-sex relationships in the United States and other countries. Vermont's law, which took effect on July 1, 2000, made same-sex civil unions equivalent to marriage with all its rights and privileges. On May 17, 2004, Massachusetts became the first and only state to make same-sex marriages legal. California's civil union statute also provides almost all the same rights for same-sex unions as are afforded through its marriage statutes to heterosexual couples. Same-sex marriage was specifically banned, but a lawsuit contested the decision through the California Supreme Court (Dolan, 2008). In May 2008, the Supreme Court struck down the ban, and over the next four-and-a-half months, an estimated 18,000 gay couples were married in California. Then, through a direct democracy process, opponents put a constitutional amendment known as Proposition 8: Eliminates Right of Same-Sex Couples to Marry on the California ballot in the November 2008 election. The amendment, which defines marriage as being between a man and a woman, was approved with 52.5 percent in favor (5,387,989 votes) and 47.5 percent against (4,883,460 votes). In chapter 9, we highlighted the importance of citizen-initiatives in view of the Arkansas statute that prevents unmarried cohabitating couples from fostering or adopting children. Here we emphasize the point that ballot-based initiatives are sometimes a way for advocacy groups to change state laws, or as in the case of same-sex marriage in California, to change a state constitution. Since the passage of Proposition 8, same-sex marriage is not legal in California. There may be, however, further challenges in the courts, or future ballot-based initiatives to amend the state constitution in the opposite direction.

Historically, Connecticut was the first state to offer an alternative to marriage for same-sex couples through civil unions. But in October 2008, the Connecticut Supreme Court struck down the civil union law for its failure to sufficiently protect the rights of gay couples and ruled that they have the right to marry (Collins, 2008). Table 11.2 shows the differences

Table 11.2 State Marriage Laws

States that issue marriage licenses to same-sex couples	Connecticut, Iowa, Massachusetts, Vermont
State where marriages legally entered into by same-sex couples in another jurisdiction are recognized	New York
States with no explicit provision prohibiting marriages between individuals of the same sex	New Jersey, New Mexico, New York, Rhode Island, the District of Columbia
States with constitutional amendments restricting marriage to one man and one woman	Alabama, Alaska, Arizona, Arkansas, California, Colorado, Florida, Georgia, Kansas, Idaho, Kentucky, Louisiana, Michigan, Mississippi, Missouri, Montana, Nebraska, Nevada, North Dakota, Ohio, Oklahoma, Oregon, South Carolina, South Dakota, Tennessee, Texas, Utah, Virginia, Wisconsin
States with a marriage law that defines marriage as only between a man and a woman	Delaware, Hawaii, Illinois, Indiana, Maine, Maryland, Minnesota, New Hampshire, North Carolina, Pennsylvania, Washington, West Virginia, Wyoming
States with a law that does or may affect other legal relationships, such as civil unions, or domestic partnerships	Alabama, Arkansas, Georgia, Kentucky, Idaho, Louisiana, Michigan, Nebraska, North Dakota, Ohio, Oklahoma, South Carolina, South Dakota, Texas, Utah, Virginia, Wisconsin

Source: Human Rights Campaign. (2008, June 3). *Relationship recognition in the U.S.* Retrieved July 21, 2008, from http://www.hrc.org/documents/Relationship_Recognition_Laws_Map.pdf.; Human Rights Campaign. (2008, May 30). *Statewide marriage prohibitions.* Retrieved July 21, 2008, from http://www.hrc.org/documents/marriage_prohibitions.pdf; Human Rights Campaign. (2008, July 15). *Proposed constitutional amendments.* Retrieved July 21, 2008, from http://www.hrc.org/documents/amendments_pending.pdf

among state marriage laws—ranging from the license to marry in Massachusetts and Connecticut to state laws and constitutions that forbid same-sex marriages. Same-sex marriages are not legally recognized in forty states, and twelve states forbid recognition of any type of same-sex civil unions (Human Rights Campaign, 2008). Excellent maps and charts on the Human Rights Campaign Web site show the various ways that same-sex relationships are recognized in seven states and the District of Columbia.

Promoting Marriage as Public Policy

Promoting marriage is a policy position no longer held only by conservatives. According to sociologist Daniel Lichter (2001), "both conservatives and liberals seem increasingly prepared to act in concrete ways to encourage marriage and to prevent divorce. This willingness to act is no longer viewed as part of a narrow family agenda of the religious right or of political conservatives, but one increasingly embraced by centrist Democrats, family and child advocacy groups, and progressive social scientists and public policy analysts" (p. 4).

Behind this interest in marriage as public policy is an accumulation of research that suggests the benefits of marriage for children and youths, women, men, and communities. In reviewing the research, Schwartz (2005) and Nock (2005) highlight some of the socioeconomic benefits of marriage:

1. Economic benefits: Marriage makes men more productive and productivity results in higher wages. Marriage encourages asset accumulation through homeownership, saving for the college education of children, and access to gifts and financial help from in-laws.
2. Health benefits: For both men and women, marriage offers lower mortality rates, better sex lives, and better mental health. For men, it leads to less involvement in risky behaviors that cause ill health and accidents (heavy drinking and driving, smoking, using drugs, and getting in fights). For women, it leads to more access to social support and higher household incomes.
3. Benefits for child rearing: Marriage creates higher household incomes and offers the benefit of two adults to supervise and help children with school work and extracurricular activities, a greater likelihood that children will go to college, and less likelihood that male children will engage in crime.

Communities with higher percentages of couples in healthy marriages than in unhealthy marriages also stand to gain. The community benefits of marriage include higher rates of educated citizens; increased involvement in schools and civic organizations; higher property values and rates of homeownership; lower teen pregnancy, crime, juvenile delinquency, and domestic violence rates; and decreased need for social services (Institute for American Values, 2005; U.S. Department of Health and Human Services, 2008). "Thus for the sake of adults, children, and society, a growing consensus is emerging that it is not just marriage per se that matters, but *healthy marriage*" (Moore, Jekielek, Bronte-Tinkew, Guzman, Ryan, & Redd, 2004, p. 1).

Figure 11.1 shows efforts at Child Trends to conceptualize a framework for measuring and defining healthy marriage. In reviewing decades of research data, theory, and commissioned papers from scholars, Moore and her colleagues identified ten constructs or elements of a healthy marriage: commitment, overall satisfaction with the marriage, ability to handle conflict, absence of family violence, faithfulness, communication, time spent together, intimacy and emotional support, commitment to children, and

Figure 11.1 Measurement Framework for Conceptualizing and Defining Healthy Marriage

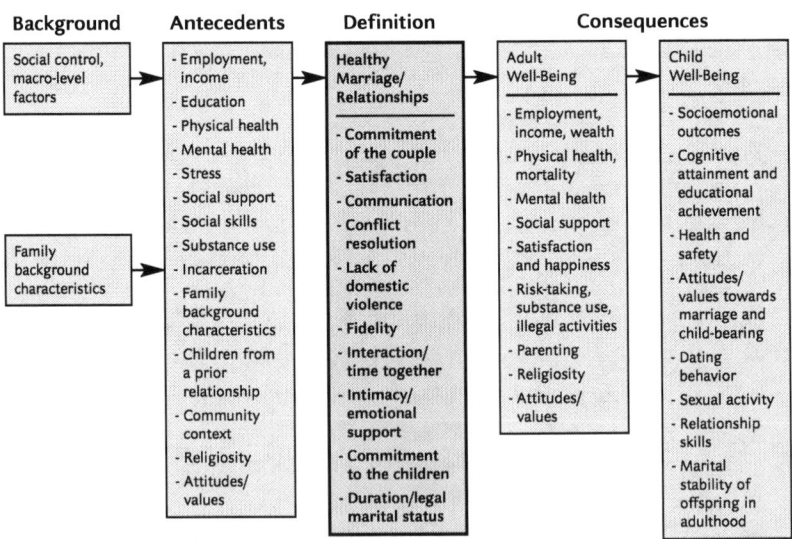

Source: Moore, K. A., Jekielek, S. M., Bronte-Tinkew, J., Guzman, L., Ryan, S., & Redd, Z. (2004). *What is "healthy marriage"? Defining the concept* (Child Trends Publication No. 2004-16). Retrieved March 3, 2009, from http://www.acf.hhs.gov/healthymarriage/pdf/Child_Trends-2004.pdf

duration and legal marital status. This conceptual model is a starting point for future research on promoting healthy marriages, but much work remains. "Of course, questions of cause and effect are very complex, and some factors appear to be both *causes* and *consequences* of marriage" (Moore et al., 2004, p. 3). For example, on one hand, those with higher incomes, few health problems, and better social skills are more likely to get married. On the other hand, as research seems to indicate, marriage contributes to higher incomes, fewer health problems, and improved social support.

The Federal Marriage Initiative

From the above discussion, it is clear that there is support among policy makers for policies that promote marriage in order to improve health and family well-being and potentially reduce the number of unmarried unions. Dion (2005) writes:

> Federal and state legislation enacted over the past decade clearly reflects a growing national interest in reducing the number of children growing up without both parents. In 1996, Congress passed a law allowing states to use part of their welfare block grants to promote the formation of two-parent families and marriage. The Administration for Children and Families . . . at the U.S. Department of Health and Human Services announced a Healthy Marriage Initiative in 2001, prompted in part by research showing that children fare best when raised by their married parents (U.S. Department of Health and Human Services, 2008). As of fall 2004, more than forty states had launched government sponsored efforts to support marriage and couple relationships (Ooms, Bouchet, & Parke, 2004). Congress is now considering legislation to provide $200 million annually in competitive grants to states and organizations to advance marriage-related activities, including demonstration programs to help couples form and sustain healthy marriages and research to determine the effectiveness of those programs. (p. 140)

Further discussion of the Federal Marriage Initiative can be found at the U.S. Department of Health and Human Services' (2008) Healthy Marriage Initiative Web site.

In constructing the history of government's involvement in marriage, Ooms (2001) shows the federal government's extensive and increasing role in legislative and programmatic involvement in marriage. For example, a stated objective of the PRWORA welfare reform legislation was "to end dependence of needy parents on government benefits by promoting job preparation, work and marriage." Since 1996, several states, including West Virginia, Arizona, Florida, Louisiana, Michigan, and Utah, have developed government-funded marriage initiatives with the goal of encouraging single parents to marry, decreasing divorce rates, and reducing the effects of absent fathers on children. Programs typically give financial bonuses to unwed parents who attend workshops and marry. Oklahoma's $10 million initiative features educational workshops for both married and unmarried couples. More recently, the Deficit Reduction Act of 2005 provides $100 million per year for five years to fund healthy marriage promotion efforts, and $50 million per year for five years to promote responsible fatherhood. Lind (2004) critiques the PRWORA as an example of heterosexual bias in social welfare policy. The law attempts to "legislate the family" by defining family and household composition in ways that preclude gay and lesbian individuals and their families from accessing their full civil rights and needed social services.

Another case in point is a marriage promotion plan authored by Senator Sam Brownback (R-KS), who is the District of Columbia Appropriations Subcommittee chairperson. In order to help readers understand the ins and outs of the dynamic policy environment, we want to point out that Congress often uses the District of Columbia as a sort of policy laboratory to test or try new initiatives. New initiatives are attached to bills that fund the District of Columbia. Of the nearly $11 billion in the District of Columbia Appropriations Bill (2005) in FY 2006, $3 million was earmarked for marriage counseling and marriage development accounts, to be matched by private foundations and individuals. Married couples with incomes up to $50,000 who save $3,000 in three years will receive a 3-to-1 match of up to $9,000 for the purchase of assets such as a home, training or education for themselves or their children, or funds to start or expand a business. Engaged couples and unmarried childless individuals taking part in marriage education receive pre-marriage development accounts and would receive up to $4,500 in matching funds when they marry.

To help people understand how getting married would positively or negatively affect their receipt of government benefits, the federal government designed an online tool called the Marriage Calculator (U.S. Department of Health and Human Services, n.d.). Users can input income, for example, for a single woman and her potential spouse and calculate how government programs such as TANF, food stamps, child care subsidies, subsidized housing, Medicaid, SCHIP, and WIC would be affected. The calculator shows the financial impacts of taxes and transfer programs in four different scenarios: a man and woman (1) living apart; (2) cohabiting, which they report to government programs; (3) cohabiting, which they do not report to government programs; and (4) getting married. State comparisons show differences in results, as well as the numerous interactions between assistance programs, income taxes, and EITC. Three state-specific tables highlight states with particularly large marriage bonuses (or small penalties), moderate or average penalties (or bonuses), and particularly low bonuses (or high penalties). The penalties and bonuses reflect relative differences in income when a couple living apart decides to marry.

In commenting on the debate about what government can do to promote marriage through public policy, Nock (2005) points out the individualistic nature of marriage promotion policy. Since researchers and helping professionals know relatively little about how to help couples enter into healthy marriages and stay married, "our expectations of policies in these areas should be modest, at best" (p. 28). At the heart of the matter is whether the problem lies within the individual or within society as a whole. In the former case, policies such as couple's education and counseling are useful; in the latter case, public discussion on the changing role of the family and the institution of marriage in modern society is required.

Summary

There is substantial evidence that there are individual and societal benefits that derive from marriage. It is not so much that policies encouraging marriage are ill advised, but rather that such an emphasis ignores the fact that the nature of family relationships is rapidly shifting, and that most families do not resemble the married two-parent family of the 1950s and 1960s. In addition, the strong bias against gay marriage and civil unions has been used to drive the development of policies focused on marriage and the nuclear family—to the exclusion of policies designed to address the growing population of families headed by unmarried couples. The effort to reestablish the married two-parent nuclear family is not supportive of the 11 million people who live with an unmarried partner, and who should have the same basic legal rights and protections as married couples. Our review covered four types of formal or quasi-formal mechanisms—marriage, common-law marriage, domestic partnerships, and civil unions—that provide various levels and different types of legal rights and protections. These laws and the policies that frame them are discussed in terms of how they apply to heterosexual and same-sex couples.

The issues that surround the debate about marriage as public policy reflect many of the themes of the book. For example, the issue of marriage for same-sex couples brings attention to our view that families in all their diversity should be afforded the same civil and legal rights. Same-sex marriage is a dynamic policy issue, particularly at the state level. Through grassroots democracy, voters in California passed a constitutional amendment that took away the right of gay and lesbian couples to marry, a right previously granted under the state's constitution by the state supreme court. We can expect that advocates for and against the legalization of same-sex marriage will continue their efforts to move the issue into public consciousness, with legal and direct democracy initiatives playing important roles.

The changing demographics of American families have also prompted a value-based debate about whether the institution of the family is declining and deteriorating, or in flux and changing. On one side of this argument, we presented contemporary myths about marriage that have not held true historically in American society. On the other side, we reported on a growing body of research that shows that healthy marriages benefit the health and well-being of women, men, children, and communities. From a research standpoint, however, relatively little is known about how to help people enter into healthy marriages and stay married, especially because factors that lead to healthy marriages may also result from healthy marriage relationships. Current policy promoting marriage is largely individualistic in nature, focusing on counseling and pre-marriage education. Nonetheless, over 1,000 federal laws determine rights, benefits, and responsibilities based on an individual's marital status, and thus the importance of marriage as a public policy issue should not be underestimated.

FOR FURTHER READING

Avery, A., Chase, J., Johansson, L., Litvak, S., Montero, D., & Wydra, M. (2007). America's changing attitudes toward homosexuality, civil unions, and same-gender marriage: 1977–2004. *Social Work, 52*(1), 71–79.

Bernstein, A. (2007). Subverting the marriage-amendment crusade with law and policy reform. *Washington University Journal of Law & Policy, 24,* 79–120.

Cahill, S., Ellen, M., & Tobias, S. (2002). *Family policy: Issues affecting gay, lesbian, bisexual and transgender families.* New York: National Gay and Lesbian Task Force Policy Institute. Retrieved November 13, 2008, from http://www.thetaskforce.org/downloads/reports/reports/FamilyPolicy.pdf

Coontz, S. (2005). *Marriage, a history: From obedience to intimacy, or how love conquered marriage.* New York: Viking.

LaSala, M.C. (2007). Too many eggs in the wrong basket: A queer critique of the same-sex marriage movement. *Social Work, 52*(2), 181–183.

Meezan, W., & Rauch, J. (2005). Gay marriage, same-sex parenting, and America's children. *The Future of Children, 15*(2), 97–115.

Nice, J. (2007). Promoting marriage experimentation: A class act? *Washington University Journal of Law & Policy, 24*, 45.

Nock, S. L. (2005). Marriage as a public issue. *The Future of Children, 15*(2), 13–32.

Waite, L. J., & Gallagher, M. (2000). *The case for marriage: Why married people are happier, healthier, and better off.* New York: Doubleday.

References

Clarkson-Freeman, P. A. (2004). The Defense of Marriage Act (DOMA): Its impact on those seeking same-sex marriages. *Journal of Homosexuality, 48*(2), 1–19.

Collins, D. (2008, October 10). Connecticut gay marriage legalized. *Huffington Post.* Retrieved November 7, 2008, from http://www.huffingtonpost.com/2008/10/10/connecticut-gay-marriage_n_133605.html

Congressional Record. (2004, July 9–14). *Proceedings and debates of the 108th Congress, second session, United States Senate.* Retrieved May 16, 2006, from http://frwebgate.access.gpo.gov/cgi-bin/getpage.cgi?dbname=2004_record&position=all&page=S7981

Coontz, S. (1997). *The way we really are: Coming to terms with America's changing families.* New York: Basic Books.

Defense of Marriage Act, Pub. L. No. 104-199, 110 Stat. (1996).

Deficit Reduction Act, Pub. L. No. 109-171, 42 U.S.C. 1396p and 1396r-5 (2005).

Dion, M. R. (2005). Healthy marriage programs: Learning what works. *The Future of Children, 15*(2), 139–156. Retrieved February 24, 2008, from http://www.futureofchildren.org/usr_doc/08_FOC15-2_fall05_Dion.pdf

District of Columbia Appropriations Bill, Pub. L. No. 109-115 (2005).

Dolan, M. (2008, March 5). Same-sex marriage has skeptics on California Supreme Court. *Los Angeles Times.* Retrieved March 5, 2008, from http://latimes.com/news/local/la-me-gaymarriage5mar05,1,1548922.story

Edin, K., & Reed, J. M. (2005). Why don't they just get married? Barriers to marriage among the disadvantaged. *The Future of Children, 15*(2), 117–137.

General Accounting Office. (1997, January 31). *Tables of laws in the United States Code involving marital status, by category.* Retrieved February 23, 2008, from http://www.gao.gov/archive/1997/og97016.pdf

Goldenberg. S. (2007, January 17). Turning point in US as more women choose not to marry. *The Guardian.* Retrieved February 25, 2008, from http://www.guardian.co.uk/world/2007/jan/17/usa.population

Human Rights Campaign. (2008). *Equality from state to state: Gay, lesbian, bisexual and transgender Americans and state legislation.* Retrieved February 29, 2008, from http://www.hrc.org/about_us/7071.htm

Institute for American Values. (2005, September). *Why marriage matters, second edition: Twenty-six conclusions from the social sciences.* Retrieved March 3, 2009, from http://center.americanvalues.org/?p=7#about

Johnson, J. L. B. (1997). The meaning of "general laws": The extent of Congress's power under the full faith and credit clause and the constitutionality of the Defense of Marriage Act. *University of Pennsylvania Law Review, 145*(6), 1611–1647.

Lawrence v. Texas, 539 U.S. 558 (2003).

Lichter, D. T. (2001, September). *Marriage as public policy.* Retrieved March 3, 2009 from http://www.ppionline.org/documents/marriage_lichter.pdf

Lind, A. (2004). Legislating the family: Heterosexist bias in social welfare policy frameworks. *Journal of Sociology and Social Welfare, 31*(4), 21–35.

Liu, F., & Macedo, S. (2005). The federal marriage amendment and the strange evolution of the conservative case against gay marriage. *Political Science & Politics, 38*(2), 211–215.

Moore, K. A., Jekielek, S. M., Bronte-Tinkew, J., Guzman, L., Ryan, S., & Redd, Z. (2004). *What is "healthy marriage"? Defining the concept* (Child Trends Publication No. 2004-16). Retrieved March 3, 2009, from http://www.acf.hhs.gov/healthymarriage/pdf/Child_Trends-2004.pdf

National Conference of State Legislatures. (2009). *Common law marriage.* Retrieved February 23, 2009, from http://www.ncsl.org/programs/cyf/commonlaw.htm

Nock, S. L. (2005). Marriage as a public issue. *The Future of Children, 15*(2), 13–32. Retrieved February 24, 2008, from http://www.futureofchildren.org/usr_doc/02_FOC_15-2_fall05_Nock.pdf

Ooms, T. (2001). The role of the federal government in strengthening marriage. *Virginia Journal of Social Policy, 9*(1), 165–191.

Ooms, T., Bouchet, S., & Parke, M. (2004). *Beyond marriage licenses: Efforts in states to strengthen marriage and two-parent families.* Washington, DC: Center for Law and Social Policy. Retrieved February 26, 2008, from http://www.clasp.org/publications/beyond_marr.pdf

Rothblum, E. D. (2005). Same-sex marriage and legalized relationships: I do, or do I? *Journal of GLBT Family Studies, 1*(1), 21–31.

Schwartz, J. (2005). The socio-economic benefits of marriage: A review of recent evidence from the United States. *Economic Affairs, 25*(3), 45–51.

Simmons, T., & O'Connell, M. (2003). *Married-couple and unmarried-partner households: 2000.* Retrieved February 26, 2008, from http://www.census.gov/prod/2003pubs/censr-5.pdf

Simpson, D. (2005). *The Defense of Marriage Act (DOMA): An analysis of discrimination toward the GLBT individuals.* Jane Addams College of Social Work, University of Illinois at Chicago. Unpublished paper.

Smith, A. M. (2004). *Same-sex marriages: Legal issues.* Washington, DC: Congressional Research Service. Retrieved March 3, 2009 from http://digitalcommons.ilr.cornell.edu/crs/13/

Suffredini, K. S. (2005). Left at the altar: Differentiating the benefits of marriage, civil unions and domestic partnerships. *Diversity Factor, 13*(1), 5–12.

Sullivan, A. (Ed.). (1997). *Same-sex marriage: Pro and con: A reader.* Toronto: Random House.

Traiman, L. (2008). A brief history of domestic partnerships. *Gay & Lesbian Review Worldwide, 15*(4), 23–24.

U.S. Census Bureau. (2000). *Bicentennial edition: Historical statistics of the United States, colonial times to 1970. Marital status of the population 15 years and over, by sex and race: 1950 to present.* Retrieved February 24, 2008, from http://www.census.gov/prod/www/abs/statab.html

U.S. Census Bureau. (2004, November). *America's families and living arrangements: 2003* (Current Population Reports, Population Characteristics, P20-553). Retrieved June 16, 2006, from http://www.census.gov/population/www/socdemo/hh-fam.html

U.S. Census Bureau. (2006). *Factfinder.* Retrieved February 25, 2008, from http://factfinder.census.gov/servlet/GRTSelectServlet?ds_name=ACS_2006_EST_G00_&_lang=enr)

U.S. Department of Health and Human Services. (2008). *The healthy marriage initiative.* Retrieved February 26, 2008, from http://www.acf.hhs.gov/healthymarriage/index.html

U.S. Department of Health and Human Services. (n.d.). *The marriage calculator: Financial consequences of marriage decisions.* Retrieved May 31, 2006, from http://marriagecalculator.acf.hhs.gov/marriage/index.php

Willetts, M. C. (2003). Exploratory investigation of heterosexual licensed domestic partnerships. *Journal of Marriage and Family, 65*(4), 939–952.

Yep, G. A., Lovaas, K. E., & Elia, J. P. (2003). A critical appraisal of assimilationist and radical ideologies underlying same-sex marriage in LGBT communities in the United States. *Journal of Homosexuality, 45*(1), 45–64.

CHAPTER 12

Family Caregiving and Aging Policy

Each of the previous six chapters has described social issues affecting families and critically examined selected policies that apply to families. Here we address policies related to aging and multigenerational caregiving across the life span. Much of this chapter illustrates a major theme of the book: that demographic trends and the changing nature of the family make it difficult to develop comprehensive family policy.

Statistics show new demographic trends, such as adult children returning home, multigenerational families, grandparents raising grandchildren, and a dramatic increase in the frail elderly. These changing patterns of living, combined with family caregiving, create special challenges for families in the twenty-first century. First, life expectancy has increased and the elderly are living longer. Second, the children of middle-aged Americans are often still living at home or are returning to live with their parents. Third, baby boomers will be reaching retirement age in record numbers in just a few years. Consequently, middle-aged adults find themselves in a peculiar situation, torn between two generations, one older and one younger. Since the bulk of responsibility for caring for family members still rests with the family, middle-aged baby boomers are squeezed in the middle. Demographers call baby boomers the sandwich generation because they provide care for dependent children and aging parents at the same time.

The baby boom, which occurred in the United States between 1946 and 1964, was a result of social forces surrounding the end of World War II, the beginning of the cold war, and the start of the nuclear age. During this era, the family became the central focus of American life and was "the place where many found a sense of security in an increasingly difficult world"

(Conner, 2000, p. 7). Seventy-six million children were born between 1946 and 1964—the most children born at any time in the nation's history. Those still living are now nearing retirement in record numbers. In 2011, the oldest baby boomers will be sixty-five years old, and by 2029, all boomers will be sixty-five or older. Consequently, by 2030, the sandwich generation will be the largest group of retirees in America's history. What makes these demographics interesting is that the boomers have had fewer children than their parents. Many boomers delayed having children until their thirties or early forties, so their children are now teenagers or young adults. This has caused the ratio of middle-aged people to younger people to drop dramatically. Because of increased life expectancy, some boomers still have parents, and sometimes grandparents, who are elderly and need increasing levels of care.

Caregiving for children, adult children, grandchildren, and aging parents creates unique challenges for the sandwich generation. The topic of this chapter, family caregiving, emphasizes what these changing patterns of living mean to families in America. We anchor our discussion by focusing on the baby boom generation, because they are the ones most likely to provide family caregiving amidst these many demographic changes. The chapter begins with a look at some of the changing trends in patterns of family living and caregiving. These changes place the baby boomer generation at the center of caregiving for family members across the life span.

The second part of the chapter looks at federal and state policies that provide services, support, or other types of assistance to multigenerational family caregivers. As with other areas of policy that relate to families in the United States, there is not a comprehensive set of policies designed to assist family caregiving in its multigenerational and kinship care forms. Thus, we have selected some federal and state policies for discussion that address the issue of care for family members: the Family and Medical Leave Act of 1993; the recently passed Fostering Connections to Success and Increasing Adoptions Act of 2008; and the Older Americans Act, which authorizes some types of caregiving services for the elderly.

The last section of this chapter covers Old Age, Survivors, Health and Disability Insurance. As an insurance program tied to work and payroll taxes, Social Security is generally considered the most successful social program in U.S. history. Our discussion looks particularly at retirement benefits and disability insurance. We also discuss cost-of-living adjustments, a policy component largely responsible for moving elderly persons out of poverty. Social Security policy also underscores another major theme of the book: the role of privatization and managed care in service delivery.

Here, we look at arguments for and against privatizing the Social Security Trust Fund and discuss the effect of several proposed models for privatizing Social Security. For example, analysts argue that policy discussions on privatizing Social Security mask the real problem with the current system's retirement and beneficiary rules. Since 1935, there have been fewer marriages and more divorces, many of those who divorce do not marry again, and cohabitation is becoming increasingly common. Two-earner families have replaced single-earner families. These analysts conclude that Social Security is out of step with the structural changes in the family that are taking place in the United States. Thus, we can expect that Social Security will be privatized in the near future, or that alternative methods of policy reform will occur. Future changes to Social Security will affect other generations of workers after the baby boomers, and therefore these future reforms are important for all working families in the United States.

Changing Patterns of Family Living

Adult Children Moving Home

The first demographic trend we will discuss is adult children moving back home to live with their parents. Generally, the baby boomer generation did not come back home to live with their parents as adults. *Empty nest syndrome* is a term used to describe the stress that the middle-aged mothers of baby boomers experienced when their children left home. Today, "boomerang kids" are young adults who move back home to live with their parents for a variety of reasons. The Census Bureau estimates that 56 percent of men and 43 percent of women ages eighteen to twenty-four live with one or both parents (Ambrose, 2004). According to Kingsmill and Schlesinger (1998), "Velcro kids" return home for emotional reasons. Although the values gap between baby boomers and their parents was quite wide, the gap between boomers and their children is much narrower. Children are closer to their parents, and this makes living at home easier. Home is a place where adult children can regroup when there is an emotional crisis; home is an environment where they feel secure.

Changes in the job market are another reason why young adults are living with their parents. In the job market of previous decades, workers expected to stay with one employer for many years—perhaps for their entire working career. The current recession, corporate downsizing, outsourcing, mergers, and layoffs all make today's employment environment unstable. Young adults are the last hired, so they are often the first to lose their jobs. It is also much more common for young people today to change jobs and return home to save money while they transition from one job to another. When adult children return to school for advanced degrees, they often go home to live with their parents.

Other changes in the labor market make it difficult for young adults to be financially independent. Wages have declined in real dollars, so young adults earn less than their counterparts thirty years ago. Declining wages combined with high rent can mean that young adults today pay as much as 50 percent or more of their monthly income for rent, and this makes it difficult for young adults to make ends meet. Many middle-class adult children are not prepared for the lower standard of living that often comes with entry-level positions. Accustomed to the standard of living of their baby boomer parents, some young adults choose to live at home. Rather than squeak by financially on their own, they prefer to have extra money to spend on consumer goods and a comfortable lifestyle. Thus, whether due to sickness or accidents, credit card debt, failed relationships or divorce, job loss, depression, a return to school, or other reasons, it is not uncommon for adult children to leave home and return several times before becoming completely independent of their parents.

The Multigenerational Family

The second demographic trend is the graying of America. People are living longer. In 1900, life expectancy at birth was forty-six years, compared to seventy-eight years in 2005. Diseases once regarded as life threatening are now being treated by advanced surgical techniques, new technology and treatments, and better medications. Thus, most boomers have at least one living parent, and some have at least one surviving grandparent. Given this increased longevity, it is not uncommon for five generations of a family to be alive at the same time, with a sixty-five-year-old grandmother caring for her eighty-five-year-old mother (Kingsmill & Schlesinger, 1998). Overall, about 10 percent of senior citizens today have children who are also senior citizens, but most of these individuals are being cared for by the members of the generation in the middle: the baby boomers. When elderly parents are not sick enough to go to a nursing home but have a difficult time living independently, baby boomers bring their parents home to live with them or relocate their parents so they are closer to family members. Almost 25 percent of American households care for their elderly family members an average of eighteen hours each week. Many of these caregivers still have children under eighteen in the home (Conner, 2000). Virtually all older persons (about 95%) living in non-institutionalized settings receive assistance from relatives and friends. About two out of three older persons (67%) who live in the community rely solely on informal help, mainly from wives and adult daughters (Family Caregiver Alliance, 2002).

There has also been a dramatic increase in grandparent-maintained families. Nearly 4 million children live in households headed by grandparents. Almost 2 million grandparent-headed households include not only grandchildren but also one or both of the biological parents. Often children and grandchildren move in with grandparents because of unemployment, divorce, or other social and economic problems, and the grandparents attempt to help stabilize the second generation and their offspring. But more and more often, grandparents are raising their grandchildren without the second generation in the home. From 1990 to 1997, grandparent-maintained households increased by 19 percent, with the most growth occurring among households with neither parent present (U.S. Census Bureau, 2003). Increases in homelessness, AIDS, drug and alcohol abuse, and child abuse have much to do with the increase in grandparent-maintained households. Relatives are much more likely to take children when a parent is incarcerated. High rates of incarceration of women are the result of harsher drug laws and mandatory sentencing, and this resulted in a sixfold increase in incarceration rates of women between 1990 and 2000 (Smith, Beltran, Butts, & Kingson, 2000).

All these issues combined have created a generation of adults who have elderly parents to care for, perhaps with their own young children still at home, older children returning home (sometimes with children of their own), and/or grandchildren to raise. The stress associated with caregiving in the multigenerational family is felt by all but is most acute for women. Kingsmill and Schlesinger (1998) estimate that women can expect to spend seventeen years looking after children, and eighteen years looking after their elders, either sequentially or at the same time. Already, the surge of women into the workforce in recent decades has put tremendous burdens on women, but since women are the traditional caregivers, they are expected to fill the caregiver role even when they work. For women, caregiving is a juggling act between balancing their careers and taking care of children and extended family members. Due to caregiving, workers miss an average of nine hours per month at work. Women tend to miss more time than men and are more likely to decrease their work hours or leave the workforce entirely due to the stress of competing work and family demands (Robinson, Barbee, Martin, Singer, & Yegidis, 2003).

Over time, caregiver stress causes conflict within families as resentment develops when caregiving impedes on the time people spend with their spouses, children, or work. Stress associated with adult children living at home comes from failure to renegotiate the child-adult relationship. In order for the arrangement to work even temporarily, the relationship must change to an adult-adult relationship of mutual respect and responsibility.

When the arrangement is more permanent, negotiating a new relationship between parent and adult child can be even more difficult. When the adult child arrives home with the grandchildren in tow, space and privacy issues may create resentment on the part of grandparents, particularly if they are the "automatic" babysitters.

There is, however, a body of research that shows that the multigenerational experience is rewarding for families who garner support from informal community networks. Caregivers tend to have less time for social activities, so the support of a friend or confidant is especially important for women. Expanding the network of caregivers within the family, sharing responsibilities, and seeking out support and respite care can decrease caregiver stress. As Bullock (2004) found in her study of rural grandparents caring for their grandchildren, social support can be provided by the extended family and community. Families who provide needed relief in child-rearing responsibilities, and who view their relationship with grandchildren positively, find the caregiving situation very fulfilling. Social workers who view the family context positively, assist with coordination of services, and mobilize community support also aid in developing positive roles for the extended family.

Compared to white families, African American families are more involved in intergenerational helping networks and are more likely to provide elders with emotional support and practical assistance through informal helping networks, particularly through church. Asian Americans have close-knit multigenerational family systems, but research on the quality of these relationships is inconclusive. Most Asian American subgroups report that they would go to their family for help in a crisis before contacting an agency (Conner, 2000). Hispanic families are most likely to live in intergenerational families. Overall, the number of minority families with aging parents is increasing at a much faster rate than that of white families with aging parents. Since the poverty rates of older people of color are high, they have less access to community care (Roots, 1998). This places a double burden on baby boomers of color.

Kinship Care

Kinship care is the third demographic trend related to caregiving by the baby boomer generation. Some kinship caregivers are official foster parents through state child protection systems. Others parent children outside the child welfare system, albeit on a full-time and sometimes lengthy basis. In order to understand these trends in kinship care, we need to look more closely at what the term means. The general term *kinship care* refers to many different types of caregiving for children. First, the word *kin* is used to refer to blood relatives, as well as others who do not have legal or blood relationships to a child. These can include godparents, family friends, and others with close emotional ties to the child. About half of the states define *kin* as individuals related by blood, marriage, or adoption, but the rest do not require a biological or legal relationship with the child for the caregiver to be considered kin. Researchers and policy makers typically use the terms *informal* and *formal* kinship care—the former referring to caregiving for children not involved in the child welfare system, and the latter referring to children in state custody who are placed with grandparents or other relatives. However, these differentiations are incorrect. For example, informal caregivers may, in fact, have legal custody, guardianship, or power of attorney to make decisions about the welfare of the child. A child placed with formal caregivers may actually not be a ward of the state but may have been placed voluntarily by the parent or parents outside the parental home after an investigation of child abuse and neglect. Yet because of the voluntary nature of the placement, the state does not go through the formal legal processes to terminate parental rights and thereby assume custody of the child. Geen (2004) suggests that the term *private kinship care* should be used to refer to care that occurs without involvement of child welfare agencies; the terms *kinship foster care* and *voluntary kinship care* should be used for care involving the child welfare system.

These different categories of kinship care make it difficult to track the exact number of children living in various family care arrangements. In 1997, a national study by the Urban Institute found that of the nearly 2 million children not living with either parent, 1.3 million children were in private kinship care arrangements, 284,000 children were living in voluntary kinship care, and 197,000 of the 1.7 million children living with relatives were in kinship foster care (Geen, 2000). Preliminary estimates for 2005 show that nearly 24 percent of the children in foster care were living in kinship foster care (Administration for Children and Families, 2006).

The growth in kinship foster care is attributed to a new emphasis among child welfare workers on child placement within the extended family or with others who are emotionally bonded with the child. Younger children are more likely than older children to be placed in kinship foster care, and African American children are more likely than members of other racial or ethnic groups to be in kinship foster care. The birth parents are more likely to be younger and less likely to be or have been married than the parents of children in traditional foster care. Most kinship caregivers are grandparents. They are most likely older, African American, low income, and female, which, as Schwartz (2002) points out, are undervalued social categories: "Both caregiver and child are often vulnerable because of their position in society, and kinship policies reinforce this vulnerability by failing to provide adequate assistance" (p. 431). The commitment of caring for grandchildren is often not temporary. Over half of grandparents who care for grandchildren will parent grandchildren for more than three years (Weber & Waldrop, 2000).

This type of grandparent-headed family is a multigenerational family in which the middle generation is physically absent, but emotionally significant. Children have a difficult time when they are separated from their parents for extended lengths of time and may act out behaviorally. Thus grandparent-headed families may experience long-term family crises because of the added stress of the child, but also because of the problems of their own children, which keep them from raising their offspring. Grandparents raising grandchildren are more likely to live in poverty and to be in poor health than their non-caregiver counterparts. Almost half still work, which adds to their stress. The social, physical, and emotional stresses that accompany the grandparent caregiver role may manifest into depression, feelings of helplessness, and isolation. Gibbons and Jones (2003) found that the grandparents most at risk are those who have cumulative stressors, low physical and emotional functioning, and few resources.

Often, grandparents and others who provide private kinship care do not want to strain family relationships by seeking guardianship or legal custody, sometimes because they hope that the parent or parents will be able to care for and raise the children on their own at some point in time. However, without legal guardianship, or at minimum a legal power of attorney, kinship caregivers may have difficulty enrolling children in school or giving permission for children to see a physician. Rather than reporting neglect or alleged abuse and risking losing children to the child welfare system, private kinship caregivers often take responsibility for raising children with little or no financial help. Box 12.1 illustrates a case

Box 12.1 Multigenerational Caregiving

Stella was a single mother who was also the caregiver for her multigenerational family. Stella had her mother, one daughter in high school, and the baby of her adult daughter living with her.

> When Sandy, my daughter, got divorced, she was out partying and didn't take care of her baby. Chloe has been with me basically since she was eighteen months old. It's just something you have to do. . . . We have a very close-knit family.

Stella experienced additional stress because her daughter showed signs of mental illness and began self-medicating with drugs and alcohol. It was difficult for Stella to watch her daughter and not be able to help. She tried to help her daughter many times but knew that ultimately she had to care for her granddaughter.

> *Where would Chloe be if I didn't take care of her? She would have been under state care. . . . I used to hope Sandy could come take care of her. But then it just got to the point where we would just thank God when she got to jail 'cause we knew she was going to have a roof over her head and food. You know? I know I did everything I could for Sandy. She has been in counseling, special schools, rehab. I finally got to the point where I've done all I can do, Chloe is my responsibility, and that's who I'm going to take care of. I wouldn't have done anything any differently, even when I think about it. I'm glad I did it. She's just like my child, she's precious to me—that's for sure. And she knows it.*

When Stella first started caring for Chloe, she did not want to get involved with the child welfare system. She decided to ask the courts for legal custody when things became complicated.

> *I have legal custody of Chloe, I didn't for quite awhile 'cause there was never any problem. I could take her anywhere, I took her to the doctor and everything and then there was a point in school and also in insurance when I had to show papers to prove that I had custody of her. Sandy knew she couldn't take care of Chloe—she's thanked me a million times for that. When I applied for guardianship, I just went to the courthouse and they sent out a social worker to see the house. I never got money and I never asked for any—that's the way you stay out of the system. I asked for nothing but custody.*

For several years, Stella's mother was a big help with the children, but in her mid-eighties she began showing signs of dementia. Stella eventually had to quit her job to take care of her.

> *Mother had Alzheimer's at the end; it was very stressful at that point. We knew she was forgetful. She'd forget to eat, forget her medicine. Finally, I couldn't work any longer, I couldn't leave her. I took care of my aunt and took my mother with me and that worked for awhile. One day we came home from the doctor and she was nervous and shaky and couldn't sleep. About midnight she was jerking on the curtains and didn't know who I was or who she was. I think she had a stroke. But anyway, she went from the hospital to the nursing home.*

of multigenerational family caregiving in which Stella is the baby boomer caregiver caught in the middle. Stella eventually took over all the caregiving for her frail elderly mother and her granddaughter when her daughter began having problems with drugs and alcohol. Stella did not want to get involved in the child welfare system but eventually applied for legal custody of her granddaughter.

Caring for the Frail Elderly

The fourth demographic trend is the dramatic growth of the number of the frail elderly, who are sometimes referred to as the "old" old within the elderly population. As we have discussed, life expectancy has increased dramatically, and along with this trend, the definition of the elderly has changed. One in every eight adults is over the age of sixty-five, but the fastest-growing segment of the population is those over eighty-five years old (Conner, 2000). The number of those over eighty-five is expected to increase from 5.4 million in 2008 to 19 million in 2050 (U.S. Census Bureau, 2008) Although African Americans have a lower overall life expectancy, they make up a larger segment of the oldest population and are more likely than white Americans to live to be one hundred years old. While African Americans make up only 12 percent of the general population, they comprise 14 percent to 21 percent of those one hundred years old and older.

Statistics show that 70 percent to 75 percent of the elderly live independent lives well into their eighties and remain at home until they can no longer cope with everyday activities. However, the longer people live, the greater the likelihood that chronic illnesses, dementia, decreased physical capacity, and other natural aging processes will occur. In the past, death occurred earlier and was often acute, but now it may be a longer process of chronic problems and frailty requiring prolonged care for longer periods of time. When families can no longer care for their senior members through family and/or community-based support, long-term care must be obtained. Medicare pays for nursing home care only under certain circumstances and only for a limited period of time after a hospital stay if rehabilitation is needed. After one hundred days, the elder or his or her family must pay anywhere from $80 to $300 per day out of pocket, depending on the level of care needed (Medicare, 2006). Medicaid will pay for long-term nursing home care after the patient's assets are "spent down," so this type of access to nursing home care is financially viable only for elders who require nursing home care for the rest of their lives.

Because of increased longevity, continuing-care retirement communities have sprung up. These retirement communities offer a full-service continuum of care with step-down housing and care options, beginning with independent living apartments or townhouses complete with nursing visits, recreational facilities, and often an on-site cafeteria (Kingsmill & Schlesinger, 1998). When individuals need more assistance with daily activities, they can move to the assisted living part of the retirement complex. These units are set up like small efficiency apartments and residents are provided with more personal care as well as nursing care. Assisted living serves as a bridge between independent living and nursing home care. The final level of care is the nursing home. Once elders enter the nursing home, they are still near their spouse or friends who are living in other parts of the retirement property. These communities are quite popular and on the rise, but they are expensive. People pay an expensive entrance fee to join the community by purchasing their apartment or townhouse, as well as a monthly service fee for the guarantee that they will be taken care of for the rest of their lives. These types of retirement communities are for upper-income families who have substantial retirement savings and/or proceeds from the sale of their homes.

Policies for Family Caregiving

In this section of the chapter, we look at policies that support or provide services for family caregiving across the life span. Some policies that we have selected focus on one generation of the family. Other policies, such as the Family and Medical Leave Act of 1993, provide general support for family caregiving. We also look at policies that support family caregiving through kinship care and the Older Americans Act, which covers some types of care for senior citizens and the frail elderly. We have grouped these caregiving and support policies together because of our focus on the caregiving functions of the multigenerational family, which are due, in part, to the changing trends in family living that we have discussed.

The Family and Medical Leave Act

The Family and Medical Leave Act (FMLA) of 1993 provides some protection to families who experience medical crises and must take time off from work. FMLA allows job-protected, unpaid leave for up to twelve weeks in any twelve-month period because of the birth of a child; care of a newborn, newly adopted, or foster child; care of a family member (child, spouse, or parent) with a serious health condition; or the employee's own health condition and inability to work. Employees who take FMLA leave are entitled to keep their employer-provided health benefits, provided they pay any shared health care premiums while on leave. Employees have the right to return to the same position or an equivalent position with equivalent pay, benefits, and working conditions. FMLA covers all public agencies, including state, local, and federal employers and schools, all private-sector employers engaged in commerce, and any industry affecting commerce with more than fifty employees who have worked at least twenty or more workweeks. Employees must also have worked at their job for the last twelve months and for at least 1,250 hours within the last year. The employer has a right to a thirty-day advanced notice from the employee when it is feasible.

The dynamic process behind the passage of FMLA shows the role that coalitions played, as well as the trade-offs and policy concessions that advocates often must make, during the policy-making process. FMLA is also a good example of a bill that lost much of its original policy intent during the years leading up to its passage. It was first introduced in 1985 as the Parental and Disability Act and provided eighteen weeks of job-protected leave and universal coverage for all employees. In 1987, the bill was reintroduced and many compromises were made. The universal component was changed to exempt employers with fifty or fewer employees, and the length of covered leave was decreased to twelve weeks. Paid leave was not even introduced in the original bill because advocates did not believe they could find a sponsor for the bill if it required paid leave. Even without the paid-leave component, lawmakers worried about the cost to businesses if workers were allowed to take time off to care for their families. Others who would have advocated the bill pointed out that the unpaid component favored the middle class because poor families would not be able to afford to take leave. The Chamber of Commerce, a major opponent of the bill, was able to garner grassroots support from businesses, but the FMLA coalition did not have the finances to organize the support needed to send letters and make phone calls to constituents. As Kaitin (1994) points out in her analysis of FMLA's legislative history, "Constituents tended to be unaware that there were no laws requiring job-protected leave until they were in the midst of a family crisis or transition. . . . On the other hand, the business community was very resourceful in making its position known to members of Congress through mailings and other grassroots activities" (p. 110). After much organizing, the bill passed in 1990 and again in 1992, but both times the legislation was vetoed by President George Bush. Finally in 1993, President Clinton signed the bill. Advocates reasoned that it was better to get a law passed that could be amended than to go on without a family leave policy in the United States.

A feminist policy analysis by Fine (2006) suggests that a variety of social and political conditions led to the final passage of FMLA. Some key factors included the fact that the legislation was intended to benefit the female members of the sandwich generation whose careers were wedged between the rearing of children and caring for aging parents. At the time the legislation was passed, there were more opportunities for higher education for women, and women also had access to new birth control methods to delay childbearing, which increased the number of women having children later in life. In the political arena, more than one hundred women ran for Congress in 1992, and politicians were more aware of the voting power of women boomers. In the early 1990s, the cold war had just ended, and there was a general view that policy attention should return to domestic issues such as education, health care, and child and family issues. In this context, FMLA was both an equal opportunity bill and a work-family accommodation bill. As an equal opportunity bill, it provided protection for employees to move from paid work to caregiving, and back to paid work. As a family accommodation bill, it allowed temporary flexibility for parents to attend to child and family care. Utilization rates, however, show that women, particularly unmarried women, are more likely than men to be among "leave-needers." Women are more likely to be part-time workers; they are more likely to work for companies with fewer than fifty employees, which are not required to permit unpaid leave. Single mothers with responsibility for the care of children are more likely than men to need leave, but less likely to be able to afford unpaid leave. Thus, FMLA "reinforces gender stereotyping and the devaluation of women's contributions. Because leave is unpaid, FMLA devalues women's work on behalf of the family unit because it suggests that such labor has no capital value" (Fine, 2006, p. 61).

Finally, FMLA is a great example of the incremental approach to policy making. The rationale behind incrementalism emphasizes the importance of getting a policy "on the books." The idea is that it is easier to change or modify current policy than it is to marshal the forces needed to get a major new policy on the agenda and passed into law in the first place. Still, incremental policy change is also often easier said than done. For example, over the fifteen-year history of FMLA, advocates have not been successful in changing the law to provide paid leave or even partial paid leave for family caregivers. The only recent change to FMLA occurred in 2008 as part of a defense spending bill related to the Iraq war. President Bush signed the National Defense Authorization Act for FY 2008, which amends FMLA to permit a "spouse, son, daughter, parent, or next of kin" to take up to twenty-six workweeks of leave to care for a "member of the Armed Forces, including a member of the National Guard or Reserves, who is undergoing medical treatment, recuperation, or therapy, is otherwise in outpatient status, or is otherwise on the temporary disability retired list, for a serious injury or illness" (U.S. Department of Labor, 2008).

Federal and State Policies on Kinship Care

Families were providing kinship care long before policies were created to assist them. The first federal legislation to give preference to kin placement was the Indian Child Welfare Act of 1978. After fifteen years of advocacy, the legislation, which requires state child welfare workers to notify the tribe of the child and give preference to the tribal authority to assume authority over the case, was passed. If the tribe does not assume authority, the worker must first attempt to place the child with a family from the same tribe, followed by placement with any Native American family, and lastly with a non–American Indian foster family (Matheson, 1996).

Several other major policies have provided some level of assistance to kinship caregivers. Prior to the 1980s, state agencies paid kinship caregivers less than non-kin foster parents. The U.S. Supreme Court decision in *Miller v. Youakim* (1979) entitled relatives of children in legal custody of the state to receive the same federal foster care benefits as those received by non-relative foster parents in cases in which the kinship placements were eligible for federal reimbursement under the AFDC-Foster Care Program through Title IV-E of the Social Security Act (Gleeson, 1999). Title IV-E was amended as part of the Adoption Assistance and Child Welfare Act of 1980, which made any foster home that met state licensing standards eligible to receive foster care maintenance payments. Thus, since the 1980s, the placement of children in foster homes with grandparents and other relatives by state child welfare agencies has increased steadily. In 1996, Title IV-A of the Social Security Act was amended as part of the PRWORA to allow for TANF payments for kinship foster care. The 1996 legislation also specified who qualifies as a relative caretaker. Those who qualify are parents, grandparents, siblings, stepparents, stepsiblings, aunts, uncles, first cousins, nephews, and nieces. The Adoption and Safe Families Act (1997) gives preference to kinship placement for foster care and adoption. In chapter 2, we pointed out the importance of implementation rules that are drawn up by agencies of the federal or state executive branch of government that are charged with monitoring a given piece of legislation. Kinship care policy is a good example of this. According to Geen (2004), the January 2000 final rule guiding the implementation of the Adoption and Safe Families Act from the U.S. Department of Health and Human Services spelled out the requirements for federal reimbursement to states for kinship foster care. Kinship foster homes must meet the same standards as non-kin foster homes. In specific cases, waivers may be requested (typically for space and training requirements), but waivers may not be requested for safety issues. In addition, temporary and emergency foster care placements with kin are not eligible for federal matching funds. In most states, sufficient income is a requirement for licensure as a foster parent. Kinship foster families often face barriers in meeting this standard, as well as requirements in space, age, and education (Templeman, 2003). The 2000 final rule is a good example of how quickly federal rules and regulations can cause states to change their policies. Between 1999 and 2001, twenty-seven states changed their licensing policies, with two-thirds of the states setting more stringent licensing criteria for kinship foster care. Thus, based on federal executive rules, funding for kinship care holds firmly to the criterion that kin foster parents must meet state licensing conditions.

Both the Adoption and Safe Families Act and the final rule allow states to set different standards for kinship care and non-kinship care, and most states have set separate criteria. Twenty states have a less stringent licensing process for kinship foster homes; twenty-three states waive some licensing requirements. Variations also occur in voluntary kinship care, with some states using such placements to divert children from state foster care without any payment to the kin caregivers. Geen (2000) points out the irony of the situation: "Kin with the resources and knowledge to become licensed receive a higher level of financial support than kin who have fewer resources" (p. 5). "For those kin who are not eligible for federal reimbursement, states have broad discretion in developing licensing requirements and determining what financial support they will provide to kinship foster parents, if any. Moreover, many states have developed multiple assessment options. As a result, the amount of financial assistance that kinship caregivers receive can vary due to the eligibility status of the children in their care, the assessment criteria and licensing requirements of individual states, and even the discretionary decisions made by child welfare line supervisors and caseworkers" (Geen, 2004, p. 139).

In addition to federal child welfare policy, AFDC/TANF cash assistance also affects the care and well-being of children in out-of-home placements with relatives. Under AFDC, a kinship caregiver could receive welfare payments for the child as a relative of the eligible family, or if the family was not eligible for welfare, it could receive a child-only grant. Under the PRWORA, states have the option of using TANF funds for child-only grants as long as the caregiver meets the state's TANF definition of a relative caregiver. Although all states have opted to provide TANF support, because of devolution, there is great variation in how states implement TANF. For example, there are variations in funding levels, and differences in rules that guide TANF assistance for children in kinship foster care. Some states combine foster care support *and* TANF cash assistance; some states provide foster care support *or* TANF; some states provide only TANF, and others only foster care support; and some states provide funds from other sources (Leos-Urbel, Bess, & Geen, 2002). Overall, TANF grants are much smaller than foster care payments. As a result, the economic well-being of grandmother-headed families faces greater risk when the grandmothers act as caregivers of children outside the foster care system. "Foster care payments often exceed TANF benefit amounts, depending on the state and the age and number of children in care. State TANF child-only rates vary from $60 to $514 a month, with the amount for each additional child prorated on a declining scale. Foster care payment rates vary from $212 to $708 a month for basic care and are the same per child, regardless of the number of children being cared for. Thus the difference in benefits becomes even greater when there are multiple children in care" (Park, 2005, p. 20).

In assessing the policy implications of welfare reform for older caregivers and kinship care in California, researchers speculate that when younger TANF recipients reach welfare-to-work time limits and lose the adult portion of TANF cash assistance, they may transfer care of their children to older adult relatives. In California, older adult caregivers, especially women age fifty to fifty-nine, are more likely to be exempt from time limits due to their age and the difficulty of finding employment for older welfare recipients. "The unresolved question is: How many parents will move their children into the homes of relatives? Some families may indeed respond to the economic incentives created by a non-time-limited environment for older relatives" (Berrick, Needell, & Minkler, 1999, p. 860).

The newest federal child welfare legislation regarding kinship care was passed in the last days of the 110th Congress, at the height of the financial crisis on Wall Street, and just before the November 2008 presidential election. The Fostering Connections to Success and Increasing Adoptions Act of 2008 was signed into law by President Bush on October 7, 2008. Although official rules and regulations on the act's implementation have not been written, the Center for Law and Social Policy (2008) provides an excellent summary of the new law:

- The notice to relatives when a child is about to enter care allows grandparents and other relatives to get involved early in the child's care, as relatives can sometimes keep the child out of foster care.
- Grants for kinship navigator programs and other activities to engage family members will help link relative caregivers both in and out of foster care to a broad range of services and supports for their children and themselves. Funding can also be used for intensive family-finding efforts, family group decision-making meetings, and residential family substance abuse treatment programs.

- State child welfare agencies will have the option to use federal funds for kinship guardianship assistance to help children leave foster care and live permanently with relatives.
- State child welfare agencies must make reasonable efforts to place siblings in the same foster care, kinship, or adoptive home or to maintain connections among siblings, unless it would be contrary to their safety or well-being to do so.
- State child welfare agencies must ensure that every school-age child in foster care or receiving kinship guardianship or adoption assistance is enrolled full time in school.
- For the first time, children older than sixteen who leave foster care for kinship guardianship will be eligible for education and training vouchers for higher education or other vocational training, as well as independent living services.
- States may waive non-safety-related licensing standards for relative homes on a case-by-case basis. Most often these rules are related to physical conditions of the home, such as requirements that there be a separate bedroom for each child or a certain amount of square footage in the home. Although such requirements can currently be waived in individual cases, the new law makes this explicit.

As we discussed in chapter 9, child welfare policy exhibits a pendulum-like swing between policy that seeks to reunify abused and neglected children with their families and policy that seeks to remove children permanently from their families of origin through foster care and adoption. Clearly, this new legislation's focus is on kinship care. In addition, as part of the managed care approach being used in child welfare, the incentive payment given to state agencies for completed adoptions has doubled from $4,000 per child to $8,000 per child. The legislation pays little, if any, attention to previous methods of family preservation. Rather, the law heralds a major policy change in support of kinship caregiving by the grandparents and other relatives of abused and neglected children.

The Older Americans Act

The Older Americans Act (OAA) was enacted in 1965 to provide nutrition programs, transportation, supportive services, and senior centers for older Americans. The OAA provides the policy foundation for agencies dedicated to advocacy, policy, and programs for older Americans, targeting people in greatest economic and social need with a series of block grant programs (Takamura, 1999). Title III of the OAA authorizes grants for community areas on aging and senior centers. Community areas on aging are agencies that coordinate many services for the elderly, including meals on wheels; transportation to doctors, pharmacies, and shopping; and case management. Senior centers are community-based programs that offer meals, recreational programs, information and referral services, health checks, opportunities for socialization, and respite for caregivers. Title VII of the OAA (added in 1992) provides grants for vulnerable elder rights protection programs. Currently, all fifty states have laws authorizing the provision of adult protective services in cases of elder abuse (National Center on Elder Abuse, 2006). All these programs are designed to assist elders to stay in their homes for as long as possible.

The Older Americans Act Amendments of 2000 included the National Family Caregiver Support Act (NFCSA), which authorized the creation of the National Family Caregiver Support Program. This program provides much more extensive caregiver assistance than the OAA. The OAA of 1965 had explicitly stated in its objectives that the government should give "support to family members and other persons providing voluntary care to older individuals needing long-term care services." In addition, the OAA included provisions for supportive services, mainly respite care, for older family caregivers of selected target populations. However, there was no comprehensive program for supporting families. The NFCSP provides additional services as follows:

- Information for caregivers about available services
- Assistance in gaining access to supportive services for caregivers
- Individual counseling, support groups, and caregiver training to assist caregivers in making decisions and solving problems related to their roles
- Respite care to temporarily relieve caregivers of their responsibilities
- Supplemental services, on a limited basis, to complement the care provided by caregivers

The National Family Caregiver Support Act also expands the definition of a caregiver and gives additional support to caregivers with children of their own. The NFCSA defines a family caregiver as an adult family member, or other individual, who is an informal provider of in-home and community care to an older individual. This broad definition allows flexibility for meeting the needs of those who care for their loved ones, acknowledging the fact that, in addition to close family members, other relatives, friends, neighbors, domestic partners, and others often share the burden of caring for their loved ones. The NFCSA gives a high priority to services for older caregivers with the greatest social and economic needs (with particular attention to low-income older individuals) and older caregivers of persons with mental retardation and related developmental disabilities. The law also allows each state to use no more than 10 percent of the total funds to provide support services to eligible caregivers raising children ages eighteen and younger.

The Family Caregiver Alliance (2002) undertook a state-by-state analysis to identify what types of supplemental services were being offered by states. The report summarizes the preliminary experiences of ten states in providing caregiver support services after the passage of the NFCSP. Respite care and supplemental services (e.g., consumable supplies) were seen as the top service needs of family caregivers. States vary in how they have designed their caregiver support services under the NFCSP, but services ranged from the provision of medical supplies, nutritional supplements, and chore services to home health aides, adult day care, companions, respite care, and support groups (see Area Agency on Aging, 2006). This program has provided much-needed resources that allow elderly family members to live in their homes for as long as possible. Social Security retirement benefits are a major factor that allow the elderly to live independently, particularly the non-frail elderly who are sixty-five to eighty-five years of age. Also, when retirees live with their children and/or grandchildren in multigenerational families, their retirement benefits from Social Security add income to the household.

Old Age, Survivors, Health and Disability Insurance

Old Age, Survivors, Health and Disability Insurance is the official name of the Social Security Act of 1935. The act represents a comprehensive package of benefits to ensure against earnings loss due to retirement, death, and disability. These benefits are an essential part of the safety net for older Americans, but spouses, dependent children, and sometimes other family members also are entitled to a wide range of benefits provided through various titles of the act. As we discussed in previous chapters, Social Security includes a variety of health and long-term care policies through Medicare and Medicaid. Supplemental Security Income is a means-tested program that provides income to adults over the age of sixty-five who have limited income, and adults and children who are blind or disabled. Although Supplemental Security Income is part of the Social Security Act, it is not financed through the Social Security Trust Fund, but through general tax revenues. Benefits for 2008 were $637 per month for a single individual and $956 per month for couples (U.S. Social Security Administration, 2007). We refer readers to a complete compilation of the Social Security laws through 2007 that is available through the U.S. Social Security Administration (2008a). An online benefit eligibility screening tool is also available to help consumers find out different benefits that they may be eligible for through various titles of the Social Security Act (U.S. Social Security Administration, n.d.).

Here we look briefly at Social Security's retirement benefits and disability insurance. The part of Social Security known as Old-Age and Survivors Insurance (OASI) is funded through payroll taxes paid by employees as part of the Federal Insurance Contributions Act, with an additional portion of the tax paid by employers. In 2008, for example, employees must pay in 7.65 percent of their income and employers must match it at 7.65 percent. Self-employed individuals are required to pay the full tax rate of 15.30 percent into the payroll tax system under the Self-Employed Contributions Act. OASI is financed by this money, which is paid into the OASI trust fund. Each year, however, there is a maximum amount of earnings that is taxable. The amount of taxable earnings in 2007, for example, was $97,500, and $102,000 in 2008. To be fully eligible for OASI benefits, workers must work a specified number of quarters of coverage, and all workers must work and pay into the system for at least six quarters of coverage. Thus, based upon these conditions of work and the payment of Federal Insurance Contributions Act or Self-Employed Contributions Act tax, OASI is a universal social insurance program. This means that its benefits apply to all who are eligible through participation in the program. Thus, as a social insurance program, it is quite different from social welfare programs that have means-tested or income eligibility requirements. Benefits are calculated based on a person's lifetime earnings, and those who pay more taxes into the system receive more benefits upon retirement. For example, the maximum retirement benefit for workers retiring at the full retirement age was $2,116 per month in 2007, and $2,185 per month in 2008. Disability insurance benefits in 2008 ranged from $670 per month for persons who are able to engage in substantial gainful activity and $940 per month for the non-blind to $1,570 per month for the blind.

OASI retirement and disability benefits can also include family benefits. This means that the following family members can receive Social Security benefits on the retiree's or disabled person's record: spouse if he or she is at least sixty-two years old (or any age but caring for an entitled child under age sixteen); children if they are unmarried and under age eighteen or under age nineteen and a full-time elementary or secondary student; children age eighteen or older who are disabled; ex-spouse if the divorce took place ten or fewer years ago. OASI survivor benefits are also payable to widows and widowers as a portion of their spouse's income or they may switch to their own lifetime earnings if it is larger than their spouse's lifetime earnings at age sixty-two. Based on certain eligibility criteria, survivor benefits can be claimed by:

- Widows and widowers, who can receive full benefits at full retirement age, or reduced benefits as early as age sixty
- Disabled widows and widowers as early as age fifty
- A widow or widower at any age if he or she takes care of the deceased's child, who is under age sixteen or disabled and receiving Social Security benefits
- Unmarried children under eighteen, or up to age nineteen if they are attending high school full time (under certain circumstances, benefits can be paid to stepchildren, grandchildren, or adopted children)
- Children at any age who were disabled before age twenty-two and remain disabled
- Dependent parents age sixty-two and older (U.S. Social Security Administration, 2008b)

An important aspect of Social Security retirement is that benefits are adjusted for inflation. This means that as the cost of living rises, retirement income rises. Although passed in 1935, Social Security did not pay out benefits until the early 1940s and did not become the dominant source of income protection for the elderly until 1950, when Congress enacted the first cost-of-living adjustment (COLA). In 1975, Congress made COLAs automatic by tying benefits to changes in the consumer price index. This means that Social Security benefits increase yearly to keep up with the rate of inflation. However, rising costs for gas and heating bills, groceries, and prescription drugs are not offset by increases in income from Social Security.

Why does this happen? If Social Security benefits are increased based on the rise in the cost of living, why don't benefits keep up with inflation? First, there are several consumer price indexes—each of which measures inflation by looking at rising costs differently. Second, although the federal government uses the Consumer Price Index for Elderly Consumers (CPI-E) to measure senior costs, it uses a very slowly growing consumer price index called the Consumer Price Index for Urban Wage Earners and Clerical Workers (CPI-W) to calculate the COLA for Social Security benefits. According to McCutchen (2006), the CPI-W "surveys the goods and services that younger workers use. But younger workers have far different spending habits than seniors, who must spend a greater percentage of their income on health care" (p. 1). Consequently, the CPI-W is not a good measure of the type of goods that seniors need to purchase. Thus, if policy required COLAs to be tied to the CIP-E, the difference would be small but substantial over time. In 2005, for example, beneficiaries received a 2.7 percent increase, but if the COLA were based on CIP-E, they would have received a 3.1 percent increase.

Despite all this, primarily because of COLAs, Social Security has been the most important anti-poverty program in the United States. "Reducing poverty among the elderly is Social Security's major accomplishment to date. The poverty rate among the elderly in 2000 was approximately 10 percent, down from a rate of 35.2 percent in 1959. Without Social Security, the poverty rate among the elderly would be 48 percent" (American Institute of Certified Public Accountants, 2005). However, the decrease in poverty among the elderly is not shared equally. Since Social Security benefits are based on previous work and contributions into the system, the anti-poverty aspect of the program has not benefited elderly persons of color as much as whites due to discrimination in employment and historically lower wages for Hispanics and African Americans. Nonetheless, Social Security has contributed to lower rates of poverty among elderly persons of color and single-parent families with children. Figure 12.1 shows the decrease in the poverty rate among the elderly from 1965 to 2002.

Figure 12.1 Percent of Individuals Sixty-Five Years of Age and Older Below Poverty by Race

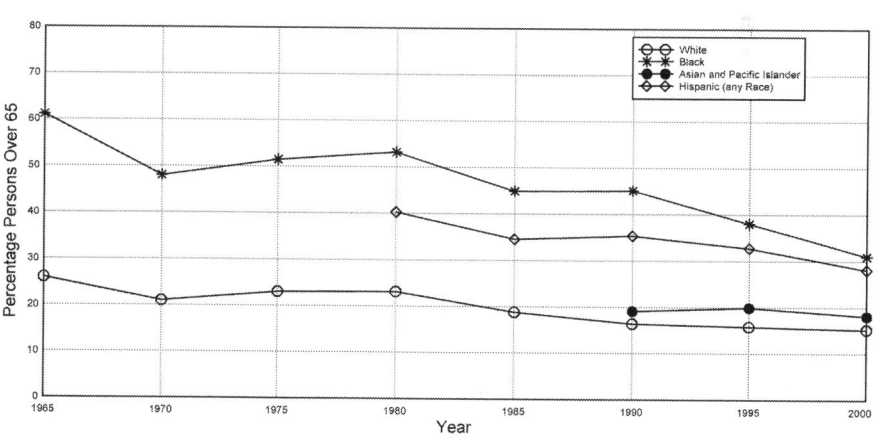

Note: Data unavailable for 1965 and 1970 for Hispanics
Source: U.S. Census Bureau. (2005). *Historic poverty tables* (Current Population Survey, Housing and Household Economic Statistics Division). Retrieved May 15, 2006, from http://www.census.gov/hhes/www/poverty/histpov/hstpov3.html

Social Security and Privatization

The issue of the solvency of Social Security illustrates how problems and policy solutions emerge in political and policy debates, recede from public consciousness and attention, and return. During the first part of the twenty-first century, there was an active policy debate on the solvency of Social Security, which revolved around the projected retirement costs of the baby boomers. The Social Security Trust Fund has been projected to run out of money by the year 2034 because the ratio of the number of workers to retirees will decrease to a level that will make it impossible to fund the system (BBC, 1999). Congress modified Social Security in 1983 to address the shrinking worker-to-retiree ratio by gradually increasing the retirement age. Before 2000, a person could retire early at age sixty-two and reduce his or her benefit level. Beginning in 2000, the age of full retirement was increased from sixty-five to sixty-seven, so people born after 1958 who retire at age sixty-five will be taking early retirement (Nuschler, 2005). Although people can still retire at age sixty-two if they wish, the penalties are much greater. Nyce and Schieber (2005) have suggested that there are other ways to address the shrinking worker-to-retiree ratio. Policy makers can find ways to maintain or enlarge the workforce or otherwise increase productivity. Shifting greater risk to higher-level earners is one policy alternative for funding the retirement of baby boomers. Instead of having incentives to retire early, policy should entice older workers to stay in their jobs longer and encourage younger workers to enter the workforce earlier. Both of these alternatives will increase labor force participation to offset projected shortfalls for paying retirees. Policy makers also suggest immigration as a way to make up for labor shortfalls and bring in more workers to supplement the tax system.

Not all agree that a major reform of the Social Security system is even needed. The Social Security Trust Fund currently has assets of $1.9 trillion (Home.att.net, 2009). During the Clinton administration, policy makers realized that the federal tax surplus would be much larger than expected, so funds were targeted to keep Social Security solvent until 2053. The Social Security Trust Fund grew from $31 billion in 1984 to $1.5 trillion by the end of 2003, and the United States holds the accumulating trust fund entirely in government bonds. The Bush administration's approach to tax surpluses, however, was to use them to finance tax cuts and government spending in other areas, rather than saving and investing in the future of Social Security (Nyce & Schieber, 2005). An analysis of the Social Security deficit and the Bush administration's tax cuts shows that the long-term size of the tax cut is more than double the entire long-term Social Security shortfall (Center on Budget and Policy Priorities, 2002).

For the most part, however, debates on reforming the country's guaranteed federal entitlement program focus on privatization. According to Fullerton and Geruso (2006), *privatization* is an ambiguous term in the world of Social Security reform: "Privatization usually means that workers get individual retirement accounts in their own names, as with a private defined contribution pension. But does privatization necessarily entail all of the aspects of a private pension? Must contributions be voluntary and accounts privately managed? Must pensioners have choice over investments or receive payouts that are actuarially fair? Or can privatization include plans where government retains control over some of those decisions?" (p. 1).

Table 12.1 compares common attributes of private pension plans to the principles upon which Social Security is currently based. None of the proposed plans make changes to all seven current principles. Thus, privatizing Social Security means many things—depending on the number of attributes that are changed, and the degree to which each is changed. Even without considering potential dependencies among the various attributes, we can see at least 127 possible plans that could emerge as alternative policy proposals. Thus, there are a myriad of ways to privatize the Social Security system, but ultimately privatization means taking some portion of the money collected through worker contributions and investing it in the private market.

Proponents of privatization argue that investments—in the stock market or other types of investment mechanisms such as bonds and annuities—would provide higher rates of return to retirees than the benefits

Table 12.1 Comparison of Seven Elements of Social Security Privatization Proposals

Current Social Security Policy	Typical Private Pension Packages
Pay-as-you-go funding	Full funding
Defined benefits	Personally defined benefits
Voluntary contributions	Voluntary contributions
Government management	Management by the private sector
No choice in investment	Choice in investment
Benefits by annuity only	Lump-sum payment option
Redistribution of wealth	Actuarial fairness based on contributions

Source: Adapted from Fullerton, D., & Geruso, M. (2006). The many definitions of Social Security privatization. *Economists' Voice, 3*(4). Retrieved March 3, 2008, from http://www.bepress.com/ev/vol3/iss4/art3

that accrue to those who pay into the trust fund system. At the same time, privatization would reduce government expenditures on Social Security (Ozawa & Yoon, 2002). Moving Social Security toward personal accounts would meet the savings and insurance goals of Social Security—without requiring government to administer the system. Lazear (2005) acknowledges that private accounts will not redistribute income but contends that Social Security was not designed for this purpose.

Critics state that privatization would not necessarily increase retirees' returns on investments. Evidence from the adoption of private 401(k) plans suggests that people are not very good at saving through voluntary savings plans or at making sound investment decisions. Simulation projections indicate that an older worker should accumulate $300,000, but in reality the amount is very low—less than $50,000. Why are these projections so far from reality? A detailed empirical analysis by Munnell (2005) offers this explanation: "The employee must now decide whether or not to join the plan, how much to contribute, how to invest the contributions and when to re-balance, what to do about company stock, whether to roll over accumulations when changing jobs, and how to withdraw money at retirement. The evidence indicates that at every decision-making step along the way, a significant fraction of participants make serious financial-planning mistakes" (p. 7). There is no way to avoid financial risks if one invests in the stock market, as "anyone who has lived through the recent collapse of stock and bond prices knows that the value of private investments fluctuates dramatically" (Shulz & Gorin, 2005, p. 75). In addition, the high costs of creating and administering private investment accounts would accelerate the depletion of the trust fund. Opponents of privatization of Social Security believe that the only winners are likely to be the investment corporations, which would gain from advising and administering retirement portfolios.

Who stands to lose the most if Social Security is privatized? Anrig and Wasow (2004) point out that young people, the generation that will bear the costs of changing the system, will be worse off because payroll taxes paid into the current system will be used to fund benefits for current retirees. Women will lose the most because they participate in the workforce for fewer years, earn less per year, and live longer after retiring than men. Under privatization, African Americans and Hispanics would also be in a weaker position. Due to lower earnings over their life span, African American and Hispanic retirees will be more at risk of poverty. Lower rates of marriage and shorter life expectancy negatively affect Social Security benefit levels among African American retirees, but the current system also benefits African Americans because they have higher rates of disability, more survivors eligible for benefits, and lower average wages.

The debate on Social Security reform in recent years has concentrated almost entirely on privatization, focusing on different ways of saving money, and how to protect the overall solvency of the trust fund. However, in view of the changing nature of work, family structure, and other economic, social, and demographic changes taking place in the United States, this disproportionate attention to privatization has overshadowed the need for policy reform addressing the outdated nature of Social Security rules. According to Stanfield and Nicolaou (2000), Social Security is out of step with the modern family:

> Since its inception in 1935, Social Security has provided both benefits to workers based on earnings and auxiliary benefits to spouses. The benefit structure reflects the era's idealized family structure—the husband as sole earner with a dependent wife who remains at home, generally to raise children. When the earner reaches retirement age, the household receives Social Security benefits totaling the earner's allotment plus half that amount for the spouse. If the earner dies, the surviving spouse gets the full earner's share.
>
> Although these provisions are decades old, they generally have not been updated to take into account two-earner households. As long as both spouses are alive, the second earner (or earner with lower lifetime earnings—usually, but not always, the wife) receives either a benefit based on her own earnings or half of the spouse's worker benefits, whichever is larger. As two-earner households become the norm and the "typical" family becomes harder to define, the failure of the Social Security system to adapt results in glaring inequalities. (p. 6)

They conclude that "Social Security rules designed mainly for the one-earner, married-couple families are out of place in today's world of two-earner families, single-parent households, short-lived marriages, and domestic relationships that don't involve marriage at all. This mismatch deters real benefit increases and may even increase poverty among the elderly—the exact opposite of what Social Security was designed to achieve" (p. 16).

Summary

The sandwich generation is reaching retirement age in record numbers. Demographic trends such as adult children returning home to live, multigenerational families, kinship care and grandparents raising grandchildren, and the growing population of the frail elderly mean that many baby boomers find themselves providing care for several generations of the family, often at the same time. Families—not institutions or service providers—provide most long-term care, and most people who need long-term care prefer to receive assistance and services at home and to stay in their communities, near family and friends, for as long as possible.

In this chapter, we discussed several policies that relate to family caregiving. These include the Family and Medical Leave Act; Title IV-A of the PRWORA, which allows TANF payments for kinship foster care; the Adoption and Safe Families Act of 1997, which allows federal reimbursement for licensed kinship foster homes; and the Fostering Connections to Success and Increasing Adoptions Act of 2008, which focuses on kinship care and increases adoption incentive funds to states. The Older Americans Act of 1965 and later amendments provide caregiving services that support family caregivers by providing meals on wheels, transportation for medical care, respite for caregivers, and a variety of other services. The National Family Caregiver Support Act defines family caregivers broadly to include non-related persons, domestic partners, friends, and neighbors who provide care to the elderly and provides services such as counseling and support groups, as well as home health aides and adult day care.

The last section of this chapter looked at Old Age, Survivors, Health and Disability Insurance. We focused on retirement benefits and disability insurance, which are funded through payroll taxes deposited in the Social Security Trust Fund. Recent policy debates on Social Security reform have centered on the privatization of Social Security, which up to this point in time has been one of the most successful—if not the most successful—anti-poverty programs in U.S. history. Unlike means-tested welfare programs, Old Age, Survivors, Health and Disability Insurance is a social insurance program that guarantees benefits provided that workers contribute to the system for a minimum number of years. Although Social Security reform based on privatization did not occur during the Bush administration, we can expect that the reform of Social Security will emerge as a policy issue again as baby boomers reach retirement age and begin to draw benefits. Researchers at the Urban Institute note that policy discussions on privatizing Social Security mask the real problems with the Social Security system that are caused by its retirement and beneficiary rules, and that Social Security is out of step with social, economic, and demographic changes in the structure of families in the United States.

For Further Reading

Beland, D. (2007). *Social Security: History and politics from the New Deal to the privatization debate.* Lawrence: University Press of Kansas.

Campbell, A. L. (2003). *How policies make citizens: Senior political activism and the American welfare state*. Princeton, NJ: Princeton University Press.

Dattalo, P. (2007). Borrowing to save: A critique of recent proposals to partially privatize Social Security. *Social Work, 52*(3), 233–242.

Lavery, J., & Reno, V. P. (2008). *Children's stake in Social Security*. Retrieved May 6, 2008, from http://www.nasi.org/usr_doc/SS_Brief_027.pdf

Messing, J. (2005). *From the child's perspective: A qualitative analysis of kinship care placements*. Berkeley: National Abandoned Infants Assistance Resource Center, University of California at Berkeley. Retrieved May 6, 2008, from http://aia.berkeley.edu/media/pdf/kinship_research_summary.pdf

U.S. Social Security Administration. (2003). *SSA's FY 2003 performance and accountability report*. Retrieved May 6, 2008, from http://www.socialsecurity.gov/finance/2003/Overview.pdf

References

Administration for Children and Families. (2006). *The AFCARS report*. Retrieved March 8, 2009, from http://www.acf.hhs.gov/programs/cb/stats_research/afcars/tar/report13.htm

Adoption and Safe Families Act, 42 U.S.C. § 671 et seq. (1997).

Adoption Assistance and Child Welfare Act of 1980, Pub. L. No. 96-272, 42 U.S.C. §§ 620-628, §§ 670-676 (1980).

Ambrose, E. (2004, February, 29). Returning to the nest. *Baltimore Sun*. Retrieved May 12, 2006, from http://www.theeagle.com/businesstechnology/022904returnnest.htm

American Institute of Certified Public Accountants. (2005, March). *Understanding Social Security reform: The issues and the alternatives* (2nd ed.). New York: Author. Retrieved May 6, 2008, from http://www.aicpa.org/download/members/socsec/SOCIAL_SECURITY_REFORM_3-2005.pdf

Anrig, G., Jr., & Wasow, B. (2004). *Twelve reasons why privatizing Social Security is a bad idea*. Retrieved March 4, 2008, from http://www.socsec.org/publications.asp?pubid=503

Area Agency on Aging. (2006). *The caregiver handbook*. Retrieved May 20, 2007, from http://www.agingcarefl.org/resources

BBC. (1999). *The trillion dollar surplus*. Retrieved May 15, 2006, from http://news.bbc.co.uk/1/hi/business/the_economy/380217.stm

Berrick, J. D., Needell, B., & Minkler, M. (1999). The policy implications of welfare reform for older caregivers, kinship care, and family configuration. *Children & Youth Services Review, 21*(9–10), 843–864.

Bullock, K. (2004). The changing role of grandparents in rural families: The results of an exploratory study in southeastern North Carolina. *Families in Society, 85*(1), 45–54.

Center for Law and Social Policy. (2008). *The Fostering Connections to Success and Increasing Adoptions Act of 2008 offers to help children raised by relatives.* Retrieved November 9, 2008, from http://www.clasp.org/publications/fctsaiaact2008resources.htm

Center on Budget and Policy Priorities. (2002). *Social Security and the tax cut.* Retrieved May 15, 2006, from http://www.Cbpp.org/8-2-01tax.htm

Conner, K. A. (2000). *Continuing to care: Older Americans and their families.* New York: Falmer Press.

Family and Medical Leave Act of 1993, 29 U.S.C. § 2601 et seq. (1993).

Family Caregiver Alliance. (2002). *Family caregiver support: Policies, perceptions and practices in 10 states since passage of the National Family Caregiver Support Program.* Retrieved February 24, 2009, from http://caregiver.org/caregiver/jsp/content_node.jsp?nodeid=451.

Fine, T. S. (2006). The family and medical leave law: Feminist social policy? *Journal of Policy Practice, 5*(1), 49–66.

Fostering Connections to Success and Increasing Adoptions Act of 2008, Pub. L. No 110-351 (2008).

Fullerton, D., & Geruso, M. (2006). The many definitions of Social Security privatization. *Economists' Voice, 3*(4). Retrieved March 3, 2008, from http://www.bepress.com/ev/vol3/iss4/art3

Geen, R. (2000). In the interest of children: Rethinking federal and state policies affecting kinship care. *Policy and Practice of Public Human Services, 58*(1), 19–27.

Geen, R. (2004). The evolution of kinship care policy and practice. *The Future of Children, 14*(1), 131–149.

Gibbons, C., & Jones, T.C. (2003). Kinship care: Health profiles of grandparents raising their grandchildren. *Journal of Family Social Work, 7*(1), 1–14.

Gleeson, J. P. (1999). Kinship care as a child welfare service: Emerging policy issues and trends. In R. Heger & M. Scannapieco (Eds.), *Kinship foster care: Practice, policy, and research* (pp. 28–53). New York: Oxford University Press.

Home.att.net. (2009). *Social Security Trust Fund—income, outgo, and balance: 1940–2009.* Retrieved March 8, 2009, from http://home.att.net/~rdavis2/ssfund.html

Indian Child Welfare Act of 1978, Pub. L. No. 95-608 (1978).

Kaitin, K. K. (1994). Congressional responses to families in the workplace: The Family and Medical Leave Act of 1987–1988. In F. H. Jacobs & M. W. Davies (Eds.), *More than kissing babies? Current child and family policy in the United States* (pp. 91–120). Westport, CT: Auburn House.

Kingsmill, S., & Schlesinger, B. (1998). *The family squeeze: Surviving the sandwich generation.* Toronto: University of Toronto Press.

Lazear, E. P. (2005). The virtues of personal accounts for Social Security. *Economists' Voice, 2*(1). Retrieved March 4, 2008, from http://www.bepress.com/ev/vol2/iss1/art4

Leos-Urbel, J., Bess, R., & Geen, R. (2002). The evolution of federal and state policies for assessing and supporting kinship caregivers. *Children & Youth Services Review, 24*(1–2), 37–52.

Matheson, L. (1996). The politics of the Indian Child Welfare Act. *Social Work, 41*(2), 232–235.

McCutchen, R. (2006). *The Social Security cost of living increase is not keeping up.* Retrieved June 11, 2006, from http://www.tscl.org/NewContent/102668.asp

Medicare. (2006). *The basics.* Retrieved February 12, 2006, from http://www.medicare.gov/publications/pubs.pdf110153.pdf

Miller v. Youakim, 44 U.S. 125, 99 S. Ct. 957 (1979).

Munnell, A. (2005). Test drive suggests Bush's "Ownership Society" may be a lemon. *Economists' Voice, 2*(1). Retrieved March 4, 2008, from http://www.bepress.com/ev/vol2/iss1/art9

National Center on Elder Abuse. (2006). *Adult protective services.* Retrieved May 12, 2006, from http://www.elderabuse.org/default.cfm?p=faqs.cfm#seven

National Defense Authorization Act for FY 2008, Pub. L. No. 110-181 (2008).

National Family Caregiver Support Act, Older Americans Act as Amended, Title III (2000).

Nuschler, D. (2005). *Social Security reform.* Retrieved May 10, 2006, from http://kohl.senate.gov/ss.pdf

Nyce, A. S., & Schieber, S. J. (2005). *The economic implications of aging societies.* New York: Cambridge University Press.

Older Americans Act Amendments of 2000, Pub. L. No. 106-501 (2000).

Older Americans Act of 1965, Pub. L. No. 89-73 (1965).

Ozawa, M. N., & Yoon, H. (2002). Social Security and SSI as safety nets for the elderly poor. *Journal of Aging and Social Policy, 14*(2), 1–25.

Park, H. (2005). Grandmothers raising grandchildren: Family well-being and economic assistance. *Focus, 24*(1), 19–27.

Robinson, M. M., Barbee, A. P., Martin, M., Singer, T. L., & Yegidis, B. (2003). The organizational costs of care giving: A call to action. *Administration in Social Work, 27*(1), 83–102.

Roots, C. R. (1998). *The sandwich generation: Adult children caring for aging parents.* New York: Garland.

Schwartz, A. E. (2002). Societal value and the funding of kinship care. *Social Service Review, 76*(3), 430–459.

Shulz, J., & Gorin, S. (2005). Let's not gamble with Social Security. *Health and Social Work, 30*(1), 75.

Smith, C. J., Beltran, A., Butts, D. M., & Kingson, E. R. (2000). Grandparents raising grandchildren: Emerging program and policy issues for the 21st century. *Journal of Gerontological Social Work, 34*(1), 81–94.

Social Security Act of 1935. 42 U.S.C.A. § 301 et seq. (1935).

Stanfield, R., & Nicolaou, C. (2000). *Social Security: Out of step with the modern family.* Washington, DC: Urban Institute. Retrieved May 6, 2008, from http://www.urban.org/UploadedPDF/out_of_step.pdf

Takamura, J. C. (1999). Getting ready for the 21st century: The aging of America and the Older Americans Act. *Health and Social Work, 24*(3), 232–238.

Templeman, A. (2003). Licensing and payment of kinship foster parents. In R. Geen (Ed.), *Kinship care: Making the most of a valuable resource* (pp. 63–94). Washington, DC: Urban Institute Press.

U.S. Census Bureau. (2003). *Complex households and relationships in the decennial census*. Retrieved May 12, 2006, from http://www.census.gov/pred/www/rpts/Complex%20Households%20Final%20Report.pdf

U.S. Census Bureau. (2008). *An older and more diverse nation by midcentury*. Retrieved March 8, 2009, from http://www.census.gov/Press-Release/www/releases/archives/population/012496.html

U.S. Department of Labor. (2008). *Family medical leave act and national defense reauthorization act of 2008*. Retrieved May 6, 2008, from http://www.dol.gov/esa/whd/fmla/NDAA_fmla.htm

U.S. Social Security Administration. (2007, October). *2008 Social Security changes*. Retrieved May 6, 2008, from http://www.ssa.gov/pressoffice/colafacts.htm

U.S. Social Security Administration. (2008a). *Compilation of the Social Security Laws, including the Social Security Act, as amended, and related enactments through January 1, 2007* (Vols. 1–2). Retrieved May 6, 2008, from http://www.ssa.gov/OP_Home/ssact/ssact.htm

U.S. Social Security Administration. (2008b). *Glossary of terms*. Retrieved May 6, 2008, from http://www.socialsecurity.gov/glossary.htm#Benefits

U.S. Social Security Administration. (n.d.). *Benefit eligibility screening tool*. Retrieved January 14, 2009, from http://connections.govbenefits.gov/ssa_en.portal

Weber, J. A., & Waldrop, D. P. (2000). Grandparents raising grandchildren: Families in transition. *Journal of Gerontological Social Work, 33*(2), 27–46.

CHAPTER 13

Family Policy in a Global Context

This chapter will give readers some idea of the global context of family policy and will reflect on the future of policies for families. Although the chapter does not cover all that one should know about family policies in the global context, we hope that it will sensitize readers to the importance of looking outside the United States for policy ideas. We also hope that the chapter provides a global context for comparative purposes. Comparing the United States to other countries is a way to expand our thinking from a U.S.-centric lens. Overall, we hope the chapter gives students and policy practitioners a beginning frame of reference for evaluating social policy in the United States.

This chapter puts domestic issues and policies in a broader perspective by looking at family well-being in the global context. The issue of globalization and the policies surrounding it create new challenges for American families. How other countries have dealt with the global marketplace and its impact on family is discussed, and social welfare policies in the United States are compared with those of other industrialized countries. Comparing the United States with other countries broadens our perspective regarding what may or may not work well. Social workers can benefit greatly from knowledge of social welfare systems in other countries and test normative claims regarding social welfare for families.

As we showed in chapter 7, globalization means different things. To many, the global economy means a chance for unlimited economic opportunity and prosperity in a market without national boundaries. To others, it is seen as the spread of unregulated capitalism and unlimited power of multinational corporations (O'Connor, 2002). To many families in the United States, globalization means a loss of jobs when heavy manufacturing and white-collar jobs move overseas or when businesses close because they cannot compete. To others, it means the ability to buy cheaper high-quality consumer products. Thus, depending on one's life experience, the effect of globalization may be positive or negative. In either case, the fact remains: globalization is here to stay. What we can learn about is whether other countries have been able to control the potentially negative effects of economic globalization on their populations, and how the United States has chosen to deal with these issues.

Like many others in the population, social workers may feel removed from the global economy, particularly since it appears that ordinary citizens have little control over it. But just as domestic policy affects human service practitioners and their clients, policies regulating the global economy do as well. The decisions that are made regarding the obligation of the state to protect its citizens in a global marketplace affect the social safety net and the money set aside for public use through social welfare programs. As we have seen in previous chapters, those decisions are inextricably linked to the values and subjective experiences of policy makers and to the interest groups inside and outside government that attempt to influence them.

This chapter begins with a discussion of devolution in the global context. We examine the concept of the social economy, which is the part of government policy and programs designed to provide social welfare programs and at the same time enable the country to compete in the global marketplace. It is clear that devolution and privatization are occurring in much of the industrialized world, but there is also evidence that the way a nation chooses to balance policies in the global context stems from the values held by decision makers and others in power, rather than scientific evidence of what the correct balance might be. The question is how to implement devolution and privatization so that the social safety net is not undermined. Next, we look at family well-being from a global perspective. Here we show how the United States ranks compared to other industrialized countries on issues such as child poverty, infant mortality, social expenditures, and income inequality. Lastly, we discuss some implications of the global economy for families and family policy in the United States.

Devolution in the Global Context

In order to limit the power of the federal government, the United States is a federalist political system in which power is divided and shared by the national government and the states. Since the 1980s the United States has adopted the philosophy of new federalism, using decentralized policies (i.e., devolution) to shift program and financial responsibility from the federal government to lower levels of government. According to the Organisation for Economic Co-operation and Development (2001), devolution and globalization are interdependent. Devolution increases local decision making and improves the competitive environment of cities and regions so that they are able to compete in the global economy. States must adapt to a new economic environment characterized by global competition and the market. Privatizing government-run programs is seen as a way to achieve efficiency and competitiveness in a global market. The prevailing belief concerning social welfare programs in the United States is that social needs in the era of globalization can be met largely by the market, rather than by government programs.

The question of how to safeguard family well-being and at the same time remain globally competitive is being debated in other industrialized nations as well. Countries have chosen various ways to try to assist families—either through the market or through government programs and policies or through some combination of the two. Countries also create different economic policies to improve their place in the global market. O'Connor (2002) states that "most countries of the world have jumped onto the capitalist bandwagon and embraced a decentralized decision making model" (p. 100) to support their global economic expansion. The reliance on decentralized or devolved government leads to a greater emphasis on the market in meeting the demands of families to ensure quality of life. Thus, the globalization of economic markets has affected national policies, practices, and politics across the industrialized world. Competing arguments of just how globalization affects various countries are both positive and negative. If nations compete in a deregulated market, then countries must shift investments in domestic welfare to the market to compete, and this action can "trigger a race to the bottom" (Beyeler, 2004, p. 2). On the other hand, some argue that if there is global market regulation, an international consensus on welfare needs can prevent competitive deregulation of the global market. The problem, of course, is that there is disagreement about the level of social regulation needed, as well as the extent to which social welfare safety nets should be funded by government expenditures.

Beyeler (2004) suggests that various countries' value systems can help explain how a nation will compete in the global market and what impact that will have on the safety net they provide for their citizens. For example, some countries such as the United States see the global marketplace as a solution for problems that the government is currently attempting to solve. Although it is generally assumed that rational scientific policy analysis shapes these types of decisions and tells us what problems can be solved through global competition, Yee (1996) points out that "politicians often shape the scientific agenda and also use science selectively to legitimate policies chosen" (p. 88). Rather than being informed by science, policies may be developed based on the "subjective perceptions colored by normative views of how the world should be organized" (Beyeler, 2004, p. 4). Thus, the way in which a globalization policy is implemented in a nation is strongly influenced by how that policy fits with the values and norms of the power holders and others of influence in that country.

The Social Economy

The Organisation for Economic Co-operation and Development (OECD) is a Paris-based organization representing thirty of the richest, most industrialized countries in the world. For years, the OECD has been advocating the devolution and privatization of the welfare state as a way for countries to compete more effectively in the global marketplace. Thus, the concepts of devolution and privatization and the ways in which they affect the welfare state have been part of international dialogue and serious policy discussions for quite some time. The OECD provides guidance on ways to implement a social economy, which is defined as a sector between the government and the market that fulfills both economic roles and social priorities (Young, 2003).

The social economy is generally thought of in terms of nonprofit agencies that use market-based approaches in order to solve social problems. Although the market is important for the success of the social economy, the federal government still has the central responsibility for overseeing and establishing universal policies that protect the well-being of its citizens. The Organisation for Economic Co-operation and Development (2001) states that the social economy can only function efficiently if there is sufficient government investment in human capital, high-quality education, and child care, and if the people have a voice and are heard. The ideal of the social economy can succeed only if government creates an infrastructure that will make it sustainable and effective (Galliano, 2003). The OECD suggests that if implemented properly, devolution and privatization can promote social policy innovation, greater stakeholder participation, increases in social inclusion, and local innovation.

In the 1980s, when the United States began to institute large-scale devolution of program responsibility to state and local governments, the federal government also began to withdraw government funding. This model of devolution is contrary to the tenets of effective development of the social economy (Young, 2003). In addition, the funneling of monies down to nonprofits through privatization was accompanied by cuts in funding. Yet the belief that nonprofit organizations are able to provide an infrastructure for social services based on market-driven approaches is risky business, especially when government funding for safety-net programs is decreasing. If the social economy becomes too dependent on the market economy, it becomes vulnerable in times of economic downturns, when more people need assistance. Thus, unless government takes the responsibility to put appropriate policies in place, globalization will increase social inequalities. "Devolution is not a panacea for all ills. When insensitive to broader issues, poorly directed, or applied to regions with unequal resources, it can generate waste and be inefficient. Centralized policies are needed to control quality" (Organisation for Economic Co-operation and Development, 2001, p. 94). In order to create safeguards in a global economy, the central government must provide a foundation of social protection, which should include education, social security, and health care, and guard against income disparities, unemployment, poverty, and social exclusion (Organisation for Economic Co-operation and Development, 2001). Devolution and privatization, in combination with decreasing federal dollars, unlimited accumulation of wealth, skyrocketing corporate profits, and unequal distribution of resources, have had negative consequences for families in the United States, compared to countries where the safety net is well integrated into the system of government (Rocha, 2007).

Family Well-Being from a Global Perspective

In view of the above discussion on globalization, devolution, privatization, and the social economy, it is important to compare family well-being across nations. This will help readers understand the effects of certain policy decisions compared to the effects of alternative policy choices. Given their unique mix of values, political systems, programs, and services, how do other industrialized countries compare with the United States? One good example is the emphasis placed on marriage as an anti-poverty strategy and the answer to social ills by U.S. welfare reform of 1996. Table 13.1 shows an interesting twist to this policy argument. While the United States' divorce rate of 49 percent is below those of both Sweden and the United Kingdom, the United States has the highest child poverty rate of all seven countries, as well as the highest infant mortality rates, the lowest life expectancy, and the greatest percentage of low-paying jobs. Although the United States has the second-highest per capita gross domestic product, which is a proxy measure of the wealth of a nation and its citizens, the nation fell short on many of the indicators of well-being shown in table 13.1.

Table 13.1 Comparisons of Social Indicators in the United States and Selected Industrialized Countries

Social Indicators	United States	Australia	Canada	Japan	Spain	Sweden	United Kingdom	Norway
Government social expenditure as a percent of GDP (gross domestic product) in 2003[2]	16.2	17.9	17.3	17.7	20.3	31.3	20.6	25.1
Per capita GDP in 2007[1]	43,267	34,154	36,243	31,696	28,079	34,457	33,191	49,606
Educational expenditures as a percent of GDP in 2004[2]	7.4	5.9	NA	4.8	4.7	6.7	5.9	NA
Percent unemployed in fourth quarter of 2008[2]	6.9	4.4	6.4	4.0	13.7	6.9	6.2	2.9
Prisoners per 100,000 persons in 2006[2]	738	126	107	62	143	78	139	68
Expenditure on health as a percent of GDP in 2005[2]	6.9	6.4	6.9	6.6	5.9	7.7	7.2	7.6
Suicides per 100,00 persons in 2004	10.2	11.1	10.6	20.3	11.9	6.7	6.3	10.5
Infant mortality per 1,000 live births in 2005[2]	6.8	5	5.4	2.8	4.1	2.4	5.1	3.1
Life expectancy (in years) in 2007[2]	77.8	80.9	80.2	82.1	80.7	80.6	79	80.1
Percent of individuals voting in an election in 2005 or latest[2]	55	79	55	62	81	77	69	75

[1]U.S. Department of Labor Bureau. (2008). *Comparative real gross domestic product per capita and per employed person 16 countries 1960–2007*. Retrieved March 9, 2009 from http://www.bls.gov/fls/flsgdp.pdf

[2]Organisation for Economic Co-operation and Development. (2007). *Selection of OECD social indicators: How does your country compare?* Retrieved March 9, 2009, from http://www.oecd.org/dataoecd/12/7/38138100.xls

The United States spends less on social expenditures as a percent of GDP than other countries. While the United States has been touted as an example of a government that has devolved responsibility down to the states (Organisation for Economic Co-operation and Development, 2001), devolution has not had the same outcomes as those expected from countries experimenting with the concept of the social economy, such as increased social inclusion and decreased inequality. In particular, voter turnout was markedly lower, as was the percentage of the population in prison.

Computing Inequality in Comparative Analyses

The Gini coefficient is the most commonly used measure of inequality. The coefficient varies between 0, which reflects complete equality, and 1, which indicates complete inequality, meaning that one person or group has all the income, while all others have none (World Bank, 2007). To calculate the Gini coefficient, one must first graph a Lorenz curve, which is simply a graphic representation of income shares of the population on the vertical access and the distribution of the population on the horizontal axis. This is the same step that we used in chapter 4 to get the share of income distribution by quintiles, which allow us to determine the poorest 20 percent up to the richest 20 percent.

The Gini index for the United States in 2005 was .489. This in and of itself does not give us much information, unless we compare the United States to other nations. Using the same countries that were analyzed in table 13.1, we can see where the United States ranks on the indicators of income translated into income inequality. Table 13.2 shows the Gini coefficients for the eight countries analyzed in table 13.1. One of the major arguments against comparing the United States with other countries is that in order for other countries to offer the increased safety-net programs that they do, they must charge exorbitant taxes, while citizens in the United States pay lower taxes. The Economic Policy Institute calculated the Gini index and the percent of median household income for the poorest 10 percent of workers and the richest 10 percent of workers and adjusted it for the amount of taxes citizens had to pay, as well as income transfers (e.g., public assistance, child and family allowance) and income tax credits (e.g., EITC) for each country (Mishel, Bernstein, & Allegretto, 2005).

According to their analysis, the United States has the greatest income inequality of all the industrialized countries analyzed, even after adjustments are made for tax transfers and income transfers. Furthermore, the

Table 13.2 Household Income Inequality Adjusting for Taxes and Income Transfers

Country	Gini Coefficient	Year
United States	.408	2000
Japan	.249	1993
United Kingdom	.360	1999
Canada	.331	1998
Australia	.354	1994
Spain	.325	1990
Sweden	.250	2000
Norway	.258	2000

Source: United Nations. (2004). *Gini-coefficient.* Retrieved March 9, 2009, from http://www.scribd.com/doc/328232/United-Nations-Gini-Coefficient

poorest 10 percent of the population receive a smaller percentage of the median income than in any other industrialized country. An analysis of the tax structure in the United States from 1979 to 2000 found that the richest 1 percent of Americans have paid fewer taxes over the years, exacerbating the growth of income inequality. Post-tax income growth increased 17 percent between 1979 and 2000 for the richest 1 percent in the United States, and only 2.1 percent and 2.6 percent for low- and middle-income earners, respectively (Mishel et al., 2005).

Another important measure that can be used to compare the well-being of industrialized nations is the number of persons who live in poverty. As we discussed in chapter 4, this concept is difficult to measure, and it is difficult to compare the official measure of poverty in the United States to that of other countries. The United States uses an absolute definition of poverty known as the poverty threshold. Other countries, however, generally use a relative poverty measure based on a percentage of the median earnings of workers. Thus, it is difficult to compare the United States with other countries because poverty is not measured the same way. Smeeding, Rainwater, and Burtless (2001) analyzed industrialized countries by creating a standardized measure of poverty of 50 percent of the median disposable personal income, adjusted for family size. Their analysis reveals that the United States has the highest relative poverty rate of the nine industrialized countries they examined. Figure 13.1 shows some of their findings for selected countries.

Figure 13.1 Percent of the Population in Relative Poverty in Selected Industrialized Countries

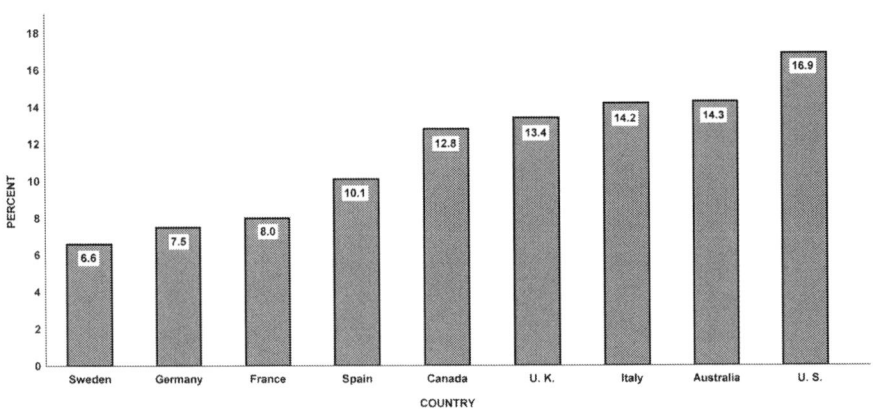

Source: Data from Luxembourg Income Study Database. (n.d.) *LIS key figures*. Retrieved July 22, 2009, from http://www.lisproject.org/php/kf/kf.php

Why is the United States behind in measures of income equality and safety-net programs when the nation clearly has more per capita income than the other industrialized nations? Two hypotheses should be considered. First, per capita income is a theoretical distribution of income across a country, assuming all things are equal. But as the data presented in this chapter show, all things are not equal. The United States has the largest income and wealth inequalities in the industrialized world. Second, other industrialized countries have not given up their investments in their social safety nets while they compete in the global market. The European Union, Canada, Australia, Japan, and the Scandinavian countries, for example, all have universal health care, paid family leave policies, family and children allowances, minimum wages that are above the poverty level, and greater protection for workers than the United States. These countries are also competing in the global marketplace but have maintained various safety nets for their citizens.

Implications of the Global Economy

One of the obvious implications of economic globalization for families in the United States is the loss of jobs that occurs when corporations outsource their production operations to countries where wages are lower and benefits fewer. Between 2000 and 2003, manufacturing industries lost 2.7 million jobs. During the same time period, professional and business services lost 669,000 jobs, and information technology lost 433,000 jobs. These shifts are due to several factors, primarily trade deficits, outsourcing, and deindustrialization. Between 1994 and 2005 the service and retail trades accounted for 96 percent of all new jobs in the United States, a phenomenon that drove down wages to an unprecedented level (Mishel et al., 2005). In the absence of policies that protect workers, such as national health care and an adequate minimum wage, families suffer from economic deprivation and the problems triggered by inadequate income. But the way the global marketplace affects domestic policy and families is more indirect: the government diverts needed domestic resources to invest in larger global market endeavors with the hopes that a strong market will assist families indirectly. However, in the quest for growth in the international market, inequalities, child poverty, and the number of low-skilled, low-paid jobs in the United States have increased.

What does the future hold for families in the age of devolution? If the United States follows the international community's suggestions for successful devolution, then it will create an infrastructure that will sustain itself in times of economic downturns, or it will give more revenue-building capacity to the states so that they are not reliant on the federal government for such a large portion of their funding. Also essential is the establishment of a federal mandate for minimum safety-net services for the sustenance and stability of the nation's citizens. Federally mandated policies also serve to decrease the current variability of assistance that now characterizes much of current state-implemented social policies.

Summary

Devolution and privatization are not unique to the U.S. experience. Experiments with devolution and privatization are occurring in various ways in every industrialized country. But how they intersect with the global economy and the welfare of their people is a values-based decision that must be made in each country. The way devolution and privatization are handled by nations competing in the marketplace is not necessarily an outgrowth of globalization but stems from entrenched values and beliefs concerning the ways in which families should—or should not—be taken care of by the central government. As this chapter illustrates, there is an interdependence between domestic family issues and globalization in terms of how the central government responds to the social/economic balance. Decentralization, privatization, and the devolution of responsibility to states, nonprofits, and for-profit businesses will likely continue as the United States competes in the global economy. But the federal government cannot simply rely on the market to replace funding diverted from social programs. Although nonprofits increasingly rely on entrepreneurship in the market to supply funding, as the economy ebbs and flows, both states and nonprofits need guaranteed federal assistance to meet the needs of families.

The United States suffers from greater income inequality, higher poverty rates, and greater percentages of poverty-level wages than almost every other industrialized economy. Are these negative social indicators caused by devolution and privatization? Or are they caused by the political choices that have been made concerning the distribution of the dollars of devolution? Or do they occur because of the choices that have been made to monitor the process and regulations of privatization? These political choices are just that—choices. Other countries are also experimenting with devolution and privatization, but they have made different choices based on their own unique cultures and values regarding families and their political decisions on how to support them. Comparing the United States to other countries is a way to expand our thinking from a U.S.-centric lens. This helps us look at other alternatives that might make it possible to expand the safety net of social programs and, at the same time, compete in the global economy.

Families require a basic social safety net in order to function in a healthy way. What is needed is a commitment by the federal government to provide this net so families can maintain a basic standard of living without having to worry about accessing health care and child care or being able to feed their children. In the richest country in the world, families should not have to struggle simply to survive. As we look at other industrialized countries, a different picture of how countries have decided to mix their economies to care for the needs of their citizens emerges. The Organisation for Economic Co-operation and Development has suggested useful ways to ensure that democratic participation and local decision making are a part of global competition. Thus there are policy alternatives that, if adopted in the United States, would provide the opportunity for the United States to compete internationally and still provide resources for social programs that benefit its citizens and support family well-being.

FOR FURTHER READING

Alesina, A., & Gianvassi, F. (2006). *The future of Europe: Reform or decline.* Cambridge, MA: MIT Press.

Bourdieu, P. (2005). *The social structures of the economy.* Cambridge: Polity.

Court, J., & Young, J. (2006). Bridging research and policy in international development: An analytical and practical framework. *Development in Practice, 16*(1), 85–90.

McDonald, C., & Reisch, M. (2008). Social work in the workfare regime: A comparison of the U.S. and Australia. *Journal of Sociology & Social Welfare, 35*(1), 43–74.

Pontusson, J. (2006). *Inequality and prosperity: Social Europe vs. liberal America.* Ithaca, NY: Cornell University Press.

Williams, C. (2003). New trends in financing nonprofit sector in the U.S.: Transformation of private capital: Reality or rhetoric? In A. Noya & C. Nativel (Eds.), *The nonprofit sector in a changing economy* (pp. 109–138). Paris: Organisation for Economic Co-operation and Development.

Wineburg, R. J., Coleman, B. L., Boddie, S. C., & Cnaan, R. A. (2008). Leveling the playing field: Epitomizing devolution through faith-based organizations. *Journal of Sociology & Social Welfare, 35*(1), 17–42.

REFERENCES

Beyeler, M. (2004). Introduction: A comparative study of OECD and European welfare states. In K. Armingeon & M. Beyeler (Eds.), *The OECD and European welfare states* (pp. 1–12). Northampton, MA: Edward Elgar.

Galliano, R. (2003). *Social economy, entrepreneurship and local development.* Milan: ASNM/Eurada.

Mishel, L., Bernstein, J., & Allegretto, S. (2005). *The state of working America, 2004/ 2005*. Ithaca, NY: ILR Press.

O'Connor, D. E. (2002). *Demystifying the global economy*. Westport, CT: Greenwood Press.

Office for National Statistics. (2003). *Measuring inequality in household income: The Gini coefficient*. Retrieved May 23, 2007, from http://www.statistics.gov.uk/about/methodology_by_theme/gini/default.asp

Organisation for Economic Co-operation and Development. (2001). *Devolution and globalization: Implications for local decision makers*. Paris: Author.

Rocha, C. (2007). *Essentials of social work policy practice*. Hoboken, NJ: John Wiley & Sons.

Smeeding, T., Rainwater, L., & Burtless, G. (2001). United States poverty in a cross-national context. *Focus, 21*(3), 50–54.

World Bank. (2007). *Measuring inequality*. Retrieved May 23, 2007, from http://go.worldbank.org/3SLYUTVY00

Yee, A. S. (1996). The causal effects of ideas on politics. *International Organization, 50*(1), 69–108.

Young, D. (2003). New trends in U.S. nonprofit sector: Toward market integration? In A. Noya & C. Nativel (Eds.), *The nonprofit sector in a changing economy* (pp. 61–78). Paris: Organisation for Economic Co-operation and Development.

APPENDIX A

Preparing a Good Fact Sheet—the Basics

What Are Fact Sheets?

Fact Sheets introduce you—and your issue—in a format useful to busy people. They come in many styles, shapes, and sizes, but every advocacy group needs at least one.

Good Fact Sheets recognize that busy people need something short and punchy to grab their attention. A good Fact Sheet says: "Read me. I'm a painless way to get acquainted with an issue." (Anything long and complicated may not just be ignored, it can be counter-productive.)

Fact Sheets can do many things:

- identify your group with a particular issue;
- set out facts—key statistics relating to a problem, issue, or group;
- provide Answers to commonly-asked Questions (Fact Sheets can use a Q&A format);
- set out information using graphics or charts;
- inform, persuade, educate (e.g., about a legislative proposal or budget request);
- make an argument for a particluar course of action.

Good Fact Sheets rely on format . . .

Nothing over 1 or 2 pages;
No long sentences or wordy paragraphs;
Something easy to read, with sub-heads, "bullets," and possibly graphics; and

Lay-out that carries the eye from basic facts to logical conclusions or the "pitch."

As well as content . . .

Your most compelling, most useful statistics;

Information arrayed to "make an argument," targeted to a particular audience;

Homey examples, or simple ways to convey complicated points;

Reflecting careful thought about the audience, and what facts will work best with *them*;

Drawing a conclusion or suggesting something the reader can do.

. . . To make a point.

In Short: good Fact Sheets include most or all of the following:

- Basic definition(s),
- basic statistics, and
- basic information,
- organized to draw a conclusion or invite the reader to take some action, plus . . .
- the name/address/telephone number and contact person of the group responsible.

Source: Alliance for Children and Families. (2006). *Mission-based advocacy: A toolkit for human service nonprofit board members and volunteers.* Washington, DC: Author. Retrieved July 21, 2008, from http://www.alliance1.org/Public_Policy/advocacyr3.pdf

APPENDIX B

The Policy Brief

Overview

The policy brief is a document which *outlines the rationale for choosing a particular policy alternative or course of action in a current policy debate.* It is commonly produced in response to a request directly from a decision-maker or an organization that intends to advocate for the position detailed in the brief. Depending on the role of the writer or organization, the brief may only provide a targeted discussion of the alternatives without arguing for a particular one, or it may focus directly on arguing for the adoption of a particular alternative. In either case, *the purpose of the policy brief is to convince the target audience of the urgency of the current problem and the need to adopt the preferred alternative or course of action outlined and therefore, serve as an impetus for action.*

As with all good marketing tools, *the key to success is targeting the particular audience for the message.* The most common audience for a policy brief is the decision-maker but, it is also not unusual to use the document to support broader advocacy initiatives targeting a wide but knowledgeable audience (e.g. decision makers, journalists, administrators, researchers). In constructing a policy brief that can effectively serve its intended purpose, it is common for a brief to be:

- *Focused*—All aspects of the policy brief (from the message to the layout) need to be strategically focused on achieving the intended goal of convincing the target audience. For example, the argument provided must build on what they do know about the problem, provide insight about what they don't know about the problem and be

presented in language that reflects their values, i.e. using ideas, evidence and language that will convince them.
- *Professional, not academic*—The audience for a policy brief is not interested in the research/analysis procedures conducted to produce the evidence, but is very interested to know the writer's perspective on the problem and potential solutions based on the new evidence.
- *Evidence-based*—The policy brief is a communication tool produced by policy analysts and therefore all potential audiences not only expect a rational argument but will only be convinced by argumentation supported by evidence that the problem exists and the consequences of adopting particular alternatives.
- *Limited*—The policy brief provides an adequately comprehensive but targeted argument within a limited space, so the focus of the brief needs to be limited to a particular problem or area of a problem.
- *Succinct*—The type of audiences targeted commonly do not have the time or inclination to read an in-depth 20 page argument on a policy problem. Therefore, it is common that policy briefs do not exceed 6–8 pages in length (i.e. usually not longer than 3,000 words).
- *Understandable*—This not only refers to using clear and simple language (i.e. not the jargon and concepts of an academic discipline) but also to providing a well explained and easy to follow argument targeting a wide but knowledgeable audience.
- *Accessible*—The writer of the policy brief should facilitate the ease of use of the document by the target audience and therefore, should subdivide the text using clear descriptive titles to guide the reader.
- *Promotional*—The policy brief should catch the eye of the potential audience in order to create a favorable impression (e.g. professional, innovative, etc.) In this way, many brief writers use the features of the promotional leaflet (use of color, use of logos, photographs, illustrative quotes, etc.).
- *Practical and feasible*—The policy brief is an action-oriented tool targeting policy practitioners. As such, the brief must provide arguments based on what is actually happening in practice with a particular policy and propose recommendations which seem realistic to the target audience.

Common Structural Elements of a Policy Brief

The policy brief is usually said to be the most common and effective written communication tool in a policy campaign. However, in balancing all of the criteria above, many analysts also find the brief the most difficult policy tool to write.

As discussed above, policy briefs directly reflect the different roles that the policy analyst commonly plays, i.e. from researcher to advocate. The type of brief that we are focusing on is one from the more action-oriented, advocacy end of the continuum. Although there is much variation even at this end of the scale, the most common elements of the policy brief are as follows:

> Title of the paper
> Executive summary
> Context and importance of the problem
> Critique of policy option(s)
> Policy recommendations
> Appendices
> Sources consulted or recommended

▪ Title of the paper

The title aims to catch the attention of the reader and compel him/her to read on and so needs to be ***descriptive, punchy and relevant.***

▪ Executive summary

The executive summary aims to convince the reader further that the brief is worth in-depth investigation. It is especially important for an audience that is short of time to clearly see the relevance and importance of the brief in reading the summary. As such, a 1 to 2 paragraph executive summary commonly includes:

> *A description of the problem addressed*
> *A statement on why the current approach/policy option needs to be changed*
> *Recommendations for action*

▪ Context and importance of the problem

The purpose of this element of the brief is to convince the target audience that a current and urgent problem exists which requires them to take action. The context and importance of the problem is both the introductory and first building block of the brief. As such, it usually includes the following:

—A clear *statement of the problem or issue* in focus.
—A short *overview of the root causes of the problem.*
—A clear statement of the *policy implications of the problem* which clearly establishes the current importance and policy relevance of the issue.

It is worth noting that the length of the problem description may vary considerably from brief to brief depending on the stage of the policy process in focus. For example, there may be a need to have a much more extensive problem description for policy at the evaluation stage than for one at the option choosing stage.

■ Critique of policy option(s)

The aim of this element is to detail shortcomings of the current approach or options being implemented and, therefore, illustrate both the need for change and focus of where change needs to occur. In doing so, the critique of policy options usually includes the following:

—A short *overview of the policy option(s)* in focus.
—An argument illustrating *why and how the current or proposed approach is failing.* It is important for the sake of credibility to recognize all opinions in the debate of the issue.

■ Policy recommendations

The aim of the policy recommendations element is to provide a detailed and convincing proposal of how the failings of the current policy approach need to be changed. As such this is achieved by including;

—A breakdown of the *specific practical steps or measures* that need to be implemented.
—Sometimes also includes *a closing paragraph* re-emphasizing the importance of action.

■ Appendices

Although the brief is a short and targeted document, authors sometimes decide that their argument needs further support and so include an appendix. *Appendices should be included only when absolutely necessary.*

■ Sources consulted or recommended

Many writers of the policy brief decide not to include any sourcing of their evidence as their focus is not on an academic audience. However, if you decide to include a short bibliography then place it at the end. Many writers prefer to include a recommended readings section.

Source: International Policy Fellowships. (2009). *The policy brief.* Retrieved April 12, 2009, from http://www.policy.hu/ipf/fel-pubs/samples/PolicyBrief-described.pdf

APPENDIX C

Guidelines for Testifying before a Committee

Introduction (75 words or less)

    Introduce yourself.
    Identify the organization you represent.
    Describe the organization.
    Note the number of members in the organization.
    Thank the committee for the opportunity to testify.

Body of the Testimony

    State your most important recommendation.
    Provide rationale behind recommendation #1.
    State the flaw in your opponent's argument.

    State your least important recommendation.
    Provide rationale behind recommendation #2.
    State the flaw in your opponent's argument.

    State your second most argument.
    Provide rationale behind your argument.
    State the flaw in your opponent's argument.

Closing Remarks

    Thank the committee for the opportunity.
    Offer to provide more information.
    Offer to take questions (oral only).

Length: Five minutes (four pages of written text)

Index

Note: Page numbers followed by "f" or "t" refer to figures or tables respectively.

Absolute measures of poverty, 96
Abuse. *See* Child maltreatment; Elder abuse; Family violence; Intimate partner violence; Women, violence against
Abused women, 334
Activism, Internet and, 83–87
Adoption, gay and lesbian parents and, 305–306
Adoption and Safe Families Act (ASFA, 1997), 324, 344–345, 395, 396
Adoption Assistance and Child Welfare Act (1980), 324, 340, 343–344, 344
Adult children, 384–385
Advantage plans, Medicare, 262
Advocacy, 47–48
  class, 53–55
  client-centered, 52–53, 60
  community-level, 60
  e-mail, 85
  family policy and, 7, 13–14
  for homeless shelter and services in St. Louis, 64–66, 65t
  Internet and, 83–87
  letters for, 75–76
  levels of practice and place of, 50–55
  media and, 79–83
  personal visits for, 76
  phone calls for, 76
  political, 88–89
  resources for, 55
  role of, 48–50

Advocacy campaigns
  persuasion skills for, 61–64
  planning, 55–60
  ten-step process for, 57–59t
African Americans, 10
  elder care and, 387
Aid to Dependent Children (ADC), 160
Aid to Families with Dependent Children (AFDC), 162, 166
  family caregiving and, 396
All Kids and Family Care programs (Illinois), 269–270
American Recovery and Reinvestment Act (2009), xxii–xxiii
Anderson, Elijah, 150
Asian Americans, elder care and, 387
Assets for the poor theory of poverty, 140–142
Auto manufacturing, globalization and, 210–211, 212t
  case study, 213–215

Baby boomers, 382–383
Bad debt care, 256–257
Ballot initiatives, types of, xxi, 77–79, 77t. *See also* Direct democracy
Barrier theories, 130, 132–133, 132t
Battered child syndrome, 338, 340
Battered women, 334
Blogs, 85
Blumenthal, Cynthia, 60
Blumer, Herbert, 20
Bogenschneider, Karen, 19, 37
Bonding capital, 146–147
Boomerang kids, 384–385

435

INDEX

Brace, Charles Loring, 338
Brian A. et al. v. Sundquist et al., 347
Bridging capital, 146–147
Brougham, Tom, 366
Bureaucracies, development of, 22–24

Campus Care and Counseling Act (2004), 281
Caregiver stress, 386–387
Carter, Rosalyn, 275, 279
Cash assistance, 161–162
Catholic Charities of the Archdiocese of Chicago, 348
Cause-versus-function debate, 48–50
  breaking out of, 87–89
Charity care, 256–257
Chicago public housing, case of, 184–186
Child abuse. *See* Child maltreatment; Family violence
Child Abuse Prevention and Treatment Act (CAPTA, 1974), 324, 339–343
Child and dependent care tax credit (CDCTC), 312–313
Child care
  arrangements for, 293, 294t
  average weekly expenditures for, 296t
  cost of, 293–298
  policies, 306–313
  quality of, 298–302
  single mothers and, 293–295
  working and, 290–293
Child Care and Development Block Grant Act (CCDBG, 1990), 307–309
Child care policies, 306–307
  child and dependent care tax credit (CDCTC), 312–313
  Child Care and Development Block Grant Act (CCDBG, 1990), 307–309
  Head Start, 310–312
Child-centered approach, to child maltreatment, 338–339
Child custody, divorce and, 302–304
Child maltreatment, 326, 327f, 328–329t, 338–351
  age trends in, 331
  child-centered approach to, 338–339
  family-centered approach to, 339
  gender trends in, 330
  intimate partner violence and, 332–335
  racial and ethnic trends in, 330
  trend data for, 328–329t
Child maltreatment policies
  Adoption and Safe Families Act (1997), 344–345

Adoption Assistance and Child Welfare Act (1980), 343–344
Child Abuse prevention and Treatment Act (1974), 339–343
Keeping Families Safe Act (2003), 346
lawsuits and, 346–348
Child protection, legal and legislative history of, 339–342
Children's Aid Society, 338
Children's Health Insurance Program Reauthorization Act (2007), 270–271
Child support, 313–316
Civil marriage, 364
Civil unions, 368–369, 371
Class advocacy, 53–55
Client-centered advocacy, 52–53, 60
Coalitions, 64–71
  building, 67–71
  formal, 67
  manual for building, 66–67
  permanent, 67
  temporary, 67
Coercive strategies, 62–64
Coleman, James, 142–147
Collaborative problem solving, 61–62
Commentaries, 81
Common-law marriage, 365
Community health centers, 271–273
Community-level advocacy, 60
Community mental health centers (CMHCs), 274–276
Concentration effects, of poverty, 150
Confrontation, 62–63
Consolidated Appropriations Act (2008), 228
Consolidated Omnibus Budget Reconciliation Act (COBRA, 1986), 267–268
Continuing-care retirement communities, 392
Cost-of-living adjustments (COLAs), 402–403
Courtney, Mark, 348
Culture, poverty and, 150–151
Custodial parents, 313–316

De facto parenthood, 306
Defense of Marriage Act (1994), 360, 369
Defense of Marriage Act (DOMA, 1996), 369–371
Deficit Reduction Act (DRA, 2005), 265–267, 272–273
Deindustrialization, 209–210
Demographics, families and, 7–8

Index

Devolution, 6, 11–12, 418t
  globalization and, 414–416
  social economy and, 416–417
  social outcomes and, 418
  TANF and, 162–163
Direct democracy, 76–79
  types of, 77t
Direct lobbying, 75
Disposable income, 120–121
Divorce, child custody and, 302–304
Dixon, Ron, 60
Dodd, Christopher, 281
Domenici, Pete V., 279, 280
Domestic abuse/violence, 325–326. *See also* Family violence
  gender trends in, 327t, 330
  racial and ethnic trends in, 330
Domestic partnerships, 365–368
Doughnut hole, 262–263

The Early Childhood Learning and Knowledge Center of the Administration for Children and Families, 312
Earned income tax credit (EITC), 237–240
Economic recessions
  globalization and, 217–223
  indicators of, 219–220
  measuring, 217–218
  National Bureau of Economic Research's definition of, 218–219
Education, families and, 10
Elder abuse, 351–354
Elder care, 391–392
Electronic activism, 83–87
E-mail, as advocacy tool, 85
Emergency Economic Stabilization Act (2008), 279
Emergency Medical Treatment and Active Labor Act (1985), 256
Emergency rooms, accessing health care through, 257
Employment. *See* Work and employment
Empty nest syndrome, 384
Entrepreneurs, policy, 26–27
Environments, families and, 35
Enzi, Michael B., 280
Equitable estoppel, 306
Ethnicity, families and, 9–10
Exits, poverty, 108–112
Ex parte Crouse, 339

Facebook, 86
Fact sheets, preparing, 425–426
Fair Labor Standards Act (1938), 231–237

Fair Minimum Wage Act (2007), 236
Families
  changing demographics of, 7–8
  education levels and, 10
  environments and, 35
  government intervention and, 5
  grandparent-maintained, 386
  lack of uniform definition of, 4
  life cycle stages of, 35
  marriage and, 360–363
  membership of, 8–9
  multigenerational, 385–387
  poverty theories and, 151–153
  race and ethnicity of, 9–10
  as social systems, 34–36
  social trends and, 7–8
  structure of, 8–9
  valuing, 1–2
Family and Medical Leave Act (FMLA, 1993), 392–395
  as example of incremental approach to policy making, 394–395
Family caregiving
  changing patterns of family living and, 384–392
  overview of, 382–384
Family caregiving policies
  Family and Medical Leave Act (FMLA, 1993), 392–394
  for kinship care, 395–398
  National Family Caregiver Support Act (NFCSA), 399–400
  Older Americans Act (OAA), 398–400
Family-centered approach, to child maltreatment, 339
Family Education Rights and Privacy Act (1974), 340
Family impact analysis, 19, 33–43
  advanced, 36
  eight steps of, 37–42
  families as social systems and, 34–36
  resources for, 37–38
  social construction of knowledge and, 36–37
  usefulness of, 42–43
Family living, changing patterns in, 384–392
Family Opportunity Act (2005), 267
Family policy
  advocacy and, 7, 13–14
  analysis and, 7, 13–14
  changing nature of U.S. population and, 6
  devolution and, 6, 11–12

elements of current and proposed measures of, 115t
globalization and, 413–414
managed care and, 6–7, 12–13
poverty theories and (*See* Poverty theories)
privatization and, 6–7, 12–13
social work practice and, 14–15
symbolic interaction and, 35–36
themes for, 2–7
in United States, xviii, 4–5
Family poverty, 5. *See also* Poverty theories
approaches to measuring, 96–103
culture of, 150–151
defining, 96
exits from, 108–112
experimental measures of, 112–114, 116f, 117f
guidelines, 100–103
overview of, 95–96
politics of, 119–125
rates of, 98–100
threshold for, 97–100
U.S. Census Bureau's use of alternative measures for, 119–121
Family problems, 5
Family roles, 8
Family structure, 8
Family Support Act (1988), 160
Family systems theory, 34
Family theory, areas lacking attention in, 151–153
Family values, 1–2, 3
Family violence, 323–325, 326f, 327t
defining, 325–327
trends, 327–332
Family well-being, 115–117, 118, 199f
global perspective of, 417–418
lack of consensus on, 4
Federal food assistance programs, 169–175
Federal Home Loan Mortgage Corporation (Freddie Mac), 188–190
Federal Marriage Initiative, 369, 375–377
Federal National Mortgage Association (Fannie Mae), 188–190
Fields, Rex, 60
Food banks, 168
Food pantries, 168–169
Food policies, 166–175
Food security, 166–169
Food Stamp Act (1964), 170
Food stamps, 169–171
eligibility requirements for, 171
participation, 172

policy changes for, 170–171
privatization of, 172–173
WIC vs., 174
Formal coalitions, 67
Formal kinship care, 388
Foster care, 338. *See also* Kinship foster care
Foster care drift, 343–344
Frail elderly, caring for, 391–392
Friendly approach, to negotiation, 61

Garret Lee Smith Memorial Act (2004), 280–281
Gay and lesbian families, 9
Gay parenting, 304–306
General Motors, legacy costs of, 211–212, 212t
Gini coefficient, 103
for United States, 418–419
Gini index, 103–104
for United States, 419
Glazier, Dan, 66
Globalization, 202, 203–204
auto manufacturing and, 210–215
definitions of, 204–205
deindustrialization era of, 206–215
effects of, economic recessions and, 217–223
eras of, 205–206
family policy and, 413–414
implications for U.S. and, 421–422
moving white-collar jobs offshore and, 215–217
steel industry and, 206–207
2.0, 205–215
3.0, 206, 215–217
United States labor market and, 204–217
Government intervention, 5
Graham v. Schoemehl, 66
Grandparent-maintained families, 386, 389
Grassroots democracy, xxi
Grassroots lobbying, 75
Greenspan, Alan, 189–190

Hayes, Karen, 48–49
Head Start, 310–312
Health care
accessing, through emergency rooms, 257
access to, 249–251
auto manufacturing industry and costs of, 211–212

changing needs for, 254
costs of, 252–255
insurance companies, 252–253
managed care and, 6–7, 12–13, 255–256, 348–351
overview of, 247–249
uncompensated, 256–258
Health care programs
  Consolidated Omnibus Budget Reconciliation Act (COBRA, 1986), 267–268
  Deficit Reduction Act (DRA), 265–267
  Medicaid, 263–265
  Medicare, 261–263
  public clinics, 271–273
  State Children's Health Insurance Program (SCHIP), 268–271
Health Centers Renewal Act (2007), 273
Health disparities
  community effects on, 258–261, 260t
  environmental effects and, 258
  neighborhood effects and, 259–261
  racial discrimination and, 258–259
Health opportunity accounts, 267
Hispanic families, elder care and, 387
Hispanics, 9
Homelessness, defining, 22, 23
Homeowner bailout, 190–193
HOPE NOW, 190
HOPE VI (Housing Opportunities for People Everywhere), 175, 183–186
Housing, 175
  drug laws and subsidized, 182–183
  federal housing assistance for, 178–180
  homeowner bailout initiatives and, 190–193
  housing affordability gap and, 176–178
  preference rules and obtaining, 180, 181–182
  procedural barriers to obtaining assistance for, 180–181
  subprime mortgage crisis and, 187–190
  types of federally subsidized assistance for, 178–180
Housing affordability gap, 176–178
Howard, Constance A., 60
Hunger, 166–167
  behavioral effects in children and, 174–175

Improving Head Start for School Readiness Act (2007), 311–312
Income deficit per capita, calculating, 103
Income elasticity of the poverty line, 112–113

Income-to-poverty ratio, 101
Independent Media Center, 86
Indian Child Welfare Act (1978), 340, 395
Individual development accounts (IDAs), 142
IndyMac Bankcorp, 188–189
Inequality, comparative analyses of, 418–421
Informal kinship care, 388
In loco parentis, 306
In re Gault, 340
Insurance companies
  health care and, 252–253
  managed care and, 255–256
Interest groups, 71–73
Internet, activism on, 83–87
Intimate partner violence, 325–326
  age trends in, 331
  child abuse and, 332–335
  gay and lesbian, trends in, 331–332

Job churning, 203
Job Opportunities and Basic Skills Training Program (JOBS), 160–161, 162
Job retraining, 208
Juvenile Justice Delinquency Prevention Act (1974), 340

Keeping Families Safe Act (2003), 324, 346
Kempe, C. Henry, 338, 340
Kennedy, Edward, 279, 280
Kennedy, John F., 274
Kennedy, Patrick J., 279
Kidcare (Illinois), 269–270
Kingdon, John W., 18, 25–28
Kinship care, 387–391
  federal and state policies, 395–398
  formal, 388
  informal, 388
  voluntary, 388
Kinship foster care, 388–389, 396. *See also* Foster care
Knowledge, social construction of, 36–37, 219

Labor market, United States, globalization and, 204–217
Latchkey kids, 292
Lawrence v. Texas, 371
Lesbian and gay families, 9, 304–306
Letters, for advocacy, 75–76
Letters to the editor, 81
LGBT parenting, 304–306
Life cycle stages, of families, 35

Lobbying, 73–76
  direct, 75
  grassroots, 75
Local 880 Service Employees International Union, 72–73
Lorenz curve, 103

Macro-practice concentrations, 88–89
Macro-versus-micro debate, of family poverty, 134–136
Madigan, Lisa, 257
Managed care, 6–7, 12–13, 255–256. *See also* Health care
  in child welfare, privatization and, 348–351
Marisol v. Pataki, 347
Marriage, 3, 359–360
  benefits of, 373
  civil, 364
  civil unions and, 368–369
  common-law, 365
  domestic partnerships and, 365–368
  families and, 360–363
  myths of, 361–363
  promoting, as public policy, 373–375
  religious, 364
  same-sex, 369–373
  state laws and, 364–365, 372t
  status, 364
Marriage Calculator, 376–377
Media
  advocacy and, 79–83
  tips for working with, 80
Medicaid, 263–265
  frail elderly and, 391
Medical care. *See* Health care
Medicare, 261–263
  Advantage plans, 262
  frail elderly and, 391
  Part A, 262
  Part B, 262
  Part D, 262
  prescription drug coverage, 54
Medicare Prescription Drug, Improvement, and Modernization Act (2003), 262
Medigap policies, 262
Mental Health Centers Construction Act (1963), 274–276
Mental Health Parity Act (1996), 276–280
Mental health policies
  Garret Lee Smith Memorial Act (2004), 280–281
  Mental Health Centers Construction Act (1963), 274–276
  Mental Health Parity Act (1996), 276–280
  Mental Health Systems Act (1980), 275
  Paul Wellstone and Pete Domenici Mental Health Parity and Addiction Equity Act (2008), 279–280
Mikells, Gloria, 60
Miller v. Youakim, 395
Minimum wage policies, 231–237
Modern welfare state, social problems and, 22–23
Mondale, Walter, 339
Multigenerational families, 9, 385–387, 389–390
MySpace, 86

National Center on Elder Abuse, 353
National Family Caregiver Support Act (NFCSA), 399–400
National School Lunch Program, 174
Native Americans, 9
Negotiation, friendly approach to, 61
Nergaard, Chris, 60
New federalism, 414–415. *See also* Devolution
News releases, 81–82
Nixon, Richard, 339
No-fault divorce, 302–303
Normandin, Heidi, 37
North American Free Trade Agreement (NAFTA), 207–208

Obama, Barack, xxi–xxii
Old-Age and Survivors Insurance (OASI), 401–402
Older Age, Survivors, Health and Disability Insurance. *See* Social Security
Older Americans Act (1965), 353, 398–400
Omnibus Budget Reconciliation Act (1981), 275–276
Omnibus Budget Reconciliation Act (1990), 307
Opinion editorials (op-eds), 81
  writing guidelines for, 82
Organization for Economic Co-operation and Development (OECD), 416
Orphan train movement, 338
Orshansky, Mollie, 97–98

Panel Study of Income Dynamics (PSID), 108–109
Part A, Medicare, 262
Part B, Medicare, 262
Part D, Medicare, 262

Part-time employment, 208
Patient Dumping Act (1985), 256
Paul Wellstone and Pete Domenici Mental Health Parity and Addiction Equity Act (2008), 279–280
Perkins, Frances, 231–232
Personal Responsibility and Work Opportunity Reconciliation Act (PRWORA, 1996), 161, 163, 307
  food stamp policies and, 170–171
Personal self-sufficiency, 164–166
Personal visits for, 76
Persuasion skills, for advocacy campaigns, 61–64
Phone calls, for advocacy, 76
Plan for Transformation, 184–185
Policy analysis
  family policy and, 7, 13–14
  model of, 25
Policy briefs, 74
  preparing, 427–431
Policy development, values, power, and politics in, 19–20
Policy entrepreneurs, 26–27
Policy implementation, modes of, 50–51
Policy making, 13–14
  role of values, power, and politics in, 122
Policy players, 25–26
Policy practice, 53–54, 88
Policy research, guidelines for, 28–33
Policy streams, 26
Policy think tanks, 124–125
Policy windows, 26–27
  preparing for opening of, 28–33
Political advocacy, 88–89
Political social work, 89
Politics
  family poverty and, 119–125
  policy solutions and, 19–20
Poverty. *See* Family poverty
Poverty exits, 108–112
Poverty gap, 102–103
Poverty guidelines, 100–103
Poverty line. *See* Poverty threshold
Poverty personalities, views of, 135t
Poverty rate, comparative analysis of, 420, 421t
Poverty theories. *See also* Family poverty
  assets for the poor theory, 140–142
  barrier, 131, 132–133, 132t
  cultural, 131
  families and, 151–153
  individual, 131

  macro-versus-micro debate and, 134–136
  overview of, 130–131
  psychology of the poor, 130, 132, 132t, 133–134
  social capital theory, 142–147
  social dislocation theory, 147–151
  structural, 131
  structural vulnerability theory, 136–140
  types of, 131–134
Poverty threshold, 97–100, 420
  dissatisfaction with usefulness of, 113–114
Power, policy solutions and, 19–20
Preference rules, housing assistance and, 180, 181–182
Prescription drug benefits, 254–255
Primary care, four Cs of, 272
Prince v. Massachusetts, 340
Private kinship care, 388
Privatization, 6–7, 12–13
  of child welfare services, 348–351
  food stamp program and, 172–173
  managed care in child welfare and, 348–351
  Social Security and, 404–407
Procedural barriers, for housing assistance, 180–181
Professions
  development of, 22–24
  "troubled persons," 24
PSAs (public service announcements), 82–83
Psychology of the poor theories, 130, 132, 132t, 133–134
Public agendas, 25
Public health clinics, 271–273
Public housing, 178
Public housing authorities (PHAs), 178–179, 180–181
  preference rules and, 181–182
Public service announcements (PSAs), 82–83
Putnam, Robert, 144–145

Quality of life, 117–118
Quintiles, 106–107

Race
  domestic violence and, 330
  families and, 9–10
Racism, health disparities and, 258–259
Ramstad, Jim, 279
Rank, Mark, 136–137

Recessions, economic
  globalization and, 217–223
  indicators of, 219–220
  measuring, 217–218
  National Bureau of Economic Research's definition of, 218–219
Relative measures of poverty, 97
Religious marriage, 364
Reproductive technologies, gay and lesbian parents and, 306
Riders, 236
Rotating credit associations, 145
Rugged individualism, 123–124

Same-sex families, 9
Same-sex marriage, 369–373
Same-sex parenting, 304–306
Satcher, David, 281
SCHIP (State Children's Health Insurance Program), 268–271
Schoemehl, Vincent, 66
School Breakfast Program, 174
Section 8 certificates, 179–180
Service systems, development of, 22–24
Sherraden, Michael, 140–142
Shishkin, Julius, 217–218
Smith, Garrett Lee, 281
Smith, Gordon, 281
Social bridges, 146
Social capital
  dimensions of, 145–146
  forms of, 143
  types of community level, 146–147
  voluntary group participation and, 144–145
Social capital theory, 142–147
  elements of, 143t
Social construction of knowledge, 36–37, 219
Social dislocation theory, 147–151
Social economy, devolution and, 416–417
Social glue, 145–146
Social problems
  collective definition process of, 20
  defining, 20–24
  development of professions, bureaucracies, and service systems and, 22–24
  dynamic policy process and, 24–28
  factors affecting the emergence of, 22
  identifying and defining, 18–19
  modern welfare state and, 22–23
  moment in history and, 22, 23t
  values and, 21–22
  welfare state and, 22–24

Social Security, 400–401
  as anti-poverty program, 403
  privatization and, 404–407
  retirement and disability benefits, 401–403
Social Security Act (1935), 400
  Title IV-A, 395
  Title IV-E, 395
Social Services Block Grant (SSBG, 1981), 308–309
Social trends, families and, 7–8
Social work, political, 89
Social work practice, family policy and, 14–15
Soup kitchens, 169
SourceWatch, 86
Special Supplemental Nutrition Program for Women, Infants and Children (WIC), 173–174
  food stamps vs., 174
State Children's Health Insurance Program (SCHIP), 268–271
Steel industry, as example of globalization, 206–207
Stewart B. McKinney Homeless Assistance Act (1990 and 2001), 341, 342
Strengths approach, 1–2
Stress, caregiver, 386–387
Structural vulnerability theory, 136–140
Subjective measures of poverty, 97
Subprime mortgage crisis, xxii, 187–190
Suicide prevention, youth, 280–281
Supplemental Nutrition Assistance Program (SNAP), 169, 170, 173
Survey of Income and Program Participation (SIPP), 108, 109
SUTA dumping, 226
Symbolic interaction theory, 35

Task forces, 64
Task groups, 64–71
Technological change, job loss and, 203
Teenagers, childbirth among, 9
Temporary Assistance for Needy Families (TANF), 161–163
  family caregiving and, 396–397
Testimony, legislative, 74–75
  guidelines, 75, 433
Think tanks, policy, 124–125
Thresholds, poverty, 97–100
Title IV-A of the Social Security Act, 395
Title IV-E of the Social Security Act, 395
Title XX, 308–309, 309t, 340
Toyota, 211–212, 212t

Index

Trade Adjustment Assistance (TAA) Reform Act (2002), 226–228
Traiman, Leland, 366
"Troubled persons" professions, 24

Uncompensated care, 256–258, 258
Unemployment, demographics of, 220–223
Unemployment compensation programs, 224–226
Unemployment insurance, 225–226
Unemployment policies, 223–230
    Trade Adjustment Assistance (TAA) Reform Act (2002), 226–228
    unemployment compensation programs, 224–226
    Worker Adjustment and Retraining and Notification Act (WARN), 229
    Workforce Investment Act (1998), 229–230
Unemployment rates, 219–223, 221f, 222f, 223f
Uninsured families, in United States, 247–248
United States
    changing nature of, family policy and, 6
    distribution of income and wealth in, 103–108
    family policy in, xviii
    Gini coefficient for, 418–419, 419t
    Gini index for, 419
    health disparities in, 247–248
    implications of globalization for, 421–422
    income and wealth distribution in, 103–108
    income inequality of, 419–421
    labor market of, globalization and, 204–217
    lack of family policies in, 4–5
    poverty guidelines, 100–103
    poverty rate of, 98–100
    prevalence of hunger in, 166–167
    uninsured families in, 247–248

Values
    defining social problems and, 21–22
    policy solutions and, 19–20
Vancouver Citizen's Committee, 72
Velcro kids, 384–385
Victims of Trafficking and Violence Protect Act (2000), 336

Violence. *See* Child maltreatment; Elder abuse; Family violence; Intimate partner violence; Women, violence against
Violence Against Women Act (1994), 324, 335–337
Violence Against Women and Department of Justice Reauthorization Act (2005), 336–337
Violence Crime Control and Law Enforcement Act (VAWA, 1994), 336–337
Viral marketing, 86
Voluntary group participation, 144–145
Voluntary kinship care, 388
    private, 388

Waiver programs, 162–164
Warren, Barry, 366
WashingtonWatch.com, 273
Wasilewski, Janina, 49
Web logs, 85
Web sites, evaluating, 84
Welfare state, social problems and, 22–24
Welfare-to-work policy, 160–166
Wellstone, David, 279
Wellstone, Paul, 279
White-collar jobs, moving offshore, 215–217
WIC (Special Supplemental Nutrition Program for Women, Infants and Children), 173–174
    food stamps vs., 174
Wilson, William Julius, 147–151
Women, violence against, 335–337
Work and employment
    introduction to, 202–204
    technological change and, 203
Worker Adjustment and Retraining and Notification Act (WARN), 229
Workforce Investment Act (1998), 229–230
Working, child care and, 290–293
Working overtime without overtime pay, 233

Youth Suicide, Early Intervention and Prevention Expansion Act (2004), 281
Youth suicide prevention, 280–281
YouTube, 86

Ziegler, John, 60

About the Authors

Alice K. Butterfield (MSW, PhD) is professor at the Jane Addams College of Social Work, University of Illinois at Chicago. She is the author of more than thirty-five journal articles and book chapters, many of which are devoted to housing policy and service delivery for homeless families, community practice, and international social work. Since 2001, Alice has been involved in the development of the School of Social Work at Addis Ababa University in Ethiopia (www.aboutsweep.org). She is on the National Board of Advisors of Influencing State Policy and the Council on Social Work Education's Commission on Global Social Work Education. In 2007, she received the Distinguished Alumni Award from Washington University in St. Louis.

Cynthia J. Rocha (PhD) is associate dean and associate professor at the College of Social Work, University of Tennessee, Knoxville. She has taught family policy and policy practice for fourteen years and has researched the plight of poor and dislocated workers throughout her career. She has published numerous articles on the family, the family well-being of dislocated manufacturing workers, economic justice, and the working poor.

William H. Butterfield (MSW, PhD) served in the South Dakota National Guard, the U.S. Navy, and the U.S. Army Reserve and worked as a juvenile probation officer in Maricopa County for seven years before returning to school at the University Michigan, where he received degrees in social work and psychology. He held a joint appointment at the University of Wisconsin in social work and at the Medical School as the director of Family Counseling in the University Family Health Service. He subsequently joined the George Warren Brown School of Social Work, where he served as associate dean and director of the PhD program.